Series 7 Securities Licensing Review

Richard P. Majka

Series 7 Securities Licensing Review Exam Cram

International Standard Book Number: 0-7897-3287-4

Library of Congress Catalog Card Number: 2004112113

Printed in the United States of America

First Printing: December 2005

08 07 4 3

Trademarks

All terms mentioned in this book that are known to be trademarks or service marks have been appropriately capitalized. Que Publishing cannot attest to the accuracy of this information. Use of a term in this book should not be regarded as affecting the validity of any trademark or service mark.

Warning and Disclaimer

Every effort has been made to make this book as complete and as accurate as possible, but no warranty or fitness is implied. The information provided is on an "as is" basis. The author and the publisher shall have neither liability nor responsibility to any person or entity with respect to any loss or damages arising from the information contained in this book or from the use of the CD or programs accompanying it.

Bulk Sales

Que Publishing offers excellent discounts on this book when ordered in quantity for bulk purchases or special sales. For more information, please contact

U.S. Corporate and Government Sales

1-800-382-3419

corpsales@pearsontechgroup.com

For sales outside the U.S., please contact

International Sales

international@pearsoned.com

Publisher
Paul Boger

Executive Editor
Jeff Riley

Acquisitions Editor
Carol Ackerman

Development Editor
Mark Renfrow

Managing Editor
Charlotte Clapp

Project Editor
Seth Kerney

Copy Editors
Cheri Clark
Kezia Endsley

Indexer
Aaron Black

Proofreader
Leslie Joseph

Technical Editor
Richard V. Hall

Publishing Coordinator
Cindy Teeters

Multimedia Developer
Dan Scherf

Interior Designer
Gary Adair

Cover Designer
Anne Jones

About the Author

Richard P. Majka has served the financial community for the past 23 years as a financial trainer. He was employed by Credit Suisse—First Boston as the director of their International Bankers School for Investment Advisors and Private Bankers. After leaving Wall Street in 1997, he was commissioned to author four financial textbooks for various New York, Boston, and international publishing firms. He has taught exclusively for many of the major financial institutions in the country. His clients include Citigroup, Paine Webber, Lloyds Bank, and HSBC, as well as numerous banks, broker dealers, and insurers. He is well versed in the field of derivative products, debt and equity securities, as well as insurance products. He is licensed by New York State as a life and health agent, as well as by the NASD as a registered representative. Rich has also authored numerous case studies on ethics in the securities industry, which are used as a training tool by many broker-dealers throughout the United States.

As a financial services representative, Rich has combined his financial background and strong desire to help people in his practice. He offers his clients clear, concise, and honest advice in meeting their financial and investment needs. Rich's philosophy is that each of his clients is a valued partner that he will work together with to build a long-term relationship. With careful evaluation, combined with educating his clients, he strives to meet their financial goals.

A lifelong resident of Long Island, Rich and his wife Christine, son Garrett, and daughter Sabrina live in Suffolk County. He is active in coaching Little League, as well as being a manager and player in the Men's Senior Baseball League. Rich also actively serves on the Board of Directors for both the Men's Senior Baseball League and the Suffolk Stan Musial Baseball League. In 1998, he became the first original inductee into the MSBL Long Island Baseball Hall of Fame.

About the Technical Editors

Jared Nishida is an investment analyst with KSM Capital Advisors, a wealth management division of Indianapolis-based accounting firm Katz, Sapper & Miller. Jared is currently a Level II candidate in the CFA program and holds his Series 7, Series 66, and Indiana Life, Accident, and Health licenses.

He began his career in the financial services industry in 2002 as a financial advisor with American Express Financial Advisors, Inc. Jared graduated from Taylor University in Upland, Indiana with a Bachelor of Science degree in business administration.

Stacy Stephenson is a planning advisor with STAR Financial Services in Indianapolis, Indiana, and has been working in the financial markets since she graduated from Purdue University in 1998 with a Bachelor of Science degree. In addition to holding Series 7 and Series 66 licenses, Stacy is licensed to sell life, health, and long-term care insurance. Over her career, Stacy has created and implemented hundreds of financial plans for individuals and managed assets in excess of ten million dollars. Prior to employment with STAR Financial, Stacy worked for Merrill Lynch. Stacy is currently pursuing her MBA at Butler University.

We Want to Hear from You!

As the reader of this book, *you* are our most important critic and commentator. We value your opinion and want to know what we're doing right, what we could do better, what areas you'd like to see us publish in, and any other words of wisdom you're willing to pass our way.

As an executive editor for Que Publishing, I welcome your comments. You can email or write me directly to let me know what you did or didn't like about this book—as well as what we can do to make our books better.

Please note that I cannot help you with technical problems related to the topic of this book. We do have a User Services group, however, where I will forward specific technical questions related to the book.

When you write, please be sure to include this book's title and author as well as your name, email address, and phone number. I will carefully review your comments and share them with the author and editors who worked on the book.

Email: feedback@quepublishing.com

Mail: Jeff Riley
Executive Editor
Que Publishing
800 East 96th Street
Indianapolis, IN 46240 USA

For more information about this book or another Que Certification title, visit our website at www.examcram.com. Type the ISBN (excluding hyphens) or the title of a book in the Search field to find the page you're looking for.

Contents at a Glance

Part V: Options

Part VI: Accounts

Part VII: Investment Vehicles

Part VIII: Market Analysis and Economics

Part IX: Appendixes

Table of Contents

Chapter 23
Mutual Funds 457

Chapter 24
Direct Participation Programs 477

Foreword

Rich Majka has been associated with James J. O'Donnell for many years. He has served the financial community for more than 20 years as a Program Manager of Credit Suisse International Bankers School and was instrumental in creating and implementing the first International Bankers Training Program. Rich has extensive experience in teaching programs in management development, selling skills, and financial courses. As a member of the management team and instructor with Global Training & Development Group, Inc. for more than five years, he successfully prepared many individuals for the Securities Qualification exams and wrote numerous securities industry educational materials.

As a teacher and author of financial licensing material, Rich Majka is outstanding. Any study materials on securities licensing written by Rich are sure to offer readers quality information. The only thing better would be to attend a class by Rich Majka.

—James J. O'Donnell, co-founder of the Series 7 Exam

James J. O'Donnell is President of Global Training & Development Group, Inc. He was a member of the NYSE Advisory and NASD Qualification Committees and a co-founder of the Series 7 examination. He is currently an arbitrator with the NYSE and the NASD and serves on the NYSE/NASD Supervisory Continuing Educational Committee.

Introduction

So you want to be a stockbroker? With all the volatility and unpredictability of the stock market, many individuals want to be part of this fast-paced, cutting-edge environment. The road to becoming a stockbroker is a challenging one, but for the right individual, it can also be a rewarding highway to success.

What Is This Book About?

Welcome to the *Series 7 Securities Licensing Review Exam Cram*! The sole aim of this book is to provide you with a review of Series 7 information that will help you learn, drill, and review for the Series 7 exam.

Who Is This Book for?

This book is for anyone studying for the Series 7 exam who is ready to test his or her knowledge before taking the real exam. If you have been preparing but you want to test yourself before taking the exam, this book is for you! Maybe you have taken other practice exams, reviewed other material, or unsuccessfully taken the real exam, and you want to try more review questions before taking the exam again: then this book is for you, too!

What Will You Find in This Book?

The *Series 7 Securities Licensing Review Exam Cram* utilizes a variety of special elements to help you best understand the material being tested. Each chapter follows a regular structure, with graphical cues about important or useful material. The special elements you will find within the book are described as follows:

- *Opening hotlists*—Each chapter begins with lists of the terms you need to understand and the concepts you need to know for the exam.

- *Topical coverage*—After the opening hotlists, each chapter covers the topics related to the exam.
- *Alerts*—We highlight throughout the material items most likely to appear on the exam by using a special Exam Alert that looks like this:

Exam Alerts are intended to help you score better on the exam, which they do by providing you with "insider information" for the particular question type/section that is being discussed where the Exam Alert appears.

Even if material isn't flagged as an Exam Alert, all the content is this book is associated in some way with test-related material. What appears in the chapter content is considered critical material.

- *Notes*—Some content opens another inquiry which is not specifically exam-related but good background. A Note looks like this:

Notes will give you supplementary information on a topic at hand, and in some cases point you to other information resources.

- *Sidebar*—A sidebar is useful information that is not tested but provides background for important information. A sidebar looks like this:

Sidebars

Sidebars are designed to give you more extensive supplementary information that is not necessarily specific to exam objectives but is background you may find useful.

- *Exam Prep Questions*—You are going to get a lot of practice questions in this book, both in the form of sample quizzes and full-length practice exams. Practice questions are not only listed, but detailed answer explanations are also provided.
- *Need to Know More?*—At the end of the book is a section titled "Need to Know More?" This section provides useful resources to help you if you need additional information on exam topics.
- *Practice Exam*—The Practice Exam is intended to test your comprehension of the material in this book. The sample questions are similar in format and degree of difficulty as the questions you will find on the real

exam. However, because the questions on the real exam are highly confidential, expect that the real exam will be new to you.

- *Answer Key*—This provides all the answers to the questions in the Practice Exam. There is a quick check key plus more in-depth explanations of the answers, explaining incorrect answers that you might find confusing.
- *Glossary*—This is an extensive list of important terms used in this book.
- *Cram Sheet*—This appears as a tear-out card inside the front cover of this book. It is a valuable tool that represents a collection of the most difficult-to-remember facts, terms, and concepts we think you should memorize before taking the test.
- *CD-ROM*—The CD contains additional questions so you can practice taking sample exams. Again, these questions are merely similar to those you will find on the real exam and are not to be thought of as "real" questions.

Hints for Using This Book

Because this book is a paper practice product, you might want to complete the Practice Exam on a separate sheet of paper so that you can reuse the questions over and over without seeing the answers. Also, as a general rule of thumb, you should make sure you score in the 80% to 90% range in all topics before attempting the real exam. The higher the percentages you score on review question products, the better your chances for passing the real exam. Of course, we can't guarantee a passing score on the real exam, but we can offer you plenty of opportunities to practice and assess your knowledge level before entering the real exam.

The Road to Becoming a Stockbroker

To become a registered representative, the qualified applicant is required to meet some demanding requirements:

- The applicant must be a minimum of 18 years old or, at some of the larger firms, a minimum of 21 years old.
- The applicant is required to possess a clean personal record, with no criminal convictions in the past.

- The applicant is required to be employed by a broker/dealer before she can actually apply to become a registered representative. The broker/dealer can be either a NYSE member firm or an NASD member firm.
- The applicant is not required to have a college degree, but many larger firms do not hire an individual without a degree.
- After employed by a broker/dealer, the applicant has a 30-day waiting period before he can apply to become licensed.
- The applicant must complete a NASD form called the U-4 application for General Securities Registration and submit the completed form to the Central Registration Depository (CRD) for investigation.
- The applicant must receive a CRD approval for her application to be qualified to sit for the Series 7 qualifying examination. Applicants with any previous criminal convictions are denied approval from the CRD. Additionally, any applicant who has previously been barred from the securities industry for past violations is also denied approval.

As the applicant prepares for the exam, the registration or compliance personnel of the firm open a "window" for the applicant to schedule her exam with a certified testing site. This window typically lasts 90 days because the applicant must sit for the examination within that time frame.

The Series 7 is a 250 multiple-choice question examination that the applicant must pass with a minimum attained grade of 70%. The applicant must answer a minimum of 175 questions correctly to attain the 70% passing grade. Then the successful applicant is licensed by the NASD to buy and sell securities. Most firms have a probationary period for new brokers.

After successfully passing the Series 7 examination, all candidates must also pass the Series 63–Uniform State Law Examination to buy and sell securities for their clients. An individual can fail the Series 7 exam and still sit for the Series 63 exam.

If an applicant fails the examination, he must wait another 30 days before he can schedule another testing date. Any applicant who has failed the Series 7 Exam three times is required to wait six months before he can refile his application to take the exam.

Many new stockbrokers are required by their firms to "build a book" of new clients. This building includes cold calling qualified leads. As the new stockbroker builds her business and a list of clients, she can expect to earn a "draw" from her employer over a period of time. This draw is considered a salary until the new stockbroker can sufficiently sustain herself from the commission business she generates.

In this age of Internet trading, it is becoming more difficult for stockbrokers to earn commission income from clients. The most successful stockbrokers must be more than just an order taker for their clients. They must know their customers and their investment profiles to make a living in this business. The better versed a broker is in the markets and products that are available to investors, the more successful he will become.

Need Further Study?

Are you having a hard time correctly answering these questions? If so, you probably need further review. Consult the sister product to this book, *Series 7 Securities Licensing Review Questions Exam Cram* (Que Publishing, 0-7897-3286-6) for further review.

Self-Assessment

I've included a Self-Assessment in this *Exam Cram* to help you evaluate your readiness to tackle the Series 7 Securities Licensing exam. It will also help you understand which topics you need to master in this book. Before you tackle this Self-Assessment, however, I address the concerns you might face when pursuing a Series 7 license and what an ideal candidate might look like.

Series 7 Securities License in the Real World

In the next section, I describe an ideal Series 7 securities license candidate, knowing full well that only a few actual candidates meet this ideal. In fact, my description of that ideal candidate might seem downright scary. But take heart; although the requirements to obtain a Series 7 license might seem formidable, they are by no means impossible to meet. However, you should be keenly aware that it does take time, requires some expense, and calls for a dedicated effort.

You can get all the real-world motivation you need from knowing that many others have gone before you. You can follow in their footsteps. If you're willing to tackle the process seriously and do what it takes to gain the necessary experience and knowledge, you can take—and pass—the Series 7 exam. In fact, the *Exam Cram* and the companion *Review Questions Cram* are designed to make it as easy as possible for you to prepare for the exam!

The same, of course, is true for other securities licensing exams, including

- The Series 6 licensing exam
- The Series 63 state licensing exam
- The Series 65 licensing exam
- Other requisite securities licensing exams

The Ideal Series 7 Securities License Candidate

Just to give you some idea of what an ideal Series 7 securities candidate is like, here are some relevant statistics about the background and experience such an individual might have. Don't worry if you don't meet these qualifications (or, indeed, if you don't even come close), because this world is far from ideal. Where you fall short is simply where you have more work to do. The ideal candidate has the following qualifications:

- Academic or professional training in the financial field. Ideal candidates have a minimum of a two-year business degree or higher, such as a BBA or an MBA.
- A minimum of one to two years experience in the securities, banking, or insurance fields. The more familiar the candidate is with the financial services field, the better position he or she is in.

Many candidates will meet these requirements, but remember, these are not mandatory prerequisites. In fact, many candidates embark on attaining the Series 7 license with little if any background in the financial field. If this describes you, rest assured that with diligence, you too can survive it, especially if you heed what this Self-Assessment tells you about what you need to learn.

Put Yourself to the Test

The following series of questions and observations is designed to help you determine how much work you face in pursuing the Series 7 Securities license and what kinds of resources you can consult on your quest. Be absolutely honest in your answers, or you'll end up wasting money on an exam that you're not ready to take. There are no right or wrong answers, only steps along the path to achieving your securities license. Only you can decide where you really belong in the broad spectrum of aspiring candidates.

Two things need to be clear from the outset, however:

- Even a modest background in finance, insurance, or banking is helpful.
- Hands-on experience with investments of some sort, such as buying or selling stocks or bonds, is an essential ingredient for certification success. Such experience can even be from creating your personal portfolio.

Educational Background

1. Have you ever taken any computer-related classes?
2. Have you taken any classes about the securities industry?
3. Do you have a working knowledge of basic financial terms, such as common stock, bonds, options, and mutual funds?
4. Have read about the securities industry and how it works?

Hands-On Experience

Another important key to success on the Series 7 examination is hands-on experience. If I leave you with only one realization after taking this Self-Assessment, it should be that there's no substitute for practical hands-on experience in the securities and investment fields.

1. Have you ever bought or sold stocks or mutual funds in your own personal brokerage account or 401k/IRA?
2. Have you dealt with finances, such as loans for mortgages, cars, and so on, with a bank or other financial firm?
3. Have you watched Bloomberg or CNN Financial Network on television and understood what they were talking about?
4. Have you read research reports on a company or mutual fund provided by an industry analyst?

Testing Your Exam Readiness

If you can answer the following questions, you are well on your way to being prepared for the real exam. If you cannot answer all these accurately, go back and study the topics you missed. Retake the practice exams as many times as needed until you fully understand the terms and concepts.

1. Which of the following security acts affects the issuance of corporate debt the most?
   - ❑ A. Security Act of 1934
   - ❑ B. Trust Indenture Act of 1939
   - ❑ C. The Investment Company Act of 1940
   - ❑ D. The Maloney Act of 1938

The correct answer is B. The Trust Indenture Act of 1939 oversees the issuance of corporate debt. It covers bond indentures and the protective covenants in the indenture. The Security Act of 1934 covers the rules of the stock market, and the Investment Company Act of 1940 covers investment companies and mutual funds. The Maloney Act governs the OTC markets.

2. T-Bills are offered each Monday by the U.S. government to competitive bidders and noncompetitive bidders. An individual has $500,000 in cash that she wants to invest in T-Bills. What type of tender would she be able to conduct?

❑ A. She can enter a competitive bid for $500,000.

❑ B. She can enter five separate noncompetitive bids for $100,000 each.

❑ C. She can enter one noncompetitive bid for $500,000.

❑ D. She can enter a bid for $500,000 on both the competitive side and the noncompetitive side and take the best price.

The correct answer is C. Individual investors can only enter a noncompetitive bid for T-Bills. An investor with $500,000 to invest would tender the entire amount in a noncompetitive bid.

3. All the following will be used by a municipal bond underwriter to determine a submitted competitive bid on a new issue, except:

❑ A. Pre-sale orders

❑ B. The credit rating of the issuer

❑ C. The municipality's debt-per-capita ratio

❑ D. The anticipated revenues from the proposed project

The correct answer is D. A competitive bid is almost always used exclusively for general obligation (GO) bond issues. In determining the bid, the underwriter will gauge investor demand by pre-sale orders that have been taken. The underwriter will also consider the credit rating of the municipality and the risk they will incur. Tax collection ratios are also used to help determine the lowest possible bid. Anticipated project revenues come from revenue bonds, and are not considered in a competitive bid (GO bond), but rather on a negotiated basis between one underwriter chosen by the issuing municipality.

4. The Standard & Poor's 500 Index tracks 500 stocks as an index for securities on which of the following markets?

I.The NYSE

II.The AMEX

III. The NASDAQ market

IV. The Bulletin Board

❑ A. I only

❑ B. I and II

❑ C. I, II, and III

❑ D. I, II, III, and IV

The correct answer is C. The S&P 500 Index is a measure of 500 select stocks from the NYSE, the AMEX, and the over-the-counter (OTC) market. Bulletin board stocks are very small stocks listed on the pink sheets or bulletin board of the OTC market, and are too small to be considered for the S&P 500 Index.

5. All option trades are settled with the Options Clearing Corporation in how many days?

   ❑ A. Same-day settlement
   ❑ B. Next-day settlement
   ❑ C. Three business days
   ❑ D. Five business days

The correct answer is B. All options must settle with the Options Clearing Corporation on the next business day. The broker can give clients up to five business days to settle their option accounts.

6. New interest rate options on Treasury Notes are issued by the O.C.C. how often?

   ❑ A. Weekly
   ❑ B. Every month
   ❑ C. Every quarter
   ❑ D. Every 60 days

The correct answer is B. Treasury note price base options are issued monthly by the Options Clearing Corporation. This coincides with their issuance from the Federal Reserve Bank.

7. A customer sells short 300 shares of GHI stock at $3.50 per share. What is the margin requirement on the transaction?

   ❑ A. $525
   ❑ B. $750
   ❑ C. $1,050
   ❑ D. $2,000

The correct answer is C. The NASD margin requirement on a short sale of a penny stock is the greater of $2.50 per share or 100% of the sale proceeds. 300 shares of GHI stock sold short at $3.50 per share has a total sale proceed of $1,050. The $2.50 requirement per share multiplied by 300 shares equals $750, so the client is required to deposit $1,050 as the margin requirement.

8. All the following are characteristics of an investment company, except:

   ❑ A. It allows investors to remain liquid.
   ❑ B. It allows investors to make their own specific investment choices.
   ❑ C. It allows investors to diversify their holdings, regardless of size.
   ❑ D. It gives investors professional management of their holdings.

The correct answer is B. An investment company allows investors to pool their funds, giving them significantly more market access and clout. This allows investors to own certain securities that might normally be out of their investment range, such as those with pre-set investment limits, like agency debt securities. An investment company also offers investors professional management of their funds and provides investors with a diversified portfolio of securities. Investment companies do not allow investors to make their own specific investment choices.

9. A mutual fund is not required to pay corporate taxes on portfolio income if it distributes what percentage of its investment income to shareholders?

- ❑ A. 75% of its income
- ❑ B. 80% of its income
- ❑ C. 90% of its income
- ❑ D. 97% of its income

The correct answer is C. Under Subchapter M of the IRS tax code, portfolio-based mutual funds are not required to pay corporate taxes on any income if they distribute 90% of their earnings to shareholders. The IRS also adds a tax surcharge to funds that do not pass on at least 97% of their dividend income and 98% of their capital gains to shareholders. Most funds will retain 2–3% of their earnings in order to meet these IRS requirements.

10. An annuity that pays an annuitant for life, but also specifies a minimum period over which payments are made, is considered which of the following?

- ❑ A. Life annuity
- ❑ B. Life annuity with period certain
- ❑ C. Joint and last survivor annuity
- ❑ D. Unit refund life annuity

The correct answer is C. A joint and last survivor annuity is held jointly by two people, and when one dies, the agreed-upon payments will continue to the other. Married couples often purchase joint and last survivor annuities.

Study Methods

Whether you attend a formal class on a specific topic to get ready for an exam or use written materials to study on your own, some preparation for the Series 7 exam is essential. At $225 a try, pass or fail, you'll want to do everything you can to pass on your first try. That's where the correct studying comes in.

I have included several practice exam questions for each chapter and two sample tests, so if you don't score well on the chapter questions, you can study more and then tackle the sample tests at the end of the book. If you don't earn a score of at least 70% on the sample tests, you'll want to review where you are deficient and retake these exams. For this subject, consider taking a structured course provided by a qualified training firm and experienced instructor. An instructor with a solid re[as]sume[as] and working knowledge of the many varied topics that are required is invaluable. Remember, this is an exam that covers numerous financial topics, including many products that you have more than likely never heard of before or have no idea how they work. Someone qualified as an instructor can prove to be your greatest asset in starting to understand the wide array of materials needed for the exam.

For information about Series 7 classes, discuss it with your operations manager. If you are attempting to pass the exam without a formal training class, you must be well-versed in the financial field. Many of the topics on the exam are so unique and varied that even MBA graduate students might not have been exposed to them.

After you have completed your formal training class, all the while studying and practicing exam questions, you'll start to get an idea of how well you understand the materials. If you are consistently achieving 80% or higher on the practice exams, you clearly grasp these topics. Remember, there is nothing wrong with taking a practice exam first and reading the answers as your initial review before attempting to "fly solo."

It is important to stress that this exam is not a sprint, but rather a marathon. You definitely need to pace yourself. The very reason for getting the Series 7 license is that you will more than likely be dealing with investors and clients in your future career. After you have passed the exam and have your license, you are best served if you actually understand the materials in depth. I often tell my students that nothing is more embarrassing than not understanding a topic or product that a client asks you about. Even after the exam is over and you have passed, you still need to study and know these materials. Your future earnings might very well depend on it!

After you've assessed your readiness, mastered the right background studies, obtained the hands-on experience that helps you understand the products and technologies at work, and reviewed the many sources of information to help you prepare for a test, you'll be ready to take a round of practice tests. When your scores are high enough, you're ready to go after the real thing. If you follow my assessment regimen, you'll not only know what you need to study, but you'll also know when you're ready to make a test date. Good luck!

PART I

Primary and Secondary Markets

The Primary Market

Terms You Need to Know

- ✓ Accredited investor
- ✓ Agreement among underwriters
- ✓ Authorized stock
- ✓ Blue sky laws
- ✓ Commitment
- ✓ Control stock
- ✓ Cooling-off period
- ✓ Due diligence meeting
- ✓ Eastern account (or undivided account)
- ✓ Effective date
- ✓ Filing date
- ✓ Final prospectus
- ✓ Freeriding
- ✓ Green shoe clause
- ✓ Hot issue
- ✓ Initial public offering (IPO)
- ✓ Investment banking
- ✓ Investors
- ✓ Issued stock
- ✓ Letter of intent
- ✓ Market issuer
- ✓ New issue
- ✓ Outstanding stock
- ✓ Over-the-counter (OTC)
- ✓ Penalty bid clause
- ✓ Preemptive right
- ✓ Preliminary prospectus (or red herring)
- ✓ Primary market
- ✓ Primary offering
- ✓ Private placement (Regulation D or Reg D placement)
- ✓ Proxy
- ✓ Public offering price
- ✓ Regulation A
- ✓ Restricted stock
- ✓ Road show
- ✓ Rule 144
- ✓ Rule 144a
- ✓ Rule 147 (or intrastate exemption)
- ✓ Secondary market
- ✓ Securities Act of 1933
- ✓ Securities and Exchange Commission (SEC)
- ✓ Securities Exchange Act of 1934
- ✓ Selling group
- ✓ Selling out
- ✓ Shelf registration
- ✓ Stabilizing bid
- ✓ Sticky issue
- ✓ Stock (or equity security)
- ✓ Stock exchange
- ✓ Syndicate of underwriters
- ✓ Taking indication
- ✓ Tombstone advertisement
- ✓ Treasury stock
- ✓ Underwriter
- ✓ Underwriting spread
- ✓ Western account
- ✓ Withholding

Concepts You Need to Understand

- ✓ The primary market
- ✓ The underwriting process
- ✓ How companies raise capital
- ✓ Which institutions make up the primary market
- ✓ What are the sources of funding
- ✓ How a company makes a public offering of securities
- ✓ What underwriting entails
- ✓ The role of the investment banker
- ✓ Who the major players are in a public offering
- ✓ How public offerings are priced
- ✓ The responsibilities of the Securities and Exchange Commission
- ✓ What a hot issue is and the restrictions placed on it
- ✓ How a sticky issue can be avoided
- ✓ Necessary conditions for a private placement
- ✓ Who qualifies as an accredited investor
- ✓ How private placement issues can enter the public market
- ✓ Other exemptions to the SEC's regulations of the primary market

The Corporation

Sometimes a business does not have enough retained earnings to finance its plans for modernization and expansion. In other instances, it might possess the necessary internal funds, but not want to commit them all at once or in one place. Investors—from individuals hoping to increase their savings, to large pension funds working to provide adequate retirement income for millions of men and women—can provide the firm with the money it needs to build a new plant or buy new equipment. Businesses and investors often meet in the primary market, where companies give up shares of their ownership in exchange for fresh capital.

When a Business Becomes a Corporation

A corporation is a business enterprise whose legal structure strictly limits the financial liability of its owners. The advantage in becoming a corporation is that a company can seek to raise capital from public investors; the disadvantage is that it must give up confidentiality and entrust its ultimate control to an elected board of directors. The board of directors, in turn, chooses a management team to oversee the day-to-day operations of the company. To form a corporation, a business must file for an article of incorporation (certificate of incorporation) in a single state. Among other things, this "corporate charter" must list:

- ➤ The corporation name
- ➤ A business description

- The amount of debt it can acquire (through bank loans and the sale of bond)
- A description of the corporate officers' duties
- The amount and type of capital stock the corporation can issue

Stock Ownership

When a corporation is formed, it can choose to sell stock to investors. This *stock*, or *equity security*, represents an investor's share in the ownership of the business. In the event of bankruptcy, stockholders (partial owners) can lose only the amount that they spent to buy the securities.

A Corporation Does Not Typically Issue All Its Stock

The corporation's charter lists the amount of shares it is authorized to sell—called *authorized stock*—but normally the board of directors keeps a portion of the total shares for possible future sales. Also, sometimes a company buys back shares of its own stock; these shares are then considered *treasury stock*. Treasury stock does not carry the same rights as *outstanding stock* (which is owned by investors). Treasury stock neither receives dividends nor possesses voting rights. A company's *issued stock* equals the amount of outstanding shares and treasury shares combined.

Shareholders Rights

Among other rights, shareholders have the right to:

- Receive dividends (a portion of the company's earnings, based on the number of outstanding shares) if and when the company decides to make a dividend payment (usually on a quarterly basis).
- Sell their shares. The right to transfer ownership.
- Vote for members of the board of directors and on certain matters before the board (such as changing the corporation's business). They can vote either in person or via a *proxy* (a written power of attorney authorizing a specific vote on behalf of the shareholder).
- Receive a share of the company's liquidated assets, should the company fail.
- Maintain the same proportion ownership of the company's stock—when a new issue has been authorized—by buying the necessary amount of new securities, generally at a discounted price. This is called *preemptive right*.

For example, Mr. Smith owns 2% of Triple Z Garment Co.'s one million outstanding securities. The company plans to sell a new issue of one million shares. Preemption gives Mr. Smith the right to purchase another 20,000 shares of the new issue so that he can maintain his overall 2% holding.

The board of directors decides if and when the corporation pays dividends to shareholders; this is *not* a matter on which shareholders get to vote.

The Primary Market

The primary market comprises two sources of funding, private and public. In a private placement, the company offers its securities directly to banks, financial institutions, and wealthy investors. In making a public offering, the company attempts to sell its stocks to more public investors with the help of an underwriter.

Publicly trading equity securities occurs in two venues:

➤ **Stock exchanges**—Actual physical locations where thousands of auctions take place every business day. Buyers "bid" the highest price they are willing to pay for securities, whereas sellers "ask" the lowest price they are willing to accept for them. Among the most dominant are the New York Stock Exchange and the American Stock Exchange.

➤ **Over-the-counter (OTC) market**—Not any specific location, but rather a system in which individual sellers can negotiate the price of securities with individual buyers. Today, most OTC trading takes place through telecommunication and computer lines.

Public Offerings Are Not Sold Through the Stock Exchanges

Underwriters sell, or place, new equity issues with their customers. By the time a stock reaches an exchange, it has moved to the secondary market. The issue has sold out of the primary market, and some of the stock's original purchasers—underwriters' clients—begin trading their shares.

Companies know beforehand on which exchange or exchanges their stock will be listed. Depending on the characteristics of an underwriting, the move from the primary market to the secondary market can occur very rapidly.

Nonetheless, the fundamental distinction remains: proceeds from sales in the primary market go to the company that issued the stock, whereas proceeds (or losses) from sales in the secondary market go to individual investors.

Participants in the Primary Market

Several parties actively participate in the primary market:

- **Issuer**—The company that wants to raise capital by issuing securities.
- **Underwriters**—Firms that assist corporations sell their securities.
- **Investment banks**—Firms that help companies perform underwritings, mergers, acquisitions, reorganizations.

Smaller underwriters, although they might not constitute full-fledged investment banks, are nevertheless practicing one of the functions of investment banking and are sometimes referred to as "investment bankers."

- **Investors**—People, institutions, and businesses that want to buy securities.
- **Securities and Exchange Commission (SEC)**—The federal agency that oversees the primary and secondary markets.

The Securities Act of 1933 established the rules that companies must abide by when issuing new securities. The Securities Act of 1934 sets the trading rules for securities after they have been issued, regulates the stock exchanges, and governs the conduct of broker-dealers. Both acts are enforced by the Securities and Exchange Commission.

How a Company Complies with the Securities Act of 1933

Principally, the company complies by registering the proposed securities sale with the SEC, and by sending a *prospectus*—a document containing information about the issuer—to potential buyers. Whenever a corporation wants to place a new issue, it must meet the registration and prospective requirements of the SEC.

New Issues

A security that has never been offered in the public market is called a *new issue*. A new issue represents a company's attempt to raise money by selling shares of equity ownership in the primary market. There are two kinds of new issues:

- **Initial public offering (IPO)**—The first attempt by a corporation to sell its stock to the public.
- **Primary offering**—Additional securities issued by a public corporation.

IPOs and primary offerings occur in the primary market. The process, for both, is essentially the same. After the fee earned by underwriters is paid, the remaining sale proceeds go to the issuing company for its investment plans and growth.

The Underwriting Process

If a business needs capital and wants to explore the possibility of "going public," it might contact an investment banker. Or the investment banker might contact the business, believing that it has good potential to raise money in the public market. Underwriting is an important source of income for investment bankers. When the company and the investment banker have agreed to look into the possibility of raising capital this way, the investment banker analyzes the company's commercial and financial situation, assesses the merits of a public offering, and advises on how best to craft the issue to meet the demands of the marketplace. If a successful public offering seems likely, the investment banker will give the company a letter of intent.

The Purpose of the Letter of Intent

A *letter of intent* is a document that describes how the investment banker intends to take the company public or to sell a new issue of the company's stock. The letter of intent outlines the investment banker's plan to underwrite the offering. If the plan is successful, the letter of intent becomes a contract, and the investment banker becomes the issuer's underwriter.

Normally, two major decisions are included within the letter of intent:

- **Commitment**—How much of a commitment does the underwriter want to make toward selling the securities? Different levels of commitment imply different levels of risk. Here the underwriter has several choices:

Firm commitment—The investment banker agrees to purchase the entire offering and keep any shares that it cannot sell. The investment banker is taking on considerable risk; it is firmly committed to the issuing corporation.

Best Effort—The underwriter will make its best effort to sell all the issue to the public, but if it is not successful, any unsold shares will be returned to the issuer.

All-or-none—Under this kind of agreement, the investment banker will try to sell the entire offering, but it makes no financial commitment. Until the issue sells out, purchased securities and sales receipts are held in escrow. If the investment banker does not sell everything, the issue is cancelled, all securities are returned to the issuer, and all money is returned to the investors. A less extreme form of an all-or-nothing agreement is the *mini-maxi commitment*. Here the investment banker strives to sell a certain minimum portion of the total offering. If it does not reach the threshold, the entire sale is cancelled. If it passes the minimum threshold, but does not attain the maximum one, the remaining shares are returned to the issuer. A company with specific capital requirements for its investment plans might pursue either of these options.

EXAMPLE: Triple Z Garment Co. hopes to build a new factory and equip it with state-of-the-art sewing machines. Company engineers estimate the total cost to be $7 million. Acme Investments analyzes the situation and writes a letter of intent, detailing its plan to take Triple Z public. Acme suggests a mini-maxi commitment of $10 million of stock, with the minimum threshold set at 70%. If successful, this will raise at least $7 million for Triple Z. Had Acme instead recommended a $7 million all-or-nothing offering, Triple Z would have lost the possibility of raising an extra $3 million.

➤ **How the securities will be sold**—The second major decision expressed in the letter of intent is how the underwriter aims to sell the offering. For most larger issues, the investment banker may decide to spread its risk by forming a *syndicate of underwriters*. In this case, the original underwriter becomes the lead (or managing) underwriter.

Before examining this syndicate and its working agreement, this chapter looks at what the issuer is doing in order to comply with the Securities Act of 1933.

The Company's Responsibilities

The company's primary responsibility is to register the stock offering with the SEC. The day that the SEC receives the registration is the *filing date*, which is followed by a *cooling-off period* (a minimum of 20 days), used by the SEC to review whether the issuer has complied with the provisions of the 1933 act, whether the registration contains any misleading claims, and whether it is complete. Among other things, the registration statement must include:

- Current stock ownership in the company by directors, officers, and underwriters
- Identification of people who already own 10% or more of the company's outstanding shares
- History of the company's past equity and bond issues
- Detailed financial statements for the company
- What the proceeds from the offering will be used for

The company must also register with any states in which the securities are to be sold. In the aftermath of the 1929 crash, states passed their own laws to help prevent future market disasters. These are called *blue sky laws*, designed to prevent unscrupulous brokers from attempting to sell appealing but worthless pieces of "blue sky" to unsuspecting investors. Besides setting registration requirements, blue sky laws require that all broker-dealers conducting business in a certain state be registered there. Thus, a broker not registered in Illinois is prohibited from selling stocks in Chicago. Depending on the state, companies can "blue sky" their proposed offering in several ways:

- Registration by coordination—The SEC helps the company meet blue sky laws by notifying the states in which the issue will be sold. Most states allow this form of registration, which is done simultaneously with an SEC registration.
- Registration by qualification—Some states require a corporation to submit a comprehensive application if it has not previously filed with them.
- Registration by filing (or notification)—A business that has previously sold its stock in a state can simply renew the earlier application.

Other Issuer Responsibilities

Working with its lead underwriter, the company must prepare a *preliminary prospectus*. This document, based largely on the registration statement, gives potential investors and underwriters the information that they will need to make an initial assessment of their interest in the offering. Because of the red-letter notice on its cover page, the preliminary prospectus is best known as a *red herring*. The notice warns that the information within the prospectus is subject to change, while emphasizing that the securities cannot yet be sold nor can offers to buy be accepted. Further, a disclaimer on the cover page states that the SEC does not endorse the offering. Although the red herring does not include the actual public offering price (POP) of the securities, it often lists a probable range, say $12–$16 per share. The red herring also describes the major points of the agreement among underwriters.

The Agreement Among Underwriters

When the underwriter has decided to spread its risk among several investment bankers, that is, to form a *syndicate*, it must establish a structure of fees and liabilities for the syndicate members. This is done in the *agreement among underwriters*. Basically, the members must agree upon what kind of commitment they will make to the stock issue and how they are going to split up the *underwriting spread*.

underwriting spread = public offering price – proceeds to issuer

Often the spread is defined in terms of "points," with each point equaling 1% of the public offering price.

EXAMPLE: If Triple Z stock is to be sold at $35 per share, and if the underwriting spread equals $1.75, or 5 points, Triple Z will receive $33.25 per share. Acme Investments, the lead underwriter, and its fellow syndicate members will make their profit from this spread.

Others Can Help Sell a Public Offering

The lead underwriter can enlist the help of other investment bankers. If so, it forms a *selling group*, whose members share a piece of the underwriter's spread, known as a *concession fee*, but who do not take on any financial liability for any unsold stock. In this case the lead underwriter formulates a selling group agreement, detailing the terms.

That Is Not It for the Sales Force

In some instances, outside broker-dealers also end up selling part of an offering. If they have interested clients, they can call one of the syndicate or selling group members and negotiate a reallowance fee to place a number of shares. Whereas syndicate and selling group members are guaranteed a place at the sales table, these outside broker-dealers get no such assurance. If anything, they receive some of the issue's leftovers. See Table 1.1.

Table 1.1 Syndicate Breakdown

Business	Earnings (Per Share)	Possible Result
Issuer	Public offering price—underwriter's spread	If the POP equals $35, and the spread is $1.75 (5 points), the issuer gets $33.25.
Lead underwriter	Management fee equals a part of the spread	1 point equals $0.35 for each share sold.
Syndicate member	Takedown fee equals spread minus the management fee	4 points equals $1.40 for each share sold by the member.
Selling group member	Concession fee equals a part of the takedown fee	2 points equals $0.70 for each share sold by the member.
Outside broker-dealer	Reallowance fee equals a smaller part of the takedown fee	½ point equals $0.175 for each share sold by the broker.

The underwriter has two possibilities:

- **Western account.** Each member takes responsibility for selling a specified portion of the offering. If unsuccessful, a member keeps its unsold shares on its own books for future sales. Western accounts limit the liability of any one underwriter.

  EXAMPLE: The underwriting firms of Capital, United, and Excelsior each make a firm commitment to place one third of Triple Z's new issue. If Capital and United meet the goal, but Excelsior only manages to sell 20% of the issue, the latter will find itself with 13.33% of Triple Z stock sitting in its own account.

- **Eastern account** (or **undivided account**). All members commit to sell a given portion of the offering. Each member is also responsible for the same portion of any stock that other syndicate members have failed to sell. (This is often the way that underwriters sell offerings of municipal bonds.)

EXAMPLE: Capital, United, and Excelsior form an Eastern syndicate to underwrite Triple Z's public offering of one million shares. Capital signs on to sell 25%, United 40%, and Excelsior 35% of the shares. On the second day of the offering, Capitol has sold 250,000 shares, United 300,000 shares, and Excelsior 350,000 shares. Although Capitol and Excelsior have met their commitments, they are still responsible for selling 25,000 and 35,000 shares, respectively, of the 100,000 shares that United cannot sell.

During the cooling-off period, the lead underwriter shops the preliminary prospectus around to investment bankers and potential investors in an effort to learn their likely response to the offering. This process is known as *taking indication*, and it is one of the lead underwriter's most important responsibilities. The "indications of interest" the lead underwriter receives help it build the team it needs to sell the issue, plus it helps determine where to set the final offering price for a share of the stock. Furthermore, the syndicate members have only one more chance to get out of the deal, so they pay very close attention to the indications of interest—or lack thereof.

The End of the Cooling-Off Period

At the end of the cooling-off period, the *due diligence meeting* is held. Here the issuer, lead underwriter, and syndicate members review their compliance with all relevant SEC and blue sky regulations. They must make sure that they have disclosed complete and accurate information in the preliminary prospectus, and that they have made a full effort to meet the requirements of state and federal securities laws.

The SEC's Options in Response to the Registration

The SEC can give one of three responses to the issuer:

- **No.** If the SEC finds too many problems in the proposed offering—if the issuer has not exercised due diligence—it can simply give a "stop order."
- **Qualified no.** If the SEC discovers deficiencies in the issuer's compliance with securities laws, but believes that they are correctable, the agency can issue a "deficiency letter" and postpone the effective date. The issuer then has the opportunity to amend the identified deficiencies, usually by disclosing more information, and later can resubmit its petition.

- **No action.** When the SEC decides that the issuer has met its obligations, it allows the offering to proceed but does not endorse the issue itself. The cooling-off period is over; the effective date has been reached.

The Effective Date

With SEC approval of the company's registration statement, the underwriter can begin actual sale of the issue on the *effective date*. A *road show* is the most common method of developing a market for a new issue. During this stage in the process, the underwriter and top managers of the issuer travel to major financial centers to present the details of the offering and answer questions from the investment community.

The lead underwriter, the members of the syndicate, and the selling group members can begin to sell the company's securities. To do so, the lead underwriter must first insert the final *public offering price* into the prospectus, remove the red lettering, and be prepared to send this *final prospectus* to customers. Usually these tasks have already been carried out, so that sales can start immediately.

The final prospectus still carries the SEC disclaimer, noting that the securities have not been "approved or disapproved" by the commission. The SEC never vouches for the accuracy of any prospectus. The SEC's responsibility is solely to ensure that the issuer has supplied the necessary information and met its due diligence requirements.

The Final Prospectus Is Not Available Indefinitely

No, in most cases, the team of underwriters can place the entire stock offering in a matter of hours. If not, they must make the final prospectus available to customers for a specified period following the effective date: These time frames are:

- 90 days—For the initial public offering of a company
- 25 days—For corporations whose securities are already listed on a stock exchange or, for over-the-counter securities, on the computer system known as NASDAQ
- 40 days—For issuers who have already sold stock to the public, but not on an exchange or through the NASDAQ

Why Underwriters Place Ads in the Business Sections of Newspapers

Tombstone advertisements are the only ads permitted for new stock issues, and although they are not a legal requirement, the syndicates of larger issues normally place tombstone ads to announce their offerings. An ad states the name of the issuer, the amount of shares to be sold, the price per share, the lead underwriter, and syndicate members. It is important to note that the selling group members arc *not* listed.

Only the underwriters and selling group members can legally sell the securities, and they must send customers a copy of the prospectus. Thus, the tombstone ad always includes the statement, "This announcement is neither an offer to sell nor a solicitation of an offer to buy these securities. The offer is made only by the prospectus." Aside from bringing attention to the prospectus, the tombstone highlights the names of underwriters.

When the Price Is Not Right

After the issuer and its lead underwriter have fulfilled their requirements under the Securities Act of 1933, the Securities and Exchange Commission declares the registration effective, and members of the underwriting syndicate can begin selling the new issue. After receiving indications of interest from potential investors about a stock offering, the lead underwriter and the issuer must decide on a final public offering price (POP). The goal is to choose a POP that accurately reflects current conditions in the stock market—and that raises the necessary capital needed by the corporation. To do so, the underwriter must assess the issuer's financial strength and competitive prospects, and then gauge the strength of investor demand for securities from such a company.

Sometimes the lead underwriter underestimates demand for the issue and thus sets the share price too low. Perhaps investors are eager to purchase the stock of a well-known company that is going public, or perhaps they are anxious to buy shares in a lesser-known company that appears to possess an exciting new product. These public offerings are called *hot issues*, and they make the work of the underwriter very easy. The sign of a hot issue is that, after quickly *selling out* of the primary market, its shares sell for a higher price in the secondary market.

When an Issue Sells Out of the Primary Market

The answer depends on the kind of commitment made by the underwriters:

After an issue has sold out of the primary market, it begins its life in the secondary market, where it is listed on a stock exchange or in one of the OTC's markets.

The sharp difference between a hot issue's POP in the primary market and its price in the secondary market raises some important questions. First, the issuing company must ask whether it might have gained more capital—or sold fewer shares—by pricing its stock higher. Second, the SEC must ask whether any person or firm associated with the offering is making illegal profits from the price discrepancy. Withholding and freeriding are violations of federal securities laws, defined as follows:

- *Withholding* is an illegal practice in which underwriters hold back shares of a hot issue, thereby enabling themselves to earn unfair profits by later selling the shares at a price above the public offering price.
- In *freeriding*, a firm illegally allocates shares of a hot issue to close associates, who in turn can earn an unfair profit. To prevent this, the SEC forbids underwriters from selling shares of hot issues to:

  Officers and employees of banks, insurance companies, and other financial institutions who might influence security sales

  Any accountants or lawyers involved in the underwriting (and their immediate family members)

  Directors, officers, partners, or employees of syndicate members (and their immediate family members)

  A broker-dealer's own account (called *withholding*)

The SEC can grant exceptions to certain members of these groups, provided that they can demonstrate a history of buying new issues and have not bought a substantial number of the hot issue's shares.

Underwriters Can Avoid the Creation of Hot Issues

Underwriters can avoid the problem of hot issues with hard work. Experienced underwriters perform a thorough "due diligence" on the issuing firm—analyzing its financial situation, investment plan, commercial prospects, and competition. By combining this information with their knowledge of current market conditions, they often can estimate a reasonable price range for the company's securities.

But, anyone can misjudge market demand, even the best of underwriters. Therefore, most underwriting agreements include a *green shoe clause*. If, while taking indication, an underwriter finds surprisingly strong interest in a public offering, it can use the green shoe clause. This allows it to increase the number of shares offered, generally by 10 to 15%. By increasing the supply of the security, the chance of the stock becoming a hot issue is reduced to some extent.

When the Offering Price Is Set Too High

When the public offering price is too high—or demand is too low—the stock can become a *sticky issue*, with several unfortunate consequences:

- The security is difficult to sell at its original price
- The issuer becomes disenchanted with its lead underwriter and syndicate members
- Customers who have already bought the stock might grow angry when they see the price faltering

Sticky issues are identified by their slow sales in the primary market. In the extreme case, a sticky issue fails to sell out of the primary market and thus does not even make it to the secondary market. When a sticky issue does move to the secondary market, its shares are likely to begin trading at a discount.

Sticky Issues Can Be Avoided

The lead underwriter can make a stabilizing bid when it sees an issue becoming sticky. A *stabilizing bid* is the underwriter's offer to buy back shares of the stock at a certain price. Stabilizing bids can be entered only at or below the public offering price, never above. Stabilizing bids cannot exceed an independent bid in the market. They are permitted under the Securities Exchange Act of 1934.

A stabilizing bid effectively places a price floor under the issue. (A "floor" is created because investors wanting to sell their shares do not have to sell them for any price less than the stabilizing bid.) Concerned investors know that, at least for the time being, their maximum potential loss is limited to the difference between the POP and the stabilizing bid.

The stabilizing bid demonstrates the underwriter's commitment to the issuer, thus boosting investors' confidence in the worth of the security. The bid is temporary—it normally concludes after the issue has sold out of the primary market. The goal is to stabilize the stock's price during its initial distribution, after which the forces of supply and demand in the secondary market take over.

Stabilizing Bids Backfire

Yes, the presence of speculative investors can make stabilizing bids dangerous. Suppose that a syndicate member has sold a large number of shares to customers who are looking for quick price increases and easy profits. Realizing that this is not going to occur, such customers might dump their securities on the lead underwriter as soon as it makes its stabilizing bid.

However, the lead underwriter can take steps to prevent this from happening. The firm wants its syndicate to sell the issue only to long-term investors, not to overnight speculators. To encourage its fellow members to pursue this goal, the lead underwriter can include a *penalty bid clause* in the agreement among underwriters. According to this clause, if the lead underwriter finds itself buying back a substantial number of shares that were originally sold by one member, that member will lose its commission on those securities.

Exemptions to the SEC Rules

Some securities are exempt from the registration and prospectus rules of the Security Act of 1933. These include the following:

- U.S. government and U.S. government agency issues.
- State and municipal issues.
- Commercial paper with maturities of 270 days or fewer.
- Nonprofit organization issues.
- Small business investment company (SBIC) issues. (SBICs, which are licensed and funded by the Small Business Administration, provide financial counseling and training, as well as loans, to small businesses owned by minorities, the poor, and the disabled.)

Other securities are exempt from the normal registration requirements because of the way they are offered. These include offerings that fall under the guidelines of private placement, Rule 144, Rule 147, and Regulation A.

Private Placements

When an underwriter privately sells a security issue to wealthy or experienced investors, such as "accredited" investors, along with limiting the number of nonaccredited investors, it is conducting a *private placement*. This is also called a *Regulation D placement* offering (or simply a *Reg D*). This lets the brokerage avoid the registration requirements of the SEC because it is not selling to the general public. Several conditions must be met:

- The issuer must give buyers an "offering memorandum," which includes the financial information normally placed in the prospectus.
- Buyers assure the issuer that they intend to hold the stock as a longer term investment.
- The issuer has to establish that the buyer is an accredited investor.
- Although the issuer can sell the stock to any number of accredited investors, it cannot sell the stock to more than 35 nonaccredited investors. (The latter group might have to enlist a "purchaser representative" in order to buy stock in a Reg D offering.)

Defining Accredited Investors

Accredited investors are:

- Financial institutions such as banks, insurance companies, and investment companies
- Nonprofit organizations with assets of $5 million or more
- Persons with a net worth greater than $1 million—or an annual income exceeding $200,000 for the two preceding years, plus a well-founded belief that this level of income will continue
- Any purchasers of at least $150,000 of the securities offered (provided the amount does not exceed 20% of the purchaser's net worth)
- Directors and officers of the issuing company

Accredited investors often have restricted stock and control stock in their portfolios:

- **Restricted stock**—Securities that have not been registered; usually bought in a private placement.
- **Control stock**—Owned by a "control" person of the issuer, that is, an officer or director of the company, or a person who owns 10% or more of the company's shares.

Private Placement Issues Entering the Public Market

In general, private placements are not available to the general public unless the issuer files a registration for public offering with the SEC. Shares of stock bought in a private placement can only be sold to other investors in private transactions. There is, however, an exception to this rule.

Rule 144 Exemption

If an accredited investor wants to sell restricted stock in the public market, he or she can obtain an exemption under SEC *Rule 144*. The SEC grants the exemption only under stringent conditions:

- The issuer must have other registered shares of the security outstanding
- The seller must file a notice (Form 144) with the SEC prior to the sale
- The seller must have held the stock, fully paid, for at least one year
- The seller can offer restricted shares only once every 90 days, and no sale can exceed the *greater* of the following two quantities:
  - 1% of the company's outstanding shares
  - Average weekly trading volume for the company's shares during the four weeks preceding the filing of the Form 144

For small companies in the OTC marketplace, weekly trading volumes are often unavailable, so the size of the sale is limited to 1% of the issuer's outstanding shares.

Control persons in a corporation often own many shares of the company's stock. Because any attempt by them to sell large blocks of their shares can hurt the security's market price, control stock is subject to Rule 144. However, control persons do not have to meet the one-year ownership condition.

> **EXAMPLE:** A vice-president of Triple Z Garments owns 6% of the company's 10 million outstanding shares (600,000 shares). He wants to sell them all. How long will it take him? If the average weekly trading volume of Triple Z stock remains under 100,000 shares (that is, less than 1% of the company's total shares outstanding), he can sell 100,000 every 90 days. It will take him a year and a half to sell his shares.

Because it allows only for the gradual sale of restricted and control securities, Rule 144 has become known as the *dribble rule*. One purpose of the dribble rule is to prevent accredited investors and insiders (officers, directors, and anyone owning 10% or more of the company's shares) from damaging a stock by selling their private holdings all at once.

Rule 144 permits an exception—Rule 144a—that allows certain investors to sell restricted and control stock more freely, although not to the general public.

Who Uses the Rule 144a Exception

Large institutional investors (with more than $100 million invested in securities) can buy and sell private placement securities under *Rule 144a*. Trading huge blocks of unregistered securities among themselves, these giants in essence create a separate market that is not considered a threat to the prices of publicly offered stocks.

Rule 147

Rule 147 is the *intrastate exemption:* public issues sold only within the borders of a certain state do not come under the purview of federal laws. The most important requirement of Rule 147 is that all the buyers reside in the state. Furthermore, the issuer must also be a state resident. Within the borders of the state, the company must:

- Locate its main office
- Keep at least 80% of its assets
- Earn at least 80% of its revenues
- Invest at least 80% of the issue's proceeds

Regulation A

Regulation A, the *small issue exemption*, permits corporations to make small public offerings—new issues of $5 million or less—each year without fulfilling the SEC's registration rules. Issuers must, however, file a notice with the SEC and provide customers with an "offering circular" for 90 days after the effective date. The offering circular does not provide as much detailed information as the final prospectus does in a regular public offering.

Exam Prep Questions

1. All the following are true about a hot issue except:
   - ❑ A. The issue sells out of the primary market quickly.
   - ❑ B. The issuer will probably gain less from the offering then it might have otherwise.
   - ❑ C. The underwriter has priced the new issue too low.
   - ❑ D. The underwriter can sell shares of the issue out of its own inventory account.

2. When a syndicate member retains shares of a hot issue in its own account, hoping to sell them in several weeks at a higher price, it has engaged in:
   - ❑ A. Withholding
   - ❑ B. Freeriding
   - ❑ C. A fire sale
   - ❑ D. A "market out"

3. All the following statements regarding stabilizing bids are false except:
   - ❑ A. The Securities Act of 1933 explicitly permits stabilizing bids.
   - ❑ B. Stabilizing bids must be entered at the public offering price or below.
   - ❑ C. Stabilizing bids are often used in the secondary market during downturns.
   - ❑ D. Stabilizing bids are a form of price manipulation and are therefore illegal.

4. If speculators purchase shares of a new issue from a syndicate member, but then dump the shares back on the lead underwriter when they fail to make quick profits, the underwriter can invoke which of the following?
   - ❑ A. Penalty bid clause
   - ❑ B. Reg A exemption
   - ❑ C. Green shoe clause
   - ❑ D. Reallowance fee revocation

5. Securities issued by which of the following entities are exempt from the SEC registration requirements under the Securities Act of 1933?

   I. Nonprofit organizations

   II. Cities and counties

   III. Small business investment companies

   IV. U.S. government agencies

   - ❑ A. I
   - ❑ B. I, II, and III
   - ❑ C. I, II, and IV
   - ❑ D. I, II, III, and IV

6. Rebus, Inc., has issued the following types of securities. Which of the following is exempt from SEC registration?
   - ❑ A. Common stock
   - ❑ B. Preferred stock
   - ❑ C. Commercial paper
   - ❑ D. Debenture bonds

7. A public offering in which the underwriter keeps whatever shares remain unsold is called:
   - ❑ A. Best efforts
   - ❑ B. All or none
   - ❑ C. Mini-maxi
   - ❑ D. Firm commitment

8. A tombstone ad has all the following information except:
   - ❑ A. The price of the new security.
   - ❑ B. A list of syndicate members.
   - ❑ C. A list of selling group members.
   - ❑ D. The number of shares offered.

9. After an equity security has sold out of the primary market, it will trade in the secondary market on which of the following?
   - ❑ A. New York Stock Exchange
   - ❑ B. OTC market
   - ❑ C. American Stock Exchange
   - ❑ D. The exchange where the company has been listed

10. The lead underwriter in a public offering earns which of the following for each share sold by the syndicate?
    - ❑ A. Markup
    - ❑ B. Management fee
    - ❑ C. Underwriting spread
    - ❑ D. Commission

11. Who attends the due diligence meeting?

    I. Lead underwriter

    II. Issuer

    III. SEC

    IV. Syndicate members

    - ❑ A. I, II, and IV
    - ❑ B. I and II
    - ❑ C. II and III
    - ❑ D. I and IV

12. Action Securities has agreed to join a Western account syndicate to place a new equity offering. Action has been allotted 1 million shares in the offering. If Action sells 700,000 shares, what happens to the remaining 300,000 shares?

- ❑ A. Action is required to place them in its own account.
- ❑ B. The shares are split evenly among the remaining syndicate members.
- ❑ C. The shares are returned to the lead underwriter.
- ❑ D. The selling group is required to purchase the 300,000 shares.

13. A corporation can register a public offering in other states through all these methods except:

- ❑ A. Registration by coordination
- ❑ B. Registration by administration
- ❑ C. Registration by qualification
- ❑ D. Registration by filing

14. Action Securities has negotiated a management fee of ¼ point, out of a total spread of one point in a public offering of Triple Z stock, with a POP of $10 per share. Syndicate member Ace Securities sells 1 million shares of the offering. What does Ace Securities receive as its takedown fee?

- ❑ A. $1,000,000
- ❑ B. $75,000
- ❑ C. $25,000
- ❑ D. $100,000

15. In the same offering, Action Securities sells two million shares directly to its clients. What fee does it earn on these shares?

- ❑ A. $500,000
- ❑ B. $75,000
- ❑ C. $200,000
- ❑ D. $150,000

Exam Prep Answers

1. The correct answer is D. An underwriter is prohibited under SEC withholding rules from selling hot issue shares out of its own inventory. A hot issue sells out of the primary market quickly, and trades above its public offering price in the secondary market, indicating that the underwriter probably priced the offering too low and that the issuer might have raised more capital or sold more shares.
2. The correct answer is A. The syndicate member is guilty of the illegal practice of withholding if it keeps shares for itself to sell later at a higher price, instead of placing them with investors. Freeriding, in contrast, occurs when an underwriter sells shares of the hot issue to an associate, friend, or family member.
3. The correct answer is B. Stabilizing bids must be entered at the public offering price, or just below it. The Securities Exchange Act of 1934, not the Securities Act of 1933, allows for stabilizing bids. Such bids can be used only by underwriters in the primary market—they are not permitted in the secondary market. Stabilizing bids are the only form of price manipulation that the SEC does allow.
4. The correct answer is A. A lead underwriter who has made a stabilizing bid can invoke the penalty bid clause against a syndicate member whose customers are selling back a substantial number of shares. This indicates that the syndicate member's customers were speculators, interested only in a quick profit. Because the syndicate member loses its takedown fee if the underwriter invokes the penalty bid clause, it has an incentive to place the issue with long-term investors rather than speculators.
5. The correct answer is D. Nonprofit organizations, municipalities, U.S. government agencies, and small business investment companies issue securities that are exempt from the registration requirements of the Securities Act of 1933.
6. The correct answer is C. Corporations that issue commercial paper, a money market instrument with a maturity of less than 270 days, do not have to file a registration statement with the SEC. They must still, however, register their issues of common and preferred stock, as well as their bond offerings.
7. The correct answer is D. In a firm commitment offering, the underwriter will keep whatever shares it has not been able to sell.
8. The correct answer is C. A tombstone ad does not list the selling group members, but does list the syndicate members, the number of shares offered, and the price per share.

9. The correct answer is D. After a security has sold out of the primary market, it is traded on the exchange where the new offering has been listed. This can be any one of the three markets given—the NYSE, the American Stock Exchange, or OTC market.
10. The correct answer is B. The lead underwriter receives a management fee—as part of the underwriting spread—for every share of stock sold in a primary offering. The entire underwriting spread is divided among the syndicate members, any selling group members, plus any outside broker-dealers.
11. The correct answer is A. The issuer and lead underwriter, plus any syndicate members, are required to demonstrate that they have exercised due diligence in complying with the provisions of the 1933 act and relevant state laws—otherwise they risk costly shareholder lawsuits. These parties sit down with their accountants and lawyers in a mandated due diligence meeting to ensure that they have complied with all regulations.
12. The correct answer is A. Because this is a Western account, the 300,000 unsold shares are the responsibility of Action, and so become part of its inventory. A Western account features separate liability for each syndicate member. In an Eastern account, liability is undivided, and any unsold shares are the responsibility of the remaining syndicate members in proportion to their commitment to the entire issue.
13. The correct answer is B. Depending on the state, a corporation can register its public offering by coordination, qualification, or filing.
14. The correct answer is B. Ace has sold 1 million shares for $10 million, and earns a takedown fee equaling the underwriter's spread, minus the management fee. Thus, Ace's takedown fee is $\frac{3}{4}$ of a point, or 0.0075%. That is, Ace will earn $75,000 ($10 million × 0.0075 = $75,000).
15. The correct answer is C. Because Action sold these shares itself, no syndicate member receives a takedown fee, and the firm keeps the entire spread of one point for 2 million shares. Thus, Action earns $200,000 ($20 million × 0.01 = $200,000).

The Secondary Market

Terms You Need to Know

- ✓ American Stock Exchange (Amex)
- ✓ Ask price (or offered price, or asked)
- ✓ Bid price (or bid)
- ✓ Broker-dealer
- ✓ Confirmation
- ✓ Dual listing
- ✓ Equity option
- ✓ First market
- ✓ Form 10-K
- ✓ Fourth market
- ✓ Insider
- ✓ Instinet Inc. commission
- ✓ Margin
- ✓ Margin requirement
- ✓ Mark-up (or mark-down)
- ✓ Market maker
- ✓ National Association of Securities Dealers (NASD)
- ✓ New York Stock Exchange (NYSE)
- ✓ Off-the-floor trading
- ✓ Proxy
- ✓ Quotation
- ✓ Regional exchange
- ✓ Second market
- ✓ Secondary market
- ✓ Selling short
- ✓ Short-sale rule (or uptick rule)
- ✓ Specialist
- ✓ Spread
- ✓ Third market

Concepts You Need to Understand

- ✓ The various markets encompassed by the secondary market
- ✓ How stocks are priced on the exchanges
- ✓ What a regional exchange is
- ✓ Who (besides the SEC) oversees trading in the over-the-counter market
- ✓ What kinds of stocks are listed on NASDAQ
- ✓ When a broker-dealer is an agent, and when it is a principal
- ✓ How a stock is quoted
- ✓ What a spread is and its significance to dealers
- ✓ Major rules and regulations of the Securities Exchange Act of 1934
- ✓ How the definition of insider trading has expanded in recent years

The Markets Within the Secondary Market

In the primary market, corporations raise capital by selling their securities to the clients of underwriters, with proceeds of sales going to the issuing company. In the secondary market, investors trade already-issued securities while trying to earn profits for themselves. The *secondary market* consists of the stock exchanges and the over-the-counter (OTC) market. It includes four arenas for trading: the first, second, third, and fourth markets.

The First Market

The *first market* includes all the stock exchanges, where competing buyers and sellers take part in thousands of daily auctions to trade securities. Individuals wanting to buy stocks bid the highest prices they are willing to pay. Others, hoping to sell, ask (or offer) the lowest price they are willing to accept. The exchanges work like an old town auction lot, whereby buyers and sellers gather together and haggle. A sugar vendor wants the highest *bid price* by any one customer; whereas a savvy sugar buyer shops for the lowest *ask price* (or *offered price*) that day in the market. In principle, the exchanges remain true to their historical marketplace roots.

The New York Stock Exchange Is Known as the "Big Board"

Exchanges list the most current *quotations*—bid and ask prices—for their stocks on a board that can be observed by all traders. A century ago, the board was a chalkboard, today it is an array of electronic display terminals. Because the *New York Stock Exchange (NYSE)* is the largest in the world, and because its board lists almost 3,000 of the largest U.S. corporations, it is commonly referred to as the Big Board. Over 60% of global corporate wealth is represented on the Big Board, and daily trading volumes have exceeded 900 million shares. For a corporation to list its stock on the NYSE, it must meet certain minimum requirements concerning its market value, number of shareholders, and annual earnings. For a securities firm to trade stocks on the floor of the NYSE, it must become a member of the exchange and adhere to its rules.

SOME STOCK HISTORY. In the United States, securities markets originated with the trading of government issues—which generally funded war debts—and bank and insurance company issues. Philadelphia opened the nation's first stock exchange in 1791. The following year, a handful of New York traders and merchants met beneath the branches of a buttonwood tree at 68 Wall Street to sign what came to be known as the Buttonwood Agreement. This accord gave birth to the first formal securities exchange in New York. Signers charged each other a standard commission for negotiating deals, whereas nonmembers were charged a higher commission. Much of their trading took place in Tontine's Coffee House. Not until 1817 did these brokers further organize themselves and create the New York Stock and Exchange Board.

The American Stock Exchange

The *American Stock Exchange*, or *Amex*, is located in New York City on Trinity Place, just a few blocks away from the NYSE. Historically, its traders called their bids and offers on the street curbs outside, hence the American Stock Exchange's nickname, the "Curb." Compared to the mammoths found on the Big Board, the corporations that list their securities on the Amex are, generally speaking, of more modest stature. The Amex has the greatest number of foreign stock listings in the United States and is also noted for its listings of oil and gas companies. The stocks of almost one thousand corporations trade on the Amex, with nearly 30 million shares changing hands daily.

The Regional Exchanges

The *regional exchanges* are located in other areas of the United States, beyond the frontiers of New York City. They tend to focus on companies with a strong presence in their particular geographical area, although many feature *dual listings*—securities that are listed on one of the major exchanges (the NYSE or the Amex) and on one of the regional exchanges. Dual listing widens the market for a security, augmenting the trading competition. About 50% of the Big Board's securities are also listed on one of the regional exchanges. However, a stock cannot be listed on both the NYSE and the Amex. Except for these dual listings, the typical corporation found on regional exchanges is of small or medium size.

The regional exchanges include stock markets located in:

- Philadelphia
- Boston
- Cincinnati
- Chicago
- Salt Lake City (Intermountain Stock Exchange)
- San Francisco and Los Angeles (Pacific Stock Exchange)

The Exchanges Trade More Than Equity Securities

At many exchanges, investors can buy and sell more than equity securities—they can also trade securities such as corporate bonds, government bonds, and options. Options markets are also considered part of the first market.

An *equity option* is a contract giving the right—but not the obligation—to buy or sell a stock at a stated price by a specified date. When investors buy options, they are not buying the underlying security, but the *right* to buy or sell it.

Some options investors think they know the direction the security's price is going to take; if they are correct, their options enable them to make a profit. Other investors use options to protect their investment portfolios from price swings.

The following exchanges trade equity options:

- ➤ American Stock Exchange
- ➤ Pacific Stock Exchange
- ➤ Philadelphia Stock Exchange
- ➤ Chicago Board of Options Exchange (CBOE)

Note that corporate stock options were listed on the NYSE until 1997, at which point the Big Board sold its option and index division to the CBOE.

The Second Market

The *second market* is the OTC market, which is distinguished from the first market by its lack of a physical "floor" for trading and by its method of arriving at securities prices. Rather than using an "open outcry" auction of competitive traders, the OTC market employs one-on-one negotiations between sellers and buyers. Trading in the OTC market is generally negotiated over computer and telephone lines.

Companies that List in the OTC Market

Many very large corporations have chosen to list their securities in the OTC market rather than on one of the major exchanges. These companies believe that certain features of a negotiated marketplace confer trading advantages on their stocks that are unavailable in a traditional auction market. Nonetheless, the average firm in the OTC market is relatively small, because the OTC market is often the easiest way for emerging companies with limited resources to go public.

Organizing OTC Trading

Quotations for many OTC stocks are posted on a computer network called *NASDAQ*, for the *National Association of Securities Dealers Automated Quotation system*. Members of the *National Association of Securities Dealers (NASD)* consult their computer terminals for the latest bid or ask prices on a security, and then they contact the appropriate buyer or seller to negotiate a deal.

THE ORIGINS OF NASD. In 1938 Congress passed the Maloney Act, which amended the Securities Exchange Act of 1934 to provide for the regulation of the over-the-counter market. The industry itself, Congress believed, should be in charge of this regulatory task. The following year, the SEC approved the formation of the first self-regulatory organization (SRO), the National Association of Securities Dealers. Today, all the securities and commodities exchanges, as well as NASD and the Municipal Securities Rulemaking Board, are self-regulatory organizations under federal law.

NASD is charged with establishing and enforcing rules of conduct for its members while overseeing the workings of the OTC market, thereby protecting the public from unfair trading practices. However, the SEC maintains a supervisory role over the NASD, and of course remains the ultimate custodian of the nation's securities laws.

Of the approximately 10,000 companies in the OTC market, about half are quoted on NASDAQ. Companies that do not meet the requirements to be listed on NASDAQ are found either in the *Pink Sheets*, a daily publication of the National Quotation Bureau, or on the *OTC Bulletin Board*, printed by NASD. A large number of the securities listed here are termed "penny stocks," because of their low price (less than $5 per share), which tends to reflect the small size of the issuer.

Equity Securities Are Not the Only Products Traded in the OTC Market

No, investors can also trade corporate bonds, foreign currencies, U.S. government bonds, and municipal bonds over the counter. Indeed, the OTC market witnesses more bond transactions than do any of the exchanges.

The Third Market

The *third market* is effectively a marriage between the first and second: the trading of exchange-listed securities by OTC firms. In the third market, an investor can purchase or sell a security listed on an exchange without being constrained by the exchange's normal trading procedures. Most stocks traded in the third market are listed on the NYSE, and are traded outside of the Big Board's business hours.

Stock exchanges have limited trading hours, which did not become a serious concern for investors until the 1980s, when financial markets became truly global. The Big Board is open to investors between 9:30 a.m. and 4:00 p.m., Eastern Standard Time. Members of the NYSE are prohibited from bidding or offering outside of those hours. Suppose an investor in Tokyo wakes up one morning and decides to purchase 100 shares of a NYSE-listed stock—immediately. Although the Big Board has closed for the day, the Tokyo investor can contact an OTC firm that remains open for business 24 hours a day and keeps an inventory of NYSE stocks. Because this OTC firm is a member of the NASD, but not of the NYSE, it does not have to abide by NYSE rules. The Japanese investor negotiates a price, buys the security from the OTC firm's accounts, and everyone is satisfied.

This is an example of *off-the-floor trading*, in which investors buy and sell exchange-listed securities away from the exchange "floor." The only way to accomplish this is through an OTC firm, because NYSE members must perform their trades on the floor, during business hours. Off-the-floor trading keeps the market for NYSE stocks open throughout the day.

The Fourth Market

Large institutional investors, such as pension funds, mutual funds, and endowment funds, make up the buyers and sellers in the *fourth market*, where exchange-listed stocks are traded in huge blocks. Before 1975, the NYSE imposed fixed commission rates on all trades, regardless of size. This system made the big trades of institutional investors expensive, so they developed a computerized trading network called *Instinet (Institutional Networks Corporation)* to enable them to deal directly among themselves, avoiding costly intermediaries. Although fixed commissions were eliminated by federal law in 1975, enabling brokers to offer discounts on large trades, Instinet has managed to maintain a portion of the securities business of mutual funds and other institutional investors. About 35 million shares change hands each day over Instinet.

Broker, Agent, or Dealer

A securities firm acts as a broker when it buys or sells securities for its customers. The securities in the transaction never belong to the brokerage firm, which charges the customer a *commission*. The broker assumes the role of an agent, carrying out the needs of its clients. This is stated on the confirmations for these transactions. A *confirmation* is a document sent by a broker-dealer to its client, describing a securities transaction.

EXAMPLE: Mr. Brown calls his broker, Mercury Securities, and places an order to buy 100 shares of Triple Z stock, now listed on the American Stock Exchange. Mercury instructs its representative at the Amex to make the purchase, which he or she does, at $20 per share. Because Mercury charges a 2% commission on such brokerage business, it sends Mr. Brown a confirmation stating the details of the trade, including the date, time, name of the stock, price, commission, and the total cost of $2,040.

When a Securities Firm Is a Dealer

Whenever a securities firm buys stocks for—or sells stocks from—its own account, it is acting as a dealer. Here, the firm assumes the role of a principal, taking on risk and following its own profit-seeking strategy. As a dealer, it charges its customers a *mark-up* (or *mark-down*) on the market price for each security it sells (or buys).

EXAMPLE: Ms. Orange wants to buy 200 shares of Sunburst Juice, Inc. She calls her broker at Mercury Securities and places the order. Mercury carries several thousand shares of Sunburst in its trading account whose current market price is $15 per share. If Mercury charges a mark-up of 25 cents per share, how much is Ms. Orange's bill? Her bill totals $3,050.

Most securities firms do business both as agents and as principals, so they are known as *broker-dealers*.

A Stock's Spread

A securities' *spread* is the difference between its lowest asked and highest bid prices.

EXAMPLE: Sunburst juice is listed on the Amex. Today at 10:15 A.M. the stock quotes at bid 20.12, asked 20.37. The spread is 25 cents on this security. Suppose a new buyer enters the market, assesses the latest quotation, and decides to pay the ask price of 20.37. The spread has been "jumped," in an upward direction. If a second buyer follows in the footsteps of the first, and then a third and a fourth, a trend might be set. Would-be purchasers might find themselves raising their bid prices, whereas would-be sellers are discovering that they can increase their ask prices. The price of Sunburst stock inches upward.

Usually, the more heavily traded a stock is, the narrower its spread tends to be. The existence of more competitors in the marketplace forces buyers to raise their bids, and sellers to lower their offers, thus shrinking the spread. Conversely, wider spreads tend to characterize stocks that are "thinly" traded.

The bid is the highest price a buyer is willing to pay for a stock, whereas the ask is the lowest price a seller is willing to accept for a stock.

How the Spread Is Determined in a Negotiated Market

In the OTC market, where prices are decided by negotiation, not auction, dealers name their own spread. With inventories of securities on hand, OTC dealers quote both bid and ask prices to create a spread. In this case, the spread provides the dealer with its gross profit margin.

> **EXAMPLE:** Apollo & Co. quotes a bid price of $13 and an ask price of $13.25 ("13 bid, .25," in market jargon) for Moonburst juice shares that it holds in inventory. In other words, Apollo is willing to buy shares of Moonburst for $13 and to sell them for $13.25, making a .25 point spread. Every time Apollo completes a "round turn," that is, buys and sells 100 shares of Moonburst, it makes a profit of $25.

An OTC dealer that is always prepared to buy or sell a certain company's stock is called a *market maker*. The market maker's role is to ensure that customers always have a place to trade their securities, thereby maintaining public confidence in the market. In the floor exchanges, the position of market maker is assumed by securities firms that deal only with other traders, not with the public. They are called *specialists*.

What the SEC Will and Will Not Permit

Less than a year after passing the Securities Act of 1933, Congress passed the Securities Exchange Act of 1934. Their goal was to restore public confidence in the stock market by eliminating practices that had made the exchanges susceptible to manipulation, corruption, and eventual collapse. You can recall the crucial provisions of the 1934 Act using the mnemonic device "MISS PERMS":

M—Manipulation of stock prices is prohibited

I—Insiders are defined and regulated

S—Short sales of securities are regulated

S—SEC is established

P—Proxy rules are set

E—Exchanges and exchange members must register with the SEC

R—Reports (quarterly and annual) must be filed by issuers

M—Margin requirements are established by the Federal Reserve Board

S—Stabilizing bids are allowed for new issues

All Securities Are Covered by the Act of 1934

Securities of issuers that are exempt from the Securities Act of 1934—the U.S. government, U.S. government agencies, states, municipalities, non-profit organizations, and small business investment companies—avoid most of the act's regulations. For example, the "short-sale rule" does not apply to municipal issues, nor do states have to file annual and quarterly reports with the SEC.

One provision of the act that *does* pertain to all securities in the secondary market is the prohibition on price manipulation. Any attempt to manipulate stock prices (with the exception of stabilizing bids) is considered to be fraud and triggers SEC investigation and prosecution.

Manipulations Prohibited by the Act

Manipulations prohibited by the act include:

- **Trading pools**—Working together, several investors artificially sell a stock back and forth among themselves, raising the price.
- **Wash trading**—The purchase and sale of the same stock by one dealer within 30 days.
- **Matched orders**—Two or more people place offsetting buy and sell orders on a security to create the appearance of trading activity. This attracts other investors, thereby raising the price.
- **Early trading by underwriters**—The underwriter of a public offering attempts to affect the course of the initial distribution by simultaneously soliciting orders in the secondary market.

- **False rumors and tips, omission of facts**—A broker-dealer sends correspondence to customers that deliberately contains untrue or misleading statements about a corporation—or that deliberately omits important facts—inducing investors to buy or sell stock in the company.

To discourage unscrupulous individuals from trying to get around the restrictions on these activities by creating entirely new schemes, the act includes a catch-all provision, Rule 10b-5, which simply forbids all fraud, whether specified in other sections or not.

Insiders Defined

Section 16 of the act defines an *insider* as:

- A director or officer of a corporation
- A shareholder with 10% or more of a corporation's stock

Insiders are prohibited from:

- Trading on the basis of "material, nonpublic information" (information about the company that is pertinent to stock prices and is not yet available to the public).
- Earning short-term profits on the stock of their corporation; that is, selling securities at a profit after owning them for fewer than six months (or, in the case of securities that *have* been held for longer than six months, selling and then rebuying them within a six-month period).
- Selling short the stock of their own company. This can indicate that the person possesses—and is acting upon—inside information concerning the company's future.

The Short-Sale Rule

Also known as the *uptick rule*, the *short-sale rule* states that short sales can be executed only on an exchange floor when the price of the security in question has risen, or not moved after a past increase. *Selling short* is the sale of *borrowed* securities in the belief that their market value will drop, at which point the borrowed securities can be replaced for less money, thus earning the investor a profit. When selling short, investors never actually own the stock. Instead, they borrow it from the account of a broker-dealer. They receive the current market price for the sale, but owe the dealer the number of shares that they have sold. If the stock's price declines, they can "cover" their short position at a profit; that is, buy the shares they need to repay their broker-dealer for less money than they sold them for. If, on the other hand, the stock's price increases, they will suffer a loss, being forced to spend extra money to replace the borrowed shares.

EXAMPLE: Sam sells 500 shares of Triple Z short, at $20 per share. He receives $10,000, but at some point he must cover his short position—replace the 500 shares of Triple Z stock that he borrowed from his broker-dealer, Mercury Securities. Sam's hunch pays off, and Triple Z stock begins to decline; two days later he purchases 500 shares at $18 per share. He repays Mercury the shares he borrowed and pockets a profit of $1,000 (less interest on the loan of the shares).

Why Congress Was Worried about Short Sales in 1934

Selling short had proven to be an effective tool for wealthy investors to make big profits from artificial price movements. J. P. Morgan's "bear raids" were famous. The technique was simple for anyone with vast financial reserves: sell a company's stock short—again and again and again—forcing its price to plummet. When the raider had driven all buyers out of the market, he can cover his short position at a fraction of what the stock cost originally.

The 1934 act permits short sales only after a stock's price has risen, an "uptick" on the exchange's price board, or has stayed the same after a past rise, a "zero plus uptick."

EXAMPLE: The most recent transactions for Triple Z stock are 20.37... 20.25... 20... 20... 19.875. Can Sam sell Triple Z short? No, because the price movements are downticks or zero downticks.

Sunburst Juice has traded at the following prices: 16.12... 16... 15.75... 15.87... 15.87. Can Sam now sell the stock short? Yes, he can, because the last trade was a zero uptick. He also could have sold Sunburst short after the preceding trade (the first at 15.87), as it constituted an uptick.

The short-sale rule effectively ended the practice of hammering a corporation's stock downward, one of the most notorious forms of manipulation prior to the establishment of the SEC.

The Securities and Exchange Commission

Section 4 of the Securities Exchange Act of 1934 officially establishes the SEC as the overseer of the nation's securities markets.

Rules for Proxies

Recall that shareholders of a corporation have a right to vote for the board of directors and certain other corporate matters. If a shareholder cannot attend the annual shareholders' meeting, he or she can vote through a *proxy*, a written power of attorney authorizing a specific vote; informed voting depends on the nature and veracity of the material supplied by the company with its proxy solicitations. The Act of 1934 specifies the kind of information that proxy solicitations must contain, ensuring that shareholders get the facts needed to make well-founded decisions. Furthermore, the 1934 Act requires that corporations file proxy solicitations with the SEC before mailing them to shareholders.

Securities that are exempt from (many of) the provisions of the Securities Act of 1933 and the Securities Exchange Act of 1934 include those issued by the U.S. government, U.S. government agencies, states, municipalities, nonprofit organizations, and small business investment companies. Nonexempt securities, then, include almost all corporate issues. Some commercial paper does fall outside of the SEC's domain.

Who Registers with the SEC

- All exchanges that trade in nonexempt securities (for example, the Philadelphia Stock Exchange)
- Other marketplaces for nonexempt securities (for example, NASDAQ and Instinet)
- Member firms and their sales staff
- Broker-dealers who conduct interstate business

The Act of 1934 requires that, after registering with the SEC, an exchange regulate *itself* in accordance with federal securities laws. The act also imposes several rules on the business practices of exchange members. For instance, member firms must maintain a minimum level of net capital and provide customers with a balance sheet and net capital calculation every six months.

Reports Issuers Must File

The Act of 1934 requires that issuing corporations file certain reports with the SEC. The most important of these is the *Form 10-K*, which is a comprehensive report of the company's financial situation, including total sales, revenue, and operating income. It is prepared by a certified public accountant and filed annually with the SEC, at which time the document becomes public information. Form 10-K, and other required reports, force companies to provide shareholders and potential investors with reliable statements about the companies' financial health.

Margin Requirement

Margin is the portion of total purchase price that a customer deposits when buying securities from a broker-dealer. A *margin requirement* is thus the minimum that customers must put up to acquire securities on credit.

Before the market crash of 1929, customers purchased new issues with just 10% margin and bought stocks in the secondary market with 10 to 20% margin. As long as the economy remained sound and public confidence in the stock market was strong, such low margin requirements were advantageous to investors—with very little cash up front, a person could enter the market and make large profits. However, during periods of economic weakness or public uncertainty, low margin requirements might sharpen a market decline.

The Act of 1934 regulates three aspects of margin:

- *Regulation T.* This provision assigns the duty of setting margin requirements to the Federal Reserve Board (the governing body of the U.S. monetary and banking system). Today, for nonexempt securities, broker-dealers are permitted to extend credit equal to 50% of a customer's purchase. Note that a stock exchange can establish a stricter margin requirement than that allowed by the Fed.
- *Regulation U.* This provision gives the Federal Reserve Board the power to control the amount of credit that they can extend to broker-dealers in order to support their customers' margin loans.
- *New issues.* The act prohibits credit for the purchase of (nonexempt) new issues; that is, the margin requirement is set at 100%.

Stabilization

The SEC allows only one form of price manipulation: To protect new issues from speculative attacks, the managing underwriter of a public offering can place a stabilizing bid during the security's initial distribution in the market. Such stabilizing bids can never be entered above the public offering price.

Do the Acts of 1933 and 1934 Constitute the Country's Securities Law?

Over the years, both congressional action and judicial decision have served to expand and amend various sections of U.S. securities law. The Insider Trading and Securities Fraud Enforcement Act of 1988 made the definition of insider trading more general in order to enable the SEC to prosecute unforeseen forms of the crime. Now, *anyone* who sells or buys securities and is privy to "material, nonpublic information" about the issuing corporation is considered an insider (and is subject to penalties of up to three times the amount of his or her ill-gotten gains). To help prevent further occurrences of insider trading, the 1988 Act requires that investment banking firms develop procedures that will stop their merger and acquisition departments from disseminating insider information to their trading departments, a process known as "building a Chinese wall."

Exam Prep Questions

1. The American Stock Exchange is noted for trading which of the following securities?

   I. Oil and gas company stocks

   II. Foreign company stocks

   III. Options

   IV. Dual-listed NYSE stocks

   ❑ A. I and III
   ❑ B. I, II, and III
   ❑ C. I, III, and IV
   ❑ D. IV

2. Which of the following constitutes a dual listing for an equity security?

   ❑ A. A stock listed on the NYSE and the Amex
   ❑ B. A stock listed on the NYSE and the OTC market
   ❑ C. A stock listed on the NYSE and the Pacific exchange
   ❑ D. All of the above

3. The second market of the secondary market consists of which of the following?

   I. NYSE

   II. Amex

   III. OTC market

   IV. Regional exchanges

   ❑ A. II
   ❑ B. III
   ❑ C. III and IV
   ❑ D. II and III

4. The over-the-counter market is:

   ❑ A. A negotiated market
   ❑ B. An auction market
   ❑ C. A specialist market
   ❑ D. A regional market

5. When the Big Board is closed, NYSE-listed securities can be traded in the:

   ❑ A. First market
   ❑ B. Second market
   ❑ C. Third market
   ❑ D. Fourth market

6. The NASD operates under the supervision of which entity?
   - ❑ A. NYSE
   - ❑ B. SEC
   - ❑ C. Federal Reserve Board
   - ❑ D. U.S. Treasury Department

7. When acting as an agent, what does a broker-dealer charge customers for executing orders?
   - ❑ A. Commissions
   - ❑ B. Mark-ups and mark-downs
   - ❑ C. Takedowns
   - ❑ D. Underwriting fees

Use the following ticker of NYSE trading to answer the next two questions:

…VRX 25… ZYX 54… ZYX 54.12… VRX 24.88… WCI 33.13… VRX 24.25… WCI 33… ZYX 54.19… VRX 24… VRX 24.63 .SLD… WCI 33.19… VRX 24… ZYX 54.25… WCI 33.25… WCI 33.06 1⁄16 .SLD… WCI 33.38… WCI 33.63… ZYX 54.25… VRX 24.38… ZYX 54.19…

8. Lee Gordon tells his broker to sell short 100 shares of World Cable (WCI) at the market price. After which transaction can Gordon's broker execute the short sale?
   - ❑ A. ZYX 54 .12
   - ❑ B. VRX 24 .63 .SLD
   - ❑ C. WCI 33 .19
   - ❑ D. WCI 33 .06 .SLD

9. Alix Ignatoff has placed an order to sell short 500 shares of Virex, Inc. (VRX), at the market with her broker. Which transaction might trigger the short sale in her margin account?
   - ❑ A. WCI 33 .19
   - ❑ B. ZYX 54 .12
   - ❑ C. VRX 24 .63 .SLD
   - ❑ D. VRX 24 .38

10. When an OTC securities firm acts as a dealer, it charges its customers a:
    - ❑ A. Commission
    - ❑ B. Mark-up or mark-down
    - ❑ C. Takedown fee
    - ❑ D. Spread

11. A trader wants to buy a NASDAQ NMS stock. The highest price she is willing to pay is known as her what?
    - ❑ A. Bid
    - ❑ B. Ask
    - ❑ C. Spread
    - ❑ D. Markup

12. The Securities Exchange Act of 1934 makes trading pools illegal. What constitutes a trading pool?
    - ❑ A. The purchase of shares of a certain security by a pool of investors, with any subsequent trading only on approval by all members.
    - ❑ B. The pooling of capital by a group of investors in order to eliminate brokerage fees.
    - ❑ C. The trading of a stock among a group of institutional investors, away from market influences.
    - ❑ D. The frequent trading of a certain stock among a pool of investors to falsely indicate market interest and give it upward price momentum.

13. The Securities Exchange Act of 1934 provides for all the following except:
    - ❑ A. Registration of nonexempt securities
    - ❑ B. Prohibition on stock price manipulation
    - ❑ C. Registration of exchanges and their member firms with the SEC
    - ❑ D. Regulation of margin accounts

14. Regarding shareholder voting and proxy rights, the Securities Exchange Act of 1934 provides that:
    - ❑ A. A shareholder not attending a shareholder meeting is allowed to vote on corporate matters via proxy.
    - ❑ B. A corporation is obligated to collect all proxies sent to shareholders.
    - ❑ C. All issuers of nonexempt securities must publish a shareholders' report on a quarterly basis about upcoming proxy matters.
    - ❑ D. Any shareholder who does not return a proxy can be denied future voting rights.

15. The Securities Exchange Act of 1934 empowered which entity to regulate margin requirements?
    - ❑ A. New York Stock Exchange
    - ❑ B. National Association of Securities Dealers
    - ❑ C. Federal Reserve Board
    - ❑ D. Securities and Exchange Commission

16. All the following statements concerning the Insider Trading and Securities Fraud Enforcement Act of 1988 are true except:
    - ❑ A. The act defines insiders as officers, directors, and 10% shareholders.
    - ❑ B. The act institutes treble damages on illegal trading gains.
    - ❑ C. The act allows shareholders to sue someone convicted of insider trading.
    - ❑ D. The act does not precisely define what constitutes insider trading.

Exam Prep Answers

1. The correct answer is B. Options are traded on the Amex, but the exchange is most noted for its listings of oil and gas companies and foreign company stocks. A dual-listed stock cannot trade on both the NYSE and Amex, but rather on a major and a regional exchange.

2. The correct answer is C. Dual-listed securities are traded on a major exchange, such as the NYSE, and on one of the regional exchanges. A stock cannot be dually listed on two major exchanges.

3. The correct answer is B. The various OTC marketplaces form the second market. The NYSE, Amex, and the regional exchanges are all part of the first market.

4. The correct answer is A. The OTC market is a national negotiated market, using a market-maker system. The NYSE and Amex are both auction markets that rely on specialists to ensure trading liquidity.

5. The correct answer is C. The third market consists of off-the-floor trading of exchange-listed stocks. Only OTC firms can conduct third-market trading, because NYSE member firms cannot trade outside of the exchange's regular business hours, according to exchange rules.

6. The correct answer is B. Although it's an independent organization, the NASD remains under the jurisdiction of the Securities and Exchange Commission.

7. The correct answer is A. A broker-dealer acting as an agent for its customers charges a commission on the execution of each trade. When acting as a dealer, the brokerage adds a mark-up to the price of a security it sells from its inventory or charges a mark-down on the price of a security it buys for its inventory.

8. The correct answer is C. A short sale can be executed only on an uptick or a zero uptick; the trade WCI 33.19. is the first such upward price movement in the World Cable stock. The entry WCI 33.06 .SLD denotes a trade reported out of time sequence; such a trade cannot trigger a short sale. The transactions WCI 33.25, WCI 33.38, and WCI 33.63 all reflect further upticks in World Cable stock.

9. The correct answer is D. The trade VRX 24.38 is the first reported uptick in Virex's stock price. Note that the trade VRX 24.63. SLD has been reported out of sequence, so it cannot be an uptick.

10. The correct answer is B. When acting as a dealer, an OTC brokerage adds a mark-up to the price of a security it sells from its inventory, or charges a mark-down on a security it buys from a customer. When acting as a broker, the firm charges a commission on its transactions (obtaining or placing customer securities with other brokerages).

11. The correct answer is A. The highest price a trader is willing to pay for a security is called his or her bid. A trader wanting to sell a security gives an offer price, or ask price, or simply ask. The difference between the highest bid and the lowest ask is the spread.

12. The correct answer is D. A trading pool is a form of stock manipulation in which a group of brokers trade a stock among themselves to create artificial volume and price movement. The aim is to draw in outside investors. When enough outside investors have bought in—and the stock's price has climbed sufficiently—the pool members sell out.

13. The correct answer is A. The Securities Act of 1933, not the Act of 1934, requires issuers to register nonexempt securities with the SEC.

14. The correct answer is A. A shareholder who does not attend a shareholder meeting can still vote on corporate matters via proxy. Issuers must send proxy solicitations to all shareholders of record for matters needing shareholder approval, but it is up to individual shareholders to respond.

15. The correct answer is C. The 1934 Act gives authority concerning margin regulations to the Federal Reserve Board.

16. The correct answer is A. The Act of 1988 expands the definition of "insider" from the previous "officers, directors, and 10 percent shareholders" to include anyone who has material, nonpublic information about a corporation. The SEC prefers to leave the definition of insider trading unspecified in order to discourage individuals from seeking legal loopholes.

PART II

Corporate Equity and Debt Securities

Equity in the Secondary Market: Common and Preferred Stock

Terms You Need to Know

- ✓ Adjustable preferred
- ✓ American depositary receipts (ADRs)
- ✓ Book-entry method
- ✓ Class
- ✓ Common stock
- ✓ Conversion parity
- ✓ Conversion ratio
- ✓ Convertible preferred
- ✓ Cum dividend
- ✓ Cum rights
- ✓ Cumulative preferred
- ✓ Cumulative voting
- ✓ Dividend
- ✓ Ex date
- ✓ Ex dividend
- ✓ Ex rights
- ✓ Market value
- ✓ Par value
- ✓ Participating preferred
- ✓ Preemptive right
- ✓ Preferred stock
- ✓ Proxy
- ✓ Record date
- ✓ Registrar
- ✓ Regular-way settlement (T+3)
- ✓ Reverse split
- ✓ Rights offering
- ✓ Shareholder of record
- ✓ Shareholder rights
- ✓ Standby commitment
- ✓ Statutory voting
- ✓ Stock split (or forward split)
- ✓ Street name
- ✓ Subscription price
- ✓ Transfer agent
- ✓ Voting trust certificates (VTCs)
- ✓ Warrant (or subscription warrant)

Concepts You Need to Understand

- ✓ Classes and kinds of common stock
- ✓ How foreign stocks are traded in the United States
- ✓ Basic rights
- ✓ When and how shareholders can vote
- ✓ Preemptive right and rights offerings
- ✓ Rules that govern the distribution of dividends
- ✓ Important dates for dividend calculations
- ✓ How stock prices are affected by the declaration of dividends
- ✓ Rights of preferred shareholders
- ✓ The relationship between interest rates and preferred stock prices
- ✓ How some preferred stock can be converted into common stock
- ✓ The purpose of subscription warrants

The Fundamentals of Common Stock

The secondary market is the scene of most securities trading. Many kinds of securities trade there, from corporate bonds, government bonds, and municipal bonds, to options and more recent financial inventions such as derivatives. Equities are the most common way for corporations to raise capital. This chapter looks at the features of common and preferred equity stock—including the rights of shareholders, the process of declaring dividends, what distinguishes subscription rights from subscription warrants, and the characteristics of convertible preferred stock.

Common stock gives shareholders an equity, or ownership position in a corporation. One of the chief characteristics of common stock is that it pays a variable dividend—or none at all—depending on the decision of the company's board of directors. A *dividend* is a periodic payment (either in cash or stock) made by the company to owners of its common or preferred stock. The corporate charter authorizes that a certain number of common shares be issued and assigns them an arbitrary *par value*. For common stock, par value is usually very low, often only one dollar. The par value of preferred stock, on the other hand, is very important.

Why So Cheap? The par value of common stock is not low for purely arbitrary reasons. States often tax corporations based on the par value of their common stock.

The *market value* of common stock is determined wherever the stock is traded. Market prices reflect investors' knowledge and beliefs about a whole range of factors, including the company's present and future profitability, the likelihood of dividend payments, the health of the industry, and even the growth prospects for the entire economy.

Types of Common Stock

In some instances a corporation might choose to issue various classes of stock to help a select group of shareholders maintain control of the company. A family-owned business that is going public, for example, might issue class A common stock to family members and class B to the public. This classification method has fallen out of favor in recent years, and Congress has reviewed proposals to prohibit it altogether. The NYSE rarely lists companies employing this kind of two-tier structure, although the American Stock Exchange continues to do so. The differences between class A and class B stock can be found in their respective prospectuses.

Categories of Common Stock

Investors and broker-dealers distinguish stocks according to their historical performance in the marketplace and the issuing company's track record. A few of the more frequent labels are:

- **Blue chip**—Stock of a big, well-known company with a long history of profits and regular dividend payments. Coca-Cola and Ford Motor Company belong to this group.
- **Income**—Stock of companies that have good records of paying relatively high and stable dividends. Telephone companies, electric utilities, and banks are often considered income stocks.
- **Growth**—Stock of a company that is expanding rapidly by investing in its own growth with profits that otherwise might have become dividend payments. In the 1980s and 1990s, the technology sector featured many growth stocks.

Investors in the secondary market have several kinds of common stock to choose from. In addition, they might want to consider purchasing shares in overseas companies. The easiest way to accomplish this is through American depositary receipts.

American Depositary Receipts

American depositary receipts (ADRs) are certificates representing shares of foreign companies. ADRs are traded in U.S. markets, whereas the actual securities remain in the vault of a U.S. bank branch in the company's home country. Holders of ADRs enjoy all the rights of common stock owners except for voting and preemptive rights. For the foreign firm, ADRs present an opportunity to tap into the vast U.S. capital market while avoiding the time and expense of registering with the SEC. Instead, the U.S. bank that is holding the securities (in its overseas branch) handles all SEC compliance.

How Dividends Are Paid to the Owners of ADRs

The foreign corporation pays dividends to the U.S. bank that is holding its securities. The bank then converts the dividends into dollars and pays the owners of the ADRs in the United States.

Where are ADRs traded? Sponsored ADRs are bought and sold on one of the major exchanges (AMEX or the NYSE), whereas nonsponsored ADRs can be found on the OTC market. In the case of a sponsored ADR, the issuing company works with one U.S. depositary bank and sends its American shareholders annual financial reports in English. The issuing companies of nonsponsored ADRs, on the other hand, play no direct role in the receipts' creation. Nonsponsored ADRs are packaged and sold by banks or broker-dealers on their own initiative. Because the company does not participate, nonsponsored ADRs can have more than one depositary bank.

All shareholders, whether of ADRs or domestic stocks, have certain rights. Generally, these rights consist of sharing in the growth and profitability of the company, and having a voice in how the company is managed.

Common Shareholder Rights

Although the specific rights and privileges of common stock shareholders can vary with each corporation's charter or bylaws, they all have the right to:

- Receive dividends (when the company declares them)
- Receive a certificate of stock ownership
- Transfer their securities (sell their stock)
- Inspect the company's financial records, plus the minutes of shareholder meetings
- Vote—either in person or by proxy—on certain corporate matters
- Maintain their proportionate share of the company's outstanding stock (known as the preemptive right)
- Partake in the division of company assets if the company is liquidated

Who decides when shareholders receive a dividend? The board of directors determines whether a dividend will be declared and, if so, how large it is.

When companies decide to declare dividends, they usually make payments quarterly.

The Process of Paying Dividends

Dividends can be paid in cash or stock. Companies might issue stock dividends in order to conserve cash for expansion or other purposes. For the shareholder, the advantage of stock dividends is that, unlike cash dividends, taxes are not owed until the shares are sold. Stock dividends are usually stated as a percentage of outstanding shares, and the price of the common stock is reduced accordingly.

> **EXAMPLE:** An investor owns 100 shares of Triple Platinum Records, Inc., which are trading at $50. The company declares a 10% stock dividend. After the distribution, the shareholder now has 110 shares, each worth $45.50. (There are now 10% more shares of stock outstanding, or 1.1 times as many as before the stock dividend. Fifty dollars divided by 1.1 equals $45.45.)

The Right of Transfer

Common stock is a negotiable security: owners can sell their shares to anyone. Among other things, this means that corporations face a challenge keeping track of their shareholders. Usually they hire an outside firm to act as a *transfer agent*, which maintains records of all shareholder names and addresses. A *registrar*, also an outside firm, makes sure that the corporation does not issue more shares than its charter authorizes. Shareholders can give their brokers permission to keep their stocks in *street name*—the name of the broker. This simplifies the transfer process after stock sales.

Shareholders have a right to receive stock certificates as evidence of ownership. Some corporations, however, use the *book-entry method*, whereby the registrar records purchases and sales, but no certificates change hands.

Shareholders of a corporation have the right to review company records. In practice, this means that they can read the company's annual reports, known as Form 10-Ks, as well as its quarterly reports (Form 10-Qs), both of which must be filed with the SEC. The SEC views the filing of annual reports as a fundamental requirement of publicly traded companies. A company that fails to file a 10-K not only compromises its reputation with investors, but also triggers an SEC investigation and risks being delisted by the exchange on which it trades.

Shareholders Influence on Company Decisions

Holders of common stock have the right to vote on many of the matters that affect their ownership interest. These include:

- Membership on the board of directors
- Stock splits and reverse stock splits
- The issuing of convertible securities (securities that can be converted into common stock)

Shareholders do not vote on whether a corporation:

- Declares a dividend
- Declares a rights offering

If shareholders cannot be present when matters affecting their ownership interest are to be decided—usually at the company's annual meeting—they have the right to vote by *proxy*. On such issues, the corporation is required to send ballots (proxies) to its shareholders. Shareholders mark their choices and return them to the corporation, where their votes are counted.

The Voting Process

Shareholder voting can be conducted on either a *statutory* or *cumulative* basis. In broad terms, the two methods are similar: shareholders get one vote per share, times the number of items on the ballot. If three board positions are to be filled, for example, a person with 100 shares has 300 votes. The difference between statutory and cumulative voting comes into play in cases such as these, where there are multiple choices for a single ballot item. Under statutory voting, shareholders cast votes equal to the number of shares they own for *each* open position on the board. The 100-share owner can vote 100 times for each of the three openings. Cumulative voting allows the shareholder to *distribute* his or her votes among the choices. Thus, the stock owner can place 150 votes for one candidate, 150 for a second, and none for the third.

EXAMPLE: An investor owns 100 shares of Satellite Technologies, which is electing six directors. The company uses statutory voting. The investor has 600 total votes (100 shares × 6 directors), but cannot cast more than 100 votes for any one candidate.

BioGen Corp, which employs cumulative voting, is also electing six directors. An investor who owns 100 shares of BioGen has 600 votes (the same as the Satellite Technologies investor), but can apportion them as he or she sees fit, even giving them all to one director.

Cumulative voting is advantageous to smaller shareholders, enabling them to amass their votes on a single candidate or policy option. Perhaps that is why statutory voting remains much more common.

In addition to electing members of the board of directors, shareholders are often asked to approve splits of the company's stock.

The Stock Split

A *stock split* multiplies the number of a company's outstanding shares by whatever ratio the company chooses. The market price of the stock drops accordingly. So, if a company's stock were selling at $30 per share, and it carried out a 3:1 split, there becomes three times as many shares outstanding after the split, each priced at $10. Companies use stock splits to make their shares more affordable to investors.

EXAMPLE: WorldScape stock is selling at $110 a share. The company wants to attract new investors and declares a 2:1 split. The number of outstanding shares doubles and the price per share drops by half. An investor with 1,000 shares now owns 2,000, each priced at $55. If WorldScape had declared a 4:1 split, the same investor would have 4,000 shares, each priced at $27.50. Note, however, that the *total* market value of the investor's shares remains the same in either scenario: $110,000.

Par value is the value arbitrarily assigned to common stock by the corporation. *Market* value is the price investors are currently willing to pay for the stock.

Although ownership interest is not affected by splits, shareholder approval is required. Why? Because stock splits change the par value of a company's stock. They might also increase the number of outstanding shares beyond the amount currently authorized in the corporate charter. Either of these changes requires an amendment of the charter and thus stockholder approval.

Different Kinds of Stock Splits

Stock splits are sometimes called *forward splits* to distinguish them from reverse splits. A *reverse split* increases the price of each share, while reducing the number of shares in circulation. Companies generally use reverse splits when they think their share price is too low to inspire investor confidence. By declaring a reverse split, companies can elevate the market price of their shares, creating an impression of higher value.

> **EXAMPLE:** Test Right Corp. has nine million outstanding shares selling at $10 a share. Trading has been slack, so the company declares a 1:3 reverse split. Now the company has only three million shares outstanding, each selling at $30. An investor who owned 90 shares of the original stock now has only 30 shares, but the total value of his shares is unchanged: $900.

Not everything that changes the number of a company's outstanding shares requires stockholder approval. A company can issue *new* shares without such approval because shareholders are protected by their preemptive right, which they can exercise through a rights offering.

Rights Offering

A *rights offering* gives stockholders the opportunity to purchase new shares of a corporation before those shares are made available to the public. Shareholders' *preemptive right*, the privilege of existing shareholders to maintain their proportionate ownership in the company, is triggered whenever a company issues new stock through a rights offering.

In a rights offering, shareholders can purchase new shares at a price less than the current market price. This lower price is known as the *subscription price*. Shareholders usually receive one right for each share they own, but the number of rights necessary to buy a new share, the subscription ratio, is determined by the corporation. For example, the corporation might decide that 20 rights are required to buy one new share at the subscription price. Rights are generally valid for 30 days and are transferable. (In some offerings, rights are valid only for two weeks; in others, for as long as three months.)

When a company stages a rights offering, it often negotiates a *standby commitment* with an investment banker, who agrees to purchase any unsubscribed shares and sell them to the public.

Performing a Rights Offering

After deciding to issue new shares, a corporation places an announcement in major business newspapers. The notice states the subscription ratio and price, the current market price of the stock, and the following deadlines:

- **Record date**—Date by which any transfer of shares must be completed in order for the new shareholder to receive rights.
- **Distribution date**—Date that shareholders of record receive the rights.
- **Expiration date**—Date the rights are no longer valid.

Any investor who has completed the purchase of shares in a corporation by the record date becomes a *shareholder of record*. Shares traded from the date of the announcement through the record date are traded *cum rights*, which means with the rights attached. After the record date, shares trade *ex rights*, which means without the rights attached.

The time between the distribution date and the expiration date is called the "standby period." After the standby period, an investment banker with a standby commitment must purchase whatever portion of the issue that remains.

> **EXAMPLE:** Based on the announcement below, a shareholder with 100 shares of Java Express stock will receive 100 rights from the company on May 28. With a subscription ratio of 5-1, that shareholder can purchase 20 new shares of Java Express, at a total cost of $480 (20 new shares times $24 per share). Companies frequently retain a rights agent to handle the mechanics of the rights offering. The stockholder who wants to exercise his or her preemptive right must notify the Java Express rights agent, plus mail a check for $480, by June 29 for 20 new shares.
>
> Java Express Corporation
> Santa Monica, California
>
> Java Express Announces Rights Distribution
>
> The Board of Directors of Java Express Corporation is planning a rights distribution to stock holders of record on
>
> May 4, 1998. Stockholders will receive one right for each share owned. The rights will be distributed May 28, 1998.
>
> Under the terms of the offer, five rights are necessary to subscribe to one new share at a price of $24 per share. The offer expires midnight of June 29, 2006. The current market price of Java Express stock is $30.

Shareholders, of course, are not obligated to purchase new shares with their rights. Rights are transferable, so holders can decide to sell their rights in the marketplace. Shareholders thus need to calculate the market value of their rights.

Determining the Value of a Right

$$\frac{\text{market price} - \text{subscription price}}{\text{number of rights required} + 1} = \text{value of right}$$

So the value of a Java Express right mentioned in the previous example is

$$\frac{30 - 24}{5 + 1} = \frac{6}{6} = \$1 \text{ per right}$$

Rights offerings are important for investors who own shares in a healthy company. But investors with holdings in an ailing corporation also have legal rights.

Shareholder Rights During Bankruptcy

As part-owners of a corporation, stockholders are entitled to their proportionate share of the company's assets in the event of bankruptcy or liquidation (provided that assets are available). Shareholders, however, are not the first group to be paid in a liquidation. Common stockholders are compensated after banks and the owners of the corporation's bonds and preferred stock—otherwise known as senior securities—have been paid.

In a liquidation, a stockholder's liability is limited to the loss of his or her investment. Limited liability is one of the cornerstones of corporate structure. Of course, companies make every effort to avoid bankruptcy. To mitigate its financial difficulties, a corporation might recall its common stock and replace it with voting trust certificates.

> **EXAMPLE:** Jefferson Adams paid $1 million for a 10% ownership position in Presidential Hotels, Inc. The company unfortunately goes bankrupt. After liquidating its assets, Presidential still has outstanding debt of $50 million. Mr. Adams, however, is not responsible for paying 10% of that debt (or $5 million). He only loses his original investment of $1 million.

Voting Trust Certificates

The board of directors of a financially distressed company can replace shareholders' common stock with *voting trust certificates (VTCs)*. Shareholders retain all their rights except the right to vote. Those voting rights are given to a group of trustees appointed by the board of directors to turn the company around. VTCs thus concentrate decision-making power in the hands of the appointed trustees, giving them more freedom to take the steps necessary to put the company back on track. If the trustees are successful in saving the company, the common shares are returned to the shareholders (along with their voting rights). VTCs are traded just like common stock.

Although companies do not receive any money from the trading of their stock in the secondary market, they do want their stock to perform well. One way a company can inspire investor confidence is by regularly distributing dividends.

When Companies Declare a Dividend

As with rights offerings, when a company decides to pay a dividend, certain dates become important. A dividend announcement might read as follows:

> Megahit Studios
> Hollywood, California
>
> **Board Announces Dividend**
>
> The Board of Directors of Megahit Studios today declared a dividend of 75 cents per share to stockholders of record on Monday, April 20, 2006. The dividend will be paid on May 4, 2006.

Megahit thus has established the

- Declaration date (April 6)—Date on which the company announced the dividend
- Record date (April 20)—Date by which any transfer of shares must be completed in order for a shareholder to be eligible for the dividend
- Payment date (May 4)—Date the corporation will pay the dividend

Who is eligible to receive dividends? Only shareholders of record on April 20, the record date in this case, receive a dividend. The buying and selling of stocks is usually completed through *regular-way settlement*, in which a transaction settles three business days after the trade date (or *T+3*). So to buy Megahit Studios stock *cum dividend* (with the dividend), an investor has to purchase the stock on or before Wednesday, April 15. The following day, Thursday, April 16, is known as the *ex date* because investors who buy

Megahit on that date or later will not have enough time to settle their trades before the record date of Monday, April 20. These investors thus buy the stock *ex dividend* (without the dividend).

The ex-dividend date is important for another reason: on this date the company's stock price is adjusted downward by the exchange on which it is listed.

Stock Adjustment on the Ex-Dividend Date

On the ex-dividend date, the stock opens at a price reduced by the amount of the dividend to be paid. For example, if Megahit stock closed at $50 per share on April 15, the stock will open at $49.25 on the morning of April 16 to account for the 75-cent dividend.

This adjustment prevents traders from making riskless profits. If there were no reduction, a trader could buy the stock for $50 on April 15 (becoming a shareholder of record for April 20), sell it for $50 on April 16 (going off the record on April 21), and receive the dividend—an essentially risk-free profit of 75 cents per share. The price adjustment eliminates that profit. As mentioned earlier, price adjustments are made for stock dividends as well. Common stock is not the only type of stock that a company can issue. Under some circumstances, corporations might choose to issue preferred stock. Preferred stock has noticeably different rights and characteristics from common stock.

The Fundamentals of Preferred Stock

Preferred stock is a hybrid security that combines characteristics of common stock and bonds. Like common stock, preferred stock is a unit of ownership in a public corporation. Like bonds, preferred stock is a fixed-income security: it pays a set dividend that is determined at the time it is issued. Typically it has a par value of $100, and the dividend is stated as a percentage of this par value. For example, 6% preferred stock pays a dividend of $6 per year, or $1.50 per quarter.

Preferred stock has limited potential for capital growth compared to common stock. Because the dividends received by preferred stockholders are fixed at the outset, the value of preferred stock is affected more by interest rate fluctuations than by the company's performance. In contrast, common stockholders can benefit from higher dividend payments when a company is successful—with the market value of their stock climbing accordingly.

More often than not, preferred stock is an investment choice of other corporations that are seeking better returns on their cash reserves. Current U.S. tax law allows corporations that own 20% or more of an issuer's preferred stock to deduct 80% of the dividend payments received. A corporation that owns less than 20% of an issuer's preferred stock can still deduct 70% of the dividend payments. On the other hand, any interest income earned by the same corporations on their bond investments is taxable.

Dividends on preferred stock are paid before dividends on common stock. As mentioned earlier, preferred stockholders also precede common stockholders in receiving a distribution from a company's liquidation, making preferred stock a senior security much like a bond.

There are drawbacks to preferred stock, however. Preferred stockholders usually do not have voting rights. Nor do they have preemptive rights, because even if the corporation issues more stock, the preferred stock's rate of return is not affected.

What determines the market value of preferred stock? Because preferred stock earns a fixed return, its value in the marketplace is affected by interest rate movements. When preferred stock is issued, its dividend rate is set to be competitive with the existing market rate of interest.

Thus, an inverse relationship exists between interest rate movements and the market value of preferred stock. If interest rates climb above the fixed rate offered by the preferred, its market price declines. If interest rates fall below the preferred stock's rate of return, the price of the stock increases.

Calculating the Market Value of Preferred Stock

To determine what an existing share of preferred stock is worth after a change in interest rates, investors use a simple formula:

$$\text{market value} = \frac{\text{market income}}{\text{market yield}}$$

Of course, there are factors other than interest rates that influence a preferred stock's attractiveness. Investors must also consider the features of different types of preferred stock.

Other Types of Preferred Stock

The most common varieties of preferred stock include

- **Callable preferred**—Stock that the issuer can call (buy back) if interest rates fall. This allows the company to issue new preferred stock at a lower rate. Callable preferred typically pays a higher dividend rate because of the call feature.
- **Participating preferred**—Stock giving the preferred shareholder the right to participate in any "special" dividends paid by the company. For example, after an especially lucrative year, a company might announce an additional year-end dividend of $2. Participating preferred stockholders receive the extra dividend along with common stock owners. This type of stock is quite rare.
- **Cumulative preferred**—Stock requiring that any dividend payments in arrears be paid before the company pays dividends to common shareholders. If a company has missed three consecutive quarterly dividends on an 8% preferred stock and wants to pay a $1 dividend on its common stock in the fourth quarter, it must first pay a total dividend of $8 to preferred stockholders. See Table 3.1 for a schedule of dividend payments for cumulative preferred stock.

Table 3.1 Cumulative Preferred Stock Dividend Payment Schedule

	First Quarter	Second Quarter	Third Quarter	Fourth Quarter
8% cumulative preferred	$2 missed	$2 missed	$2 missed paid before common stock dividend	$8 must be paid
Common stock	None	None	None	$1 paid after payment of cumulative dividend

- **Adjustable preferred**—Stock with a dividend rate that is reset every six months to match movements in market interest rates.
- **Convertible preferred**—Stock that can be converted into shares of common stock. Convertible preferred generally pays a lower dividend rate because of the conversion feature. Also, because any conversion dilutes the ownership interest of existing common stock owners, a company must get shareholder approval before issuing this type of security.

How Does Preferred Stock Become Common Stock?

Owners of convertible preferred stock can exchange their shares for common stock according to a set conversion price, which determines the *conversion ratio:*

$$\frac{\text{par value of preferred stock}}{\text{conversion price}} = \text{number of common shares received}$$

EXAMPLE: Cyclops Vision, Inc., convertible preferred stock ($100 par value) is convertible at $40. The conversion ratio is thus 2½:1. One share of the preferred stock can be converted into 2½ shares of Cyclops common stock.

The conversion feature becomes valuable when the price of common stock is equal to or greater than the preferred stock's price, divided by the conversion ratio.

EXAMPLE: Cyclops preferred stock, which is trading at $93, can be converted at $40. The conversion ratio (par value divided by conversion price) is 2½:1. To find the threshold for profitable conversion, divide $93 by 2.5. The answer, $37.20, is the price of *conversion parity*. At this level, preferred stock can be converted for common stock of equal value. If the market price of Cyclops common stock trades at $34, the company's convertible preferred stock will trade at $85, regardless of what interest rates are doing, in order to achieve parity with the common stock.

An investor wanting to know whether a convertible preferred share is more valuable than the corresponding shares of common stock can use this formula:

parity price of preferred stock = conversion ration × market price of common stock

EXAMPLE: An investor wants to know if she should convert her Cyclops preferred stock. The preferred stock is trading at $95; the common stock at $36½.

Parity price of preferred stock = conversion ratio × market price of common stock

= 2.5 × $36.50

= $91.25

At current market prices, the investor will probably want to hold on to her Cyclops preferred.

The conversion feature is one of several features that companies use to make preferred stock more attractive to investors. Companies can also issue warrants along with their preferred stock.

Subscription Warrants

Warrants (or *subscription warrants*) give investors the chance to buy a company's common stock at a specified price, at some point in the future. Often they are packaged with a bond or preferred stock, as a "sweetener," to make the fixed-income security more attractive to investors. Warrants are freely transferable and are traded on the major exchanges or over the counter, depending on where the underlying stock is listed.

Warrants resemble rights offerings because they permit investors to buy stock at a set price. They differ from rights in two important ways:

- Whereas rights generally have terms of 30 to 60 days, warrants commonly last for many years or even for perpetuity. (Warrants also often include initial waiting periods, during which they cannot be exercised.)
- Warrants have a subscription price that is *higher* than the stock's market price. Warrants, therefore, have a low value at the outset; they increase in value when the market price of the company's stock climbs above the subscription price—or when investors expect it to.

> **EXAMPLE:** B. Mulligan Publishers, Inc., issues a warrant with its new preferred stock. The warrant has a subscription price of $40, whereas Mulligan's common stock is selling at $30. The current value of the warrant is $2. If the stock's market price rises to $45, however, the value of the warrant increases to at least $5. It might sell for much more than $5, depending on how investors judge the prospects of the company and its stock.

Companies sometimes give warrants to their top executives as an incentive to improve the company's performance and drive up the price of its stock. If the price of the common stock rises above the subscription price, an executive can then exercise his or her warrants for a substantial profit. See Table 3.2 for an example of executive warrants and rights schedule.

Table 3.2 Warrants and Rights Schedule

	Warrants	Rights
Term	Long (often 5 years) or perpetual	Short (weeks)
Waiting period	Yes	No
Subscription price	Higher than current market price	Lower than current market price
Value	Low at outset; increases if stock price rises above subscription price	Immediate value
Transferable	Yes	Yes
Traded on exchanges	Yes	Yes
Availability	All investors	Shareholders of record

Exam Prep Questions

1. Why do companies typically set the par value of common stock at a low arbitrary value?

   ❑ A. Many states tax common stock—a taxable corporate asset—on the basis of the stock's par value.

   ❑ B. Stockholders can deduct the difference between par and market value on their income tax statements.

   ❑ C. A low par value makes it easier for the company to issue additional shares.

   ❑ D. Low par value enables a company to issue inexpensive long-term warrants to its executives.

2. Which of the following are rights of common-stock owners?

   I. To receive dividends

   II. To receive a stock certificate

   III. To stand second in seniority to bondholders for a claim on the company's assets in the event of a liquidation

   IV. To maintain proportionate ownership in a company when it issues additional stock

   ❑ A. I and II

   ❑ B. I, II, and III

   ❑ C. I, II, and IV

   ❑ D. I, II, III, and IV

3. Argus Co. shares are trading at $60 when it declares a 10% stock dividend. Harold Cross, who owns 100 shares:

   ❑ A. Receives a $600 dividend

   ❑ B. Owns 110 shares worth $54.55 each

   ❑ C. Owns 100 shares worth $66 each

   ❑ D. Receives 10 additional shares valued at $60 each

4. Harry Green owns 300 shares of DDT, Inc., which uses the cumulative method of voting. What is the maximum number of votes that Green can cast for one candidate when stockholders vote to fill three open positions on the DDT board?

   ❑ A. 100

   ❑ B. 300

   ❑ C. 900

   ❑ D. 1,200

5. Which procedures favor investors with smaller holdings over investors with larger holdings?

   I. Statutory voting rights

   II. Cumulative voting rights

   III. Forward stock splits

   IV. Reverse stock splits

   ❑ A. I
   ❑ B. II
   ❑ C. II and III
   ❑ D. I and IV

6. Which are true about rights offerings?

   I. Companies price rights above the market price of their existing shares.

   II. Companies price rights below the market price of their existing shares.

   III. Through rights offerings, existing shareholders have the choice of maintaining proportionate ownership in a company.

   IV. Companies can use rights to dilute the holdings of existing owners.

   ❑ A. I
   ❑ B. II
   ❑ C. I and IV
   ❑ D. II and III

7. Zyxon Corporation declares a rights distribution with a subscription price of $30 and a subscription ratio of 10:1. When Zyxon trades at $34, what is the market value of rights to purchase 20 shares of Zyxon?

   ❑ A. $6,000
   ❑ B. $800
   ❑ C. $72.72
   ❑ D. $680

8. Millenium Corporation has petitioned the courts for bankruptcy protection to attempt a restructuring. Millenium's board appoints a group of trustees and issues voting trust certificates (VTCs), replacing its outstanding stock. Existing shareholders:

   I. Retain all of their common-stock rights.

   II. Might eventually get their common shares back.

   III. Cannot sell their holdings.

   IV. Lose their voting rights to the appointed trustees.

   ❑ A. I
   ❑ B. II and III
   ❑ C. II and IV
   ❑ D. III and IV

9. Tuscarora Light and Gas issues 100,000 shares of 6.4% preferred stock at $100 par value. Megabyte Corp. buys 30,000 shares of the Tuscarora preferred. Assuming that the utility makes all scheduled dividend payments, what amount must Megabyte claim as taxable dividend income on the preferred each year?

   ❑ A. $48,000
   ❑ B. $38,400
   ❑ C. $192,000
   ❑ D. $57,600

10. Last year, Rocky Falls Power issued 7% preferred stock at a par value of $100. Since then, interest rates have risen from about 7% to about 9%. The Rocky Falls preferred stock now:

   ❑ A. Trades at about par
   ❑ B. Trades at about 78
   ❑ C. Trades at about 128
   ❑ D. Pays a 9% dividend

11. Logical Decisions, Inc. (LDI), has omitted payment of the last two dividends on its 6.6% cumulative preferred stock, a one million share issue with a par value of $100. Based on strong sales of its new database software, the LDI board decides to pay a $1.40 dividend in the next quarter to owners of its five million outstanding shares of common stock. What sum does LDI's treasurer set aside to pay the quarter's dividends?

   ❑ A. $7 million
   ❑ B. $10.3 million
   ❑ C. $11.95 million
   ❑ D. $8.4 million

12. The common stock of Online Auctions, Inc., trades at $23. The company's convertible preferred shares, issued at a par of $100 with a conversion ratio of 4:1, trade at parity with the common stock at:

- ❑ A. 92
- ❑ B. 25
- ❑ C. 48
- ❑ D. 100

13. Jordan purchased 1,000 shares of Virex common stock when the biotech firm went public with an offering price of 12. Each share had one warrant attached that gave the holder the right to purchase the stock at 35. Virex now trades at 38. What is the minimum market value of Jordan's warrants?

- ❑ A. $105,000
- ❑ B. $78,000
- ❑ C. $3,000
- ❑ D. $72,000

14. Which of the following are true about warrants?

I. Warrants often exist in perpetuity.

II. Companies use warrants as an incentive to attract investors in common-stock offerings.

III. Investors must use European-style execution to exercise warrants.

IV. Warrants issued by NYSE-listed companies trade over the counter.

- ❑ A. I
- ❑ B. I, II, and IV
- ❑ C. I, II, and III
- ❑ D. I and II

15. Regular-way settlement for preferred-stock transactions occurs on:

- ❑ A. The same day
- ❑ B. The next day
- ❑ C. T+3
- ❑ D. T+5

Exam Prep Answers

1. The correct answer is A. Many corporations set the par value of their stock at an arbitrary and low level because states have historically taxed this asset on the basis of its par value.
2. The correct answer is C. Shareholders of common stock have the right to receive dividends, to take physical delivery of the stock from the transfer agent, and to maintain their proportionate ownership by exercising the preemptive right. Owners of common stock stand last in seniority for a claim on assets of a liquidating firm.
3. The correct answer is B. After the stock dividend, Cross owns 110 shares of Argus at 54.55. Argus issues its shareholders 10% additional shares; the exchange on which Argus is listed adjusts the stock's price downward to keep the value of the shares unchanged.
4. The correct answer is C. Using cumulative voting, Green can pool the 900 votes to which his 300 shares entitle him, and he can distribute them as he desires among the three candidates for the board.
5. The correct answer is C. Cumulative voting rights and forward stock splits best serve the interest of small investors. Cumulative voting gives smaller shareholders the capability to apportion their voting in favor of candidates they prefer. A forward stock split lowers a stock's price, making its shares more affordable to smaller investors.
6. The correct answer is D. Corporations price the shares in rights offerings below the market price of their existing shares to provide current shareholders with the chance to protect themselves, at a discount, from dilution of their ownership.
7. The correct answer is C. The market value of a right is

   $$\frac{\text{market price} - \text{subscription price}}{\text{number of rights required} + 1}$$

   One Zyxon right thus equals

   $$\frac{\$34 - \$30}{10 + 1} = \$0.3636$$

   Two hundred rights, at the subscription ratio of 10:1, enable an investor to purchase 20 shares, so $200 \times \$.3636 = \$72.72$.
8. The correct answer is C. The Millenium shareholders retain all of their rights except their voting rights. They can still sell their holdings, now in the form of VTCs, which trade just as common stock does. Or, if the trustees turn the company around, they can wait for the board to return their shares of common stock, along with their voting rights.

9. The correct answer is B. Corporations that own more than 20% of another company's preferred stock can claim an 80% exemption on the dividend income they earn from the preferred. Megabyte earns \$192,000 a year from the Tuscarora preferred (30,000 × 0.064 × \$100 = \$192,000). Because 80% of this amount is exempt from taxation, Megabyte must claim \$38,400 as dividend income subject to taxation (\$192,000 × 0.20 = \$38,400).
10. The correct answer is B. Because the market value of preferred stock moves inversely to interest rates, investors can calculate the approximate market value of preferred stock by dividing the fixed income they receive each year by the current level of interest rates. As interest rates have risen to 9%, the Rocky Falls preferred stock, issued at par when interest rates (and thus its dividend) were 7%, now trades at \$77.78 (\$7 ÷ 0.09 = \$77.78).
11. The correct answer is C. Cumulative preferred stockholders are entitled to receive all dividends they have missed before the company pays any common-stock dividend. LDI has to pay the cumulative preferred shareholders the two quarters of omitted dividends, or \$3.3 million (1 million × \$100 × 0.066 ÷ 2 = \$3.3 million), plus the next quarter's cumulative preferred dividend of \$1.65 million. The common stock dividend equals \$7 million (\$1.40 × 5 million = \$7 million). The total dividend bill equals \$11.95 million.
12. The correct answer is A. The parity price of convertible preferred stock equals the conversion ratio multiplied by the current market price of the common stock. The parity price of the Online Auctions convertible is thus \$23 × 4, or \$92.
13. The correct answer is C. A warrant's market value equals at least the difference between the price of the underlying stock and the subscription price. As Jordan owns 1,000 warrants, and the underlying Virex stock trades three dollars above his subscription price, his warrants are worth a minimum of \$3,000. If investors believe that the underlying Virex stock has significant upside potential, the warrants might trade at a premium to this minimum value.
14. The correct answer is D. Warrants, often issued by unproven companies as an inexpensive way to attract additional investors in a new stock issue, generally exist in perpetuity. Because warrants trade on the exchange where the issuing company's underlying stock is listed, the warrants issued by an NYSE-listed stock trade on the Big Board. Investors can exercise warrants any time after the initial waiting period—if one exists—for the life of the security.
15. The correct answer is C. Regular-way settlement for all corporate issues, including preferred stock, is T+3.

Corporate Debt: Bonds and Yields

Terms You Need to Know

- ✓ Basis point
- ✓ Bond
- ✓ Bond rating
- ✓ Call premium
- ✓ Call protection
- ✓ Call provision
- ✓ Coupon (coupon rate)
- ✓ Current yield
- ✓ Defeasance
- ✓ Discount bond
- ✓ Indenture
- ✓ Maturity date
- ✓ Nominal yield
- ✓ Original issue discount bond
- ✓ Par value (face value)
- ✓ Point
- ✓ Premium bond
- ✓ Present value
- ✓ Protective covenant
- ✓ Put provision
- ✓ Refunding
- ✓ Sinking fund
- ✓ Trust Indenture Act of 1939
- ✓ Yield
- ✓ Yield to call (YTC)
- ✓ Yield to maturity (YTM)
- ✓ Yield to put (YTP)

Concepts You Need to Understand

- ✓ How companies raise capital without relinquishing ownership
- ✓ Why issuing bonds might be better than borrowing from a bank
- ✓ How indentures protect bondholders
- ✓ Common features of bonds
- ✓ Effect of interest rate changes on bond prices
- ✓ Inverse relationship of price and yield
- ✓ Nominal yield
- ✓ Reasons for calculating current yield and yield to maturity
- ✓ What yield to call and yield to put are
- ✓ The importance of corporate bond ratings
- ✓ How bond maturities affect prices

Why Companies Issue Debt

When corporations want to raise capital, they might decide to issue debt securities instead of stock—borrowing money from investors rather than taking on new owners. Because a company's cash needs are often relatively long-term, it commonly sells bonds, which are debt securities that guarantee a fixed rate of return. This chapter discusses why a corporation issues bonds, how bonds work, and what factors influence bond prices and yields.

When companies want to finance new investments or expansion activities, they can choose to borrow money by issuing *bonds*—securities that guarantee to pay the bondholder a fixed rate of interest and to repay the principal on a specific date in the future. Bonds offer several advantages to the issuing corporation. First, they confer tax advantages, because the company can deduct a bond's yearly interest costs. Second, the company does not relinquish ownership of its business, as it does when issuing equity stock. Third, the company can enhance its standing in the financial marketplace by establishing a credit history and earning a credit rating. A strong credit rating enables the company to raise capital more easily in the future.

Why Companies Don't Just Borrow from a Bank

Banks often charge a higher interest rate than companies need to set on their bonds to attract investors. Also, bank loans tend to have variable interest rates, thus exposing borrowing companies to interest rate risk. Furthermore, banks can require that borrowers provide collateral. Finally, banks generally prefer not to make loans for very long terms, whereas bond maturities often range between 20 and 30 years. By issuing bonds, a company is able to borrow money on its own terms and meet its specific needs.

To issue bonds, however, companies must think about more than just prevailing interest rates. Most corporate bond issuers fall under the jurisdiction of the SEC, which imposes regulations on the issuers.

How Corporate Bonds Work

Under the *Trust Indenture Act of 1939*, all bonds with an aggregate value greater than $5 million must be issued under an *indenture*. The indenture is a legal agreement that spells out the terms of the bond and appoints a trustee (typically a commercial bank) to protect the interests of bondholders. For example, if a corporation issues bonds using a mortgage on its property as collateral, the trustee holds the lien. If the company defaults on interest or principal payments, the trustee then liquidates the property to pay the bondholders.

Provisions of Bond Indentures

Indentures specify all the terms and features of the bond, including:

- Total amount of the issue
- Par value of each bond
- Rate of interest (coupon)
- Maturity date
- Property pledged as collateral, if any
- Protective covenants
- Call or put provisions

Par Value

Par value (or *face value*) is the principal amount of the bond, typically $1,000. Expressed differently, investors pay par value for the bond at the time of original issue—and receive par value from the company at the bond's maturity.

How Interest Payments Are Made

Like preferred stock, bonds pay a fixed rate of interest, sometimes referred to as the *coupon* or *coupon rate*. The coupon is expressed as a percentage of par value. Therefore, a $1,000 bond with a coupon of 8% pays the bondholder $80 per year. Interest is usually paid semiannually, so in this case the bondholder receives $40 in interest every six months on each bond owned.

The Significance of the Maturity Date

The *maturity date*, which is named in the indenture, establishes the date on which the issuer must repay the entire principal of the bond to the bondholder. Some bonds, however, have redemption features that allow the company or the bondholder to redeem the bond before the maturity date.

How a Company Retires a Bond Before Maturity

Companies sometimes issue bonds with a *call provision*, which allows them to buy back the bonds prior to their maturity date. Callable bonds protect companies from unexpected falls in interest rates, by allowing them to refinance their debt at the new, lower rate. Investors might be reluctant to buy callable bonds. Few want to risk losing a security that pays 10% when they can replace it with one yielding a rate of 8%. Thus, companies generally must offer two provisions to make their callable bonds more appealing:

- **Call protection**—The length of time that must elapse before a company can call its bonds, generally 10 or more years after the issue date.
- **Call premium**—The amount over par value that a company will pay to buy back its bonds before maturity.

EXAMPLE: In 1998, Tidewell Corp. issues $10 million of 8% 20-year bonds with a face value of $1,000. They are callable after 2008 at a premium of $50; that is, at $1,050. In 2010, interest rates have fallen to 6%. Tidewell calls its bonds in order to issue new ones at the lower rate. Although the company pays out an additional $500,000 in premiums ($50 × 10,000 bonds), it saves $1.6 million in interest payments over the last eight years of the original bond ($20 × 10,000 bonds × 8 years).

Other Ways for Companies to Remove Bonds from Their Books Early

Companies can retire their bonds through either a *sinking fund* or *defeasance*. A sinking fund is a pool of cash created specifically to redeem bonds. In many cases, indentures include a *protective covenant* requiring the issuing company to make annual contributions to a sinking fund. Protective covenants are provisions in the indenture that protect the bondholder's interest. A sinking fund provision might stipulate that the fund be used to retire some bonds each year—known as a sinking fund call—or that the fund grow at a rate sufficient to repay the entire principal at maturity.

Defeasance is similar to a sinking fund, except that new debt securities—rather than cash—are used to cover the bonds. A company with outstanding low-coupon bonds can purchase higher-yielding government securities to cover the principal and interest payments of its original bond issue. Sometimes the company issues new bonds in order to acquire the money needed to buy the government securities. These securities are held by a trustee who makes all required interest and principal payments. This step is known as *refunding* the first bond issue. The final step is defeasance—when the original bonds are actually removed from the company's balance sheet.

Example of Profiting from Defeasance

Exxon was the first U.S. company to practice defeasance. In 1982 the oil giant used $312 million worth of government securities (paying 14%) to defease $515 million of its own bonds with rates of about 6 to 7%. Because the new securities were sufficient to defease its old bonds, Exxon was actually able to declare an after-tax earnings on the procedure of $132 million.

Companies that defease a bond issue are taking advantage of compounding interest. The interest income that Exxon earned from its government securities was more than enough to cover the interest payments it owed on its bonds. The excess cash was then reinvested at the higher interest rate—and eventually grew sufficiently to cover the difference between the two principal amounts. Two important financial concepts are at play here:

- **Compounding of interest**—By reinvesting interest earned on a security, investors earn interest on their interest, compounding their gains.
- **Future value**—An investment today will be worth more tomorrow, given a market rate of return. Exxon understood that the value of $312 million in 1982, with reinvestment at current rates and compounding, would grow to $515 million 25 years later.

Defeasance, like sinking funds, can work in two ways. The original bonds can be repaid at maturity, in which case they are said to be escrowed to maturity, or they can be retired before maturity, in which case they are considered prerefunded.

Bondholders Can Redeem Bonds Before Maturity

Some companies issue bonds with a *put provision*, giving investors the right to sell the bond back to the issuer, usually at par. Put provisions offer clear benefits to investors in a time of rising interest rates, when bond prices are falling. Bondholders can put their bonds back to the issuer, receive the principal, and reinvest it at the higher prevailing interest rates.

Although many features within a bond indenture can influence an investor's decision to purchase the bonds, the single most important factor—all else being equal—is the promised return.

Bond Yields

The return that an investor earns on a bond is known as the bond's *yield*. Yield is expressed as a percentage, such as 6.25%. Each one-hundredth of a percent (0.01%) is referred to as a *basis point;* 100 basis points equal 1 *point*. Therefore, compared to 6%, 7% is 100 basis points—or a point—higher, and compared to 9.75%, 9.5% is 25 basis points—or a quarter of a point—lower. Investors commonly use three yields when comparing bond issues: nominal yield, current yield, and yield to maturity. Of these, *nominal yield* is the simplest: It is the coupon rate on the bond. As such, it never changes over the life of the bond. To calculate the remaining two yields, you need to factor in the current market price of a bond.

Effects of Bond Prices After It Has Been Issued

Interest rates are by far the most crucial influence on bond prices. Interest rates and bond prices have an inverse relationship, which should not be surprising, because bonds pay fixed rates of return, as coupon income.

This inverse relationship is the most important key to understanding bond price movements. Suppose that market interest rates are currently hovering around 7%. All companies with a certain credit rating might then be issuing bonds with coupons of 7.5%. Next year, however, interest rates climb to 8%. Companies with the same rating then issue bonds with coupons of 8.5%. The question is, why would anyone purchase the old 7.5% bonds on the secondary market when they can buy new bonds paying 8.5%? The answer to this question is that the 7.5% bonds will cost the buyer less than the par value of $1,000 on the new 8.5% bonds. Investors are always looking for a return on their investment that matches what is currently available in the market for similar securities. Because the coupon on a bond never changes, bond prices must move to bring the bond's yield in line with the market.

Are actual movements in interest rates the only factors that influence bond prices? In the short run, the basic forces of supply and demand determine fluctuations in bond prices. Clearly, the expectation of changes in interest rates plays a big role in the day-to-day movements of bond prices. If investors perceive signals of potential inflation—and, hence, higher future interest rates—they are likely to move funds out of bonds, leading to an immediate decline in prices. On the other hand, if they see signs of an economic slowdown, which would probably lower the rate of inflation, they will purchase more bonds. Thus, bond prices will tend to rise. Other considerations, such as the relative risk presented by different kinds of bonds, are also important determinants of bond prices in certain situations.

Bond Price Quotes

Corporate bond prices are given as a percentage of their par value, which is generally $1,000. For example, a price of 93 means the bond is selling for 93% of par, or $930. Table 4.1 shows some sample bond prices and their dollar equivalents.

Table 4.1 Sample Bond Prices and Their Dollar Equivalents

90.25	$902.50	102.125	$1,021.25
90.375	$903.75	103.375	$1,033.75
92.625	$926.25	104.625	$1,046.25

Investors use two terms to indicate the price at which a bond is selling (when it is different from par):

- **Premium bond**—The bond costs more than its face value.
- **Discount bond**—The bond costs less than its face value.

> **EXAMPLE:** Canaan Steel Co. bonds are quoted at 96.375, which means they are selling at 96.375% of par, or $963.75. So Canaan bonds are selling at a discount. Two years later, interest rates have plummeted and the same Canaan bonds are priced at 107.75. Thus, an investor would pay 107.75% of par, or $1,077.50 per bond, buying the bonds at a premium.

Companies wait until the last minute to set the rate on their new bonds. By matching their rate with the market rate, they can issue the bonds at par. Having decided to issue bonds at a given rate, however, a company sometimes sees market rates move up, but chooses to stick with its original coupon rate. This is one of the rare cases when bonds are sold at a discount at the time of issue. For example, although the bonds have a face value of $1,000, the issuing company can sell them for $990. These bonds are known as *original issue discount bonds.*

A Bond's Current Yield

Current yield is the rate of return based on the bond's current market price. It is a more accurate measure of the investor's gains because it takes into account the actual cash invested instead of the bond's par value. Investors buying already issued bonds in the secondary market rarely pay par, because interest rates are always changing. Current yield is calculated as follows:

$$\text{current yield} = \frac{\text{total annual interest income}}{\text{current market price}}$$

For example, a 7.50% bond selling at 87.5 has a current yield of 8.57%.

$$\text{current yield} = \frac{\$75 \text{ annual interest income}}{\$875 \text{ market price}} = 8.75\%$$

Of course, this formula can be manipulated to determine what a bond should sell for. Assume that market rates are currently around 6.50%. What is a fair price for this bond? By rearranging the equation, you can see that:

$$\text{current market price} = \frac{\text{total annual interest income}}{\text{current yield}}$$

$= \$75/0.065 = \$1{,}153.85$

So, the bond should be quoted somewhere about 115.375.

When bonds sell at a premium or discount, the difference from par, over the life of the bond, either subtracts from the investor's returns or adds to them. Remember, a bondholder receives exactly the par amount at maturity, no matter the price originally paid. Holders of discount bonds make a capital gain, whereas holders of premium bonds suffer a capital loss. Interest payments therefore are no longer the only source of return. As a result, the most common way of measuring bond return is yield to maturity.

Why is Yield to Maturity a better measure of a bond's return? *Yield to maturity (YTM)* accounts not only for the interest income earned on a bond, but also for the accretion of any capital gain or amortization of any capital loss realized by the investor. For example, if George Kramer buys $1,000 par bonds at $912.50 and holds them to maturity, he realizes a capital gain of $87.50 per bond. Similarly, had Mr. Kramer purchased the bonds at $1,068.75, he would have incurred a capital loss of $68.75 per bond. YTM calculates the total return to the investor, including interest income and the present value of any capital gain or loss.

Present Value

In its most simple terms, *present value* is an estimate of what receiving a dollar at some date in the future is worth to an investor today. Clearly, most of us would rather receive $100 today than wait 10 years for it. Present value calculations determine how many dollars one would accept today in lieu of the $100 in 10 years. Given certain market conditions, for example, an investor might decide that $35 today is the same as $100 10 years later. The concept of present value—sometimes also referred to as the time value of money—underlies most investment choices, but it is especially important to understanding yield to maturity.

How Yield to Maturity Is Calculated

Investment analysts find a bond's yield to maturity with a financial calculator. For those without a financial calculator or basis book, the following thumbnail approximation of the formula for YTM is useful:

total annual interest + annual capital gain

OR

– annual capital loss

(purchase price + par value) ÷ 2

This formula does not arrive at exactly the same result as a financial calculator, but it provides a result in the same ballpark.

EXAMPLE: Treetops Airlines issues 4.75% 30-year bonds in 2000. In 2010, the bonds are quoted at 108.125. The purchase price, therefore, is 108.125% of par, or $1,081.25. Buyers in 2010 suffer a capital loss of $81.25 on every bond they hold to maturity. Meanwhile, they are earning $47.50 in annual interest on each bond. The YTM on Treetops bonds can now be estimated. First, calculate the annual capital loss: $81.25 ÷ 20 years = $4.06. Now proceed with the YTM formula:

$$\frac{\$47.50 - \$4.06}{(\$1{,}081.25 + 1{,}000) \div 2} = \frac{43.4}{2{,}081.25 \div 2} = \frac{43.44}{1{,}040.63} = 4.17\%$$

The YTM of Treetops bonds is less than the nominal yield because investors are taking a capital loss by purchasing the bonds at a premium. Note that the same formula can be used if they had purchased the bond at a discount. The only difference is that you add the capital gain to the numerator (instead of subtracting the capital loss).

Earlier, bonds were discussed with put or call features. Often bondholders do not keep these bonds all the way to maturity, which means that the YTM formula must be amended slightly.

How Yield to Call or Yield to Put Is Determined

For both *yield to call (YTC)* and *yield to put (YTP)*, start with the YTM formula, and adjust the time frame for calculating the annual capital gain or loss. Then use the call or put price instead of the par value in the second numerator.

total annual interest + annual capital gain

OR

– annual capital loss

(purchase price + call or put price) ÷ 2

EXAMPLE: The same Treetops Airlines bonds are callable in 2020 at 110 and can be put at par that same year. Assume that the bonds were purchased in 2005 at 92.375. The call price is $1,100, the put price is $1,000, and the purchase price was $923.75. The total annual interest is still $47.50. What are the YTC and YTP for these bonds? Remember to use the number of years remaining until the bonds can be called—or put—to calculate the annual capital gain or loss.

Yield to call:

$$\frac{47.50 + 11.75}{(923.75 + 1{,}100) \div 2} = \frac{59.25}{1{,}011.88} = 5.86\%$$

Yield to put:

$$\frac{47.50 + 5.08}{(923.75 + 1{,}000) \div 2} = \frac{52.25}{961.88} = 5.47\%$$

Is one measure of bond yield always greater than the others? Depending on whether a bond was purchased at a discount, at par, or at a premium, the nominal yield, current yield, and YTM rank differently against each other. The best way to observe this is with an example.

EXAMPLE: Swank Clothing, Inc., issues 9% 20-year bonds in 2000. In 2002, the bonds are selling at a discount, quoted at 95.875. What are the nominal yield, the current yield, and the YTM? The nominal yield is simply the coupon rate of 9%. The current yield is $90 divided by $958.75, or 9.39%. Finally, the YTM equals 9.42%.

$$\frac{90.00 + 2.29}{979.38} = \frac{92.29}{979.38} = 9.42\%$$

So here, the YTM is the highest measure of returns, followed by the current and nominal yields. But what if the bond had been quoted at 106.625—that is, if it were selling at a premium? The nominal yield hasn't changed. The current yield is now the same $90 divided by $1,066.25, or 8.44%. And the YTM is 8.36%.

When bonds sell at a premium, the ranking of the yields reverses—nominal is now greatest, followed by current and YTM. For bonds purchased at par, there is no capital gain or loss, so interest payments are the only concern. But those are fixed for the life of the bond, so all three yields are exactly the same. Table 4.2 shows the difference between the types of yield and the types of bonds.

Table 4.2 Difference Between Types of Yield and Types of Bonds

	Discount Bond	Par Bond	Premium Bond
Nominal Yield	Lowest	Same	Highest
Current Yield	Middle	Same	Middle
YTM	Highest	Same	Lowest

Because they profoundly influence bond prices and their yields, interest rate changes are a primary consideration for bond investors. But they are not the only one.

Other Factors That Affect Bond Prices

Not all bonds are created equal. Investors must look beyond yields to the question of bond *quality*—that is, the capability of the issuer to make interest and principal payments throughout the life of the bond. Basically, investors must consider the bond's credit risk. Bondholders expect a return on their investment that is commensurate with the associated risk. Thus, a company with a strong credit history can issue bonds at a lower rate than another company with a shakier financial past.

How do investors judge the quality of a bond? Investors rely on the corporate credit ratings released by such independent agencies as Standard & Poor's, Moody's, and Fitch's, which assess the creditworthiness of bond issuers. Corporations pay the agencies to review their records, total debt, and business practices, and then to rate their capability to repay the debt arising from the proposed bond offering. The *bond rating* assigned to any given bond issue reflects the credit rating of the company and the particular characteristics of the issue. Often a corporation's bonds will carry the same rating as the corporation itself. However, if the company issues unsecured bonds, or if the indenture does not contain sufficiently stringent provisions concerning redemption, a rating agency might assign a lower rating to the bond than the one it has given to the issuing company. If the rating agency later upgrades or downgrades the corporation's rating, the bond rating changes accordingly.

Table 4.3 shows bond ratings for Standard and Poor's, Moody's, and Fitch's. The top four ratings for each agency are considered "investment grade" quality. Any ratings below those are deemed "speculative" and are often referred to as junk bonds.

Table 4.3 Bond Ratings by Agency

	S&P's	Moody's	Fitch's
Investment Grade	AAA	Aaa	AAA
	AA	Aa	AA
	A	A	A
	BBB	Baa	BBB
Speculative (Junk Bonds)	BB	Ba	BB
	B	B	B
	CCC	Caa	CCC
	CC	Ca	CC
	C	C	C
	D		DDD
			DD
			D

These basic ratings can be modified. S&P's and Fitch's both use a plus (+) or minus (–) to further distinguish quality. Moody's adds a 1, 2, or 3, with A1 ranking higher than an A2 or A3, both of which are higher than a Baa.

The Importance of Ratings to Companies

Just as consumers need good credit histories to finance major purchases on reasonable terms, companies need good credit histories to issue bonds at favorable rates. If a company has no credit history, it might have a hard time attracting investors, and thus be forced to offer a higher coupon than other companies. Similarly, if a company's ratings are poor—because of too much debt, poor market performance, or other reasons—it needs to pay a higher coupon rate. Most companies, therefore, work hard to establish and maintain good corporate ratings.

Companies issue bonds with a fixed rate of interest, or coupon. Even if a company's rating is subsequently raised or lowered, the coupon does not change. The bond's market price, however, is affected by a change in ratings, as investors reevaluate the creditworthiness of the issuing company.

What is an important consideration for bond market investors? Time. A bond's maturity date influences what investors are willing to pay for the bond. The longer a bondholder waits to receive the repayment of his or her principal, the greater the interest rate risk and repayment risk the bondholder assumes. Even strong companies can experience problems. All else being equal, bond investors demand higher yields for bonds with longer maturities.

Exam Prep Questions

1. Debt securities offer all the following benefits except:
   - ❑ A. The issuing company can deduct the interest payments, reducing its taxes.
   - ❑ B. The issuer raises money without relinquishing any ownership.
   - ❑ C. The company can establish or enhance its credit history.
   - ❑ D. The issuer's common stock increases in value.

2. Bricco Construction wants to borrow $5 million from MetroBank. Which statements are true?

   I. The interest rate that MetroBank charges Bricco will be less than the rate Bricco would have to pay bondholders.

   II. MetroBank will probably require collateral for the loan.

   III. MetroBank will allow Bricco to structure the loan for its convenience.

   IV. After Bricco repays the loan, it will receive a triple-A credit rating.
   - ❑ A. I
   - ❑ B. II
   - ❑ C. II and III
   - ❑ D. III and IV

3. Which act of Congress provides the regulatory framework for issuing corporate bonds?
   - ❑ A. Security Exchange Act of 1934
   - ❑ B. Trust Indenture Act of 1939
   - ❑ C. Investment Company Act of 1940
   - ❑ D. Maloney Act of 1938

4. What is the largest bond issue a corporation can sell without an indenture?
   - ❑ A. $5 million
   - ❑ B. $1 million or 5% of total net assets, whichever is smaller
   - ❑ C. $10 million
   - ❑ D. None; all corporate debt issues require an indenture

5. A corporate bond indenture includes which of the following?

   I. Interest rate

   II. Total amount borrowed

   III. Maturity date

   IV. Market value of the corporation's outstanding equity
   - ❑ A. I and II
   - ❑ B. I and III
   - ❑ C. I, II, and III
   - ❑ D. I, II, III, and IV

6. Jack Noyre owns five Healthco bonds with a coupon of 6%. How much does he receive on each coupon date?
   - ❑ A. $60
   - ❑ B. $150
   - ❑ C. $300
   - ❑ D. $5,000

7. What happens on a corporate bond's maturity date?
   - ❑ A. Bondholders continue to earn interest until they redeem the bond.
   - ❑ B. The issuer pays bondholders the current market price of the bond.
   - ❑ C. The issuer repays the par value to bondholders.
   - ❑ D. The issuer calls in the bond.

8. Which yield does not change over the life of a bond?
   - ❑ A. Nominal yield
   - ❑ B. Current yield
   - ❑ C. Yield to maturity
   - ❑ D. Yield to put

9. Nominal yield is known by all the following names except:
   - ❑ A. Coupon rate
   - ❑ B. Interest rate
   - ❑ C. Issue rate
   - ❑ D. Market price

10. Tidewell Corp. issued $50 million of 7.2% 20-year bonds in 1995. Since then, corporate bond rates have risen 100 basis points. What can be said about the Tidewell bonds?

    I. They should be selling at a discount.

    II. They should be selling at a premium.

    III. Their nominal yield remains at 7.2%.

    IV. Their current yield is higher than their coupon.

   - ❑ A. I
   - ❑ B. II
   - ❑ C. II and III
   - ❑ D. I, III, and IV

11. Valerie Comeau, who wants to buy a 9% Virex bond quoted at 102¼, will pay
   - ❑ A. $102.25
   - ❑ B. $113.36
   - ❑ C. $1,020.25
   - ❑ D. $1,022.50

12. Burgertron Corp.'s 7% bonds are trading at 93. What is their current yield?
   - ❑ A. 13.29%
   - ❑ B. 7.527%
   - ❑ C. 6.510%
   - ❑ D. 7.0%

13. When a bond sells at a premium, which measure of its yield is the greatest?
   - ❑ A. Nominal yield
   - ❑ B. Current yield
   - ❑ C. Yield to maturity
   - ❑ D. Yield to call

14. The most accurate measure of an investor's return from a bond is which of the following?
   - ❑ A. Nominal yield
   - ❑ B. Current yield
   - ❑ C. Yield to call
   - ❑ D. Yield to maturity

15. Thurston Marclay is considering buying 10 Sonic Devices 7.50% bonds, which have 20 years remaining until maturity, at 110. Marclay, who does not own a financial calculator, wants to make a quick estimate of the bonds' yield to maturity. He finds that they yield:
   - ❑ A. 6.67%
   - ❑ B. 7.50%
   - ❑ C. 6.82%
   - ❑ D. 8.25%

Exam Prep Answers

1. The correct answer is D. The factors that affect the prices of equity and debt securities are distinct; a debt offering normally does not have any influence on a company's stock.
2. The correct answer is B. Bricco might want to issue bonds rather than borrow from MetroBank because the construction company will not need to tie up part of its assets as collateral for the loan. More importantly, if it is a solid, profitable company, Bricco can likely pay bondholders a lower interest rate than it would pay to MetroBank.
3. The correct answer is B. The Trust Indenture Act of 1939 establishes the key regulations for corporate bonds, requiring that most issues come with a bond indenture, which must appoint a trustee to protect the interests of bondholders.
4. The correct answer is A. The Trust Indenture Act of 1939 requires that all corporate debt issues in excess of $5 million establish a trust indenture, which outlines the legal relationship between the issuer and its bondholders.
5. The correct answer is C. An indenture does not include information about the corporation's other securities—only the terms and conditions for the offering in question.
6. The correct answer is B. Corporate bonds, which normally have a face value of $1,000, pay interest semiannually, so Noyre will receive $150 each coupon date ($5,000 × 0.06 ÷ 2 = $150).
7. The correct answer is C. On the maturity date of any debt security, the issuer repays the principal of the loan—the par value of the bonds.
8. The correct answer is A. The nominal yield (or coupon rate) does not change during the bond's lifetime. This percentage of par determines the actual amount of money that bondholders will receive each coupon date.
9. The correct answer is D. A bond's market price, which changes as interest rates change, is not a form of yield.
10. The correct answer is D. As interest rates rise, the price of existing bonds falls. The Tidewell bond, issued with a 7.2% coupon, will now trade at a discount. Its nominal yield, of course, remains at 7.2%. So its current yield—the annual interest income divided by the current price—will have increased.

11. The correct answer is D. Each point in the price of a corporate bond quote represents 1% of par, or \$10, so a bond priced at 102¼ is worth \$1,020 plus \$2.50, or \$1,022.50.

12. The correct answer is B. Current yield equals the annual interest income (the coupon payments), divided by the bond's current market price. A Burgertron bond pays holders \$70 in each year. If the Burgertron bond is trading at \$930, its current yield equals 7.527% (\$70 ÷ \$930 = 7.527%).

13. The correct answer is A. The nominal yield, or coupon rate, of a bond never changes. Because bond yields fall when bond prices rise, the yield of a premium bond, no matter whether measured by current yield, YTM, or yield to call (or put), is always lower than the coupon.

14. The correct answer is D. The most accurate measure of the return on a bond is yield to maturity, because it takes into consideration any premium paid (or discount saved), plus the time remaining until maturity.

15. The correct answer is A. An investor can make a good approximation of YTM on a premium bond with the following formula:

$$\text{YTM} = \frac{\text{total annual interest} - \text{annual capital loss}}{(\text{purchase price} + \text{par value}) \div 2}$$

The Sonic devices bonds are selling at \$1,100, so their annual capital loss is \$5 (\$100 ÷ 20 years). Marclay thus calculates:

$$\text{YTM} = \frac{\$75 - 5}{(\$1{,}000 + 1{,}100) \div 2} = \frac{\$70}{\$1{,}050} = 6.67\%$$

Corporate Bonds

Terms You Need to Know

- ✓ Accretion
- ✓ Accrued interest
- ✓ Adjustment bond (income bond)
- ✓ Arbitrage
- ✓ Call risk
- ✓ Collateral trust certificate
- ✓ Convertible bond (or convertible debenture)
- ✓ Conversion ratio
- ✓ Credit risk
- ✓ Debenture
- ✓ Equipment trust certificate (ETC)
- ✓ Eurobond
- ✓ Eurodollar bond
- ✓ First mortgage bond
- ✓ Forced conversion
- ✓ Interest rate risk
- ✓ Junk bond
- ✓ Legislative risk
- ✓ Liquidity risk
- ✓ Market risk
- ✓ Marketability risk
- ✓ Nine-bond rule (NYSE Rule 396)
- ✓ Parity price of bond
- ✓ Parity price of stock
- ✓ Phantom interest
- ✓ Reinvestment risk
- ✓ Second mortgage bond
- ✓ Secured debt
- ✓ Subordinated debenture
- ✓ Unsecured debt
- ✓ Yellow Sheets
- ✓ Zero coupon bond

Concepts You Need to Understand

- ✓ Inverted yield curve
- ✓ Yield curve
- ✓ Normal yield curve
- ✓ Payment of accrued interest
- ✓ Risks faced by bondholders
- ✓ How investors use yield curves

Different Kinds of Corporate Bonds

Companies have a range of options when issuing bonds. As mentioned in Chapter 4, "Corporate Debts: Bonds and Yields," bonds often permit companies to structure their debt in a manner that better suits their needs than bank loans do. Certain companies can issue bonds with lower coupon rates by pledging some of their assets as collateral. Other companies find it advantageous to issue unsecured bonds—debt not backed by collateral but by the issuer's good name. Many unsecured bonds are issued with a conversion feature that enables investors to turn bonds into shares of the issuer's common stock. After examining the differences between secured and unsecured corporate bonds, this chapter will look at how bonds are traded, how they are taxed, and how to interpret their yield curves.

The bond market offers a variety of bonds to meet corporations' financial needs. Bonds also vary because they reflect the financial situations and track records of the specific companies. An important preliminary distinction is whether a bond represents secured or unsecured debt. In general, companies prefer to issue bonds that do not require them to pledge collateral. Companies with weaker credit ratings might have to provide some form of collateral to issue their debt at a favorable rate.

Secured Debt

Secured debt is any debt, such as a bond, for which the issuer pledges land, buildings, or other tangible assets as collateral. If a company cannot make the required payments on its secured bond issue, the trustee named in the indenture sells the pledged asset and uses the proceeds to repay bondholders. Secured bonds often receive higher ratings from the ratings agencies, as bondholders' risks have been mitigated. Better ratings enable the issuer to pay lower interest rates. Note that the company is potentially giving up control over its pledged assets.

There are three main kinds of secured bonds:

- **Mortgage bonds**—These bonds are backed by some or all of the issuer's real estate holdings. The company can issue *first mortgage bonds* and *second mortgage bonds*, both secured by the same property. If the company fails and its assets are liquidated, first mortgage bondholders have priority over second mortgage bondholders.
- **Equipment trust certificate (ETC)**—ETC bonds are secured by the same equipment that the company purchases with the proceeds of the bond offering. For example, a railroad company needing to purchase

railcars can sell ETCs that pledge the new cars as collateral. ETCs are common among utilities, truckers, airlines, and railroads.

- **Collateral trust certificate**—These are bonds backed by a portfolio of negotiable securities, instead of real estate or equipment. Frequently, the pledged securities are issued by subsidiaries of the issuer.

Unsecured Bonds

Unsecured bonds—called *debentures*—are issued on the strength of a company's name and credit history. By purchasing debentures, investors face greater risks and therefore generally receive higher interest rates. Purchasers of *subordinated debentures* experience even more risk, because their claims come after debenture holders in the event of bankruptcy. Hence, subordinated debentures typically pay a higher interest rate than debentures.

Debentures compare to consumer credit cards, which offer unsecured lines of credit to individuals. Companies with strong track records of debt repayment often choose to issue debentures—their good name alone acts as security for investors. But companies at the other end of the financial spectrum—those with weak repayment records and speculative ratings—also issue unsecured debt. The difference is that the latter companies have to pay significantly higher coupons (interest) to attract investors.

One way for companies to make their unsecured bonds more attractive to investors is to offer a conversion feature.

A *convertible bond* (or *convertible debenture*) can be exchanged for common stock of the issuing company, much like convertible preferred stock. Although the exact features of convertible debentures vary, they all establish a conversion price—the price per common share at which the bonds can be converted.

Like convertible preferred stock, convertible bonds are issued with a conversion price, from which the conversion ratio is determined. The *conversion ratio*, below, tells the investor how many common stock shares each bond can be exchanged for.

$$\text{conversion ratio} = \frac{\text{bond's par value}}{\text{conversion price}} = \text{shares per bond}$$

EXAMPLE: AM Global issues $1,000 par bonds, convertible at $40 per common share. The conversion ratio—the number of common stock shares the bond is exchanged for—is found by dividing the par value of the bond by the conversion price. Thus, the conversion ratio for these bonds is 25:1.

$$\text{conversion ratio} = \frac{\$1{,}000}{\$40} = 25 \text{ shares per bond}$$

The value of this conversion feature depends on the market price of the common stock. Assume that the previous AM bonds are trading at par, whereas AM shares are trading for $32 in the marketplace. If a bondholder converts at this time, he or she receives only $800 worth of stock (25 shares × $32 = $800), a loss of $200.

An investor begins to think about converting a debenture into common stock when the price of the stock multiplied by the conversion ratio is equal to or greater than the value of the bond. If the market value of the shares received equals the current market value of the bond, the stock and the bond are trading at parity.

Calculating Parity Price

Investors use the following formula to determine the *parity price of stock*:

$$\text{parity price of stock} = \frac{\text{market price of bond}}{\text{conversion ratio}}$$

EXAMPLE: Returning to the AM Global bonds, the conversion ratio remains at 25:1. Suppose the bonds are currently quoted at 102 7/8. At what stock price might conversion be attractive to an AM bondholder?

$$\text{parity price of stock} = \frac{\$1{,}028.75}{25} = 41.15$$

So, for the conversion to benefit the investor, AM's common stock has to trade at a price greater than 41.15.

Sometimes investors want to determine the selling price of their convertible bonds, given the current stock price. The parity price of a bond can be found using the following formula:

parity price of bond = conversion ratio × share price of stock

EXAMPLE: The AM Global bonds have a conversion ratio of 25:1, whereas AM common stock is selling at $45 per share. At what price should the bonds be trading?

parity price of bond = 25 × $45 = $1,125

To achieve parity with AM stock, the bonds need to trade around 112.5. If the bonds are selling for a lower price, bondholders can make money by converting.

An opportunity exists when bonds sell for less than their parity price. This situation can arise because a company's bonds do not trade in the same market as its stocks. Further, bond prices respond to interest rate movements, whereas stock prices are affected by news about companies and their profitability. Occasionally, convertible bonds fall out of synch with their common stock. Any time a bond sells at a discount to its parity price, an arbitrage opportunity exists.

Arbitrage

In an *arbitrage* transaction, an investor makes a profit by trading the same security in different markets, taking advantage of price differences. In the case of convertible debentures, the bonds and their related common stock are considered different forms of the same security because of the conversion feature. What is a bond on Monday can become shares of common stock on Tuesday.

> **EXAMPLE:** Unitech bonds have a conversion ratio of 40:1. They are currently quoted at 110. Unitech stock is selling at $27.75. Does an arbitrage opportunity exist? Yes, because the parity price of the bond is $1,110 (40 × $27.75). A canny investor can buy bonds at $1,100, convert each one into stock worth $1,110, immediately sell the stock, and make $10 per bond on the transaction.

Whenever the market price of a convertible bond falls below its parity price, investors can profit by arbitrage. Holders of convertible bonds also need to be concerned about the effect of stock splits and stock dividends.

Most convertible bond indentures contain a protective covenant that lowers the conversion price in the event of a stock split or stock dividend, which put more shares in circulation. After the split or dividend, each share has a lower market price. A convertible debenture, therefore, will lose value if the conversion price is not similarly adjusted.

Convertible Bonds

An issuer can usually pay a lower coupon rate because of the conversion feature—investors are willing to give up some interest income for the advantage of convertibility. Also, when bondholders convert, the company no longer has to pay interest on the bond. It swaps required interest payments for discretionary dividend payments. This, however, can be a mixed blessing. The more bondholders who convert, the more common stock ownership is diluted, lowering the company's earnings per share (EPS). Investors often use EPS as a benchmark for judging stocks, so companies try to avoid events that might seriously lower the figure. Finally, because of the potential dilution of common stock, companies must get shareholder approval before issuing convertible bonds, making the entire process more cumbersome.

Most convertible debentures are callable, thus presenting investors with call risk. An investor might never profit from the conversion feature. Depending on conditions in the bond market, owners of convertible debentures might actually be forced to convert their bonds.

Other types of unsecured bonds include

- **Adjustment bond (income bond)**—Bond issued by a company facing bankruptcy. The company replaces its existing bonds with new adjustment bonds, which typically trade flat—that is, without interest—and are considered speculative.
- **Eurobond**—Bond issued in the currency of one country and sold in another country. Investors buying these bonds face foreign currency risk in addition to the normal risks associated with bonds. *Eurodollar bonds* are dollar-denominated bonds issued outside of the United States.
- **Guaranteed bond**—Bond issued by one company and backed by another (usually the parent company). This enables the subsidiary to take on the credit rating of the stronger parent company.
- **Junk bond**—Bond that is deemed speculative by ratings agencies. Junk bonds normally pay a significantly higher coupon than investment grade bonds, because of their greater risk of default.
- **Zero coupon bond**—Bond that pays no periodic interest and is thus sold at a discount. The investor's return comes strictly from receiving the bond's par value at maturity. Zero coupon bonds have interest rate risk. Although owners of zero coupon bonds receive no interest payments, they must pay taxes every year as if they did. From the time of purchase until maturity, the owners of zero coupons accrete their phantom interest.

Moody's begins its speculative grades with Ba, whereas Standard & Poor's and Fitch's Investors Service start their "junk" bonds with BB. Moody's lowest rating is Baa, S&P's and Fitch's go down to BBB.

How Corporate Bonds Are Traded

Although corporate bonds are found on several exchanges, the vast majority of them trade in the OTC market. Member firms of the New York Stock Exchange must observe what is called the *nine-bond rule (NYSE Rule 396)*—when executing orders for nine bonds or fewer, they have to place the order on the exchange floor for one hour before taking the order to the OTC market. The nine-bond rule is designed to help small investors find a wider market, and perhaps a better price, for their bonds. Investors, however, can request that the rule be waived.

For bonds traded over the counter, bid and asked prices can be found in the *Yellow Sheets*, which are published by the National Quotation Bureau every business day. Bonds appearing in the *Yellow Sheets* can be listed on an exchange, but the trades reported have taken place in the OTC marketplace. Trading activity on the NYSE and AMEX is found in the financial pages of most newspapers. Corporate bonds are quoted on a percentage of par basis.

How Bonds Are Transferred and Interest Accrued

In general, bonds are transferred according to the same settlement schedule as stocks—regular way settlement is three business days after the trade date (T + 3). However, bond sales involve an extra step—determining the accrued interest.

Accrued interest is the interest earned on a bond from the date of the last interest payment until the time of the sale. The seller is entitled to this accrued interest.

Interest income on a corporate bond is computed on a 30-day month/360-day year basis. To calculate accrued interest, count how many days have passed since the last coupon payment. Make sure to include the day interest was paid, but not the settlement date of the bond sale. Finally, find the amount of interest the bond earns each day, and multiply this amount by the correct number of days.

> **EXAMPLE:** On Monday, October 6, Mr. Murphy sold Dr. Melville 10 bonds with a coupon of 8% at a price of 94. The bonds pay interest on January 1st and July 1st. How much does Dr. Melville owe Mr. Murphy? First, she owes $9,400 for the principal portion ($940 × 10). To calculate accrued interest, she needs to determine how many days have passed since the last interest payment. She includes the day that interest was paid, but not the settlement date.

July = 30 days

August = 30 days

September = 30 days

October = 8 days (T + 2, not T + 3)

Total = 98 days of accrued interest

Now she calculates how much interest the bonds earn per day. With an 8% coupon, the 10 bonds pay $800 per year. Dividing $800 by 360 days, she gets a daily interest income of $2.22. Dr. Melville thus owes $217.56 in accrued interest ($2.22 × 98), for a total of $9,617.56 on the settlement date ($9,400 + $217.56).

Do all bonds pay interest January 1st and July 1st? Although companies issue bonds throughout the year, they observe the same calendar for payments—first they make a partial interest payment covering the period from the date of issue to either January 1st or July 1st (whichever is closer), and then they make regular, semiannual payments thereafter.

How Corporate Bonds Are Taxed

State governments and the federal government tax interest income from corporate bonds as ordinary income for the tax year in which it is received. Holders of corporate bonds must also factor in capital gains or losses. When a bond is purchased at a discount and held to maturity, a capital gain is realized. This capital gain is spread over the life of the bond in a process known as *accretion*. The accreted value for each year is treated as taxable interest income. Because no cash is actually received, however, the income is usually referred to as *phantom interest*. At maturity, the entire capital gain is accreted and no additional taxes are due.

EXAMPLE: A bond with a face value of $1,000, a 10% coupon, and 20 years remaining until maturity is purchased for $800. The bondholder realizes a capital gain of $200 over 20 years. For tax purposes, he or she must report $10 per year for the accretion of that gain ($200 ÷ 20), plus $100 per year in interest income, for a total annual income from the bond of $110.

How Premium Bonds Are Taxed

Premium bonds are treated like discount bonds, except that in this case capital losses *reduce* bondholders' annual taxable income. Over the life of their bonds investors can *amortize* the premiums they paid.

EXAMPLE: A bond with a par value of $1,000, an 8% coupon, and 12 years until maturity is purchased for $1,120. The bondholder incurs a capital loss of $120 over 12 years. So, the purchaser amortizes a $10 loss each year ($120 ÷ 12), partially offsetting the $80 of annual interest income, for a total annual income of $70.

Risks Are Associated with Bonds

The fundamental risk is *credit risk*—the risk that the company will default on its interest and principal payments. Investors can rely on ratings agencies to provide accurate assessments of the degree of credit risk present in particular bonds. Other risks to keep in mind include:

- **Interest rate risk**—Risk that a bond will lose value because interest rates rise.
- **Call risk**—Risk that a bond will be called and reduce the investor's expected gains.
- **Marketability risk**—Risk that a bond will be difficult to sell in the future. This depends on the market demand for the bond.
- **Liquidity risk**—Risk that selling the bond will involve above-average transaction costs (similar to marketability risk). Generally, short-term and highly rated bonds are more liquid than long-term and low-rated bonds.
- **Legislative risk**—Risk that state or federal governments will change, in an adverse way for investors, such as how interest income or capital gains and losses are taxed.
- **Reinvestment risk**—Risk that an investor cannot reinvest bond earnings at an equal or higher rate of return.
- **Market risk**—Risk that a bond's value will vary greatly with movements in interest rates. This risk is particularly strong for bonds with long maturities or low coupons because their prices move more dramatically with changes in interest rates.

The more time left until a bond's maturity, the greater the danger that one or more of these risks will hurt bondholders. Time itself thus becomes a crucial factor in the degree of risk associated with any bond. The longer a bond's maturity, the higher its yield normally is. Market analysts use yield curves to interpret bond earnings relative to their maturity dates.

Yield Curve

A *yield curve* is a line graph that shows the relationship between bond maturities and yields, helping investors evaluate interest rate trends over time. A *normal yield curve* shows that yields increase as bond maturities lengthen. Normal yield curves generally reflect an expanding economy, in which investors can anticipate greater returns for long-term investments.

Investors sometimes face flat or inverted yield curves. If the monetary policymakers of the nation fear that economic expansion has peaked and inflation is threatening, they will take steps to tighten the money supply. But because the market for short-term debt is much larger than that for long-term, the impact of higher interest rates are felt more immediately in the short-term market. Short-term rates become closer to long-term rates, creating a *flat yield curve*.

Inverted yield curves are rare—short-term rates have to rise above long-term rates to produce an inverted yield curve. This occurs if the economy becomes "overheated" and inflation threatens to break into a destructive spiral, leading monetary authorities to reduce available credit in the marketplace.

The *Wall Street Journal* regularly publishes a yield curve based on Treasury securities.

Exam Prep Questions

1. Roundway Transport's debentures are backed by
   - ❑ A. Roundway's assets
   - ❑ B. Roundway's name and good credit
   - ❑ C. Property Roundway has pledged against the bond
   - ❑ D. Roundway's plant and equipment
2. Roundway Transport has issued all the following types of securities. On which does it pay the highest rate of interest?
   - ❑ A. First mortgage bonds
   - ❑ B. Debentures
   - ❑ C. Subordinate debentures
   - ❑ D. Second mortgage bonds
3. Hudson Hills, Inc., issues bonds at par that are convertible to common stock at $25. What is the conversion ratio of the bonds?
   - ❑ A. 25:1
   - ❑ B. 50:1
   - ❑ C. 40:1
   - ❑ D. 4:1
4. Norbert has purchased a convertible bond for Locust, Inc., at 120 and has a conversion ratio of 30. If Locust is trading at 38, when is Norbert most likely to convert his bond?
   - ❑ A. Immediately
   - ❑ B. When Locust falls to 33 3/8 or lower
   - ❑ C. When Locust rises to 40
   - ❑ D. When Locust rises above 40
5. Zyxon convertible bonds, which have a conversion ratio of 25, are selling at 110. The parity price for Zyxon is which of the following?
   - ❑ A. 41.38
   - ❑ B. 42
   - ❑ C. 44
   - ❑ D. 44.37
6. The Mirabelle Company issues convertible bonds with a coupon of 6.50% and a conversion ratio of 18. Mirabelle shares are currently trading at 57.25, so the bonds should be trading at which of the following?
   - ❑ A. 100
   - ❑ B. 103.50
   - ❑ C. 67
   - ❑ D. 158.50

7. Graceland Tchotchkes, Inc., has issued convertible bonds with a conversion ratio of 22. Steven notices that the bonds are priced at 114.50, whereas Graceland's stock sells at 52.50. Steven should

   - ❑ A. Wait for Graceland stock to drop before taking any action.
   - ❑ B. Buy the bond and convert it to stock.
   - ❑ C. Buy the bond and hold it for later conversion.
   - ❑ D. Sell the stock short and buy the bonds.

8. On the brink of bankruptcy, Fuchsia Fashions decides to restructure its debts. It issues

   - ❑ A. Moral obligation bonds
   - ❑ B. Zero coupon bonds
   - ❑ C. Adjustment bonds
   - ❑ D. Promissory notes

9. Each of the following is an example of a Eurobond except:

   - ❑ A. A dollar-denominated bond issued in Germany by Ameri-Tours, a U.S. company.
   - ❑ B. A Euro-denominated bond issued in the United States by Funk-Werner, a German company.
   - ❑ C. A pound-sterling-denominated bond issued in the United States by Wessex Motor Cars, an English company.
   - ❑ D. A French franc-denominated bond issued in France by Hat Trick Trading, a Canadian company.

10. Joey Manufacturing issues guaranteed bonds. These bonds are which of the following?

    - ❑ A. AAA-rated
    - ❑ B. Backed by Kangaroo Industries, Joey's parent company
    - ❑ C. Guaranteed by government subsidies
    - ❑ D. Issued by blue-chip companies only

11. Karen enters an order with Matt, her broker, to purchase Circle, Inc., corporate bonds. Under the NYSE nine-bond rule, what must Matt do?

    - ❑ A. He must keep the order open on the NYSE floor for one hour before moving it to the OTC market.
    - ❑ B. If the order is for nine bonds or more, he must keep it open on the NYSE floor for one hour before moving it to the OTC market.
    - ❑ C. If the order is for nine bonds or fewer, he must keep it open on the NYSE floor for one hour before moving it to the OTC market.
    - ❑ D. If the order is for nine bonds or fewer, he must place it in the OTC market rather than on the exchange.

12. In the financial newspaper *Business Battery*, Marilyn sees the listing "WrldCorp 7s02-10 8.4 350 96.13 unch." What does this tell her about the WorldCorp bond?

    I. The bond is callable.

    II. Trading is active.

    III. The bond is selling at a premium.

    IV. The bond closed at the previous day's close.

    - ❑ A. I and II
    - ❑ B. I and III
    - ❑ C. I, III, and IV
    - ❑ D. I, II, and IV

13. All the following statements about accrued interest on corporate bonds are false except:

    - ❑ A. The seller pays it.
    - ❑ B. It is paid on settlement date.
    - ❑ C. It is computed on an actual/actual basis.
    - ❑ D. It is computed on an actual/360 basis.

14. Julie sells Tex 10 WorldCorp bonds on June 15. The trade settles regular way. How many days of accrued interest does she receive?

    - ❑ A. 165 days
    - ❑ B. 169 days
    - ❑ C. 167 days
    - ❑ D. 13 days

15. Which of the following bonds has the highest market risk?

    - ❑ A. A 10-year 8% subordinated debenture
    - ❑ B. A 20-year 5% corporate
    - ❑ C. A 30-year 9% debenture
    - ❑ D. A 30-year 5% first mortgage bond

Exam Prep Answers

1. The correct answer is B. Debentures are unsecured bonds issued on the strength of a company's name and credit history. Investors who purchase Roundway debentures have faith in Roundway's management and financial prospects.

2. The correct answer is C. Subordinated debentures are both unsecured and junior to debentures in their claim on the firm's assets. To attract investors, they must pay a higher rate of interest than other types of corporate bonds.

3. The correct answer is C. The conversion ratio—the number of common shares for which the bond can be exchanged—is the bond's par value divided by the conversion price. Investors can exchange Hudson Hills' $1,000 bond for 40 shares of common stock ($1,000 ÷ $25 = 40).

4. The correct answer is D. Norbert paid $1,200 for the bond ($1,000 × 120). It thus has a parity price—the price at which the value of the shares he will receive is equal to the market value of the bond—of 40 ($1,200 market price ÷ 30 conversion ratio). Norbert will want to convert his bond when the stock rises above 40.

5. The correct answer is C. The Zyxon bond is currently selling for $1,100 ($1,000 × 110). Because the parity price of the stock is the market price of the bond divided by the conversion ratio, the parity price for Zyxon stock is $44 ($1,100 ÷ 25).

6. The correct answer is B. The parity price of Mirabelle's bonds—the amount at which they should currently be trading, given the price of its stock—is the conversion ratio times the price per share. Mirabelle's bonds should thus be trading at 103.50 (18 × $57.25 = $1,030.50).

7. The correct answer is B. The parity price of the stock is the market price of the bond divided by the conversion ratio. Graceland stock's parity price is thus slightly higher than 52 ($1,145 ÷ 22 = 52.05). Put another way, if Steven converts the bond, he can purchase the shares at 52 when they are selling in the market at 52.50.

8. The correct answer is C. A company facing bankruptcy issues adjustment bonds. Fuchsia will replace its existing bonds with these, which will probably have a higher par value than the original bonds. The new bonds pay interest only if Fuchsia has sufficient income to do so. (Municipalities issue moral obligation bonds. Zero coupon bonds are issued at a deep discount and mature at par. Companies issue

promissory notes to guarantee payment of a specific sum, either on demand or at a specific date.)

9. The correct answer is D. Bonds denominated in French francs which are sold in France are not Eurobonds. Companies issue Eurobonds denominated in their own currency and sell them in a foreign market. Investors who buy these bonds expose themselves to exchange risk in addition to the risks normally associated with bonds.

10. The correct answer is B. A company can issue guaranteed bonds, or bonds backed by another company. As in Joey's case, the backer is usually the parent company of the issuer. This arrangement enables Joey's bonds to take on the credit rating of Kangaroo Industries.

11. The correct answer is C. The nine-bond rule, also known as NYSE Rule 396, was established to help small investors find a wider market and perhaps a better price for their bonds. It requires that member firms executing orders for nine bonds or fewer place the order on the floor of the NYSE for one hour before taking it to the OTC market. However, investors can request that the rule be waived.

12. The correct answer is D. Because the bond closed at 96.13, it is trading at a discount, not a premium. (The coupon of 7.0%—7s, with the "s" separating the coupon from the maturity—coupled with the current yield of 8.4% indicates this.) The closing was unchanged from the previous day. The figures 02-10 show that the bond is callable in 2002 and due in 2010, whereas the figure 350 indicates a trading volume of 350,000 bonds, a considerable amount.

13. The correct answer is B. The buyer of a corporate bond pays the accrued interest to the seller on the settlement date. It is computed on a 30/360 basis.

14. The correct answer is C. The trade settles on June 18. Julie must receive the interest earned up to this date. Because interest is paid on January 1st and July 1st, Tex owes Julie the interest for five months (January 1st–June 1st = 5 months × 30 days = 150), plus 17 days. Tex will recover this amount on July 1st when he receives six months' interest as the owner of the bond.

15. The correct answer is D. Market risk is the risk that a bond's value will vary greatly with movements in interest rates. This risk is particularly strong for bonds with long maturities or low coupons. Although the debenture and subordinated debenture have a higher credit risk, they have a lower market risk.

The Money Market

Terms You Need to Know

- ✓ Banker's acceptance
- ✓ Call rate (or broker loan rate)
- ✓ Commercial paper
- ✓ Discount rate
- ✓ Eurodollars
- ✓ Federal funds
- ✓ Federal funds rate (or Fed funds rate)
- ✓ Federal Open Market Committee (FOMC)
- ✓ Federal Reserve System (the Fed)
- ✓ LIBOR (London Interbank Offered Rate)
- ✓ Matched sale (or match)
- ✓ Money center bank
- ✓ Money market
- ✓ Money market fund
- ✓ Money market instrument
- ✓ Negotiable certificates of deposit (or jumbo CDs)
- ✓ Open market operations
- ✓ Primary dealers
- ✓ Prime rate
- ✓ Repurchase agreement
- ✓ Reserve requirement
- ✓ Reverse repurchase agreement
- ✓ Treasury security (or Treasury)

Concepts You Need to Understand

- ✓ The importance of the money market
- ✓ The major players and what they seek
- ✓ The mechanics of a repurchase agreement
- ✓ How the Fed can adjust the nation's money supply
- ✓ Why use repos
- ✓ Why corporations issue commercial paper
- ✓ The purpose of banker's acceptances
- ✓ Which highly mobile funds compose the heart of the money market
- ✓ How an individual investor enters the money market

Market Overview

Businesses can raise capital by issuing securities, such as stocks and bonds, but the underwriting process can be lengthy and costly. Often a company or a bank needs a quick infusion of cash; to obtain it, the enterprise can enter what is called the *money market*, where it sells debt securities for the short run. Other companies might have extra cash on hand—and be looking for ways to earn a return on these unused funds. They can enter the money market as buyers. The money market is really composed of two things: a variety of short-term debt securities and a number of special arrangements for trading them. Together, the securities and the trading arrangements are referred to as "instruments." A distinguishing characteristic of money market instruments is their relative safety, because the issuers are usually large corporations, banks, and the U.S. government.

The *money market* is where businesses, the U.S. government, and institutional investors meet to buy and sell various debt securities for short periods of time. Some of the instruments are found exclusively in the money market, whereas others enjoy a wider existence in the debt market

A Money Market Instrument

A *money market instrument* is a debt security that typically matures in one year or less, and is traded by banks, corporations, investment companies, and the federal government. The issuer has sold the instrument specifically to raise money in the near term. More generally, a money market instrument can be a method or agreement for trading such securities in the short run. So the phrase "money market instruments" refers both to securities and to ways of selling them. Within the money market's short time frame, most instruments have negotiable maturity dates, a benefit to both seller and buyer. Furthermore, they are judged to be extremely safe, because they are backed either by the U.S. government or by a major corporation or bank.

A money market instrument is a debt security that matures in less than a year, usually only overnight or a few days. They are traded by banks, corporations, investment companies, and the federal government.

The Importance of the Money Market

The money market plays a crucial, and threefold, role in the economy. First, businesses can acquire short-term cash—or invest surplus cash in interest-bearing securities—through money market transactions. Second, the money market provides the *Federal Reserve System* (or *Fed*), the central bank of the United States, with a means of controlling the money supply. Third, through pension funds and certain mutual funds, the money market gives individual investors an opportunity to make safe, short-term investments with relatively stable rates of return.

The Fed

Congress created the Federal Reserve System in 1913 to regulate the money supply and solidify the country's banking system. All nationally chartered banks are members; state-chartered banks can choose to apply for membership. Member banks have to buy stock in one of the 12 regional Federal Reserve Banks, whose responsibilities include ensuring that banks abide by the Federal Reserve Board's regulations, such as maintaining proper reserve requirements and overseeing the issue of currency.

The money supply is controlled by the Federal Reserve Bank by buying and selling certain negotiable securities.

The money market does not have a "location" or "floor" like the stock markets. Buyers and sellers conduct their business over–the-counter, meaning by phone, fax, or computer. They simply are not fact-to-face in any sense of the term. Some of the most important players are the money center banks, which are large commercial banks located in the world's major financial cities (such as New York, Chicago, Tokyo, or London). Money center banks not only issue some of the instruments in the money market but they are also major traders of the rest of the securities found there. They, like all banks, must meet the Fed's reserve requirements. The Fed carries out its direct interventions in the money market through the trading desk of the Federal Reserve Bank of New York. Finally, most big brokerage firms maintain money market desks.

Practically speaking, the small individual investor can only enter this market indirectly, by investing in one of the money market funds established by broker-dealers, or by saving in a pension fund that purchases money market instruments. It takes huge amounts of cash to enter this market and few individuals have it.

How Money Market Funds Work

As a type of mutual fund (or open-end investment firm), money market funds must register with the SEC and can only sell their shares by prospectus.

Customers do not acquire actual shares in the underlying securities, but rather shares in the fund itself. These shares are maintained in $1 denominations. Based on the returns the fund is earning from its current portfolio, the firm pays interest to its investors in the form of additional $1 shares and fractional shares totaling up to $1.00.

Money market funds provide customers with a relatively safe place to store their money while earning a higher rate of return than they get from a regular savings account. Further, they offer considerable liquidity—most money market funds provide check-writing privileges. When a person writes a check for $1,000, the fund simply sells 1,000 shares to cover the amount of the check.

The Federal Reserve's Role in the Money Market

Whereas corporations and banks are interested in the money market as a place to acquire and dispose of cash in the short run, the Federal Reserve uses the money market to help regulate the pace of economic activity. From the perspective of the country's overall economic performance, the Fed's actions in the money market are profoundly important. The Fed accomplishes its objectives in three main ways:

- **The discount rate.** This is the interest rate at which the Federal Reserve allows banks (and other depository institutions) to borrow money when they cannot obtain funds elsewhere to meet their reserve requirements or liquidity needs. The discount rate functions as a floor for interest rates; commercial banks set their lending rates above it. When the *Federal Open Market Committee* adjusts the discount rate, it is signaling a significant change in its economic outlook. Although infrequent, a change in the discount rate leads banks to adjust their rates accordingly, therefore affecting the overall amount of borrowing.

- **Reserve requirements.** The Federal Reserve sets the percentage of customer deposits that banks (and other depository institutions) must keep either in a Federal Reserve Bank or in their own vaults. These cash reserves are called *Federal funds.* If the Fed wants to decrease the amount of money that banks have available for lending—thereby shrinking the money supply and slowing the economy—it can raise the reserve requirement. Lowering the reserve requirement has the opposite effect.

WHAT'S IN RESERVE?

Which customer deposits does a bank count when calculating its reserves? For the purpose of meeting the Fed's reserve requirements, banks must total their transaction deposits (checking and other accounts from which transfers can be made to third parties) and their nonpersonal time deposits (such as CDs and savings accounts not held by individuals). The Fed establishes a percentage of each of these categories that banks must maintain as reserves.

- **Open market operations.** Through its open market desk at the Federal Reserve Bank of New York, the Fed buys and sells government securities. When it buys securities from banks and brokerage firms, the Fed indirectly boosts banks' reserves, helping lower a key short-term interest rate. Conversely, when the Fed sells securities, it reduces banks' available reserves, thereby raising the Fed funds rate.

For day-to-day fine-tuning of market interest rates, the Fed relies on an open market transaction called the repurchase agreement.

The Fed regulates the money market in three main ways: through the discount rate, reserve requirements, and open market operations. A clear understanding of these actions by the Federal Reserve is paramount to exam success and to broker dealer performance.

Money Market Instruments

Money market instruments are short-term debt instruments that mature in one year or less. This is the financial market in which banks borrow from and lend to each other via short-term instruments such as commercial paper, CDs, banker's acceptances, and government securities. They also enter into agreements such as repurchase agreements as well as forward rate agreements and short-term interest rate futures. For the purpose of this book, however, the important instruments to know are described next.

Commercial Paper

Commercial paper consists of short-term debt—in the form of promissory notes—issued by corporations and banks. Because commercial paper matures in 270 days or fewer, issuers do not have to register their offerings with the SEC. Unlike repurchase agreements, which are backed by government securities, commercial paper is unsecured, meaning that buyers depend solely on the good faith of the issuing companies for repayment. Normally, however, the issuers of commercial paper are highly regarded firms with excellent credit ratings, so repayment is not a great concern.

EXAMPLE: Xyron Corporation must find almost $7 million to pay for unexpected cost overruns at its chemical plant in Texas. Company officers figure they will need the extra cash just until fertilizer sales pick up in the spring, about three months away. Banks offer to loan Xyron the money at 8% interest, which is the *prime rate,* or what they charge their best corporate customers. Instead, Xyron issues commercial paper with a par value of $7 million for 90 days. It sells the paper at a discount to various investors, who pay a total of $6,900,000. In other words, Xyron is obligated to pay its creditors $100,000 for the three-month loan. How much money will the company save? Xyron will save $36,110. (8% of $6.9 million equals $552,000. Divide this amount by 365—the number of days in a year—and multiply by 90—the maturity of Xyron's commercial paper—to arrive at $136,110.)

Why do corporations issue commercial paper? As the previous example illustrates, established companies with good credit ratings can usually issue commercial paper more cheaply than they can borrow money from banks. Most commercial paper is sold at a discount and then redeemed for its par value at maturity. Some commercial paper bears interest. In either case, the borrower ends up paying a rate of interest (actual or implied) on the loan. If this rate beats the current bank rate for short-term loans, the company is well-advised to issue commercial paper rather than take out a bank loan. An issuer with high creditworthiness increases its chances of securing a low-priced loan through the sale of commercial paper.

Corporations issue commercial paper to raise cash cheaper than borrowing from a bank. Commercial paper is sold at a discount and repurchased at par value.

As with bonds, both Moody's and Standard & Poor's rate the prospects of repayment for offerings of commercial paper. Two other important rating agencies for commercial paper are Fitch and Duff & Phelps. Ratings are based on the issuer's repayment record for short-term debt. Even though most issuers are blue-chip corporations, commercial paper does carry some risk.

How important is the market for commercial paper? Within the money market, the trading volume of commercial paper is exceeded only by T-Bills. For blue-chip companies and banks, commercial paper offers an affordable way to raise cash quickly. Because commercial paper is usually issued in large denominations, purchasers are generally institutional investors and banks, who view "paper" as a good way to earn a return on excess cash reserves.

The biggest players in the money market have another means of raising money—the jumbo CD.

Jumbo CDs

Jumbo CDs—also known as *negotiable certificates of deposit*—are short-term debt securities that pay interest to the investor and are traded in the money market. "Jumbo" is the key word; these CDs are not of the same magnitude as the ones you buy at your local bank. The minimum size of a jumbo CD is $100,000, but amounts of $1 million and more are common. Large commercial banks sell them to raise money, whereas large institutional investors buy them to earn a fixed rate of interest. Because they are considered to be safe and are easily traded, jumbo CDs are a favorite investment for managers of money market funds.

Typically, jumbo CDs mature in one to three months. The shortest maturity is seven days and, although there is no maximum maturity, most mature in less than a year.

Banks play several key roles in the money market. The banker's acceptance is yet another banking instrument commonly traded here.

Banker's Acceptances

A *banker's acceptance*, a time draft written by a business and guaranteed by its bank, enables the business to import or export goods. In effect, the bank is lending its customer the money needed to pay for imports—against the collateral of the goods that are to be imported. The procedure is fairly complicated:

1. The U.S. company and the foreign exporter agree on a price for the goods. Because the transaction is made with a time draft (a check payable in the future), the foreign company must consider what the discounted value of the check is.

2. The U.S. company goes to its bank and secures a conditional loan. The bank agrees to write a letter of credit guaranteeing the company's time draft, provided that it (the bank) receives the shipping documents for the imported goods, plus temporary title to them. The letter of credit and time draft are sent to the foreign exporter.

3. The foreign exporter sends the requested documents to the U.S. bank, which guarantees or "accepts" the time draft. The exporter can now safely ship the goods. For payment, it can either hold the time draft until maturity or take the check and the letter of credit to a domestic bank, where it can sell the check at a discount. In the latter case, the

time draft, guaranteed by the U.S. bank, becomes a full-fledged banker's acceptance. It is now a tradable money market instrument.

4. At the date of maturity on the banker's acceptance, two things happen:
   - The U.S. company pays the holder the instrument's face value.
   - The U.S. company pays its bank a commission for providing the line of credit.

The banker's acceptance instills business confidence. Because of the time draft , the foreign exporter knows that its goods will be paid for and can proceed to ship them. On the other side, the U.S. importer knows that it will receive the goods because its check is post-dated and because its bank holds temporary title to the goods. The importance of banker's acceptances to the flow of world trade is apparent.

Repurchase Agreements

In a *repurchase agreement (repo)*, the seller of a debt security, usually a *Treasury security*, agrees to buy the security back within a short period of time for a specified amount. In effect, the buyer is making a short-term loan to the seller. Of course the buyer makes a profit by setting the "sell-back" price higher than the original purchase price. Both business and government engage in repurchase agreements, although for markedly different reasons.

Through the Federal Reserve, the U.S. government can enter into repo agreements with a special group of broker-dealers called *primary dealers*. These large investment houses and banks have to meet a stringent set of financial and operational criteria, as well as maintain a presence in the money market at all times. In return, they gain the privilege of being the only brokerage firms that deal directly with the Fed, thus serving as a "transmission belt" between the Fed and the financial markets. The Federal Open Market Committee takes indications of interest from the primary dealers and sets a daily intervention rate for the day's repo auction. This rate induces the primary dealers to buy or sell the amount of Treasuries that the Fed wants to trade.

To temporarily expand bank reserves, the Fed will buy Treasury securities with an agreement to sell them. Dealers deposit their receipts in commercial banks, which boosts the banks' reserves, making it easier for the banks to meet their reserve requirements. The Fed pays interest for the transaction, at the intervention rate set for the auction. If, on the other hand, the Fed wants to temporarily shrink bank reserves, it can enter into *reverse repurchase agreements*. Here it will *sell* Treasury securities to primary dealers, agreeing to buy them back at the conclusion of the agreed-upon period. This latter procedure is called, from the perspective of the Fed, a *matched sale* (or a *match*) because sales are matched to later purchases. To pay for the securities, dealers must draw down their accounts at commercial banks, thereby making it more difficult for banks to meet their reserve requirements. Again, at the end of the period, the Fed pays interest to the dealers at the intervention rate.

EXAMPLE: The economy is cranking along at a good rate, business inventories are low, exports are booming, and unemployment is falling. The only problem is that short-term interest rates are creeping upward. Banks need an infusion of cash, at least until the end of the month, when employees will be depositing their paychecks. So the Fed negotiates a large block of repos: it buys $40 billion worth of Treasury bills from primary dealers, agreeing to sell them back in 15 days. Dealers are soon depositing the $40 billion in their bank accounts. Now banks find it much easier to meet their reserve. Banks also have roles in the money market. The very heart of the money market is composed of overnight borrowing of Federal funds between banks. Recall that Fed funds are the reserves that banks must maintain, by law, in a Federal Reserve Bank or in their own vaults. Depending on their transactions for the day, banks are bound to find themselves either with too little cash on hand to meet their reserve requirements, or with more than they need. The solution is for the banks with excess money to lend to those without enough. This flow of "overnight" money is loaned at what is called the *Federal funds rate*.

Borrowing between banks is the basis for the money market. In order to meet Fed reserve requirements, banks must keep a certain amount of money on hand; literally, in the vault. If they cannot meet this requirement, they must borrow it from another institution. They then find an institution with more cash than they need and enter into a repo agreement to borrow the necessary funds, usually only for overnight. The rate at which money is loaned is called the Federal funds rate.

Because of the last-minute, yet inescapable, nature of these overnight loans, the Fed funds rate tends to be volatile. Banks lacking sufficient reserves must find money quickly. Banks with too much money in reserve are anxious to loan it out and earn a return. Further, because it changes daily and reflects the amount of money available in the banking system, the Fed funds rate is the most sensitive indicator of the current interest rate environment.

If a bank in need of federal funds cannot find a domestic lender offering an attractive rate of interest, it can also turn to banks outside the United States, which often have large reserves of dollars, called Eurodollars.

The Origin of Eurodollars

When a U.S. company imports goods or services from another country, it pays for them with dollars; the foreign producer (or exporter) then changes those dollars into local currency at its bank. The dollars, now entered in the financial accounts of the bank overseas, become *Eurodollars*.

Foreign banks can, and do, trade their Eurodollar deposits among themselves, much as U.S. banks trade Fed funds. U.S. banks can also borrow Eurodollars to meet their reserve requirements. Whereas Fed funds are loaned overnight, Eurodollars might be loaned for longer periods. The rate for Eurodollar lending among big international banks is called *LIBOR*, which stands for the *London Interbank Offered Rate*. It is an average of the interest rates for Eurodollar loans made by five large London-based banks.

The money market, populated by various instruments of different characteristics, risks, and maturities, has an array of interest rates. Another important rate is known as the call rate.

The Call Rate

The *call rate* (or *broker loan rate*) is the interest rate that banks charge broker-dealers for loans to back the margin accounts of their customers. When individual investors buy stocks on margin, their brokers are giving the investors loans to carry out the transactions. The name "call rate" comes from a distinguishing feature of such broker loans: normally they are redeemable—callable—at any time. So broker loans create yet more flows of funds within the money market, where short-term cash is the ultimate product.

The average individual investor might appear to have a difficult time buying a stake in the money market. After all, not many investors are prepared to plunk down $100,000 for a jumbo CD. Most can, however, own a small piece of a jumbo CD by purchasing shares in a *money market fund*, which is a mutual fund dedicated to investing in the various instruments of the money market.

Exam Prep Questions

1. All these investors participate directly in the money market except:
   - ❑ A. The U.S. government
   - ❑ B. Institutional investors
   - ❑ C. Businesses
   - ❑ D. The general public

2. Which statements describe money center banks and their role in the money market?

   I. Money center banks are large banks found in major cities around the world.

   II. Money center banks issue many of the instruments that are traded in the money market.

   III. Money center banks are major traders of money market instruments.

   IV. Money center banks must be members of the Federal Reserve System.

   - ❑ A. I and II
   - ❑ B. I and III
   - ❑ C. I, II, and III
   - ❑ D. I, II, III, and IV

3. Commercial banks set their lending rates:
   - ❑ A. Above the discount rate
   - ❑ B. Below the discount rate
   - ❑ C. Equal to the discount rate
   - ❑ D. At a rate determined by the Federal Open Market Committee

4. The securities that institutional investors most often use when entering repurchase agreements and reverse repurchase agreements are:
   - ❑ A. Commercial paper
   - ❑ B. Negotiable CDs
   - ❑ C. Treasury securities
   - ❑ D. Banker's acceptances

5. Cedar Point Bank needs to meet its monthly payroll shortly before some large loans mature, so it plans to enter into a repurchase agreement with Acme Corp. Which of the following statements are true about the transaction from Cedar Point's perspective?

   I. Cedar Point Bank sells securities to Acme Corp.

   II. Cedar Point Bank purchases securities from Acme Corp.

   III. Cedar Point Bank receives a short-term loan.

   IV. Cedar Point Bank buys stock in Acme Corp.

   ❑ A. I
   ❑ B. II
   ❑ C. I, II, and III
   ❑ D. II and IV

6. Which of the following statements is true regarding commercial paper issued by corporations?

   I. It is a money market instrument.

   II. It has a minimum maturity of one year.

   III. It is secured by a bank guarantee.

   IV. It is usually sold at a discount.

   ❑ A. I
   ❑ B. I and II
   ❑ C. I and III
   ❑ D. I and IV

7. Commercial paper is which of the following?

   ❑ A. Unsecured debt
   ❑ B. Secured debt
   ❑ C. Long-term debt
   ❑ D. Regulated by the FOMC

8. Which statement regarding commercial paper is false?

   ❑ A. Companies with good credit ratings issue commercial paper.
   ❑ B. Corporations generally sell commercial paper at a discount and redeem it at par value.
   ❑ C. Commercial paper matures in 270 days or fewer.
   ❑ D. Corporations normally find that borrowing from a bank at the prime rate is less expensive than issuing commercial paper.

9. The minimum denomination of a jumbo certificate of deposit is:

   ❑ A. $100,000
   ❑ B. $1,000,000
   ❑ C. Set by the Federal Reserve Board
   ❑ D. Dependent on market interest rates

10. Which money market instrument does Erin's Woolens use to finance its imports of Irish sweaters?
    - ❑ A. Commercial paper
    - ❑ B. Eurodollar loans
    - ❑ C. Banker's acceptances
    - ❑ D. Repurchase agreements

11. Which interest rate does the Federal Reserve target with its open market operations?
    - ❑ A. Prime rate
    - ❑ B. Fed funds ratc
    - ❑ C. Broker loan rate
    - ❑ D. Discount rate

12. Which statements concerning bank reserve requirements are true?

    I. Reserves earn interest.

    II. Reserves earn no interest.

    III. Reserves must meet levels sct by the Fed.

    IV. Banks' commercial needs determine the amount of reserves they must hold.

    - ❑ A. I
    - ❑ B. II
    - ❑ C. II and III
    - ❑ D. I and IV

13. Banks that need to borrow funds for longer than overnight and cannot meet their reserve requirements by borrowing from domestic sources can:
    - ❑ A. Borrow from the Federal Reserve discount window.
    - ❑ B. Enter a reverse repurchase agreement with a foreign corporation.
    - ❑ C. Sell banker's acceptances.
    - ❑ D. Borrow in the Eurodollar market.

14. Which money market rate changes daily?
    - ❑ A. Discount rate
    - ❑ B. Fed funds rate
    - ❑ C. Prime rate
    - ❑ D. Call rate

15. Money market funds must register with:
    - ❑ A. The Federal Reserve
    - ❑ B. The SEC
    - ❑ C. The Treasury department
    - ❑ D. None of the above; they are exempt securities

Exam Prep Answers

1. The correct answer is D. The general public does not usually participate in the money market, because most money market instruments are too large for the average person to buy. Small investors can participate indirectly in the money markets by buying shares in mutual funds or saving through pension funds with money market instruments in their portfolio.
2. The correct answer is C. Money center banks are large banks located in major financial centers around the world, such as New York and London. The banks actively issue and trade many money market instruments, but they do not have to be members of the Federal Reserve System.
3. The correct answer is A. Commercial banks set their lending rates above the discount rate. The discount rate is the rate the Fed charges banks and other depository institutions for advances from the discount window.
4. The correct answer is C. Investors fund repos and reverse repos with Treasury securities—bills, notes, and bonds.
5. The correct answer is C. By first selling securities to Acme Corp., under an agreement to repurchase them at a later date, Cedar Point Bank effectively receives a short-term loan from Acme.
6. The correct answer is D. Commercial paper is a money market instrument. It is usually sold to investors on a discounted basis. The maturity is less than one year and it is not guaranteed by any bank.
7. The correct answer is A. Corporations or bank holding companies issue commercial paper, a short-term, unsecured debt. Commercial paper matures in 270 days or fewer and is backed only by the good faith of the issuing company.
8. The correct answer is D. Established corporations with good credit ratings usually find it cheaper to issue commercial paper than to borrow from banks at the prime rate.
9. The correct answer is A. Jumbo CDs are bank-issued certificates of deposit with a minimum denomination of $100,000, although CDs of $1 million or more are frequent.
10. The correct answer is C. Erin's Woolens uses banker's acceptances to import sweaters from Ireland. A banker's acceptance is a time draft, accepted by a bank, enabling the business to guarantee its payment to an exporter.
11. The correct answer is B. The Fed uses its open market operations to adjust the Fed funds rate. If the market rate has drifted too far from the Fed's desired target, the FOMC fine-tunes the rate through repos or matched sales.

12. The correct answer is C. The Fed pays no interest on reserve balances, for which it sets requirements that banks must meet.
13. The correct answer is D. Banks can meet their reserve requirement by borrowing Eurodollars at LIBOR from banks outside the United States. The Fed discourages repeated borrowing from the discount window, which only funds overnight loans.
14. The correct answer is B. Overnight borrowing of Federal funds among banks determines the Fed funds rate, which changes every day.
15. The correct answer is B. Money market funds must register with the SEC, as they are a type of mutual fund (or open-end investment company). The funds may only sell shares via prospectus.

PART III
Public Sector Debt

Debt Securities of the U.S. Government

Terms You Need to Know

- ✓ Bond (or coupon) equivalent yield
- ✓ CATS (Certificates of Accrual on Treasury Securities)
- ✓ Competitive bid
- ✓ Direct obligations
- ✓ Discount yield
- ✓ Noncompetitive bid
- ✓ Noninterest-bearing securities
- ✓ Percentage of par
- ✓ Primary dealer
- ✓ Repackaging of government securities
- ✓ STRIPS (Separate Trading of Registered Interest and Principal of Securities)
- ✓ TIGERS (Treasury Investment Growth Receipts)
- ✓ Treasuries
- ✓ Treasury bills (T-bills)
- ✓ Treasury notes (T-notes)
- ✓ Treasury bonds (T-bonds)
- ✓ Treasury receipts

Concepts You Need to Understand

- ✓ Why and how the U.S. government issues debt securities
- ✓ The characteristics of Treasury bills, notes, and bonds
- ✓ Auction procedures
- ✓ Pricing methods
- ✓ Interest accrual
- ✓ Taxation
- ✓ How Treasury bonds are repackaged
- ✓ The benefit to investors of repackaged Treasury bonds
- ✓ What products were created by brokerages (CATS and TIGERS)
- ✓ The government's response to these products (STRIPS)

Government Securities

The U.S. government issues debt securities to pay expenses that are not necessarily covered by tax revenues, such as military spending. For the most part, the proceeds from these issues cover the costs of entitlement programs such as Medicare and Social Security. U.S. government securities are known as Treasury bills, notes, and bonds—each differs in terms of maturity, pricing, and interest payments. This chapter focuses on the characteristics of the various government securities, how they are priced and sold, and how the securities are often repackaged for sale to the public.

The U.S. government issues debt to meet its financial obligations. Although the federal government can levy income taxes, tax revenues are sometimes not sufficient to meet its total fiscal needs. Moreover, entitlement programs, such as Social Security and Medicare, are not completely funded through taxes. When these programs need extra money, the government borrows from investors by issuing a variety of debt securities. The government also uses these debt securities to even out their cash flow. While the U.S. government frequently runs a deficit, it can always issue new debt securities. The market for U.S. government debt is the largest and most actively traded securities market in the world.

Does the deficit make government debt a risky investment? No. The U.S. government can never default on any issue, because it can always raise money to cover its debts through tax increases. Therefore all government debt issues are rated AAA. The SEC does not regulate the trading of government securities, although the Federal Reserve does oversee this market to some extent.

Obligations of the Government Issue

The federal government issues three kinds of debt securities, collectively referred to as Treasuries: Treasury bills, notes, and bonds. (The government also issues U.S. savings bonds, but they are not negotiable instruments.) Because Treasuries are issued directly by the federal government, they are also referred to as *direct obligations.*

Treasury Bills

Treasury bills (T-Bills) are the government's direct obligations with the shortest maturities: of three months, six months, and one year. Treasury bills make up the largest part of total government debt.

Treasury bills make no interest payments—as they are considered *noninterest-bearing securities.* The Treasury encourages investors to buy bills by selling them at a discount and paying the investor the full face value at maturity. In addition, the Treasury does not issue physical certificates for bills; transactions are done strictly on a book-entry basis.

Because of their short maturities, bills generally provide a lower yield than notes and bonds. Investors and analysts watch the Treasury bill market closely because price changes in this market often signal coming changes in interest rates. Also, the interest rate on some loans—such as variable-rate mortgages—is often tied to the changes in T-bill prices. The minimum denomination on a T-Bill is $1,000 for an investor.

Treasury Notes and Treasury Bonds

Treasury notes (T-notes) and *Treasury bonds (T-bonds)* are the government's intermediate- and long-term debt securities, respectively. Treasury notes have maturities ranging from two to ten years; bonds mature anywhere from 11 years up to 30 years. T-bond returns are frequently used as benchmarks for other types of long-term investments. Like bills, both notes and bonds are issued in book-entry form only. Unlike bills, however, both notes and bonds pay interest semiannually.

Not only do the various Treasuries have different maturities, but they also are priced and sold in different ways.

Selling, Bidding, and Pricing of Treasuries

The federal government sells Treasuries in auctions at regular intervals, according to the following schedules:

- **T-bills**—The Treasury auctions three-month and six-month bills every Monday. The bills trade w.i. (when issued); they mature on a Thursday, 13 or 26 weeks later, making it easy for investors to roll their money into a new bill at the next auction. The Treasury auctions 1-year bills every four weeks. These auctions are held on Tuesdays; the bills are issued the following Thursday.
- **T-notes and T-bonds**—Currently, the Treasury auctions two-year notes every month, five- and ten-year notes quarterly (in February, April, August, and November), and the long bond three times a year (in February, August, and November).

The Federal Reserve oversees all government securities auctions.

The Bidding Process

There are two types of bids, or tenders, at Treasury auctions: competitive and noncompetitive. This system was designed to meet the government's goal of arranging the least expensive financing possible. *Competitive bids* are placed by large securities firms and financial institutions. Each firm states the price it is willing to pay for the issue, along with the dollar amount it wants to buy. Given the large amounts that are sold at each auction, no individual firm can purchase an entire issue. The bidders whose prices are most favorable to the government win the auction. Each winning bidder then pays the average price of the winning bids for the dollar amount it offered to buy.

One set of large fixed-income dealers, called *primary dealers*, ensures a strong market for Treasury securities. Primary dealers, who are appointed by the Federal Reserve, need to show both the capacity and the commitment to participate in all Treasury auctions. Also, they must make a secondary market for the securities they buy.

Noncompetitive bids come from individual investors. Here, the term "bid" is somewhat misleading. A noncompetitive bid is actually an investor's way of indicating interest in purchasing a certain dollar amount of a given issue. The government will honor all noncompetitive bids before any competitive bids. The amounts specified in the noncompetitive bids, are sold at the average yield of the winning competitive bids. Recently, the Treasury has turned to a different kind of auction, the Dutch auction, in which all successful bidders—no matter what they bid—pay the yield that proves high enough (that is, the price low enough) for the Treasury to sell all the bills it wants to issue. In this process, noncompetitive bidders also pay that same high yield (that is, the lower price).

> **EXAMPLE:** The government decides to issue $10 billion in T-bills at the Monday, August 10 auction. Noncompetitive bids totaling $4 billion are placed for that bill issue. Those investors are guaranteed to receive the amounts for which they bid. Next, the best (or lowest) competitive bids adding up to the remaining $6 billion are accepted and filled. Finally, the prices of the winning competitive bids are averaged and the resulting average price is used to fill all noncompetitive bids.

Can investors place bids for any amount? The minimum purchase for all Treasury securities is $1,000, with increments of $1,000 thereafter. Bills are issued on the Thursday following the auction, whereas coupon-bearing Treasury securities are issued on the 15th of the auction month. These issues then pay coupon interest semiannually on the 15th of the appropriate month.

The government auctions, however, are not the only place that investors can purchase Treasuries, which are widely traded over the counter in the secondary market.

Treasuries are traded strictly on the OTC market. The major players in that market are the securities firms and financial institutions that the government has designated as primary dealers. Primary dealers must make a market in Treasuries for smaller broker-dealers (secondary dealers), who, in turn, trade the securities with individual and institutional investors.

Pricing of Treasuries

Treasuries are priced in two ways:

- T-bills are sold on a discounted yield basis.
- T-notes and T-bonds are quoted as a percentage of par.

Let's look at T-bills. Dealers quote bills on a *discount yield* basis, meaning the annualized amount of the price is discounted from the par value of the bill. Because bills have no coupon rate, dealers use the percentage amount of the discount as a measure of the bill's yield. When the bill matures at par, the holder receives the discount as accreted income.

> **EXAMPLE:** Helen Carter earns a year-end bonus and wants to invest it. She asks her broker to buy $10,000 of the 1-year bill that the Treasury is about to auction. The broker submits a noncompetitive bid for her, and she purchases the bill at the average discount yield, 4.50%. The discount means that her purchase price is 4.50% less than $10,000, or $9,550. Thus, the yield and price of the bill are directly related. Carter will earn the $450 discount if she holds the bill to maturity.
>
> Several months later, Carter decides to sell the bill. Her broker quotes a discount yield of 4.35% on her 1-year bill. Does she then receive $9,565? No, because she has earned some of the income that the bill has accreted as it moves toward maturity. The discount yield is an annualized number, so to determine the price Carter gets for the bill, she needs to factor in the time that has passed. Thus, she must multiply the par value of the bill by the discount yield, and then by the time remaining to maturity (on a 360-day basis). Assuming that the bill matures in 235 days, she determines the discount using the formula:
>
> $= \$10,000 \times 0.0435 \times 235/360$
>
> So, Carter receives $10,000 – 283.96, or $9,716.04, for her 1-year bill. Her profit of $166.04 reflects the value of the discounted yield she has earned over the four months she owned the bill.

Current bill bid and asked prices are quoted in online services, electronic quote services, and in many daily newspapers. See Figure 7.1.

TREASURY BILLS

Maturity			Days to Mat.	Bid	Asked	Chg.	Ask Yld.
Sep	10	'98	52	4.91	4.95	−0.02	5.01
Sep	17	'98	59	4.91	4.95	−0.03	5.02
Sep	24	'98	66	4.90	4.92	−0.02	5.01
Oct	01	'98	73	4.97	4.95	−0.02	5.07
Oct	08	'98	80	4.97	4.95	−0.02	5.07
Oct	15	'98	87	5.01	5.00	−0.02	5.13

Figure 7.1 Treasury bill trading.

As shown in Figure 7.1, the financial section of a newspaper provides information about the current issues, including days to maturity and the price change from the previous day.

The most important data, however, are in the Bid, Asked, and Ask Yield columns.

First, consider the bill maturing on October 1, 1998. Note that the bid (4.97) is higher than the ask (4.95).

Remember that the bids quoted represent yields, not dollar amounts: the higher the yield, the lower the dollar price.

For the most part, the difference between the bid and asked prices—the spread—is very small. This reflects the highly competitive nature of the Treasury trading market.

The ask yield represents the bond (or coupon) *equivalent yield* of a bill. It enables investors to compare the yield on a T-bill with those of T-notes, T-bonds, and other similar interest-bearing securities.

Two factors make it difficult to compare bill yields to yields of coupon-bearing instruments. First, yields on Treasury bills are computed on a

360-day year basis, whereas Treasury notes and bonds use a 365-day year. Second, bill yields are stated in terms of their discount. The bond equivalent yield computes a bill's yield based on the amount invested. Whereas the discounted yield on the bill Ms. Carter purchased is based on the face value of $10,000, the bond equivalent yield is based on the $9,460 she actually paid. In this way, the bond equivalent yield better matches the yield to maturity used for corporate and Treasury bonds.

It is important to recognize that a bill's bond equivalent yield is always higher than its discounted yield. Treasury notes and bonds are sold on a percentage of par basis, not on a discount yield basis.

Next are the T-notes and T-bonds, which are calculated as a percentage of par. *Percentage of par* is the same method of calculating yields used for corporate bonds. To review, when using percentage of par ($1,000) dealers quote prices for a security as a percent of the face value of the security—versus stating a dollar price or a discounted yield. So a quote of 100 means that the note or bond is selling for face value ($1,000); a quote of 96 tells an investor that the bond is selling for 96% of face value ($960).

Corporate bonds, T-notes, and T-bonds all use percentage of par for price quotes; however, the notation used for note and bond quotes can differ from that of corporate bonds.

How T-Note and T-Bond Prices Are Written

As shown by the excerpt from a newspaper's financial section in Figure 7.2, some market participants separate the fractional part of a point for note and bond prices with colons, as opposed to decimal points or fractions.

The numbers after the colon in the bid and asked prices represent an additional 30 seconds of a point in the price of a given security. For example, the bid quote above the $9\frac{3}{8}$% bond maturing in February 2006 is 123:09. So that bond is selling for 123 and $\frac{9}{32}$% (or 123.28%) of par. For five February 2006 bonds (with a face value of $5,000), an investor pays $6,164.06.

$123.28 \times \$5,000 = \$6,164$

$+(\frac{9}{32} \times 0.01 \times \$5,000) = \$14.06$

The other data in the note and bond quotes is as follows:

- The Rate column states the coupon interest rate on the security. Remember that, unlike Treasury bills, notes and bonds pay interest semiannually.

- The Maturity column is largely self-explanatory. The letter "n" at the end of a maturity distinguishes a note from a bond. Also, the letter "i" identifies one of the inflation-indexed bonds introduced by the Treasury in 1997. Finally, a listing with a maturity date such as the $7\frac{7}{8}\%$ "Nov 02-07" denotes that the bond is callable.
- The Change column shows the change in the bid price from the previous day. Changes are noted in 30 seconds of a point, so "–3" for the October 2006 note means the note's closing bid price on that day was $\frac{3}{32}$ of a point lower than the previous day's close.
- The Ask Yield column states the yield to maturity (YTM) on the note or bond. YTM is calculated the same way for Treasury notes and bonds as it is for corporate bonds.

GOVT. BONDS & NOTES

Rate	Maturity Mo/Yr	Bid	Asked	Chg.	Ask Yld.
5 5/8	Feb 06n	100:01	100:03	– 2	5.61
9 3/8	Feb 06	123:09	123:15	– 2	5.54
6 7/8	May 06n	107:29	107:31	– 2	5.60
7	Jul 06n	108:25	108:27	– 2	5.61
6 1/2	Oct 06n	105:22	105:24	– 3	5.62
3 3/8	Jan 07i	96:26	96:27	– 1	3.81
6 1/4	Feb 07n	104:09	104:11	– 3	5.60
7 5/8	Feb 02-07	106:16	106:18	– 1	5.57
6 5/8	May 07n	106:30	107:00	– 3	5.61
6 1/8	Aug 07n	103:19	103:21	– 3	5.60
7 7/8	Nov 02-07	109:10	109:12	– 1	5.41
3 5/8	Jan 08i	98:25	98:26	– 1	3.78
5 1/2	Feb 08n	99:17	99:18	+ 1	5.56

Figure 7.2 Trading for government bonds and notes.

How Interest Payments Affect the Way T-Notes and T-Bonds Are Sold

As with corporate bonds, interest on Treasury notes and bonds accrues to whomever is holding the security, so buyers are required to pay sellers the interest accrued since the last interest payment. The method for calculating accrued interest on Treasuries is different from corporate bonds in two ways:

- Regular-way settlement for Treasuries (including bills) occurs the business day after the trade—trade date plus one, or "T + 1"—not the trade date plus three days that is used for corporate bonds.
- Interest on Treasury notes and bonds is computed on an actual-day month/365-day year basis, versus the 30-day month/360-day year basis for corporate bonds.

EXAMPLE: On September 14, Mr. C. F. Kane purchased $20,000 of the 6% July 2002 bonds. How much accrued interest does Mr. Kane owe the seller? The issue last paid interest on July 15, so the number of days since then equals:

September = 14 days (Remember not to count the settlement date) Then, use the following formula to calculate the accrued interest:

Accrued interest = face value × interest rate × (# of days ÷ 365)

= $20,000 × 0.06 × (76 ÷ 365)

= $20,000 × 0.06 × (0.16712)

= $200.54

How Income from Treasuries Is Taxed

The federal government taxes income from all Treasuries as ordinary income. This income is exempt from state and local taxes, because different levels of government cannot tax each other—because of the "reciprocal immunity doctrine" of the U.S. Constitution. For bills, the federal government treats the amount of the discount as an interest payment. An investor who buys a bill at a discount of $700 pays tax on $700 of interest income. For Treasury notes and bonds, the semiannual interest payments are considered income in the year the investor receives them.

Other Important Differences Among Bills, Notes, and Bonds

Some T-bonds are callable. The federal government can redeem bonds it issued during a high-inflation era, such as the late 1970s and early 1980s, beginning five years before the scheduled maturity date. Recall that, in the newspaper excerpt with bond quotes earlier in this chapter, some bonds' maturity dates seemed to have two dates, such as the "Nov 02-07." This means that the maturity date is November 2007, but that the bond can be called as of November 2002.

You can study the unique features of each kind of Treasury security in Table 7.1.

Table 7.1 Distinctions Among Treasury Bills, Bonds, and Notes

	Treasury Bills	Treasury Notes	Treasury Bonds
Length of term	3 mos., 6 mos., 1 year	1 to 10 years	Over 10 years; up to 30 years
Minimum denomination	$1,000	$1,000	$1,000
Increments	$1,000	$1,000	$1,000
Interest paid	Noninterest-bearing	Yes; semiannually	Yes; semiannually
Accrued interest method	None	Actual-day month/365-day year	Actual-day month/365-day year
Quoted in	Discount yield	Percent of par; in 32nds	Percent of par; in 32nds
Callable	No	No	Some; usually five years prior to maturity

Debt securities of the government have unique features; study the table and become very familiar with them.

Repackaged Government Securities

Although these issues seem to present a complete range of choices for investors, broker-dealers created new investment options for investors. In the 1980s, some of the largest Treasury dealers invented ways to *repackage* Treasury bonds to offer new products to investors. These dealers created varied series of zero-coupon bonds by stripping the interest and principal payments from large pools of bonds they had purchased.

Typically, a primary dealer buys a large number of bonds that mature at the same time. Each of these bonds has two distinct cash streams: the semiannual interest payments and the principal repayment at maturity. What firms like Merrill Lynch and Salomon Brothers did was to sell each individual stream, at a discount, to investors. They didn't just sell all the interest payments as a block. They sold each separate interest payment as a zero-coupon bond to investors. So, a 30-year bond theoretically can be broken into 61 zero-coupon bonds: one for the principal repayment at maturity and 60 for the semiannual interest payments.

The best-known of these hybrid securities include:

- **CATS (Certificates of Accrual on Treasury Securities)**—Created by Salomon Brothers, this product created a zero-coupon bond from the principal portion of the underlying Treasury bond.
- **TIGERS (Treasury Income Growth Receipts)**—Created by Merrill Lynch, TIGERS created zero-coupon bonds from both the interest and principal portions of the underlying bond.

These repackaged securities, or Treasury receipts, were attractive to investors because they eliminated both credit and reinvestment risk. Although investors were not buying the actual bonds on which CATS and TIGERS were based, the fact that the hybrid securities were created from Treasury bonds essentially provided investors a guarantee from the U.S. government against possible default.

Second, one of the risks that investors face with bonds is reinvestment risk: the chance that the income from interest payments cannot be reinvested at an equal or higher rate. By creating zero-coupon bonds out of the individual interest payments on a bond, the Treasury provides investors with a way to lock in a return for a given time period. No matter what happens to interest rates, the final principal repayment on a zero-coupon is known. This is especially attractive to pension fund managers, whose future cash needs are relatively predictable, and who thus are more comfortable locking in a specific return on an investment. These fund managers can now buy individual future interest payments according to when they needed the income and what kind of return they required—a degree of flexibility that is not available by buying the Treasuries themselves.

In response to these products, the Treasury Department decided to eliminate the profits generated by dealers creating CATS and TIGERS by making its own hybrid security—*STRIPS (Separate Trading of Registered Interest and Principal)*. STRIPS create zero-coupon bonds from the interest and principal payments of bonds, just as TIGERS did. By eliminating dealers from the sales chain, the government can sell STRIPS at lower prices than CATS and TIGERS, effectively killing the market for new CATS and TIGERS. Today, the only CATS and TIGERS available for purchase are those that were sold before the introduction of STRIPS.

STRIPS compare with regular Treasuries in the following ways:

- Like all Treasuries, STRIPS are issued only in book-entry form.
- Like bills, STRIPS are noninterest-bearing securities, but the discount earned is taxable by the federal government.

Exam Prep Questions

1. Which programs does the U.S. government fund by issuing debt securities?

   I. Social Security

   II. Medicare

   III. Medicaid

   IV. Military spending

   ❑ A. I and II
   ❑ B. II and III
   ❑ C. I, II, and III
   ❑ D. I, II, III, and IV

2. Which statements are true regarding government debt?

   I. U.S. Treasury securities have no credit risk.

   II. The SEC regulates government debt trading.

   III. Government debt obligations must be registered with the SEC.

   IV. The Federal Reserve oversees all auctions of government securities.

   ❑ A. I and II
   ❑ B. I, II, and III
   ❑ C. I and IV
   ❑ D. I, II, III, and IV

3. Which instrument makes up the largest portion of government debt sales?

   ❑ A. Treasury bills
   ❑ B. Treasury notes
   ❑ C. Treasury bonds
   ❑ D. Strips

4. Which direct government obligation does not pay interest?

   ❑ A. Treasury bills
   ❑ B. Treasury notes
   ❑ C. Treasury bonds
   ❑ D. All of the above

5. Which statement is true regarding Treasury bill auctions?

   ❑ A. They occur every Monday.
   ❑ B. All competitive bids are filled first.
   ❑ C. All noncompetitive bids are filled first.
   ❑ D. Competitive bidders are awarded securities at a lower price than noncompetitive bidders.

6. All these statements are true about Treasury bonds except:
   - ❑ A. Bonds pay interest semiannually.
   - ❑ B. Bonds are always callable five years before maturity.
   - ❑ C. The minimum purchase price for bonds is $1,000.
   - ❑ D. Bonds have a maximum maturity of 30 years.

7. Which statements are true regarding U.S. government debt securities?

   I. They are direct obligations of the government.

   II. All government debt is guaranteed by the government.

   III. They carry little, if any, credit risk.

   IV. All government securities pay interest on a semiannual basis.

   - ❑ A. I and III
   - ❑ B. II and III
   - ❑ C. I, II, and IV
   - ❑ D. I, II, III, and IV

8. Melvin Stoute purchases a $10,000 6-month T-bill due April 15, 1999, on December 11, 1998, at a discounted yield of 5.22%. What does Stoute pay?
   - ❑ A. $10,000
   - ❑ B. $9,637.50
   - ❑ C. $9,818.75
   - ❑ D. $9,821.23

9. Angela Moiseyer buys $1,000 of a Treasury note priced at 94. She pays:
   - ❑ A. $1,000
   - ❑ B. $1,063.83
   - ❑ C. $940
   - ❑ D. $906

10. What does Anna Scottini pay to buy $10,000 of a Treasury bond quoted at 107.18?
    - ❑ A. $9,330.10
    - ❑ B. $9,296.92
    - ❑ C. $10,705.63
    - ❑ D. $10,756.25

11. What is a large pool of 30-year Treasury bonds sold as individual securities with separate interest and principal payments called?
    - ❑ A. Zero-coupon bonds
    - ❑ B. Flower bonds
    - ❑ C. STRIPS
    - ❑ D. Long bonds

12. A Treasury bond quoted at 105.13 in the paper is worth which amount?
    - ❑ A. $1,051.13
    - ❑ B. $1,054.06
    - ❑ C. $1,005.41
    - ❑ D. $1,050.41

13. Jason owns 10 T-bonds with a coupon rate of 7.00%. These bonds pay interest semi-annually for a total of $700 per year. Which statements are true of how Jason's bond income will be taxed?

    I. It is ordinary income for federal tax purposes.

    II. It is ordinary income for state tax purposes.

    III. It is ordinary income for local tax purposes.

    IV. All interest income on T-bonds is tax-free.
    - ❑ A. I only
    - ❑ B. II and III
    - ❑ C. I, II, and III
    - ❑ D. IV only

14. Roger owns $15,000 worth of 10-year T-notes paying 6% and selling at 110 in the market. What is the semi-annual interest payment on these bonds?
    - ❑ A. $900
    - ❑ B. $818
    - ❑ C. $450
    - ❑ D. $409

15. Which of the following entities can bid on T-bills in a competitive bidding process known as a Dutch auction?

    I. Primary dealers

    II. Secondary dealers

    III. The general public

    IV. All of the above
    - ❑ A. IV only
    - ❑ B. I only
    - ❑ C. I and II
    - ❑ D. I and III

Exam Prep Answers

1. The correct answer is C. When the government runs a deficit, it funds entitlement programs such as Medicaid, Medicare, and Social Security by selling debt obligations. The government funds discretionary expenses, such as defense spending, through taxes.
2. The correct answer is C. Because Treasury securities are direct obligations of the government, they carry no credit risk—investors consider them the safest securities in the world. The Federal Reserve oversees all auctions of government securities. The SEC does not regulate government debt trading nor is it a requirement to register with the SEC.
3. The correct answer is A. Treasury bills make up the largest part of government debt sales because the Treasury uses them to supply the government with short-term operating cash. T-bonds and T-notes make up a much smaller portion of government debt and STRIPS even less.
4. The correct answer is A. T-bills do not pay periodic interest, but rather are sold at a discount and later redeemed at par. Investors receive the difference between the two amounts as their return. Both T-bonds and T-notes pay interest semi-annually.
5. The correct answer is C. The government fills all noncompetitive bids before filling any competitive bids. Noncompetitive bidders buy securities at a price that equals the weighted-average yield of the accepted competitive bids. The Treasury auctions 3-month and 6-month bills every Monday, but auctions the 1-year bill every four weeks, on a Tuesday.
6. The correct answer is B. The Treasury issued some callable bonds during the high-inflation era of the early 1980s, but has not issued callable bonds since then. The remaining callable bonds, most of which investors still actively trade, usually have a call period beginning five years before they mature.
7. The correct answer is A. Government debt consists of direct obligations (bills, notes, and bonds), and the obligations of government agencies and government-sponsored entities. The government does not guarantee most agency obligations; nonetheless, this debt carries little (if any) credit risk because of its association with the government. Bills pay no interest, whereas notes and bonds pay semi-annual interest.

8. The correct answer is C. Stoute paid $9,818.75. The purchase price of a T-bill equals the face value less the discount, which investors calculate by multiplying the discount rate, the par value, and fraction of the year remaining until maturity. The discount on this bill equals 5.22% × $10,000 × $12^{125}/_{360}$, so Stoute's purchase price equals $9,818.75.
9. The correct answer is C. A Treasury note quoted at 94 sells for 94% of its par value. Because she is buying $1,000 of the note, Moiseyev pays $940.
10. The correct answer is D. A T-bond quoted at 107.18 sells for 107 $^{18}/_{32}$% of par value. Scottini pays $10,000 × 1.075626%, or $10,756.25.
11. The correct answer is C. STRIPS is an acronym for Separate Trading of Registered Interest and Principal. These are large pools of government securities that have been stripped of coupons and issued as zero coupon securities. They are sold directly to investors by the government. Zero coupon bonds have no coupons, are sold at a deep discount, and mature at face value. STRIPS are, in fact, zero-coupon bonds. Flower bonds are sold at discount mainly to create income to pay estate taxes. Long bonds are any bond with a maturity of ten years or more; usually referring to a 30-year bond.
12. The correct answer is B. Each point on a T-bond quote is worth $10.00. A T-bond quoted at 105.13 equals = $1054.06. The 105 equals $1050 and the 13/32 equals $4.06, for a total of $1054.06.
13. The correct answer is A. U.S. Direct obligations do not pay state and local taxes on interest earned. This is from a reciprocating agreement between the federal government and state governments approved by the U.S. Supreme Court. All interest income is taxed on the federal level as ordinary income.
14. The correct answer is C. $15,000 worth of T-notes with a coupon of 6% earns $900 a year in interest to the holder ($15,000 × 6% = $900). Treasury Notes pay interest on a semi-annual basis, thus each payment totals $450.00. The coupon rate will not change on the notes regardless of the market price on the notes.
15. The correct answer is C. Treasury competitive bids are held in a Dutch auction process. Both primary and secondary dealers can bid on a competitive basis. The public, however, bids in a noncompetitive process, because it's willing to accept the average winning bid on the competitive side.

Agency Debt

Terms You Need to Know

- ✓ Agency
- ✓ Average life
- ✓ Collateralized mortgage obligation (CMO)
- ✓ Companion tranche
- ✓ Export-Import Bank (Eximbank)
- ✓ Extension risk
- ✓ Federal Farm Credit System (FFCS)
- ✓ Federal Home Loan Bank System (FHLBS)
- ✓ Federal Home Loan Mortgage Corporation (Freddie Mac)
- ✓ Federal National Mortgage Association (Fannie Mae)
- ✓ Fiscal agents
- ✓ Government National Mortgage Association (Ginnie Mae)
- ✓ Government-sponsored entity
- ✓ Guaranteed mortgage
- ✓ Modified pass-through
- ✓ Mortgage loan (mortgage or conventional mortgage)
- ✓ Mortgage pool
- ✓ Pass-through certificate
- ✓ Plain vanilla CMO
- ✓ Planned amortization class bond (PAC)
- ✓ Prepayment risk
- ✓ Public Securities Association (PSA) model
- ✓ Securitization
- ✓ Straight pass-through
- ✓ Student Loan Marketing Association (Sallie Mae)
- ✓ Targeted amortization class bond (TAC)
- ✓ Tranche
- ✓ Yield–spread basis

Concepts You Need to Understand

- ✓ The various agencies created by the federal government
- ✓ Characteristics and missions of the agencies
- ✓ How agency securities are issued and traded
- ✓ What pass-through certificates are and how they work
- ✓ Straight versus modified pass-throughs
- ✓ Prepayment and extension risk
- ✓ What CMOs are and how they work
- ✓ The tranche system
- ✓ PACs, TACs, and companion tranches

Agencies and Agency Debt

As a matter of policy, the U.S. government encourages Americans to farm, to own property, and to pursue higher education. Washington believes each of these goals is vital to keeping the country and its economy strong. To support these objectives, the government has founded several agencies to help finance activities in these areas, hoping to keep borrowing costs as low as possible and make funds widely available. This chapter explores the missions of the various agencies and the securities each one issues to fund its respective sector of the economy.

Why the U.S. Government Created Agencies

By creating various agencies, policymakers in Washington have attempted to make it easier for Americans to farm, get an education, or own property. In most cases, people must borrow money to pursue these activities. Thus, to lower the cost of funds in these important sectors, the federal government created a number of dedicated *agencies*.

Agencies or Government-Sponsored Entities? All the entities discussed are referred to as "agencies"—that is, agencies of the U.S. government. In reality, however, the title applies to only two entities:

- The Government National Mortgage Association (Ginnie Mae), which is part of the Department of Housing and Urban Development
- The Export-Import Bank (Eximbank), which, although it is an independent entity, can borrow from the Treasury Department to finance its operations

Hence, only debt securities issued by Ginnie Mae and the Eximbank are directly guaranteed by the U.S. government. All other entities discussed are more accurately referred to as *government-sponsored entities*. They support some of the government's policy objectives, but are neither part of the government nor directly backed by it. In fact, entities such as the Student Loan Marketing Association (Sallie Mae) and the Federal National Mortgage Association (Fannie Mae) are publicly traded corporations.

How Agencies Help Fund Their Respective Sectors of the Economy

In broad terms, agencies issue debt securities to investors, and then use the proceeds to buy loans that private lenders have made to homeowners, farmers, and students. This frees up cash at the local level and enables those private lenders to make more loans. The agency debt securities are collateralized by the mortgages purchased from private lenders. Some agencies also fund themselves by selling stock.

Remember, in most cases, agency debt is **not** guaranteed by the federal government.

Nevertheless, given the importance of the policy goals represented by agencies, agency debt is considered to have the implicit backing of the government. So for rating purposes, agency securities are treated as if they were a direct obligation of the U.S. government and receive triple-A ratings.

Agencies That Support Farming

The *Federal Farm Credit System (FFCS)*, created by the Farm Credit Act of 1971, oversees all farm-related financing activities. The FFCS operates through 12 Farm Credit districts, each of which has three agencies:

- Federal Land Bank
- Federal Intermediate Credit Bank
- Bank for Cooperatives

The FFCS has yet another arm, the Federal Farm Credit Bank (FFCB), which coordinates financing for the district-level agencies. Through the FFCB, the FFCS issues short-term notes (maturing in 5 to 270 days) in increments of $50,000, and Consolidated Systemwide Bonds (6- to 9-month maturities) in increments of $5,000. Rates for all these securities are set by the FFCB. Notes are quoted on a discount–yield basis, whereas bonds are quoted on a percentage of par basis. Income from FFCS notes and bonds is taxed at the federal level, but not at the state and local levels. The government does not provide a guarantee for any farm agency debt securities. However, investors believe these securities have the implicit backing of the government and consider them very safe investments.

Functions of Each Farm Agency in Its District

In general, the Federal Land Banks (FLBs) take care of the longer-term financing needs of people in farming or farm-related businesses, whereas the

Federal Intermediate Credit Banks (FICBs) and Banks for Cooperatives (BCs) fund shorter-term needs.

More specifically, FLBs extend long-term, mortgage-backed credit to both crop and livestock farmers for purchasing land and other farming-related purposes. FLBs fund these loans by issuing 1 to 15-year notes and bonds. To qualify for such loans, farmers are required to purchase stock in a local land bank association, in an amount equal to 5% of the loan. The local land banks, in turn, purchase stock in their district's FLB. The stock is retired when the underlying loan is repaid.

Federal Intermediate Credit Banks buy intermediate-term farm loans that have already been extended by local commercial banks and credit corporations or associations. These loans typically finance activities such as storage and transport. Farmers own the stock in the various FICBs. FICBs fund their activities by issuing notes on a discounted basis. Finally, Banks for Cooperatives finance the activities of farming cooperatives, which are owned by local farmers. BCs get cash for their operations by issuing short-term notes (7 to 270 days) at a discount. Income from securities issued by FLBs, FICBs, and BCs is taxed by the federal government, but not by state and local governments.

How the Federal Government Promotes Higher Education

On the education side, The *Student Loan Marketing Association*, founded in 1972, and commonly known as *Sallie Mae*, purchases educational loans from private financial institutions or universities and finances state student loan agencies. Its primary goal is to increase the number of loans made through the federal Guaranteed Student Loan Program or Health, Education Assistance Loan Program. By buying up loans made at the local level, Sallie Mae enables local lenders to give more loans.

Sallie Mae is a publicly traded corporation whose stock is listed on the NYSE. Nevertheless, its debt obligations are implicitly backed by the government and are rated triple-A. Sallie Mae finances its activities by issuing notes and bonds, some of which carry floating-rate coupons, that pay interest semiannually. Income from Sallie Mae securities is taxed at the federal level, but not at the state and local levels.

Agencies That Help Finance Home Ownership

Four federal agencies are charged with making mortgage loans easier to obtain:

- Federal Home Loan Bank System
- Federal National Mortgage Association
- Government National Mortgage Association
- Federal Home Loan Mortgage Corporation

Each of these agencies helps private local lenders extend more mortgage loans to more people at better rates. In practice, however, each of these agencies has a different charter and achieves its goals in a different manner.

Banks and other financial institutions issue *mortgage loans* (*mortgages*) to buyers of property who cannot, or do not want to, pay the entire purchase price at once. These loans are secured by the property being financed. Borrowers agree to amortize (pay back) the loan by making a series of monthly payments over 15 to 30 years. At first, most of each monthly payment is applied to the interest charged on the loan, but over time, more of each payment reduces the principal amount. At maturity, the mortgage is paid off and the borrower owns the property. These mortgages are sometimes called *conventional mortgages* to distinguish them from *guaranteed mortgages*, which are backed by the U.S. government.

The federal government guarantees the following mortgages:

- Veterans Administration (VA) mortgages, available to military veterans or their surviving spouses
- Farm Service Agency mortgages, offered in low-income rural areas (the FSA was formerly known as the Farmers' Home Administration, or FmHA)
- Federal Housing Administration (FHA) mortgages, provided more widely for residential properties

The Federal Home Loan Bank System

The *Federal Home Loan Bank System (FHLBS)*, created in 1932, provides credit reserves for the nation's savings and loan (S&L) institutions, cooperative banks, and other mortgage lenders. It is very similar to the Federal

Reserve, which provides a similar service to private sector banks. Also, like the Fed (and the FFCS), the FHLBS is made up of 12 regional *Federal Home Loan Banks.* These regional banks lend money to the local savings and loans, cooperative banks, and mortgage lenders. Unlike the housing-related agencies discussed later in this section, the FHLBS does not purchase mortgages from regional lenders; rather it uses the mortgages as collateral to extend loans to the lenders.

The FHLBS generates funds for its activities by issuing both short-term notes and long-term bonds. The notes generally have terms of less than one year and are quoted on a discount-yield basis. FHLBS bonds pay interest semiannually, are not callable, have a minimum par value of $10,000, and are quoted on a percentage of par basis. FHLBS securities are not guaranteed by the U.S. government. Income from FHLBS issues is taxed only by the federal government.

The Federal National Mortgage Association

The *Federal National Mortgage Association*, frequently referred to as *Fannie Mae*, was established by the government in 1938 to purchase mortgages from private sector lenders and repackage them for sale to investors. Like Sallie Mae, Fannie Mae is a corporation whose stock trades on the NYSE. Initially, Fannie Mae dealt only with FHA-guaranteed mortgages, but today the majority of Fannie Mae business is based on conventional mortgages. Fannie Mae finances its operations by issuing both debt and equity securities. Its debt securities consist of:

- Short-term notes (maturing in less than one year), quoted on a discount–yield basis
- Bonds that pay interest semiannually, are not callable, have minimum value of $10,000, and are quoted on a percentage of par basis, in 32nds
- Pass-through certificates, which are securities created from repackaged mortgages

Debt securities issued by Fannie Mae do not carry a direct government guarantee. Still, Fannie Mae can borrow money directly from the discount window of the Fed, making the government's support of Fannie Mae something more than implicit. Income from these securities is taxed at the federal, state, and local levels. The rationale for this difference in tax treatment rests on the nature of Fannie Mae—a privately owned, for-profit corporation issuing mortgages for which the majority of homeowners have already enjoyed a tax exemption.

The Government National Mortgage Association

The *Government National Mortgage Association (Ginnie Mae)* is the only agency that is actually part of the U.S. government, specifically the Department of Housing and Urban Development.

Created in 1968, Ginnie Mae issues debt securities backed by pools of residential mortgages guaranteed by the FHA, the FSA, and the VA. Ginnie Mae securities are direct obligations of the U.S. government, and they are quoted on a percentage of par basis in 32nds. Although Ginnie Mae is part of the U.S. government, income from its securities is taxed at the federal, state, and local levels. In this case, the lack of tax benefits is because of the tax deductions already taken by the mortgage holders.

The Export-Import Bank

The *Export-Import Bank (Eximbank)* is another agency whose debt obligations are directly guaranteed by the U.S. government. The Eximbank is an independent bank established in 1934 to promote trade between the United States and other nations. In addition to issuing its own debt securities, Eximbank can borrow from the Treasury Department to finance, guarantee, or provide insurance for trade transactions, as well as to offer credit to non-U.S. entities.

The Federal Home Loan Mortgage Corporation

The *Federal Home Loan Mortgage Corporation (Freddie Mac)*, established in 1970, is a corporation that provides a secondary market for conventional residential mortgages.

Unlike Fannie Mae and Ginnie Mae, Freddie Mac does not purchase government-guaranteed mortgages.

It buys conventional mortgages, places them in a trust, and issues mortgage-backed securities based on the interest and principal payments from the underlying mortgages.

Freddie Mac stock is owned by savings institutions in the United States and held in trust by the FHLBS. Freddie Mac securities have only the implicit backing of the U.S. government. Like those of Fannie Mae, its securities are taxed by federal, state, and local governments.

Just as the Treasury uses primary dealers to sell its securities to the public, government agencies use another group of broker-dealers to make their securities available to investors.

How Agency Securities Are Issued and Traded

Agency securities are issued through select broker-dealers, known as *fiscal agents*. Each agency puts together a group of fiscal agents who are responsible for marketing the agency's debt issues. Fiscal agents sometimes buy up a portion of an issue for subsequent sale on the secondary market, but they mostly find institutional investors who want to purchase parts of the given issue. For this service, fiscal agents charge about a 1% fee on the issue's value.

The broker-dealers who purchase Treasury securities directly from the government are called *primary dealers*. Primary dealers can also serve as fiscal agents for agency debt.

All government agency securities trade exclusively in the OTC market. Agency debt settles the next business day after the trade date (Trade Date+ 1) in Fed funds that have been deposited at a Federal Reserve Bank. Institutional investors purchase the vast majority of agency securities and tend to hold them. Nevertheless, these big investors give individual investors access to agency securities. Typically, agency debt is sold in large increments—$25,000 and up is very common. Broker-dealers, however, often repackage these securities by breaking them into smaller pieces and reselling them on the secondary market.

Most agency issues are quoted on a percentage of par basis, in 32nds of a point. Figure 8.1 lists the quotations for nine Fannie Mae issues on July 17, 1998.

The system of recording agency quotes is similar to that used for Treasury bonds. Look at the issue maturing in October of 1998. The asterisk means that it is callable. Its coupon is 4.88%, whereas its yield to maturity is 5.28%. The highest bid price is 99:26, or 99 and $^{26}/_{32}$% of the issue's par value. Thus, if the par value is $10,000 (a bond), the bid is equal to $9,981.25 ($10,000 × 0.998125).

Rate	Mat.	Bid	Asked	Yld.
5.35	8-98	100:00	100:02	4.44
4.70	9-98*	99:28	99:30	5.07
7.85	9-98	100:10	100:12	5.05
4.95	9-98	99:28	99:30	5.12
4.88	10-98*	99:26	99:28	5.28
5.77	11-98	100:02	100:04	5.22
5.30	12-98*	99:29	99:31	5.35
5.75	12-98*	100:02	100:04	4.96
7.05	12-98	100:18	100:20	5.36

Figure 8.1 Quotes for Fannie May issues. (Trading in U.S. Government Agency Securities. Reprinted by permission of the *Wall Street Journal* 1998 Dow Jones & Co., Inc. All rights reserved worldwide.)

Pass-Through Certificates

In much the same way that ingenious broker-dealers used Treasury bonds to create CATS and TIGERS, housing-related agencies realized that mortgages can be pooled, repackaged, and sold to the public as collateralized securities.

Mortgages are often pooled. Because mortgages have a standardized structure, it is simple to create groups (or pools) of similar mortgage loans. Mortgages make equal monthly payments for the term of the loan and most mortgages have fixed interest rates. Thus, to create a pool of similar mortgages, one need only find mortgages with the same maturity and same interest rate.

Securitization is the process of turning an illiquid (nonnegotiable) asset, such as a mortgage, into a liquid (negotiable) one like a bond. This is what housing-related agencies did in creating pass-through certificates. In general, a securitized asset is tangible property, has a known resale value, produces steady cash flow, and is of high quality. Securitization has proved to be one of the most influential changes in the investment world. As broker-dealers have searched for new ways to serve the investment market, a variety of debt instruments have been securitized.

A *pass-through certificate* is a security purchased from Fannie Mae, Ginnie Mae, or Freddie Mac, representing an investor's ownership interest in a *mortgage pool* and the cash flows arising from that pool. With pass-through certificates, money flows from homeowners to investors, as shown in Figure 8.2.

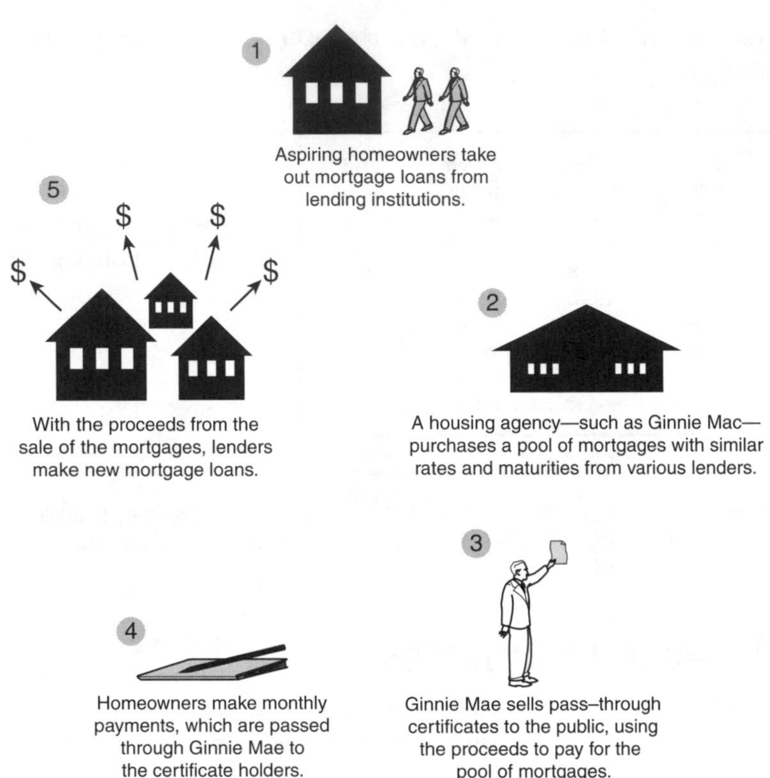

Figure 8.2 The pass-through creation process.

In practice, the creation of a pass-through is more complex than the process outlined in Figure 8.2. Having purchased a pool of mortgages, pass-through issuers then place those mortgages in a grantor trust. This effectively passes ownership of—and tax liability for—those mortgages into the hands of investors. (This is a crucial distinction between pass-throughs and collateralized mortgage obligations.) The most important concept is how cash moves in a pass-through. Pass-through certificates are sold in increments of $25,000 and quoted on a percentage of par in 32nds.

Pass-through certificates issued by Ginnie Mae are guaranteed by the U.S. government. Also, Fannie Mae pass-through certificates—which are backed by FHA-, FmHA-, or VA-guaranteed mortgages—are effectively guaranteed. In any of these cases, defaults by mortgagees do not affect the cash flows (and hence return) received by the investor. These types of pass-throughs are called *modified pass-throughs*—the modification consisting of the guarantee.

An "unmodified" pass-through is any Freddie Mac pass-through, or one issued by Fannie Mae that is not government backed. They are known as straight pass-throughs.

In a basic sense, everyone benefits from pass-throughs. First, local lenders use the cash from the sale of the mortgages to create more loans, thereby earning more fees and profits. Second, aspiring homeowners have greater access to financing. Third, housing-related agencies achieve their policy goal of making home ownership more available, and earn a servicing fee on the pass-through. Finally, the owners of the certificates have a very secure investment, for these reasons:

- Agency pass-throughs are directly or implicitly backed by the U.S. government
- To a degree, pass-throughs are collateralized by real property—the mortgaged homes

So, are pass-throughs essentially risk-free? No. As mentioned previously, there is always the risk of defaults by mortgagees with straight pass-throughs. More important, however, the very nature of mortgage loans introduces two risks to owners of pass-throughs:

- Prepayment risk
- Extension risk

Prepayment Risk

Prepayment risk is the risk that a pass-through's underlying mortgages will be paid off prior to maturity, thus exposing investors to reinvestment risk. Few mortgage loans are held to maturity. Homeowners often move to new residences, paying off their original mortgages with the proceeds from their new mortgages. Also, in a scenario of falling interest rates, homeowners seek to refinance their original mortgages with new mortgages at lower interest rates. In the latter scenario, investors in pass-throughs are forced to reinvest at a lower rate than they were earning.

Prepayment risk has an inverse relationship with interest rate movements. Prepayment risk rises as interest rates fall because more homeowners seek to refinance their higher-rate mortgages.

Do pass-through investors want all mortgages held to maturity? Not necessarily, because that scenario exposes them to *extension risk*. Assume that interest rates are rising. Homeowners will not seek to refinance their mortgages, because they are better off with their existing mortgages at a lower rate. On the other hand, investors want to get their money out of a pass-through and into a newer, higher-yielding security. When interest rates rise, holders of pass-through certificates desire prepayments.

Extension Risk

In this context, extension simply refers to the risk that mortgage holders will take longer than expected to pay off their mortgages. As mentioned, very few mortgages are held to maturity. In fact, securities analysts have developed a statistical model, the *Public Securities Association (PSA) model*, which accurately predicts how many mortgages with the same maturity date will be prepaid for any given period of time. Unlike prepayment risk, extension risk has a direct relationship with changes in interest rates.

Collateralized Mortgage Obligations

Using the PSA model, analysts at Freddie Mac and some private dealers realized that mortgage pools can be viewed in terms of expected cash flows instead of "contractual" cash flows—the payments dictated by the terms of a mortgage loan that is held to maturity. In other words, even if Freddie Mac assembles a pool of 30-year mortgages, it knows in advance that the expected life of that pool is less than 30 years. Hence, the cash flows from that pool are not expected to extend to 30 years either. In fact, the PSA model provides a relatively accurate picture of the amount and timing of the expected cash flows from that pool. With this knowledge, Freddie Mac invented the collateralized mortgage obligation.

Collateralized mortgage obligations (CMOs) are mortgage-backed bonds that represent discrete portions of the cash flows from an underlying pool of mortgages. CMOs resemble pass-throughs in that they are based on the cash flows from a group of mortgages. Nevertheless, CMOs are unlike pass-throughs in one very important respect: investors in CMOs do not have an ownership interest in either the underlying mortgages or in the cash flows generated by those mortgages. Issuers of CMOs place the mortgages in a limited-purpose finance subsidiary, which retains ownership of the mortgages and issues bonds collateralized by those mortgages. For that reason, CMOs are sometimes known as *pay*-through bonds.

CMOs are divided into different maturity classes called *tranches*. For example, a CMO based on a group of 15-year mortgages might be divided into five tranches—tranche 1 representing maturity years 1 to 3, tranche 2 for years 4 to 6, and so on. Cash flows from the mortgages are disbursed to CMO investors in the following manner:

- Regular monthly payments are distributed pro rata to each of the five tranches.
- Prepayments of principal are paid first to tranche 1, and then to tranche 2, and so on.

It is important to recognize that CMOs pay bondholders on a schedule that differs from that of the underlying mortgage pool. Mortgage payments received from the pool are broken into various cash flow streams, as shown in Figure 8.3, creating a series of bonds that have different rates and maturities. Because the value of CMOs is based on this management of mortgage payments, CMOs are known as a derivative product.

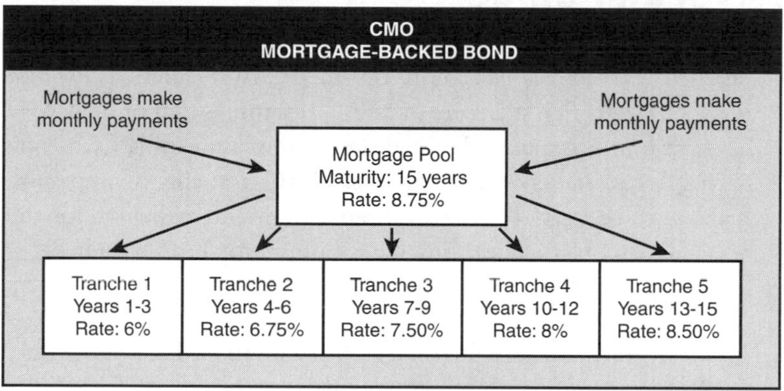

Figure 8.3 Cash flow streams for mortgage payments received.

How does a CMO benefit investors? CMOs provide investors with greater flexibility than pass-through certificates and reduce the prepayment and extension risk associated with pass-throughs. Based on their unique objectives, some investors might want to purchase a mortgage-backed security with a three-year investment horizon—instead of being locked into a 15-year pass-through certificate.

Moreover, if actual prepayments don't match expected prepayments, investors who buy CMO tranches are less likely to be hurt than owners of pass-throughs. To see how this works, assume that interest rates are falling and that Mr. Pink owns tranche 1 of the CMO in Figure 8.3. Tranche 1 was expected to be paid out in three years, but movements in interest rates accelerate prepayments and tranche 1 is actually fully repaid in two and a half years. Although exposed to some reinvestment risk, Mr. Pink will suffer less than another investor who bought a normal pass-through certificate that has been repaid years early. Similarly, by directing prepayments to the earlier tranches first, CMOs provide some protection against extension risk.

Rules for Playing the CMO Game

Please note that CMOs are the only agency security that are not exempt from the Securities Act of 1933. Technically, CMOs qualify as unit investment trusts, which brings them under the supervision of the SEC. Additionally, any advertising of CMOs must be reviewed by the National Association of Securities Dealers before it can be released. Certain boilerplate statements are required in every such ad, and restrictions exist as to the claims that can be made for a CMO.

The general CMO structure is referred to as a plain vanilla CMO. There are a variety of other CMO "flavors," or structures, discussed next.

Other Types of CMOs

To give investors an additional layer of protection against prepayment and extension, agencies created a variation on the CMO called a *Planned Amortization Class (PAC)*. The structure of a PAC resembles that of the CMO in that both are split into tranches. PACs differ from plain vanilla CMOs by virtue of having *companion tranches* for each PAC tranche. Companion tranches are specifically created to absorb prepayment and extension for the PAC tranche. Companion tranches thus act as buffers for PAC tranches.

Cash flows in a PAC are distributed as follows:

- Regular monthly payments are distributed pro rata to all PAC and companion tranches.
- Earlier-than-expected prepayments of principal are paid first to companion tranche 1, then to PAC tranche 1, then to companion tranche 2, then to PAC tranche 2, and so on.
- Later-than-expected prepayments of principal are paid first to PAC tranche 1, then to companion tranche 2, then to PAC tranche 2, and so on.

In other words, companion tranche 1 of a PAC absorbs prepayment risk for PAC tranche 1. Companion tranche 2 absorbs extension risk for PAC tranche 1, as well as prepayment risk for PAC tranche 2, and so on. Figure 8.4 illustrates this principle.

So PACs give investors even greater flexibility with regards to investment horizon and additional cover against prepayment and extension risk. An investor looking for a mortgage-backed security with a specific maturity might opt for a PAC over a pass-through or even a plain-vanilla CMO.

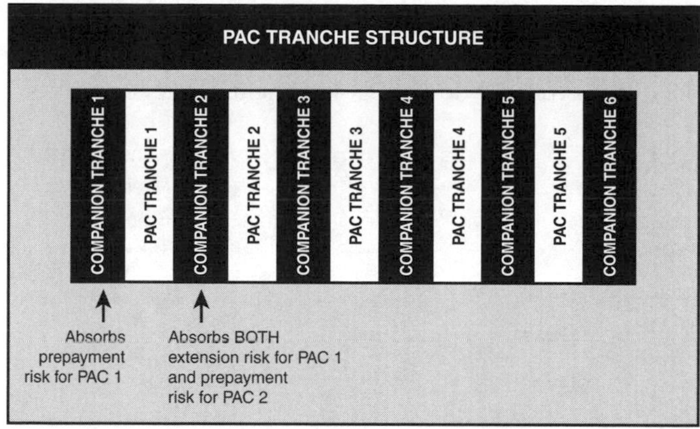

Figure 8.4 Companion tranches acting as buffers for PAC tranches.

Another type of CMO is a TAC. A *Targeted Amortization Class (TAC)* is virtually the same as a PAC, except that investors receive no additional extension risk protection in a TAC. That is, each TAC tranche still has a companion tranche, which absorbs its prepayment risk, but no similar companion tranche exists to absorb its extension risk.

CMOs (including PACs and TACs) have the additional advantage of being sold in increments of $1,000, which makes them more affordable to individual investors. Generally, CMOs are quoted on a *yield-spread basis*, using Treasury issues as benchmarks. A CMO bond quoted at "50 basis points over the Treasury" is being offered at a yield half a percentage point above a Treasury issue with the same maturity as the CMO bond.

Exam Prep Questions

1. Which sectors of the economy do U.S. government agency securities support?

   I. Farming

   II. Housing

   III. Higher education

   IV. Foreign trade

   ❑ A. I and II
   ❑ B. II and III
   ❑ C. I, II, and III
   ❑ D. I, II, III, and IV

2. Which agencies does the government sponsor?

   I. Government National Mortgage Association

   II. Federal National Mortgage Association

   III. Student Loan Marketing Association

   IV. Export-Import Bank

   ❑ A. I
   ❑ B. I, II, and IV
   ❑ C. I, II, and III
   ❑ D. I and IV

3. Which statements are true of U.S. government agencies?

   I. Securities issued by agencies are rated triple-A.

   II. The federal government guarantees all agency securities.

   III. The agencies sell stock to fund their operations.

   IV. All agencies are publicly-traded corporations.

   ❑ A. I
   ❑ B. I and II
   ❑ C. III and IV
   ❑ D. I, II, III, and IV

4. Federal Land Banks have all these characteristics except:

   ❑ A. They finance the long-term needs of the farming sector.
   ❑ B. They fund their lending programs by issuing bonds with maturities of 1 to 15 years.
   ❑ C. They require that farmers purchase stock in a local land bank before receiving a loan.
   ❑ D. They are privatized companies.

5. Which type of mortgages does the federal government guarantee?

   I. Veterans Administration mortgages

   II. Farm Service Agency mortgages

   III. Federal Housing Administration mortgages

   IV. Conventional mortgages at commercial banks

   - ❑ A. IV
   - ❑ B. I and III
   - ❑ C. I, II, and III
   - ❑ D. I, II, III, and IV

6. Bonds issued by the Federal Home Loan Bank System have all these characteristics except:

   - ❑ A. They pay interest semiannually.
   - ❑ B. They are callable five years prior to maturity.
   - ❑ C. They are issued with a minimum par value of $10,000.
   - ❑ D. Dealers quote them in 32nds.

7. Which statements are true about the Federal National Mortgage Association?

   I. Fannie Mae purchases private-sector mortgages.

   II. Fannie Mae purchases FHA-guaranteed mortgages.

   III. Fannie Mae purchases VA-guaranteed mortgages.

   IV. Fannie Mae securities are guaranteed by the federal government.

   - ❑ A. I
   - ❑ B. II and III
   - ❑ C. I, II, and III
   - ❑ D. I, II, III, and IV

8. The following statements are true regarding the Government National Mortgage Association except:

   - ❑ A. GNMA is part of the federal government.
   - ❑ B. Income from GNMA securities is exempt from state and local taxes.
   - ❑ C. GNMA only purchases government-guaranteed mortgages.
   - ❑ D. GNMA places mortgages in a grantor trust to form pass-through certificates.

9. The following statements are true regarding the Federal Home Loan Mortgage Corporation except:

   - ❑ A. Freddie Mac provides a secondary market for conventional mortgages.
   - ❑ B. Freddie Mac purchases government-guaranteed mortgages.
   - ❑ C. Freddie Mac issues stock to savings institutions.
   - ❑ D. Freddie Mac issues mortgage-backed securities.

10. Government agencies sell their debt issues to the public:
    - ❑ A. Directly
    - ❑ B. Through broker-dealers known as fiscal agents
    - ❑ C. Through the Federal Reserve
    - ❑ D. Through the United States Treasury
11. Government agency securities have all these characteristics except:
    - ❑ A. They trade only on the OTC market.
    - ❑ B. Agency transactions settle on T+3.
    - ❑ C. Dealers generally sell agencies in increments of at least $25,000.
    - ❑ D. Institutional investors provide most of the market for agencies.
12. For investors, the advantages of CMOs over standard pass-throughs include all the following except:
    - ❑ A. CMOs receive a Freddie Mac guarantee not available to pass-through investors.
    - ❑ B. CMOs give some protection from prepayment and extension risk.
    - ❑ C. Investors in CMOs do not have tax liability for the underlying mortgages.
    - ❑ D. Investors in CMOs can choose the maturity of their investment more precisely.
13. Straight pass-through certificates are backed by the:
    - ❑ A. Guarantee of the federal government
    - ❑ B. Real property underlying the debt
    - ❑ C. Guarantee of the issuing agency
    - ❑ D. Guarantee of the Federal Reserve
14. The greatest risk of pass-through certificates is:
    - ❑ A. Interest rate risk
    - ❑ B. Extension risk
    - ❑ C. Prepayment risk
    - ❑ D. Call risk
15. The following actions by homeowners decrease the average life of the mortgage pool (on which pass-through securities are based) except:
    - ❑ A. Defaulting on a mortgage
    - ❑ B. Selling a home
    - ❑ C. Refinancing at a lower interest rate
    - ❑ D. Taking on a second mortgage

Exam Prep Answers

1. The correct answer is D. The government has created agencies to support its policy objectives in many sectors of the economy, including farming, housing, higher education, and foreign trade.
2. The correct answer is D. The Government National Mortgage Association and the Export-Import Bank are the only two agencies that the U.S. government directly sponsors. Ginnie Mae is part of HUD, Eximbank, although an independent entity, can borrow directly from the U.S. Treasury.
3. The correct answer is A. Agency debt is rated triple-A; although, in most cases, agency debt does not carry a government guarantee. Investors generally consider that the securities carry the implicit backing of the government.
4. The correct answer is D. Federal Land Banks are not privatized companies, even though they issue stock. To qualify for loans from FLBs, farmers must purchase stock equaling 5% of the loan in a local land bank association. The local land bank, in turn, purchases stock in the district FLB.
5. The correct answer is C. The federal government guarantees VA, FSA, and FHA mortgages. VA mortgages are available to military veterans and surviving spouses, FSA mortgages are offered to families in low-income rural areas, and FHA mortgages are provided to people purchasing residential properties.
6. The correct answer is B. The Federal Home Loan Bank System, which provides credit to savings and loan institutions, cooperative banks, and other mortgage lenders, does not issue callable bonds.
7. The correct answer is C. Fannie Mae issues do not carry a direct government guarantee. The agency can borrow from the Fed's discount window however, providing government support for Fannie Mae.
8. The correct answer is B. Although Ginnie Mae is part of the Department of Housing and Urban Development, income from its securities is taxed at the federal, state, and local levels, because the mortgagees of the underlying loans have already taken tax deductions.
9. The correct answer is B. Freddie Mac does not purchase government-guaranteed mortgages, but rather conventional mortgages, which it places in a trust, issuing mortgage-backed securities (based on the cash flows from the underlying mortgages).
10. The correct answer is B. Agency securities are issued through broker-dealers called fiscal agents. Each agency assembles a group of fiscal agents, which then markets the agency's debt issues.

11. The correct answer is B. Agency securities settle the regular way on Trade Date +1.
12. The correct answer is A. Although Freddie Mac issued the first CMOs, it does not provide a government guarantee for any of its issues. Savings and loan institutions, not the government, own the agency.
13. The correct answer is B. Straight pass-throughs—pass-throughs not backed by government-guaranteed mortgages such as Freddie Mac—represent ownership interest in the real property underlying the debt. Modified pass-throughs do carry a U.S. government guarantee, either directly or through the government's guarantee of the underlying mortgages.
14. The correct answer is C. The greatest risk associated with pass-through certificates is prepayment risk—the risk that investors will repay the underlying mortgages prior to maturity. This exposes pass-through investors to reinvestment risk, because prepayments occur most frequently in an environment of falling interest rates, making it less likely that the investors can find another investment vehicle yielding as much as their original pass-throughs.
15. The correct answer is D. When homeowners take out a second mortgage, they become more likely to amortize their mortgage at a prepayment speed slower than that predicted by the PSA model—extending the average life of the associated mortgage pool. This action increases extension risk for pass-through investors, rather than prepayment risk.

Municipal Debt

Terms You Need to Know:

- ✓ *Ad valorem* taxes
- ✓ Adjusted cost basis
- ✓ Assessed valuation
- ✓ After-tax yield
- ✓ Bank-qualified issues
- ✓ Constant yield method
- ✓ Cost basis
- ✓ Discount
- ✓ Feasibility study
- ✓ Flow-of-funds
- ✓ General obligation (GO) bond
- ✓ Gross revenue pledge
- ✓ Mill rate
- ✓ Municipal bond (or muni)
- ✓ Net revenue pledge
- ✓ Original issue discount (OID)
- ✓ Premium
- ✓ Private activity bonds
- ✓ Protective covenants
- ✓ Revenue anticipation note (RAN)
- ✓ Revenue bond
- ✓ Short-term municipal debt (municipal notes)
- ✓ Straight-line method
- ✓ Tax anticipation note (TAN)
- ✓ Tax assessment
- ✓ Taxable equivalent yield (or tax-equivalent yield)
- ✓ Triple tax exemption

Concepts You Need to Understand

- ✓ Reasons issuers find municipal bonds desirable
- ✓ Special features that make municipal bonds an attractive investment
- ✓ The different structures of general obligation bonds and revenue bonds
- ✓ How municipalities assess the taxes that support general obligation bonds
- ✓ The range of municipal projects funded by revenue bonds
- ✓ Features that protect investors in revenue bond issues
- ✓ How municipalities can address cash-flow problems
- ✓ The variety of notes available for addressing specific cash-flow needs
- ✓ How to compare yields of tax-exempt issues with yields of taxable issues
- ✓ The tax consequences of selling municipal bonds before maturity
- ✓ The tax implications of selling municipal bonds that were bought at a discount or premium

Municipal Bonds

Private corporations can raise capital in the stock and bond markets, and the federal government can fund its operations by offering a smorgasbord of debt instruments. State and local governments needing to raise capital can also enter the debt market, issuing securities in what is known as the municipal bond market. This chapter introduces municipal bonds (commonly called "munis"), some of the features that make them attractive to both issuers and investors, and the distinctions among different kinds of munis.

A *municipal bond* (commonly called a *muni*) is a long-term loan made by the purchaser to a local or state government. Most municipal bonds mature in five years or more. All municipalities and states—from the smallest towns to the largest states—need money to build and maintain their infrastructure. A school district wanting to construct a new high school might not have the necessary funds in its normal operating budget. Thus, it must borrow money to finance the project. To do this, the district sells bonds—essentially small pieces of the debt—to various lenders, often middle-class citizens. Over the life of the loan, the school district pays interest to its bondholders, and, at the end of the loan period, pays back the bond's purchase price.

Municipal bonds are exempt from the registration and prospectus rules of the Securities Act of 1933. Munis are also exempt from most of the regulations set down in the Securities Exchange Act of 1934, although they *are* subject to its antifraud and antimanipulation provisions.

Who can issue municipal bonds? Any town, city, county, state, or U.S. territory can issue bonds. Local political authorities such as school districts, water districts, and public utilities can also issue municipal bonds.

A *municipality* is a self-governing political unit, including everything from water districts to states. The term "municipal bond" covers all bonds issued within the United States by political jurisdictions other than the federal government.

Munis finance all sorts of capital intensive projects that state and local governments carry out in their year-to-year business: building roads, bridges, sewers, schools, public housing, and government offices, to name a few.

Different Uses for Municipal Bond Proceeds

Not all municipal bonds are issued to finance public infrastructure. In one famous case, a municipality issued bonds merely to pump up its own investment fund. In 1993 and 1994, Orange County, California, issued almost $1 billion of munis through one of their favorite brokers, the proceeds of which went into the county treasury's ill-famed investment pool. Unfortunately, the county treasurer invested most of the money in highly leveraged securities to take advantage of an interest-rate trend that then suddenly reversed. The investment pool collapsed, and Orange County declared bankruptcy.

Municipalities Offer Competitive Yields

Municipalities can offer competitive yields by offering tax-exemption to bond investors. Through a reciprocal agreement, federal and state governments pledge not to tax the interest earned on each other's bonds. For the owners of U.S. Treasury securities, this means that they do not pay state and local income taxes on their interest income. For the owners of state and locally issued bonds, this means that they pay no federal income tax on their interest income. This tax shelter strongly enhances the attraction of municipal bonds. State and local governments generally take this tax-exempt status a step further for in-state residents by making the interest earned on municipal bonds free from all state and local taxes as well. Thus, most municipal bonds enjoy *triple tax exemption*—freedom from income tax at all levels.

Who gains from a triple tax-exempt status? Typically, only those municipal bond buyers who reside in the state where the bond is issued can benefit from triple tax exemption. Bonds issued by U.S. territories—including Puerto Rico, Guam, Samoa, the U.S. Virgin Islands, and even Washington, D.C.—constitute an exception. Territory-issued bonds are triple-tax-exempt for *all* U.S. buyers, regardless of where they live.

Those citizens who get the greatest relative benefit from triple tax exemption are of course those who reach the highest tax brackets. Taxpayers in a 30% tax bracket keep an extra $30 for every $100 in interest income they earn on triple-tax-exempt bonds. Taxpayers in a 48% tax bracket, though, keep an extra $48 for every $100 in interest they earn.

All municipal bonds are not triple-tax-exempt. Since the Tax Reform Act of 1986, one category of municipal bond is no longer shielded from federal income tax: the *private activity bond*. The 1986 Act classifies a bond that meets *both* of the following criteria as a private activity bond:

- More than 10% of its proceeds are earmarked for a project used by a private entity, such as a sports team.
- The facility for the private entity serves as collateral to secure more than 10% of the bond issue.

EXAMPLE: Twenty-five percent of the proceeds from the sale of a Mudville urban renewal bond are going toward the construction of a baseball stadium that, city managers hope, will attract a major league franchise to Mudville's downtown area. After it's built, the stadium itself will secure 25% of the bond issue's principal. Because this bond meets both of the criteria for a private activity bond, the future Mudville bondholders have to pay federal income tax on their interest income.

Even here, however, lawmakers left some wiggle room. The 1986 act establishes seven categories of "qualified" private activity bonds that remain tax-exempt, provided that they meet a set of technical requirements. Private activity bonds that can fall into these seven categories include those financing facilities like airports, housing for veterans, and universities.

Triple tax exemption enables munis to compete with corporate bonds that usually offer a higher—although taxable—yield.

In spite of the benefits of triple tax exemption, municipal bonds can be like molasses—illiquid and slow to move. Issuers can make their munis more attractive to a large potential customer—commercial banks—if they can designate the bonds as *bank-qualified issues.* Buying bank-qualified issues give banks a significant tax break: they can deduct 80% of the interest they pay to depositors whose savings they have invested in the bonds. Not only does the bank save by investing in tax-free bonds, it also saves by deducting a major portion of its interest payments to customers. Municipalities issuing bank-qualified bonds must meet two conditions:

- The bonds cannot be private activity bonds.
- Generally, no municipality can issue more than $10 million of bank-qualified bonds per year.

Municipal bonds, then, share many features that make them attractive to both large and small investors. But not all munis are the same—a city or water district that wishes to issue bonds must choose the kind of bond that best fits its needs.

General Obligation Bonds Versus Revenue Bonds

The two primary classes of municipal bonds are defined as follows:

- *General Obligation bonds* (or *GO bonds*) are backed by the full faith and taxing capability of the issuing municipality. In practical terms, this means that GO bonds are serviced with revenues from state or local taxes.

- *Revenue bonds* are serviced with income from the projects funded by the bonds (for instance, tolls collected at a bridge whose construction was financed by a bond sale).

The main advantage for GO bonds for the investor is government backing. Because a governmental taxing authority backs general obligation bonds, they are the safest of municipal issues. If a town runs into trouble paying its bondholders, it can usually raise taxes to avoid default on the bonds. Angry GO bondholders can even compel a municipality to levy higher taxes or to appropriate other funds for payment of the debt.

Municipalities normally service the interest and principal payments of GO bonds with taxes on commercial and residential properties—commonly known as *ad valorem* ("to the value") property taxes. A municipality assesses each parcel of property within its boundaries, assigning each a dollar value. This *assessed valuation* is the basis for the computation of property taxes. The tax rate applied to the assessed valuation is known as the *mill rate*, measured in units of 1/10 of 1%, called *mills*. The mill rate multiplied by the assessed valuation gives the total *tax assessment*, or the amount of property tax owed.

> **EXAMPLE:** The Mervin family's home is visited by the county tax assessor, who inspects the abode and gives it an assessed valuation of $120,000. The county's finance officer has set the mill rate at 15 mills, or 1.5%. The Mervins will owe $120,000 × 1.5%, or $1,800 in property taxes on their home for the year. A considerable chunk of that $1,800 can go to paying interest and principal on the county's general obligation debt.

Property tax revenues don't back all general obligation bonds, because some jurisdictions, such as counties and states, do not levy property taxes, whereas most levy general taxes of other types. The market distinguishes three classes of GO bonds, according to the kind of tax revenue available to back them:

- Regular GO bonds are backed by the unlimited taxing power of the issuer and can be serviced by property taxes, sales taxes, income taxes, or any other tax a municipality collects.
- Limited obligation bonds have a more narrow tax base, being serviced only by *ad valorem* property taxes, sometimes with a maximum mileage cap.
- State-issued GO bonds are serviced by any tax revenue that a state can collect, including gasoline and alcohol taxes. Generally, states and counties do not collect property taxes; only local governments do.

Taxes, then, provide municipalities with the wherewithal to pay back their GO bond debts.

Revenue Bonds Differ from GO Bonds

Revenue bonds differ from general obligation bonds in that they are not backed by taxes, but by income generated from the project that the bond itself has funded. Municipalities often issue revenue bonds to finance construction projects that eventually are supported by users' fees. These projects include bridges, roads, hospitals, sewer and water systems, and airports. Revenue bonds are self-supporting—the bond issue and the project depend on each other for success.

Buying a revenue bond is somewhat akin to buying a corporate bond. In both cases, the bondholder invests money to help an entity create a product that must sell. The bondholder's return depends on the entity making sufficient revenue from sales to pay the interest and principal. Because revenue bond payments are contingent on the project's success, and because the issuing municipality has little recourse to taxpayers' money if things go awry, revenue bonds as a class are riskier than GO bonds. However, a municipality can take measures to assure potential bond buyers that its revenue bond issue will present a sound investment opportunity.

Factors That Lower Revenue Bond Risk

Three sets of safeguards lower the risk of owning revenue bonds, giving investors greater confidence that they will receive their promised payments:

- **Feasibility study**—The municipality hires an independent engineering firm to perform a feasibility study for the proposed project. The firm, which has no vested interest in the undertaking of the project, completes the study before the bonds are issued. The feasibility study tries to determine whether the project can earn the revenues necessary to service the debt and also includes a detailed engineering report on the proposed facility.
- **Protective covenants**—The bond contract must incorporate protective covenants to protect investors' interests. These covenants can include:
    - **Maintenance covenants**—The issuer guarantees that it will set funds aside to maintain the facility in good working order
    - **Rate covenants**—The issuer insures that it will keep user fees for the facility at a level high enough to service the debt
    - **No-sale covenants**—The issuer promises that it will not sell the funded facility to another party, or saddle it with a mortgage
    - **Insurance covenants**—The issuer promises to purchase sufficient insurance to protect against loss of, or damage to, the facility
    - **Additional bond covenants**—Prohibit the issuer from diluting the investors' collateral by issuing future bonds against the facility
    - **Nondiscrimination covenants**—The issuer promises not to grant specific groups special rates to use the facility
    - **Audit covenants**—Mandate regular audits to protect the facility against fraud or mismanagement
- **Flow-of-funds**—The municipal issuer establishes a flow-of-funds, setting the priorities for disbursement of the money produced by its revenue-generating project. There are two basic flow-of-funds structures that provide very different levels of protection; a net revenue pledge and a gross revenue pledge.

A *net revenue pledge* promises that the issuer will meet the facility's operation and maintenance costs before it allocates money to servicing the bond issue.

A *gross revenue pledge* promises that the issuer will make interest and principal repayment to bondholders its top funding priority, making such payments from gross revenues *before* setting aside money for operations, maintenance, or project improvements.

Note that net revenue pledges are much more common than gross revenue pledges, and for good reason. Gross revenue pledges, in difficult economic times, can lead to a project falling into disrepair, while bondholders continue to enjoy regular interest payments.

Money generated by a revenue-bond project typically cascades through several levels of funds:

- **Revenue fund**—Gathers all gross revenues for disbursement
- **Debt service fund**—Pays coupon and principal to bondholders
- **Debt service reserve fund**—Holds one year's coupon and principal payments; must be replenished if drawn down
- **Operating and maintenance fund**—Pays normal business expenses
- **Sinking fund**—Allows retirement of a percentage of the issue each year
- **Renewal and replacement fund**—Pays for repairs and new equipment
- **Surplus fund**—Collects all excess; useful for emergencies

Short-Term Municipal Debt

Essentially, a municipality issues short-term debt for the same reasons consumers might take cash advances against their credit cards to pay for home improvements. A municipality's needs don't always match the timing of its income receipts. By selling *short-term municipal debt*, or *municipal notes*, a town or state can smooth out uneven cash flows, thus permitting its operations or projects to continue without interruption.

Muni notes, which mature within five years (and usually in less than one), can take several forms. Property owners tend to wait until the final hour to mail their property tax checks, but municipalities must pay their employees year-round. *Tax anticipation notes (TANs)* solve this problem. TANs are backed by the expected receipt of future property taxes, and are backed by a GO pledge.

Tax anticipation notes (TANS) are short-term debt obligation issued by state or municipal governments in 'anticipation' of future tax collections.

But what about cash-flow difficulties with revenue projects? TANs have a sibling known as *revenue anticipation notes*, or *RANs*. Jurisdictions awaiting the first income stream from a facility under construction often issue RANs. RANs are typically backed by a GO pledge of revenue other than *ad valorem* taxes. Sometimes, a town or county might find that it owes payments on both GO and revenue bonds during a period when it does not have sufficient tax or revenue receipts. In this case, it can issue a hybrid note, named a tax and revenue anticipation note (TRAN). Most local units of government get some funding from the federal government and from voter-approved bond issues, both of which can lead to uneven income streams. In response, municipalities might issue grant anticipation notes (GANs) or bond anticipation notes (BANs). These instruments are backed by the full faith and taxing power of the jurisdiction, and thus are considered general obligations. BANs enable work to start on a project before the municipality completes its long-term financing, and are "taken out," or retired, by the long-term bonds when those are issued, after the completion of the project.

Revenue anticipation notes (RANS) are securities issued in anticipation of future revenue that will be used for repayment of the security.

Many cities have also taken advantage of two short-term debt instruments specifically designed to foster construction in the housing sector. Construction loan notes (CLNs) help finance multifamily apartment buildings, whereas project notes (PNs) are used to build subsidized housing for low-income families. Project notes are guaranteed by the U.S. Department of Housing and Urban Development (HUD). Because of this, buyers consider PNs to be investment-grade paper. As with BANs, after the project is completed and tenants begin paying rent, the city takes out the CLNs and PNs by issuing long-term bonds.

Other Types of Muni Bonds

An investor in the bond market is likely to find the following munis being traded:

- **Public housing bond (Section 8 bonds)**—No longer issued, but still traded on the secondary market, these bonds were used to fund the building of low-cost subsidized housing. They have the backing of the federal government, so investors consider them quite desirable. Rents paid by tenants of the public housing service the issue.
- **Double-barreled bond**—A muni backed both by the revenue raised from the funded project and taxes (other than *ad valorem*): a GO-revenue hybrid. These issues finance projects that will charge fees (toll bridges, water and sewer facilities, or convention centers, for instance), but if the project fails to generate the expected level of income, the municipality pledges tax revenues to cover interest and principal payments.

- **Special tax bond**—Municipal bond backed by the proceeds of a tax that is unrelated to the project financed by the issue. The assessment is often a so-called "sin tax" on liquor, tobacco, or gambling.
- **Special assessment bond**—An issue backed by an *ad valorem* tax assessed only on those areas or properties that benefit from the bond project. For example, a municipality might propose a bond to raise funds to renovate streetlights and sidewalks in a particular neighborhood. Only property owners in that part of town pay the tax levied to support the bond.
- **Moral obligation bond**—A bond issued by a municipality and backed by a pledge from the state government to pay off the debt if the municipality cannot. However, because no pledge can legally compel a future state legislature to vote for the needed funds, bondholders must rely solely on moral persuasion—and the power of the market, via the ratings agencies—to secure their investment.
- **Tax allocation bond**—This bond finances commercial redevelopment, typically in older urban districts. Often subsidized property taxes on the refurbished real estate secure the issue. In contrast, a *municipal utility district bond* provides for construction of water, sewer, power, and roadways into both commercial and residential undeveloped areas.

So a person wanting to invest money in the muni bond market has a number of bonds to choose from.

Municipal Bonds and Taxes

To compare a municipal bond's tax-exempt yield with a corporate bond's taxable yield, investors must compute the municipal bond's *taxable equivalent yield* (or simply, *tax-equivalent yield*). For any muni, the tax-equivalent yield equals what a taxable bond has to earn in order to equal the muni's tax-exempt yield.

The tax-equivalent yield is thus the tax-exempt yield divided by the percentage of income left to an investor after he or she pays income taxes.

$$Yt = \frac{Ye}{(1 - 8)}$$

Where Yt = tax-equivalent yield, Ye = tax-exempt yield, and B = income tax bracket—combining local, state, and federal taxes

Formulas and Notation

Some people find the ideas presented in the next few sections to be clearer if they can see a few simple arithmetic formulas. To make the material as useful as possible, the formulas are presented in the text and in shortened form, using the following abbreviations:

Y = yield-to-maturity

Yt = tax-equivalent yield

Ye = tax-exempt/after-tax yield

B = tax bracket

P = par value

V = market value

A = principal amount

Ta = time of accretion (or amortization)

C = cost basis

Ca = adjusted cost basis

M = life of bond, in years

An example can help clarify the concept.

EXAMPLE: Ms. Quigley, who lives in Deaf Smith County, Texas, and pays 28% of her earnings in income taxes, is interested in buying bonds. She is looking at a new-issue 5.5% Deaf Smith County bond, and a taxable Xyron Corp. bond. What yield does she need to get on the Xyron bond to pocket the same amount she would earn on the Deaf Smith bond? To find out, she computes the muni's taxable equivalent yield.

$$Yt = \frac{Ye}{(1 - B)}$$

$$Yt = \frac{.055}{(1 - 0.28)} = \frac{.055}{0.72} = 7.64\%$$

So the Deaf Smith tax-exempt bond has a taxable equivalent yield of 7.64% for Ms. Quigley. That is, if she were to buy the Xyron bond, she needs to get a yield of at least 7.64% in order to equal the return of the municipal bond.

Determining the After-Tax Yield on a Taxable Bond

Investors can use the same method to compute the after-tax yield on a taxable bond. The *after-tax yield* on a taxable instrument such as a corporate bond simply equals the bond's yield multiplied by the portion of income left after an investor pays income taxes. Rearrange the previous equation as so:

$Ye = Yt(1 - B)$

Ye now stands for the after-tax yield.

> **EXAMPLE:** Mr. Greenglass buys a Zenon Corp. bond with a yield-to-maturity of 7.16%. If he is in a 26% tax bracket, what is his after-tax yield on the bond?
>
> $$\begin{aligned} Ye &= Yt\ (1 - B) \\ &= 0.0716 \times (1 - 0.26) \\ &= 0.716 \times 0.74 \\ &= 5.30\% \end{aligned}$$
>
> So Mr. Greenglass realizes an after-tax yield on the Zenon bond of 5.30%. In other words, a triple-tax-exempt municipal bond yielding 5.30% would give him the same effective return.

Although tax exemption clearly provides a higher real return for munis than they might otherwise enjoy, investors do have to be aware of some tax considerations. When investors buy bonds at a *discount*—below redemption value—or at a *premium*—above redemption value—they can record capital gains or capital losses, which can affect their tax situation and their overall returns.

The Tax Consequences of Buying Municipal Bonds at a Discount or Premium

There are two broad cases. Municipal bonds bought at a discount or premium and *held until maturity* usually do not have tax consequences, but current tax laws provide exceptions under some circumstances. Munis bought at a discount or premium and *sold before maturity* usually record a capital gain or loss—with any capital gain being taxable.

To help keep the ideas clear, the rest of this section is broken into three parts. First, I introduce the needed terms; second, I examine the cases of bonds held to maturity; third, I look at the cases of bonds sold before maturity.

Terms

Cost basis is an accounting term that simply means the purchase price of an asset, such as a muni bond. The term is used for tax purposes. Cost basis is the starting point for figuring the capital gain or loss when an investor sells or redeems a bond.

Accretion is the accumulation of additional tax-exempt interest on a bond that has been issued for less than its redemption value. If a municipality sells a $1,000-face-value bond for $950, buyers receive the extra $50 upon redemption. An investor spreads the $50 profit evenly over the life of the bond as additional tax-exempt interest.

Amortization is the analogous concept for premium bonds. An investor only gets the redemption value of the bond at maturity, so the additional amount he paid is not considered interest income; for tax purposes, it must be discounted.

The *adjusted cost basis* is the cost basis increased or decreased by accretion or amortization. The investor makes a sliding adjustment over time, most often using the *straight-line method*, which prorates the adjustment by the percentage of time that has passed toward the maturity date.

Bonds Held to Maturity

Again, there are two cases. Munis bought at a *premium* and held to redemption have no capital gains or losses. Over the life of the bond, the investor amortizes the premium paid, and the adjusted cost basis of the bond decreases until at maturity it equals the bond's redemption value.

Munis bought at a *discount* provide a more complicated situation; much depends on whether the investor purchased the bond in the secondary market, or as an *original issue discount (OID)*—a bond sold below par by the issuing municipality. The accretion on an OID is part and parcel of the tax-free interest income of the muni, not a capital gain, and is not taxable. This is not the case for discounted bonds in the secondary market. An investor who buys a discount bond in the secondary market and holds it until maturity realizes a taxable capital gain on the bond.

> **EXAMPLE:** In 1986, Dr. Burton bought $10,000 of the Chesapeake Bridge and Tunnel Authority bond with a 5% coupon and a 1998 maturity in the secondary market at a price of 92. She holds the munis for 12 years, until maturity, when she redeems them for their $10,000 face value. Dr. Burton has realized a capital gain of $800 on the bonds ($10,000 redemption price – $9,200 purchase price). Although the $6,000 of interest she has earned (0.05 × $10,000 × 12 years) remains tax-free, she must pay capital gains tax on this $800.

As market conditions change, investors frequently trade munis in the secondary market rather than hold them to the redemption date. When they do, more complicated tax situations arise.

Bonds Sold Before Maturity

An investor who sells a premium bond before maturity might record a capital gain or loss, depending on the difference between the bond's selling price and its adjusted cost basis. The premium is amortized using the straight-line method to arrive at the adjusted cost basis. If the investor sells the bond for more than its adjusted cost basis, he or she realizes a taxable capital gain. If, on the other hand, the investor sells the bond for less than its adjusted cost basis, he or she suffers a capital loss that can be applied toward a tax credit. Thus, when investors sell a premium muni in the secondary market, they need to calculate the adjusted costs basis to determine whether they have a tax liability or credit.

Calculating Adjusted Cost Basis

The adjusted cost basis is the sum of the price originally paid for the bond (cost basis), and the difference between the cost basis and the redemption price after factoring in its maturity date.

$Ca = C + [(Ta \div M) \times (P - C)]$

where

Ca = adjusted cost basis

C = cost basis

Ta = time of accretion (or amortization) was issued

M = life of the bond

P = par value

EXAMPLE: Mr. Tong bought 10 Municipal Assistance Corp. (MAC) bonds with an 8% coupon, maturing in 1999. MAC had issued them in 1979 with a 20-year maturity, and Mr. Tong bought them at a price of 110 in 1981, but, he chose to sell his bonds after only eight years. He calculated his adjusted cost basis:

$= \$11{,}000 + [0.4 \times (-\$1{,}000)]$

Mr. Tong's adjusted cost basis per bond is $10,600. He tells his broker to sell them.

- If his broker sells the bonds for $10,000, Mr. Tong will realize a capital loss of $600.
- If the broker sells the bonds at $10,600, Mr. Tong will realize no capital gain or loss.
- If the broker sells the bonds for $10,750, Mr. Tong earns a capital gain of $150.

Notice that although investors' tax liability for premium bonds depends on the market price actually paid, that liability is not adjusted for the lower yield-to-maturity resulting from the premium. The amortization of the premium continues as if the investor still earned the higher yield of the coupon rate. The IRS eventually responded to bondholders' complaints by revising the amortization calculation.

Calculating the Amortization on a Premium Bond

Investors must now use the *constant-yield method* to compute amortization. (Bonds issued before September 1985 still take the straight-line method.) With the constant-yield method, the premium amortizes on a yield-to-maturity basis. The bondholder must repeat this process for each coupon period, using the result of each step as part of the next step, for the entire period in question. This "iteration" process, although more complicated, enables investors to track their real amortization more closely.

For tax purposes, discount bonds sold in the secondary market are treated just like premium bonds sold. Keep in mind that additional tax-free income is accreting to the cost basis, rather than amortizing from it. Again, the key is whether the investor sells the bond for more or less than its adjusted cost basis.

Calculating the Adjusted Cost Basis of a Discount Bond

You can use the same formula as for premium bonds:

$Ca = C + [(Ta \div M) \times (C - P)]$

Where

Ca = adjusted cost basis

C = cost basis

Ta = time of accretion

M = life of the bond

P = par value

A discounted bond sold before maturity has an adjusted cost basis that is less than its redemption value, and the seller uses this adjusted cost basis to compute any capital gain or loss. Bondholders always use the straight-line method to do the calculation.

EXAMPLE: Mr. Nunez buys a $10,000 OID Marin County 10-year bond at 95, a cost of $9,500. He decides to sell his bond after seven years have passed. He computes the adjusted cost basis of the OID at that time based on the amount of the discount that has accreted thus far.

$$\begin{aligned} Ca &= C + [(Ta \div M) \times (P - C)] \\ &= \$9{,}500 + [(7 \div 10) \times (\$10{,}000 - \$9{,}500)] \\ &= \$9{,}500 + [0.7 \times \$500] \\ &= \$9{,}850 \end{aligned}$$

So the adjusted cost basis on Mr. Nunez's bond after seven years is $9,850.

- If he sells the bond for $10,000, he has a $150 capital gain.
- If he sells the bond for $9,850, he has no capital gain or loss.
- If he sells the bond for $9,650, he has a $200 capital loss.

Exam Prep Questions

1. Which statements are true about municipal bond issues?

   I. Municipalities use the proceeds from municipal bond issues to build and maintain their infrastructure.

   II. Municipalities use the proceeds from municipal bond issues for general purposes.

   III. States, cities, and other political subdivisions issue municipal securities.

   IV. Municipal bonds are exempt from SEC registration requirements.

   - ❑ A. I and III
   - ❑ B. II and III
   - ❑ C. I, II, and III
   - ❑ D. I, II, III, and IV

2. Interest investors earn on most municipal securities is generally exempt from:

   - ❑ A. Federal taxes
   - ❑ B. State taxes
   - ❑ C. Local taxes
   - ❑ D. Federal, state, and local taxes

3. Angie Davis is a resident of California. She bought a municipal bond issued by the Washington, D.C., Sewer District. What is the tax treatment of the interest Davis earns?

   - ❑ A. Davis must pay state and local taxes on the interest, because she is not a resident of Washington.
   - ❑ B. Davis must pay federal tax, but not state and local taxes on the interest.
   - ❑ C. Davis must pay federal, state, and local taxes on the interest.
   - ❑ D. Davis is exempt from federal, state, and local taxes on the interest.

4. Which statements are true about bank-qualified municipal issues?

   I. A municipality cannot issue more than $10 million of bank-qualified bonds per year.

   II. Bank-qualified issues cannot be private activity bonds.

   III. Banks get significant tax breaks relative to the interest expense on the deposits they use to buy such bank-qualified issues.

   IV. Bank-qualified bonds must be general obligations.

   - ❑ A. I and II
   - ❑ B. II and III
   - ❑ C. I, II, and III
   - ❑ D. I, II, III, and IV

5. Which statements are true concerning general obligation bonds?

   I. Revenue from municipal projects services GOs.

   II. Revenue from municipal tax services GOs.

   III. GOs must be approved by the voters of the municipality issuing them.

   IV. Municipalities can issue an unlimited amount of GO bonds.

   ❑ A. I
   ❑ B. I and IV
   ❑ C. II and III
   ❑ D. III and IV

6. Joe Davos owns a home in Dade County, Florida, which the county assesses at $200,000. If the county property tax rate is 18 mills, how much does Davos pay in property taxes each year?

   ❑ A. $360
   ❑ B. $1,800
   ❑ C. $3,600
   ❑ D. $18,000

7. Which taxes do municipalities use to service limited-obligation bonds?

   I. Property taxes

   II. Sales taxes

   III. Income taxes

   IV. Gasoline taxes

   ❑ A. I
   ❑ B. I and II
   ❑ C. I, II, and III
   ❑ D. I, II, III, and IV

8. The city of Muncie issues a revenue bond for construction of a municipal swimming complex with a provision that ensures that the city can keep user fees for the facility high enough to service the debt. This provision is called:

   ❑ A. A maintenance covenant
   ❑ B. A rate covenant
   ❑ C. An insurance covenant
   ❑ D. A nondiscrimination covenant

9. Kings county issues a revenue bond with a net revenue pledge to fund construction and operation of Kings County Municipal Hospital. The county has thereby promised to:

❑ A. Make payment of the hospital's operating and maintenance costs top priority.

❑ B. Make interest payments on the bond top priority.

❑ C. Make sinking fund payments for the bond top priority.

❑ D. Equally split profits between operational costs and bond service costs.

10. Which statements are true about industrial revenue bonds and industrial development bonds?

I. Municipalities use both to attract new corporate business to their locale.

II. Industrial revenue bonds carry the credit rating of the issuing municipality.

III. Industrial development bonds carry the credit rating of the issuing municipality.

IV. Both are general obligation bonds.

❑ A. I and II

❑ B. I, II, and IV

❑ C. I, III, and IV

❑ D. II and III

11. Property taxes back which municipal notes?

❑ A. TANs

❑ B. RANs

❑ C. BANs

❑ D. CLNs

12. Which statement is false concerning special assessment bonds?

❑ A. The issuing municipality backs the bond with *ad valorem* taxes.

❑ B. Only property owners who benefit from the improvement pay increased tax to service the bond.

❑ C. They are a type of revenue bonds.

❑ D. The issuing municipality backs the bond with tax revenue unrelated to the project financed by the issue.

13. Bexar County issues a Riverwalk improvement bond backed by a pledge by the State of Texas to pay off the debt if the county cannot. This is a:

❑ A. Double-barreled bond

❑ B. Limited obligation bond

❑ C. Special delivery tax bond

❑ D. Moral obligation bond

14. Section 8 (public housing) bonds have a unique attraction for investors because:
    - ❑ A. Government-subsidized property taxes secure them.
    - ❑ B. Both the income from the tenants and *ad valorem* revenue from the state secure them.
    - ❑ C. Short-term notes provide investors with bridge funding for them.
    - ❑ D. They are the only muni bond that the federal government backs.

15. Ivan Varbo, an investor in the 32% tax bracket, considers buying a muni yielding 5.40%. What yield must a taxable security have for Varbo to equal the return he would earn on the muni?
    - ❑ A. 5.40%
    - ❑ B. 7.94%
    - ❑ C. 16.875%
    - ❑ D. 4.09%

Exam Prep Answers

1. The correct answer is D. Any state, city, or political subdivision can issue municipal bonds. They use the proceeds to support either their general financing needs or for specific projects. Municipal securities are exempt from the registration rules of the Securities Act of 1933.
2. The correct answer is A. Interest on most municipal securities is free from federal taxes. For the interest to be exempt from state and local taxes, the bondholder must reside in the jurisdiction that issued the muni, or in Washington, D.C., or U.S. territories such as Puerto Rico.
3. The correct answer is D. Interest that U.S. residents receive from municipal bonds issued by Washington, D.C. (and U.S. territories), is exempt from all taxes, regardless of the bondholder's residence. U.S. territories include Puerto Rico, Guam, Samoa, and the U.S. Virgin Islands.
4. The correct answer is C. Bank-qualified issues need not be GOs, and in fact can be any kind of muni except private activity bonds, from which more than 10% of the benefit goes to nongovernment activities.
5. The correct answer is C. Revenue from municipal taxes, such as property and sales taxes, services GO bonds. The residents of the municipality must approve the bond issue—usually through a referendum—before the municipality can borrow. Through either a referendum or by statute, the residents of a municipality can also mandate a ceiling on the public debt burden of the municipality.
6. The correct answer is C. Davos owes $3,600 in property taxes each year. He calculates the tax assessment by multiplying the mill rate (18 or 1.8%) and the assessed valuation of the home ($200,000).
7. The correct answer is A. Municipalities service limited-obligation bonds only with *ad valorem* (usually property) taxes, often with a maximum mileage cap.
8. The correct answer is B. Muncie used a rate covenant to assure investors that the swimming complex generates enough revenue that the city can service the revenue bond.
9. The correct answer is A. Kings county's net revenue pledge means that it will meet the hospital operation and maintenance costs before it allocates any money to service the bond issue.
10. The correct answer is A. Municipalities use both industrial revenue bonds and industrial development bonds to finance new business facilities. They employ industrial revenue bonds to pay for the construction of new industrial parks, backed by their own credit rating. Municipalities with more bargaining leverage usually offer industrial development bonds, which are backed by the corporations' credit rating, rather than that of the municipality.

11. The correct answer is A. The expected receipt of future property taxes back tax anticipation notes. TANs serve as a temporary bridge to smooth out cash flow for municipalities.
12. The correct answer is C. *Ad valorem* taxes back special assessment bonds, so they are GOs, not revenue bonds. Only those property owners who benefit from the project that the bond funds pay the special assessment.
13. The correct answer is D. Bexar county has issued a moral obligation bond, under which the state will make interest on principal payments if the county defaults.
14. The correct answer is D. Public housing bonds (Section 8 bonds) are the only muni bonds to carry the backing of the federal government. Housing authorities no longer issue them, but they still trade on the secondary market, where investors find the guarantee attractive enough to keep yields on them relatively low.
15. The correct answer is B. Varbo must earn a 7.94% taxable yield to equal the return he can earn from the muni. He computes this by dividing the yield on the municipal bond (5.4%) by the percentage of his income he has left after paying taxes (100% minus the tax bracket of 32%, or 68%).

Issuing and Trading Municipal Debt

Key Terms You Need to Know

- ✓ Accrued interest
- ✓ Basis point
- ✓ Bond buyer index
- ✓ Bond counsel
- ✓ Brokers' broker
- ✓ Brokers' wire
- ✓ Competitive bid
- ✓ Concession fee
- ✓ Designated orders
- ✓ Dollar bonds
- ✓ Eastern account (undivided account)
- ✓ Financial advisor
- ✓ Firm offer
- ✓ Firm offer with recall
- ✓ Good faith deposit
- ✓ Group net orders
- ✓ Lead underwriter
- ✓ Management fee
- ✓ Member takedown orders
- ✓ Municipal workable
- ✓ Munifacts wire
- ✓ Negotiated bid
- ✓ Net interest cost (NIC)
- ✓ Notice of sale
- ✓ Official bid form
- ✓ Official statement
- ✓ Placement ratio
- ✓ Point
- ✓ Pre-sale orders
- ✓ Qualified opinion
- ✓ Reallowance fee
- ✓ Reoffering rate
- ✓ Round lot
- ✓ Scale
- ✓ Selling group
- ✓ Settlement date
- ✓ Spread
- ✓ Takedown fee
- ✓ *The Blue List*
- ✓ *The Bond Buyer*
- ✓ True interest cost (TIC)
- ✓ Trustee
- ✓ Underwriting syndicate
- ✓ Unqualified opinion
- ✓ Visible supply
- ✓ Western account
- ✓ When issued (w.i.)

Concepts You Need to Understand

- ✓ Basic pricing and trading terminology
- ✓ Details of the bidding process for munis
- ✓ Duties of the syndicate manager
- ✓ Features of negotiated bids and competitive bids
- ✓ Steps the underwriter takes after a bid is awarded
- ✓ The nature of underwriting syndicates in the muni market
- ✓ The steps a municipality must take to issue GO or revenue bonds
- ✓ Where traders find information on muni issues and trades

Issuing Bonds

Issuing municipal bonds is a lengthy and complex process. Many municipalities do not have the professional or financial resources to watch every detail of their bond issues. To maintain control of the financing, municipalities rely on outside expertise to deal with some parts of the process. The complications involved in issuing general obligation bonds, in particular, require such expertise.

Hiring a *financial advisor* to take care of the details is the most important step for a municipal bond issuer to take. The financial advisor is usually a firm that has worked with the issuer before. The financial advisor to a municipality that is seeking to issue new bonds:

- Analyzes the municipality's debt statement to ensure that it has room under its debt ceiling to issue new bonds
- Reads and interprets the standard barometers of the municipality's fiscal well-being: the per capita debt ratio, the debt to assessed valuation ratio, and their tax collection ratio
- Advises the municipality on how the new bond issue might affect the community's credit rating
- Recommends the type of bond to be issued, a call schedule for the bonds, and a target interest rate
- Suggests the denominations in which the bonds will be issued

The results of this process give the municipality a good idea of whether it should go ahead with the bond issue. Remember that a GO bond issue also has to be approved by the voters in a referendum. If the municipality chooses to forge ahead, it first must consult its bond counsel.

Underwriting and the Bidding Process

The process of municipal underwriting is more complicated than corporate underwriting, because revenue bonds and GO bonds take different forms.

In a general obligation issue, the underwriter is almost always chosen by competitive bid. For revenue bonds, the municipality usually chooses an underwriter in a negotiated bid.

General obligation bonds use a competitive bid
Revenue bonds use a negotiated bid

Because it is noncompetitive, the negotiated bid is more straightforward.

In a *negotiated bid*, a municipality commits to one underwriter and negotiates directly with that underwriter to set the bond issue's parameters—the call schedule, bond denominations, interest rates, spread, and protective covenants. Generally, the underwriter is a broker-dealer whom the municipality has worked with before.

The situation is slightly different for GO bonds, because voters must approve any new issue. Thus the municipality needs to be able to demonstrate to the public that it has secured the best possible financing package. To do this, most municipalities require a *competitive bid*, with interested dealers trying to make the lowest bid to the municipality.

The Competitive Bid Process

After a municipality that wants to issue general obligation bonds has consulted with its financial advisor and has received the necessary documents from its bond counsel, it advertises for underwriting bids in *The Bond Buyer*, the major muni trade paper.

The advertisement, or *notice of sale*, includes information about:

- The amount of the sale
- The type of bonds offered
- The date on which interest will start accruing (also called the dated date)
- The kinds of taxes that are backing the issue
- The process for submitting bids, including location and deadline

The muni market is a thin market, so dealers will regularly peruse *The Bond Buyer* in search of promising new issues on which to bid. Interested muni dealers place sealed bids on a new GO issue, and the lowest bid generally wins the underwriting contract.

Therefore, to win new business, potential underwriters need to construct a careful bid that balances the competing interests of issuers and investors. A successful bid must keep the municipality's debt service costs as low as possible, at the same time offering bond purchasers a yield high enough to attract their investment.

Determining an Appropriate Bid

Dealers attempt to set a realistic bid by collecting as much information as possible on the issue itself, the bids of competitive underwriters, and the likely demand for the issue. First the dealer examines the bond and the issuing municipality. What is the municipality's current credit rating? What is its per capita debt ratio? How will it use the capital raised by the issue? What taxes will be used to service the bond debt? The dealer must examine the issue the same way as a savvy investor.

Next, the dealer must study the competition and the profit margin that they need to operate. Because munis offer triple tax-exemption only to citizens of the state of issue, usually only dealers from the same state submit bids. Because banks can also underwrite municipal issues, they might be among the competitors for the underwriting contract. Finally, prospective broker-dealers need to gauge investor demand, which helps determine the bond's coupon rate, perhaps the key factor for winning the underwriting. Dealers can obtain insight into the demand for an issue through a process that the muni market shares only with the agency market.

How Dealers Gauge the Market for an Unissued Bond

Because munis are exempt from the Securities Act of 1933, muni underwriters are allowed to take *pre-sale orders* from clients. The pre-sale client agrees to buy bonds from the dealer in the event that the dealer wins the bid on the issue. Such pre-sale orders are essential to a muni underwriter because they indicate the potential market demand for the issue—and what interest rate the market will bear.

Pre-bid response also gives potential underwriters an indication of whether they should submit a bid at all. If a dealer takes enough pre-sale orders to sell out an entire new issue, it can make a very competitive bid, confident that market demand supports its position. Suppose, on the other hand, that pre-sale orders leave the issue greatly undersubscribed. If the dealer still takes on the issue, it might find itself with many unmarketable bonds, a highly unprofitable situation. Thus, if pre-sale interest is sluggish, a dealer might choose to bow out before even placing a bid.

If the dealer is encouraged by its pre-sale orders, it then structures and submits a formal bid.

How a Dealer Makes a Bid

Once the dealer has made the decision to bid on an issue, it constructs the *scale*, or schedule of interest rates, for pre-sale orders. This rate (or set of rates, for a serial bond) is sometimes called the *reoffering rate*, and represents the underwriter's assessment of the market's demand for the offering.

> **EXAMPLE:** The Home Surety Brokerage Corporation of Texas has been gathering pre-sale orders for a $350 million Texas serial GO bond due in 2015. The bonds have a 10-year maturity and are callable in five years according to the call schedule shown next. Following is HSBC's list of pre-sale orders and the corresponding scale (see Tables 10.1 and 10.2).

Table 10.1 Scale of Interest Rates			
Maturity	**Amount**	**Pre-Sale Orders**	**Interest Rate**
2011	$ 50,000,000	$ 40,000,000	5.77%
2012	$ 50,000,000	$ 45,000,000	5.85%
2013	$ 50,000,000	$ 50,000,000	5.90%
2014	$ 50,000,000	$ 50,000,000	5.95%
2015	$ 150,000,000	$ 100,000,000	6.15%

Now Home Surety must decide how much profit it wants to make on the spread. Remember that an underwriter profits by purchasing from the municipality at one price and selling to the public at a slightly higher price. After the dealer determines its spread, it assembles the final bid, which includes the amount issued at each maturity, the interest rate, price or yield, and amount of profit.

Table 10.2 Pre-sale Orders			
Maturity	**Amount**	**Pre-Sale Orders**	**Interest Rate**
2011	$ 50,000,000	$ 40,000,000	5.85%
2012	$ 50,000,000	$ 45,000,000	5.95%
2013	$ 50,000,000	$ 50,000,000	6.05%
2014	$ 50,000,000	$ 50,000,000	6.10%
2015	$ 150,000,000	$ 100,000,000	6.20%

The bid determines the selling price, which is the issuer's expected cost. This is either the issuer's net interest cost or true interest cost. The *net interest cost (NIC)* is the total of the interest payments the issuer makes over the life of the bond. It's the amount of each maturity multiplied by the corresponding interest rate, and then multiplied by the appropriate number of years. The results are summed up for all the maturities. The *true interest cost (TIC)* takes into account the time value of those payments, discounting their future value into current dollars.

The bid, entered on the *official bid form* provided by the municipality, is sealed along with a *good faith deposit*—generally a check for 2% of the bid's value. The bid must be submitted by the deadline given in the notice of sale. Of course, dealers want to have their bids reflect the most current market conditions, so it is standard procedure to submit competitive bids as close to the deadline as possible.

It is time for the issuer to collect the bids and select an underwriter.

How Does the Municipality Award the Bid?

Once the deadline has passed, the municipality opens the bids and awards the offering to the lowest bidder. The municipality announces, in the notice of sale, whether it decides the lowest bid on the basis of TIC or NIC. All good-faith deposits attached to losing bids are immediately returned. The municipality must then have the bonds printed with the appropriate coupon rate information, a process that can take several weeks. In the meantime, the underwriter can fill pre-sale orders for the bond on a *when issued (w.i.)* basis, meaning that the sale becomes final as soon as the printed bonds are delivered by the municipality. At that point, pre-sale buyers are also entitled to the interest that has accrued on the bonds from the purchase to the settlement date.

For munis, the *settlement date* is not a fixed period from the purchase, but rather a date upon which the municipality and underwriter exchange bonds and money. Along with the printed bonds, the municipality delivers sufficient copies of the legal opinion and the *official statement*—the document that spells out the legal details of the bond contract. For muni issues of $1 million or more, underwriters must have performed due diligence by reviewing the official statement prior to submitting a bid. They must also receive the final official statement from the issuer within seven business days of winning the underwriting, and provide it to any potential buyer within one business day. Both the legal opinion and the official statement must be provided to all bond purchasers.

Because of the highly competitive, narrow-margin nature of the muni market, GO bond offerings are usually awarded to a syndicate of dealers who have joined together to bid on the underwriting contract.

Underwriting Syndicates

As with corporate bonds, an *underwriting syndicate* for municipal bonds is a group of broker-dealers who work together to place bids on competitive muni issues. In fact, for most muni offerings, prospective underwriters find it in their best interest to establish or join syndicates.

The bidding process for GO offerings is highly competitive, yet the syndicate system aligns the interests of several potential bidders. To balance these contrasting forces, a syndicate needs a strong organizational hand.

Two primary benefits make syndicates enticing for broker-dealers bidding on munis:

- Greater resources of the combined firms make it possible to bid on more and larger issues.
- Larger client lists and sales forces of the syndicate typically lead to more presale orders.

A municipal underwriting syndicate is organized by a *lead underwriter* (or syndicate manager), who generally has the largest stake in the endeavor. It is also the lead underwriter who searches *The Bond Buyer* and maintains contacts with various municipalities to discover new issues on which to bid. Upon choosing an issue, the manager distributes a syndicate letter to potential syndicate members. This letter outlines the obligations of each member, the way in which bond orders are handled, the means for splitting the underwriting spread, and whether the syndicate functions as an Eastern or Western account.

Municipal bond underwriting syndicates are generally *Eastern* (*undivided*) *accounts*—each member is responsible for the percentage of any *unsold* bonds that is equal to their participation in the issue, regardless of whether they have fulfilled that commitment. (*Western accounts* are more common in equity underwritings.)

In a Western account, a syndicate member is responsible for a specific portion of the security offering. If the offering is unsuccessful, the member must place the unsold securities on its books. In an Eastern account, any unsold bonds are the responsibility of *all* members.

Before the syndicate can bid on a municipal issue, its members need to assemble a list of customers and arrive at an agreement on the terms of the particular deal.

The first major task of the syndicate members is to assemble as many presale orders as they can. As the bidding deadline for an issue approaches, the syndicate members then meet to set the scale and decide on their commitments to the syndicate—what percent of the total issue each member will commit to sell. They must also determine how the underwriting spread will be apportioned.

How the Syndicate Shares the Spread

Remember that the spread is the difference between the public offering price of an issue and the price paid by the underwriter to the municipality. The members' *takedown fee* can be further divided as shown in Table 10.3 when a member of a selling group decides to join the effort after the municipality has awarded the bid.

Table 10.3 Breakdown of an Underwriting Spread

MOTLEY COUNTY 5.5% GO'S OF 2005				
public offering price: $5,000 per bond				
price paid to Motley County: $4,975 per bond				
(spread = public offering price – price paid to municipality)				
½ point = $25.00 per bond				
Bond sold by syndicate member	management fee	takedown fee		
	= ⅛	**= ⅜ point**		
	= $6.25	**= $18.75**		
Bond sold by selling group member	management fee	additional takedown fee	concession fee	
	= ⅛ point	**= ⅛ point**	**= ¼ point**	
	= $6.25	**= $6.25**	**= $12.50**	
Bond sold by broker-dealer	management fee	additional takedown fee	concession fee	reallowance fee
	= ⅛ point	**= ⅛ point**	**= ⅛ point**	**= ⅛ point**
	= $6.25	**= $6.25**	**= $6.25**	**= $6.25**

Selling Groups

To reach a larger set of investors, a syndicate sometimes agrees to let another group of broker-dealers do some of the selling on a new issue of munis. Members of this *selling group* have not taken on the same level of risk as the syndicate members, so their profit, or *concession fee*, is smaller than the profit of full syndicate members. The relationship between the syndicate and the selling group is laid out in full legal detail in the selling group agreement. Even beyond the selling group members, other outside broker-dealers can also attempt to place the new bonds. For each bond sold, they receive a *reallowance fee*, which is a further split of the concession fee.

EXAMPLE: Burnham, Howe, & Dewey recruits Cashe Securities to help sell the latest Mudville GOs. Cashe Securities sells $4 million worth of the bond, generating an aggregate profit of $20,000. Cashe earns a concession fee of 1/4 point, worth $10,000. BHD earns a management fee of 1/8 point, or $5,000. The remaining syndicate members split the additional takedown fee of ? point, or $5,000.

THE LARGEST MUNICIPAL OFFERING IN HISTORY. In the summer of 1998 a new utility, the Long Island Power Authority (LIPA), took over most of the functions of the Long Island Lighting Co. (Lilco), the troubled utility serving Long Island, New York. Lead underwriter Bear, Stearns & Company, which had also served as one of the authority's financial advisors, headed a syndicate of more than 50 underwriters that took the $5 billion issue public. The syndicate made about $21 million on its spread, while Bear, Stearns also split an additional $8 million fee with Goldman, Sachs, the other financial advisor. Muni bond insurance companies guaranteed over half of the issue, thereby earning the largest single sum from the deal, about $28 million.

Rates on the $3.5 billion fixed-rate and $1.5 billion variable-rate notes ranged from 3.90% to 5.60%, high enough to attract strong retail demand. One selling group member took more than $25 million of orders within a day and a half of the LIPA bonds going public, with many sales at the minimum $5,000 denomination, and many more between $25,000 and $50,000. Notably, the yields were high enough that even non-New York residents—that is, people not eligible for triple tax-exemption—showed interest in the LIPA bonds. Nationwide, retail volume totaled $807 million in the first two days of the offering, boding well for the additional $2 billion in follow-on financing due through the rest of the year. The LIPA offering was by far the largest muni ever, totaling $7 billion.

Note that the lead underwriter, or syndicate manager, turns a profit on every bond sold. The manager earns this *management fee* not only for taking the greatest risk, but also for handling most of the administrative duties required to manage the syndicate.

The Syndicate Manager's Duties

Beyond searching out promising new issues on which to bid and putting together the syndicate letter, the syndicate manager's duties include:

- Issuing announcements of the syndicate's winning bids—and the corresponding offer of new municipal bonds on the market—via the Munifacts wire service
- Closing the books on a sold-out issue and paying syndicate and selling group members their share of the spread
- Collecting information on who has purchased the bonds to ensure that no single customer purchases too many of them (wide distribution induces a more active secondary market)
- Ensuring that orders for the new bonds are filled in the proper order

How the Lead Underwriter Fills the Orders

The lead underwriter follows the distribution priority agreed to in the syndicate letter. Of course, pre-sale orders are filled first, because having those orders in hand helped the syndicate win the offering. Then come the *group net orders*, sales made by syndicate members at the public offering price during the "order period" immediately after issuance. These are the sales for which all syndicate members receive a takedown fee. In most muni new issues, the offering has been completely sold out at this point. If that has not happened, the lead underwriter next fills the *designated orders*, placed by customers through a syndicate member of their choice. Finally, the lead underwriter allocates whatever *member takedown orders* exist for syndicate members who want bonds for their own inventory or for "related" accounts, which are usually municipal investment trusts (mutual funds) sponsored by the syndicate member. The syndicate structures the order priority this way to ensure that the entire group gets the greatest possible benefit before any of the syndicate members profit individually.

After the lead underwriter finishes the order distribution, secondary market trading begins.

Trading Bonds

The basic facts for trading in the municipal bond market can quickly be summarized:

- Municipal bonds trade in increments of $5,000. A *round lot* (the normal trading unit) for retail investors is five bonds ($25,000).
- A round lot of munis for institutional traders is $100,000, compared to a round lot of corporate bonds, which is $5,000.
- Prices of municipal bonds are quoted in *points*, with each point equal to 1% of the bond's par value, or $50; thus, 1 point = $50.

  A bond quoted at 96 has a price of $4,800

  A bond quoted at 103? has a price of $5,175
- Yields on municipal bonds are quoted in *basis points*, whereby 1 basis point = of a percent, or .0001.
- As with all fixed-income securities, interest rates and prices are inversely related. When interest rates rise, existing bonds become less valuable—their prices drop. When interest rates drop, existing bonds become more valuable—their prices rise.

- Interest rate changes have a more pronounced effect on short-term municipal debt prices than on long-term ones.

Some characteristics of munis differ from those of corporate and Treasury bonds, but many are the same. Because of the state-by-state nature of the muni market and the resulting illiquidity, the actual trading of munis can be quite different from that of other fixed-income instruments.

Because the muni market is relatively thin, muni dealers do not have a trading floor, electronic exchange, or real-time service to facilitate bond trading. Therefore, they must depend on the telephone to find the best bids and offers. This labor- and knowledge-intensive system has given rise to a unique set of techniques for buying and selling munis.

A dealer bidding for a bond wants to canvas as many other dealers as practical to find the lowest offering price, and might not necessarily commit to the first offer another dealer makes. The bidding dealer contacts another dealer, who makes a *firm offer*. If the bidding dealer wants to purchase at the offered price, the two parties close the deal. However, if the bidding dealer wants to shop around, the offering dealer might modify the firm offer to a *firm offer with recall*. This sets a time limit on the offer and permits the offering dealer to entertain higher bids.

> **EXAMPLE:** Burnham, Howe, & Dewey wants to buy some Alaska 4.7% GOs due in 2009 for a customer planning to move from Key West to Juneau. Henri, the BHD broker, calls Glacier Securities in Anchorage, who quotes a yield of 5.21%, firm. Henri says, "I want to get some other quotes," and the Glacier Securities broker replies, "I'll offer them firm to you for 40 minutes with a 5-minute recall." This means that the 5.21% offer is good for 40 minutes, but that Glacier reserves the right to sell them to another dealer if it gets a better bid (say for 5.205%) in the meantime—unless Henri accepts the original 5.21% offer within five minutes of Glacier notifying him of the competing bid.

Dealers use a similar process to sell muni bonds.

How Does the Selling Process Work?

A dealer offering bonds contacts other dealers; again, those dealers might not want to finalize a trade at the first offering price they hear. Instead of a firm bid, a willing buyer can make a *municipal workable*, a price near which it is willing to buy the bonds, depending on other dealers' offers. The potential buyer then calls some other dealers to get more workables before deciding from whom to buy the bonds, and at what price.

EXAMPLE: The Burnham, Howe, & Dewey customer has now moved from Key West to Juneau, leaving the firm with some Florida GOs in inventory. Henri, the BHD broker, gets on the phone to try to sell the bonds, first approaching Everglades Securities. Ivy, the Everglades broker, although willing to buy the bonds, is unsure of exactly where they have been trading; she bids 5.50%; workable. Henri calls around to other Florida municipal firms to get a better perspective on the market for the GOs. Several other firms bid workables that cluster around 5.53%, so Henri quickly decides to try getting a firm bid from Ivy before she has had a chance to sound out other dealers and notice that her bid is above the market.

Even using these techniques, dealers sometimes have trouble trading muni bonds for customers. This is especially true for well-known customers who have large blocks of bonds to buy or sell. The broker's broker provides a way to solve this problem.

The Brokers' Broker

Brokers' brokers serve as go-betweens for large institutional investors and maintain no bond inventories of their own. Through their services, they buffer large clients from the price fluctuations that can result when large blocks of bonds enter the market. The two largest and most established broker's brokers, J. J. Kenny and Chapdelaine, provide a private wire service over which they list the munis available for bid, a listing composed of bonds owned by their subscribers. Widespread knowledge of the institutional sale of a large block of bonds puts downward pressure on the bond's price, because usually the entire block cannot trade all at once. Knowing that a seller *needs* to continue unloading the bonds enables other dealers to bid lower than they otherwise might. A broker's broker solves this problem by marketing bonds bit by bit, without revealing the seller's identity, thereby maintaining market stability.

Again, this trading activity does not take place at any physical location, but over the telephone. The muni market does not exist on the floor of an exchange, nor does any firm distribute real-time price information electronically. Thus, muni dealers have developed another set of resources to trade effectively.

Where Municipal Bonds Are Actually Sold

In the secondary market, municipal bonds are traded over the counter (OTC), generally on the basis of information listed in one of the industry's standard newspaper, wire, or online publications. Broker-dealers use all these sources to stay abreast of the market.

There are four important sources for municipal bond information:

- ***The Blue List:*** A daily Standard & Poor's publication (printed on blue paper) in which dealers advertise their available municipal offerings for other dealers.

The Blue List is important to know for the exam.

- **Munifacts wire:** A wire service created by *The Bond Buyer* that includes dealer information on new issues and on the secondary market.
- **Brokers' wires:** Electronic wire systems listing bonds available for subscribers to bid. Brokers' wires are maintained by J. J. Kenny and Chapdelaine, the major brokers' brokers.
- ***The Bond Buyer:*** The trade paper for muni issues. It also tracks the visible supply of bonds, supplies information on new issues, and gives placement ratios for all issues that dealers have placed in the secondary market. *The Bond Buyer visible supply* reflects the total of known competitive and negotiated offerings of 13 months or longer expected to reach the market within the next 30 days. The *placement ratio* compares the dollar volume of bonds sold each week to the volume of the week's new competitive issues of $5 million or more.

Each week, *The Bond Buyer* lists four indices that traders watch closely:

- Bond Buyer Index—Average yield of 20 municipals, each with a maturity of 20 years and a rating of single-A or better
- Eleven Bond Index—Average yield of 11 bonds from the 20-bond index, with an average rating of double-A
- Revenue Bond Index—Average yield of 25 revenue bonds, each with a maturity of 30 years
- Municipal Bond Index—Average dollar price of 40 heavily traded municipals, both GO and revenue, with maturities more than 19 years and a minimum rating of single-A

Over the years, muni trade publications like *The Blue List* have come up with concise shorthand to signify the important aspects of the munis they list.

What a Muni Quote Looks Like

Municipal bond quotes generally include the number of bonds offered, the name of the issuer, the coupon rate, the maturity date, the yield basis, the amount of the dealer's concession, and any call provisions on the bonds. Serial bonds are quoted on a yield-to-maturity basis, and term bonds on a price basis. For this reason, term bonds are sometimes called *dollar bonds*.

EXAMPLE: Here is what an offering in *The Blue List* might look like:

	50	New York State	6.675%	1/1/20	C15	7.51%	Goldman
Key:	**A**	**B**	**C**	**D**	**E**	**F**	**G**

A. Face value of $50,000 of bonds (not 50 bonds) on offer

B. Issuing municipality is New York State

C. Coupon is 6.675%

D. Maturity date is January 1, 2020

E. Bonds are callable in 2015

F. Yield-to-maturity is 7.510%

G. Offering broker is Goldman

These bonds are selling at discount because they yield 7.51% while carrying a 6.675% coupon. Buyers can compute the cost of one of these bonds by calculating the actual interest ($5,000 × .06675 = $333.75) and dividing it by the yield, 0.0751.

$333.75 ÷ 0.0751 = $4,444.07

So, to return a yield of 7.51%, these bonds have to be sold at $4,444 each. Remember, though, that the dealer gets the concession. If the dealer receives a concession of 5/8, how much does one bond sell for? The bond sells for $4,475.32. Recall that each point equals $50, so 5/8 of a point equals $31.25, which must be added to $4,444.07.

Municipals almost always pay bond interest semiannually.

How Interest Is Calculated When a Bond Is Sold

This interest on muni bonds is computed on a 30-day month, 360-day year basis, just as with corporate bonds. However, interest on municipal notes, just as with other short-term instruments, is computed according to the actual number of days elapsed and the actual number of days in the year. *Accrued interest* is computed for all the days up to, but not including, the settlement date. Municipal bond sales settle the regular way, three business days from date of purchase.

EXAMPLE: Inez sells a $5,000 Mudville GO, carrying a 5.95% coupon, on May 17. If she last received interest on the bond January 1, how many days of interest have accrued to her?

The sale date is May 17, so the settlement date is three days later—May 20. Interest accrues to Inez through May 19.

January	30 days
February	30 days
March	30 days
April	30 days
May	19 days
Total	139 days of accrued interest

How much interest must the purchaser add to the settlement price? The buyer must add $114.87 in accrued interest to the settlement check to Inez ($5,000 × 0.0595 = $297.50 annual interest; $297.50 ÷ 360 = $0.8264 daily interest; $0.8264 × 139 = $114.87).

Exam Prep Questions

These questions help you review the chapter's material in more detail, ensuring that you have remembered the key facts and getting you ready for the practice exams (see *Series 7 Preparatory Exams*).

1. First Nation Bank has an extremely large block of municipal bonds that they want to sell in the market. Where can they go to get the best possible price for their bonds?

   ❑ A. They need to offer the bonds for sale in the OTC market.

   ❑ B. They need to go to a municipal broker's broker to have them sell the bonds.

   ❑ C. They need to offer the bonds for sale in the Blue List.

   ❑ D. They need to offer the bonds for sale in the Pink Sheets.

2. When considering a bond issue for a municipality, the financial advisor to a municipality will perform which of the following duties?

   I. Analyze the municipality's debt statement.

   II. Advise the municipality on how the bond issue will affect its credit rating.

   III. Recommend the type of bonds the municipality should issue.

   IV. Recommend the interest rate at which the municipality should offer the bonds.

   ❑ A. I and II

   ❑ B. II and III

   ❑ C. I, II, and III

   ❑ D. I, II, III, and IV

3. The role of a bond counsel in a municipal bond underwriting includes which of the following characteristics?

   I. Render a legal opinion on the bond issue.

   II. Draw up the bond contract between the municipality and bondholder.

   III. Appoint a trustee for the bond issue.

   IV. Become the trustee for the bond issue.

   ❑ A. I only

   ❑ B. I and II

   ❑ C. I, II, and III

   ❑ D. I, II, and IV

4. A municipality has decided to build a new bridge to service a connecting area. Which of the following statements are true of the bond issue that will finance the new bridge?

I. The municipality needs a referendum vote of residents before they can issue bonds to finance the project.

II. A feasibility study will be commissioned to study the project.

III. The cost of the project will need to be determined.

IV. Property taxes will be re-assessed in the community.

- ❑ A. I and II
- ❑ B. II and III
- ❑ C. I, II, and III
- ❑ D. I, II, III, and IV

5. In a negotiated bid for a municipal bond offering, which of the following statements are considered true?

I. It is conducted for a revenue bond issue.

II. It is conducted for a GO bond issue.

III. The municipality commits to one underwriter to issue the bonds.

IV. The municipality is guaranteed the lowest possible interest rate.

- ❑ A. I and III
- ❑ B. II and III
- ❑ C. II, III, and IV
- ❑ D. I, III, and IV

6. The notice of sale placed by a municipality in *The Daily Bond Buyer* has all of the following information except for?

- ❑ A. The amount of the bond issue
- ❑ B. The type of bonds to be offered
- ❑ C. The interest rate for the bonds
- ❑ D. The type of taxes backing the issue

7. Which of the following statements is considered true of pre-sale orders for a municipal bond offering?

I. Pre-sale orders can be taken on municipal bond issues, but not on corporate issues.

II. Pre-sale orders give the underwriter a better gauge of investor interest.

III. Pre-sale orders must be filled by the municipal bond underwriter.

IV. Pre-sale orders enable the underwriter to make a competitive bid on the issue.

- ❑ A. I and II
- ❑ B. I, II, and III
- ❑ C. I, II, and IV
- ❑ D. II, III, and IV

8. When municipal bond underwriters "write the scale," they are in effect doing which of the following?
   - ❑ A. Comparing interest rates with other municipal bond issues.
   - ❑ B. Determining whether taxes collected by the municipality can meet the debt obligation.
   - ❑ C. Assessing the market demand for the bond offering.
   - ❑ D. Comparing their submitted bid to other underwriter's bids.

9. Lead underwriters for a municipal bond underwriting syndicate have which of the following characteristics?

   I. They are considered the syndicate manager.

   II. They make all investment decisions for the bond underwriting.

   III. They earn a management fee on each bond sold.

   IV. They choose all syndicate members.
   - ❑ A. I and II
   - ❑ B. II and III
   - ❑ C. I, II, and III
   - ❑ D. I, II, III, and IV

10. Which of the following statements is considered true of Western Account Municipal Bond offerings?

    I. Western accounts are considered divided accounts.

    II. Western accounts are considered undivided accounts.

    III. In a Western account, any unsold bonds are the responsibility of all syndicate members.

    V. In a Western account, a syndicate member is only responsible for the amount they have been allocated.
    - ❑ A. I and III
    - ❑ B. I and IV
    - ❑ C. II and III
    - ❑ D. II and IV

11. Cord & James is a large municipal bond underwriter and the lead manager of a $100 million municipal bond offering. The bond offering has a 1/2 point spread. The lead underwriter receives a management fee of 1/8 of a point for each bond sold. Lakeland Securities is a syndicate member that has sold $10 million worth of the issue. What will Cord & James earn on the amount of the issue that Lakeland has sold?
    - ❑ A. $12,500 management fee
    - ❑ B. $37,500 management fee
    - ❑ C. $50,000 management fee
    - ❑ D. $50,000 takedown fee

12. All of the following are responsibilities of the syndicate manager in a municipal bond syndicate, except for
    - ❑ A. Announcing the syndicate's winning bid on the munifacts wire
    - ❑ B. Closing the books on the sold-out issue, and paying syndicate members their share of the spread
    - ❑ C. Making sure that any one customer did not purchase too many bonds of the issue
    - ❑ D. Becoming a market maker of the sold issue in the secondary market

13. Which of the following statements are true of municipal bonds that trade in the secondary market?

    I. Municipal bonds trade in increments of $5,000 minimums

    II. A round lot for institutional traders is $100,000

    III. A round lot for retail investors is five bonds

    IV. Municipal bonds are quoted in points

    - ❑ A. I and II
    - ❑ B. II and III
    - ❑ C. I, II, and III
    - ❑ D. I, II, III, and IV

14. A municipal bond dealer gives what type of quote for bonds they are willing to buy or sell?
    - ❑ A. Firm offer
    - ❑ B. Firm offer with recall
    - ❑ C. Municipal workable
    - ❑ D. Nominal bid

15. Municipal bond dealers looking to find the best possible price for their retail customers look in which of the following?
    - ❑ A. *The Pink Sheets*
    - ❑ B. *The Yellow Sheets*
    - ❑ C. *The Blue List*
    - ❑ D. *The Bond Buyer*

Exam Prep Answers

1. The correct answer is B. A municipal broker's broker helps assist large institutional clients sell municipal bonds in the market. Because the municipal market is a thinly traded market, a large block of bonds for sale by an institutional client can drive the price on the bonds down. A broker's broker represents the institution on an anonymous basis, and moves the bonds bit by bit. By providing this service, the broker's broker can get the possible price for the bonds.

2. The correct answer is D. The financial advisor for a municipality is a firm that has typically worked with the municipality in the past. They analyze the municipality's debt statement to ensure that it has room under its debt ceiling to issue additional bonds. They advise the municipality on how the issue will impact their credit rating. They also recommend the target interest rate the municipality should seek in the bond issue, and the type of bonds that they should issue to meet their needs.

3. The correct answer is C. A bond counsel is a law firm with which the municipality has conducted business in the past. The primary charge of the bond counsel is to render an impartial legal opinion on the bond. The bond counsel also draws up the bond contract between municipality and bondholder, and appoints a trustee, which is typically a bank to oversee the issue.

4. The correct answer is B. A municipality considering a revenue producing project finances the project with revenue bonds. The first thing that a municipality does is to commission a feasibility study to determine the cost, expected use, and determine whether the revenue producing project can service the debt. Revenue bonds are backed by project revenues, and are not backed by property taxes. GO bonds are backed by taxes, and often need a voter approval to be issued.

5. The correct answer is A. In a negotiated bid, the municipality issues a revenue bond. In doing so, the municipality has committed to one underwriter that they have done business with in the past. The negotiated bid determines the call schedule, protective covenants, bond denominations, spread, and other parameters of the issue between the underwriter and municipality. Conversely, GO bond issues are conducted on a competitive bid basis.

6. The correct answer is C. The notice of sale for a General Obligation bond that has been placed in *The Daily Bond Buyer* by a municipality

states the amount of the issue, the type of bonds being offered, and the type of taxes that back the bonds. It does not state the interest rate of the bonds, because this is yet to be determined by the bidding process.

7. The correct answer is C. Pre-sale orders are permitted on municipal bond issues and not corporate issues. This allows an underwriter to pre-sell bonds prior to even winning the bid for the bonds. The pre-sale orders help an underwriter gauge investor demand for new bonds. It will help the underwriter determine the lowest possible bid on the issue, when entering their final competitive bid. Obviously, pre-sale orders are not required to be filled, in the event that the underwriter does not win the bond issue with their bid.

8. The correct answer is C. Writing the scale is a process used by municipal bond underwriters when entering a bid for a General Obligation bond issue. The scale is a schedule of interest rates for pre-sale orders. This rate represents the underwriter's assessment of the market demand for the bond issue. It shows the rate that investors are willing to buy the bonds at. It is not the final submitted bid that the underwriter submits to the issuer.

9. The correct answer is D. The lead underwriter for a municipal bond syndicate is considered the syndicate manager. They choose all members of the syndicate and make all investment decisions on the issue. For each bond that is sold, the lead underwriter earns a management fee as part of the total spread charged.

10. The correct answer is B. In a Western account for a bond underwriting the account is considered to be divided. This means that each syndicate member is only responsible for the allocated amount of the total offering they have been assigned. Any unsold bonds remain the responsibility of the member who was unable to sell the bonds. Each syndicate member knows exactly their total commitment to the overall issue.

11. The correct answer is A. Cord & James will earn ¼ of the ½ point spread that Lakeland will earn on the sale of their bonds. $10 million × ½ point spread = $50,000 takedown on the bonds. The lead underwriter is Cord & James, who earn 1/8th on each bond sold. Remember that ⅛th is ¼ of the ½ point spread. $10 million × .125 = $12,500.00 management fee earned by Cord & James for the bonds that Lakeland has sold.

12. The correct answer is D. Syndicate managers are not necessarily required to become market makers in the underlying bonds that they have brought to the public. In many cases, they will hold some bonds in inventory if they remain unsold. Otherwise, there is no obligation to be a market maker for the bonds.

13. The correct answer is D. Municipal bonds trade in increments of five bonds with a round lot for retail customers being five bonds, and a round lot for institutional investors being 100 bonds. Prices for municipal bonds are quoted in points, with each point equaling to one percent of the bond. Most municipal bonds will trade in increments of $5,000. Thus one bond will actually total $5,000.

14. The correct answer is A. A firm offer by a municipal dealer is a good price at which they are willing to buy or sell the bonds at. The firm quote is honored by the quoting dealer, if it is accepted.

15. The correct answer is C. *The Blue List* is a daily publication by Standard & Poor's that is printed on blue paper, in which dealers advertise their available municipal offerings to other dealers. These dealers often find bonds for their retail clients in *The Blue List*.

PART IV

Auction and Negotiated Markets

The Municipal Securities Rulemaking Board (MSRB)

Key Terms You Need to Know

- ✓ Arbitration
- ✓ Associated person (AP)
- ✓ Bona fide quote
- ✓ Cash settlement
- ✓ Churning
- ✓ Confirm
- ✓ Conflict of interest
- ✓ Control relationship
- ✓ Customer suitability
- ✓ Discretionary account
- ✓ Duplicate confirms
- ✓ Financial operations principal (FINOP)
- ✓ Good delivery
- ✓ Municipal investment trust (MIT)
- ✓ Municipal securities principal
- ✓ Municipal Securities Rulemaking Board (MSRB)
- ✓ Nominal quote
- ✓ Power of attorney
- ✓ Reciprocal dealing
- ✓ Reclamation
- ✓ Registered representative (registered rep)
- ✓ Regular way settlement
- ✓ Series 52
- ✓ Subject quote
- ✓ Unsolicited trade

Concepts You Need to Understand

- ✓ The composition of the Municipal Securities Rulemaking Board (MSRB)
- ✓ Which agencies enforce the MSRB's regulations
- ✓ What qualification standards municipal bond brokers must meet
- ✓ What practices ensure fair treatment of customers
- ✓ How municipal bonds are traded, and how trades are reported
- ✓ How long a broker-dealer must store records
- ✓ What standards of truthfulness and accuracy advertising must meet
- ✓ What potential conflicts of interest and ethical problems broker-dealers face
- ✓ How MSRB arbitration procedures resolve dispute

The Structure of the MSRB

Regulation of the municipal securities market has increased in recent decades. Congress passed the Securities Act Amendment of 1975, which established the Municipal Securities Rulemaking Board (MSRB), a self-regulating organization that sets the rules governing the muni market. Although MSRB rules must be approved by the SEC, their enforcement is left mainly in the hands of the National Association of Securities Dealers (NASD) and various bank regulatory bodies.

Established under the Securities Act Amendment of 1975, the *Municipal Securities Rulemaking Board (MSRB)* is the self-regulatory organization (SRO) assigned with the primary responsibility for overseeing the municipal securities market. As a self-regulatory organization, the MSRB falls under the SEC's jurisdiction. The board devises standard practices and norms of conduct for brokers, dealers, and banks that deal in municipal bonds and notes. It is comprised of 15 members—five each from the securities industry, the banking industry, and the public.

The MSRB does not oversee municipalities themselves. Neither does the MSRB enforce the rules; rather it interprets them, leaving the enforcement to other agencies.

So who does enforce the rules? Enforcement of MSRB rules falls to five separate agencies, each of which supervises a certain group of dealers. For instance, commercial banks often deal in large quantities of municipal bonds, so bank regulatory agencies must enforce MSRB rules for them. Table 11.1 shows the division of responsibility among these five agencies.

Table 11.1 Enforcement Agencies for MSRB Rules

Enforcement Agency	For Muni Departments Within
SEC	Securities broker-dealers
NASD	Securities broker-dealers who are NASD members
Comptroller of the Currency	Commercial banks chartered by the Comptroller of the Currency
Federal Reserve Board	Commercial or savings bank members of the Federal Reserve System
Federal Deposit Insurance Corporation	State-chartered banks that are not members of the Federal Reserve System

MSRB rules, which cover the relations between dealers and the public, are exactly the same for all these dealer groups. Given the complexity of the municipal securities market, the MSRB has focused its attention on those areas that it believes has the greatest potential for abuse.

Besides the Federal Reserve Board, the U.S. government has other agencies that regulate different sectors of the banking system. The most important of these are

- The Comptroller of the Currency, a Treasury department agency headed by an official appointed by the president and confirmed by the Senate that charters, oversees, and examines all national banks.
- The Federal Deposit Insurance Corporation (FDIC), established by the Securities Act of 1933, guarantees the funds of its members, banks, and thrifts (savings and loans). It also provides federal regulation for banks that have not joined the Federal Reserve System but are chartered by the states.

The MSRB has identified seven areas of concern in the municipal debt market. They are as follows:

- Setting qualification standards for brokers in the municipal debt market
- Ensuring fair treatment of customers
- Providing rules for primary and secondary market
- Setting guidelines for maintenance of records by broker-dealers
- Regulating advertising by broker-dealers
- Delineating ethical standards for all market participants
- Providing for arbitration to resolve disputes

In each of these areas, the MSRB has developed detailed standards and rules. Let's examine each one individually.

Setting Qualification Standards for Brokers in the Municipal Debt Market

The MSRB sets requirements for brokers wanting to become municipal securities principals and financial operations principals. A *municipal securities principal* (often someone who heads a branch office) supervises the issuing, trading, or clearing of municipal securities and the training of municipal representatives within a firm. A principal must pass the *Series 53* exam, proving familiarity with regulatory issues in the muni market. A *financial operations principal* (FINOP) supervises the production of required financial reports, the work of the personnel who produce them, and the proper maintenance of supporting records. The FINOP must pass the *Series* 27 exam, proving familiarity with the capital and reporting requirements of their SRO.

The Series 27 exam qualifies FINOPS for all types of securities firms, not just muni firms. Most broker-dealers operating in any part of the financial markets must keep their SRO regularly informed of their basic financial condition. They submit a balance sheet and profit-and-loss statement to prove that they are financially well managed and have the capital necessary to operate in their chosen market. Muni firms must submit the required reports to both the MSRB and the SEC.

The MSRB does modify its regulations from time to time. Those licensed employees known collectively as *associated persons* (APs) who have not worked in the industry for an extended time period risk, if they return, using outdated information.

Ensuring Fair Treatment of Customers

To ensure that broker-dealers treat their customers with fairness, honesty, and integrity, the MSRB specifies uniform practices of fair dealing to be followed. A broker-dealer must:

- Deliver securities on a timely basis and send confirms listing the details of a trade by the next business day
- Treat partial calls of serial bond issues impartially, avoiding preferential treatment of customers
- Pay accrued interest to customers who buy w.i. (when issued) bonds
- Notify customers of any put or call provisions on bonds that they are considering purchasing
- Accept the MSRB's arbitration procedure in lieu of court action if a dispute with a customer (or with another broker) cannot be resolved directly
- Not give any customer gifts worth more than $100 in any year

- Limit business entertainment expenses to those normally allowed by the IRS
- Supervise the activities of its associated persons, and establish a written supervisory procedures manual in addition to a continuing education program

In order for registered reps to fulfill these requirements, their key responsibility is to follow the "know your customer" rule. That process begins when a new customer wants to open an account.

All the SROs operating under the SEC have a "know your customer" rule. The NYSE regulation is called Rule 405, whereas the NASD incorporates the concept in Article 3 of its Rules of Fair Practice. The intent of these rules is identical: Brokers must gather all information necessary for judging their customers' financial goals, tolerance for risk, and capability to evaluate potential investments.

Providing Rules for Primary and Secondary Market Transactions

The principle underlying the MSRB's rules for bond trading is fair dealing. Broker-dealers must make every reasonable effort to get their clients a fair and equitable price, based on their knowledge and feel for the market. At times, it can be difficult for the broker to know at what price a bond should trade, so they must take advantage of workables and offers with recall to "feel out" the market. They also rely on their judgment and experience. The broker charges a commission based on the cost of the transaction, the price of the security, and the difficulty of executing the transaction. If the bond is difficult to obtain or the market is illiquid, the broker charges a higher commission than if the bond is a commonly traded, well-known issue.

Setting Guidelines for Maintenance of Records by Broker-Dealers

The length of record storage depends on the document. There are three classes of historical records; each class, listed in Table 11.2, is defined by how long a broker-dealer must keep it on file. All records must be readily accessible—in files at the broker-dealer's office, and not in long-term storage—for at least two years.

Table 11.2 Records Storage Requirements

Keep Readily Accessible for Three Years	Keep Readily Accessible for Six Years	Keep Permanently
Transaction records	Daily purchase and sales ledgers	Articles of incorporation
Correspondence	Syndicate records	Corporate charter
Order tickets	Account records	Corporate minute book
Advertising	Securities records Customer complaints	

Beyond requiring that broker-dealers retain a paper trail of their actions, the MSRB also requires active monitoring of the production of documents, especially those that can influence the public. Most importantly, the board oversees advertising, which it defines broadly.

Regulating Advertising by Broker-Dealers

The MSRB requires that all advertising by a broker-dealer be approved by a principal of the firm, who must ensure that it is true and accurate. Any literature a broker-dealer sends to the public, *except* for official statements and offering circulars, is considered advertising.

The MSRB holds all statements in advertising to strict standards of truthfulness.

For example, a firm can claim that bonds are tax-exempt only if they actually *are* tax-exempt, meaning that bonds such as those that are subject to the alternative minimum tax (AMT) must be disclosed in advertising as such. Because of the illiquidity of the muni market, a broker-dealer can advertise bonds that it does not hold in its inventory provided that they are labeled "subject to availability." The broker-dealer must also point out that bond prices and yields might change by the time the dealer actually acquires the bonds.

Advertising can contain price information that is current as of its publication date. For new issues, an ad must give information on the issue's yield, along with a disclaimer reminding customers again that the price or yield is subject to change.

For secondary issues, an ad must give prices that are valid as of the publication date of the advertisement, and, if listing a yield, use yield-to-maturity, a more accurate indicator of the bond's value, rather than the current yield. Advertising must identify whether the bonds are discounted; if they are, it must explain that the stated yield to maturity might be reduced by taxes due on the discounted amount that accretes over the life of the bond.

The MSRB is concerned not only with how broker-dealers interact with the public, but also with the relations between issuers and underwriters, an area that might remain opaque to most investors without the board's intervention. To prevent unfair deals between municipalities and underwriters, the board has designed rules to uphold ethical standards.

Delineating Ethical Standards for All Market Participants

Muni broker-dealers can face ethical problems in dealing with their customers, with issuers, and with other dealers. Ethical problems with customers include actions that come under the heading of fair dealing, such as customer suitability, sharing in or guaranteeing against loss, and incomplete disclosure of the terms of an issue.

Another ethical problem in customer relations is *churning,* an action by which a broker generates commissions through trading that is excessive in size or frequency given a customer's means or goals.

Ethical problems between broker-dealers and issuers, or other dealers, usually involve conflicts of interest. Several situations can bring about a *conflict of interest*, in which a broker-dealer plays two roles but finds that fulfilling one role often frustrates fulfilling the other.

Providing for Arbitration to Resolve Disputes

The MSRB requires that all parties—broker-dealers, bankers, and customers—agree that they are bound by the decisions of an arbitration panel, if a dispute arises. When clients open an account with a broker-dealer, they sign an agreement to resolve disputes not through the courts, but through *arbitration*, a process that is less expensive and less time-consuming, but one that also means abandoning the due-process and appeals protections of the legal system. Both written customer complaints and disputes between dealers that the broker-dealer cannot resolve are settled through arbitration.

A municipal securities arbitration panel comprises three to five members, and its decisions are binding. The process follows rules set by the NASD, the securities exchanges, and the MSRB. Disputes involving amounts of $10,000 or less can be submitted to a simplified arbitration procedure. A broker-dealer who refuses arbitration in the event of a dispute can be sanctioned by the MSRB.

Conflict of Interest

Broker-dealers can face two kinds of conflict of interest. One develops when a broker-dealer serves as financial advisor to a municipality while also underwriting a new bond issue in a negotiated bid for that municipality. The other conflict of interest occurs when a broker-dealer has a *control relationship* with an issuing municipality while also acting as a dealer, selling the bonds to customers. Control relationships can exist under several guises. The most common occurs when the broker-dealer is owned by a firm benefiting from a bond issue or when an employee of the broker-dealer has influence over the issuing or servicing of debt, by virtue of his or her position as an officer of a municipality. In any control relationship, it is the broker-dealer's responsibility to resolve the conflict of interest.

How can dealers avoid "new issue" conflicts of interest? When a broker-dealer who is serving as financial advisor to a municipality that is about to issue bonds wants to underwrite the issue in a negotiated bid, the broker-dealer must take several steps to avoid a conflict of interest. First, the dealer must resign as the municipality's financial advisor, and then it must get written consent from the municipality to negotiate to be the underwriter of the bonds, and finally it must disclose its underwriting fee to the municipality.

If the new muni is issued in a competitive bid, there is inherently less potential for conflict, because the bidding process helps ensure that the former financial advisor does not have an undue advantage. In a competitive bid, the broker-dealer, after resigning as the financial advisor, must simply get the municipality's written approval to bid on the issue. In either case, the dealer winning the bid must let its customers know, in writing, of its relationship to the issuing municipality before it sells any bonds.

It is important to avoid control relationships in conflict of interest. If a broker-dealer is in a control relationship with a municipality, it is not free to trade the bonds in a discretionary account unless it receives written authorization from the customer before trading. It must disclose to the customer, in writing, the nature of the control relationship.

EXAMPLE: Worldwide Corp., which has just built the Global Financial Center in downtown Houston with the help of industrial development bonds (IDBs) issued by the city, is acquiring a presence in regional financial markets, primarily by merging with Cashe Securities. Subsequently, Jim Hogg, the Cashe broker, recommends Worldwide IDBs to some of his customers. Hogg must reveal in writing Cashe's control relationship: that is that his employer has a stake in the bonds he is trying to sell.

Interestingly, the MSRB does not prohibit a broker-dealer from using information it has gleaned in a fiduciary capacity, even if the information is not available to other broker-dealers—as long as it has permission to do so from the issuer. As long as the dealer secures permission, the MSRB does not view this as trading on inside information.

Beyond the question of a control relationship lies the thorny problem of indirect control or influence over municipal authorities. Political contributions are one area of influence that the MSRB has scrutinized in recent years.

Political Contributions

There are limits to the amount of money a broker-dealer can contribute to any political campaign.

If a broker-dealer makes a campaign contribution of more than $250 to an elected official of a municipality, it cannot act as financial advisor or as a negotiated bid underwriter to that municipality for the next two years.

After making a campaign contribution, a broker-dealer can, though, still participate in competitive bid underwritings. Gift donors who must obey this rule (MSRB Rule G-37) include any dealer, any municipal securities employee of a broker-dealer, and any political action committee (PAC) associated with a broker-dealer. The $250 limit also applies to all contributions to a campaign that are funneled through another person, an anonymous donor, or a political party. Rule G-37 grew out of a 1994 SEC directive to the MSRB to prevent undue influence by political campaign contributions on the awarding of municipal issues to underwriters. This prohibition on campaign contributions to politicians who are in a position to influence negotiated bond offerings constitutes another attempt to avoid conflicts of interest. The MSRB also keeps a watchful eye on the relationships among brokerage firms.

Rules for the Delivery of Munis

The customer is entitled to receive good delivery of the securities by the settlement date. *Good delivery* means, if the bonds are in bearer form, that they arrive together, with all unpaid coupons attached. The bond counsel's legal opinion must also be attached, and the bonds must not be retired. If the bonds are in registered format, delivery must include a valid assignment transferring ownership to the buyer.

If the delivered bonds do not meet the criteria for a good delivery, the customer has the right to reject delivery. If the customer, after having accepted delivery, later discovers that the delivery is bad, the customer has the right to *reclamation*, or recovery of losses upon returning the bonds to the dealer.

All these trading rules concern the secondary market. However, the MSRB also regulates how underwriters function in the primary market.

Primary Market Rules

The MSRB sets rules for municipal dealers (including banks). The bulk of these rules concern underwriting syndicates.

As a syndicate member, a dealer who buys bonds in a new issue must disclose to the syndicate manager the destination of the bonds—whether they are going into the dealer's own account, a related account controlled by the dealer (a "related portfolio"), or a unit trust municipal pool, such as a municipal investment trust. *Municipal investment trusts* (or MITs) are funds that specialize in muni bond investments. The disclosure determines where confirms for the sale are sent, because they should go directly to the owner rather than to the dealer. It also gives the syndicate manager a method to track the identity of the bond owners.

The syndicate manager must fill orders for the new bonds in the following sequence: pre-sale orders, group net orders, designated orders, and finally member takedown orders. Syndicate members must disclose to the manager the identity of all group net customers. This ensures that no one buyer has accumulated too much of the issue. Syndicate managers try to ensure that an issue is fairly well distributed, which helps to develop a healthy secondary market.

Within two days of winning the bid, the syndicate manager must report in writing to the members about which bonds were allocated before the member takedown orders were filled. Within 60 days of settlement, the manager must report to the members the identity and size of the group orders,

Municipal Investment Trust orders, related portfolio orders, the aggregate of all syndicate account orders, and the breakdown of all syndicate expenses.

The completion of a competitive offering involves a good deal of reporting, and generates a substantial amount of documentation. The MSRB has developed standards for recordkeeping so that any questions about past deals can be easily resolved.

The MSRB also regulates interdealer conduct. MSRB rules prohibit one broker-dealer from getting a second broker-dealer's business in exchange for selling products of the second firm to its own clients. In other words, the MSRB prohibits *reciprocal dealings*.

Qualifying to Work in Munis

To qualify as a *registered representative* (registered rep) in municipal bonds, a candidate must meet two requirements:

- Pass the *Series* 7 (to become a general securities representative) or the *Series 52* (to become a municipal securities representative)
- Complete a 90-day apprenticeship in a municipal securities firm, while preparing for one of these exams

Individuals serving their muni apprenticeship cannot represent their firm to customers and cannot work on commission, but they can represent the firm to other broker-dealers. Individuals who have previously been registered with a Series 7 license for more than 90 days are exempt from the apprenticeship requirement.

Even after meeting these qualifications, the registered rep of a broker-dealer needs to meet requirements for continuing education and ethics training. Also, the MSRB requires employees with greater responsibility in municipal bond firms pass additional licensing examinations.

The MSRB Regulates AP Qualifications

The MSRB states that all associated persons (APs) who have qualified for any of these roles, but who later spend more than two years unregistered, must re-qualify before working in that capacity again. The MSRB also requires that someone disqualified or expelled from *another* self-regulatory body (such as the NASD), or someone who has made a false statement on an application, cannot be an associated person at a municipal securities firm.

This helps provide customers with some assurance that an unqualified or disqualified broker cannot simply find a new job at a different brokerage house.

Other MSRB Rules

One of the responsibilities of a broker is opening new accounts. The broker must first fill out a new account form, which includes the customer's name, address, and social security number. The form includes information concerning the ultimate beneficiary of the account. The customer's employer is also entered on the form. If the account is a margin account, the application must include the customer's written authorization for the margin agreement.

Finally, if the customer wants to open a *discretionary account*, that is, an account giving the broker authority to choose specific investments without explicit permission from the customer, the new account form must include a notarized power of attorney and a trading authorization. In the future, the broker has to judge whether any particular investment is proper for a given customer. A new account form allows the broker to collect the needed information to make this judgment.

Know Your Customer's Financial Situation

A broker must be able to fairly assess a *customer's suitability* for investing in municipal bonds. To do so, he or she has to learn the customer's approximate income and net worth, tax situation, and investment objectives. The tax information is particularly important, because it allows the broker to gauge how appropriate and beneficial tax-exempt investments are for that customer.

Customers who withhold information about investment objectives, tax status, or financial holdings are perfectly within their rights. A broker, although still free to open the account, cannot make trading recommendations to this customer. Because a broker needs to have reasonable grounds for believing that an investment is in the customer's best interest, a broker who does not possess the required financial information is in no position to make such a judgment. Thus, customers who want to retain their privacy by not revealing financial information have to make their own investment decisions.

Broker Discretion in Trading

If a customer wants to make a trade that the broker considers unsuitable, he must tell that customer that he or she thinks the trade is unsuitable. If the customer wants to proceed, the broker notes the trade as unsolicited on the order ticket, making it an *unsolicited trade*.

A broker has some discretion in making trades. Customers with discretionary accounts prefer that their broker, who is in closer touch with the minute-to-minute fluctuations of the market, make whatever investment decisions the broker thinks best.

A broker always has the authority to choose the timing and purchase price of a trade.

A discretionary account gives the broker even broader responsibility, which is why the customer must sign and have notarized both a *power of attorney* and a *trading authorization*, which enable the broker to choose which securities to purchase and the size of trades. The MSRB stipulates that, by the end of every trading day, a principal at the firm must review all orders that brokers process for discretionary accounts.

People who work in the securities industry often feel confident about their ability to judge the market and make their own trading decisions. Because they are also well-situated to trade on the basis of insider information, and might try to hide from watchful eyes by trading through another firm, the MSRB has established careful regulations for this situation.

Regulating Employee Accounts of Other Trading Firms

The MSRB has established a set of rules, similar to those in other sectors of the financial world, to regulate how a broker-dealer manages an account held by an employee of another broker-dealer. Trading in these accounts must be transparent to the employer of the account holder. To accomplish this, the broker in charge of the account must notify the account holder's firm that its employee has opened an account, must send *duplicate confirms* of all trades to that firm, and follow any written instruction from the employer regarding the account.

In addition, broker-dealers cannot guarantee a customer's account against losses, nor participate in profits or losses along with customers. MSRB rules thus set standards and limits on both the buyer and seller involved in the muni markets. They have established other rules to regulate the actual trading between buyers and sellers.

Brokers must also deal fairly with other brokers when they seek bonds for their customers. The unique variety of quotes used in the muni market provides a mechanism for maintaining fairness.

Providing Quotes

A quote published by a dealer must be a *bona fide quote*, meaning that it is based on the broker's best judgment of what is fair and equitable, and that the broker-dealer is prepared to provide the security at the quoted price at the time the quote is made. Because the market for municipal bonds is generally illiquid, it might be nearly impossible for a broker to ascertain an exact price ahead of time. So, a bona fide quote can still change before the trade is completed.

Nominal quotes, or quotes made for informational purposes such as workables, and *subject quotes*, quotes made subject to certain conditions, are appropriate as long as the broker explicitly labels them as such. Quotes made by a broker's broker must also be bona fide quotes.

Sometimes, a group of firms comes together in a joint account to trade a large block of municipal bonds. They do so to try to secure a better price. After they have formed the account, they must make a joint quote, usually done through the account manager. If each firm were to make separate quotes, it might give the false impression that more bidders than actually exist were interested in the issue, which can artificially manipulate prices. Just as broker-dealers cannot give the impression of a false number of bidders for a bond, they cannot imply that bonds have traded if they have not (a process known as "painting the tape").

Reporting Trades

A broker can report a trade only if it actually occurred, and at the price stated. Given that municipal trades do not take place on a floor or exchange, and no real-time electronic ticker exists, brokers carry a strong responsibility to report all trades accurately. Whenever a broker reports a trade, he or she must have a reasonable basis for believing the bond was in fact traded, and traded at the reported price.

In addition to reporting accurate information to the rest of the market, brokers need to verify information with their clients. Brokers must send customers a confirmation, known as a *confirm*, of every trade by the settlement date, so that no question remains about the exact nature of the trade. See Figure 11.1.

The customer confirmation should include these particulars:

- Transaction date
- Settlement date, including whether the transaction is a *regular way settlement* (three days after the trade, or T+3) or a *cash settlement* (the next day, or T+1)
- Description of the traded security, including its par value, name of the issuer, interest rate, maturity date, type of bond, and any call or put provisions
- The price and/or yield of the traded security. Here there are three possibilities:

  If the security is sold on a price basis, the lowest yield: to call, to par, or to maturity

  If the security is sold on a yield basis, the lowest price: to call, to par, or to maturity

  If the security is sold at par, the yield only
- Total amount the customer owes on the transaction, including any accrued interest
- Whether the broker served as principal (dealer) or agent (broker)
- The broker's commission or dealer's takedown on the transaction

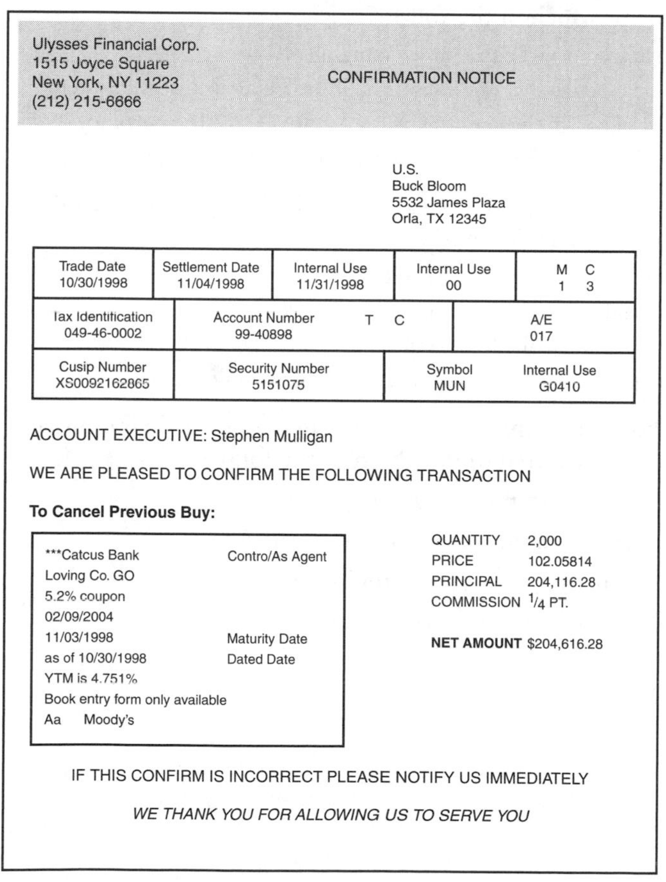

Ulysses Financial Corp.
1515 Joyce Square
New York, NY 11223
(212) 215-6666

CONFIRMATION NOTICE

U.S.
Buck Bloom
5532 James Plaza
Orla, TX 12345

Trade Date	Settlement Date	Internal Use	Internal Use	M C
10/30/1998	11/04/1998	11/31/1998	00	1 3

Tax Identification	Account Number T C	A/E
049-46-0002	99-40898	017

Cusip Number	Security Number	Symbol	Internal Use
XS0092162865	5151075	MUN	G0410

ACCOUNT EXECUTIVE: Stephen Mulligan

WE ARE PLEASED TO CONFIRM THE FOLLOWING TRANSACTION

To Cancel Previous Buy:

***Catcus Bank — Contro/As Agent
Loving Co. GO
5.2% coupon
02/09/2004
11/03/1998 — Maturity Date
as of 10/30/1998 — Dated Date
YTM is 4.751%
Book entry form only available
Aa Moody's

QUANTITY	2,000
PRICE	102.05814
PRINCIPAL	204,116.28
COMMISSION	1/4 PT.
NET AMOUNT	$204,616.28

IF THIS CONFIRM IS INCORRECT PLEASE NOTIFY US IMMEDIATELY

WE THANK YOU FOR ALLOWING US TO SERVE YOU

Figure 11.1 Customer confirmation.

Brokers must, for bonds in bearer form, deliver the physical securities after sending the confirm.

Exam Prep Questions

1. The rules and regulations that the MSRB has created for the Municipal securities market apply to which of the following?

   I. Municipal brokers and dealers

   II. Commercial banks that deal in municipal underwriting

   III. Thrift institutions

   IV. Municipalities bringing new issues to the market

   - ❑ A. I only
   - ❑ B. I and II
   - ❑ C. I, II, and III
   - ❑ D. I, II, III, and IV

2. The Federal Deposit Insurance Corporation has enforcement power of MSRB rules for which of the following?

   - ❑ A. State-chartered non-Fed member banks
   - ❑ B. Commercial banks that are members of the Federal Reserve System
   - ❑ C. Commercial banks chartered by the Comptroller of the currency
   - ❑ D. None of the above, because banks cannot deal in municipal bonds

3. Which of the following is not considered MSRB's concern in regulating the Municipal Securities market?

   - ❑ A. Ensuring fair treatment of customers
   - ❑ B. Setting qualification requirements for licenses
   - ❑ C. Regulating municipal advertising
   - ❑ D. Regulating the amount of debt that a municipality can issue

4. Individuals who are currently participating in a municipal apprenticeship program are permitted to do which of the following?

   I. Represent their firm to public customers

   II. Receive remuneration in the form of commissions

   III. Represent their firm to other municipal broker-dealers

   IV. None of the above, because they are apprentices

   - ❑ A. I and II
   - ❑ B. II and III
   - ❑ C. III
   - ❑ D. IV

5. A Municipal Securities Principal under MSRB rules is best described by which of the following?

❑ A. A supervisor at a broker-dealer who supervises the issuing, trading, and clearing of municipal securities

❑ B. An agent who deals in the sale of municipal securities

❑ C. An agent who is in charge of the back office of a broker-dealer

❑ D. A supervisor who is in charge of producing financial reports for the broker-dealer

6. A municipal bond dealer is thinking of advertising a certain municipal issue for additional business. The dealer currently does not have any of the bonds they are planning on advertising in their current inventory. Under MSRB rules, what is permitted?

❑ A. The dealer can advertise the bonds with no restrictions.

❑ B. The dealer can advertise the bonds, as long as they are labeled "subject to availability."

❑ C. The dealer is not permitted to advertise the bonds.

❑ D. The dealer needs to make a market in the bonds in order to advertise them.

7. Which of the following information is required by a municipal dealer when advertising municipal bonds according to MSRB rules?

I. The price of the bonds on publication date

II. The current yield

III. The nominal yield

IV. The yield to maturity

❑ A. I only

❑ B. I and II

❑ C. I and III

❑ D. I and IV

8. Which of the following information is required when opening a new municipal bond account?

I. Customer name and address

II. Customer social security number

III. Customer's suitability for investing in municipal bonds

IV. Customer's beneficiary for the account

❑ A. I and II

❑ B. II and III

❑ C. I, II, and III

❑ D. I, II, III, and IV

9. A municipal dealer had served as a financial advisor to a municipality, and then later resigned so that it could place a bid on a competitive basis. The same dealer was then awarded the bond issue from the municipality. Before selling bonds to its customers, the dealer is required under MSRB rules to do which of the following?
   - ❑ A. Disclose to the customer its relationship with the municipality
   - ❑ B. Disclose to the customer the amount of its winning bid
   - ❑ C. Disclose to the issuer their control relationship with other municipalities
   - ❑ D. Disclose to the MSRB its relationship with other municipalities

10. A municipal dealer who has made a political contribution to the campaign of an elected official in excess of MSRB rules can be censured in which of the following ways?
    - ❑ A. Fined 100 times the amount of the contribution
    - ❑ B. Fined 1,000 times the amount of the contribution
    - ❑ C. Prevented from being a negotiated bid underwriter for the next five years
    - ❑ D. Prevented from being a negotiated bid underwriter for the next two years

11. Trenton Securities recently made a $1,000 contribution to an elected official of Union City. Union City has a $20 million revenue bond due out in three weeks. Under MRSB rules, which of the following statements are true?

    I. Trenton can bid on the issue because it is below the maximum contribution allowed.

    II. Trenton is prohibited from bidding on the issue due to an excessive contribution.

    III. Trenton is suspended from conducting business with Union City for two years.

    IV. Trenton can enter a competitive bid to the municipality.

    - ❑ A. I only
    - ❑ B. II only
    - ❑ C. II and III
    - ❑ D. II, III, and IV

12. Arco Securities is serving in the role of financial advisor to the city of Hallendale. The municipality has decided to issue $200 million worth of revenue bonds to construct a new water treatment plant. Arco Securities, Jordan Securities, King Securities, and Rice Securities are all interested in becoming the sole underwriter in a negotiated offering for the new bond issue. Which of the following statements are true?

    I. Arco can underwrite the bonds.

    II. Jordan, King, and Rice can underwrite the bonds.

    III. Arco and King can join together to underwrite the bonds.

    IV. Arco has to resign as financial advisor and receive municipal approval to underwrite the bond issue.

    ❑ A. I and II
    ❑ B. II and III
    ❑ C. II and IV
    ❑ D. I, II, and III

13. Which of the following statements are considered true of a customer opening a discretionary account with a broker dealer?

    I. Duplicate confirms must be sent to the client's employer

    II. The customer is prohibited from working for another broker dealer

    III. The customer must sign a Power of Attorney

    IV. A Power of Attorney gives the broker the right to the security and size of a trade

    ❑ A. I and II
    ❑ B. II and III
    ❑ C. I, II, and III
    ❑ D. I, III, and IV

14. Under MSRB rules, a municipal securities principal is best described as what?

    ❑ A. A broker who supervises the issuing, trading, and clearing of municipal securities for the company.
    ❑ B. An agent who deals in the sale of municipal securities.
    ❑ C. An agent in charge of the back office.
    ❑ D. A supervisor in charge of producing financial reports for the company.

15. Which of the following is not considered MSRB concerns in regulating the municipal securities market?

    ❑ A. Ensuring fair treatment of customers
    ❑ B. Setting qualification requirements for licenses
    ❑ C. Regulating municipal advertising
    ❑ D. Regulating the amount of debt that a municipality can issue

Exam Prep Answers

1. The correct answer is B. The MSRB rules and regulations that have been established apply only to those entities that deal in municipal securities. These rules do not apply to the issuing municipality. The municipal market is different than the corporate market when it applies to underwriting. Municipal securities can be underwritten by both securities dealers as well as commercial banks and savings banks. Thrift institutions do not underwrite municipal issues, thus the MSRB rules do not apply to them. Issuers are not subject to MSRB rules, either by design or by inference.
2. The correct answer is A. The Federal Deposit Insurance Corp. is the enforcement arm of the MSRB rules for state-chartered banks that are not members of the Federal Reserve System.
3. The correct answer is D. MSRB rules are not designed to regulate the amount of debt that a municipality can issue. The MSRB covers a wide spectrum in the municipal market. This includes the treatment of customers, the qualifying of municipal dealers and brokers by licensing exams, and the type of advertising that municipal dealers are permitted.
4. The correct answer is C. The apprenticeship program allows individuals to represent their firms to other municipal dealers, as long as they are not earning a commission on any business they bring to the firm. They can be paid by salary, but not on commission while participating in an apprentice program.
5. The correct answer is A. A municipal securities principal is a supervisor, manager, or senior individual who supervises other municipal brokers in the trading, issuing, or clearing of municipal securities. A principal must pass the Series 53 exam to be considered qualified to act in this capacity.
6. The correct answer is B. A municipal broker-dealer is permitted to advertise bonds that they do not maintain in their own inventory account as long as in the advertisement they state the bonds are subject to availability.
7. The correct answer is D. When advertising municipal bonds, a broker-dealer is required to list the price of the bonds as of the date of the advertisement, as well as the yield to maturity, which is a more accurate indicator of a bond's value in the market.
8. The correct answer is D. All of the choices are correct. All are record-keeping necessities except option IV. Learning the customer's suitability to invest in municipal bonds is very important. A broker needs to know the customer's approximate income and net worth, tax situation, and investment objectives in order to assess the best investment. If the broker does not have this information, he cannot

adequately judge what investments are in the customer's best interest. Customers can refuse to give financial information, but the broker can only open the account. He cannot advise about investments; the customer is on his or her own.

9. The correct answer is A. If a broker-dealer had acted as a financial advisor to a municipality and then resigned so that they might bid on a competitive GO bond offering, they are required to disclose to their customer's the relationship they had with the municipality.
10. The correct answer is D. Any excessive political contribution made by a broker-dealer to a political candidate (in excess of $250) prohibits the broker-dealer from being a negotiated bid underwriter for that municipality for a period of two years.
11. The correct answer is D. A municipal broker who has made a political contribution in excess of $250 has violated MSRB rules. Trenton is prohibited from bidding on a negotiated issue as well as being suspended from additional negotiated offerings for two years. Trenton can, however, still underwrite and bid on a competitive offering. In theory, they would not have an inside track on a competitive bid because municipalities almost always award the issue to the lowest bidder.
12. The correct answer is C. Arco would have to resign as financial advisor to Hallendale and receive permission from the city to act as their negotiated underwriter. All others can underwrite the issue without receiving permission because they have no standing relationship with the city.
13. The correct answer is D. By definition, a discretionary account is one in which the broker dealer is given the authority to trade on behalf of the client; therefore, it is a requirement that the client sign a Power of Attorney. The client is not prohibited from working for another broker dealer. In such cases, MRSB rules are very strict about broker personal accounts and all trades must be watched by the principle of the firm in charge of the account and duplicate confirms sent to the employer.
14. The correct answer is A. A municipal securities principal supervises, manages, or is the senior individual who oversees the other brokers in the trading, issuing, or clearing of municipal securities. A principal must pass the Series 53 exam to be considered qualified to act in this capacity.
15. The correct answer is D. MSRB rules are not designed to regulate the amount of debt that a municipality can issue. The MSRB covers a wide spectrum of appropriate conduct for brokers, including the fair treatment of customers, the qualifying of municipal dealers and brokers with licensing exams, and the type of advertising that municipal dealers are permitted.

The New York Stock Exchange

Terms You Need to Know

- ✓ All or none (AON)
- ✓ At the close
- ✓ At the opening
- ✓ Away from the market
- ✓ Blanket fidelity bond
- ✓ Block trade
- ✓ Circuit breakers
- ✓ Competitive (registered) trader
- ✓ Consolidated tape system (CTS)
- ✓ Day order
- ✓ Designated Order Turnaround (DOT)
- ✓ Dow Jones Industrial Average (the Dow)
- ✓ Either/or (OCO)
- ✓ Fill or kill (FOK)
- ✓ Floor broker
- ✓ Good till canceled (GTC or open) order
- ✓ Immediate or cancel (IOC)
- ✓ Limit order
- ✓ Market order
- ✓ Not held (NH)
- ✓ Odd-lot trades
- ✓ Order ticket
- ✓ Program trading
- ✓ Round-lot trades
- ✓ Seat
- ✓ Size of the market
- ✓ Specialist
- ✓ Specialist's book
- ✓ Stop-limit order
- ✓ Stopping stock
- ✓ Stop order
- ✓ Stock index
- ✓ Super DOT
- ✓ Trading post
- ✓ Two-dollar (independent) broker

Concepts You Need to Understand

- ✓ How the New York Stock Exchange is organized
- ✓ Listing requirements
- ✓ Reasons for delisting
- ✓ Membership requirements
- ✓ Rules of conduct and trading
- ✓ Who the key players are in a stock transaction
- ✓ The trading process
- ✓ Different types of orders
- ✓ How to read the ticker tape
- ✓ How to read an order ticket
- ✓ Stock indexes

The New York Stock Exchange

The largest stock market in the world is the New York Stock Exchange, where more than 700 million shares change hands every day. This chapter takes a look at how the NYSE works—how companies come to be listed on the exchange, who belongs to the exchange, the key participants in stock transactions, and the types of trades made.

The roots of the New York Stock Exchange (NYSE) go all the way back to the first years of the nation, when merchants and brokers gathered regularly in Tontine's Coffee House in lower Manhattan to trade government, bank, and insurance company securities. Twenty-four individuals signed the famed Buttonwood Agreement in 1792, whereby they pledged to meet daily for trading and to charge each other a smaller commission on deals than they charged to nonmembers. In 1817, this trading association took the name New York Stock and Exchange Board, which was shortened to its current form in 1863.

The NYSE is an unincorporated business that nevertheless operates much like a corporation. It is governed by a board of directors, with an elected chairman and 20 board members who are drawn from the public and from the exchange's membership. The NYSE also has a variety of departments and affiliated organizations that pursue its business objectives in areas such as market operations, regulation and surveillance of member firms, and product development.

The importance of the NYSE as a securities market is abundantly clear in the staggering numbers it produces. Currently some 2,900 common stocks and 480 preferred stocks, representing around 3,100 companies, are listed on the exchange. All told, approximately 236 billion shares are listed on the Big Board. As of the late 1990s, close to half of the common shares traded on exchanges in the United States were found on the NYSE.

To be listed on the Big Board, companies must meet requirements as to their earnings, number of shareholders, tangible assets, and the total market value of their stock.

The NYSE generally requires that each company meet the following minimum thresholds:

- Earnings of at least $2.5 million before taxes in the latest fiscal year
- A minimum of 1.1 million publicly held common shares, with a market value of at least $18 million
- No fewer than 2,000 shareholders, who each own 100 or more shares
- A monthly average of 100,000 shares traded over the past six months

Listings on the Big Board are not necessarily perpetual. A company must also meet certain criteria to maintain its listing. These criteria are not as stringent as the entrance qualifications.

The NYSE will consider delisting a company if the company falls below one or more of the following limits:

- Fewer than 1,200 shareholders with 100 or more shares each
- Fewer than 600,000 outstanding publicly held shares
- Total market value of less than $5 million

Please note that there is no profitability requirement for remaining listed, as there is for *becoming* listed. The NYSE understands that companies can suffer through lean years for a wide variety of reasons.

Can a company voluntarily delist its stock? Yes, occasionally a corporation decides that its stock can better attract investors on another exchange, and so voluntarily removes its stock from the Big Board. The process is becoming easier. The NYSE previously required that a company get approval from two-thirds of its shareholders to move its listing to another exchange. As of December 1997, the exchange requires that companies wanting to delist get approval only from their boards and audit committees, and allow at least 45 days for their shareholders to object. It is still rare for a company to voluntarily delist itself.

Just as companies must meet certain requirements to be listed on the NYSE, individuals who want to trade on the Big Board must also meet a series of requirements.

Members of the NYSE

Membership on the NYSE is currently fixed at 1,366 seats. The right to conduct business on the NYSE floor is commonly called a *seat.* Some brokerage firms have more than one seat, so there are only about 440 member firms. Seats become available only when an existing member decides to sell one, at which point it is auctioned off to the highest bidder.

The price of a seat at auction is a good indicator of how business is doing on Wall Street. In 1987, just before the October market crash, a seat sold for a record $1.15 million. Within a few years, seats were selling for as little as $250,000. But by the end of 1997, the price was once again in record territory—more than $1.5 million. In 1998, seats commonly sold for about $1.3 million. Recently a seat went for over $2.5 million.

The requirements of membership are no less stringent than for companies wanting to be listed.

Rules Governing NYSE Member Firms

The rules governing the NYSE are extremely important to know, especially Rule 405: Know Your Customer.

The four most important rules governing member firms are explained here.

Rule 77—Prevents member firms from doing any of the following:

- Betting on movements in the market
- Buying or selling dividends
- Buying or selling privileges to receive or deliver securities
- Buying or selling stock at the closing price
- Buying or selling stock at a stop price away from the market

Rule 78—Prohibits firms from buying or selling stocks for their customers with a prearranged agreement to sell or buy them back at the same price.

Rule 405—The "know your customer" rule. The NYSE demands that brokers recommend investments that are suitable for each client.

Rule 435—Similar to Rule 405 in requiring the ethical treatment of clients. It prohibits:

- Excessive trading in a customer's account (churning), whether in frequency or amount
- Misleading a customer by artificially exaggerating trading activity in a stock
- Manipulating a security to suggest price movement
- Initiating rumors about a security
- Altering a transaction confirmation report
- Violating Federal Reserve requirements on extending credit to customers

All NYSE member firms must post a *blanket fidelity bond*, which provides a firm's customers with insurance against fraud or embezzlement by the firm's employees.

Firms must be truthful and complete in all communications with the public.

The Big Board, however, does not limit its jurisdiction to member firms. It also has specific rules of conduct for representatives of nonmember firms.

NYSE Rules Governing Individuals

The following NYSE rules govern representatives of nonmember firms:

- All sales representatives and brokers must be registered to conduct business on the NYSE.
- Anyone registered with the NYSE must be investigated by his or her employer for past improper conduct.
- Anyone registered with the NYSE must receive approval from his or her firm to take on a second job elsewhere.
- Gifts to clients or other NYSE members must not exceed $100 in value.

A comparatively recent set of NYSE regulations tells a great deal about how both the mechanics of trading and public access to the markets have changed in the 20th century. In the late 1980s, the Big Board instituted a series of rules, known as *circuit breakers*, which limit trading under certain circumstances.

Circuit Breakers

Circuit breakers are a series of exchange regulations (Rules 80 and 80B) that prohibit trading after significant swings in the market. For the most part, circuit breakers deal with drastic drops in the Dow, but they can also be triggered by sudden advances.

Why were circuit breakers adopted? The advent of circuit breakers can be traced to the October 1987 stock market crash. That year, on October 19, the Dow fell 508 points, or 22.6%—the third largest point loss and the largest percentage loss in its history. Some of the day's sell-off resulted from the widespread use of program trading by mutual and pension funds. *Program trading* uses computers to trigger either sales or purchases, based on pre-established indicators in the market. For example, the managers of a mutual fund might program their computers to sell a portfolio of stocks if the Dow drops 200 points, and then yet more stocks if the Dow falls another 100 points.

Perhaps even more of the sell-off can be ascribed to the flawed implementation of a device called portfolio insurance. To hedge, or insure, broad-based equities portfolios, many fund managers sold index futures, which are contracts to trade a financial instrument in the future at a set price. At the time, computer systems could not keep up with large trading volumes, and managers with portfolio insurance could not use futures successfully. Instead, their interventions in the market tended to exacerbate price swings. The new regulations were designed to break the "circuit" that allowed program trading to create such trading avalanches. Still, program trading does not tell the entire story of October 19, 1987.

The October 1987 crash did affect the general public. More than at any previous time, movements in the stock market in 1987 seriously affected a new class of investors in the United States—middle-class Americans, people who were not professional investors or dealers. In earlier decades, average citizens rarely invested a large portion of their savings in the stock market. Since the early 1980s, more and more Americans have placed their savings into stock mutual funds and pension funds, which, in turn, invest in Wall Street securities. Indeed, the nation plowed almost $5 trillion into such funds in the 15 years after 1982. One consequence is that sudden, large drops in the stock market are felt by a much larger portion of the country than in the past.

In addition, because of the growth of discount brokerage houses like Charles Schwab, many more Americans participate in the stock market directly. As word spread about the steep drop in the Dow, members of the general public—with their savings at stake—sought to limit their losses by selling as soon as possible. Predictably, this only sent stock prices further south.

Circuit breakers, then, aim to achieve two purposes:

- Mitigate the multiplier effects of program trading in sudden market downturns
- Protect the general public (and the market) from panic-driven downturns

Have circuit breakers ever been used? Before the end of the trading day on October 27, 1997, the Dow had fallen 350 points on fears of economic downturns in Asia. A circuit breaker was tripped, and the NYSE was shut down for 30 minutes. But a few minutes after trading reopened, the Dow dropped another 200 points, which triggered another circuit breaker, this time closing trading for the day. The Dow finished 554 points down.

At the time, circuit breakers were keyed to specific point changes. The NYSE has since realized that circuit breakers are more effective (and realistic) when tied to percentage changes in the Dow. Although the 554-point loss that day was the largest ever in absolute terms, it represented a decline of only 7.2%—not even one of the top 10 largest percentage losses in history. As a result, in

April 1998, circuit-breaker rules were fine-tuned, and trading is halted only when the Dow falls 10%, 20%, and 30%. The length of the stoppage depends on the time of day, but a 30% drop ends trading for the day.

Other Limits on Trading

When the Dow rises or falls 50 points from the previous day's close, curbs are placed on certain types of computerized trading. Specifically, the NYSE's Super DOT system is shut off to large institutional traders, with trades going directly to specialists. In the late 1990s, this circuit breaker kicked in almost every day and did not prevent large swings in the market, so its usefulness is questionable. Other restrictions on computerized trading go into effect if the futures contract on the Standard & Poor's 500 Stock Index rises or falls by 12 points or more.

Rules about who can trade on the NYSE and when trading must stop are well and good, but other rules are best understood after examining how an actual trade happens.

The Trading Process

Although seemingly a simple matter, a stock transaction is a complex chain of events that can involve dozens of people. And not only do trades have to happen quickly they must also be accurate and well documented. The NYSE is distinguished by being a securities auction market, which requires that the primary participants in a transaction have clearly defined roles.

There are several key players on the exchange floor. They are specialists, floor brokers, competitive or registered traders, and two-dollar brokers.

- *Specialists* maintain a fair and orderly market in one or more specific securities. They must be ready to buy or sell those securities at any time to maintain a balance of supply and demand. If there are no buyers or sellers available for that security, the specialist takes on whatever role is necessary. This makes the market more efficient and helps to control volatility. Specialists work from one of the various *trading posts* on the exchange floor; they can trade more than one security from each post. The specialist also executes limit orders, which are orders to buy stock at a specific price away from the current market price.
- *Floor brokers* execute trades on behalf of the member firm's clients. They receive a trade order by telephone or computer and move to the appropriate trading post to execute the trade.

- *Competitive traders*, also known as *registered traders*, buy and sell securities for their own account, hoping to profit from price fluctuations in an actively traded stock. The NYSE requires that 75% of their trades be made in a stabilizing fashion. That is, they can buy a stock only if it fell on its last trade, and they can sell a stock only if it rose on its last trade. Because registered traders are privileged insiders in the NYSE market, this requirement is necessary to maintain an equitable market. Occasionally, competitive traders take orders from clients, in which case the orders take precedence over their own trading account. In fact, NYSE Rule 92 demands that all customer orders be given priority over any trades for a member firm's account.
- *Two-dollar brokers* execute orders for floor brokers who are inundated with market orders and cannot handle their own volume, or for member firms that do not currently have a representative on the floor. At one time, these brokers received $2 for each round-lot trade executed. Today, their commission is negotiated, based on the size of the transaction. Two-dollar brokers are also called *independent brokers* because they handle trades for any firm on the exchange.

How a Trade Works

A trade starts with a decision to buy or sell a security. Although mutual funds and large institutional investors play a big role in the market, many trades are initiated by small investors.

Say John Miller wants to buy 5,000 shares of Coca-Cola Co. He calls his brokerage firm and places an order to buy at the current market price. The information is written on an order ticket and passed on to a floor broker, who proceeds to the trading post where Coca-Cola is traded.

The floor broker then asks the specialist what the market is on Coca-Cola. The specialist gives a price of, say, 64.25 bid and 64.62 ask. In other words, the most anyone is willing to pay is 64.25 and the least anyone is willing to sell for is 64.62. The broker also might ask the *size of the market*: how many will buy at 64.25 and how many will sell at 64.62. The specialist can respond 64.25 – 64.62, 900 by 600—meaning buyers exist for 900 shares at 64.25 and sellers exist for 600 shares at 64.62. In this particular case, the specialist must step in: he becomes the seller of 4,400 Coca-Cola shares and matches the existing offers for 600 shares, all at 64.62, to Mr. Miller's order for 5,000 shares.

Notification of the trade is then given to a NYSE floor reporter, who sees that it is displayed within 90 seconds on the NYSE's consolidated tape for the benefit of all market participants. It is also sent to various NYSE departments to ensure that it is recorded properly.

NYSE Rules for Reporting Trades

Two NYSE rules pertain specifically to the reporting and recording of transactions:

Rule 410—Requires that member firms maintain records of all transactions they execute on the floor for three years. In addition, auditors have access to those records for the first two of those years.

Rule 411—States that if a firm incorrectly reports a trade to a customer, the firm is liable for the actual price of the trade and must make up any difference to the customer.

Specialists provide other services as well. As a courtesy to a floor broker, a specialist can guarantee the best price currently available on a stock for a short period of time, usually 15 minutes. This is called *stopping stock*. The broker (and only that broker) is free to obtain a better price, but can return to the specialist to execute the trade at the stopped price. If other brokers enter the market for that particular stock, the specialist has no obligation to offer them the stopped price.

Specialists also handle all *odd-lot trades*—any trades for 99 shares or fewer. These transactions are distinguished from those in multiples of 100 shares, which are called *round-lot trades*. Specialists charge an additional fee, usually ⅛ of a point, for odd-lot trades; this is known as an odd-lot differential.

Trading Through a Specialist or a Floor Broker

If two floor brokers have matching buy and sell orders, they can complete the trade by themselves. The broker and "contra broker" complete the trade in front of the specialist, and report the trade to the floor reporter. Note, however, that NYSE Rule 76 prohibits brokers from crossing orders between their own clients. That is, a broker cannot match one client's order to buy 1,000 shares of Disney with another client's order to sell 1,000 shares of Disney.

All trades do not have to go through a floor broker. The NYSE has a computerized system called *Designated Order Turnaround (DOT)*, which enables member firms to send an order directly to the specialist, speeding the trading process. DOT can be used for market orders up to 30,999 shares. A related system, *Super DOT*, is used for limit orders of up to 99,999 shares.

Orders are ranked first by price: the highest price for a buy order or lowest one for a sell order is executed first. If the two orders have the same price, the order that arrived first at the trading station is processed first. When orders have the same price and arrived at the same time, the larger order is completed first.

EXAMPLE: An order to buy 600 shares of Motorola, Inc., at $58.62 arrives at the trading post at the same time as another order to buy 300 shares of Motorola at $58.62. They have the same bid and arrived at the same time; the 600-share order is executed first because it is larger.

Investor Orders

Investors can place different types of orders. The most common order is a *market order*.

A *market order* is one in which a customer directs a broker to buy or sell a security at the best price currently available. A market order is completed quickly, but the customer does not know the actual transaction price until the trade is made.

When an investor wants to specify a price for a transaction, they place a *limit order*.

A *limit order* can be executed only at the limit price or better. These orders are always placed away from the market, with no guarantee they will be filled. A buy limit order is always at a price lower than the current market price, whereas a sell limit order is always at a price higher than the market price.

EXAMPLE: James Hitchcock places a buy limit order for 100 shares of Better Banking at $20 a share. The stock is currently trading at $21 per share, so the shares are purchased only when the stock falls to $20 or lower. If Clark Capra were to place a sell limit order for 100 shares of Better Banking at $22 per share, that order is completed only when the stock price rises to $22 or higher.

A *stop order* enables a customer to specify a price at which the order is activated. It then becomes a market order. After a stop order is activated, prices can move for or against the investor—unlike a limit order, which is executed only at the limit price or better. Stop orders have a further distinction from limit orders: the stop price is always *above* the market price in a buy stop order, and *below* the current market price in a sell stop order.

EXAMPLE: Sturges McGinty places a buy stop order for 100 shares of Consolidated Chemical at $25 per share. The stock is currently trading at $20 per share, so Mr. McGinty's order is completed only if the stock reaches $25. Should it do so, the original buy stop order is treated as a market order and filled at the best prevailing price.

Who might use a stop order and why? Buy stop orders are frequently used to protect an investor's profit, or limit his loss, on a short sale. Assume that Jay Fitzgerald had sold 500 shares of Green Light Courier Co. short at $30 per share. Green Light is now trading at $30. Although Mr. Fitzgerald would obviously like the stock price to go down so he can realize a profit, he wants to be sure that he won't lose more than $1,000 on the transaction. He therefore places a buy stop order for 500 shares at $32 per share.

Conversely, sell stop orders protect profits and limit losses when investors have long stock positions. For instance, Gertrude Toklas owns 100 shares of Pound Publishing, Inc., which she purchased at $10 per share. The stock is now trading at $15 per share. In order to lock in a 20% profit, Ms. Toklas places a sell stop order for 100 shares at $12.

Can you combine a stop order and a limit order? Yes, it's called a *stop-limit order*.

As with a stop order, the order is activated only if the stock trades at the stop price. But instead of becoming a market order, it becomes a limit order. That is, the trade is executed only at the stop price or *better*.

In the same fashion as stop orders, buy stop-limit orders are often employed by short sellers, and sell stop-limit orders by holders of long positions. As with limit orders, investors placing stop-limit orders risk not completing the trade. For example, if the stock plunges below the limit price in a sell stop-limit order, the order is not executed unless the stock later rebounds.

EXAMPLE: Thomas H. Wyeth has purchased 10,000 shares of American Retailers at $65 per share. To limit any potential losses, Mr. Wyeth places a sell stop-limit order for 10,000 American Retailers shares at $60. So, if the stock price drops to $60, the order is triggered. However, it now becomes a limit order and is executed only at $60 or higher—if the stock continues to fall below $60, the order is not filled.

Table 12.1 lists the types of orders a broker-dealer must be very familiar with for daily trading.

Table 12.1 Types of Stock Orders

Orders placed above current market price:	Sell limit order	Investor wants to sell a stock at a favorable price. No guarantee of execution.
	Buy stock order	Investor probably wants to protect a profit or limit a loss on a short sale. After stop price is price reached, order becomes a market order, so no guarantee of price.
	Buy stop-limit order	Investor might want to protect a profit or limit a loss on a short sale. After stop price is reached, order becomes a limit order. No guarantee of execution.
Orders placed at current market price:	Market order	Investor wants to buy or sell security at current market price, whatever it is.
Orders placed below current market price:	Buy limit order	Investor wants to buy a stock at a favorable price. Can be executed at limit price or lower. No guarantee of execution.
	Sell stop order	Investor probably wants to protect a profit or limit a loss on a long stock position. After stop price is reached, order becomes a market order, so no guarantee of price.
	Sell stop-limit order	Investor might want to protect or limit a loss on a long stock position. After stop price is reached, order becomes a limit order. No guarantee of execution.

Who keeps track of all the orders? The specialist keeps a *specialist's book* of all orders that are *away from the market*, meaning above or below the current market price. These orders cannot be executed immediately and include all stop, limit, and stop-limit orders. It's important to write these orders down, because some can remain in place for days, even weeks, before they are either executed or canceled.

Qualifying an Order

The NYSE also enables investors to qualify orders so that they can tell brokers how long to keep an order in place or how an order should be filled.

The following are some types of order qualifiers:

- **Day order**—Good for one day only. If not executed by the end of the trading day, it is canceled. This is used typically with limit orders, because they are placed away from the current market price and might take time to be completed.
- **Good till canceled (GTC** or **open) order**—Remains in place until it is executed or the customer cancels it. Theoretically, a GTC order can be in place for weeks, even months, but the broker will periodically check to make sure the customer still wants to execute the trade at the specified price.
- **All or none (AON)**—If the entire order cannot be executed at the dictated price, it is not filled. The broker normally has several chances to fill the entire order.
- **Fill or kill (FOK)**—Similar to an AON order, except that the FOK order must be completed on the first attempt by the floor broker, or it is canceled.
- **Immediate or cancel (IOC)**—The floor broker must fill either a part or all the order on the first attempt, or it is canceled. If only a portion of an IOC order is filled, the remainder is canceled.
- **Either/or (OCO)**—Also known as a "one cancels the other," instructs the broker to execute one of two orders, and then cancel the other one. For example, assume Paul Cassidy places an order to buy either 100 shares of Sundance Railroads stock at $75 a share or 50 shares of Redford National Bank at $65 a share. If the floor broker fills the order for Sundance Railroads first, the Redford buy order is canceled.
- **Not held (NH)**—Gives the broker discretion over when to execute a market order, in hopes of finding the best possible price. An NH order can wait until later in the day if the broker believes the price will move in the investor's favor. By issuing an NH order, an investor is stating that he or she will not hold the floor broker responsible if the transaction price is not up to the investor's expectations.
- **At the opening**—To be executed as close to the opening price of a security on a given day. This can be either a limit order, in which case the order might not be completed, or a market order, in which the price is not guaranteed.
- **At the close**—To be executed as close to the closing price of a security as possible. This is a market order, with no price guarantee.

All instructions given to the floor broker are written on an *order ticket*, which must be retained for a certain period after the trade is completed to ensure proper settlement.

In addition to the type of order and any special instructions, the order ticket must include the following information:

- The security to be purchased and the number of shares
- Whether the customer is executing a short sale
- The customer's name and account number

- The executing broker's name
- Whether the broker is acting as agent or principal
- Whether the broker has discretion over the customer's account
- Whether the order was solicited by the customer

How NYSE Trades Are Recorded

In 1975, the NYSE and the American Stock Exchange began reporting their transactions jointly, on a single system called the *consolidated tape system (CTS)*. The CTS has two parts:

- Network A reports trades of NYSE-listed securities.
- Network B reports trades of all Amex-listed securities, as well as those listed on regional exchanges.

Each security listed on the NYSE has a ticker symbol of up to three letters. For example, General Motors is GM, Ford is F, and Exxon is XON. Occasionally the ticker symbols are harder to recognize—Quaker State is KSF and General Mills is GIS—so it helps to have a good memory.

Transactions cross the ticker tape with the number of round lots traded. A round lot is 100 shares. If exactly 100 shares were traded, no volume is given. A trade of 200 shares is accompanied by a 2, a trade of 2,000 shares is accompanied by a 20, and so on. The volume and the price are then separated by an "s."

> **EXAMPLE:** Say Emma Peale bought 100 shares of Ford at $65 a share. The trade crosses the ticker as F 65. However, if Ms. Peale had purchased 200 shares, the tape reports F 2s65.

There are two exceptions to the round-lot rule: If the number of shares is 10,000 or more, the entire volume is written out in full. Transactions of this size are called *block trades*. On the other end of the spectrum, trades of fewer than 200 shares are sometimes shown in 10-share lots for stocks that are not actively traded. In these cases, the trade is accompanied by the symbol $\frac{s}{s}$.

It is also possible for two trades for the same security to be combined on the same tape. However, only when they happen right after one another. In such cases, the company's ticker symbol is listed only once, and the whole number portion of the trading price is dropped after the first trade.

EXAMPLE: John Stied bought 200 shares of GM at $66.20 a share and James Baund bought 500 shares of GM at $66.25 immediately afterward. The trades are reported as follows: GM 2s66.20 5s25. Note that the $6 portion of the price is not listed twice.

Ticker Tape Abbreviations

The ticker tape also specifies the type of security being traded, using one of the following abbreviations after the ticker symbol. If there is no such abbreviation, the security is assumed to be common stock.

Pr—Preferred stock

WT—Warrants

WI—When-issued

RTS—Rights

The following abbreviations indicate special conditions. They are separated from the ticker symbol by a period.

SLD—The trade happened earlier and is being reported out of its proper sequence

OPD—The first trade on a security for which the opening was delayed

LAST—Trading in the security was halted after this trade

S/T—The trade reported was for stopped stock

If a trade occurred on a market other than the NYSE or AMEX, the following abbreviations are used and are separated from the ticker symbol by an ampersand (&).

B—Boston Stock Exchange

C—Cincinnati Stock Exchange

M—Midwest Exchange, in Chicago

O—Other markets, including Instinet

P—Pacific Stock Exchange

T—Third market, or over-the-counter trading

X—Philadelphia Stock Exchange

Having purchased a given company's stock, investors and broker-dealers need to be able to track and judge its performance relative to other stocks and to the market as a whole. Stock indexes are perhaps the most useful tools for judging overall market performance, thus providing a good yardstick for measuring individual companies' successes or lack thereof. Of the many stock indexes available, the Dow Jones Industrial Average is the best known. Changes in the value of the Dow over time also offer a good way of examining the history of the NYSE.

Stock Indexes

A *stock index* is a number whose movement over time reflects the price changes in a pool of stocks. The index is constructed in such a way as to gauge how the overall stock market (or a section within it) is performing—a carefully selected group of stocks can reflect trends in the overall market. The Dow Jones Industrial Average is the best-known of the many market indexes.

The *Dow Jones Industrial Average (the Dow)* is a stock index that tracks price changes in 30 stocks. The corporations in the Dow are mainly huge industrial companies such as Boeing, 3M, GE, and Coca-Cola, but it also includes some financial giants like J. P. Morgan and American Express. Every Dow company is considered to be a blue-chip stock, ranks among the largest in the United States, and is listed on the NYSE. The Dow is published by the Dow Jones Co., which also publishes the *Wall Street Journal.* Please note that Dow Jones publishes several indexes, but that the industrial average is by far the most widely quoted. When network news anchors talk about movements in the Dow, they are referring to the industrial average.

When the Dow was first published in 1884, it tracked 11 stocks, most of which were railroad and steel companies. At the time, railroads were the main means of commercial transportation in the United States. If railroads were thriving, it was assumed that other businesses had to be shipping lots of goods, and therefore were doing well themselves. In 1896, the Dow grew to 12 stocks; it expanded again in 1928 to its current size of 30 stocks.

Despite its title, the Dow is not a straight arithmetic average; it is a price-weighted average. That is, in calculating the value of the industrial average, Dow Jones weighs the prices of the individual stocks, so that they are all at roughly the same "price." Also, when the Dow expanded in 1928, the methodology used to derive its value was changed. Instead of dividing the market value of the selected stocks by the number of stocks, a "special divisor" was used. This divisor is adjusted to eliminate distortions that arise from stock splits or the substitution of new companies into the Dow pool. So, strictly speaking, the industrial average is an index, not an average; its title has been retained for tradition's sake.

In spite of its name recognition and pervasive use, academics and analysts do not consider the Dow to be the best indicator of the strength of the stock market. First, the Dow tracks stocks of only 30 of the some 3,100 companies listed on the NYSE.

Second, the Dow Jones Industrial Average takes only one share from each of its constituent companies. Those corporations, however, do not have equal numbers of outstanding shares. For example, Coca-Cola had approximately 2.5 billion outstanding common shares in 1998, whereas 3M had around 404 million. Investors in the stock market, therefore, owned six times as many shares in Coca-Cola as they did in 3M. Thus, the Dow tends to misrepresent the market by holding an equal number of shares in each company.

Other Indices

There are a large number of indices available to track the stock market. After the Dow, perhaps the most popular is the S&P 500. As its name suggests, the S&P tracks 500 companies, not all of them are on the NYSE—thus providing a more accurate picture of the state of the entire stock market. Other more specialized indexes appeal to certain types of investors or investment theories, for example:

- Dow Jones also publishes indices tied to utility and transportation companies.
- The Russell 2000 tracks mid-sized companies, on the theory that these entities are more representative of American business in general than the McDonalds or Coca-Colas.
- The NYSE Composite restricts itself to the companies appearing on the Big Board, but measures the total market capitalization of every stock listed.
- NASDAQ's Composite Index and the NMS Composite Index enable investors to gauge the strength of the over-the-counter market, which is the subject of the next chapter.

Exam Prep Questions

1. To qualify for listing on the NYSE, a company must have all the following except:
   - ❑ A. A minimum of 1.1 million publicly held common shares.
   - ❑ B. Earnings of at least 2.5 million dollars before taxes in the latest fiscal year.
   - ❑ C. No fewer than 2,000 shareholders who each own 100 or more shares.
   - ❑ D. A monthly average of 200,000 shares traded over the past six months.

2. The NYSE can delist a company for which of the following reasons?

   I. The company has fewer than 1,200 shareholders who own 100 or more shares of stock.

   II. The company has fewer than 600,000 outstanding publicly held shares.

   III. The company's total market value is less than $5 million.

   IV. The company has losses for the current or previous year in excess of $10 million.
   - ❑ A. I and II
   - ❑ B. II and III
   - ❑ C. I, II, and III
   - ❑ D. I, II, III, and IV

3. NYSE Rule 77 forbids all the following except:
   - ❑ A. Buying or selling dividends
   - ❑ B. Betting on movements in the market
   - ❑ C. Owning more than one seat on the exchange
   - ❑ D. Buying or selling privileges to receive or deliver securities

4. New York Stock Exchange Rules 80 and 80B:
   - ❑ A. Act as circuit breakers for the market.
   - ❑ B. Prevent brokers from buying and selling dividends.
   - ❑ C. Require that brokers know their customers.
   - ❑ D. Govern the opening of margin accounts.

5. The Dow Jones Industrial Average falls to 9922, from 9972 at the previous day's close. Which of the following conditions occurs?

   I. The market is closed to institutional investors.

   II. The Super DOT system is shut off to large institutional traders.

   III. The floor reporter handles all orders.

   IV. The specialist handles all orders.
   - ❑ A. I
   - ❑ B. II
   - ❑ C. I and III
   - ❑ D. II and IV

6. As a specialist on the floor of the NYSE, Marie Matisse:
   - ❑ A. Maintains a market in all NYSE-listed securities.
   - ❑ B. Maintains a market in certain NYSE-listed securities.
   - ❑ C. Trades securities only at the prices bid and offered by investors.
   - ❑ D. Sets her own prices for all NYSE-listed securities.

7. Van Gold is a competitive trader on the NYSE floor. When he trades for his own account, he must:

   I. Make 50% of his purchases after a fall in a stock's price.

   II. Make 75% of his purchases after a fall in a stock's price.

   III. Make 50% of his sales after a rise in a stock's price.

   IV. Make 75% of his sales after a rise in a stock's price.

   - ❑ A. I
   - ❑ B. II
   - ❑ C. I and III
   - ❑ D. II and IV

8. Specialist Marie Matisse quotes the price of American Retailers as 70.62 – 70.75, 800 by 500. This means that the price of the stock is:
   - ❑ A. 70.62 bid, with sellers for 800 shares; and 70.75 ask, with buyers for 500 shares.
   - ❑ B. 70.62 ask, with sellers for 800 shares; and 70.75 bid, with buyers for 500 shares.
   - ❑ C. 70.62 bid, with buyers for 800 shares; and 70.75 ask, with sellers for 500 shares.
   - ❑ D. 70.62 ask, with buyers for 800 shares; and 70.75 bid, with sellers for 500 shares.

9. A specialist stops Allied Tin for broker James Hitchcock at an ask of 60.88. Ten minutes later, Allied rises to 61. Hitchcock returns immediately to the specialist to purchase the stock and finds Lois Olsen, another broker, also purchasing it. At what price did each purchase the stock?
   - ❑ A. Both purchased the stock at 61.
   - ❑ B. Both purchased the stock at 60.8.
   - ❑ C. Hitchcock purchased the stock at 60.88; Olsen purchased it at 61.
   - ❑ D. Hitchcock purchased the stock at 60.88; Olsen purchased it at 61.12.

10. Holly Lyme enters an order to purchase 500 shares of Vienna Pharmaceuticals at 48. Vienna is currently at 45.75. What type of order has she entered, and what happens when Vienna reaches 48?
    - ❑ A. She has entered a buy order, which will become a market order at 48.
    - ❑ B. She has entered a buy stop order, which will become a market order at 48.
    - ❑ C. She has entered a stop limit order, which will become a limit order at 48.
    - ❑ D. She has entered a market order, which will become a limit order at 48.

11. Lifeline, Inc., declares a dividend of $1 per share. During the two days Lifeline trades ex dividend, specialists will adjust prices downwards by $1 for which orders?

    I. Buy limits

    II. Buy stops

    III. Sell stops

    IV. Sell stop-limits

    - ❑ A. I and II
    - ❑ B. II and III
    - ❑ C. I, II, III, and IV
    - ❑ D. I, III, and IV

12. Hugh Plath enters an IOC order to purchase 800 shares of Bellwether at 77. Which trade fills his order?

    - ❑ A. The floor broker makes three attempts to fill the order. He fails all three times, so the order is canceled.
    - ❑ B. On his first attempt to fill the order, the floor broker buys 600 shares at 77. Later that day, he buys the remaining shares at 76.50.
    - ❑ C. On his first attempt to fill the order, the floor broker buys 600 shares at 77. The remainder of the order is canceled.
    - ❑ D. On his first attempt to fill the order, the floor broker finds only 600 shares available at 77. He buys nothing and the entire order is canceled.

13. Order tickets must include all the following except:

    - ❑ A. The customer's account number.
    - ❑ B. The executing broker's name.
    - ❑ C. Whether the order was solicited by the customer.
    - ❑ D. The terms of payment for the transaction.

14. On the consolidated tape, the report UGH 2s34.12 S/T means:

    - ❑ A. 2,000 shares of UGH sold short at 34.12.
    - ❑ B. 200 shares of UGH sold short at 34.12.
    - ❑ C. 2,000 shares of UGH sold as stopped stock at 34.12.
    - ❑ D. 200 shares of UGH sold as stopped stock at 34.12.

15. The Standard & Poor's 500:

    I. Tracks the stocks of 500 companies.

    II. Tracks exclusively NYSE-listed stocks.

    III. Provides a more accurate picture of the market than the Dow.

    IV. Tracks the top 500 stocks on the NYSE.

    - ❑ A. I only
    - ❑ B. I and II
    - ❑ C. I and III
    - ❑ D. I, II, III, and IV

Exam Prep Answers

1. The correct answer is D. A company must have a monthly average of 100,000 shares traded over the past six months to qualify for listing on the NYSE.
2. The correct answer is C. The NYSE does not delist companies on the basis of financial losses, but only for failure to maintain adequate ownership distribution and capitalization.
3. The correct answer is C. Member firms can own as many seats on the NYSE as their volume of business requires.
4. The correct answer is A. Rules 80 and 80B restrict trading after significant swings in the market, thereby acting as "circuit breakers" to prevent a destabilizing acceleration of trading.
5. The correct answer is D. If the Dow falls by 50 points from the previous day's close, the NYSE's Super DOT computerized trading system for large institutional traders shuts down, and all trades go directly to the specialists for handling.
6. The correct answer is B. Specialists on the NYSE floor maintain a fair and orderly market in one or more specific securities, buying and selling the securities to balance supply and demand.
7. The correct answer is D. Competitive traders are privileged insiders in the NYSE market, so exchange rules require that they make 75% of all trades for their own accounts in a stabilizing fashion. Therefore, in 75% of his transactions, Gold can buy a stock only if it fell on its last trade or can sell a stock only if it rose on its last trade.
8. The correct answer is C. All traders and brokers quote the bid price first, so buyers exist for 800 shares of American Retailers at 70.62. Matisse quotes the ask price second, so sellers exist for 500 shares of American Retailers at 70.75.
9. The correct answer is C. Specialists usually stop stock—guarantee a broker the best price available—for 15 minutes. Because Hitchcock returned within that time, he can purchase Allied Tin at the stopped price of 60.62. Olsen's order was filled in the normal manner, at the current market price of 61.
10. The correct answer is B. Because Lyme is not buying at 45.75 but will buy at the higher price of 48, the order is neither a simple buy nor a limit order. She is evidently protecting a short position—hoping for a fall in the stock's price so that she can realize a profit, but limiting her losses in case of a rise. She has entered a buy stop order. When Vienna Pharmaceuticals reaches 48, Lyme's order will become a market order.

11. The correct answer is D. When Lifeline is trading ex-dividend, the specialist adjusts downwards any order placed below the market. They do not adjust buy stop orders, with which investors enter to buy at a price above the current market.
12. The correct answer is C. A floor broker must fill as much of an IOC (immediate or cancel) order as possible on the first attempt; the remainder of the order is canceled. If the broker cannot fill any of the order on the first attempt, the entire order is canceled. (If Plath had entered an FOK [fill-or-kill] order, the floor broker would buy all 800 shares of Bellwether at 77 or would cancel the entire order.)
13. The correct answer is D. Terms of payment are regulated by industry and brokerage rules. They do not vary from transaction to transaction.
14. The correct answer is D. The tape reports trade size in 100-unit round lots. The designation S/T means that the trade occurred in stopped stock. The price of stopped stock can differ from the current market price because the specialist had stopped the price for a broker.
15. The correct answer is C. The Standard & Poor's 500 Index tracks the stocks of 500 companies, not all of them are on the NYSE—providing a more accurate picture of the strength of the entire stock market than the Dow, which tracks only 30 blue-chip, NYSE-listed companies.

NASDAQ and the OTC Market

Terms You Need to Know

- ✓ 5% policy
- ✓ Agent
- ✓ American Stock Exchange (Amex)
- ✓ Arbitrage trade
- ✓ Ask quote
- ✓ Auction market
- ✓ Backing away
- ✓ Bid quote
- ✓ Bid wanted (BW)
- ✓ Code of Arbitration
- ✓ Commission
- ✓ Crossed trade
- ✓ District Business Conduct Committe (DBCC)
- ✓ Dual agency transaction
- ✓ Front running
- ✓ Inside market
- ✓ Interpositioning
- ✓ Level One, Two, and Three of the NASDAQ system
- ✓ Markdown
- ✓ Market maker
- ✓ Markup
- ✓ NASDAQ (National Association of Securities Dealers Automated Quotation System)
- ✓ NASDAQ National Market System (NMS)
- ✓ NASDAQ SmallCap Market
- ✓ NASDAQ Stock Market
- ✓ National Arbitration Committee
- ✓ National Association of Securities Dealers (NASD)
- ✓ Negotiated (dealer) market
- ✓ Offer wanted (OW)
- ✓ Office of Supervisory Jurisdiction (OSJ)
- ✓ OTC Bulletin Board
- ✓ Penny stocks
- ✓ Philadelphia Stock Exchange (PSE)
- ✓ Pink Sheets
- ✓ Principal
- ✓ Registered representative
- ✓ Riskless trade
- ✓ Rules of Fair Practice (Conduct Rules)
- ✓ Simplified arbitration
- ✓ Small Order Execution System (SOES)
- ✓ Spread
- ✓ Subject quote
- ✓ Uniform Practice Code
- ✓ Workout quote

Concepts You Need to Understand

- ✓ How the OTC market works
- ✓ Similarities and differences between the OTC market and the major exchanges
- ✓ The National Association of Securities Dealers
- ✓ Different types and categories of stocks traded over the counter
- ✓ How stocks are offered and traded
- ✓ Computer systems that track and deal stocks over the counter
- ✓ The roles of agents and principals
- ✓ NASD bylaws
- ✓ Dos and don'ts regarding trading in OTC stocks
- ✓ Procedures for arbitration and resolving complaints
- ✓ Penny stocks and their misuses

The Over-the-Counter Market

Historically, the term "over-the-counter" identified all stocks not traded on the floor of an exchange in the United States—particularly that of the New York Stock Exchange. Perhaps more importantly, the term refers to a method of trading stocks. The over-the-counter (OTC) marketplace is a negotiated market, as opposed to an auction market such as the NYSE. The OTC market consists of several submarkets. NASDAQ, which is run by the National Association of Securities Dealers (NASD), serves each of these submarkets in some capacity. This chapter discusses the differences between dealer and auction markets, the various submarkets within the OTC market, NASDAQ's structure and role in those submarkets, and how stock transactions are conducted over the counter.

The over-the-counter-market, usually referred to as the OTC market, is a catch-all term for upwards of 10,000 stocks—as well as other types of securities—and the manner in which they are traded. OTC securities are not listed or traded on any securities exchanges. Whereas exchanges deal primarily in stocks and options, the OTC market offers corporate, government, agency, and municipal bonds, in addition to stocks. The primary distinguishing characteristic between the over-the-counter market and an exchange like the New York Stock Exchange is the manner in which trades are executed.

The OTC market is a *negotiated* (or *dealer*) *market*, whereas floor exchanges are auction markets. Recall that at the NYSE, prices are established by a competitive bidding and offering process between brokers. In contrast, over-the-counter trades are negotiated one-on-one between two dealers, one of whom is a market maker in that security.

Like specialists at a stock exchange, market makers are dealers who "make a market" for a certain company's stock or a type of bond. A market maker is always willing to buy or sell that particular company's stock. Unlike exchange-listed stocks, which have only one specialist, OTC-listed stocks can have multiple market makers. A typical over-the-counter stock will have about 10 market makers. The result is a system with less centralization and more flexibility.

Over-the-counter trades take place anywhere a broker or dealer has access to a telephone or computer. Whereas stock exchanges have a physical space, a "floor" on which business is transacted, the OTC market does not. Instead, it is a network of computers and telephones through which securities are bought and sold. In a sense, the over-the-counter market was a "virtual marketplace" long before the Internet made that term common. Although the OTC market lacks a trading floor, it is highly structured and firmly regulated.

The National Association of Securities Dealers (NASD) writes and enforces the rules governing OTC securities. To conduct business OTC, a broker or dealer must be a member of the NASD.

A dealer becomes an NASD member by agreeing to follow the NASD bylaws outlined later in this chapter. All representatives of an NASD company must be registered under the NASD Code of Registration. The NASD further distinguishes between the roles played by principals and registered representatives of member firms. *Principals* are those individuals who manage the member firm's business, whereas *registered representatives* are the ones responsible for soliciting and conducting that business, as well as training other employees who do so. Principals must not only have a Series 7 license, but must also be licensed as managers or supervisors under Series 24. Finally, NASD member firms must have supervisory personnel (who are also registered representatives) to make certain that branch offices keep appropriate records, review orders entered by account executives, approve new customer accounts, and record and follow up on complaints against the firm.

Historically, the OTC market has differentiated itself from the nation's exchanges by the types of companies whose stocks are traded over the counter.

In the past, most companies whose stocks traded over the counter were small start-up companies that hoped to grow large enough to eventually earn a listing on the NYSE or one of the other exchanges across the United States. Their lack of size and prestige as well as the OTC market's status as a negotiated marketplace led to a negative public perception of the OTC market. Over-the-counter securities were in some ways viewed as inferior to those listed on an exchange. Recently, however, many large blue-chip companies have chosen to maintain their OTC listing despite being able to qualify for an NYSE listing. Microsoft and Intel, for instance, currently trade over the counter.

Some companies feel that the OTC market's decentralized trading system benefits their stocks more than an exchange's auction system does, so they keep an OTC listing. There is also something to be said for being a large fish in a small pond. With the exception of the occasional Microsoft or Intel, the largest OTC companies do not necessarily stand out among those listed on the NYSE.

Any company that issues stock is eligible to be traded over the counter. There are, however, different categories of stock, or submarkets, within the larger over-the-counter marketplace. These submarkets have different requirements for listings.

Submarkets in the OTC Marketplace

The more than 10,000 stocks that trade over the counter belong to one of three submarkets:

- NASDAQ's National Market System (about 2,500 stocks)
- NASDAQ's SmallCap Market (about 3,000 stocks)
- Pink Sheets or OTC Bulletin Board market (about 4,500 stocks)

NASDAQ

NASDAQ (National Association of Securities Dealers Automated Quotations System) began as a computerized system for carrying price quotes on over-the-counter securities. It is a subsidiary of the NASD and, as such, is governed by that organization. In the mid to late 1990s, NASDAQ began to reposition itself as a securities market unto itself, not merely a quotation service. In fact, NASDAQ commonly refers to the National Market System and the SmallCap Market as forming what it calls the *NASDAQ Stock Market.* Clearly, this distinction is intended to present NASDAQ as a serious challenger to the NYSE for company listings.

The National Association of Securities Dealers Automated Quotations System is a computerized system established by the NASD for brokers/dealers to trade on over-the-counter stocks and some listed stocks. Unlike the Amex and the NYSE, the NASDAQ does not have a physical trading floor nor does it employ market specialists. All trading on the NASDAQ exchange is done over a network of computers and telephones. Orders for stocks are sent out and transactions are executed electronically.

NASDAQ's *National Market System (NMS)* provides a market for the stocks of the approximately 2,500 largest OTC-listed companies, including such giants as Microsoft. Although NASDAQ offers several options for qualifying for the NMS, the basic requirements are:

- Net tangible assets of more than $6 million
- Total assets and total revenue of $75 million each
- Pretax income of at least $1 million
- Total market value of outstanding stock of more than $8 million
- Minimum of 1.1 million outstanding shares
- Minimum of 400 shareholders with a minimum of 100 shares each
- At least three market makers in the corporation's stock
- Minimum bid price of $5

The NASDAQ SmallCap Market

Another 3,000 or so over-the-counter stocks are listed on NASDAQ's *SmallCap Market*. Companies traded on the SmallCap Market are smaller than those traded on the NMS, thus the listing requirements are less stringent:

- Net tangible assets of more than $4 million
- Net income of at least $750,000
- Total market value of outstanding stock of more than $5 million
- Minimum of one million outstanding shares
- Minimum of 300 shareholders with a minimum of 100 shares each
- At least three market makers in the company's stock
- Minimum bid price of $4

The Pink Sheets Market

The Pink Sheets market is named for the National Quotation Bureau's *Pink Sheets,* a daily publication of dealer quotations for non-NASDAQ OTC stocks.

The Pink Sheets are named for the color of the paper on which they are printed. Pink Sheet stocks—which currently number about 4,500—attract less interest than those on the NMS and SmallCap Market. Included in the Pink Sheets market are so-called penny stocks, which have very low bid prices and are considered highly speculative. Quotations for Pink Sheet stocks are also carried on the *OTC Bulletin Board,* a computerized system which is operated by NASDAQ.

Despite the existence of three submarkets in the OTC market, all over-the-counter trading is conducted in similar fashion, which differs markedly from trading on the floors of the securities exchanges.

The OTC Trading Process

The over-the-counter marketplace is a dealer, or negotiated, market because trades are negotiated one-on-one by broker-dealers and market makers—via telephone or computer. Unlike the auctions that take place at exchanges, there is no competitive bidding process between brokers. Moreover, OTC stocks have multiple market makers, as opposed to one specialist at an exchange.

Any firm can become a market maker in a particular stock, if it is willing to commit the funds and resources to do so. Dealers simply have to meet the capital requirements and promise to buy and sell their chosen stock as the market dictates. They also need to register with the NASD.

Market makers supply bid and ask quotes for the stock(s) they deal in. Other firms contact them and make transactions based on these listed prices.

Market makers are independent of each other, so they can quote their own bids and asks. This is where, claim its supporters, the negotiated market can outperform its auction house competitors. Brokers, acting on behalf of their clients, and dealers, trading for their own accounts, are always on the lookout for the best possible price. Because they can buy from or sell to different market makers, the market makers are under constant pressure to improve their quotes, narrowing their spreads. The narrower the spread, the more efficient the market.

Quotations for Pink Sheet stocks, along with the name and telephone number of their market makers, appear either in the daily Pink Sheets or on the OTC Bulletin Board. The latter gives the same information as the Pink Sheets, but in electronic form, and is updated by market makers. The Bulletin Board's gaining popularity might eventually make the Pink Sheets obsolete.

NASDAQ stock quotes, on the other hand, appear on NASDAQ's three-level computerized system. Subscriptions to the system are available only to traders and brokers at NASD-member firms.

Level One of the NASDAQ System

Level One of the NASDAQ system provides the least amount of information and is used by brokers solely to get the highest bid price and the lowest ask price offered by the market makers in a particular stock. This is called the *inside market.* Level One, however, does not identify the market makers. In the initial stages of a transaction, neither the broker nor the customer need to know which dealers act as market makers in the stock.

> **EXAMPLE:** Brooks Palmer wishes to buy stock in Oriole Industrials. Mr. Palmer visits a branch office of Ace Securities and talks to a broker, who brings up the Level One screen. The Level One screen displays the following:

Oriole Industrials 11.50 .62

So, if Mr. Palmer wishes to buy Oriole Industrials, the most favorable price he can obtain is 11.62. If Mr. Palmer decides to purchase the stock at that price, the Ace broker will send an order ticket to the brokerage's OTC trader, who has access to Level Two.

Level Two of the NASDAQ System

Level Two identifies the market makers and provides their bid and ask prices. Access to Level Two is generally limited to OTC traders at NASD member firms.

A typical Level Two screen offers the information shown in Table 13.1.

Table 13.1 A Typical NASDAQ Level Two Screen

Oriole Industrials		
Market Makers	**Bid**	**Ask**
Angel Securities	11.375	.75
Twin Investments	11.25	.62
Ranger Portfolios	11.50	.75
Jay Securities	11.37	.87

From this list, it's apparent that the highest bid price is Ranger Portfolios' 11.50 and the lowest ask price is Twin Investments' 11.62. Remember, some of the larger NASDAQ companies have many more than four market makers, whereas some smaller NASDAQ-listed stocks have only two. Although a company's stock must have three market makers for the company to be listed on NASDAQ, only two market makers are required for the company to maintain its listing.

Level Three of the NASDAQ System

Level Three is open only to market makers in a particular stock. It enables market makers to enter new quotes as market conditions change. The new quotes appear on Levels One and Two.

Executing OTC Trades

A trader at an OTC brokerage contacts the market maker it wants to deal with, and then, negotiates the transaction at an agreed-upon price and number of shares. For small numbers of shares—under 1,000—NASDAQ uses an automated system called the *Small Order Execution System (SOES)*. Simply by touching the computer screen in response to various prompts, the trader can complete the deal with a market maker. Larger orders must be confirmed by telephone. In either case, the seller must report the deal to NASD within 90 seconds.

> **EXAMPLE:** Mr. Palmer decides to purchase 100 shares of Oriole Industries. Ace's OTC trader could contact Twin Investments and strike a deal to buy the stock at 11.62. Rather than carry out the negotiation person-to-person, however, the Ace trader quickly uses SOES before the market moves away from the customer's desired price.

Market makers must honor their bid and ask quotes on the NASDAQ system—the "firm quote rule." The situation is somewhat different with Pink Sheets quotations. Because quotes cannot be instantly updated, *Pink Sheet* quotations must be confirmed with the market maker by the broker.

Quoted prices aren't good for any number of shares, but market makers must agree to sell a certain number of shares of the security when posting their bid and ask prices. For NASDAQ NMS stocks, these numbers vary according to the trading volume of the stock being traded, as shown here:

Average Daily Trading Volume	Minimum Shares/Quote
More than 3,000 shares	1,000
1,000–3,000 shares	500
Fewer than 1,000 shares	200

Although some exceptions exist, the minimum quote size for NASDAQ SmallCap Market stocks is 500 shares. Pink Sheet quotations are for a minimum of 100 shares.

> **EXAMPLE:** Mariner Seafood Restaurants is an NMS stock whose average daily trading volume is about 1,600 shares. A market maker in Mariner Seafood quotes a bid price of 9.87. The securities firm is required to buy at least 500 shares of Mariner Seafood from any individual buyer at 9.87.

As an exception to the "firm quote rule," dealers sometimes offer either subject quotes or workout quotes, neither of which commits the dealer to buying or selling at the quoted price. A dealer who is not a market maker in a stock can offer a *subject quote* on that stock. This means that the quote is good "subject to" confirmation or negotiation with the market maker. If a dealer is contacted about buying or selling a given amount of a particular stock and has a client who has already expressed interest in the opposite side of such a transaction, the dealer offers a *workout quote*, which is pending a check to determine whether the client is still interested. Dealers must always state when they are providing a subject or workout quote.

Finally, sometimes dealers actually seek quotes from prospective sellers and buyers. When a dealer decides to sell, he or she can ask a potential buyer to suggest a price—this is known as a *bid wanted (BW)*. An *offer wanted (OW)* arises when a dealer asks a possible seller for a price.

Making Money from Trading

Market makers profit from the spread between their bid and ask prices. Specifically, broker-dealers earn money in three distinct ways: markups, markdowns, and commissions. Which of these fees they actually earn depends on the position of the dealer within the trade and on the type of trade.

A firm that buys stock for or sells stock from its own inventory is the *principal* in the transaction. Principals can charge a *markup* when they sell securities. Just as a retail store adds a profit margin to every item it sells, dealers add a markup to every share of stock they sell from inventory.

> **EXAMPLE:** Carlton Williams wants to purchase stock in Fenway Wallpapers, Inc. His brokerage house has some of the Fenway stock in its inventory, for which it is quoting 4.62. When Mr. Williams purchases the stock, the final price is 4.75 (4.62 plus .12 markup). Notice that the inside market price of 4.62 is applicable only to other NASD firms, not to the general public.

When a client buys an over-the-counter stock directly from a principal, the markup is reported on the confirmation given to the customer.

Markdowns

Markdowns are the dealer firm's margin of profit when buying stock for its inventory.

> **EXAMPLE:** Cardinal Securities is a market maker for Big Red Heating and Cooling (BRHC). Cardinal Securities offers a bid price of 9.87 for BRHC stock on the NASDAQ system. Audrey Concepcion wants to sell her Big Red stock directly to Cardinal. Because Cardinal charges a markdown of a .12, it pays Ms. Concepcion 9.25 (9.87 – .12 markdown) for each share of Big Red she sells to Cardinal.

The Commissions Process

Commissions are earned by broker-dealers who bring trades to a market maker.

Besides buying and selling stocks for investors, brokers and dealers engage in a wide variety of other transactions in the OTC market, some of which have specific names.

Broker-dealers execute the following transactions:

- A broker-dealer performs a *riskless trade* when it buys a stock into its inventory and then sells it immediately to a customer at a profit.
- A *crossed trade* arises when a broker has a customer who wants to sell a certain amount of a particular stock, and another who wants to buy the same amount of the same stock. The dealer buys the first customer's shares (earning a commission) and then sells them to the second customer (earning another commission). Crossed trades must be executed at the prevailing market price.
- A *dual agency transaction* refers to a trade in which a customer directs a broker to sell one stock and use the proceeds to buy another. Again, because there are two separate transactions, the dealer earns two commissions.
- A broker-dealer engages in an *arbitrage trade* when it takes advantage of a negative spread between the ask quote of one market maker and the bid quote of another. Ask quotes are normally higher than bid quotes. With transactions taking place as rapidly as they do on NASDAQ, however, it is possible that one market maker's ask price might actually be lower than another's bid price. An astute broker-dealer can profit from the difference: buying at the lower ask price and immediately selling at the higher bid price. Arbitrage trades are only possible with securities that have sufficient liquidity to enable the broker-dealer to buy and sell quickly.

As mentioned, NASD serves two functions in the OTC market, facilitating transactions and regulating participants in those transactions. In fact, NASD essentially has two operating arms: the NASDAQ Stock Market, which includes the NMS and the SmallCap Market; and NASD Regulation, Inc., which writes and enforces the rules that govern over-the-counter trading.

Rules and Regulations for OTC Trading

When the Securities Exchange Act was passed in 1934, it did not cover over-the-counter trading. As part of its Depression-era initiative to regulate the securities industry, Congress passed the Maloney Act in 1938, establishing rules for the OTC market. With the Maloney Act, Congress chose not to put the OTC market under the direct control of the SEC, but instead opted for self-regulation. The following year, broker-dealers formed the NASD to implement this policy.

The NASD governs the OTC market through a series of rules and regulations known as the NASD bylaws. These bylaws pertain primarily to ethics and procedures, and are divided into four categories:

- Uniform Practice Code
- Rules of Fair Practice (or Conduct Rules)
- Code of Procedure
- Code of Arbitration

Uniform Practice Code

The *Uniform Practice Code* covers business dealings between member firms, with the purpose of ensuring that all such business is handled in an orderly fashion. The Uniform Practice Code covers all transactions for nonexempt securities between NASD member firms.

Rules of Fair Practice

The *Rules of Fair Practice* (*Conduct Rules*) govern the dealings of member firms with their customers, calling for high standards of integrity and honesty among NASD members. Conduct Rules require, for example, that a broker know the investment background, capacity, and goals of his or her customers. The rules also demand that dealers not tolerate dishonest conduct by other dealers. Finally, the rules also establish guidelines for how much dealers can charge for markups, markdowns, and commissions.

Perhaps the most important element of the Conduct Rules is the requirement that each member firm effectively monitor and supervise its personnel. This is the responsibility of the firm's *office of supervisory jurisdiction (OSJ)*. In each OSJ, a principal of the firm, who must be licensed under Series 24, is responsible for ensuring that proper procedures are followed by the firm's registered representatives and other employees. An OSJ can oversee the operations of a number of the brokerage's branch offices, or, if the firm is relatively small, the OSJ can simply be the firm's main office, with one principal in charge of supervising the firm's compliance with securities rules. Each OSJ establishes and enforces the firm's written procedures regarding all applicable securities laws and regulations.

The best-known example of other acts covered by fair practice is probably the NASD's 5% policy, which states that member firms need to aim for a 5% markup or commission on transactions. Note, however, that this is a guideline, not a strict rule. The NASD recognizes that exceptions arise and that a dealer's markup is influenced by the type of security, the availability and price of the security, and the size of the transaction. The following instances can justify a higher markup:

- Trades of very small numbers of shares
- Stocks with very low share prices
- Stocks that are not actively traded

The NASD also states that the 5% markup be based on a security's current market value, not on the dealer's cost. Obviously, this can work either for or against a dealer, depending on how prices have moved since the dealer purchased the security.

Member firms must make every effort to secure the best possible price for their customers, chiefly by identifying the inside market. Nevertheless, broker-dealers can consider the following when determining the "best" price:

- Current market for the stock
- Size of the transaction
- Number of market makers a dealer has contacted
- Difficulty of executing the transaction

As established by the Rules of Fair Practice, dealers are expressly forbidden from engaging in the following activities:

- *Interpositioning*—A broker is guilty of interpositioning when he or she needlessly places another broker in the transaction chain, thereby increasing the customer's fees unfairly.
- *Front running*—Front running occurs when a broker-dealer trades stock for its own inventory despite holding a customer order for the same amount of the stock. Customer orders always take precedence over the firm's transactions for its account.

- *Acting as broker and dealer on the same trade*—A brokerage can act as either principal or agent on a trade, but not both. This is similar to the prohibition on interpositioning, because it forbids dealers from double-charging (earning both a markup and a commission) on the same transaction.

Remember that a brokerage can act as either principal or agent on a trade.

- *Backing away*—A broker-dealer backs away when it fails to honor a firm price quote. Brokers must specifically state when they are offering subject or workout quotes, as opposed to firm quotes.

The Code of Procedure outlines the NASD's disciplinary procedures with regard to member firms and their employees. The Code of Procedure guides the NASD's District Business Conduct Committees (DBCC) in hearing and adjudicating complaints filed between member firms and complaints against member firms from customers. Brokerage firm clients who feel they have been treated unfairly, in violation of the NASD Rules of Fair Practice, can enter formal complaints with the DBCC in their locality. (The NASD is divided into 15 districts covering different regions of the country.)

Complaints must be made in writing to the local DBCC, which has the power to penalize a firm or to dismiss the complaint. DBCC decisions are not necessarily final. Respondents (the member firms named in complaints) can appeal DBCC rulings to the NASD National Adjudicatory Council, which can affirm or reverse the decision and increase or reduce any penalties. Even then, respondents have recourse to two more venues for appeals: the SEC and the federal courts.

The Code of Procedures allows for censures, fines, and suspensions or expulsions from the NASD. Suspensions and expulsions are used against entire firms or against individuals connected with those firms—depending on which rules and procedures have been violated.

Not all disputes in the OTC marketplace are so severe; many can be resolved more cheaply and informally through arbitration. The NASD has developed a special Code of Arbitration for these cases.

The *Code of Arbitration* establishes rules for arbitrating disputes between firms and customers, or between firms. Member firms can bring customers to arbitration, but only when the customer has given prior written consent.

Disputes covered by the Code of Arbitration do not involve rules violations, but focus instead on monetary disputes. Such disagreements are brought before the *National Arbitration Committee*, which provides three arbitrators to hear the case. When less than $10,000 is at stake, customers employ *simplified arbitration*, which uses only one arbitrator.

One more set of regulations, which are not part of the NASD bylaws, apply uniquely to broker-dealers in the OTC market: the SEC's rules pertaining to the solicitation and processing of transactions involving *penny stocks*, which are securities whose market value generally does not exceed $5 a share. Most penny stocks are issued by companies new to the market, with a short or spotty history of revenue and earnings. Thus, buying a penny stock is a highly speculative venture. Penny stock quotations are found either in the *Pink Sheets* or on the OTC Bulletin Board.

From market makers to markdowns, from the National Market System to the SmallCap Market, from firm bids to workout quotes, from Conduct Rules to the Uniform Practice Code—the OTC world is indeed vast and complex. Soon it might become even bigger and more complicated.

Exam Prep Questions

1. The publication that reports quotes for non-NASDAQ OTC securities each day is called what?
   - ❑ A. The Financial Times
   - ❑ B. The OTC Bulletin Board
   - ❑ C. The Pink Sheets
   - ❑ D. The Blue List

2. Which facilities of the NASDAQ system do NASD traders use?

   I. Level One

   II. Level Two

   III. Level Three

   IV. SOES
   - ❑ A. II and IV
   - ❑ B. I and IV
   - ❑ C. I, II, and III
   - ❑ D. II and III

3. Paul Westworld wants to purchase 50 shares of Redford Banking (REDB), a NASDAQ-listed security, at 15.12. To find the inside market for REDB, Westworld's broker uses the:
   - ❑ A. Pink Sheets firm quote
   - ❑ B. Small Order Execution System (SOES)
   - ❑ C. NASDAQ system Level One
   - ❑ D. OTC Bulletin Board

4. Chaotic Industries has a daily trading volume of 5,000 shares on the NASDAQ National Market System. Market makers posting bid and ask prices for Chaotic must be willing to buy or sell, at these prices, a minimum of:
   - ❑ A. 100 shares
   - ❑ B. 200 shares
   - ❑ C. 500 shares
   - ❑ D. 1,000 shares

5. How does a riskless trade occur in the OTC market?
   - ❑ A. A broker-dealer sells stock from its own inventory to a customer.
   - ❑ B. A broker-dealer buys stock for its own inventory, and then sells it immediately to a customer at a profit.
   - ❑ C. A customer goes short against the box.
   - ❑ D. A customer purchases a married put along with a stock.

6. Charlene Clement, an OTC broker, receives an order from Peter Rocke to sell 100 shares of Big Red stock, and a second order from Paula Oldman to buy 100 shares of Big Red. If she crosses the orders, what will she earn on the trade?
   - ❑ A. Nothing, because the NASD prohibits crossed trades for OTC securities.
   - ❑ B. She will earn a single cross-trade commission.
   - ❑ C. She will earn two commissions, one from each customer.
   - ❑ D. She will earn a dual-agency markup.

7. The NASD bylaws include which of the following?

   I. Uniform Practice Code

   II. Net Capital Rule

   III. Code of Procedure

   IV. Customer Protection Rule
   - ❑ A. I
   - ❑ B. II and IV
   - ❑ C. III and IV
   - ❑ D. I and III

8. The section of the NASD bylaws that governs the dealings of member firms with their customers is the:
   - ❑ A. Customer Protection Rule
   - ❑ B. Code of Procedure
   - ❑ C. Rules of Fair Practice
   - ❑ D. Uniform Practice Code

9. Dealers on the OTC market charge a markdown when they:
   - ❑ A. Want to move hard-to-sell securities
   - ❑ B. Sell Pink Sheets securities
   - ❑ C. Buy stock for their inventory
   - ❑ D. Sell stock from their inventory

10. NASD-member firm Ace Securities buys 30 shares of Greenwater Properties for its customer Charles Smith. What facts can Ace use to justify charging Smith a commission of 10%?

    I. Smith purchased an odd lot.

    II. Ace had to contact an unusually large number of market makers to find an ask.

    III. Greenwater was selling for $2 a share.

    IV. Ace had difficulty obtaining the stock because Greenwater is not widely available.

- ❑ A. I
- ❑ B. I and III
- ❑ C. II and IV
- ❑ D. I, II, III, and IV

11. Broker Herbert Dannemayer receives an order from a customer to buy 1,000 shares of California Fruits and Nuts. Although he can purchase the shares directly from the market maker, he instead calls fellow broker Lily LaMarr, a personal friend, and asks her to buy the shares from the market maker and then sell them to him. Dannemayer is guilty of:
    - ❑ A. Reclamation
    - ❑ B. Interpositioning
    - ❑ C. Front running
    - ❑ D. Marking to the market

12. Claire Eauclaire files a complaint of front running against Diamondback Brokerage with her District Business Conduct Committee. The DBCC can respond to Eauclaire's complaint in any of the following manners except:
    - ❑ A. By acting as legal counsel for Eauclaire in civil court
    - ❑ B. By fining Diamondback
    - ❑ C. By dismissing Eauclaire's complaint as unwarranted
    - ❑ D. By expelling Diamondback from the NASD

13. Joan Neumann believes that her Ace Securities broker, Herbert Dannemayer, has defrauded her of $11,000. The quickest way for her to resolve this dispute is to:
    - ❑ A. Submit it to simplified arbitration
    - ❑ B. Submit it to the National Arbitration Committee
    - ❑ C. File a complaint against Dannemayer in civil court
    - ❑ D. File a complaint against Ace with the Better Business Bureau

14. OTC broker-dealer Atlas Securities suggests that customer Uschi Schwarz purchase 1,000 shares of TinyMinds at $3.38. Before Atlas can execute the trade, Schwarz must sign which of the following?

    I. Suitability form

    II. Margin agreement

    III. Hypothecation agreement

    IV. Broker loan agreement

    - ❑ A. I
    - ❑ B. II
    - ❑ C. II, III, and IV
    - ❑ D. I and III

15. The NASDAQ Level 1 screen shows which of the following information?

I. Dealer quotes

II. The highest bid and lowest ask

III. The lowest bid and highest ask

IV. The same as Level II except for the quote changeability

- ❑ A. I only
- ❑ B. II only
- ❑ C. II & III
- ❑ D. IV only

Exam Prep Answers

1. The correct answer is C. The National Quotation Bureau publishes the Pink Sheets, which contains daily dealer quotations for non-NASDAQ OTC stocks. NASDAQ's OTC Bulletin Board carries the same quotes electronically.
2. The correct answer is A. Traders use Level Two, which lists the market makers and their individual bid and ask prices, and SOES, through which they execute trades for fewer than 1,000 shares.
3. The correct answer is C. Brokers find the best quote for a NASDAQ-listed stock on NASDAQ system Level One.
4. The correct answer is D. Market makers for NASDAQ NMS stocks with a daily trading volume of more than 3,000 shares must agree to buy or sell at least 1,000 shares at their quoted prices. For securities with a daily trading volume of 1,000 to 3,000 shares, they must agree to buy or sell at least 500 shares; for securities with a volume of fewer than 1,000 shares, the minimum is 200 shares.
5. The correct answer is B. A broker-dealer performs a riskless trade when it buys stock for its own inventory and then sells it immediately to a customer at a profit.
6. The correct answer is C. Clement earns one commission buying the stock and a second one reselling it. The NASD permits brokers to execute such trades only at the prevailing market price.
7. The correct answer is D. The NASD bylaws include four categories of rules and regulations. The Uniform Practice Code covers dealings between member firms. The Code of Procedure outlines NASD's disciplinary procedures for member firms and their employees. Also, the Rules of Fair Practice (or Conduct Rules) govern the dealings of member firms with their customers, and the Code of Arbitration establishes rules for arbitrating disputes between firms, or between firms and their customers.
8. The correct answer is C. The Rules of Fair Practice govern the dealings of member firms with their customers. The rules require that brokers "know their customer," establish guidelines for customer fees, and also require that each member firm effectively monitor and supervise its personnel.
9. The correct answer is C. Dealers earn profits through markdowns when buying stock for their inventories. For instance, a firm seeking a stock for inventory might offer a customer the current market price of 18, but actually pay the customer only 17.75, using the .25 markdown as its profit on the trade.

10. The correct answer is D. A dealer can justify an unusually high commission if a security is illiquid or not widely available, or if a transaction occurs at a low price or at a small volume. The NASD's 5% policy provides a guideline for fair practice, stating that members charge a 5% markup or commission on most transactions.
11. The correct answer is B. A broker is guilty of interpositioning when he or she needlessly places another broker in the transaction chain, thereby increasing the customer's fees.
12. The correct answer is A. After a full investigation, the District Business Conduct Committee of the NASD has the power to dismiss Eauclaire's complaint against Diamondback or to penalize the firm. Potential penalties include censure, fines, and suspension or expulsion from the NASD. DBCCs do not act as legal counsel for member firms or customers.
13. The correct answer is B. Customers and member firms use the NASD Code of Arbitration to resolve monetary disputes. Neumann needs to submit her claim of fraud to the National Arbitration Committee. (If her claim is under $10,000, it goes to simplified arbitration.)
14. The correct answer is A. Penny stocks are highly speculative investments, so the SEC has imposed special requirements on penny stock dealers. Customers must sign a written suitability form, and dealers must approve customers as suitable for this high-risk investment—based on the customer's investment goals and financial status—before executing any penny stock orders.
15. The correct answer is B. The NASDAQ Level I screen shows the highest bid price and the lowest ask price. Dealer quotes appear on the Level II screen and the capability to change quotes is on the Level III screen.

PART V
Options

Call Options

Terms You Need to Know

- ✓ At the money
- ✓ Breakeven point
- ✓ Call option
- ✓ Closing purchase
- ✓ Closing sale
- ✓ Covered call writer
- ✓ Derivative
- ✓ Exercise
- ✓ Holder
- ✓ In the money
- ✓ Intrinsic value
- ✓ Long position (or simply long)
- ✓ Open interest
- ✓ Opening position
- ✓ Opening purchase
- ✓ Opening sale
- ✓ Option
- ✓ Options Clearing Corporation (OCC)
- ✓ Out of the money
- ✓ Premium
- ✓ Put option
- ✓ Short position (or simply short)
- ✓ Strike price (or exercise price)
- ✓ Time value
- ✓ Uncovered call writer (or naked writer)
- ✓ Underlying security
- ✓ Writer

Concepts You Need to Understand

- ✓ How call options work
- ✓ How the holder's point of view differs from that of the writer
- ✓ Which terms define a call option contract
- ✓ How and why premiums change
- ✓ How the intrinsic and time values define the premium
- ✓ When call options are in the money, at the money, and out of the money
- ✓ What holders and writers of call options stand to gain or lose
- ✓ How holders and writers open and close their positions
- ✓ What open interest is

Options

In addition to trading stocks, bonds, and other financial instruments, sophisticated investors can make money by buying and selling the *option* to trade securities before a specific date and at a specific price. Options have become an increasingly important and complicated "derivative" security in the past 15 years. With options, investors are betting that an underlying security will move in a certain direction, or they are protecting themselves from losses on other investments. This chapter and the next describe the basics of equity options by explaining *calls* (the option to buy) and *puts* (the option to sell). Chapters 18 through 20 will describe the rules of options trading and some common strategies, and Chapters 21 through 23 will introduce options based on stock indexes, interest rates, and foreign currencies.

An *option* is the right to buy or sell a number of shares of a security at a fixed price at any time until a certain date. It is a legal and binding agreement between the seller of the option, known as the *writer*, and the buyer of the option, known as the *holder*, in which the holder pays a premium to the seller in return for control over the security for a limited time. Rather than trading the shares outright, the holder is purchasing the *option* to trade them. (Note that all rights conferred by stock ownership remain with the registered owner until the security changes hands. Chapter 17 covers the consequences of dividends and stock splits on option contracts.) Options are divided into two basic types. *Call options* give holders the right to *buy* the security at the specified price (and require the writer to sell at that price), whereas *put options* give holders the right to *sell* the security at the specified price (and require the writer to buy them for the same price). In order to avoid confusion, puts and calls are introduced separately—this chapter only discusses call options. The next chapter deals with put options.

Compared to other securities, options are a strange breed. Rather than representing partial ownership in a corporation—as an equity security does—or a creditor relationship—as do bonds—an option sets the terms of a contract about a *possible* future transaction involving an underlying security. Because the value of the option depends upon, or is derived from, the value of that underlying security, options are called *derivatives*.

How Options Work

A call option gives the holder the right to *purchase* a certain number of shares of an underlying security at a fixed price. It is termed a "call" because the holder can "call in" the stock from the writer. The writer is obligated to sell the stock to the holder at the agreed-upon price. When the holder makes use of the right granted by the option, he or she *exercises* the option. If, for example, a call option gives the holder the right to buy 100 shares of stock for $65, the holder can exercise this option by paying $6,500 to the writer. The holder can choose to do this at any time before the expiration of the option—or can choose not to exercise the option at all. Note that only the holder can exercise the option; the writer has no choice in the matter. Remember that the holder controls the shares of stock covered by the option, and not the writer (seller). In simplest terms, a call option is a bet between the holder (buyer) and the writer (seller). The holder is betting that the market price will go up (bullish). If that happens, the holder can buy the stock at the specified price and then make money by reselling it at the higher, market price. The *writer* of a call, on the other hand, is betting that the market price will stay roughly the same or decline (bearish). In that case, the option will not be exercised. The seller keeps the money he or she earned by writing the option without having to sell any stock.

EXAMPLE: Stella believes that the price of Acme stock will rise in the next three months, whereas Joseph believes that it will decline. Currently, Acme is trading at $48. Stella buys a call option from Joseph, giving her the right to purchase 100 shares of Acme at $50 per share any time in the next three months. She pays Joseph a premium of $200 for this option. One month later the price of Acme has risen to $54. With her option, Stella can now buy 100 shares of Acme stock from Joseph at $50 and sell it for $54. If the market price of Acme had instead dropped to $47, Stella simply would not have exercised the option.

(In practice, option investors rarely transfer shares of the underlying security, but rather just settle the difference between the security's current price and the option's strike price.)

Information on an Option Contract

An option contract includes all the essential facts, which can be described in one succinct line, as explained in Table 14.1.

Table 14.1 Option Contract Information

Buy	**2**	**QVC**	**May**	**55**	**Calls**	**@ 3**
(Buy or sell)	(Number of contracts)	(Underlying security)	(Expiration month)	(Strike price)	(Type of option—call or put)	(Premium)

- Buy or sell: Whether the person placing the order wants to become a buyer (holder) or a seller (writer).
- Number of option contracts: For equity options, one contract covers 100 shares of stock. So in this example, the "2" means two contracts, or 200 shares of stock.
- Underlying security: The name of the company whose stock the option controls.
- Expiration month: The month the option expires.
- Strike price (or exercise price): The price at which the holder has the right to purchase the stock.
- Type of option: Call or put.
- Premium: The price the buyer must pay for the contract, expressed in dollars per share of the underlying security.

EXAMPLE: Sue places an order: Buy 2 QVC May 55 Calls @ 3. She is buying two option contracts of QVC stock, which gives her the right to purchase (call) 200 shares at $55 any time before the expiration date in May. Her total premium, or settlement amount, is $600 ($3 × 200 shares = $600).

Except for the premium, which rises and falls according to market forces, all these elements in an option contract are standardized and set by the Options Clearing Corporation (OCC). The only part of the option contract that changes is the premium.

How Options Are Traded

Options are traded by auction on exchanges, including some of the stock exchanges. Unlike stocks, however, options are not issued by individual companies. Ford Motor Company does not issue Ford options. Instead, the *Options Clearing Corporation (OCC)*, which is jointly owned by the exchanges and is regulated by the SEC, issues all options. The OCC sets the standardized terms of the options, including the expiration date, the strike price, and the initial premium. It then keeps track of buyers and sellers and guarantees that both parties meet their obligations. A more detailed description of this process and the rules of trading are described in Chapter 16.

Premiums: Intrinsic and Time Values

Option premiums change for the same reasons that the prices of other securities change. If a call option appears more valuable—that is, if the privilege of purchasing the underlying stock at the strike price seems like a better deal—people pay more for it, and the premium rises. If it appears less valuable, the premium falls. Thus the same option purchased on a different day can cost a different premium.

A premium is a combination of two components: the option's intrinsic value and its time value. Intrinsic value is the amount the holder stands to gain by exercising the option. It depends directly upon the price of the underlying stock. For example, a call option granting the right to purchase QVC stock at $55 will become quite attractive if the stock rises from $52 to $60, because it means the holder can buy at $55 and sell at $60. This $5 difference is defined as the option's intrinsic value. If QVC stock fails to pass the $55 threshold, the option never acquires any intrinsic value.

> **EXAMPLE:** Mark is happy with the options he bought last week—8 QVC Nov 55 Calls @ 2. The stock's market price has risen to $59, meaning that Mark can gain $4 per share if he exercises his option now. Instead he decides to buy the same option on another 800 shares of QVC. But the option's premium has increased to reflect the higher market value of the underlying stock. Mark now purchases 8 QVC Nov 55 Calls @ 4.50. What part of the $4.50 premium represents intrinsic value? With QVC stock trading at $59, the intrinsic value equals $4 per share ($59 – $55 strike price). The remaining part of the premium (.50) is the option's time value.

An unexpired option always has time value. An option derives *time value* from the time left before its expiration—and what investors believe might happen to the underlying security during that period. An option expiring in eight months has more time value than the same option expiring in five months, because there is more time for the stock's price to change.

Behind intrinsic and time values are a whole host of economic and market factors, as well as investors' expectations about them. Options traders must pay especially close attention to the volatility and quality of the underlying stock: How healthy is the issuing company? How stable is its stock price?

How the Intrinsic Value of a Call Option Is Calculated

For a call option, the intrinsic value is the difference between the stock's market price and the option's strike price.

If the stock price is the same—or lower than—the strike price, the intrinsic value equals zero, because the holder cannot benefit from exercising the option.

EXAMPLE: Consider the option QVC Nov 55 Call. What happens if the share price QVC drops from $59 to $54? The stock price is now lower than the option's strike price. There is no advantage in exercising the option and purchasing the stock at $55 if it can be had on the market for $54. Thus the option has no intrinsic value.

How the Time Value of a Call Option Is Calculated

You can determine the time value from the premium. It is simply the portion of the premium that is not intrinsic value.

time value = premium – intrinsic value

EXAMPLE: The option RCE Dec 70 Call is trading for a premium of $3 per share, whereas Rice's stock is trading at $72. What is the option's time value? Because its intrinsic value is $2, its time value is $1 ($3 premium – $2 intrinsic value = $1 time value).

As an option nears expiration, its time value decreases because the underlying stock has less chance of experiencing significant price changes. Until expiration, however, even those options with no intrinsic value do retain some time value, although it might be as little as a few cents.

EXAMPLE: Sue holds one RCE Dec 70 Call. It is now late November, and Rice's stock has not moved above $68 for months. Sue's option has no intrinsic value. Nevertheless, she sees in the newspaper that the option still costs .75 per share—pure time value. Then Special Foods, Inc., makes tender offer to buy Rice Enterprises. Sue is in luck. Rice's share price soars to $79, whereas the premium for her option rises to $12. Not much time remains until the option's expiration, but its time value has in fact *risen* to $3 ($12 premium – $9 intrinsic value = $3 time value).

When Is a Call Option In the Money, At the Money, or Out of the Money?

A call option is *in the money* when it has intrinsic value, that is, when the market price of the stock is higher than the strike price of the option.

A call option is *at the money* when the stock's market price is the same as the option's strike price.

A call option is *out of the money* when the stock's market price is lower than the option's strike price.

These terms provide a clue as to whether the holder stands to gain from exercising the option, but they can be misleading. A call option in the money does not necessarily guarantee the holder a profit. Nor does an option at the money mean the holder will break even. Option traders must take into account the premium payment in order to determine how much they will gain or lose.

Potential Gains and Losses

The *breakeven point* is the point at which an investor neither makes nor loses money on an option trade. The threshold occurs at the point at which the holder's gains from exercising exactly equal the premium he or she paid. Thus, the breakeven point on a call occurs when the market price of the underlying stock equals the strike price plus the premium. It is important to note that the breakeven point is the same for the writer. When the price of the underlying stock equals the strike price plus the premium, the writer must sell the stock (if someone exercises the contract) for a loss equal to the amount he or she earned from the premium. Thus, at the breakeven point, all gains and losses balance out for *both* the holder and the writer.

breakeven point = strike price + premium

(This is the same for both the buyer and the seller.)

EXAMPLE: David holds the option, QVC Dec 55 Call @ 3. At first glance, it might seem that his breakeven point is $55. Remember, though, that David has paid $3 per share for his option. Thus, he cannot break even until QVC stock rises to $58, at which point he will make $300 ($58 – $55 = $3; $3 × 100 shares = $300), which exactly cancels out the $300 he paid for the option. Similarly, Margaret, the writer, earned $3 per share by selling the option. Her gain will disappear if David exercises when the stock price rises to $58.

How Much Can the Holder of a Call Gain Or Lose?

The holder of a call can make an unlimited amount of money, depending on how high the stock's market price moves. Take, for example, the option QVC Dec 55 Call @ 3. If QVC's stock goes to $59 (one point above the breakeven point of $58), the holder can earn $1 per share. If the stock rises to $78, the holder can make $20 per share. Theoretically, there is no limit on how much the holder can gain. On the other hand, the most that a holder of a call can *lose* is the premium paid.

How Much Can the Writer of a Call Gain Or Lose?

The most the writer of an uncovered call can gain is the premium received for selling the option. If the writer has bet correctly, and the stock price declines, or stays roughly the same, the holder will not exercise, and the writer keeps the premium without selling any stock. However, there is no limit to the amount an uncovered writer can lose. Remember the stock has no limit on how high it can go.

So, what is a covered and an uncovered call writer? A *covered call writer* already owns (is long) the shares of stock covered by the option. Thus, a writer of 5 RCE Mar 70 Calls @ 3 who owns 500 shares of Rice Enterprises stock is covered. If a holder decides to exercise the option, this writer can sell his or her shares rather than purchase them in the market at a loss.

The breakeven point for a covered-call writer depends on what he or she paid for the underlying stock:

breakeven point (covered writer) = cost of stock – premium

Similarly, the most a covered call writer can gain is the strike price of the option, plus the premium, minus the cost of the stock.

EXAMPLE: Diane owns 400 shares of Rice Enterprises, which she bought at $60 per share. Currently, the stock is trading around $68. She writes 4 RCE Mar 70 Calls @ 2. No matter how high the price of Rice stock rises, she can cover her position with her own 400 shares. She has earned $800 from the option premiums. What is Diane's breakeven point? Diane will break even if Rice stock dropped to $58 ($60 – $2), and she were then forced to sell. However, with this option, Diane has nothing to fear, because no holder will exercise if Rice stock stays at or below $70.

What is Diane's largest potential gain? The most she can gain is $12 per share ($70 + $2 – $60).

Does Diane have any risks with this option? She risks losing her Rice shares and potentially larger profits. Suppose the price of Rice stock increases to $76, and her option is exercised. She must sell her shares at the strike price of $70. Without the option, she could have enjoyed an additional $2,400 in appreciation on her long Rice stock position.

An *uncovered call writer* (or *naked writer*), by contrast, does not own the stock covered by the call. This is a risky position, because the writer's loss is theoretically unlimited. If the holder decides to exercise the option, the writer has to obtain the stock at its current market price. Because there is no limit to how high the market price can climb, there is no limit to the writer's potential loss.

EXAMPLE: Marianne has written 5 BAR Mar 35 Calls @ 4. When BAR stock unexpectedly soars to $84, Marianne is informed that her option has been exercised. Because Marianne is uncovered, she must now buy 500 shares of Barbecue Industries at $84 and sell them to the holder at $35. She loses $22,500 on the transaction ($84 – $39 breakeven = $45; $45 × 500 shares = $22,500 loss).

Writers—and holders—are not entirely at the mercy of the market. They can lock in profits or limit losses by buying or selling a second option to offset their first position. This is known as closing an open position.

Openings, Closings, and Open Interest

Buying or selling a new option contract is referred to as *opening a position*. The holder of the option is said to have opened a *long position* or to be *long*, whereas the writer of the option is said to have opened a *short position* or to be *short.* The holder opens a long position through an *opening purchase,* whereas the writer opens a short position through an *opening sale.*

Someone with a long position has three possible courses of action:

- Allow the option to expire without exercising it. The holder does this when the market price of the stock remains at or below the strike price.
- Exercise the option. The holder does this when the market price climbs above the strike price, particularly when the price then starts to fall or if the option will soon expire.
- Close the position with a *closing sale.* To do this, the holder switches roles, becoming a *writer* of the same option. By selling the same option at a higher premium, the investor can protect a profit.

  EXAMPLE: It is the first week of March and Mr. Smith holds 5 TFU Mar 70 Calls @ 1. Tofu, Inc., shares are trading at about $80. Most investors expect the stock to go even higher, and the option is now selling for a premium of $13. Mr. Smith, however, fears the market price will fall, and therefore he wants to close his position. If he exercises, he will earn $4,500 ($80 – $71 breakeven = $9; $9 × 500 = $4,500).

  Instead, he becomes a writer. For writing the same option (5 TFU Mar 70 Calls), he receives a premium of $13 per share or $6,500 total. Because Mr. Smith paid only $500 for his original options, he has effectively locked in a profit of $6,000. Now, suppose Tofu soars to $90. Mr. Smith might wish that he had waited longer to close out his position, but he will still have his $6,000 profit. Eventually, he will be forced to sell 500 shares at $70, but he holds an equivalent contract, entitling him to buy 500 shares at $70. The two contracts cancel each other out, and he simply pockets the difference between the premium he received and the one he paid.

A Closing Purchase

A *closing purchase* occurs when a writer closes (or reduces) a short position by purchasing the same option contract. Closing purchases work just like closing sales.

EXAMPLE: Peter is a writer of 3 QVC Mar 55 Calls @ 3. When QVC's stock rises to $63, Peter, who is uncovered, faces a loss of $1,500 ($63 – $58 breakeven = $5; $5 × 300 shares = $1,500). If the stock keeps rising, he will lose even more. As a writer, Peter has no control over when the option is exercised, and he is becoming nervous. He decides to protect himself from further loss. He buys the same option, 3 QVC Mar 55 Calls, which is now trading for a premium of $9. With this closing purchase, he has canceled out his original position, and limited his losses to $1,800 ($9 premium paid – $3 premium received = $6; $6 × 300 = $1,800).

Closing purchases can also be used to lock in profits.

EXAMPLE: Marianne has written 2 LTD Mar 55 Calls @ 5, earning $1,000 in premiums. Although the option is now out of the money, Marianne is concerned that the stock will rise. She wants to lock in her profit, so she makes a closing purchase. Today the option is trading at .50. How much has she made? She has guaranteed herself a profit of $900, no matter how much LTD stock rises before her option expires ($5 – $0.50 = $4.50; $4.50 × 200 = $900).

Because many holders and writers, over the life of an option, open and close their positions, traders want to make sure that there are plenty of open contracts left to provide market liquidity. They want to know what the open interest is on each available option contract.

Open Interest

Open interest measures liquidity—the number of contracts that have not yet expired, been exercised, or been closed out. The volume of options transactions gives one indication of the difficulty an investor might have finding a buyer or a seller, but the fundamental determinant is the open interest.

The greater the open interest, the easier it is to open and close positions.

Open interest changes in response to a variety of transactions.

- When a buyer makes an opening purchase of one contract against a seller making an opening sale, *open interest increases by one.*
- When a holder exercises an option of one contract, *open interest decreases by one.* This is one reason why open interest tends to decrease as the option's expiration nears, because holders become more likely to exercise.

- When a holder makes a closing sale of one contract against a writer making a closing purchase, *open interest decreases by one.* Both positions on the contract, the writer's and the holder's, have been closed. Note that closing sales and closing purchases do not always decrease open interest—whereas purchases must match sales, *closing* purchases do not necessarily have to match *closing* sales.
- When an investor makes a closing purchase against another investor's opening sale, or a closing sale against an opening purchase, *open interest remains unchanged.* In both cases the closing transaction is offset by an opening transaction, leaving the overall open position unchanged.

Table 14.2 shows the potential gain and loss for the holder, the uncovered writer, and the covered writer, as well as their breakeven point.

Table 14.2 Open Interest Gain and Loss

Investor	Max. Gain	Max. Loss	Breakeven Pt.
Holder	Unlimited	Premium	Strike + premium
Uncovered writer	Premium	Unlimited	Strike + premium
Covered writer	Strike + premium – cost of stock	Cost of stock – premium	Stock price – premium

Exam Prep Questions

1. Martin Bowne purchased 10 call option contracts at a premium of 4. How much did he pay for them?

 ❑ A. $40

 ❑ B. $4

 ❑ C. $250

 ❑ D. $4,000

2. Doreen Gray holds 1 GOL Nov 40 Call @ 5. This means she:

 I. Has the right to sell 100 shares of GOL for 40.

 II. Has the right to buy 100 shares of GOL for 40.

 III. Paid $500 for this option.

 IV. Received $500 for this option.

 ❑ A. I

 ❑ B. I and II

 ❑ C. II and III

 ❑ D. I and V

3. Paula Oldman sells 2 Zyxon Apr 60 Calls @ 4. If Zyxon stock currently trades at 60.75, what are the total intrinsic and time values of this option?

 ❑ A. The intrinsic value is $75 and the time value is $325.

 ❑ B. The intrinsic value is zero and the time value is $400.

 ❑ C. The intrinsic value is $150 and the time value is $650.

 ❑ D. The intrinsic value is $600 and the time value is $200.

4. Joan Neuman owns 1 Cellnet May 50 Call @ 3. Cellnet trades for 48. Which statement is true?

 ❑ A. The option is in the money by 2 points.

 ❑ B. The option's breakeven point is 47.

 ❑ C. The option is out of the money by 2 points.

 ❑ D. The option is out of the money by 5 points.

5. When Blue Star Airline trades at 56.37, what is the breakeven point for a purchaser of Blue Star Aug 55 Calls, which sell for a 3.12 premium?

 ❑ A. 51.87

 ❑ B. 52.12

 ❑ C. 58.12

 ❑ D. 59.50

6. Peter Hobbs wrote five Netraider Oct 35 Calls @ 3. In his portfolio, he owns 500 Netraider shares, which he bought at $29. What is his breakeven price, and what is the holder's?
   - ❑ A. Hobbs' breakeven point is 32; the holder's breakeven point is 38.
   - ❑ B. Hobbs' breakeven point is 38; the holder's breakeven point is 32.
   - ❑ C. Hobbs' breakeven point is 26; the holder's breakeven point is 32.
   - ❑ D. Hobbs' breakeven point is 26; the holder's breakeven point is 38.
7. Red Hughs purchased 1 Biofuels Oct 60 Call @ 4. What is his maximum potential loss?
   - ❑ A. $400
   - ❑ B. $5,600
   - ❑ C. $5,800
   - ❑ D. It is unlimited
8. Carmen Verandah holds 2 Chief Corp. May 60 Calls @ 4. Chief has rallied to 74. If she exercises now, what is Verandah's profit on her option position?
   - ❑ A. $1,000
   - ❑ B. $2,000
   - ❑ C. $2,800
   - ❑ D. She doesn't make a profit, but a loss of $800
9. Paula Devito wrote one uncovered Digital Design (DDI) Apr 70 Call @ 3; later, Suzi Symanski bought a DDI Apr 70 Call @ 3.25. What is the most Devito can gain and the most Symanski can lose?
   - ❑ A. Devito can gain up to $300; Symanski can lose up to $6,675.
   - ❑ B. Devito can gain up to $6,700; Symanski can lose up to $325.
   - ❑ C. Devito can gain up to $300; Symanski can lose an unlimited amount.
   - ❑ D. Devito can gain up to $300; Symanski can lose up to $325.
10. Joan writes 10 NHI Jun 50 Calls @ 3. She has 1,000 shares of National Hotel, Inc., in her portfolio, which she bought at 42.50. What is the most she can gain or lose on this option?
    - ❑ A. The most Joan can gain is $300; the most she can lose is $4,700.
    - ❑ B. The most Joan can gain is $10,500; the most she can lose is $39,500.
    - ❑ C. The most Joan can gain is $3,000; the most she can lose is $47,000.
    - ❑ D. The most Joan can gain is $10,500; her losses are potentially unlimited.
11. Jeanne Meltor, who holds no unexpired options, writes two World Cable Jun 45 Calls @ 3. All the following are true except:
    - ❑ A. She has a short option position.
    - ❑ B. She controls 200 shares of World Cable stock.
    - ❑ C. She has made an opening sale.
    - ❑ D. Her potential gains on the option position are limited.

12. Ms. Chang holds 3 MMC July 55 Calls @ 2.25. The option expires in two weeks, and the stock of Mountain Motor Corporation has risen to 61.50. The same option is now trading for an $8 premium. Chang wants to lock in her gains. If she acts today, what is her maximum profit?

    ❑ A. $1,275
    ❑ B. $1,950
    ❑ C. $1,725
    ❑ D. $2,400

13. In early April, Jeremy exercises his Weldtite May 50 Call. Open interest on Weldtite May 50 Calls:

    ❑ A. Increases by one
    ❑ B. Remains the same
    ❑ C. Decreases by one
    ❑ D. Decreases by 100

14. An investor who has purchased the following option is performing which of the following: Buy 1 EDS Jun 70 Call @ 3?

    ❑ A. An opening purchase
    ❑ B. An opening sale
    ❑ C. A closing purchase
    ❑ D. A closing sale

15. What are the intrinsic and time values for the following option?

    2 JTD Apr 60 Calls @ 4 with JTD selling at 60½ in the market

    ❑ A. Intrinsic value is $50 and time value is $350
    ❑ B. Intrinsic value is $0 and time value is $400
    ❑ C. Intrinsic value is $100 and time value is $700
    ❑ D. Intrinsic value is $0 and time value is $800

Exam Prep Answers

1. The correct answer is D. Each call option contract gives the holder the right to buy 100 shares of stock. Because the premium expresses the option price in dollars per share, Bowne paid $4,000.

2. The correct answer is C. A call option contract gives the holder the right to purchase 100 shares of the underlying security at the strike price. The holder pays an amount equal to the premium times the number of shares for the option. Thus Gray owns the right to buy 100 shares of GOL at the strike price of 40, and she paid $500 to buy this call.

3. The correct answer is C. The intrinsic value of the option is the difference between the market price and the strike price, in this case .75. The remaining 3.25 of the premium equal the contract's time value. Oldman therefore received $150 (.75 × 200 shares) based on the option's intrinsic value and $650 ($3.25 × 200 shares) based on the time value, for a total premium of $800.

4. The correct answer is C. A call option is out of the money when the stock's market price is lower than the option's strike price. In this case, Cellnet's market price is 48, two points lower than the strike price of 50.

5. The correct answer is C. An option's breakeven point is the price at which an investor neither makes nor loses money on the trade. The holder's breakeven point on a call option thus occurs when the underlying stock's price equals the strike price, plus the premium. For this Blue Star option, the breakeven point equals 58? (55 + 3?).

6. The correct answer is D. Hobbs, the writer of the covered call will break even when the stock drops to the price at which he originally purchased it, minus the premium he received for the option ($29 – $3 = $26). Because the option will be out of the money at that level, he doesn't have to worry—he will do better than break even. In this example for the call holder, breakeven equals the option's strike price, plus the premium, $38.

7. The correct answer is A. Hughs can lose at most the premium he paid, which equals $400 ($4 × 100 shares).

8. The correct answer is B. Verandah will earn $2,800 by exercising the Chief options ($74 – $64 breakeven = $10; $10 × 200 shares = $2,000).

9. The correct answer is D. The most Devito can gain is the premium she earned by selling the option, or \$300. The most Symanski can lose equals the premium she paid to buy the option, or \$325.

10. The correct answer is B. The most Joan can gain is \$10,500 (\$50 strike + \$3 premium – \$42.50 purchase price = \$10.50; \$10.50 × 1,000 shares = \$10,500). This will happen if NHI stock rises past the strike price, and her option is exercised. The most she can lose is her cost for the 1,000 NHI shares, minus the premium she received, or \$39,500 (\$42,500 – \$3,000). This happens only if National Hotel shares drop to zero—before Joan can sell them.

11. The correct answer is B. Meltor has a short option position and thus does not control the underlying shares. As she holds no unexpired options, she has made an opening sale. (She can make a closing sale only by selling an option that she previously bought.)

12. The correct answer is C. Ms. Chang can maximize her gains at \$1,725 by closing out her option position—making a closing sale of 3 MMC July 55 Calls @ 8. To calculate her profit, subtract the premium she earned from the premium she paid, and then multiply by 300 shares (\$8 – \$2.25 = \$5.75; \$5.75 × 300 = \$1,725). If Chang had exercised her option, she would have profited only \$1,275 (\$61.50 – \$57.25 breakeven = \$4.25; \$4.25 × 300 = \$1,275).

13. The correct answer is C. When Jeremy, who is long, exercises one contract, open interest in the option decreases by one.

14. The correct answer is A. The purchase of 1 EDS Jun 70 Call @3 is an opening purchase; the purchase of an option that has no offsetting option in case of loss. The seller of the same option is conducting an opening sale. A closing purchase means closing an open position, such as writing or purchasing a second option to offset the first one in case of loss. A closing sale means the holder becomes a writer by selling the same option for profit.

15. The correct answer is C. 2 JTD Apr 60 Calls @ 4 is in the money by ½ point if the market price of the stock is 60½. There are two contracts or 200 shares: 200 × .5 (½ point) = \$100 intrinsic value. The remaining premium paid of 3½ points represents the time value: 200 × 3.5 = \$700 time value.

Put Options

Terms You Need to Know

- ✓ At the money
- ✓ Breakeven point
- ✓ Call option
- ✓ Closing purchase
- ✓ Closing sale
- ✓ Covered put writer
- ✓ Exercise
- ✓ Holder
- ✓ In the money
- ✓ Intrinsic value
- ✓ Long position
- ✓ Opening purchase
- ✓ Opening sale
- ✓ Options clearing corporation (OCC)
- ✓ Out of the money
- ✓ Premium
- ✓ Put option
- ✓ Short position
- ✓ Stock dividend
- ✓ Stock split
- ✓ Strike price (or exercise price)
- ✓ Time value
- ✓ Uncovered put writer (or naked writer)
- ✓ Underlying security
- ✓ Writer

Concepts You Need to Understand

- ✓ How a put differs from a call
- ✓ How the holder's point of view differs from that of the writer
- ✓ Which terms define a put option contract
- ✓ How intrinsic value is calculated for a put
- ✓ When put options are in the money, at the money, and out of the money
- ✓ What holders and writers of put options stand to gain or lose
- ✓ How holders and writers of put options open and close positions
- ✓ How an option is adjusted when the underlying stock splits
- ✓ What happens to an option when a dividend is declared for the underlying stock

Put Options

Put options are the reverse of call options. Whereas call options give the holder the right to buy a security, put options give the holder the right to *sell* one. Although puts are described in the same terms and involve the same issues as calls, the differences between the two classes of options make it useful to discuss them separately. This chapter introduces put options and illustrates the ways in which they are both similar to and different from calls, thus completing the introduction to stock options. The chapter then takes a look at how stock splits and stock dividends affect options, both puts and calls. Subsequent chapters cover the rules and strategies of option trading as well as options based on securities other than stocks.

In essence, a *put option* is the reverse of a call option. It gives the buyer the right to sell a number of shares of some security at a fixed price at any time until the expiration date. It is termed a "put" because the buyer of the option can "put," or place, the stock with the seller, who is obligated to purchase the shares at the strike price. Like *call options*, put options essentially involve a bet between the buyer and the seller. In this case, however, the buyer (or *holder*) is betting that the price of the underlying security will fall (bearish). The holder can then purchase the stock at the market price and make a profit by selling it to the writer at the higher exercise price. The seller (or *writer*) is betting the price will rise or stay roughly the same (bullish). If this occurs, the option will expire worthless, and the writer doesn't have to buy any stock. No matter what happens, the writer earns a premium for selling the option.

> **EXAMPLE:** TNT stock is currently trading at $56, and Mike thinks the price is going to fall. He buys a put that enables him to sell 200 shares at $55 at any time in the next three months. Alicia thinks the price is going to rise, so she sells an identical put. Mike pays $400 for the option, and Alicia receives $400. If the price of the stock stays at or above $55 for the next three months, Mike will not exercise the option, and Alicia earns the $400 premium without having to buy any stock. However, if the price of TNT falls to $48, Mike can buy the stock at the market price of $48 and sell it at $55, earning $1,000 ($55 – $48 = $7; $7 × 200 shares = $1,400; $1,400 – $400 cost of the option = $1,000). Alicia, meanwhile, is forced to buy 200 shares at $55, even though the market price is now $48.

Although put holders and call writers are generally considered bearish, there are crucial differences between their situations. Put holders buy the right to sell stock, whereas call writers sell the right to buy stock. Thus put holders pay a premium for the option and are granted control over the shares of stock—they decide whether and when to *exercise*, or sell, the stock. The writers of calls, however, receive a premium and have no control over when the option is exercised. If the price of the underlying security falls, both kinds of traders have bet correctly, but they make money in different ways.

Put orders look very much like call orders, as shown in Table 15.1.

Table 15.1 Put Option Order

Buy	3	TNT	Jun	35	Puts	@ 2
(Buy or sell	(Number of option contracts)	(Underlying security)	(Expiration month)	(Strike price)	(Type of option—call or put)	(Premium)

- **Buy or sell**—Whether the person placing the order wants to become a buyer (holder) or a seller (writer).
- **Number of option contracts**—For equity options, one contract covers 100 shares of stock. The "3" in the example indicates three contracts, or 300 shares of stock.
- **Underlying security**—The name of the company whose stock the option covers.
- **Expiration month**—The month the option expires. (More information on expirations appears in the next chapter).
- **Strike price (exercise price)**—The price at which the holder of the put can sell the stock.
- **Type of option**—Call or put.
- **Premium**—The price the buyer pays for the option, expressed in dollars per share of the underlying security.

EXAMPLE: David places the order, Buy 3 TNT Jun 35 Puts @ 2. This means he is buying an option that controls 300 shares of Tonight, Inc., stock. It gives him the right to sell (put) the shares to a writer at $35 per share at any time before the expiration in June. His total premium, or settlement amount, is $600 ($2 × 300 shares).

Premiums: Intrinsic and Time Values

Premiums work the same way for puts as they do for calls. The initial premium is set by the *Options Clearing Corporation (OCC)*, and, as the option trades, the premium rises or falls. As with a call, a put's premium is a combination of the option's *intrinsic value* and its *time value*. However, the intrinsic value must be calculated differently, because a put becomes more valuable as the stock price falls.

Again, the intrinsic value is the difference between the strike price and the market price. For a put, if the market price is the same as, or higher than, the strike price, the intrinsic value is zero.

Remember: intrinsic value = strike price – market price

EXAMPLE: Consider the option, 1 TNT Jun 35 Put @ 3. If the market price falls to $31, the holder of the option can buy the stock in the market at $31 and sell it to a writer at $35, earning $4 per share. The option therefore has an intrinsic value of $4 ($35 – $31 = $4). Suppose the market price rises instead to $38. The market price is now higher than the strike price. There is no advantage to buying the stock at $38 and selling it at $35. The option therefore has no intrinsic value. Table 15.2 shows the intrinsic values for each stock price.

Table 15.2 Price Versus Value

	Tonight, Inc., Stock Price	Option's Intrinsic Value
Stock price above	38	0
	37	0
	36	0
Strike price	35	0
Stock price below	34	$1
	33	$2
	32	$3

Stock price versus the option's intrinsic value is an important concept to understand. Remember, a put option only has intrinsic value for the holder if the stock price remains *lower* than the strike price.

The time value of a put is determined by the time left until expiration as well as by investors' beliefs about the volatility, quality, and market conditions of the underlying stock. Thus, two options that expire on the same day can have different time values. Once again, the time value is simply the portion of the premium that is not the intrinsic value. All options theoretically have some time value until they expire.

EXAMPLE: Anna holds the option, 3 VAN Dec 45 Puts, which she purchased for a premium of $2. In November, Vanity Pharmaceuticals comes out with a cure for baldness, and its stock rises to $65. Having lost all intrinsic value, the put trades for a premium of $1/16$. Then a side effect is discovered—the product may cure baldness, but it also causes irregular heartbeats and may have led to a number of strokes. Lawsuits are filed. The company's stock falls to $39, and Anna finds that her option is now selling for a premium of $14.

What are the option's intrinsic and time values? If Anna exercises today, she will gain $6 per share, which is the intrinsic value ($45 strike – $39 stock price). Subtract the intrinsic value from the premium to find the time value of $8. The time value has increased because traders are betting that Vanity's stock will continue to decline before the option expires.

A Put Option In the Money, At the Money, and Out of the Money

A put option is *in the money* when it has intrinsic value, that is, when the stock price is lower than the strike price. It is *at the money* when the stock price is the same as the strike price, and *out of the money* when the stock price is higher than the strike price. Note that these are the reverse of the situations for calls.

EXAMPLE: Consider the option TNT Dec 35 Put.
If TNT's share price is $32, the option is in the money by 3 points.
If TNT's share price is $35, the option is at the money.
If TNT's share price is $39, the option is out of the money by 4 points.

Being in the money does not necessarily mean that the holder makes a profit. The premium must be taken into account to find the breakeven point and to determine how much the holder and seller stand to gain or lose.

Potential Gains and Losses

As with calls, the *breakeven point* for puts is the stock price at which the investor neither makes nor loses on the option contract. However, it is calculated differently for puts than for calls. For the holder of a put—and the uncovered writer of a put—the breakeven point is reached when the market price of the stock falls below the option's strike price by an amount equal to the premium. To break even, the holder of the put must be able to sell the shares at a strike price high enough to make back the money he or she spent on the premium, whereas the writer must be forced to buy the shares at a price high enough to wipe out his or her premium earnings. Once again, the breakeven point is the same for both holder and writer.

For uncovered calls, the breakeven point occurs when the market price equals the strike price *less* the premium, or the strike price minus the premium.

breakeven point = strike price – premium

EXAMPLE: John holds 1 ADV Dec 42½ Put @ 1¼. He paid $1.25 per share for the option, and so he cannot break even until the stock price falls to $41.25. Similarly, an uncovered writer of the same option has earned $1.25 per share in premium, a gain that is not wiped out until the stock falls to at least $41.25. In this case, breakeven point for both the holder and the writer is the same

The Most the Holder Can Gain or Lose on a Put

Because the holder of a put makes money when the market price of the stock falls, the holder gains the most when the stock price plummets all the way to zero. Then the holder's profit is equal to the strike price multiplied by the number of shares, minus the total premium. Of course, it is rare for a stock to collapse to zero.

EXAMPLE: Reginald purchased the option 4 LLP Dec 80 Put @ 3. In the last two months, Long Lighting Products has lost most of its major domestic and international customers, and the company's stock has fallen to $25. How much will Reginald gain if he exercises now? How much will he gain if he waits, and LLP stock crashes to zero? Today Reginald will profit $20,800 by exercising ($77 breakeven – $25 = $52; $52 × 400 shares = $20,800. If he waits until LLP stock reaches zero, he earns $30,800 ($77 – 0 × 400).

On the other hand, the most that a put holder can lose is the premium he or she paid for the option. If the option remains out of the money, the holder simply does not exercise it, allowing it to expire worthless, losing the premium paid.

The Most the Writer Can Gain or Lose on a Put

The most an uncovered put writer can gain is the premium received for the option. If the price of the underlying stock stays at or above the strike price, the option will not be exercised and the writer does not have to purchase any shares. If the stock price falls, however, the writer loses money. Covered put writers however, face a riskier scenario.

An investor who sells short is selling shares that he or she does not own, hoping that the price falls and that the short sale can be covered later with shares bought at a lower price.

A *covered put writer* is short the underlying shares of stock (or has cash deposits at his or her brokerage equal to the aggregate strike price). In other words, he or she has sold borrowed shares of the stock at the market price. Compare this with the situation of a covered call writer, who owns the underlying shares of stock. For a put writer, owning the stock is of no advantage, because he or she has to *buy* the stock if the option is exercised. Being short the stock, however, does cover the writer (protecting them from unlimited loss).

> **EXAMPLE:** Lucy sold short 100 shares of XPP Corporation at $50. She writes the option 1 XPP Jan 45 Put @ 2. XPP begins to fall almost immediately. A few days before expiration, the option is exercised, with XPP trading at $26. Lucy must buy 100 XPP shares at $45, but she can use them to replace the borrowed shares, which she originally sold at $50. Also, she earned a $2 premium per share.

Notice that the covered put writer sells an option with a strike price below, not above, the short sale price that he or she received for the stock. This is because the short sale proceeds represent income, whereas the aggregate strike price represents a possible payment. Under normal circumstances, option writers of course prefer to keep the former amount greater than the latter.

For a covered put writer, breakeven occurs when the underlying stock price equals the short sale price, plus the option premium received.

Remember: breakeven point (covered writer) = short sale price + premium

EXAMPLE: Jack wrote the option 5 UPP Aug 50 Puts @ 3. He has also sold short 500 shares of Undertakers Prime Products at $54, making him a covered writer. What is Jack's breakeven point? At the breakeven point, his gains must offset his losses. This happens when UPP's share price reaches $57 ($54 + $3). If the option expires then, it is worthless, but Jack still has to replace the 500 shares of borrowed UPP stock, which costs him $57 per share.

The maximum gain for a covered put writer is limited, equaling the short sale price, plus the premium received, minus the option's strike price. This occurs when the price of the underlying stock falls below the option's strike price.

EXAMPLE: Jill sold short 100 shares of Apple Motors Company stock at $48. She writes the option 1 AMC Jan 40 Put @ 5. What is her maximum gain? The most she can gain is $1,300. Suppose AMC stock falls to $33, and her option is exercised. Jill must purchase the stock at $40, but she has sold it at $48 and she has earned a $5 premium. Thus, $48 + $5 – $40 = $13; $13 × 100 = $1,300.

On the other hand, a covered put writer faces potentially unlimited losses, although not from the option itself. The short position on the underlying stock is the risky element.

EXAMPLE: Maude sells short 100 shares of CBC stock at $23, and then writes the option 1 CBC Feb 20 @ 1. When two conglomerates begin a bidding war to purchase Consolidated Beer Company, the stock jumps. By early February, the share price has reached $79, and it is still climbing. If the trend continues, Maude's option will of course expire worthless; however, she must at some point replace the 100 shares of CBC that she shorted for $23. To cover her short position now, she will lose $5,600 ($79 – $23 = $56; $56 × 100 = $5,600). But CBC stock might theoretically rise indefinitely, and her losses might also.

Who Faces the Greater Risk: A Covered Or Uncovered Put Writer?

The covered writer has a potentially greater risk. An *uncovered put writer* (or *naked writer*) has not sold short the requisite shares of the underlying stock, and thus does not experience the unlimited risk of the short sale. At worst, an uncovered put writer loses the total strike price of his or her option, minus the premium. This happens only when the underlying stock falls to zero, a rare event. Table 15.3 shows the maximum gain, maximum loss, and the breakeven point for each type of investor.

Table 15.3 Investor Gain, Loss, and Breakeven Points

Investor	Max. Gain	Max. Loss	Breakeven Pt.
Holder	Total strike – Premium	Premium	Strike price – premium
Uncovered writer	Premium	Total strike – premium	Strike price – premium
Covered writer	Short sale + premium – strike	Unlimited	Short sale price + premium

Put writers (and holders) can protect their profits and limit their losses through closing purchases (and sales), just as call writers and holders can.

Openings and Closings

Opening purchases and sales are the same for puts as for calls. When someone buys a new put option, this is known as an *opening purchase.* The buyer has opened a *long position* by purchasing the option. When someone writes a new put contract, this is known as an *opening sale.* The writer has opened a *short position* by selling the option.

A Closing Sale with a Put

A put holder makes a *closing sale* by writing the same option in order to offset or reduce the original long position. The closing sale enables the buyer to lock in a profit or limit a loss.

> **EXAMPLE:** When the stock of Lifetime Books drops to $40, the option's premium rises to $14. But the company publishes a new star biography in early December, and Bruce is afraid that increased sales might lead the stock to rebound. How much does he make by exercising the option? He earns $2,400 ($48 breakeven – $40 stock price = $8; $8 × 300 shares = $2,400).
>
> Instead, Bruce closes out his position, writing the option 3 LFT Dec 50 Puts @ 14. This way, he earns a profit of $3,600. Calculating the gain is easy—simply subtract the premium paid from the premium earned, and multiply by the number of shares ($14 – $2 = $12; $12 × 300 = $3,600).
>
> With this closing transaction, Bruce has locked in the $3,600 profit. If the stock of Lifetime Books remains in the money, he will eventually both

purchase and sell 300 shares at $50. If the underlying stock were to rise past the strike price—move out of the money—both options expire worthless. In either case, Bruce's profit from the difference between the two premiums remains unchanged.

A Closing Purchase with a Put

A put writer makes a *closing purchase* by purchasing the same option to offset or reduce his or her original short position. Closing purchases enable writers to protect profits or put a cap on losses.

EXAMPLE: Catherine has written the uncovered option 2 PUG Feb 38 Puts @ 3½. Unfortunately, Pacific Undergarments fails to secure several important contracts with national retailers, and its stock begins to decline. When PUG shares reach $29 and are still falling, Catherine decides to close her position. She buys the option 2 PUG Feb 38 Puts @ 11½. With this closing purchase, she has limited her losses to $1,600 ($11.50 premium paid – $3.50 premium earned = $8; $8 × 200 shares = $1,600). Even if PUG stock continues to fall, Catherine cannot lose any more money. However, if the company's stock were to rebound, her $1,600 loss remains equally locked in.

When the stock controlled by an option splits or pays dividends, the option itself must be adjusted. This is true for both calls and puts.

If a company believes its stock has become too highly priced, it can declare a *stock split,* whereby the number of its outstanding shares is multiplied by a certain ratio, and the market price of stock is adjusted downward accordingly.

Stock Splits and Dividends

Let's start with splits. Because the value of the option is derived from the value of the underlying security, when the price of the stock is adjusted after a split, the option's price must also be modified. For an even split, the repercussions in the options market are simple. If a stock splits 2:1, for example, there are twice as many shares after the split, and each one is half as valuable. An investor with 200 shares trading at $40 before the split owns 400 shares at $20 afterward. To retain its value, an option on this stock must match the price change: Its strike price must be halved, whereas the number of contracts is doubled. As a result, the total value of the stock controlled by the option remains the same. Also, the exchange where the option trades reduces the current premium by half.

EXAMPLE: Gary holds 2 ADV Jun 40 Puts @ 3. The option, which cost him $600, gives him the right to sell 200 shares of Adventure stock at a total price of $8,000. The board of directors of Adventure, Inc., declares a 2:1 split. After the split, the Options Clearing Corporation (OCC) adjusts the terms of all Adventure options. Now Gary's option gives him the right to sell 400 shares at a strike price of $20. Thus, the aggregate strike price stays the same—$8,000. The options exchange must then adjust the premium. If Gary's option was trading for a premium of 4 1/2 before the split, afterward the premium will be 2 1/4. Table 15.4 shows the adjustment for a 2:1 stock split.

Table 15.4 A 2:1 Stock Split Adjustment

	Option	Total Strike	Total Premium
Before 2:1 split	2 ADV Jun 40 Put @ 4 1/2	$8,000	$900
After 2:1 split	4 ADV Jun 20 Put @ 2 1/4	$8,000	$900

*1 contract equals 100 shares

For an odd split, the process is slightly more complicated. Say TNT, Inc., stock splits 5:4. The number of shares is multiplied by 5/4, whereas the stock price is multiplied by 4/5.To match the price change of the stock, a TNT option must be similarly adjusted. At first it might seem that the adjustment should be the same as for an even split—multiply the number of contracts by 5/4 and the strike price by 4/5—but that would leave the number of contracts as a fraction. Instead, the number of shares represented by each contract is adjusted.

EXAMPLE: Jessica holds the option, 1 TNT Jun 80 Call @ 5, when TNT announces a 5:4 stock split. The new strike price becomes $64 ($80 × 4/5 = $64) and the new premium becomes $4 ($5 × 4/5 = $4, assuming that the premium was five before the split). In order for the option to retain its prior value, the number of shares in the contract must be adjusted. Each contract now covers 125 shares of TNT stock (100 × 5/4 = 125). Jessica's adjusted option is 1 TNT Jun 64 Call @ 4. The option keeps its value—it still controls $8,000 worth of stock, and it is still worth a total of $500.

Table 15.5 explains the relationship of the strike price to the premium before and after the split.

Table 15.5 A 5:4 Stock Split Adjustment

	Option	Total Strike	Total Premium
Before 5:4 split	1 TNT Jun 80 Call @ 5	$8,000	$500
After 5:4 split	1* TNT Jun 64 Call @ 4	$8,000	$500

*1 contract now equals 125 shares

Adjusting options—both calls and puts—after stock dividend payments is like adjusting them after stock splits. With a *stock dividend*, a corporation gives each stockholder a certain number of new shares, in proportion to his or her holdings, whereas the exchange lowers the price of the stock so that the total market value remains the same. A 10% stock dividend, for instance, increases a company's outstanding shares by 10%, at the same time decreasing its share price by 10%. (It is the equivalent of an 11:10 stock split.) Options on the company's stock must be changed accordingly.

> **EXAMPLE:** Nighttime Corp. declares a 15% stock dividend. Tom holds 1 NTC May 60 Call @ 4. Before the dividend payment, the option is still trading for a $4 premium. How is his option affected by the stock dividend? First, the number of shares per contract must be increased by 15%, to 115. Then the strike price and the premium must by lowered by 15%. The new strike price is approximately $52 ($60 ÷ 1.15), and the new premium is about $3.50 ($4 ÷ 1.15). So after the stock dividend payment, the option reads as: 1 NTC May 52 Call @ 3½.

Table 15.6 shows the strike and premium of the stock before and after the dividend.

Table 15.6 Dividend Change of Underlying Stock

	Option	Total Strike	Total Premium
Before 15% stock dividend	1 NTC May 60 Call @4	$6,000	$400
After 15% stock dividend	1* NTC May 52 Call @ 3½	$6,000	$400

* 1 contract = 115 shares (which, in this case, requires that the strike and premium be rounded off)

Until an option is exercised, all shareholder rights remain with the owner of the underlying stock.

New shares resulting from stock splits and stock dividends go to the registered owner of the stock, not to the holder of the option. Because cash dividends do not automatically affect the value of the underlying stock, no adjustments are made to the option. The dividend simply belongs to whoever owns the underlying security on the record date. If a put holder, for example, exercises the option three or more business days before the record date (giving the trade time to settle regular way), the writer receives the dividend.

Exam Prep Questions

1. What do a buyer and an uncovered writer of a put option want to happen to the price of the underlying security?
   - ❑ A. Both want the price of the underlying security to fall.
   - ❑ B. The buyer wants the price to fall and the seller wants it to rise.
   - ❑ C. Both want the price of the underlying security to rise.
   - ❑ D. The buyer wants the price to rise and the seller wants it to fall.

2. Karen Cottonwood holds 1 Zyxon Aug 60 Put, for which she paid a premium of 3. Cottonwood has:

   I. The right to buy 100 shares of Zyxon at 60.

   II The right to sell 100 shares of Zyxon at 60.

   III. Paid $18,000 for the option.

   IV. Paid $300 for the option.
   - ❑ A. I and III
   - ❑ B. I and IV
   - ❑ C. II and III
   - ❑ D. II and IV

3. Sara Northland purchases 5 Global Oil Apr 50 Puts @ 4. If Global trades at 51, what is the put's intrinsic value?
   - ❑ A. Zero
   - ❑ B. 1 point
   - ❑ C. 3 points
   - ❑ D. 4 points

4. Donald Oldman buys a Cellnet Aug 45 Put @ 2. When Cellnet trades at 47 3/8, Oldman's put is:
   - ❑ A. At the money
   - ❑ B. Out of the money by 2 points
   - ❑ C. Out of the money by 2 3/8 points
   - ❑ D. Worthless

5. Enzo Reina sold short 200 shares of Burgertron Corp. at $59. He writes 2 BGC Apr 50 Puts @ 4 1/4. What is Reina's breakeven point?
   - ❑ A. 63 1/4
   - ❑ B. 59 1/4
   - ❑ C. 55 3/4
   - ❑ D. 45 3/4

6. Devon Green purchases 5 RMC Feb 50 Puts @ 3. What is her maximum profit on the trade?
   - ❑ A. $1,500
   - ❑ B. $25,000
   - ❑ C. $23,500
   - ❑ D. Potentially unlimited

7. Jack Bayley buys 5 Treetops Airlines Oct 65 Puts @ 4. What are his maximum possible gains and losses on this position?
   - ❑ A. Bayley can gain a potentially unlimited amount; and he can lose up to $6,100.
   - ❑ B. Bayley can gain up to $6,100; he can lose up to $400.
   - ❑ C. Bayley can gain up to $30,500; he can lose up to $2,000.
   - ❑ D. Bayley can gain up to $32,500; he can lose up to $6,500.

8. Becky Orlov writes 10 TMI Jun 75 Puts @ 2. She has also sold short 1,000 shares of Tiny Minds, Inc., at $81. What is her maximum possible profit on this covered put position?
   - ❑ A. Potentially unlimited
   - ❑ B. $8,000
   - ❑ C. $4,000
   - ❑ D. $2,000

9. Tyrone Washington writes 5 uncovered WCC Oct 40 Puts @ 3. When World Cable Co. stock falls to $34, all these statements are true except:
   - ❑ A. Washington will lose $1,500 if the option is exercised.
   - ❑ B. The option is in the money.
   - ❑ C. Washington's breakeven point is $37.
   - ❑ D. Washington can make a profit by closing out the position.

10. What is the time value of a put with a strike price of $60 and a premium of $10, when the market value of the underlying stock is $52?
    - ❑ A. $10
    - ❑ B. $8
    - ❑ C. $0
    - ❑ D. $2

11. Jerry buys 3 BTG May 90 Puts @ 8¾. On the news of weak sales in the first quarter, Bohr Tunneling stock continues to decline. By the second week of May, the company's shares are trading at $79, and Jerry's option sells for a premium 12½. If Jerry thinks that BTG stock might rebound shortly, what should he do?
    - ❑ A. Make a closing purchase
    - ❑ B. Exercise his option
    - ❑ C. Make a closing sale
    - ❑ D. Sell BTG short

12. Veronika Haas buys 15 TDI Jul 60 Puts @ 5¼. When Tofu Distributors announces a 3:1 stock split, Haas now owns:
   - ❑ A. 5 TDI Jul 60 Puts @ 15¾
   - ❑ B. 5 TDI Jul 180 Puts @ 5¼
   - ❑ C. 45 TDI Jul 20 Puts @ 5¼
   - ❑ D. 45 TDI Jul 20 Puts @ 1¾

13. What is the maximum profit a seller can make for the following put option? Sell 10 HTH Jun 75 Puts @ 4
   - ❑ A. Unlimited
   - ❑ B. $4,000
   - ❑ C. $7,500
   - ❑ D. $71,000

14. What is the maximum possible gain and the maximum possible loss for the holder of the following put option? Buy 5 TNT Oct 65 puts @4
   - ❑ A. Maximum gain is unlimited; maximum loss is $6,100
   - ❑ B. Maximum gain is $6,100; maximum loss is $400
   - ❑ C. Maximum gain is $30,500; maximum loss is $2,000
   - ❑ D. Maximum gain is $32,500; maximum loss is $6,500

15. Frank purchased 2 TNT Oct 50 puts @ 3½ with a market price of TNT stock at $49 at the time. What was the intrinsic value and time value of this option contract?
   - ❑ A. Intrinsic = 1 point / Time = 3½ points
   - ❑ B. Intrinsic = 0 / Time = 3½ points
   - ❑ C. Intrinsic = 3½ points / Time = 0
   - ❑ D. Intrinsic = 1 point / Time = 2½ points

Exam Prep Answers

1. The correct answer is B. The buyer and the uncovered writer of a put are on different sides of the market. The buyer makes money when the market price of the underlying security falls below the strike price, whereas the writer wants the price to stay at or above the strike price.
2. The correct answer is D. As a put holder, Cottonwood has the right to sell 100 shares of Zyxon at the strike price any time until the option's expiration date. She paid \$300 (\$3 × 100 shares) to buy the put.
3. The correct answer is A. Because the strike price is lower than the stock price, the put has no intrinsic value. Northland will not exercise her option to sell Global Oil at \$50 if she must buy it in the market at \$51.
4. The correct answer is C. Because Cellnet's price is 2⅜ points higher than the strike price of Oldman's put, his option is out of the money by that amount. The option will only become worthless at expiration.
5. The correct answer is A. As a covered put writer, Mr. Reina will break even when Burgertron stock rises to a price of \$63.25—which equals his short sale price plus the premium he received. At that price, he can cover his short position without gaining or losing money.
6. The correct answer is C. In the event that RMC stock falls to zero, Ms. Green will make her maximum gain of \$23,500. This equals the total strike price on the five contracts (\$25,000), minus the total premium she paid (\$1,500).
7. The correct answer is C. If Treetops falls to zero, Jack will make his maximum gain of \$30,500 (\$61 breakeven × 500). The most he can lose is the total premium he paid, or \$2,000, which will happen if the option stays out of the money.
8. The correct answer is B. Orlov's maximum profit comes if the underlying stock drops below the strike price and the option is exercised. At that point, she will make \$8,000 (\$81 short sale price + \$2 premium – \$75 strike price = \$8; \$8 × 1,000 shares = \$8,000). With the 1,000 shares that have been put to her by the option holder, she can replace the shares that she borrowed for the short sale.
9. The correct answer is D. With a closing purchase of the same option, Washington can limit his losses but he cannot turn a loss into a gain. Suppose that the option is now trading for a premium of 7?. By closing out his position, Washington locks in a loss of \$2,125 (\$7.25 premium paid – \$3 premium received = \$4.25; \$4.25 × 500 shares = \$2,125). Even though this amount is more than he loses if the option was exercised today, it might be a good move, because World Cable

stock might fall even further, and he has no control over when the option is exercised.

10. The correct answer is D. The time value of an option is calculated by subtracting its intrinsic value from the current premium. This put's intrinsic value is $8 ($60 strike price – $52 stock price). Therefore, the time value equals $2 ($10 premium – $8 intrinsic value).
11. The correct answer is C. Jerry should make a closing sale. If he were to exercise his option now, he will earn a profit of $675 ($81.25 breakeven – $79 stock price = $2.25; $2.25 × 300 shares = $675). With a closing transaction, Jerry can lock in a gain of $1,125 ($12.50 premium received – $8.75 premium paid = $3.75; $3.75 × 300 = $1,125).
12. The correct answer is D. When TDI stock splits 3:1, the OCC changes the parameters of TDI options to retain their value. Remember that three times as many TDI shares are in the hands of investors, and that each share is worth just one third of its original value. So the OCC will multiply the number of contracts by 3/1, and multiply both the strike price and premium by 1/3. Veronika's option now reads: 45 TDI Jul 20 Puts @ 1 3/4. Her aggregate strike price ($90,000) and aggregate premium ($7,875) remain unchanged.
13. The correct answer is B. The maximum profit of a 10 HTH Jun 75 put @ 4 is $4,000. The calculation is the premium at $4 × the shares (10 × 100 = 1,000) = $4,000. The writer hopes that the stock will increase in value above the strike price of $75 so that the option expires worthless and the writer can keep the premium received.
14. The correct answer is C. The holder of a 5 TNT Oct 65 puts @ 4 has a maximum potential gain is $30,500 and the maximum possible loss is $2,000. The gain is calculated by subtracting the premium paid from the ask price times the number of share (65 – 4.00 × 500 = $30,500). The loss is calculated by multiplying the premium by the number of shares ($4 × 500 = $2,000).
15. The correct answer is D. 2 TNT Oct 50 puts @ 3 1/2 with a market price of $49 means that the option is in the money by 1 point (50 – 49 = 1). If the option is in the money by 1 point, it has an intrinsic value of 1 point. The remaining premium paid of 2 1/2 equals the time value of the option. The intrinsic value of 1 + time value of 2 1/2 = 3 1/2 total premium.

Equity Options and Trading Rules

Terms You Need to Know

- ✓ American-style exercise
- ✓ Assignment
- ✓ Board broker
- ✓ Chicago board options exchange (CBOE)
- ✓ Class
- ✓ Clearing member
- ✓ Compliance registered options principal (CROP)
- ✓ Cycle
- ✓ European-style exercise
- ✓ Exercise
- ✓ Exercise limit
- ✓ F floor broker
- ✓ Long-term equity anticipation securities (LEAPS)
- ✓ Margin
- ✓ Market maker
- ✓ Minimum maintenance requirement
- ✓ Next month
- ✓ Options clearing corporation (OCC)
- ✓ Order book official (OBO)
- ✓ Position limit
- ✓ R registered options principal (ROP)
- ✓ Senior registered options principal (SROP)
- ✓ Series
- ✓ Spot
- ✓ Type

Concepts You Need to Understand

- ✓ What the OCC is and what it does
- ✓ How investors are approved for trading
- ✓ Which stocks are issued options
- ✓ How options are standardized
- ✓ Where options are traded
- ✓ How trading takes place
- ✓ What position limits are
- ✓ The margin requirements for equity options
- ✓ What happens when a holder decides to exercise
- ✓ How options are assigned
- ✓ Exercise limits

Before Trading Takes Place

In many ways, trading options is similar to trading equity securities. Most options are bought and sold on exchanges in an auction process, with premiums rising and falling as investors try to gauge their worth. One crucial difference is the role of the Options Clearing Corporation. Not only does the OCC issue all options and standardize the contracts, it also sets most of the rules for options trading and guarantees that holders and writers meet their obligations. This chapter discusses the rules for trading equity options and explains the procedures for trading, step by step.

The *Options Clearing Corporation (OCC)* began in 1973 as an offshoot of the Chicago Board Options Exchange but now it is owned jointly by all the options exchanges. It is governed by a board that includes nine representatives from the brokerage firms that trade options and one representative from each of the options exchanges.

The OCC plays a crucial role in every step of the trading process, standardizing the terms of options; setting parameters such as strike prices, expiration dates, and original premiums; and then issuing the options themselves.

During trading it acts as the intermediary, clearing all trades and guaranteeing all options. The OCC also sets position limits and keeps records of positions to ensure that investors do not exceed them. Finally, when a holder wants to exercise, the OCC plays the matchmaker, checking its records for writers of the same option and assigning the contract to an appropriate brokerage house.

The fundamental purpose of the OCC is to ensure that the obligations of options contracts are met. Before the OCC existed, options were traded over-the-counter, and each individual investor had to determine the creditworthiness of his or her trading partner. Given the possibility of high losses in options trading, it was difficult to guarantee payment. The OCC eliminates this risk by essentially taking the opposite side of every transaction.

Clearing Members

A *clearing member* is a brokerage firm that belongs to a clearing corporation, which is an organization created by an exchange to facilitate trading, settlement, and delivery of its securities. In the case of options, clearing members belong to the OCC and are required to maintain a prescribed minimum of net capital and to deposit and maintain margins for all the options transactions they broker. If a customer defaults, the firm is responsible for meeting that customer's obligations up to a certain limit. Each clearing member must also appoint a *senior registered options principal (SROP)* to see that all OCC rules are followed. Because options are transferable securities that can result in profits and losses, the OCC itself is regulated by the SEC.

Which leads to the question: Can anyone invest in options? Because options trading involves substantial risks, the OCC screens prospective investors to make sure that they are fully prepared and informed. Options are traded through accounts with brokerage firms, and it is these firms that must approve investors before they can open options accounts. Brokers need to determine whether the investor understands options trading and the risks involved, and can afford the potential losses. Investors are asked about their annual income, their net worth, as well as their experience with different kinds of investments before they are approved for trading.

Approving the Application

A *registered options principal (ROP)* at the brokerage firm must approve the application before the investor can begin trading options. By the time of approval, the firm sends the investor a risk disclosure document, entitled, "Characteristics and Risks of Standardized Options." This booklet describes the basic features of options issued by the OCC, as well as the rules for exercise and settlement, plus the various risks associated with options trading. An investor has 15 days from the time of approval to sign and return the options account agreement. If the investor does not return the form in time, he or she is limited to closing transactions.

EXAMPLE: Jeff has been an avid investor in the stock market for years and wants to try his hand at options trading. He has a net worth of over $2 million and an annual income of $200,000. Still, before he can begin trading he must be approved by the ROP at Secure Investments, his brokerage firm. Jeff is quickly approved and receives a copy of "Characteristics and Risks of Standardized Options." He carefully files it away and begins buying options. Fifteen days later, Jeff is informed that he can no longer open new options positions since he has failed to sign and return his account agreement. The OCC regulates new accounts. It also regulates member firms to ensure that all educational and sales materials present a balanced view of the risks of options trading. He can now only make closing transactions in his account.

How the OCC Regulates Educational and Sales Material

Before a member firm can place advertisements about options or send educational material to customers, the documents must be approved by the *compliance registered options principal (CROP)*, who has been designated by the brokerage to guarantee compliance with OCC rules. Such material, which cannot mention past or future performance, must also be sent to the appropriate exchanges before it is used.

Sales literature, which *can* mention recommendations and past or future performances, need not be submitted to the exchanges. However, the literature must still be approved by the brokerage's CROP, and it must be mailed to customers in conjunction with the OCC's risk disclosure document. Further, this kind of material (worksheets explaining different options strategies, for example) must be supported with factual statements from the firm.

Who decides which equity securities can offer options? The individual exchanges choose the companies that are eligible to have options issued on their stock.

The OCC, not the company itself, issues the options. Companies have no say as to whether options are issued on their stock.

Each exchange makes a business decision, trying to determine whether or not the corporation's stock attracts enough attention to make an option a viable enterprise. Not surprisingly, most options are issued on securities from larger, better-known companies, like those listed on the NYSE.

The SEC must also approve options before they are issued. The commission looks closely at the issuer of the underlying security, studying the number of outstanding shares, the number of shareholders, the movement of share prices, and most importantly, trading volume. After the SEC decides that a company meets its requirements, the OCC can issue the option.

Why are options contracts standardized? Standardization makes options trading feasible. If a buyer were to bid for an option on 27 shares of a certain stock at a strike price of $33 expiring on the last day of the year, he or she might have a hard time finding a seller who will agree to all those terms. By setting guidelines for the terms of options, the OCC has greatly improved the prospects for efficient trading, thus expanding the market.

Options are classified by type, class, and series. *Type* simply refers to the kind of option, either a call or a put. A *class* of options includes all the options of the same type issued for a given company. For example, all call options for Hudson Real Estate constitute one class of options. All put options for Hudson Real Estate are another class. Finally, all options in a class that have the same expiration date and strike price are termed a *series*. Hudson Real Estate calls that expire in April and have a strike price of $55, for example, are one series. The same option, but with an expiration in July, constitutes another series.

How the OCC Standardizes Contracts

This list shows how contracts are created for an underlying security:

- *Number of shares per contract*—One equity option contract represents 100 shares of stock.
- *Strike prices*—The OCC standardizes strike prices by setting them at fixed intervals; see Table 16.1. The strike prices of stocks trading below $25 come in increments of 2½, those of stocks trading between $25 and $200 in increments of 5, and those of stocks trading above $200 in increments of 10. When issued, an option class is generally given one strike price above the current price of the underlying stock, one close to the current stock price, and one below the current stock price.

Table 16.1 Strike Prices

Price of Hudson Stock = $14	**Price of Yellowfin Stock = $112**	**Price of Pinnacle Stock = $300**
Possible Option Strike Prices	Possible Option Strike Prices	Possible Option Strike Prices
$17.50	$115	$310
$15	$110	$300
$12.50	$105	$290
($2.50 increments)	($5 increments)	($10 increments)

Number of shares represented, strike prices, premiums, bid, and ask prices are must-know terms for the exam.

- *Premiums*—Like strike prices, premiums are quoted in standard amounts. Of course, the actual level of any premium is set by the competing demands of buyers and sellers, and not by the OCC.
- *Expiration dates*—The OCC also standardizes expiration dates. All options for a given month expire at 11:59 p.m. eastern time (ET) on the Saturday following the third Friday of the month. However, expiring options cease trading at 4:02 p.m. ET on the Friday before they expire, and holders must apply to exercise by 5:30 p.m. ET on the same Friday, even though the options do not actually expire until the following night.

All equity options trade with contracts specifying *American-style exercise,* which permits the holder to exercise at any time until the Friday before expiration. Some non-equity options, such as stock index options, employ *European-style exercise,* which enables the holder to exercise only on the last business day before expiration (normally a Friday).

EXAMPLE: Consider the option HRE Jul 55 Call. It expires on the Saturday following the third Friday of July 2001, which is July 20. Thus the deadline for making a closing sale or closing purchase is 4:02 p.m. Friday, July 20. A holder who wishes to exercise the option must do so by 5:30 p.m. on the same day. And, at 11:59 p.m. on Saturday July 21, the option officially expires.

The calendar of options trading is yet further standardized. At any given moment, only options with certain expiration dates can be traded. A person might not be able to buy an HRE Aug 55 Call in April. Trading depends on the cycle to which the option has been assigned.

Option Cycles

The OCC issues options in *cycles,* which are regular schedules for trading and expiration. All options on an underlying security are assigned to one of three cycles as shown in Table 16.2.

Table 16.2 The Three Option Cycles

Cycle	Options Will Expire In
1	January, April, July, October
2	February, May, August, November
3	March, June, September, December

For an underlying security, the OCC can issue options for the current month (known as *spot*), for the following month (known as *next month*), and for the next two months in the option's cycle. Therefore, at any one time, options on a given stock can have only four possible expiration dates. A month is considered to be over as soon as the month's contracts have expired. So at the beginning of July, spot is July and next month is August. But as soon as the Saturday following the third Friday rolls around, spot jumps to the following month (in this case August), and next month jumps ahead also (to September).

Trading

The trading of options occurs on various exchanges, including the following.

Where Options Are Traded

Nearly all options trading takes place on exchanges. Although the roots of options trading lie in the OTC market, very little trading occurs over the counter today. In order of size, the major options exchanges are:

- Chicago Board Options Exchange (CBOE)
- American Stock Exchange (Amex)
- Pacific Stock Exchange (PSE)
- Philadelphia Stock Exchange (PHLX)

Because most options trading is done on exchanges, it takes place Monday through Friday, from 9:30 a.m. to 4:02 p.m. ET. (Closing time was changed from 4:10 p.m. in 1997.) Remember that the CBOE is in the Central Time Zone, so trading happens there between 8:30 a.m. and 3:02 p.m. local time.

How an Options Trade Begins

An options trade begins with an order. After a customer places the order with his or her broker, the broker fills out an order ticket to be sent to the floor of the exchange and executed. The order ticket contains the standard information about the option—number of contracts, name of the underlying stock, expiration date, exercise (strike) price, whether it is a put or a call—as well as information about the sale—whether the order is for a purchase or sale, whether it is an opening or closing transaction, and what kind of an order it is (such as market, limit, or stop).

How Options Trading Is Organized by the Exchanges

The options exchanges are auction markets, with buyers bidding the highest price they are willing to pay, and sellers asking the lowest price they are willing to accept. At the three smaller exchanges—the American, Pacific, and Philadelphia Stock Exchanges—trading procedures are very similar to those of the NYSE (see Chapter 12). The CBOE, however, uses a system closer to that of the Chicago futures markets. Unlike the NYSE, there are no specialists on the CBOE trading floor. Specialists at the NYSE accept public orders, manage the public order book, and deal from their own accounts—they are market makers. The CBOE divides these tasks among a number of positions:

- **Floor broker**—Exchange member used by a brokerage firm to execute orders from investors (public orders) or for the firm's own account.
- **Market maker**—Exchange member registered to trade specific options for his or her own account. If needed, market makers must take the opposite side of public orders, ensuring that the options have a continuous market.
- **Order book official (OBO)**—Employee of the exchange who holds public limit orders that cannot be filled immediately at the current market price. The OBO executes the orders later, if and when the market price moves to the desired level.
- **Board broker**—Exchange member who helps OBOs with trades for the most active options.

How a Trade Takes Place

In the simplest situation, one floor broker simply finds another floor broker in front of the appropriate market maker. If they both have matching orders at the same price, the trade is made. A number of rules guide their actions, including:

- Public orders have priority over orders for the accounts of member firms.

Public orders have priority over member firm orders.

- If there are buyers but no sellers (or sellers but no buyers), a floor broker goes to a market maker to sell or buy the option contract. The market maker, whose job it is to make sure that the option keeps trading, completes the transaction from his or her own account.
- If the market maker's bid is too low (or if the asked is too high), the floor broker goes to an OBO, who keeps track of orders to execute when the price rises or falls to the desired level. OBOs are employees of the exchange and handle only public orders; they do not keep orders for member firms' accounts. Board brokers, in turn, act as agents for the OBOs, helping them execute orders and keeping their own records of the orders received. Board brokers assist in trading only the most active options.

  EXAMPLE: Margaret's limit order, Buy 3 HRE Jan 60 Put @ 5.25, is given to Amy, one of Secure Investment's floor brokers. First Amy tries to find another floor broker with a matching sell order. When her search fails, Amy goes to one of the market makers for Hudson Real Estate options, who informs her that the current spread for HRE Jan 60 Put is 5.87 bid, 6.12 ask. Because Margaret's limit order can only be executed at 5.25, Amy takes it to the OBO who enters it on the list of limit orders waiting to be filled. The following day HRE Jan 60 Put falls to 5.25, and Margaret's order is executed.

Position Limits

A position limit is the maximum number of options contracts that an investor (or a group of investors acting together) can have on a given stock on a single side of the market. These limits are intended to keep investors from extending their positions too far and thus risking too much of their capital on the rise or fall of a single stock. Position limits also keep a single investor from influencing the price of the stock by betting too heavily on its rise or fall. Remember that one contract gives a holder control over 100 shares of stock, so 10,000 contracts give someone control over one million shares. Position limits apply both to the total number of contracts an investor can buy or sell, and to the number of contracts the investor can have on a single side of the market for a given security. Buying calls and selling puts are considered to be on the same side of the market (bullish), whereas buying puts and selling calls are on the other side (bearish).

For options, bullish is the upside of the market, whereas bearish is the downside of the market.

The OCC has set five possible position limits, ranging from 4,500 to 25,000 contracts, based on the underlying stock's trading volume and its number of shares outstanding. Twice a year, the OCC reviews each underlying stock and assigns a position limit.

EXAMPLE: Margaret is so happy with her 3 HRE Jan 60 Puts that she goes on to buy 2,497 more contracts, bringing her total to 2,500. Hudson Real Estate's volume of trading is comparatively small, so the position limit is 4,500. Convinced that HRE stock will fall, but wanting to vary her bearish strategy somewhat, how can Margaret maximize her position? She can write calls, earning income from the premiums (and betting that the option will never be exercised). Because writing calls places her on the same side of the market as her earlier purchases of puts, she can sell only 2,000 of the new contracts, which brings her up to the 4,500 limit.

When Margin Is Required

It is important to note that options cannot be purchased on margin; the entire premium must be paid in full for the purchase of an option contract.

Writers, on the other hand, can lose much more than the premium received, and must therefore deposit *margin* with their brokers as a guarantee against possible losses. Remember: Options can be purchased in a margin account, but they cannot be purchased on margin.

The specific sum depends on whether the writers are covered or uncovered.

Under Regulation T, the Federal Reserve Board sets the margin requirements for securities trades. Because options are securities, these requirements extend to them as well.

When a Call Writer Is Covered

A call writer is covered if he or she owns the shares of stock controlled by the option—or can provide some type of equivalent guarantee. To qualify as covered, a writer must meet one of the following requirements:

- Must own the underlying stock in an account with the broker.
- Must own convertible bonds or warrants equal to the shares controlled by the option.
- Must have an escrow receipt stating that the underlying stock is held in a bank.
- Must have a letter of guarantee from a bank stating that the bank will pay for losses if the writer cannot.
- Must hold a call for the underlying stock at the same strike price with the same expiration. This is simply a closing purchase (described in Chapter 16).
- Must hold a call for the underlying stock at a lower strike price with the same or a later expiration date.

When a Put Writer Is Covered

A put writer is covered if he or she is short the stock controlled by the option, or can demonstrate the capability to purchase the stock if the put is exercised. (See Chapter 15 for more on covered put writers.) Put writers are covered when they can meet one of the following requirements:

- They have an equivalent short position in the underlying stock.
- They have a cash escrow receipt for the total cost of the shares at the strike price.
- They have a letter of guarantee from a bank stating that the bank will pay for losses if the writer cannot.
- They hold a put for the underlying stock at the same strike price with the same expiration date. This is simply a closing purchase (described in Chapter 15).
- They hold a put for the underlying stock at a higher strike price with the same or a later expiration date.

The Margin Requirement for a Covered Writer

Since covered writers can fully meet the obligations represented by their contracts, they do not have to deposit margin for the options themselves. However, they might have to meet margin requirements on the transactions that cover the options. For example, if a writer covers a call option by purchasing stock, there is no margin requirement for the option, but the requirement for the stock purchase is 50% of the purchase price. Because the writer receives a premium for writing the option, that dollar amount can be subtracted from the total margin deposit required on the stock purchase.

EXAMPLE: Mr. Smith feels moderately bearish about Excellent Television stock and writes 2 XTV 45 Aug Calls @ 3. To cover himself, he also purchases 200 shares of XTV in his margin account, paying $42 per share. As the option is covered, he deposits no margin on it. However, he must meet the normal Regulation T 50% margin for the stock purchase, or $4,200. But the total he must deposit in his account is only $3,600 ($4,200 – $600 premium received).

Similarly, a covered put writer does not have to deposit margin for the option, but must meet the Reg T margin requirement on the short sale. Again, the premium received can be subtracted from the required margin.

EXAMPLE: Marnie sells short 300 shares of Pacific Undergarments at $38. The next day she writes 3 PUG 32.50 Sep Puts @ 4. How much must she deposit in her margin account to satisfy the Reg T requirement? Marnie must deposit $4,500. She does not have to deposit any margin on the option, because it is covered. But she does have to deposit 50% of the proceeds from her short sale, or $5,700. She can apply the premium she earned to this amount, arriving at a total margin deposit of $4,500 ($5,700 – $1,200 premium received).

The Margin Requirement for an Uncovered Writer

Like the NYSE and the NASD, the options exchanges require that customers initially deposit $2,000 in their margin accounts before they can begin trading. After trading begins, the customer must always meet the *minimum maintenance requirement* for margin, which the CBOE has set as the basic requirement or the minimum requirement, whichever is greater.

- Basic requirement—Total current premium of the option plus 20% of the current market value of the stock, minus any amount that the option is out of the money.
- Minimum requirement—Total current premium of the option plus 10% of the current market value of the stock.

A call is out of the money when the option's strike price is higher than the underlying stock's market price, and a put is out of the money when the strike price is lower than the security's market price.

EXAMPLE: Big Machine Co.'s stock price is currently $37. Jeff writes an uncovered call, 1 BMC Oct 45 Call @ .50 . The option is thus $8 out of the money. What is his margin requirement?

Basic Requirement		**Minimum Requirement**	
$0.50 premium	$50	$4 premium	$50
$3,700 market value × 20% value × 10%	+$740	$5,700 market value × 10%	+$370
	$790		$420
$8 out of the money amount	–$800		
	$10		

So Jeff must deposit the minimum requirement of $420. He already has $50 in his account from the premium, so he now needs to deposit another $380.

Marnie writes an uncovered put, 1 HRE May 60 Put @ 4. HRE stock is selling for $57. Therefore the option is in the money, and she cannot subtract any "out-of-the-money" points. What is her minimum margin requirement?

Basic Requirement		**Minimum Requirement**	
$4 premium	$400	$4 premium	$400
$5,700 market value × 20%	+$1,140	$5,700 market value × 10%	+$570
	$1,540		$970
Out of the money	–0		
	$1,540		

Because Marnie has received $400 in premium income, she now needs to deposit an additional $1,140 (basic requirement) in her margin account.

If the investor does not make a closing transaction, the final phase of the process occurs when a holder exercises the option or when the option expires.

Exercising and Assignment

Options can be exercised at the holders discretion. It is important to understand the process of exercising an option contract.

When a Holder Decides to Exercise

When a holder *exercises* an option, the Option Clearing Corp. acts as the intermediary. First, the holder must send a notice to his or her broker. Again, this notice can be sent anytime before 5:30 p.m. EST on the Friday before expiration. The broker must then send the notice to the OCC before 11:59 p.m. Saturday (when the option expires). Recall that the holder is not linked to any particular writer, hence, a writer must now be selected to complete the transaction. This process is called *assignment*. The OCC randomly assigns the exercise notice to a broker whose accounts show a matching writer, and that broker in turn selects an appropriate writer, either randomly or on a "first-in, first-out" basis. (According to the latter procedure, the first customer to write a particular option contract is the first to be exercised.) In the case of a call, the writer must deliver the stock within three business days (T+3), because this is an equity transaction. In the case of a put, the writer has three business days to buy the stock from the holder at the strike price. Note that if an option is in the money by at least 3/4 of a point at expiration, the OCC automatically exercises it.

Shares do not always change hands when an option is exercised. Often, it is more efficient for call and put writers simply to deliver the difference between the option's strike price and the stock's market price—which equals the profit the holder can earn by purchasing or selling the underlying stock. Covered writers, of course, might prefer to transfer the actual shares of stock.

Shares are not always transferred when options are exercised. It is often more efficient to deliver the profit to the holder rather than transferring shares.

To prevent option holders from unduly influencing market prices for particular stocks, the OCC establishes *exercise limits*. These limits prevent traders from exercising more than a certain number of option contracts on a given underlying stock during five consecutive business days, on a single side of the market. Exercise limits, like position limits, depend on the trading volume of the underlying security.

Exam Prep Questions

1. Joyce holds 10 QXP May 60 Puts @ 5. When QXP's stock falls to 40, she exercises the option. Against whom does she exercise?

    ❑ A. The writer who sold her the option

    ❑ B. A matching writer assigned by her broker

    ❑ C. A matching writer assigned by a broker, who has, in turn, been assigned by the OCC

    ❑ D. An exchange specialist, who acts as the other side of public trades

2. Larry is approved for an options account at Solid Securities but has not yet signed the options agreement. Which of the following statements is true?

    ❑ A. Solid will not open the account until he signs the form.

    ❑ B. Larry can begin trading upon approval but will be limited to closing transactions if he does not sign and return the agreement within 15 days.

    ❑ C. Solid opens the account but will not make trades for him until he has signed the form.

    ❑ D. He must observe a 30-day waiting period before he can begin trading, during which he can sign the form.

3. All the call options issued on one company constitute:

    ❑ A. A series

    ❑ B. A type

    ❑ C. A class

    ❑ D. A cycle

4. Trading for equity options ceases on:

    ❑ A. The Saturday after the third Friday of the expiration month

    ❑ B. The third Saturday of the expiration month

    ❑ C. The Friday after the third Saturday of the expiration month

    ❑ D. The third Friday of the expiration month

5. Option transactions settle on:

    ❑ A. The first business day after the trade

    ❑ B. The third business day after the trade

    ❑ C. The fifth business day after the trade

    ❑ D. The exercise date

6. Bill is an active trader of options on Quality Express. The total number of QEX contracts he can trade at any one time depends on:

   I. How many shares of Quality Express stock are outstanding

   II. The trading volume of QEX stock

   III. Whether his contracts are on one or both sides of the market

   IV. The cycle on which the OCC issues QEX options

   ❑ A. I only
   ❑ B. I and II
   ❑ C. I, II, and III
   ❑ D. I, II, III, and IV

7. George writes an uncovered option, 10 HTE May 50 Calls @ 4. The stock of Hubert Tin Enterprises currently trades at $51.75. How much must he deposit in his margin account to make this trade?

   ❑ A. $9,175
   ❑ B. $10,350
   ❑ C. $2,000
   ❑ D. $51,750

8. Helen writes 1 DZG May 40 Call @ 3. Which of the following positions makes her a covered writer?

   I. She is long 100 shares of DZG.

   II. She is short 100 shares of DZG.

   III. She is long 4 DZG convertible bonds with a 25:1 conversion ratio.

   IV. She is long 1 DZG May 40 Put.

   ❑ A. I only
   ❑ B. II only
   ❑ C. I and III
   ❑ D. II and IV

9. Jordan writes 2 QXP Jun 70 Calls @ 4. To cover, he also purchases 200 shares of QXP stock at 68 in his margin account. How much cash must he deposit to satisfy Reg T?

   ❑ A. $800
   ❑ B. $6,000
   ❑ C. $6,800
   ❑ D. $13,600

10. A customer with no prior options experience, who now wants to begin trading options, would probably be allowed to engage in:

    I. Covered call writing

    II. Uncovered call writing

    III. Uncovered put writing

    IV. Purchases

    ❑ A. I and III
    ❑ B. I and IV
    ❑ C. I, III, and IV
    ❑ D. II, III, and IV

11. Who at an OCC member firm has responsibility for approving applications for option accounts?

    ❑ A. Registered options principal
    ❑ B. Registered representative
    ❑ C. Compliance registered options principal
    ❑ D. Specialist

12. Norton writes 1 DZG Oct 50 Put @ 2. If DZG is selling at $55.50, and Norton is uncovered, how much margin must he maintain in his account?

    ❑ A. $2,775
    ❑ B. $880
    ❑ C. $760
    ❑ D. $755

13. Secure Investments, an OCC member firm, has prepared educational material about options investing for its customers. Before mailing the material, what must the brokerage do?

    I. Notify the SEC

    II. Notify the options exchanges

    III. Get approval from the OCC

    IV. Have the material approved by the firm's compliance registered options principal (CROP)

    ❑ A. I only
    ❑ B. I and IV
    ❑ C. II, III, and IV
    ❑ D. II and IV

14. The OCC sets limits on the number of contracts an investor can:

    I. Trade at any one option exchange

    II. Trade on one underlying stock on one side of the market

    III. Exercise on one stock during a five-day period on a single side of the market

    IV. Exercise in one month

    ❑ A. I and II

    ❑ B. II only

    ❑ C. II and III

    ❑ D. I, II, and IV

15. Ms. O'Grady holds 2 QXP Mar $57\frac{1}{2}$ Puts @ 16. What is the last possible moment for her to close out this position?

    ❑ A. 11:59 p.m. on the Saturday following the third Friday in March

    ❑ B. 4:02 p.m. on the third Friday of March

    ❑ C. 5:30 p.m. on the third Friday of March

    ❑ D. 4:30 p.m. on the third Friday of the spot month

Exam Prep Answers

1. The correct answer is C. Joyce is not linked to any particular writer, because the OCC effectively takes the other side of every purchase or sale. When she exercises, she sends a notice to her brokerage, which informs the OCC, which randomly assigns the notice to another brokerage whose accounts show a matching writer. This firm in turn selects a writer, either randomly or on a first-in, first-out basis.
2. The correct answer is B. Larry can begin trading after his account has been approved. He has 15 days from the time of approval to sign and return the options agreement. If he does not do so, he will be limited to closing transactions.
3. The correct answer is C. The OCC issues options in three cycles; it classifies them by type, class, and series. A class of options includes all options of the same type (puts or calls) issued for a given company. All options in a class that have the same strike price and expiration date are a series.
4. The correct answer is D. Trading for equity options stops at 4:02 p.m. Eastern time on the third Friday of the expiration month. The options expire the next day, one minute before midnight.
5. The correct answer is A. Option transactions settle on the next business day (T+1).
6. The correct answer is C. The OCC limits the number of contracts an investor can have on a single stock on either side of the market. If Bill holds calls and writes puts, for example, he is considered bullish. If all his contracts are on the same side of the market, they cannot exceed the position limit for that option. The OCC establishes five possible position limits, based on the underlying stock's trading volume and number of shares outstanding.
7. The correct answer is B. George must maintain in his margin account either the basic or minimum margin requirement, whichever is greater. In this case, the basic amount, $14,350, is larger than the minimum amount, $9,175. The basic requirement equals the total premium plus 20% of the current stock value, minus any out-of-the-money amount ($4,000 + $10,350 – $0 = $14,350). The minimum requirement equals the total premium plus 10% of the current stock value ($4,000 + $5,175 = $9,175). He can apply the $4,000 premium received to the basic requirement, thus he only needs to deposit an additional $10,350.
8. The correct answer is C. Helen is covered if she owns the shares of stock controlled by the option or can provide some type of equivalent guarantee. She is covered, then, if she is long 100 shares of DZG or if she owns bonds that can be converted into 100 shares of DZG.

9. The correct answer is B. For the stock purchase, Jordan must put up 50% of the price of the shares, in this case \$6,800 (\$68 × 200 shares × 50%). However, because his account contains the \$800 premium he earned for writing the call, he must deposit only \$6,000 more. Because he now owns the 200 shares of QXP controlled by the option, he is a covered writer and does not have to deposit margin for the option.
10. The correct answer is B. Brokerages typically limit inexperienced traders to the least risky options transactions, covered call writing and purchases. For covered call writers, the risk is that the underlying stock will rise and the option will be exercised—the writer loses the stock and its appreciated value. For purchasers, the risk is limited strictly to the premium paid.
11. The correct answer is A. The registered options principal (ROP) must approve all applications for option accounts—no transaction can be executed in the account until the ROP has approved the application.
12. The correct answer is C. Uncovered writers must deposit either the basic or the minimum requirement, whichever is greater. The basic requirement is the current premium plus 20% of the stock's current value, minus any amount that the option is out of the money, or \$760 (\$200 + \$1,110 – \$550). The minimum requirement is the current premium plus 10% of the stock's current value, or \$755 (\$200 + \$555). So Norton needs to maintain \$760 in his margin account (note that his \$200 premium can be applied to this amount).
13. The correct answer is D. Before using any educational material (or advertisements), the firm needs to have its CROP approve the documents. As well as send them to the options exchanges.
14. The correct answer is C. The OCC sets position limits on the number of contracts an investor can have on an underlying stock on a single side of the market. It also sets exercise limits—for five-day periods on any underlying stock, on one side of the market—to prevent traders from unduly affecting a security's price.
15. The correct answer is B. To close out the position, Ms. O'Grady must make a closing sale. The last possible moment to purchase or sell any option is 4:02 p.m. Eastern time on the third Friday of the expiration month.

Options Strategies

Terms You Need to Know

- ✓ Bear spread
- ✓ Breakeven point
- ✓ Bull spread
- ✓ Call option
- ✓ Combination
- ✓ Covered call
- ✓ Covered put
- ✓ Diagonal spread
- ✓ Hedging strategy
- ✓ Horizontal spread (calendar spread)
- ✓ Long call spread
- ✓ Long put spread
- ✓ Long spread (debit spread)
- ✓ Long straddle
- ✓ Married put
- ✓ Protective call
- ✓ Protective put
- ✓ Put option
- ✓ Short call spread
- ✓ Short put spread
- ✓ Short spread (credit spread)
- ✓ Short straddle
- ✓ Spread
- ✓ Straddle
- ✓ Uncovered writer (or naked writer)
- ✓ Vertical spread (price spread)

Concepts You Need to Understand

- ✓ Why long and short straddles are used to bet on the volatility or stability of a stock
- ✓ How combinations enable investors to tailor straddles for particular market conditions
- ✓ How spreads limit the risks and profits of the basic options positions
- ✓ Whether a spread is long (debit) or short (credit)
- ✓ The difference between vertical, horizontal, and diagonal spreads
- ✓ When investors profit from changes in premiums
- ✓ What side of the market the investor is taking
- ✓ Breakeven points
- ✓ Why investors write covered options
- ✓ The difference between a strategy's breakeven and the option's breakeven
- ✓ Maximum gains and losses
- ✓ How investors protect stock positions with options
- ✓ When a hedging strategy begins to pay off

Basic Strategies

The basic option strategies involve bets that the market price of a particular stock will rise or fall in the near future. By holding two of these simple options positions at the same time, however, more complicated strategies can be created. Investors make money with options in a variety of ways. Holders can profit from differences between stock prices and strike prices; writers earn premiums; and both holders and writers can close out their positions, earning a profit on the difference in premiums. Investors also earn profits (or limit their losses) by combining options with stock positions. They can write options to increase their portfolio income, with the stock position covering the option, or they can purchase options to protect a stock position from adverse changes in market prices. With straddles, for example, investors bet that the price of a stock will either fall outside of—or stay within—a certain range. With spreads, traders hedge the risk of one option position by opening another option position on the same stock. Pairing up options in this way leads to a wide array of strategies, enabling investors to tailor their options positions to a variety of market situations with varying degrees of risk.

These are the four simplest options strategies. Holders and writers are making a clear bet on the direction of future changes in the market price of the underlying stock. Each of the four strategies has a distinct potential for gains and losses, as illustrated in Table 17.1.

Table 17.1 Basic Strategies

	Buy a Call	Buy a Put	Sell a Call	Sell a Put
Objective	Stock price > strike price	Stock price ≤ strike price	Stock price ≤ strike price	Stock price ≥ strike price
Market side	Bullish	Bearish	Bearish	Bullish
Maximum gain	Unlimited – premium	Total strike	Premium	Premium
Maximum gain	Unlimited	Total strike – premium	Premium	Premium
Maximum gain when	Stock price rises indefinitely	Stock price falls to zero	Stock price ≤ strike price	Stock price ≥ strike price
Breakeven point	Strike + premium	Strike – premium	Strike + premium	Strike – premium
Maximum loss premium	Premium	Premium	Unlimited	Total strike –
Maximum loss when	Stock price ≤ strike price	Stock price ≥ strike price	Stock price rises indefinitely	Stock price falls to zero

The possible results of options strategies can be visually presented by graphing the investor's potential gains and losses against the market price of the underlying stock. Breakeven points are a useful signpost for options traders, indicating the price of the underlying stock at which the investor will neither make nor lose money.

Buying a Call

The vertical axis shows the investor's potential gains and losses, whereas the horizontal axis shows possible market prices for the underlying stock. Like all option holders, the purchaser of the option graphed in Figure 17.1, 1 DDA Jul 50 Call @ 3, has three choices: exercise, close out the position, or let the option expire. If the holder decides to close out the position (with a closing sale), any gain or loss simply equals the difference between the premium paid and the premium received. For the other two choices—exercise and expiration—the holder can calculate gains and losses from the graph. Whenever the company's stock price lies when the option is exercised (or expires), the holder simply looks at the associated point on the "profit-loss line."

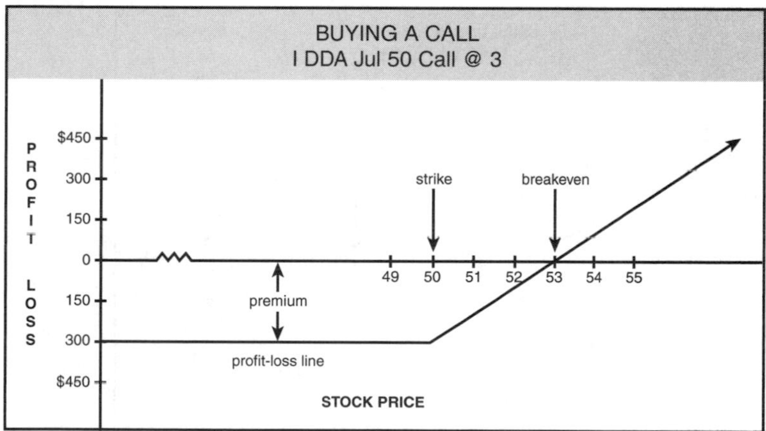

Figure 17.1 Buying a call.

A call option gives the holder the right to buy shares of the underlying stock at the strike price, until the expiration date.

Anywhere below the strike price of $50, the holder loses the amount of the full premium, $300. In this range, of course, the option can expire. At the breakeven point of $53, the holder neither gains nor loses money. When the company's stock price is greater than the breakeven point, the holder can exercise and earn a profit; a profit that can, in theory, grow indefinitely.

Buying a Put

The vertical axis shows the investor's potential gains and losses, whereas the horizontal axis shows possible market prices for the underlying stock. Like all option holders, the purchaser of the option graphed in Figure 17.2, 1 ABG Oct 60 Put @ 4, has three choices: exercise, close out the position, or let the option expire. If the holder decides to close out the position (with a closing sale), any gain or loss simply equals the difference between the premium paid and the premium received. For the other two choices—exercise and expiration—the holder can calculate gains and losses from Figure 17.2. Wherever the company's stock price lies when the option is exercised (or expires), the holder simply looks at the associated point on the profit-loss line.

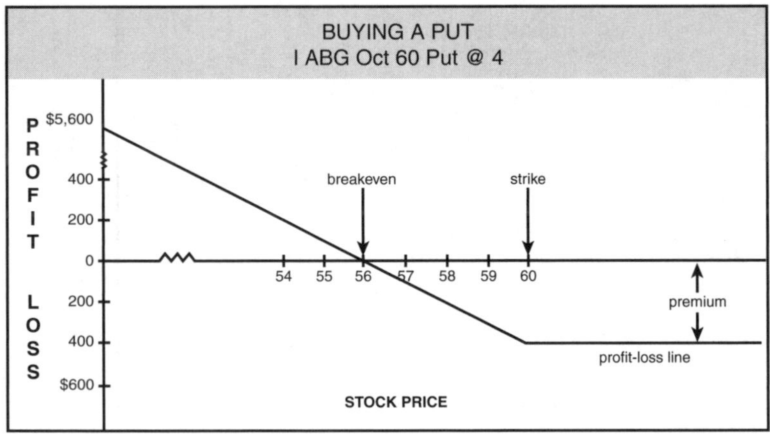

Figure 17.2 Buying a put.

A put option gives the holder the right to sell shares of the underlying stock at the strike price, until the expiration date.

Anywhere above the strike price of $60, the holder loses the amount of the full premium, $400. In this range, of course, the option can expire. At the breakeven point of $56, the holder neither gains nor loses money. When the company's stock price is less than the breakeven point, the holder can exercise and earn a profit. If ABG stock falls all the way to $0, the holder makes the maximum profit of $5,600 (total strike – premium paid).

Selling a Call

Like all option writers, the seller of the option graphed here, 1 FKX Nov 45 Call @ 2, can either close out the position or wait for the option to be exercised (or expire). If the writer decides to close out the position (with a closing purchase), any gain or loss simply equals the difference between the premium received and the premium paid. If the option is exercised, the writer can calculate gains or losses from the graph in Figure 17.3.

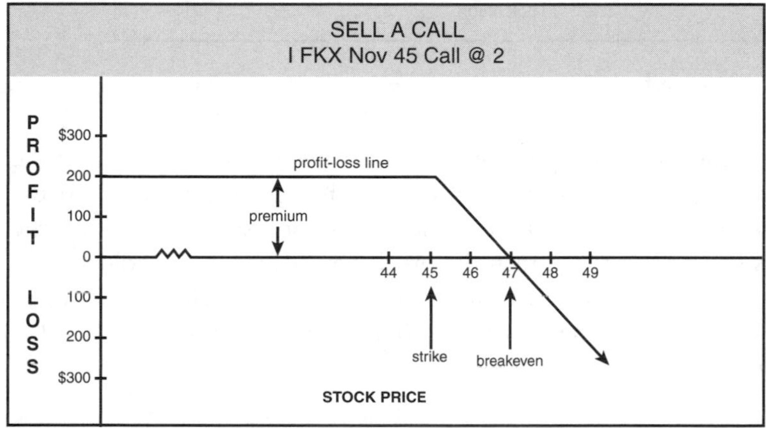

Figure 17.3 Selling a call.

Anywhere below the strike price of $45, the writer gains the amount of the full premium, $200. In this range, of course, the option can expire. At the breakeven point of $47, the writer neither gains nor loses money. When the company's stock price is greater than the breakeven point—and a holder exercises—the writer loses money. Because the price of FKX stock can, in theory, rise indefinitely, so too can the writer's losses.

Selling a Put

Like all option writers, the seller of the option graphed here, 1 JGL Jan 30 Put @4, can either close out the position or wait for the option to be exercised (or expire). If the writer decides to close out the position (with a closing purchase), any gain or loss simply equals the difference between the premium received and the premium paid. If the option is exercised, the writer can calculate gains or losses from the graph in Figure 17.4.

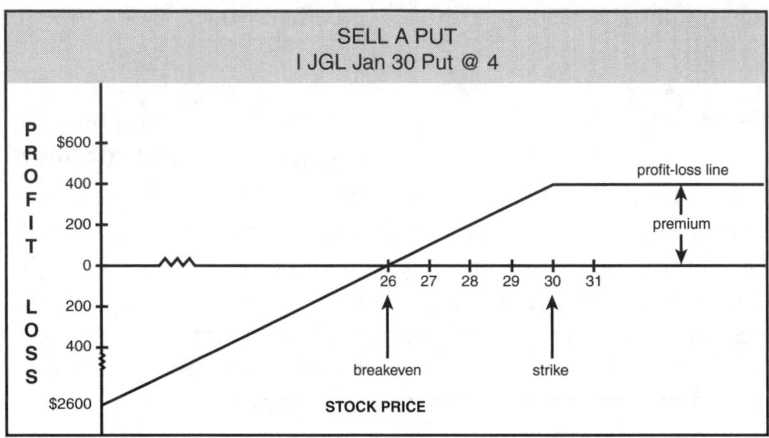

Figure 17.4 Selling a put.

Anywhere above the strike price of $30, the writer gains the amount of the full premium, $400. In this range, of course, the option can expire. At the breakeven point of $26, the writer neither gains nor loses money. When the company's stock price is less than the breakeven point—and a holder exercises—the writer loses money. If the price of JGL stock falls all the way to $0, the writer suffers the maximum loss of $2,600 (total strike – the premium).

Covered Writing Strategies

Investors who own stock long—or who have sold stock short—can increase their portfolio income by writing covered options. If a covered option is exercised, the underlying stock position limits their potential gains or losses. If a covered option remains out of the money and expires, the writer has earned premium income even though they might not have earned money from the underlying stock position.

Covered Writers, Naked Writers, and Margin

Because option writers can potentially lose much more than the amount they earn from the premiums received, they must deposit margin—or guarantee their losses. The writer of a *covered call* generally owns the underlying stock, but also might own securities that can be converted into the stock, or present a bank letter promising to pay any losses. The writer of a covered put has generally sold the stock short, but also might have sufficient cash to buy the stock, or present a bank letter promising to pay any losses. Covered writers do not have to deposit margin on their options. Naked, or uncovered, writers however cannot guarantee their losses and must therefore deposit margin.

It is important to distinguish between the overall breakeven point for the strategy (option and stock position combined) and the breakeven point for the option alone. Covered call writers and covered put writers make their maximum gain—and not lose any potential profits—when the price of the underlying stock remains in a range that is bounded by the option's breakeven point and its strike price. Table 17.2 illustrates some covered writing strategies.

Table 17.2 Covered Writing Strategies

	Sell a Covered Call	Sell a Covered Put
Objective	Strike price ≤ stock price ≤ option's breakeven point	Option's breakeven point ≤ stock price ≤ strike price
Market side	Moderately bullish	Moderately bearish
Maximum gain	Strike + premium – cost of stock	Short sale + premium – strike
Maximum gain when:	Stock price rises to strike price	Stock price falls to strike price
Overall breakeven point	Purchase price of stock – premium	Short sale price + premium
Maximum loss	Total cost of stock – premium	Unlimited
Maximum loss when:	Stock falls to zero	Stock price rises indefinitely

Writing a Covered Call

The investor bought 100 shares of Zooplankton Industries Marine at $34, and wrote the option 1 ZIM Sep 40 Call @ 3. Like all option writers, the investor can either close out the option position or wait for the option to be exercised (or expire). If the option is exercised, the writer can calculate gains or losses from the graph in Figure 17.5.

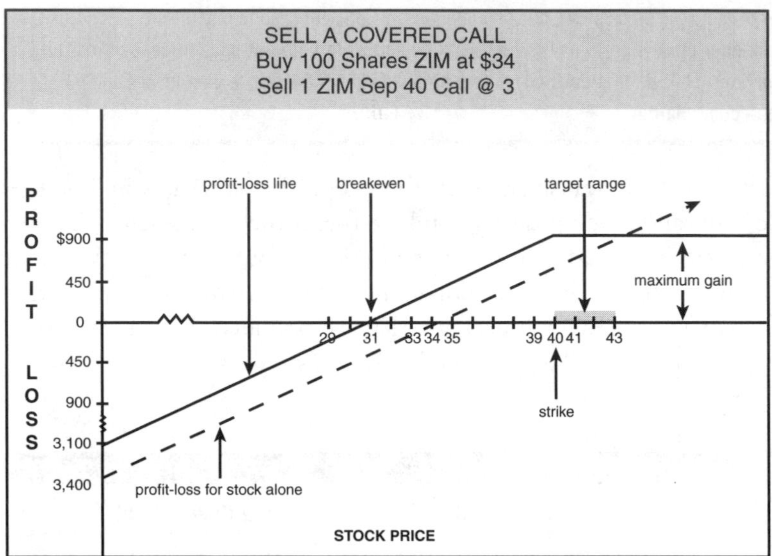

Figure 17.5 Selling a covered call.

Anywhere above the strike price of $40, the investor gains the maximum amount of $900. This gain is composed of two elements: stock appreciation and premium earnings. Suppose that ZIM stock rises to $42 and the option is exercised. The investor must sell 100 ZIM shares to the holder at the strike price of $40, earning $600 in appreciation, which adds to his or her premium income of $300.

Does the covered call writer hope that the stock price rises indefinitely? The investor does not necessarily want Zooplankton stock to increase past $43, which is the option's breakeven point. If the stock does rise past the option's breakeven, the investor would have made more money without the option. For example, at a ZIM share price of $44, the investor can earn $1,000 in appreciation, rather than the $900 earned from the combined strategy. The dashed line in Figure 17.5 represents hypothetical profits and losses resulting from the stock position alone. Thus, when writing this covered call, the investor's target range for the stock price lies between $40 and $43.

The strategy's breakeven point is $31 ($34 purchase price of stock – $3 premium). When the company's stock price is less than the breakeven point, the option is of course out of the money and can expire. The investor begins to lose money on the stock position. If the price of ZIM stock falls all the way to $0, the investor suffers the maximum loss of $3,100 (total cost of stock – premium).

Writing a Covered Put

The investor sold short 100 shares of Jupiter Medical Devices at $86, and wrote the option 1 JMD May 70 Put @ 4. Like all option writers, the investor can either close out the option position or wait for the option to be exercised (or expire). If the option is exercised, the writer can calculate gains or losses from the graph in Figure 17.6.

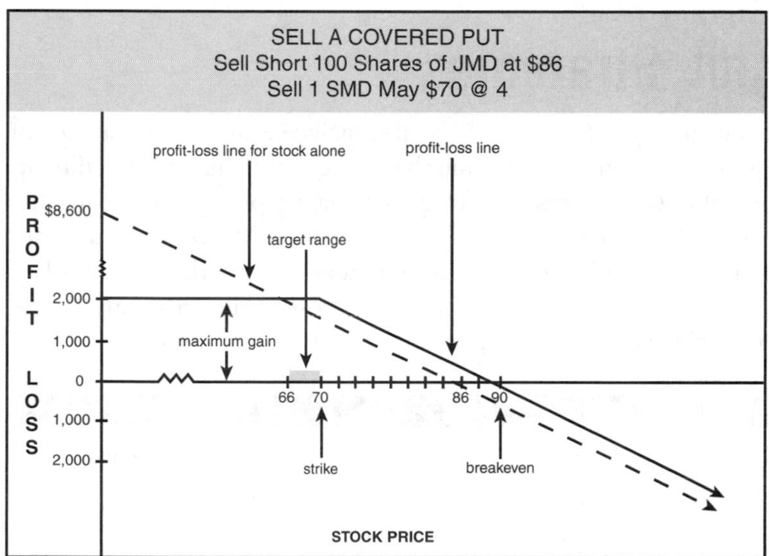

Figure 17.6 Selling a covered put.

Anywhere below the strike price of $70, the investor gains the maximum amount of $2,000. This gain is composed of two elements: short sale profits and premium earnings. Suppose that JMD stock falls to $67 and the option is exercised. The investor must buy 100 JMD shares from a holder at the strike price of $70, which he or she then uses to replace the borrowed stock, making $1,600 on the short sale transaction. In addition, the investor has earned premium income of $400.

Does the covered put writer hope that the stock price falls to zero? The investor does not necessarily want JMD stock to fall past $66, which is the option's breakeven point. If the stock does fall past the option's breakeven, the investor would have made more money *without* the option. For instance, at a JMD share price of $65, the investor can earn $2,100 on the short sale, rather than the $2,000 earned from the combined strategy. The dashed line in Figure 17.6 represents hypothetical profits and losses resulting from the short stock position alone. Thus, when writing this covered put, the investor's target range for the stock price lies between $66 and $70.

The strategy's breakeven point is $90 ($86 short sale price + $4 premium). When the company's stock price is greater than the breakeven point, the option is of course out of the money and is allowed to expire. The investor begins to lose money on the stock position. Eventually the investor must replace the borrowed shares of JMD—at a price higher than that received for the short sale. In theory, the price of JMD can rise indefinitely, as can the investor's losses.

Hedging Strategies

Hedging strategies, listed in Table 17.3, also include a stock position and an option, but in this case the investor purchases the option instead of selling it. Investors employ *hedging strategies* to guard against price movements that otherwise might hurt the value of their stock position. The option thus functions as insurance—or a hedge—against potential losses in the stock market. Insurance always come at a cost, though. The cost of the "insurance" provided by a hedging strategy is the premium paid for the option.

Table 17.3 Hedging Strategies

	Sell a Covered Call	Sell a Covered Put
Objective	Strike price ≤ breakeven point	Stock price > breakeven point
Market side	Bearish	Bullish
Maximum gain	Short sale – premium	Unlimited
Maximum gain when:	Stock price falls to zero	Stock price rises indefinitely
Overall breakeven point	Short sale price – premium	Stock purchase price + premium
Maximum loss	Strike + premium – short sale price	Purchase price + premium – strike
Maximum loss when:	Stock price ≥ strike price	Stock price ≤ strike price

Buying a Protective Call

The investor sold short 100 shares of Dirt Resources Company at $42, and bought the option 1 DRC Mar 45 Call @ 2. Like all option holders, the investor has three choices: exercise, close out the position, or let the option expire. The investor will exercise only if the price of the stock rises rather than falls. By calling the 100 DRC shares from a writer, the investor can then replace the shares borrowed for the short sale.

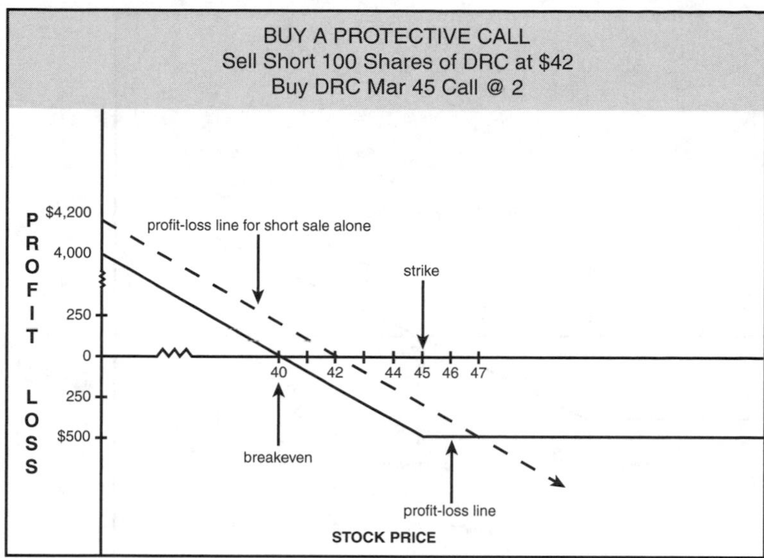

Figure 17.7 Buying a protective call.

Anywhere below the strategy's breakeven point of $40 ($42 short sale price – $2 premium), the investor earns a profit. If stock falls all the way to zero, the investor makes the maximum gain of $4,000. Above the option's strike price, the investor suffers his or her maximum loss, $500. In this range, he or she can purchase DRC shares from a writer at $45 to replace the shares originally sold short at $42. In addition to this loss of $3 per share, the investor has lost $2 per share on the option's premium.

The dashed line in Figure 17.7 represents hypothetical profits and losses resulting from the short stock position alone. Note that until the underlying stock price climbs past the option's breakeven point of $47, the investor would actually fare better *without* the protective call. At that point, however, the hedging device pays off, limiting the investor's losses.

Buying a Proctective Put

The investor bought 100 shares of Metropolitan Lighting Company at $34, and purchased the option 1 MEL Jun 32 Put @ 3. Like all option holders, the investor has three choices: exercise, close out the position, or let the option expire. The investor will exercise only if the price of Metropolitan stock falls rather than rises. By putting the 100 shares to a writer, the investor can then avoid a significant loss on the stock position. Figure 17.8 shows the profit and loss point.

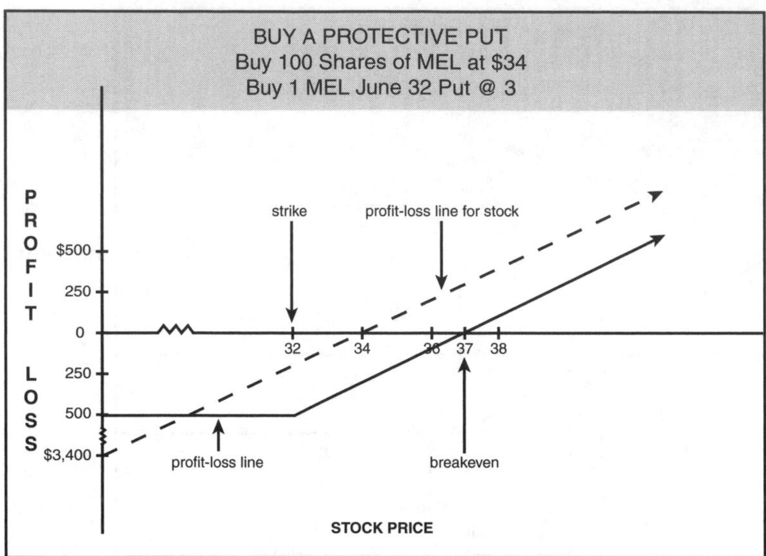

Figure 17.8 Buying a protective put.

Anywhere above the strategy's breakeven point of $37 ($34 stock purchase price + $3 premium), the investor earns a profit. Theoretically, the stock price can increase indefinitely, and the investor's profit can too. Below the option's strike price, the investor reaches his or her maximum loss, $500. In this range, he or she can sell 100 MEL shares to a writer at $32, shares originally purchased at $34. In addition to this loss of $2 per share, the investor has lost $3 per share on the option's premium.

The dashed line in Figure 17.8 represents hypothetical profits and losses resulting from the stock position alone. Note that until the underlying stock price falls past the option's breakeven point of $29, the investor would actually fare better without the protective put. At that point, however, the hedging device pays off, limiting the investor's losses.

When a protective put is purchased on the same day as the underlying stock, it is known as a *married put* for tax purposes. To calculate capital gains or losses, the investor adds the premium paid for the option to the purchase price of the stock to calculate the tax basis of the stock.

EXAMPLE: Diane bought 500 shares of XYP at $40. On the same day, she bought 5 XYP Oct 39 Puts @ 3. The tax basis of her stock is $3,500 ($40 purchase price + $3 premium paid = $43; $43 × 500 shares = $3,500).

Straddles and Spreads

Stock prices do not always behave in the same way. Depending on current conditions within a company, a sector, or the economy as a whole, an equity security can be stable, declining, or rising. If the price is moving, it can move at different rates from week to week, and it might move in one direction one month, and in the opposite direction the following month. In other words, stocks exhibit different degrees of volatility over time, and different stocks can show various degrees of volatility in the same period.

Straddles enable investors to bet on a stock's volatility. A straddle is the pairing of a call and a put on the same underlying stock, with both options having the same strike price and expiration. Straddle strategies come in two varieties, long and short. The first cousin of a straddle is the combination.

The Long Straddle

With a *long straddle*, the investor buys both a call and a put with the same strike price and expiration. He or she is betting that the stock's price is highly volatile—likely to make a significant move—but is not sure whether the movement will be upward or downward.

EXAMPLE: If Daylight stock is currently trading at $54, an order entered for a long straddle might look like this:

Buy 1 DAY Jun 55 Call @ 4

Buy 1 DAY Jun 55 Put @ 1

If the stock rises significantly, the investor exercises the call. If it falls significantly, the investor exercises the put. If the stock moves substantially in either direction, the investor makes a profit. The possibilities for profits and losses are illustrated in the graph in Figure 17.9:

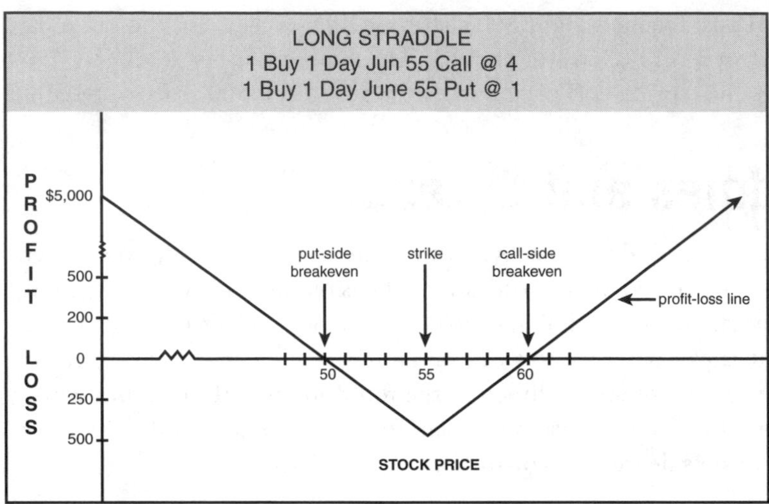

Figure 17.9 The long straddle.

Take a closer look. If the market price rises above the $55 strike price, the put will be out of the money, but the call will be in the money. Because the holder paid premiums for both the call ($4) and the put ($1), he or she will break even when the market price rises to $60 ($55 strike price + $5 total premium = $60). Further increases in the stock's market price translate into steadily increasing profits. But if the market price remains stable at $55, neither the call nor the put are in the money, and the holder loses the entire premium paid, $500. Finally, if the market price falls below $55, the call will be out of the money, but the put is now in the money. Again, the breakeven point is $5 away from the strike price; this time below it. As the stock price continues to fall toward zero, profits continue to mount.

EXAMPLE: Skyway Entertainment has sunk much of its resources into a new technology intended to be the next wave in Internet access. If it succeeds, the previous technology will likely become obsolete, and Skyway will sell its product to millions of users. If it fails, Skyway might also fail. Skyway stock is currently trading at $73, so Rebecca chooses a long straddle strategy by purchasing the following options:

Buy 3 SKY Mar 75 Calls @ 5
Buy 3 SKY Mar 75 Puts @ 1

The total premium paid is $6 ($5 call premium + $1 put premium), giving her a breakeven point of $81 ($75 strike price + $6 premium) on the call and $69 ($75 strike price – $6 premium) on the put. Skyway's new technology enjoys a more moderate success than Rebecca expected: home users love it; business users do not. Six months later, Skyway has barely risen to $83, when Rebecca exercises her call and earns $2 per share ($83 market price – $81 breakeven point = $2).

The Short Straddle

In a *short straddle*, the trader sells both a call and a put with the same strike price and expiration. Here, the investor is betting that the price of the stock will remain relatively stable. A correct bet means that neither option is exercised, and the writer keeps the full amount of both premiums received. For example, if Hudson Real Estate is selling at $85 per share, an order entered for a short straddle might look like this:

Sell 1 HRE Jan 85 Call @ 3

Sell 1 HRE Jan 85 Put @ 2

The seller's possibilities for profit and loss are illustrated in the in Figure 17.10:

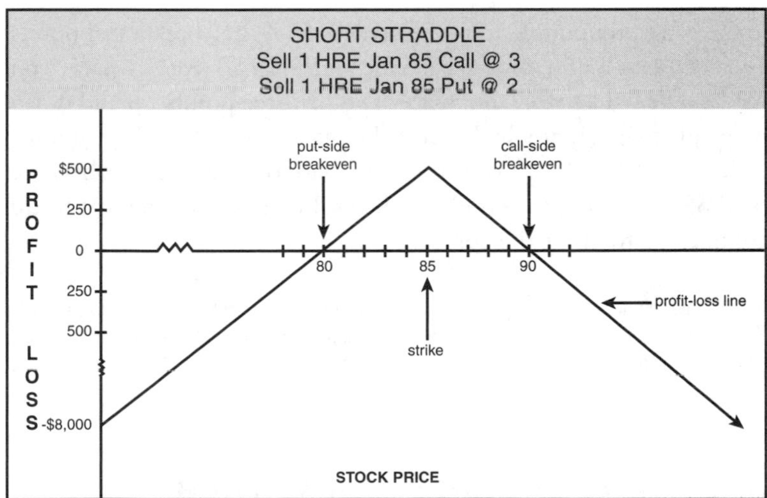

Figure 17.10 The short straddle.

If the market price stays exactly at $85, both the call and the put expire worthless, and the writer keeps the total premium of $500 ($3 call premium + $2 put premium = $5; $5 × 100 shares = $500). If the stock price rises above $85, however, the call will eventually be exercised, and the straddle writer will lose on the sale of the stock. When the market price hits $90, he or she will break even because at that point the losses from the sale ($90 market price – $85 strike price = $500) exactly equal the total premium received. The exact opposite situation occurs if the stock price declines rather than rises. In this direction, the breakeven point is $80 ($85 strike price – $5 premium received = $80), so below a share price of $80, the straddle investor suffers a net loss. Note that the maximum gain on a short straddle is limited to the total premium received, whereas the potential losses can be large (with a falling stock price) or theoretically unlimited (with a rising stock price). Not surprisingly, this is not a very popular strategy. It is only appropriate for very experienced traders investing in options on very stable stocks.

EXAMPLE: Bigness Bank is a large, stable, well-run institution, having served the community for more than 100 years. Connie believes that Bigness stock will remain roughly stable at its current price of $125 through July. She decides to try a short straddle strategy, writing the following options:

Sell 1 BIG Jul 125 Call @ 3
Sell 1 BIG Jul 125 Put @ 2.50

Because the total premium Connie receives is $5½, her breakeven points are $130.50 ($125 + $5.50) on the call side and $119.50 ($125 – $5.50) on the put side. The bank's stock fluctuates two or three points up and down and finally falls to $121, at which point the put is exercised. Connie must buy the shares at $125. She has lost $4 per share on the sale, but because she earned $5.50 writing the straddle, she still makes a net gain of $1.50 per share or $150 total for the contract.

The two options that compose a straddle have the same strike price and expiration. It is also possible, however, to buy a call and a put with different strike prices or expirations. This arrangement is called a combination.

A Combination Straddle and Spread

A *combination* works in roughly the same way that a straddle does, but the investor is able to shape the strategy according to what he or she thinks might happen to the price of the underlying stock. For example, an investor might decide that a certain company is risking a moderate-to-large decline in its stock price if it fails to bring a new product to market before Christmas, but might enjoy a spectacular rise in its stock price if it succeeds. In this case, a combination with a higher strike price on the call option might make sense.

Under different circumstances, an investor might expect a stock to take longer to fall than to rise, so he or she might choose a later expiration for the put option.

EXAMPLE: In January, Bob, who is also watching the introduction of Skyway's new Internet technology, wants to buy a combination. He thinks that if a setback occurs, the stock will fall immediately, but that the company will recover. The time to exercise the put is soon or not at all, because he does not want to pay more for an option with a later expiration. His feeling about the call, however, is different. Even if the new technology is good, it might take a while for it to make an impact in the market. With Skyway at $75, he buys the following combination:

Buy 3 SKY Dec 80 Calls @ 3

Buy 3 SKY Mar 75 Puts @ 1

His combined premium paid is $4, giving him a breakeven point of $84 on the call and $71 on the put. His possible profits and losses are illustrated in the graph in Figure 17.11:

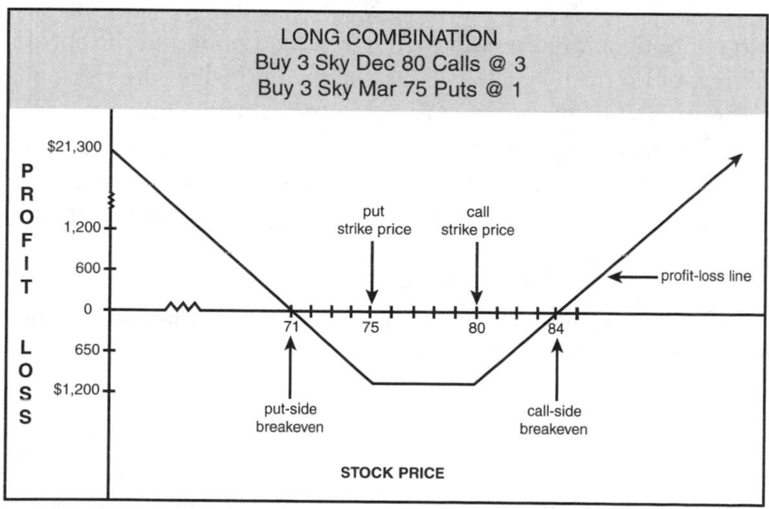

Figure 17.11 The long combination.

As long as the stock's market price stays between $75 and $80, both of Bob's options will be out of the money, and he will lose $1,200 ($4 total premium × 300 shares = $1,200). He will begin to make money on the call when the stock's price rises above $80, breaking even at $84, and making increasing profits as the price rises. Steep declines in the price of Skyway stock will also be profitable. If the market price falls below $75, he can make money on the put, breaking even at $71. His profits can reach $21,300 on this side of the market, if Skyway stock were to collapse entirely, to zero. However Skyway's stock behaves more moderately, rising only to $83 by late March when Bob's put expires worthless. He begins to fear that he has made an incorrect bet. However, as the months pass, Skyway stock slowly rises to a high of $85 in November. Bob exercises his call option, earning a net profit of $1 per share, or $300 total. Although the combination worked to some extent, Bob's profit is rather small.

Spreads

Like combinations, spreads also pair options with different strike prices or expirations. However, whereas combinations involve the purchase (or sale) of both a put and a call, spreads combine the sale and the purchase of a put—or the sale and the purchase of a call.

When an investor buys a call option on an underlying stock and simultaneously sells another call on the same stock, but with a different strike price and/or expiration, he or she has created a spread. The investor also can buy and sell two put options to form a *spread*. The second option in the spread reduces the risk of the first (much as a protective call hedges the risk on a short stock position). Of course, this insurance comes with a price: the second option limits the possible profits from the first option. For this reason, spreads are good strategies for cautious investors, or for those who expect moderate rather than extreme movements in the price of the underlying stock.

Spreads can be good strategies for some investors, especially those who are cautious or expect moderate changes in stock prices

Because the premiums for the two options in a spread are almost certain to be different, the investor's account will have either a net debit or a net credit. When the option purchased has a higher premium than the option sold, the result is a *debit spread*. When the option sold has the higher premium, the investor has formed a *credit spread*. The option with the higher premium is the primary option; it determines whether the spread is a net purchase (*long spread*) or a net sale (*short spread*). The primary option also gives its name to the spread and indicates the investor's market outlook (bullish or bearish).

The second option limits the potential gains and risk under the first. There are four basic types of spreads, each based on one of the four fundamental options positions, as listed in Table 17.4.

Table 17.4 The Four Basic Types of Spreads

Type of Spread	Buy	Sell	Credit or Debit Spread	Side of Market
Long call spread	Call with higher premium	Call with lower premium	Debit	Bull
Short call spread	Call with lower premium	Call with higher premium	Credit	Bear
Long put spread	Put with higher premium	Put with lower premium	Debit	Bear
Short put spread	Put with lower premium	Put with higher premium	Credit	Bull

With each spread, the investor's market outlook is similar to that of the simple option with the same name. The holder of a long call spread, for example, is bullish, as is the holder of a long call. Long call spreads are therefore known as *bull spreads*. However, because they also include a short call, their potential gains and losses are limited compared to those of a simple long call. Similarly, short call spreads are similar to short call options. They are credit spreads because the premium on the option sold is higher than the premium of the option purchased, and they are *bear spreads* because the investor is bearish on the underlying stock. The attached long call option merely serves as a hedge against possible losses on the short call.

A Long Call Spread

As with long calls, investors use *long call spreads* when they expect the market price of the underlying stock to rise. Buyers of long call spreads, however, expect only a modest rise in the stock's price. They therefore buy one call and then sell another at a higher strike price, expecting that the stock will rise above the lower strike price, but not past the higher one. They can then exercise the first call option and make a profit as a holder, while receiving a premium from the second option without having to sell any stock. The long call has the higher premium, giving the investor a net debit in his or her account.

EXAMPLE: Daylight stock is currently priced at $47 per share. Sue believes it will rise above $50, but not above $60, so she establishes the following long call spread:

Buy 1 DAY Jun 50 Call @ 4
Sell 1 DAY Jun 60 Call @ 1

Profits and losses on Sue's long call spread (compared to the long call alone) are represented on the following graph :

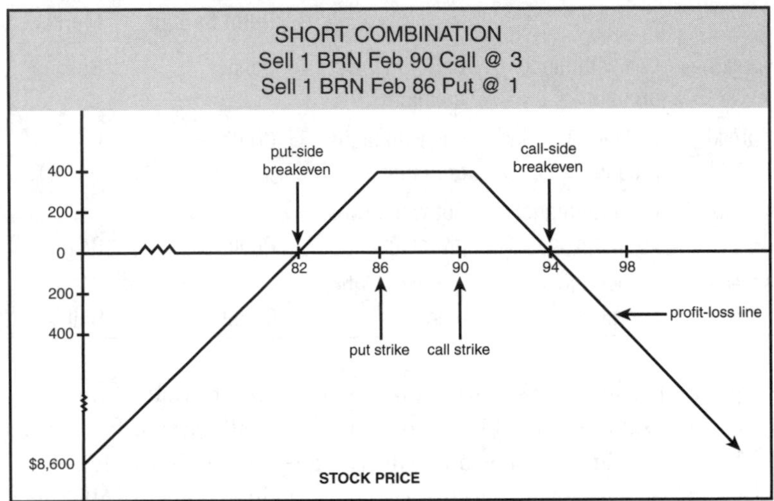

Figure 17.12 The short combination.

This is a bull spread because the long call (which is bullish by itself) is the more expensive option. Sue paid a premium of $4 for the long call, but she received a premium of $1 for the short call, giving her a net debit of $3. As long as the market price stays below $50, both calls will be out of the money, and Sue will lose the net premium. If the market price rises above $50, the long call will be in the money, and Sue can earn a profit by exercising it. When the market price rises above $60, however, her profits are capped. Somewhere above that point the short call will eventually be exercised, and Sue will be forced to sell her Daylight stock at $60 per share. Then, using her long call to buy the shares at $50, which must be sold at $60, she will earn a net profit of $700 ($1,000 gained from sale of stock – $300 premium paid = $700). Of course, without the short call, Sue's profits might have continued to rise without limit. She sacrificed the possibility of increased profits (in the event that the market price of the stock rose above $60) for higher profits (when the price stayed between $53 and $60) or for smaller losses (if the stock price remained below $53).

A Short Call Spread

Like short calls, investors use *short call spreads* when they expect market prices to fall or to remain steady. With a short call spread, the investor earns a premium by selling a call, but also buys a call with a higher strike price. The premium paid for the long call reduces the net premium received, but the long call serves to limit potential losses. If the price of the stock rises above the short call strike price, the investor loses increasing amounts of money, but when the price of the stock reaches the higher, long call strike price, he or she can exercise to obtain the stock needed to cover the short call.

> **EXAMPLE**: Mark believes that Rice stock, now at $85 per share, will fall slightly before the end of December, so he sells a call with a strike price of $80. As insurance against a possible rise in the price of Rice stock, he also buys a call with a strike price at $90:
>
> Sell 1 RCE Jun 80 Call @ 4
> Buy 1 RCE Jun 90 Call @ 1
>
> Profits and losses on Mark's short call spread compared to those of a short call alone are represented in the following graph

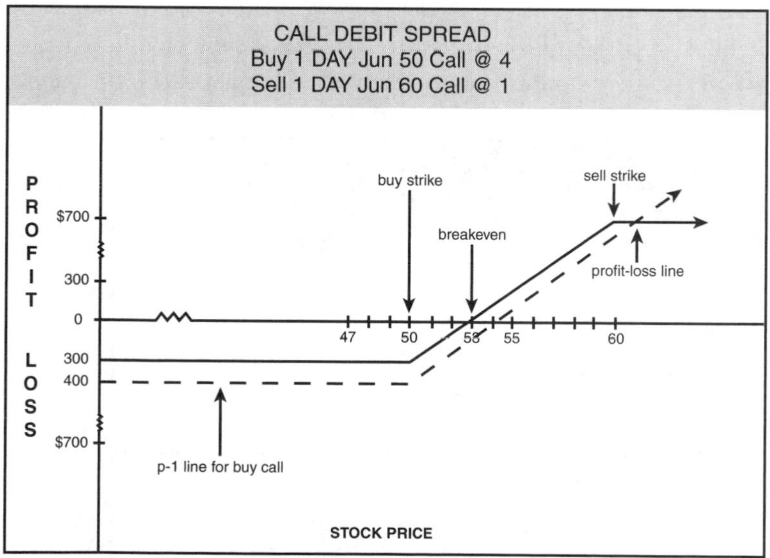

Figure 17.13 The call debit spread.

Mark received a net premium of $3 ($4 short call premium – $1 long call premium), giving him a profit of $300 as long as the market price of the stock stays below $80. If the stock price rises above $80, Mark's short call will eventually be exercised, and he will begin to lose money. However, he can limit his losses if the price of the stock reaches $90 by exercising his long call. Thus, the most he can lose is $700 ($1,000 lost on stock sale – $300 premium received = $700). With a short call alone his losses can rise indefinitely, but his profits also can be higher ($400) if the price of the stock falls below $80.

A Long Put Spread

A *long put spread* is used by investors who believe that the price of the underlying stock will fall, but not by too much. They buy a put option, and then sell another one at a lower strike price, hoping the market price of the stock will remain between the two strike prices. They can then exercise the long put and make a profit without having to fulfill their obligations as a writer of the second put.

EXAMPLE: Expecting Hudson Real Estate to fall slightly from its current price of $94, Marianne creates the following spread:

Buy 1 HRE Aug 95 Put @ 4

Sell 1 HRE Aug 85 Put @ 1

Her potential profits and losses, compared to those she would have made with only the primary option, are represented in Figure 17.14.

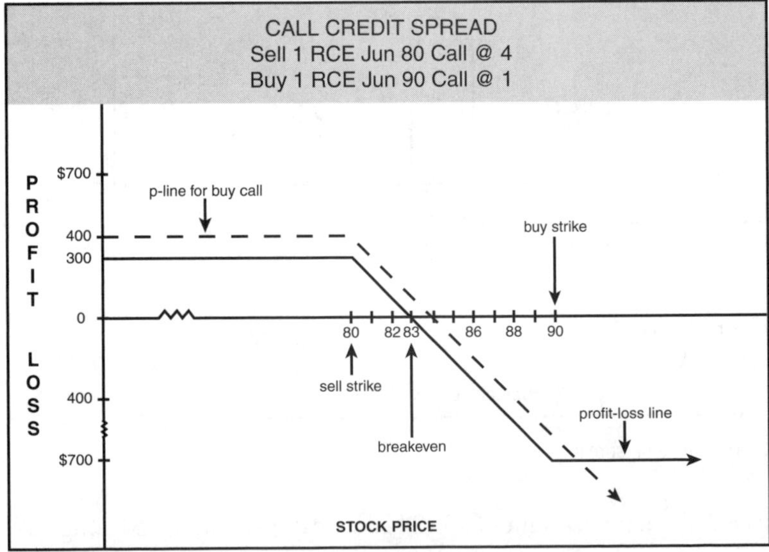

Figure 17.14 The call credit spread.

Having paid $4 for the long put and having received $1 for the short put, Marianne's net debit is $3. If the market price moves above $95, both puts will be out of the money, and she will lose her $300. Once the price falls below $95, she may exercise her long put, and she will earn a steadily increasing profit until the market price drops to $85. At this point, her short put may be exercised, effectively capping her profits. Even if this does occur, however, she still makes $7 per share ($95 long put strike price – $85 short put strike price – $3 net premium paid = $7) for a total profit of $700. Of course, without the short put, her profits would have continued to increase as the market price of Hudson fell, reaching a maximum of $9,100. But then Marianne would also have faced slightly greater losses ($400 instead of $300) if the market price had risen above $95.

A Short Put Spread

Short put spreads are used by investors who are moderately bullish. These investors sell a put at one strike price, expecting the market price of the stock to rise or remain the same. However, just in case the stock price falls, they also buy a secondary put with a lower strike price, which they can exercise to limit their losses.

EXAMPLE: With Adventure, Inc.'s, stock trading at $64, Peter establishes the following short put spread:

Sell 1 ADV Sept 65 Put @ 4

Buy 1 ADV Sept 55 Put @ 1

His possible profits and losses on the spread compared to the short put alone appear in the following graph:

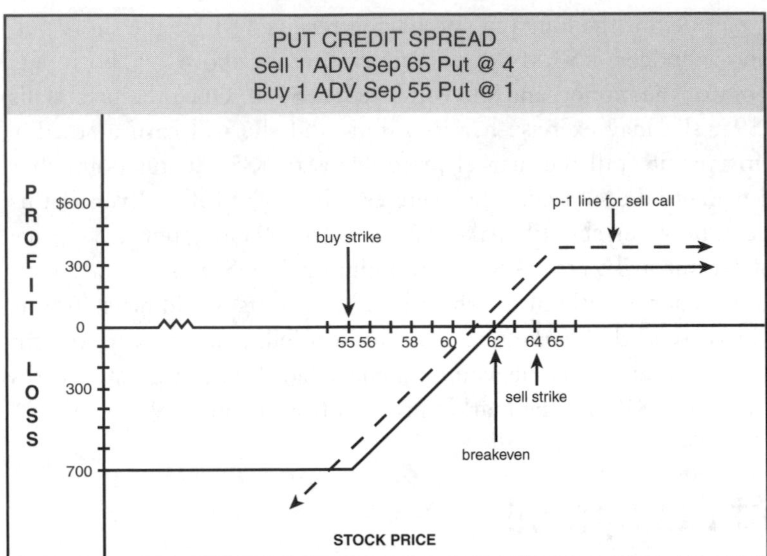

Figure 17.15 The put credit spread.

> Peter has earned a net premium of $3 per share ($4 received for short put – $1 paid for long put). If the price of the stock stays above $65 he will keep this sum, and both puts will expire out of the money. However, if the stock price falls below $65, Peter's short put will eventually be exercised, and he will begin to lose money. When the price of the stock falls below $55, he can exercise his long put, thus capping his losses at $700.

Note that in all the spreads described so far, the two options have identical expirations but different strike prices. These are known as vertical spreads, but there are other kinds of spreads as well.

Vertical, Horizontal, and Diagonal Spreads

The three kinds of spreads are vertical spreads, horizontal spreads, and diagonal spreads, as listed in Table 17.5. In a *vertical spread,* the strike prices of the two options differ but their expirations are the same. A *horizontal spread,* in contrast, includes two options with the same strike prices but different expirations. *Diagonal spreads* combine the two, their options taking both different strike prices and different expirations.

Table 17.5 Three Types of Spreads

	Strike Prices	Expirations
Vertical spread	Different	Same
Horizontal spread	Same	Different
Diagonal spread	Different	Different

Horizontal Spreads

With a horizontal spread, the investor hopes to profit from a change in the main option's time value, rather than from any change in the underlying stock's market price. Time value, you will recall, decreases as an option nears its expiration. For this reason, an investor can write an option early in its trading cycle when it has a relatively high time value and then make a closing purchase just before expiration when the time value is close to zero. The option contract is sold for a high premium and then repurchased at a lower premium just before expiration (somewhat analogous to selling stock short). Horizontal spreads are always credit spreads. That is, the option sold always has a higher premium than the option purchased. It does not make sense for an investor to buy at a high premium and sell at a lower premium.

Horizontal spreads actually involve four options contracts, because the primary and secondary options are meant to be offset with closing transactions at some later date. The key to the horizontal spread is that the gains from the premium of the option written must be larger than the loss on the option held as protection. This is accomplished by purchasing an option with a later expiration date than the option written. Because of the way time values change, the option with the later expiration loses less time value than the option that expires sooner. The investor can make a profit on the change in the primary option's premium even while holding the protective option. Of course, selling the option opens the writer to the risk of being exercised. By holding another option with the same strike price, however, the investor can minimize possible losses (see Figure 17.16).

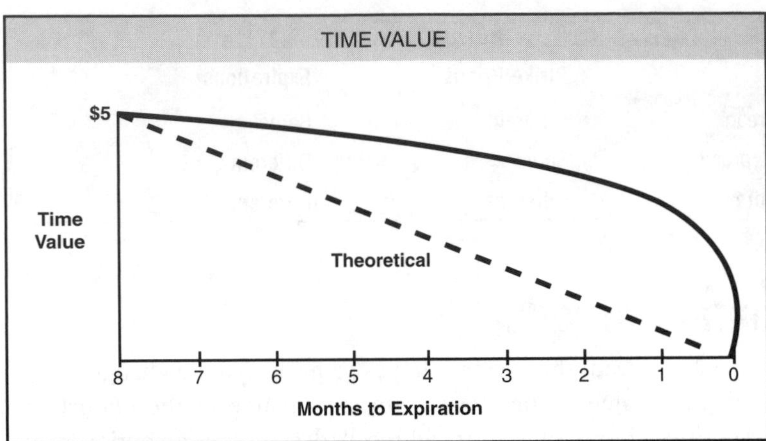

Figure 17.16 Time value.

In theory, the time value of an option should decrease at an even rate, say, half a point per month. If this in fact were the case, both options' time values would change by the same amount, and no profit can be made on the difference. In fact, time values decrease very little at the beginning of an option's life and remain relatively high until the last moment, when they then fall sharply. For options with an eight-month expiration, the difference between the actual time value and the theoretical time value is illustrated in Figure 17.16.

The time value falls by only $1 in the first four months in which the option is traded, but it falls $2 in the last month alone.

EXAMPLE: Jerry acquires the following horizontal spread in late March:

Sell 1 ADV Jun 90 Call @ 4
Buy 1 ADV Sept 90 Call @ 6

By mid-June, Adventure is at $89, and no holder has exercised against Jerry. He closes out his spread as follows:

Late March (Opening Transactions)		Mid-June (Closing Transactions)
Sell 1 ADV Jun 90 Call @ 4	→	Buy 1 ADV Jun 90 Call @ ½
Buy 1 ADV Sept 90 Call @ 6	→	Sell 1 ADV Sept 90 Call @ 5
Net loss = 2		Net gain = 4½

Because in mid-June the first option is about to expire out of the money, its premium has fallen to 1/2. The second option is also out of the money, but it is far from expiration and still retains most of its time value. The different changes in the two time values are illustrated in the graph in Figure 17.17.

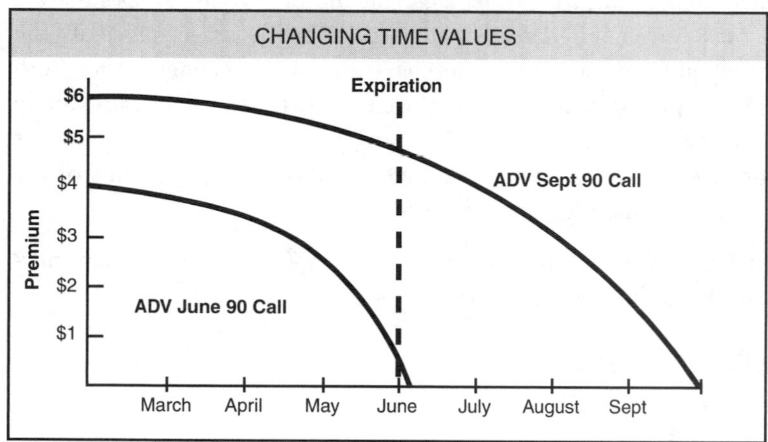

Figure 17.17 Changing time values.

Even though the same amount of time has passed, the premiums of the two options have changed by different amounts. Jerry sold the first option for $4 and can now close it for $0.50, making a profit of $3.50 per share. He purchased the second option for $6 but can sell it now for $5, losing only $1 per share. His net gain is therefore $2.50 per share or $250. What might have happened if Jerry's short call had been exercised? If this does occur, he has to sell the stock at a price of $90 per share, but he can then exercise his long call to obtain the stock at $90. His only loss is the $2 net premium.

It should be clear from the previous example that for investors with horizontal spreads, the maximum potential loss is the net premium. This is also the maximum potential gain. The investor cannot earn more than the initial net premium because he or she always has to pay some net premium for the closing transaction.

A Diagonal Spread

A *diagonal spread* combines the strategies of the vertical and horizontal spreads by using options with different strike prices and different expirations. At first this might sound like trying to add apples and oranges, because vertical spreads attempt to profit on changes in the underlying stock's market price, whereas horizontal spreads attempt to profit on changes in the options' time value. In fact, the differences are easily reconciled, for both types of spreads profit from changes in premiums. Diagonal spreads simply enable investors to profit from the changing time values of two options as well as from their changing intrinsic value (because of rises or falls of the market price of the underlying stock).

EXAMPLE: With the price of QVC stock at $67 per share, Alan purchases the following long call spread:

Buy 1 QVC Dec 65 Call @ 4

Sell 1 QVC Dec 75 Call @ 2

At the December expiration date, the price of QVC stock has risen to $74. Alan can exercise the Dec 65 Call and make $7 per share ($74 market price – $65 strike price = $9; $9 – $2 net premium paid = $7). Alternatively, Alan can close out his position. The Dec 65 Call is 9 points in the money, so its premium just before expiration is around $9 1/8. The Dec 75 Call is out of the money, so its premium is approximately $1/8. Alan can close his position with the following transaction:

Opening Transaction		Closing Transaction
Buy 1 QVC Dec 65 Call @ 4	→	Sell 1 QVC Dec 65 Call @ 9 1/8
Sell 1 QVC Dec 75 Call @ 2	→	Buy 1 QVC Dec 75 Call @ 1/8
Net loss = 2		Net gain = 9

Closing yields Alan a profit of $7 per share ($9 net gain – $2 net loss), exactly the same as exercising.

How Investors Profit from Premiums

Remember that investors do not need to exercise an option to make a profit. In fact, the options that make up a vertical spread are rarely exercised.

Because of the high fees involved in actually purchasing or selling stocks, most options positions are closed and profits are made on differences in premiums. Option premiums rise and fall depending on whether the option is in the money or out of the money. Because premiums mirror changes in the market price of the underlying stock in this way, profits on premiums should reflect the profits that could have been made by exercising the option.

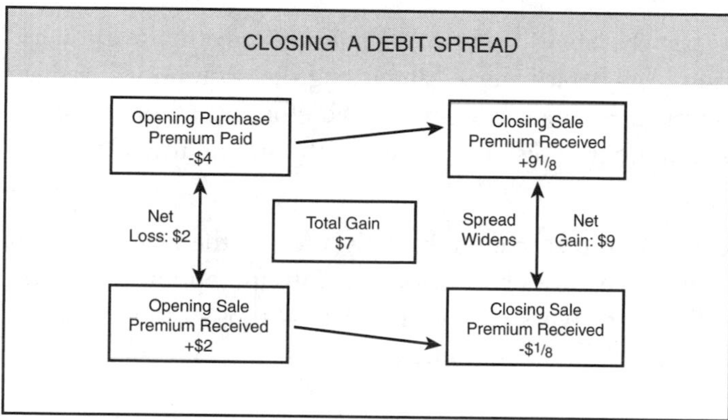

Figure 17.18 Closing a debit spread.

EXAMPLE: Rita acquires a short call spread by selling a call for a premium of $7 and buying another call for $2. She now has a net credit in her account of $5 per share. Her goal is therefore to close out both options for a net debit of less than $5. She closes the short call at a premium of $2 and closes the long call for a premium of $1. On her closing transaction she has a net debit of $1 per share. Her total profit on the entire transaction is therefore $4 per share.

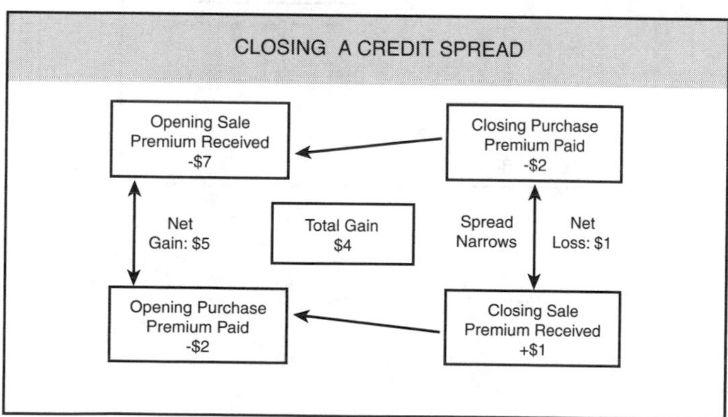

Figure 17.19 Closing a credit spread.

In the same way, you can examine every spread in terms of changing premium values rather than in terms of the possibility for exercising the option. For a debit spread like the one described here, the investor wants the difference between the two premiums to increase in order to be able to sell the position for a net credit larger than the net debit already in his or her account. Alan opened his position with a net debit of $2. In order to make a profit, he must close his position for a net credit of more than $2.

A credit spread is just the opposite. With a credit spread, the investor has received a net credit. Any debit incurred in closing the position will reduce that profit. The investor with a credit spread therefore wants only a small debit, so he or she wants the distance between the premiums of the two options to narrow.

The strategies described in this chapter are only a few of the many varieties of advanced options strategies. They work not only for options based on equities, but also for other types of options such as those based on stock indexes, interest rates, and foreign currencies.

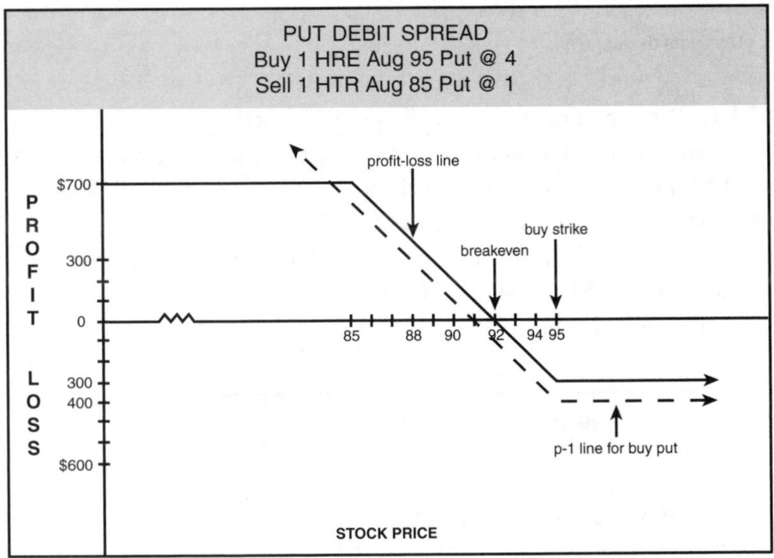

Figure 17.20 A put debit spread.

Exam Prep Questions

1. Which of the following is an order for a long straddle?
   - ❑ A. Buy 1 AKK Jul 50 Call, Sell 1 AKK Jul 50 Call
   - ❑ B. Buy 1 AKK Jul 50 Call, Sell 1 AKK Jul 50 Put
   - ❑ C. Buy 1 AKK Jul 50 Call, Buy 1 AKK Jul 50 Put
   - ❑ D. Buy 1 AKK Jul 50 Put, Sell 1 AKK Jul 50 Call

2. Joyce purchases 4 AKK May 35 Call @ 3 and 4 AKK May 35 Put @ 2. AKK falls to 19. What has Joyce gained or lost?
   - ❑ A. She has gained $1,400.
   - ❑ B. She has gained $4,400.
   - ❑ C. She has lost $2,000.
   - ❑ D. She has lost $5,600.

3. Brian purchases 5 BQB May 55 Call @ 4 and 5 BQB May 55 Put @ 3. He will lose money if BQB:

   I. Rises to 60

   II. Rises to 63

   III. Falls to 48

   IV. Falls to 44
   - ❑ A. I only
   - ❑ B. I and II
   - ❑ C. I and IV
   - ❑ D. I, II, III, and IV

4. Gail purchases 1 TFU Jun 65 Call @ 5 and 1 TFU Jun 60 Put @ 2. TFU rises to 63. What has Gail gained or lost?
   - ❑ A. She has lost $200.
   - ❑ B. She has lost $300.
   - ❑ C. She has lost $700.
   - ❑ D. She has gained $700.

5. An investor who creates a long straddle:
   - ❑ A. Is bullish on the stock.
   - ❑ B. Is bearish on the stock.
   - ❑ C. Believes the stock will remain relatively stable.
   - ❑ D. Believes the stock will move drastically, but isn't sure which way.

6. Cord purchases 1 HZH May 75 Call @ 5 and 1 HZH May 75 Put @ 2. What is his breakeven point on the call option?
   - ❑ A. 75
   - ❑ B. 77
   - ❑ C. 80
   - ❑ D. 82

7. Julia sells 1 FTZ May 60 Call @ 4 and 1 FTZ May 60 Put @ 3. What is the most she can gain?
   - ❑ A. There is no limit to the amount she can gain.
   - ❑ B. $700
   - ❑ C. $5,700
   - ❑ D. $6,700

8. Vince sells the straddle 10 HZH Oct 75 Call @ 6 and 10 HZH Oct 75 Put @ 4. What is the most Vince can gain?
   - ❑ A. $4,000
   - ❑ B. $6,000
   - ❑ C. $10,000
   - ❑ D. There is no limit to the amount he can gain.

9. Jennifer writes 1 GBZ Apr 70 Call @ 5 and 1 GBZ Apr 70 Put @ 4. Jennifer will make a profit in all the following instances except:
   - ❑ A. GBZ rises to 83
   - ❑ B. GBZ rises to 77
   - ❑ C. GBZ falls to 64
   - ❑ D. GBZ falls to 62

10. Jay writes 15 HZH Feb 110 Call @ 5 and 15 HZH Feb 110 Put @ 6. What is the most Jay can make on this short straddle?
    - ❑ A. $7,500
    - ❑ B. $9,000
    - ❑ C. $16,500
    - ❑ D. There is no limit to the amount he can make.

11. Arthur writes 2 XTP Aug 65 Call @ 6 and 2 XTP Aug 65 Put @ 4. What is his breakeven point on the put if XTP is currently at 64?
    - ❑ A. 61
    - ❑ B. 60
    - ❑ C. 59
    - ❑ D. 55

12. Which of the following orders is for a debit bull spread?
    - ❑ A. Buy 1 AKK May 60 Call @ 6, Sell 1 AKK May 70 Call @ 3
    - ❑ B. Buy 1 AKK May 60 Put @ 5, Sell 1 AKK May 50 Put @ 2
    - ❑ C. Buy 1 AKK May 60 Call @ 2, Sell 1 AKK May 70 Call @ 5
    - ❑ D. Buy 1 AKK May 60 Put @ 2, Buy 1 AKK May 50 Put @ 4

13. Grady receives a tip that VTV stock will increase in value shortly. Wary, but reluctant to lose a good opportunity, Grady creates:
    - ❑ A. A long call spread
    - ❑ B. A long put spread
    - ❑ C. A short call spread
    - ❑ D. A short put spread

14. Rose purchases 1 FTZ May 55 Call @ 4 and sells 1 FTZ May 65 Call @ 2. What is her breakeven point on this long call spread?
    - ❑ A. 57
    - ❑ B. 59
    - ❑ C. 60
    - ❑ D. 61

15. George purchases 1 HZH Jul 70 Put @ 6 and sells 1 HZH Jul 60 Put @ 2. What is his breakeven point on this long put spread?
    - ❑ A. 58
    - ❑ B. 64
    - ❑ C. 66
    - ❑ D. 74

Exam Prep Answers

1. The correct answer is C. A *straddle* is the pairing of both a call and a put on the same underlying security, with both options having the same strike price and expiration. With a long straddle, the investor buys both options; with a short straddle, the investor sells both options.
2. The correct answer is B. Because Joyce purchased both a call and a put on the same stock, with the same strike prices and expirations, she has created a straddle. With AKK at 19, Joyce's call is worthless. She will not buy AKK from a writer at 35 if she can buy it on the market at 19. However, her put is in the money. She can buy AKK at 19 and sell it to a writer at 35 for a profit of $16 per share (35 – 19). However, because she paid premiums for the two options, $3 for the call and $2 for the put, she also has a loss of $5 per share. She will therefore gain $11 per share or $4,400 ($16 – 5 = 11 × 400 shares).
3. The correct answer is A. Because Brian paid a premium of $4 for the call and $3 for the put, for a total loss of $7 ($4 + 3), he will break even when the market price rises to 62 (55 + 7) or falls to 48 (55 – 7). Between these two prices, he will have a loss; beyond them he will have a profit. With BQB at 60, his put will be out of the money and he will not yet have broken even on his call. If BBQ rises to 63, he will make money on the call. If it falls to 48, he will have broken even. If it falls to 44, he will make money on the put.
4. The correct answer is C. Gail paid a premium of $5 for the call and $2 for the put, for a total loss of $7 per share ($5 + 2). Her breakeven points on this straddle are therefore 72 (65 + 7) on the call and 53 (60 – 7) on the put. Between these points she will lose money; beyond them she will make money. Because TFU at 63 is below the strike price of the call, and above the strike price of the put, both options are out of the money. She will not exercise either, and will thus lose both premiums, a loss of $7 per share or $700 ($7 × 100 shares).
5. The correct answer is D. An investor who creates a long straddle—who buys both a call and a put on the same stock, with the same strike price and expiration—believes the stock is likely to make a significant move, but isn't sure whether the move will be upward or downward.
6. The correct answer is D. Cord paid two premiums for this straddle, $5 on the call and $2 on the put, for a total loss of $7 per share ($5 + 2). In order for him to break even on the call, then, the price of the stock must rise to at least 82 (75 + 7).

7. The correct answer is B. Julia has written a straddle—she sold both a call and a put on the same stock, with the same strike prices and expirations. The most a writer can gain on a short straddle is the two premiums, in this case $4 on the call and $3 on the put, for a total gain of $7 per share or $700 ($4 + 3 = 7 × 100 shares).
8. The correct answer is C. Vince created a short straddle, by selling both a call and a put on the same stock, with the same strike prices and expirations. As the writer of a straddle, the most Vince can gain is the two premiums, $6 on the call and $4 on the put, for a total gain of $10 per share or $10,000 ($6 + 4 = 10 × 1,000 shares).
9. The correct answer is A. Jennifer earned two premiums, $5 on the call and $4 on the put, for a total gain of $9 per share ($5 + 4). Her breakeven points on this straddle are therefore 79 (70 + 9) on the call and 61 (70 – 9) on the put. In between these two points she will keep at least some of her profit; beyond them, she will lose money. If GBZ remains between 79 and 61 (at 77, 64, or 62), she will keep at least some of her profit. If GBZ rises to 83, the holders of the call she wrote exercise and she loses money.
10. The correct answer is C. The most an investor can make on a short straddle is the two premiums. In this case, Jay earned premiums of $5 on the call and $6 on the put, for a total of $11 per share or $16,500 ($5 + 6 = 11 × 1,500 shares).
11. The correct answer is D. Arthur earned two premiums, $6 on the call and $4 on the put, for a total gain of $10 per share (6 + 4). Because the breakeven point on a put is the strike price minus the premium, Arthur's breakeven point on this put is 55 (65 – 10). The current price has no influence on the breakeven point.
12. The correct answer is A. The option with the higher premium is the primary option; it indicates the investor's outlook. A bull spread, then, is one where the investor is bullish—where the primary option is either a long call or a short put. Answer A is the only bull spread. On a debit spread, the premium paid is higher than the premium earned; in this case, the investor is paying a premium of $6 to purchase one call and earning a premium of $3 for writing the other, for a net debit of $3.
13. The correct answer is A. Because Grady is moderately bullish, he creates a long call spread, buying a call on the stock and then selling another with a higher strike price. The premium he gains in writing the second call reduces his loss in buying the first. If the stock does not rise, he will lose less than he might have with a simple long call option. If the stock does rise, he will have a modest gain, limited by the second call.

14. The correct answer is A. Rose paid a premium of $4 for the call she bought and received a premium of $2 for the one she sold, for a net debit of 2 points per share. In order for her to recover this loss, FTZ will have to rise 2 points above the strike price. Her breakeven point on the call is thus 57 (55 + 2).
15. The correct answer is C. George paid a premium of 6 points for the put he bought and earned a premium of 2 points for the one he sold, for a net debit of 4 points. The primary option is the one with the higher premium, in this case the long put. Because the breakeven point for a put is the strike price minus the premium, George's breakeven point on this long put spread is 66 (70 – 4).

Stock Index Options

Terms You Need to Know

- ✓ American-style option
- ✓ Beta
- ✓ Broad-based index
- ✓ CAPS (Capped Index Options)
- ✓ Dow Jones industrial average
- ✓ European-style option
- ✓ Index
- ✓ Index option
- ✓ LEAPS (Long-Term Equity AnticiPation Securities)
- ✓ Major market index
- ✓ Narrow-based index
- ✓ Standard & Poor's 100
- ✓ Standard & Poor's 500 (Standard and Poor's composite)
- ✓ Stock index
- ✓ Systematic risk (market risk)
- ✓ Unsystematic risk

Concepts You Need to Understand

- ✓ How indexes reflect changes in the prices of large groups of items
- ✓ What the major stock indexes are
- ✓ How broad-based indexes differ from narrow-based indexes
- ✓ How stock index options are exercised
- ✓ The difference between American-style and European-style options
- ✓ How LEAPS and CAPS work
- ✓ How portfolio managers use stock index options for hedging
- ✓ Why stock index options do not protect investors from all risks
- ✓ How beta measures stock volatility

Indexes

Even though stock options are based on the right to buy or sell a certain number of shares of stock, they are usually settled by closing out the position or by simply making a cash payment (equal to the difference between the stock's price and the option's strike price). Index options take this idea one step further, abandoning the premise of an underlying asset that can be bought or sold. That is, index options do not confer the right to buy or sell the stocks of the underlying index, rather, they simply give the holder the right to the cash value of the difference between the option's strike price and the current index value. Because a stock index represents the changing values of a wide range of stocks, index options are a way for investors to bet on (or hedge against) the rise and fall of the entire market or of a certain sector of the market.

An *index* is a statistically derived number designed to measure changes in a larger group of data. A *stock index*, for instance, is a single number whose daily movement reflects changes in the prices of a large group of stocks. The Standard & Poor's 500 Index is a good example. It tracks the prices of 500 stocks on the New York Stock Exchange. If the index rises, it means that the total value of the 500 stocks has risen. If it falls, it means that all the stocks grouped together are now worth less than before. The index therefore indicates the current state of the market.

There are two main types of indexes: broad-based and narrow-based. All the major stock indexes are *broad-based*, that is, they include a small number of stocks from very large companies, or a large number of stocks from a variety of companies and sectors. These indexes attempt to mirror the movements of the market as a whole. *Narrow-based indexes* track stock movements in only one segment of the market. They include stocks for one sector or industry, such as airlines, gold and silver mining, the Internet, or pharmaceuticals. Other narrow-based indexes include stocks for a single country or economy, such as Japan, Hong Kong, or Mexico. Options on these narrow-based indexes are less popular than the more active broad-based indexes. Table 18.1 lists the major indexes for both broad-based and narrow-based indexes, their option symbol, and where they are traded.

Table 18.1 Major Index Options

Index	Option Symbol	Traded On
Broad-Based:		
Dow Jones Ind. Avg.	DJX	CBOE
Major Market Index	XMI	AMEX
S&P 100 Index	OEX	CBOE
S&P 500 Index	SPX	CBOE
NYSE Composite	NYA	NYSE
Value Line Index	XVL	PHLX
Narrow-Based:		
Mexico Index	MEX	CBOE
Technology Index	DSE	PSE
Internet Index	IIX	AMEX
Hong Kong Index	HKO	AMEX
Pharmaceutical Index	DRG	AMEX
Gold/Silver Index	XAU	PHLX

Let's look at the broad-based indexes first. These are the better known indexes; the ones you hear about every day. They give you a good indication of the state of the market at any given moment. It is important to remember, though, that the ups and downs of the indexes also reflect the investor's attitudes and fears of the moment and are not necessarily indicative of the overall health of the economy at any given moment.

- The *Dow Jones Industrial Average* is probably the most famous stock index. The Dow is calculated from the prices of 30 blue-chip stocks, each of which is given equal weight. It is considered broad-based even though it is based on only 30 stocks because the companies represented are very large. Options on the Dow have been traded on the CBOE since October of 1997 under the symbol DJX.
- The *Major Market Index* was created by the American Stock Exchange as a substitute for the Dow. It comprises 20 stocks, 15 of which are included in the Dow, which it mimics with nearly 99% accuracy. Options traded on the Major Market Index are referred to by the symbol XMI. Now that options are available on the Dow itself, the Major Market Index has declined in popularity with investors.

- The *Standard & Poor's 100* is calculated from 100 stocks that are listed on the NYSE and that have options listed on the CBOE. In the index, each stock price is weighted in proportion to the number of shares outstanding. Options on this index are designated by the letters OEX.
- The *Standard & Poor's 500*, or the *Standard & Poor's Composite*, is even more broadly based, comprising 500 NYSE-listed stocks in the industrial (381 stocks), financial (56 stocks), transportation (16 stocks), and utility sectors (47 stocks). Together, these stocks represent about 75% of the value of all issues traded on the NYSE. Stock prices are weighted according to the number of shares outstanding, and current prices are compared to those in the base period 1941–1943. Options on this index are traded under the symbol SPX or the CBOE.
- The New York Stock Exchange Composite Index includes all common stocks listed on the NYSE. Options on this index, designated by the letters NYA, have been less successful than those on other major indexes.
- The Value-Line Index is the Philadelphia Exchange's selection of 1,700 NYSE, AMEX, and OTC common stocks. Represented by the letters XVL, options on this index have also met with less success than those on other major indexes.

Next are the narrow-based indexes; they provide you an idea of the state of an individual market, such as technology, or an international market.

- Mexico Index
- Technology Index
- Internet Index
- Hong Kong Index
- Pharmaceutical Index
- Gold/Silver Index

Stock Index Options

With *index options*, investors bet on the rise or fall of an index rather than on the rise or fall of an individual stock price. Suppose the Standard & Poor's 500 Index is at 905. Bullish investors are expecting this number to go up. That is, they expect that the aggregate value of the 500 stocks represented by the index to rise, and they therefore buy calls or sell puts on the index.

Bearish investors expect the index value to fall, so they buy puts or sell calls. The index takes the place of the underlying stock, and the index value functions as the market price.

Because investors in index options are not dealing in shares of stock, one option contract no longer represents 100 shares. Instead, each contract is used as a multiplier of 100 in calculating the total premium and the total amount due at settlement. Two contracts mean a multiplier of 200, and so on.

EXAMPLE: Leah has watched the S&P 500 fall steadily for the past few weeks in response to news of a growing economic crisis in the Far East. When the index hits 900, she believes it will soon rebound, so she purchases 2 SPX Jun 920 Calls @ 4.50. Leah must pay $900 for these options ($4.50 premium × 2 contracts × 100 multiplier = $900).

When the holder of an index option exercises, no stocks will change hands. The writer instead delivers the cash difference between the closing value of the index and the strike price.

EXAMPLE: When the S&P 500 hits 981 in early June, Leah decides to exercise her options, 2 SPX Jun 920 Calls @ 4.50. She receives $12,200 in cash (981 closing index value – 920 strike price = 61; 61 × 2 contracts × 100 multiplier = $12,200), giving her a net return of $11,300 ($12,200 cash received – $900 premium paid = $11,300).

Of course, investors can also sell index options in order to earn premiums.

Index Options Rules

Index options generally follow the same terms as equity options, but there is some variation between the different indexes. For broad-based indexes such as the Major Market Index, the S&P 100, and the S&P 500, options contracts have the following characteristics:

- Strike prices are set at five-point intervals.
- Settlement is the next day.

Remember that strike prices are set at five-point intervals and settlement is always the next day.

- Expiration occurs at 11:59 p.m. EST on the Saturday following the third Friday of the month. Buyers and sellers can trade narrow-based index options until 4:02 p.m. EST and broad-based options until 4:15 p.m. EST on the day before expiration. Holders can exercise until 5:30 p.m. EST on that day.
- Expiration cycles are different for index options. Options on the Major Market Index, the S&P 100, and the S&P 500 are issued for the current month and the following three months. In January, for example, index options are traded with expirations in January, February, March, and April.

Exercising Index Options

There are two primary differences between exercising stock options and exercising index options. First, the exercise settlement value for an index option (the equivalent of the market price) is the closing value of the index for the day, not its value at the moment of exercise. That is, if a holder exercises at 10:00 a.m. when the index is at 500, and the index rises to 510 at closing, the option is exercised with a current value of 510. If a holder exercises early in the day, and the option goes out of the money when the market closes, he or she could actually owe the writer money.

Exercise settlement value for an index option (or market price) is the *closing value* for the day, *not* the value at the moment of exercise.

EXAMPLE: Carl holds options on the Major Market Index, 5 XMI Jun 930 Calls @ 8. He expects the index to rise, but it remains low. One morning, it spurts to 940, its highest point since Carl purchased the option. He gets excited and exercises. By that afternoon, however, the index has dropped again, closing at 925. Because the option was out of the money at closing, Carl owes a writer $2,500 (930 strike price – 925 closing index value = 5; 5 × 5 contracts × 100 multiplier = $2,500).

The second major difference between equity options and index options involves the time at which they can be exercised. All equity options are *American-style options*, meaning that the holder can exercise at any time before expiration. Some index options, however, are *European-style options*, whereby the holder can only exercise at expiration. Index options can also come in one of two special types, LEAPS or CAPS.

LEAPS

LEAPS, or *Long-term Equity AnticiPation Securities*, have terms of up to three years, enabling investors to create long-term options strategies. They are traded on the CBOE on a variety of stocks and on the Dow, the S&P 100, and the S&P 500. LEAPS can be American-style or European-style, but they have expirations only in December of each year. They are available with expirations in the current year and the two following years. In January of 2006, for example, LEAPS can be purchased that expire in December 2006, December 2007, and December 2008. Index LEAPS have a multiplier of 100.

EXAMPLE: The economy has been stagnant for awhile, but Allen has noticed a number of positive signs. In March of 2006, he thinks that recent trade agreements, a government tax cut, and some technological breakthroughs that put the United States in the forefront of medical and computer markets will revive the economy. However, the effects are likely to take some time to be felt. He therefore buys a LEAPS call option on the S&P 500 with an expiration in December 2008.

CAPS

CAPS, or *capped index options*, are a fairly new European-style option, traded on the CBOE for the S&P 100 and the S&P 500. If the underlying index reaches a set value, known as the cap price (generally set at 30 points in the money), CAPS options are automatically exercised. If the index does not reach the cap price, the holder cannot exercise—even if the option is in the money—until the last business day before expiration. A CAPS option is therefore similar to a vertical spread because it has limited profits and limited losses. However, CAPS have lower commissions than spreads because they involve only the purchase of a single contract (with just one commission), whereas spreads involve two.

EXAMPLE: Expecting the S&P 100 to rise, Matt buys the CAPS option 1 OEX Jun 450 Call @ 6, which has a cap of 30 points. When the index goes to 475, Matt wants to exercise, but because this is a European-style option, he cannot. He bites his nails as the index falls, and then rises again. At the end of May, the index rises suddenly, closing at 482. Matt's option is automatically exercised because the index has passed the cap price of 480, giving Matt a profit of $2,600 (480 cap price – 450 strike price = 30; 30 × 100 multiplier = $3,000; $3,000 – $600 premium = $2,400).

Hedging with Index Options

While stock options may be used to hedge individual stock purchases, they are impractical for investors who manage very large portfolios, such as pension funds. It would be difficult (and rather expensive) to hedge every stock in a large portfolio with an individual option. For large portfolio managers, index options offer a means to hedge against the broader movements of the market. With put options on the Major Market Index, for example, an investor could offset a drop in portfolio value with the returns from the options. Hedging with index options protects a portfolio from what is known as *systematic risk*, or *market risk*. This is the risk that the value of a stock (or portfolio of stocks) may decrease as part of a more general market movement. However, index options do not protect investors against *unsystematic risk*, or the risk that the stock price might fall for other reasons. A company can suffer a decline in its stock value for a whole host of reasons, from poor management decisions to the introduction of newer and better products by competitors. This kind of decline will not be mirrored in the market as a whole, or in the indexes, so hedging with index options would not provide adequate protection.

There are two basic steps that a portfolio manager must take to protect a portfolio of stocks. First, he or she needs to select an index with a make-up similar to that of the portfolio. If the portfolio consists primarily of computer technology stocks, for example, the manager might choose a narrow-based computer technology index. Because most large portfolios are diverse, the manager is likely to select a more broadly based index. Next, the manager needs to decide how much coverage is necessary—in other words, how many contracts are needed to protect the portfolio. If the manager assumes that the value of the portfolio will fall at the same rate as the value of the index, the manager will need an *aggregate* strike price for all the put contracts that equals the value of the portfolio.

> **EXAMPLE:** George manages a portfolio worth $5 million. Because his portfolio includes a broad range of mostly blue-chip stocks, he decides to buy options on the Major Market Index with a strike price at 400. To hedge his stocks, he must purchase enough contracts so that the aggregate strike price of the options is equal to the total worth of his portfolio, or 125 put contracts (400 index value × 125 contracts × 100 multiplier = $5,000,000). Now any losses on his overall portfolio are exactly offset by gains on the put options. If the index falls by 10%, to 360, the value of George's portfolio will also fall by 10%, to $4.5 million. He can exercise

his 125 puts, however, and receive \$500,000 (400 strike price – 360 closing index value = 40; 40 × 125 contracts × 100 multiplier = \$500,000), making up for his losses with the profit from the puts.

In the example, George assumed that his portfolio would rise and fall at exactly the same rate as the market. This is not generally true for all portfolios. The manager must therefore adjust the coverage according to the portfolio's volatility, measured by the coefficient beta.

Betas

In simple terms, *beta* is a measure of the price volatility of a stock or a group of stocks. It indicates how much the price of this stock (or group of stocks) changes when the stock market as a whole rises or falls. A stock's beta is calculated by tracking the price movement of the stock over a period of time and comparing it to the movement of the market as a whole. If, in a given period, the market rises by 10% and the price of the stock (or the value of the portfolio) also rises by 10%, the stock has a beta of 1. If, on the other hand, the market falls by 10% and the price of the stock falls by 20%, the stock has a beta of 2—the stock is twice as volatile as the market. When a portfolio has a beta higher than 1, the manager needs more coverage to hedge against a falling market than when the portfolio's beta is equal to 1.

EXAMPLE: Rebecca manages an investment portfolio worth \$1 million. The portfolio has a broad base similar to that of the S&P 500 Index, but Rebecca likes to buy the stocks of smaller and emerging companies, giving her entire portfolio a beta of 2. When the S&P 500 falls, Rebecca's portfolio tends to fall twice as fast. If she buys SPX options with a strike price at 950, she will need to buy 210 put contracts (\$10,000,000 ÷ 950 strike value = 10,526; 10,526 ÷ 100 multiplier = 105 contracts; 105 contracts × 2 beta = 210 contracts) to cover her portfolio, twice what she would need to cover a portfolio with a beta of 1. When the index falls 10 points (or 1.05%), Rebecca finds that her stocks have indeed fallen twice as fast, for an overall average loss of 2.1%. Since she has hedged with twice the dollar value of her stocks in index put contracts, the \$210,000 gain on the options (950 strike price – 940 index value = 10; 10 × 210 contracts × 100 multiplier = \$210,000) offsets the \$210,000 loss in value of the stocks (\$10,000,000 × 2.1% = \$210,000).

Exam Prep Questions

1. All the following are true except:

    ❑ A. An index is a statistically derived number designed to measure changes in a larger group of data.

    ❑ B. The daily movements of a stock index reflect changes in the prices of a group of stocks.

    ❑ C. Indexes weigh all stocks equally.

    ❑ D. An index can be a good indicator of a market as a whole.

2. Which of the following statements are true of most stock indexes?

    I. A rise in a stock with many outstanding shares has as much impact as an equal rise in a stock with few outstanding shares.

    II. A fall in a stock with many outstanding shares has greater impact than an equal fall in a stock with few outstanding shares.

    III. The index value is the average of the prices of all the stocks in the index.

    IV. The index represents the percentage change of the stock's value from a point in the past.

    ❑ A. I and III

    ❑ B. I and IV

    ❑ C. II and III

    ❑ D. II and IV

3. Which of the following statements are true of narrow-based stock indexes?

    I. They track stock movements in one segment of the market.

    II. They attempt to mirror the movements of the market as a whole.

    III. They include stocks from one sector or industry.

    IV. They include stocks for a single country or economy.

    ❑ A. I and II

    ❑ B. II and III

    ❑ C. I, III, and IV

    ❑ D. I, II, and III

4. All the following are true of stock index options except:

    ❑ A. At exercise, the seller purchases or delivers the underlying stocks.

    ❑ B. At exercise, the seller makes a cash payment.

    ❑ C. The writer earns a premium for writing the option.

    ❑ D. At exercise, it is possible for the holder to owe the writer money.

5. Strike prices for index options are set at:
   - ❑ A. 2½-point intervals
   - ❑ B. 5-point intervals
   - ❑ C. 10-point intervals
   - ❑ D. $1 intervals

6. Which of the following statements are true of stock index options?

   I. Strike prices are set at 2½-point intervals.

   II. Premiums rise in increments of 1/8 and 1/16.

   III. Settlement is trade date plus three days.

   IV. Expiration occurs on the Saturday after the third Friday of the expiration month.

   - ❑ A. II and IV
   - ❑ B. I, III, and IV
   - ❑ C. I, II, and III
   - ❑ D. I, II, III, and IV

7. Which of the following statements are true of American-style index options?

   I. The holder can exercise only at expiration.

   II. The holder can exercise only when the option is 30 points in the money.

   III. The holder can exercise at any time.

   IV. At exercise, the holder receives the difference between the closing value of the index and the strike price.

   - ❑ A. I and II
   - ❑ B. III only
   - ❑ C. III and IV
   - ❑ D. I and IV

8. Claire holds an OEX index option with a strike price of 500. At 10 a.m., with the index value at 510, she exercises. The index closes at 535. The option settles at an index value of:
   - ❑ A. 500
   - ❑ B. 510
   - ❑ C. 530
   - ❑ D. 535

9. All the following statements are true of LEAPS except:
   - ❑ A. They have terms of up to three years.
   - ❑ B. They are American-style options.
   - ❑ C. They are European-style options.
   - ❑ D. Expirations occur four times a year.

10. For index option LEAPS, each contract is a multiplier of:
    - ❑ A. 1
    - ❑ B. 10
    - ❑ C. 100
    - ❑ D. 1,000

11. Ralph holds a CAP on the S&P 100 with a strike price of 510. The index soars to 555 early in the day and closes at 550. How many points has Ralph earned?
    - ❑ A. 30
    - ❑ B. 40
    - ❑ C. 45
    - ❑ D. None; he cannot exercise yet

12. Madeline decides to hedge her portfolio with an index option. She does this to protect against:
    - ❑ A. Systematic risk
    - ❑ B. Unsystematic risk
    - ❑ C. Interest rate risk
    - ❑ D. Liquidity risk

13. Hedging with index options does not protect an investor against:
    - ❑ A. Systematic risk
    - ❑ B. Interest rate risk
    - ❑ C. An overall fall in the market
    - ❑ D. Unsystematic risk

14. Susan Saranrap, an investment advisor, manages a portfolio of computer technology stocks. To hedge this portfolio, she buys:
    - ❑ A. Options on a broad-based index
    - ❑ B. Options on a narrow-based index
    - ❑ C. LEAPS
    - ❑ D. CAPS

15. Grant Favors, an investment advisor, manages a diversified portfolio. If the S&P 500 Index decreases by 10% and Favors' portfolio decreases by 20%, which of the following is true?
    - ❑ A. His portfolio has a beta of 2.
    - ❑ B. His portfolio has a beta of –2.
    - ❑ C. His portfolio has a beta of $\frac{1}{2}$.
    - ❑ D. He should not hedge this portfolio with S&P 500 Index options.

Exam Prep Answers

1. The correct answer is C. Many indexes weigh stocks differently; that is, they give some stocks more significance than others. For example, some indexes weigh stocks according to the volume of outstanding shares, because changes in the price of a stock with many outstanding shares has more impact than changes in the price of a stock with few outstanding shares.
2. The correct answer is D. For most indexes, changes in the prices of stocks with many outstanding shares have a greater impact than changes in the prices of stocks with few outstanding shares. The index value is not simply the current value of the stock in the group nor is it usually a straight average of share prices. Instead, it represents the percentage change in the stocks' value from a base point in the past, which is assigned a value of 100.
3. The correct answer is C. Narrow-based indexes track stock movements in only one segment of the market. They include stocks for one sector or industry, such as airlines or gold and silver mining, or stocks for a single country or economy, such as Japan or Hong Kong.
4. The correct answer is A. Investors in index options are betting on the rise or fall of an index. They are not dealing shares of individual stocks. When the holder exercises, no stocks change hands. Instead, the writer delivers the cash difference between the closing value of the index and the strike price. Because the exercise settlement value is the closing value of the index for the day, not the value at the moment of exercise, a holder who exercises too early in the day might actually owe the writer money if the index falls significantly before closing.
5. The correct answer is B. Strike prices for index options are set at five-point intervals. The index value does not represent dollars but the percentage change in prices from the base year.
6. The correct answer is A. Strike prices are set at five-point intervals. Settlement is the next day.
7. The correct answer is C. Holders of American-style options can exercise at any time. When the holder of an index option exercises, holders receive the difference between the strike price and the closing value of the index that day.
8. The correct answer is D. The exercise settlement value for an index option is the closing value of the index for the day, not its value at the moment of exercise.
9. The correct answer is D. LEAPS, or Long-term Equity AnticiPation Securities, can be American-style or European-style options. Expirations occur only in December of each year.

10. The correct answer is C. For all index options, including LEAPS and CAPS, each contract acts as a multiplier of 100 in calculating the total premium and the total amount due at settlement.
11. The correct answer is A. CAPS, or capped index options, are automatically exercised when the index reaches a set value, generally 30 points in the money. When the index passed Ralph's 30-point cap at 540, it was exercised automatically. If the index does not reach the cap price, the holder cannot exercise until the last business day before expiration.
12. The correct answer is A. Hedging with index options protects a portfolio from systematic risk, or market risk. This is the risk that the value of the stocks in the portfolio might decrease as part of a more general market movement.
13. The correct answer is D. Hedging with index options protects an investor against systematic risk, or market risk. This is the risk that the value of the investments might decrease as part of a more general market movement. Index options do not protect investors against unsystematic risk, or the risk that the stocks' value might fall for other reasons.
14. The correct answer is B. The first step a manager must take in hedging a portfolio is to select an index with a make-up similar to that of the portfolio. Narrow-based indexes track stock movements in only one sector or market, such as airlines, gold and silver, or computer technology. Neither LEAPS (which are long-term options) nor CAPS (which are automatically exercised when the index reaches a certain value) have any particular connection with computer technology.
15. The correct answer is B. Beta is a measure of price volatility, indicating how much the price of a group of stocks changes when the market rises or falls. If the market as a whole falls by 10% and the stocks fall by 20%, the stocks have a beta of 2. A beta of 1/2 indicates that when the market rises by 10%, the stocks rise by 5%. A beta of –2 indicates that when the market falls by 10% the stocks rise by 20%. Because Favors's portfolio is diversified, he can hedge it with S&P 500 Index options, but he needs to purchase twice as many contracts.

Foreign Currency Options

Terms You Need to Know

- ✓ Current account balance
- ✓ European Currency Unit (ECU)
- ✓ Exchange rate
- ✓ Fiscal policy
- ✓ Fixed exchange rate
- ✓ Floating exchange rate
- ✓ Foreign currency option
- ✓ Forward rate
- ✓ Interbank market
- ✓ Monetary policy
- ✓ Spot rate

Concepts You Need to Understand

- ✓ Why exchange rates are important
- ✓ What the interbank market is
- ✓ How exchange rates are quoted
- ✓ How foreign currency options are used
- ✓ The standard terms of foreign currency options

The Foreign Currency Market

As the world's economy becomes increasingly global, corporations and governments alike must confront the problem of fluctuating currency values. Changes in exchange rates can mean the difference between profits and losses for multinational corporations and can greatly affect a country's balance of trade and domestic economy. Foreign currency options, like other kinds of options, allow investors to protect their assets from future changes in price, in this case, the price of one currency compared to another. Options on exchange rates therefore provide an important way to hedge against the risks inherent in international commerce. Investors can also use them to speculate on the constantly fluctuating values of the world's most important currencies.

To understand the purpose and mechanics of foreign currency options, it is first necessary to take a brief excursion into the realm of international trade and finance. Exchange rates are the crux of the matter.

Individual firms commonly conduct business in a number of countries. A company might design a product in one country, purchase parts or raw materials in another, manufacture or assemble the items in a third, and sell the finished product in four or five other countries. At each stage in the process, payments and receipts are involved, and foreign currency exchanges must take place. Profits and losses can be greatly affected by changes in the exchange rates.

> **EXAMPLE:** American car manufacturer Speedia Motors agrees to sell 10,000 of its most popular model to a British distributor, Empire, Ltd. The car normally sells for \$14,000. The two companies agree on a price of £8,550 per vehicle at a time when the British pound is worth \$1.64. At the time of the agreement, £8,550 is therefore worth \$14,022 (£8,550 × \$1.64 per pound = \$14,022). Six months later, when Empire actually makes its payment to Speedia, the price of the pound has fallen to \$1.58. The agreed-upon £8,550 is now worth only \$13,509 (£8,550 × \$1.58 per pound = \$13,509). Speedia is losing \$513 per vehicle or \$5,130,000 on the total deal. Of course, if the pound had risen instead, Speedia would have made an unexpected profit. Such are the risks of international trade without taking advantage of hedging instruments like foreign currency options.

Companies that need foreign currency go to the commercial banks that make up the interbank market. The *interbank market* is the international market in currencies between banks. It is an unregulated market with no specific geographic location. Large banks and some multinational corporations have trading rooms where currencies are bought and sold, with each transaction involving amounts equivalent to millions of U.S. dollars. The interbank market is simply the sum of these individual transactions, just as the OTC market for stocks comprises all stock transactions that are executed on the NASDAQ computer system. In the course of daily trading, the value of each currency fluctuates. One day traders might exchange 17,720,000 German marks for $10,000,000 U.S. dollars. On another day, they might trade 16,994,000 German marks for 10 million U.S. dollars. The prevailing rate at which one currency is exchanged for another is the *exchange rate* between the two currencies. Because all the major currencies are traded freely on the interbank market, their rates change continuously in response to a wide range of economic and political factors. These are known as *floating exchange rates*.

Exchange Rates

Exchange rates are determined by the forces of supply and demand in the interbank market. Of course, a wide range of factors lies behind the tides of supply and demand. Look at the dynamics of foreign trade, for example. In order to buy American goods, foreigners must obtain U.S. dollars. The more demand that exists for goods and services produced in the United States, the more demand there is for U.S. dollars, tending to increase the value of the dollar. On the other side of the equation, the supply of dollars depends on how much Americans want to purchase foreign goods and services. If Americans import more goods and services than they export, the supply of dollars available to other countries increases (because Americans are, in effect, sending more dollars overseas than they are receiving). All other things being equal, dollars tend to decrease in value relative to other currencies. As the dollar loses value, however, American products eventually tend to become less expensive for consumers in other countries. At a certain point, American exports become cheap enough that the current *account balance* (the nation's total value of goods and services exported minus the total value of goods and services imported) shifts again.

Trade balances, however, are only one factor affecting exchange rates. The national government's *fiscal policies*, that is, its decisions about taxation and spending programs, are also important. Even factors such as political instability or war can play a role. *Monetary policy*, or how the central bank manipulates interest rates and the money supply in pursuit of economic objectives, often plays a decisive role in determining exchange rates. In general, any factor that changes expectations about a country's future economic performance can have an effect on the value of its currency.

Exchange rates can be quoted in two ways, depending on which of the currencies is chosen as the base. For example, in exchanging U.S. dollars and French francs, one can express the exchange rate either in terms of the number of U.S. dollars needed to purchase one franc or in terms of the number of francs needed to purchase one dollar.

Note that these styles are simply two ways of stating the same fact. To switch between the styles, simply take the reciprocal. For the case of U.S. dollars and French francs, see the example below:

Number of U.S. dollars in one franc = number of francs in one dollar

Number of francs in one U.S. dollar = number of dollars in one franc

Exchange rates can be stated in two ways; one is the reciprocal of the other.

One U.S. dollar = the units of a foreign currency it will purchase, or

One foreign currency unit = the number of U.S. dollars it will purchase.

EXAMPLE: While cycling in France, Marcus exchanged dollars for francs. The first exchange gave him 5.81 francs for each dollar. His next exchange was 5.55 francs for one dollar. Marcus is confused by this, however, and wants to know how many dollars are in one franc. To calculate the number of dollars per franc, he simply takes the reciprocal of 5.55 and finds that one franc is equal to 18.01 cents (1 ÷ 5.55 = .1801 dollars = 18.01 cents).

The rates posted at the local bank for small transactions like Marcus's are less favorable than the rates listed in the major financial newspapers, because the latter rates record the transactions of customers trading millions of dollars worth of currencies on the interbank market.

Spot Rates Versus Forward Rates

Spot rates are the exchange rates for immediate foreign currency transactions, which are settled within two days. Most foreign currency exchanges are spot transactions. *Forward rates* are the exchange rates for currency transactions that are scheduled to take place on a future date.

Foreign Currency Derivatives

As with interest rate options, foreign currency options trade in the shadow of their more popular relatives. Today four kinds of currency derivatives exist: currency forwards, currency futures, options on currency futures, and currency options. Forwards are simply agreements to buy or sell currencies at a certain price (or rate) on a specific date in the future. Futures are standardized forward contracts that trade on an exchange. Currency futures began trading at the Chicago Mercantile Exchange (CME) in the early 1970s, after the collapse of the Bretton Woods Agreement on fixed exchange rates. Options on currency futures (options whose underlying asset is a futures contract) were introduced in the early 1980s. Foreign currency options, the subject of this chapter, are options whose underlying security is the foreign currency itself. These have been traded on the Philadelphia Exchange since the mid-1980s.

Foreign Currency Options

The Options Clearing Corporation (OCC) issues options on foreign currencies that are traded on the Philadelphia Stock Exchange 24 hours a day. Strike prices are based on exchange rates quoted in terms of the number of U.S. dollars needed to purchase one unit of foreign currency.

EXAMPLE: Farley is bullish on the Canadian dollar: he believes that it is currently undervalued compared to the U.S. dollar and that its exchange rate will soon rise. Right now, the exchange rate is 0.7321. In this case it costs a little more than 73 U.S. cents to buy one Canadian dollar. Because Farley believes the Canadian dollar is going to increase in price, that means he thinks the exchange rate, in terms of U.S. dollars per Canadian dollars, is going to rise. He therefore purchases a call option that will allow him to buy 50,000 Canadian dollars at an exchange rate of 0.75. Two months later the Canadian dollar has indeed risen, and the exchange rate is now 0.7987. Farley exercises his option, buys the 50,000 Canadian dollars for $37,500 (50,000 Canadian dollars × 0.75 U.S. dollars per Canadian dollar = $37,500), and sells them in the foreign currency market for $39,935 (50,000 Canadian dollars × 0.7987 U.S. dollars per Canadian dollar = $39,935). He has earned a gross profit of $2,435, which will, of course, be reduced by the amount he paid for the option premium.

Investors who expect the price of a currency to increase (that is, they expect the number of dollars per unit of foreign currency to rise) are bullish. They tend to buy calls or sell puts. Bearish investors expect the price of the currency to decrease (they expect the exchange rate to fall). They tend to buy puts or sell calls. If the price of the currency does fall, the holder of a put can purchase the currency in the market and sell it at the higher strike price. The writer of a call can then pocket the premium he or she received without fear of the option being exercised.

Using Foreign Currency Options for Hedging

Companies that engage in foreign trade need to be able to protect their projected profits from currency fluctuations, thus they might want to hedge their international transactions by buying foreign currency options that lock in a satisfactory exchange rate. Put options, allowing holders to sell the currencies at a specified price, are often the instrument of choice.

> **EXAMPLE:** California Sun Sports draws up a contract for the sale of swimwear, sunglasses, in-line skates, and other gear to La Vie Californienne, a French retail chain. The contract specifies a price of 1,265,000 French francs for the first shipment. At the time the contract is signed, the exchange rate is at 0.1583 dollars per franc—a payment of $200,249.50 (1,265,000 francs × 0.1583 dollars per franc = $200,249.50). California Sun, however, is afraid the value of the franc might fall before it receives the payment in two months, so it buys five put options allowing it to sell a total of 1,250,000 French francs at the rate of 0.1590. If the franc does fall, the company has locked in an exchange rate that gives it at least $198,750 in earnings (1,250,000 francs × 0.1590 dollars per franc = $198,750).

Because an exchange rate is the price of one currency in relation to another, it is therefore affected by the price movements of *both* currencies. If the value of the French franc on the world market rises, California Sun might expect a gain in its dollar profits. If the U.S. dollar rises even faster, the rate for exchanging francs for dollars might still fall. It is therefore important to consider not only the strength of the foreign currency, but also the strength of the domestic currency, and how the *relationship* between the two is likely to change.

An exchange rate is the price of one currency in relation to another; therefore, price movements affect *both* currencies.

The best way to study the options market for foreign currencies is to examine a typical listing from a financial newspaper.

Foreign Currency Options Listings

Figure 19.1's excerpts of a foreign currency option table came from the *Wall Street Journal*.

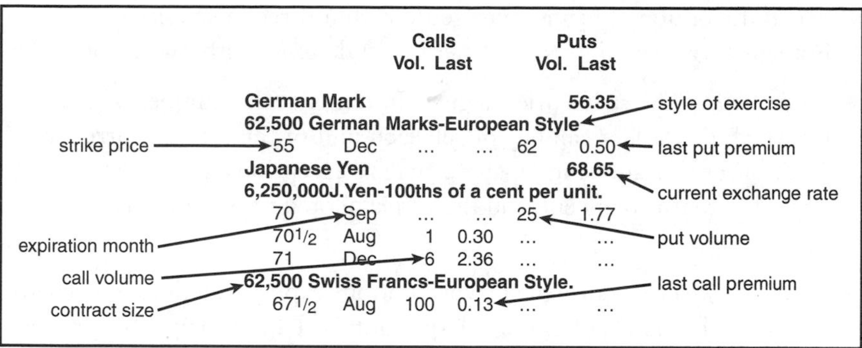

Figure 19.1 Options newspaper listing.

For each currency, the listing provides a number of crucial facts:

- *Current exchange rate*—The current exchange rate for the currency is stated directly across from the name of the currency. Rates are quoted in cents per unit of foreign currency. French francs, however, are listed in tenths of a cent per unit, whereas Japanese yen are listed in hundredths of a cent per unit. Note that this system differs from exchange rate charts, whereby prices are listed in *dollars* per unit.
- *Contract size*—The number of units of currency in each standard contract. Each currency has a different contract size, illustrated in Table 19.1.

Table 19.1 Foreign Currency Options

Currency	Contract Size	Symbol
Australian dollars	50,000	AD
British pounds	31,250	BP
Canadian dollars	50,000	CD
European currency units	62,500	ECU
French francs	250,000	FF
German marks	62,500	DM
Japanese yen	6,250,000	JY
Swiss francs	62,500	SF

- *Style of exercise*—Currency options can be European-style or American-style. Holders of American-style currency options can exercise at any time, and settlement is within four business days of the exercise date. Holders of European-style options can exercise only on the last business day of the option's life and must settle within three business days. Foreign currency options are American-style unless otherwise noted.

- *Strike price*—The strike price is given in terms of the number of cents for which the holder can buy or sell each unit of the foreign currency. Again, French francs and Japanese yen are exceptions: the franc is quoted in tenths of a cent, and the yen is quoted in hundredths of a cent.
- *Expiration month*—Foreign currency options expire on a different schedule than other kinds of options. Expiration is at 11:59 p.m. EST on the Friday before the third Wednesday of the expiration month. Options can be traded from 8:00 a.m. until 2:30 p.m. EST. They stop trading at 2:30 p.m. EST on the last business day before expiration and can be exercised until 5:30 p.m. EST on that day. Options are traded for the current month, the following month, and the last month in the coming quarter. For example, at the beginning of March, options are traded with expirations in March, April, and June (the last month of the year's second quarter).
- *Volume*—The number of call contracts and put contracts bought or sold on the previous trading day are listed separately.
- *Last (premium price)*—This column indicates the final premium at which the call or put can be bought or sold on the last trading day. The premium is stated in terms of the number of cents per unit of foreign currency.

EXAMPLE: To protect a business deal for which his company is receiving DM70,000 (German marks), Mr. Wolf wants to buy a put option on the German mark. He determines that the mark is currently at 0.5635, so he buys 1 DM 55 Sep Put @ 0.50. The strike price of 55 indicates an exchange rate of 55 cents per mark, or $0.55 per mark. Therefore, the put option gives Mr. Wolf the right to sell DM62,500 (the standard contract size) to a writer for $34,375 (DM62,500 × $0.55 per mark = $34,375) at any time before the expiration date in September. The premium for Mr. Wolf's option is 0.50 cents per mark, or $0.005 per mark, for a total premium of $312.50 (62,500 marks × $0.005 per mark = $312.50). By the time Mr. Wolf's company is paid, the mark has fallen to 0.5401, and Mr. Wolf exercises the option. He can exchange DM62,500 of the total received by the company at an exchange rate of 0.5500. The remaining DM7,500 marks must be exchanged at the market rate of 0.5401.

How much has Mr. Wolf saved his company? Without the option, his company would have to exchange the entire DM70,000 at a rate of

0.5401, for $37,807. With the option, his company receives $34,375 (DM62,500 × 0.55 = $34,375) plus $4,050.75 (DM7,500 × 0.5401 = $4,050.75), for a total of $38,425.75. Subtracting the premium paid, Mr. Wolf's company is still ahead $306.25.

Margin Requirements for Currency Options

Because writers of foreign currency options face the possibility of large, unpredictable losses, they must deposit margin unless they already hold the currency underlying the option written. Covered writers do not need to deposit margin.

EXAMPLE: Carla's company does a lot of business with France, receiving monthly remittances in French francs. Carla thinks that the French franc is going to fall, so she sells a call option on the franc on the company's behalf. If the exchange rate for the franc remains the same or falls, the company will earn a profit on the premium received. If it rises, however, and Carla is forced to sell francs, she can use the substantial receipts of her company to cover the option.

Uncovered writers must deposit margin. As with equity options, the writer pays either the basic or the minimum requirement, whichever is greater. Calculating the basic requirement takes some math.

1. Premium times the number of units
2. 4% of contract value times the number of units
3. Market rate minus the strike price, times the number of units
4. Add 1 and 2, and then subtract 3 for the basic margin requirement

The minimum requirement is a little simpler.

1. Premium times the number of units
2. 3/4% times the number of units, times the current spot rate
3. Add 1 and 2 to get the minimum margin requirement

EXAMPLE: When the Australian dollar is trading at 0.6048 (U.S. dollars per Australian dollar), Sheila writes a call, 1 AD May 60 Call @ 0.10. (One contract covers 50,000 Australian dollars). Because Sheila is an uncovered writer, she must deposit margin. She first needs to calculate the basic requirement and the minimum requirement, and then choose the larger of the two amounts. Table 19.2 shows the differences between the basic and minimum margin requirements.

Table 19.2 Margin Requirements	
Basic Requirement	
Premium = $0.0010 × 50,000 units =	$50.00
4% of contract value = 0.04 × 50,000 units × $0.6048 per unit (current spot rate) =	+$1,209.60
Out of the money amount = 0.6048 (market rate) – 0.60 (strike price in dollars per unit) = 0.0048; 0.0048 × 50,000 units =	–$240.00
$50 + $1209.60 – $240 = **$1,019.60** margin required	
Minimum Requirement	
Premium = $0.0010 *× 50,000 units	$50.00
3/4% contract value = 0.0075 × 50,000 units × 0.6048 (current spot rate) =	+$226.80
$50 + $226.80 = **$276.80** margin required	

To meet her margin, Sheila must deposit the higher of the two amounts, which is $1,019.60.

Exam Prep Questions

1. Which of the following statements would be considered true about the European Currency Unit, or ECU?

   I. The contract size is 62,500.

   II. It is used by 10 European countries.

   III. It was created in 1979.

   IV. It does not trade on the interbank market.

   - ❑ A. I only
   - ❑ B. I and II
   - ❑ C. I, II, and III
   - ❑ D. I, II, III, and IV

2. Because all major currencies trade freely on the interbank market, they have:

   - ❑ A. Floating exchange rates
   - ❑ B. Fixed exchange rates
   - ❑ C. Economic exchange rates
   - ❑ D. Lead exchange rates

3. If the German Deutsche mark changed from .5640 to .5670, which of the following statements are true?

   - ❑ A. The mark increased in value to the dollar.
   - ❑ B. The mark decreased in value to the dollar.
   - ❑ C. The mark was unaffected by the dollar.
   - ❑ D. The mark is a fixed rate of currency.

4. Paula Oldman, an American importer of fine woolen goods, believes the English pound is going to increase in value. She therefore buys:

   - ❑ A. A put option on British pounds.
   - ❑ B. A call option on British pounds.
   - ❑ C. A call option on U.S. dollars.
   - ❑ D. A put option on U.S. dollars.

5. The strike price of a foreign currency option is generally given:

   - ❑ A. As the number of cents per unit of foreign currency.
   - ❑ B. As the number of dollars per unit of foreign currency.
   - ❑ C. In tens of dollars per contract.
   - ❑ D. In hundreds of dollars per contract.

6. David writes one Australian dollar May 55 Call @ 0.27. He is uncovered. Because the Australian dollar is trading at 0.5577, his margin requirement is:
   - ❑ A. $135
   - ❑ B. $865
   - ❑ C. $1,115.40
   - ❑ D. $1,250.40

7. Robert purchases 5 DM Dec 55 Call @ 1.56. Each contract covers 62,500 German marks. The mark goes to 53.44. What has Robert gained or lost?
   - ❑ A. He has gained $4,875.
   - ❑ B. He has gained $975.
   - ❑ C. He has lost $4,875.
   - ❑ D. He has broken even.

8. Mario purchases 2 FF Apr 195 Call @ 1.57. Prices for French francs are quoted in tenths of a cent per unit, and each contract covers 250,000 francs. The franc rises to 197.11. What has Mario gained or lost?
   - ❑ A. He has gained $527.50.
   - ❑ B. He has gained $1,055.
   - ❑ C. He has gained $270.
   - ❑ D. He has lost $135.

9. Silver Steel ships steel to Germany. Owed 9.8 million marks for a recent order, Silver wants to protect itself against a fall in the mark. How many contracts of a German mark put must Silver purchase to hedge this amount?
   - ❑ A. 157 contracts
   - ❑ B. 196 contracts
   - ❑ C. 211 contracts
   - ❑ D. 314 contracts

10. Joel wants to purchase a Mercedes-Benz while he is in Germany and have it shipped to the United States. The car costs 60,000 marks. Because the mark is currently trading at 0.6630 U.S. dollar equivalent, this is the same as:
    - ❑ A. $21,062.50
    - ❑ B. $39,780
    - ❑ C. $41,437.50
    - ❑ D. $60,000

11. Joel is afraid that the German mark will rise before he buys his car. To lock in an exchange rate, he buys 1 DM Mar 67 Call @ 1.77. This costs him:

- ❑ A. $885
- ❑ B. $1,077
- ❑ C. $1,106.25
- ❑ D. $1,770

12. Which of the following are true of the interbank?

I. It is the international market in currencies between banks.

II. The interbank operates in a special building in Zurich.

III. It is the sum of the individual transactions.

IV. The value of each currency fluctuates daily.

- ❑ A. I and II
- ❑ B. II and III
- ❑ C. I, III, and IV
- ❑ D. II and IV

13. What factors affect exchange rates?

I. Trade balances

II. Margin requirements

III. Fiscal policy

IV. Monetary policy

- ❑ A. I only
- ❑ B. II and III
- ❑ C. I, III, and IV
- ❑ D. II, III, and IV

14. Each of the following comprises one contract except:

- ❑ A. 62,500 ECUs
- ❑ B. 62,500,000 Japanese yen
- ❑ C. 250,000 French francs
- ❑ D. 50,000 Canadian dollars

15. Which of the following statements is considered true about spot transactions?

I. Settlement occurs within two business days.

II. Settlement occurs months in the future.

III. Spot transactions are for a fixed rate currency.

IV. Spot transactions are for immediate settlement.

- ❑ A. I only
- ❑ B. II only
- ❑ C. II and III
- ❑ D. I and IV

Exam Prep Answers

1. The correct answer is C. The European Currency Unit was created in 1979 and is commonly used by ten European countries. It actively trades on the interbank market and has a contract size of 62,500 units, quoted in cents.
2. The correct answer is A. Because all major currencies trade freely on the interbank market, their rates change continuously in response to a wide range of economic and political factors. They thus have floating exchange rates. The Bretton Woods Agreement established fixed exchanges rates in 1944, but most countries had abandoned them by 1973.
3. The correct answer is A. At .5640, the mark equals 1.77 U.S. dollars. At .5670, the mark equals 1.764 U.S. dollars. So the mark has increased in value to the dollar because you are now getting fewer U.S. dollars for each mark. To find the amount of U.S. dollars, divide $1.00 by the D-mark value of .5640, which equals $1.77; or $1.00 divided by .5670 = $1.76.
4. The correct answer is B. Investors who expect the price of a currency to increase are bullish. They tend to buy calls or sell puts. Oldman therefore buys a call option on British pounds.
5. The correct answer is B. The strike price of a foreign currency option is given as the number of U.S. dollars needed to buy one unit of foreign currency. French francs and Japanese yen are the exceptions: the franc is quoted in tenths of a cent, and the yen is quoted in hundredths of a cent.
6. The correct answer is D. As with equity options, uncovered writers of foreign currency options deposit either the basic or the minimum margin requirement, whichever is greater. The current contract value is the total number of currency units covered by the option multiplied by the current rate, in this case $27,885 (50,000 units × 1 contract × 0.5577). The basic requirement, then, is:

$135.00	current premium ($0.0027 × 50,000)
+ $1115.40	(4% of the current contract value)
– $0.00	(amount option is out of the money)
= $1250.40	

The minimum requirement is:

$135.00	current premium ($0.0027 × 50,000)
+$209.14	(3.4% of the current contract value)
= $344.14	

The basic requirement is higher; David must deposit $1,250.40 into a margin account.

7. The correct answer is C. Robert paid a premium of 1.56 or $0.0156 per mark. He therefore paid $975 per contract (0.0156 × 62,500) or a total of $4,875 (975 × 5 contracts). Because the mark's market price is below the strike price, Robert's call is worthless: He will not purchase marks at 55 if he can get them on the market for 53.44. He has therefore lost the premium he paid, or $4,875.
8. The correct answer is C. The premium is 1.57, or $0.00157 per franc. Mario therefore paid a total premium of $785 (0.00157 × 250,000 = $392.50 × 2 contracts). Because the call is in the money by 2.11 tenths of a cent (195 – 197.11) or $0.00211 per franc, Mario exercises. He earns a profit on the francs of $1,055 ($0.00211 × 250,000 = $527.10 × 2 contracts). He has therefore made a net gain of $270 ($1,055 – 785).
9. The correct answer is A. Because each contract covers 62,500 marks, the company must purchase 157 contracts to cover the outstanding 9.8 million marks (9,800,000 (62,500 = 156.8).
10. The correct answer is B. At 0.6630 U.S. dollar equivalent, each German mark equals 0.6630 dollars. To find the cost of the car in dollars, multiply the 60,000 marks by this dollar equivalent. The car costs $39,780 (60,000 × 0.6630).
11. The correct answer is C. The premium is 1.77 cents, or $0.0177 per mark. Each contract covers 62,500 marks. Joel therefore pays a total premium of $1,106.25 ($0.0177 × 62,500 marks).
12. The correct answer is C. The interbank is an international market in currencies between banks. It is the sum of the individual transactions where the value of each currency fluctuates daily. There is no special building housing the interbank in Zurich.
13. The correct answer is C. Trade balances, fiscal policy, and monetary policy all have an effect on exchange rates. Margin requirements pertain to options trading and the amount of money an uncovered trader must deposit to cover a portion of the value of the trade.
14. The correct answer is B. One Japanese yen contract covers ¥6,250,000.
15. The correct answer is D. Spot transactions are intended for immediate settlement, which most often occurs within two business days. Forward contracts settle months in the future.

PART VI
Accounts

Customer Accounts

Terms You Need to Know

- ✓ Administrator account
- ✓ Beneficial owner
- ✓ Cash account
- ✓ Cashier's department
- ✓ Churning
- ✓ Confirmation (or confirm)
- ✓ Conservator account
- ✓ Corporate account
- ✓ Custodian account
- ✓ Discretionary account
- ✓ Executor account
- ✓ Fiduciary
- ✓ Fiduciary account
- ✓ Guardian account
- ✓ Insider
- ✓ Interest and dividend department
- ✓ Investment adviser
- ✓ Joint account
- ✓ Joint tenants with rights of survivorship account (JTWROS)
- ✓ Kiddie tax
- ✓ Legal list
- ✓ Margin account
- ✓ Numbered account
- ✓ Omnibus account
- ✓ Option account
- ✓ Partnership account
- ✓ Power of attorney
- ✓ Proxy department
- ✓ Prudent man rule
- ✓ Purchase and sales (P&S) margin department
- ✓ Receivership account
- ✓ Reorganization department
- ✓ Rule 405 ("Know Your Customer" rule)
- ✓ Securities Investor Protection Corporation (SIPC)
- ✓ Street name
- ✓ Tenancy-in-common account
- ✓ Trust account
- ✓ Wire and order department

Concepts You Need to Understand

- ✓ What brokers are required to know about customers
- ✓ What is required to establish an account
- ✓ Types of accounts
- ✓ Limits on investors' trading, given their account type
- ✓ The difference between a beneficial owner and a trader
- ✓ Rules and requirements for each account
- ✓ The departments within a broker-dealer and their duties
- ✓ How broker-dealers maintain, transfer, and close accounts for customers
- ✓ How customers are partially protected against the bankruptcy of their brokerage house

Opening an Account

Investors trade stocks, bonds, and options through broker-dealer accounts. Because trading involves risks, and because different investors have different goals and different tolerances for risk, broker-dealers must review and approve potential customers before allowing them to open accounts. A wide variety of customer accounts exist; each is distinguished by the kind of trading it allows, and by the people who are permitted to execute trades in the account (or benefit from the trading). This chapter examines the requirements for opening each type of account, the rules for maintaining them, and the process for closing them.

Needless to say, trading is inherently risky. Securities transactions can involve large amounts of money, and some instruments, like options, involve future obligations much larger than the original investment. All can result in serious losses. For these reasons, brokers must take great care when setting up new accounts for their customers, and when trading on their customers' behalf. The greatest protection afforded customers—and brokers—springs from the New York Stock Exchange's Rule 405, which specifies that brokers must know their customers.

Rule 405 was established by the NYSE to guide the conduct of member broker-dealers. Also called the *"Know Your Customer" rule*, it recognizes that what is suitable for one investor might not be suitable for another. The rule requires that brokers obtain enough information about their customers—including financial status, investment experience, and aims—to know which investments are appropriate for each. Brokers who cannot obtain this information about a customer cannot recommend trades to that customer.

Rule 405: Know Your Customer! Such information as financial status, investment experience, and goals are essential to advising any client. Brokers who do not have this information should not recommend trades to that customer.

To set up accounts for clients, then, broker-dealers must obtain certain basic information. Much of this is obtained through the application, or new account form.

The information and documentation required depends somewhat on the type of account, but the broker-dealer has to get certain basic information for all clients:

- Customer's legal name and address
- Kind of account—Cash, margin, options, or arbitrage account, each of which enables customers to trade different securities on different terms (these accounts are discussed later in this chapter)
- Age
- Tax identification number (for an individual, social security number)
- Occupation and employer—To gauge the customer's income level, and to determine whether he or she works for another broker-dealer or financial institution (in such cases, special reporting procedures are required)

In addition, some securities exchanges require the following information:

- Citizenship
- Insider status—Customers must reveal if they are officers, directors, or 10% shareholders of any publicly traded company. Each of these is considered an *insider*, a person who potentially has access to privileged information and is subject to limitations on trading.
- Tax bracket
- Bank reference

The primary purpose of the information on the new account form is to enable a registered rep to assess the suitability of investments for the customer. Know Your Customer!

What happens if a customer wants to execute a trade that the broker does not recommend? When a customer requests a trade that the registered rep believes is unsuitable, the rep must so inform the customer. If the customer nevertheless wants to proceed, the registered rep can execute the trade (it is, after all, the customer's money) but must mark the order ticket "unsolicited"—and can even record the conversation with the customer, as protection against liability. Brokers have been sued by customers who lost substantial amounts in unsuitable trades.

Such risks can be exacerbated because, in some accounts, customers can purchase securities that have a value greater than the balance in the account. This exposes them to potentially catastrophic losses. It is also of the utmost importance that the registered rep and customer carefully select the type of account. Not only should trades be suitable to the customer, but so should the account itself.

Types of Accounts

Brokerage accounts contain customers' cash deposits and the securities purchased by the broker-dealer on customers' behalf. Different kinds of accounts have different privileges; customers might be able to trade on different terms, or to trade different kinds of securities. A customer requests the type of account from the four basic choices available: cash, margin, arbitrage, and option.

- A *cash account* is the most basic type of account—customers pay for each transaction in full by the settlement date. This is the lowest risk for the broker, but it can present inconveniences for the investor, who might have to pass up opportunities because of a lack of ready funds. Margin accounts offer the investor some advantages.
- *Margin accounts* permit investors to buy securities on margin—an amount that is less than the total value of the securities. The broker-dealer extends credit to the customer for the remainder.
- An *arbitrage account* is a margin account in which investors perform arbitrage transactions; that is, they simultaneously buy and sell the same security to exploit riskless profit.
- An *option account* is an account that allows for the trading of options. Options, because they leverage relatively small premium payments into contracts controlling large numbers of securities, constitute potentially risky investments; they involve future obligations that can expose the investor to large losses. Broker-dealers must therefore ensure that customers who want to trade options have more investment experience and tolerance for risk than customers who trade only equities and bonds. Customers who want to open options accounts need to provide additional information, including their financial situation and needs, their net worth and liquid net worth, annual income, and investment objectives.

Types of Accounts by Ownership and Control

An individual account, in which a person trades on his or her own behalf, is the simplest type of account. But many other arrangements are possible. The owner of an account might be a company, for example, with one or two designated officers allowed to make trades. For many accounts, the person controlling the account is not the beneficial owner. In other cases, ownership is spread among two or more parties.

In addition to individual accounts, three kinds of accounts provide for different kinds of ownership:

- *Joint accounts* are owned by more than one person. A joint account can be a *joint tenancy with rights of survivorship* (or *JTWROS*) *account*, which means that if one of the owners dies, the other owner (or owners) takes control of the assets. For married couples, this is the most common arrangement. Alternatively, a *tenancy-in-common account* stipulates that if one of the owners dies, his or her portion of the account becomes part of that person's estate.
- *Partnership accounts* are available for legal partnerships. The partnership agreement must contain a clause allowing this type of account, and must also specify the persons who can trade on behalf of the partnership. All the partners have to sign the new account form and provide their legal names, addresses, and social security numbers.
- *Corporate accounts* can be opened only by incorporated businesses. For a cash account, the corporation must present a copy of the corporate resolution authorizing the account. The resolution specifies the persons allowed to trade in the account.

In all the previously mentioned accounts, owners—or their stated representatives—trade for their own benefit. Four other kinds of accounts permit a different person to trade on behalf of the beneficial owner:

- Custodian accounts
- Discretionary accounts
- Omnibus accounts
- Fiduciary accounts

Custodian Accounts

A *custodian account* is an account that gives an adult the right to make trading decisions on behalf of a beneficial owner who is a minor. Because minors are not considered legally responsible, they cannot open their own accounts or make trades. Under the federal *Uniform Gifts to Minors Act (UGMA)*, however, adults can give money or property (such as securities) to a minor. The UGMA also permits adults to open custodian accounts, using either gifts to the minor or the minor's earnings to establish the account, and regulates the taxation of income from the account.

Any adult can open a custodian account on behalf of a minor—the adult and the minor do not have to be related—but, there can only be one custodian and one minor per account. Custodian accounts cannot be margin accounts, nor can they keep securities in street name: all securities must be registered in the name of the custodian and the minor. Gifts of securities or cash given to the minor are irrevocable, that is, cannot legally be retracted. Also, when the minor comes of age (reaches majority), the custodian must reregister the account in the name of the new adult.

The custodian must manage the account according to the *prudent man rule*, a regulation adopted by some states that says that custodians cannot make any investment that a prudent person would not make for his or her own account. States that do not employ the prudent man rule maintain a *legal list* of investment-grade (triple-B rated or higher) securities that can be traded for custodian (or fiduciary) accounts.

The prudent man rule states that custodians trading on behalf of the client's account must invest in a prudent manner, or as the custodian might do for his own account.

Are custodian accounts taxed? Yes, the minor's social security number is used for the account, and taxes are paid by the minor. To prevent parents from evading their own tax obligations by transferring assets to their children, the Tax Reform Act of 1986 established what is called the *Kiddie tax*. This specifies that income of more than $1,300 from custodian accounts is taxed at the parents' top tax rate.

Discretionary Accounts

In a *discretionary account*, the owner grants a registered rep the right to trade in the account. Trades are considered discretionary if the registered rep has to decide on more than just the time and price of the trade. A limited authorization grants the registered rep the right to buy and sell securities for the account. A full authorization grants the registered rep the right to move assets among different accounts of the beneficial owner and to pay proceeds from trading to the owner. The right to make discretionary trades is granted to the registered rep only through a legal document known as a *power of attorney*.

Brokers who are given such broad powers over an account might at times be tempted to make trades that are unsuitable. In particular, they might be tempted to boost their own commissions by engaging in a practice known as *churning*, whereby they make too frequent or too large trades for the account. Both the SEC and the exchanges prohibit churning. To prevent churning, a principal must review all discretionary trades on a daily basis. The principal reverses trades deemed inappropriate, charging any losses to the broker's account, and can also discipline the broker.

Omnibus Accounts

An *omnibus account* groups a number of accounts under an umbrella account, allowing one investment adviser to trade more efficiently on behalf of several clients. In effect, the money of various individuals is pooled. *Investment advisers*, who must register with the SEC, manage other people's money and can make trades on behalf of many clients. Usually, the advisor charges his or her customers a yearly fee, rather than a commission per trade. Thus, omnibus accounts are often called "wrap accounts," because the one annual fee wraps all trading and account services into one package.

A customer who wants to remain anonymous can request to open a *numbered account*, whose order tickets and other records only identify the customer by a number or code. The brokerage firm must have on file a document signed by the customer stating that he or she owns the account and is responsible for any taxes due.

> **EXAMPLE:** LeRon, a young and successful hip-hop entrepreneur, has begun to invest some of his assets with Verdura Securities. Because a good deal of his investing takes place in the entertainment business that he knows best, LeRon wants to be discrete. He asks Fred, his broker, to establish a numbered account so that no rumors can leak out to competitors—or the media—about which companies this trend-spotting industry leader favors.

Fiduciary Accounts

Fiduciary accounts are accounts in which the beneficial owner does not control the trading in his or her account. Instead, a *fiduciary*, an individual authorized to manage or distribute another person's assets, controls the account on behalf of the beneficial owner. To establish a fiduciary account, a registered rep must first obtain a copy of the legal documents, such as the will or court order, appointing a fiduciary and authorizing the arrangement. The documents establishing the account generally do not permit the fiduciary to trade on margin, but on occasion can explicitly allow it.

Fiduciary accounts are authorized, often by a court, in a variety of situations, labeled by the role that the fiduciary performs. There are six types of fiduciary accounts:

- *Trust accounts* provide for the fiduciary, called a trustee, to manage the assets of a person either living (in which case it is called a "living trust") or dead (a "testamentary trust"). The trust agreement specifies the transactions that the trustee can perform.
- *Guardian accounts* are established by a judge for a minor or incompetent adult who earns or inherits a substantial amount of money. The fiduciary, called a guardian, is appointed by the judge and need not be a parent of the minor.
- *Conservator accounts* serve to protect an individual's assets and personal affairs if a court deems that he or she is mentally or physically incompetent. In this case, a judge appoints a conservator to oversee the preservation of the person's estate.
- *Executor accounts* are set up through a will. The person writing the will appoints an executor, which can be a person or a trust company, who will carry out the will by paying estate taxes, settling debts, and distributing assets to the heirs.
- *Administrator accounts* come into play when a person dies intestate (without a will). A court appoints an administrator, similar to an executor, to settle the affairs of the deceased.
- *Receivership accounts* are also court-established. Here a judge appoints a receiver for persons, companies, or estates in bankruptcy. The receiver manages the affairs of the estate until the court makes a final disposition of the estate's assets. The receiver does not take possession of the account's assets at any time.

Because their role is often to preserve another individual's assets, fiduciaries do not have the freedom to invest as they might wish. Like custodians, fiduciaries must follow the prudent man rule or make investments according to the legal list, depending on the state in which they manage the beneficial owner's assets.

Fiduciaries of all types must of course rely on broker-dealers to provide the usual customer services for the beneficial owner by executing orders, sending statements and confirmations, and otherwise maintaining the account. Over time, most large broker-dealers have created departments that specialize in each of these functions.

Maintaining an Account

Brokerage houses typically have the following departments in their "back office" that provide administrative services for customers:

- **Wire and order departments** transmit orders entered by brokers to the appropriate exchanges for execution.
- **Purchase and sales (P&S) departments** send confirmations to customers after their orders have been executed, by the first business day after the trade takes place.
- **Margin departments** keep track of margin accounts, making sure that customers meet maintenance requirements.
- **Cashier's departments** accept deposits from customers, make out receipts, and issue checks when a customer withdraws funds from an account.
- **Proxy departments** administer the accounts of beneficial owners whose shares are being held in street name. Although securities purchased on margin are held in street name until the customer pays the full amount due, the beneficial owner is still entitled to privileges such as voting rights and the receipt of dividends, interest, and annual reports.
- **Reorganization departments** notify a customer when there is a change in the corporate ownership of securities held in the customer's account.

These departments perform the detailed mechanics of keeping customer accounts running. From the time a customer deposits funds to start an account until the time he or she takes money back out, the customer likely deals with many departments at his or her chosen brokerage.

Ensuring Trades Are Properly Executed

The day after a transaction is completed, the P&S department sends the customer a *confirmation* (or *confirm*). Confirms contain all important details of the trade, including:

- Whether the transaction was a purchase or a sale
- The name of the security and the amount or number of shares
- The execution price (price paid or received) and the total price, including any commission, markup, or markdown
- The trade and settlement dates
- Whether the broker-dealer acted as agent or principal

Customers who find errors in the confirmation must notify their broker, who will contact the P&S department. If the error is in the confirmation, the P&S department sends a corrected confirmation. If the registered rep executed the trade incorrectly, and the trade can be executed as ordered, the wire and order department corrects the transaction at the broker-dealer's expense.

> **EXAMPLE:** When Azimuth Enterprises' stock dips sharply, Martin places an order asking his broker to buy 150 shares at $25. A few days later, he receives a confirmation saying that 100 shares were purchased at $25. Martin calls his broker, who contacts the P&S department, which finds that the error is not in the confirmation but in the execution of the order. By that time, Azimuth stock has climbed back to $28, so the wire and order department must purchase the additional 50 shares at $28 and resell them to Martin at $25.

The P&S department sends customers regular *statements*, which list not only the transactions performed but all the securities held in the accounts and their closing values as of the date of the statement. Any account with activity in a given month receives a month-end statement. Inactive accounts receive statements once a quarter.

Transferring an Account to Another Broker

If the customer wants to move an account to a registered rep who works at another firm, the customer must fill out and sign an account transfer form at the new firm, listing all holdings in the account. The new firm sends a copy of the account transfer to the customer's current firm. When this firm receives the notice, it freezes the account and cancels all open orders in it. It then has three business days to check the customer's holdings and validate the form, and must then transfer the customer's assets to the new firm within four business days of validation. If any holding is not physically available (for example, stock that was lent for short sales), it must be delivered within 10 days of validation.

Losing Assets if a Broker-Dealer Fails

Customers at most broker-dealers are partially insured against the bankruptcy of a brokerage. All broker-dealers that are registered with the SEC or with national stock exchanges must be members of the *Securities Investor Protection Corporation (SIPC)*, a nonprofit corporation created by Congress to insure investors for up to $500,000. However, only $100,000 of this amount is paid in cash. If an investor has both cash and margin accounts, the accounts are combined for $500,000 total coverage. If an investor has both an individual account and a joint account, the two are covered separately.

> **EXAMPLE:** Ziggie's Discount Brokerage, at which Marla has both a margin account and cash account, unexpectedly folds. The cash account contains $50,000 in cash and $100,000 worth of securities. The margin account contains $75,000 in cash and $200,000 worth of securities. Marla recovers a total of $400,000: all her securities ($100,000 + $200,000 = $300,000) and the maximum in cash ($50,000 + $75,000 = $125,000; but the SIPC limit is $100,000). Steven has an account at Ziggie's as well, containing $440,000 in securities and $75,000 in cash. He recovers the full $440,000 in securities but only $60,000 of his cash, because this brings him to the SIPC ceiling of $500,000.

Most broker-dealers provide higher insurance coverage than the SIPC maximums for their customers. Unfortunately, if a broker-dealer fails, customers have no easy recourse for collecting on that insurance.

Exam Prep Questions

1. The "Know Your Customer" rule is:
   - ❑ A. Rule 405 of the New York Stock Exchange.
   - ❑ B. Rule 410 of the New York Stock Exchange.
   - ❑ C. Rule 411 of the New York Stock Exchange.
   - ❑ D. Rule 450 of the New York Stock Exchange.

2. Ray Mann, a broker, is opening an account for investor Leila Clapton. About which of the following must Mann obtain information?

   I. Her net worth

   II. Her financial objectives

   III. Her age

   IV. Her marital status

   - ❑ A. I only
   - ❑ B. I and II
   - ❑ C. I, II, and III
   - ❑ D. I, II, III, and IV

3. Elizabeth wants to purchase 1,000 shares of Fly By Night Industries. Her broker Fred feels that the investment is too risky for her and attempts to talk her out of the trade. Elizabeth insists. Fred needs to:
   - ❑ A. Refuse the order.
   - ❑ B. Tell Elizabeth that he cannot enter the order but that she can try to make the purchase through another brokerage.
   - ❑ C. Refer the matter to a senior representative.
   - ❑ D. Mark the trade "unsolicited" and enter the order.

4. Erin opens a custodian account for eight-year-old Eamon. Which of the following statements are true?

   I. Erin must be related to Eamon.

   II. The securities Erin places in the account are irrevocable.

   III. When Eamon comes of age, Erin must reregister the account in his name.

   IV. Erin can make margin trades in the account.

   - ❑ A. II and III
   - ❑ B. I, II, and III
   - ❑ C. III only
   - ❑ D. I, II, III, and IV

5. The custodian account Erin established for her son Eamon generates $6,000 in income for the year. Erin is in the 36% tax bracket; Eamon has no other income. Which statement is true about Eamon's tax liability?

❑ A. Eamon has no tax liability because he is a minor.

❑ B. His income is taxed at his mother's rate of 36%.

❑ C. A portion of his income is taxed at his tax rate, and the balance at his mother's rate of 36%

❑ D. His mother pays taxes on the full amount at her rate of 36% because the income is attributed to her.

6. Charles wants his registered rep Wanda to trade in his account on his behalf. He therefore gives Wanda:

I. A trading authorization.

II. A power of attorney.

III. A legal list.

IV. A trust indenture.

❑ A. I only

❑ B. I and II

❑ C. I, II, and III

❑ D. I, II, III, and IV

7. Famed British entrepreneur Gloria Mundy wants to open an account with Discreet Brokerage, but she does not want her name to appear on the account. How does Discreet respond to this request?

❑ A. It denies her request because customer names must appear on all accounts.

❑ B. It opens a numbered account for her.

❑ C. It opens an anonymous account for her because she is a foreign national and not subject to the IRS tax code.

❑ D. It can open a numbered account for her only if she is an accredited investor.

8. Bernie is the fiduciary for his great-aunt Alice's fiduciary account. Aunt Alice, a victim of Alzheimer's disease, is the beneficial owner. All the following are true except:

❑ A. Aunt Alice does not control the trading in the account.

❑ B. The account was opened through a court order appointing Bernie as fiduciary and authorizing the arrangement.

❑ C. Bernie makes whatever trades he deems right and profitable.

❑ D. Bernie must observe the prudent man rule.

9. Sarah receives a confirmation of her latest trade from Volume Brokerage. Which of the following items appear on the confirmation?

   I. The name of the security and number of shares traded

   II. The trade and settlement dates

   III. The role of the broker as agent or principal

   IV. The commission she paid

   ❑ A. I and II

   ❑ B. I, II, and III

   ❑ C. II, III, and IV

   ❑ D. I, II, III, and IV

10. Eugene wants to move his account from Blankshine Brokerage to Gem Deals. During this transfer, which of the following must take place?

    I. Eugene must complete an account transfer form at Gem.

    II. Blankshine must cancel all open orders on the old account.

    III. Blankshine must validate the account transfer form.

    IV. Blankshine must transfer the account within three business days.

    ❑ A. I and II

    ❑ B. I, II, and III

    ❑ C. I, III, and IV

    ❑ D. I, II, III, and IV

11. Dewey, Cheatham, & Howe brokerage has failed because of fraud on the part of its management. Maureen has an account at the firm containing $125,000 in cash and $200,000 in securities. SIPC insurance covers her for:

    ❑ A. $125,000 in cash and $200,000 in securities.

    ❑ B. $100,000 in cash and $100,000 in securities.

    ❑ C. $100,000 in cash and $200,000 in securities.

    ❑ D. $50,000 in cash and $100,000 in securities.

12. If an individual dies leaving a detailed will, which of the following types of accounts distributes the estate?

    ❑ A. An Intestate account

    ❑ B. An Executor account

    ❑ C. A Receivership account

    ❑ D. A Conservator account

13. Which of the following would govern the investments in a fiduciary account?

I. The prudent man rule

II. The Legal list

III. The Probate list

IV. The NYSE approved list

- ❑ A. I only
- ❑ B. I and II
- ❑ C. I, II, and III
- ❑ D. I, II, III, and IV

14. Which statement is true regarding a joint tenancy with rights of survivorship and a tenancy in common?

- ❑ A. A joint tenancy with rights of survivorship is a co-ownership that passes jointly owned property to the survivor if one dies, whereas jointly owned property does not pass to the survivor in a tenancy in common.
- ❑ B. Both joint tenancy with rights of survivorship and tenancy in common provide for property jointly owned to pass to the survivor if one co-owner dies.
- ❑ C. Neither joint tenancy with rights of survivorship or tenancy in common allow jointly owned property to pass to the survivor if one dies.
- ❑ D. A joint tenancy with rights of survivorship does not allow co-owned property to pass to a survivor, whereas tenancy in common does.

15. In establishing a partnership account what requirements are needed of the partnership?

I. A copy of the partnership agreement

II. Instructions on who can trade in the account

III. Each partner's signature on the new account form

IV. The social security number of each partner

- ❑ A. I only
- ❑ B. I, II, and III
- ❑ C. I, III, and IV
- ❑ D. I, II, III, and IV

Exam Prep Answers

1. The correct answer is A. Also called the "Know Your Customer" rule, Rule 405, recognizes that what is suitable for one investor might not be suitable for another. It requires that brokers obtain enough information about customers—including financial status, investment experience, and aims—to know which investments are appropriate for each.
2. The correct answer is C. When setting up an account, a broker must obtain enough information about such things as the customer's financial status (including net worth), investment experience, and objectives to know which investments are appropriate for him or her. The broker must also ascertain that the customer is of legal age.
3. The correct answer is D. Fred must inform Elizabeth that he believes the trade is unsuitable for her. If she still wants to proceed, he can execute the trade but must mark the order ticket "unsolicited." He can even record the conversation—as protection against liability.
4. The correct answer is A. Any adult can open a custodian account on behalf of a minor; the two do not have to be related. Gifts of securities or cash given to the minor are irrevocable, that is, they cannot be legally retracted. Custodian accounts cannot be margin accounts.
5. The correct answer is C. Kiddie tax rules are designed to prevent parents from shifting investments into their children's accounts to reduce their own income taxes. The tax applies to children under the age of 14 who have unearned income, such as income from investments. The first $700 is exempt from income taxes. The second $700 is taxed at the child's tax rate, which is usually 15%. Everything more than $1,400 is taxed at the parents' tax rate.
6. The correct answer is B. Charles must give Wanda two documents. First, he needs to define the limits of her authority through either a limited trading authorization (granting her the right to buy or sell securities for his account), or a full trading authorization (granting her the right to move assets among accounts and to pay him the proceeds from trades). Second, he needs to give her the legal right to make the trades through a document known as a power of attorney.
7. The correct answer is B. A customer who wants to remain anonymous can request a numbered account, whose order tickets and other records identify the customer by a number or code. Discreet can open a numbered account for Mundy, but she must sign a document stating that she owns the account and is responsible for all taxes due.

8. The correct answer is C. Fiduciary accounts are accounts whereby the beneficial owner does not control the trading in the account. To establish a fiduciary account, Bernie must present a copy of a legal document, such as a court order, appointing him fiduciary and authorizing the arrangement. Like custodians, fiduciaries must follow the prudent man rule or make investments according to the legal list, ensuring that they make only high quality, nonspeculative investments.
9. The correct answer is D. Confirmations contain all important details of the trade, including all those listed, as well as whether the trade was a purchase or a sale, the execution price, and the total price. This permits customers to check all important details of the trade for errors.
10. The correct answer is B. If Eugene wants to move his account to Gem, he must fill out and sign an account transfer form with the new firm. When Blankshine receives the notice from Gem, it must freeze Eugene's account and cancel all open orders on it. It then has three business days to check Eugene's holdings and validate the form, and four business days after validation to transfer Eugene's assets to Gem.
11. The correct answer is C. The Securities Investor Protection Corporation insures investors for up to $500,000. However, this insurance covers only $100,000 worth of cash deposits. Maureen's coverage therefore includes only $100,000 of her cash and the full amount of her securities.
12. The correct answer is A. An executor account is set up with the will. The individual appoints an executor who is named in the will. An executor can be a person or a trust company that will carry out the terms of the will by paying estate taxes, settling debts, and distributing assets to the heirs. An intestate is known as an administrator account and handles the estates of individuals who die without a will; a receivership account is handled through the courts for persons in bankruptcy; and a conservator account provides for individuals who are mentally or physically incapable of handling their own affairs.
13. The correct answer is B. Fiduciary accounts are required to follow the Prudent Man rule or the Legal list of the corresponding state in respect to the investments that can be made in the account. A fiduciary account is controlled by someone other than the beneficial owner, and restrictions are placed on the account as to the investments that can be made.

14. The correct answer is A. A joint tenancy with rights of survivorship, JTWROS, is typical of a husband and wife property relationship. If one dies, the other becomes the sole owner of any jointly owned property. A tenancy in common is another form of co-ownership in which a survivor does not become the sole owner of jointly owned property.
15. The correct answer is D. A partnership account requires a copy of the agreement; instructions on who can trade on the account; the name, address, and social security number of each partner; and each partner's signature.

Margin Accounts

Terms You Need to Know

- ✓ Borrowed security
- ✓ Buying power
- ✓ Credit balance (CR)
- ✓ Debit balance (DR)
- ✓ Equity
- ✓ Excess
- ✓ Loan value
- ✓ Long margin account
- ✓ Long market value (LMV)
- ✓ Maintenance margin
- ✓ Margin call
- ✓ Mark to market
- ✓ Minimum maintenance requirement
- ✓ Phantom SMA
- ✓ Restricted account
- ✓ Retention requirement
- ✓ Same-day substitution
- ✓ Short margin account
- ✓ Short market value
- ✓ Short selling power
- ✓ Special memorandum account (SMA)

Concepts You Need to Understand

- ✓ Why long and short margin accounts are useful
- ✓ Minimum maintenance requirements for long and short margin accounts
- ✓ How long margin accounts are valued
- ✓ How Reg T limits purchases
- ✓ What SMA is and how it works
- ✓ How short margin accounts are valued
- ✓ How Reg T and SMA affect short margin accounts
- ✓ Calculating the equity in a total margin account
- ✓ Margin for nonequity securities, exempt securities, and options

Margin Accounts

To simplify their calculations, broker-dealers keep long margin and short margin transactions separate in each customer's account. Securities continually change in value, and the minimum margin requirements for long margin and short margin transactions are different. When an account exceeds margin requirements, the customer effectively establishes a line of credit with the brokerage, which he or she can use for additional margin transactions. When an account falls below the margins requirement, the customer faces certain restrictions.

Market prices for securities change continually. After an investor buys or sells short a security on margin, the NYSE and NASD require that he or she maintain a certain minimum amount of margin against the security to protect the brokerage against sharp changes in its value. The customer must keep this *maintenance margin* until he or she pays for the security.

For most long transactions (purchases) in stocks, the NYSE and NASD have established a minimum maintenance margin of 25%. For short transactions (short sales), the NYSE and NASD require 30% minimum maintenance margin.

Minimum maintenance requirements cover the value of all securities in accounts acquired through margin transactions.

If an account falls below the minimum maintenance requirement, the brokerage firm issues a *margin call*, requiring the customer to deposit enough funds to bring the account up to the 25 or 30% level, depending on the kind of transaction. However, under the Fed's Reg T "five hundred dollar rule," brokerages do not need to send out margin calls for amounts less than $500; in fact, most firms follow a practice of not issuing margin calls for amounts under $1,000. If the customer does not deposit the additional requested funds (usually within three business days of the margin call), the firm can sell securities from the customer's account to reach the required maintenance margin levels.

Because minimum maintenance requirements differ depending on whether it's a short transaction or a long transaction, broker-dealers keep these two kinds of transactions separate. They distinguish between a customer's *long margin account*—including all margin purchases—and the *short margin account*—including all short sales. Although the customer actually has just a single margin account, this separation makes it easier to calculate the maintenance requirements for the two kinds of transactions.

Long Margin Accounts

Every long margin account has a *long market value* (*LMV*), which is the current market value of the securities in the account. Every day, the brokerage firm revalues these securities, at the closing market rate, in a process called *marking to market*. The LMV of an account thus rises and falls as the market prices of the securities fluctuate.

> **EXAMPLE:** Sam buys 800 shares of Perpetual Motion, Inc., on margin. As the stock is trading at 50, the long market value of his account on that day is $40,000. The following week, the value of his Perpetual Motion stock rises to $53.75. Although Sam has neither spent more money nor added securities to his account, its long market value has increased to $43,000.

The amount that the customer borrows from the broker is called the *debit balance* (*DR*). As the market value of the securities, and thus the LMV, fluctuates, the debit balance remains constant. Except for the interest charged to the customer, which accrues to the DR, the debit balance does not change until the customer pays off all or a portion of the loan (or buys additional securities, thus increasing the DR).

As the market value of a security fluctuates, the debit balance remains constant.

> **EXAMPLE:** When Sam bought Perpetual Motion on margin, he deposited margin of $20,000, half of the purchase price. Verdura Securities loaned him the remaining $20,000. This $20,000 debt is the debit balance of his account. One month later, Perpetual Motion has dropped to $39 per share. Although the long market value of his account has fallen to $31,200, Sam's debit balance is still $20,000.

The difference between an account's LMV and DR is called the *equity* (*EQ*). The equity is what would be left if the account were liquidated—the assets sold off and the loan paid back.

Equity (EQ) = long market value (LMV) – debit balance (DR)

As the LMV fluctuates, so does equity.

EXAMPLE: Six months have passed and Perpetual Motion shares have risen to 58.75. The LMV of Sam's account climbs to $47,000 (800 shares × 58.75 = $47,000). Sam hasn't paid back any of his Verdura loan, so the debit balance remains at $20,000 (ignoring interest charges). How has Sam's equity changed?

Month 1: Perpetual Motion at $50

EQ = $40,000 – $20,000 = $20,000

Month 2: Perpetual Motion at $39

EQ = $31,200 – $20,000 = $11,200

Month 6: Perpetual Motion at $58.75

EQ = $47,000 – $20,000 = $27,000

If Sam liquidates his account today, $20,000 goes to Verdura to pay off the loan, and the remaining $27,000, the equity, is his.

As the value of securities in an account rise and fall, the equity also increases and decreases.

When Equity Falls Below the Reg T Requirement

When the long market value of the securities decreases to the point that the equity in the account drops below the Reg T 50% level, the account becomes restricted. In a *restricted account*, future purchases are not affected—the customer must simply deposit the required 50% for any new securities. The customer is not obligated to bring the entire account up to Reg T.

However, when a customer sells securities from a restricted account (or covers short sales), he or she must apply 50% of the proceeds toward reducing the debit balance—until the equity again reaches 50% of the LMV. After meeting this *retention requirement*, the customer can use the remaining proceeds from the sale as margin for new purchases.

If a customer's account equity falls below the NYSE and NASD minimum maintenance requirements (25% of the LMV), the brokerage issues a margin call to the customer.

A margin call is issued if the account equity falls below the NYSE and NASD minimum maintenance requirements of 25% of the LMV.

EXAMPLE: Cecilia purchases $24,000 of Robot Maids, Inc., in her Verdura Securities margin account. Her debit balance and equity both stand at $12,000. When the value of her Robot Maids position falls to $20,000, her equity drops to $8,000. Cecilia's account is now restricted because its equity is less than 50% of its LMV. Will Verdura issue Cecilia a margin call? No, Verdura will not issue a margin call, because Cecilia's equity is still well above 25% of the LMV. Table 21.1 shows Cecilia's account balance before and after the price of her stock falls.

Table 21.1 Equity Below Debit Balance

Cecilia's Account Balance When She Purchases Robot Maids		Cecilia's Account Balance After the Price of Robot Maids Falls	
LMV	$24,000	LMV	$20,000
DR	–$12,000	DR	–$12,000
EQ	$12,000	EQ	$8,000

Recall that the debit balance remains constant, even as LMV and EQ are falling. To calculate the LMV at which a brokerage must issue a margin call, an investor can simply divide the debit balance by 0.75.

EXAMPLE: Cecilia does not yet need to add funds to her account, but she's worried that Robot Maids might keep falling. She divides her debit balance of $12,000 by 0.75 to find that her account LMV can fall as low as $16,000 before she will receive a margin call. If her Robot Maids position drops any lower than that, she cannot meet the minimum maintenance requirement, and she will have to deposit more cash or fully paid securities.

In a procedure called *same-day substitution*, an investor can purchase and sell the same amount of securities on the same day in a restricted account. If the purchase price and sales price are equal, no additional margin deposit is required. If the purchase price is greater than the sale proceeds, the investor must of course deposit the Reg T 50% on the net amount. Finally, if the sales proceeds exceed the purchase price, the investor must apply 50% of the net proceeds to the debit balance, and then receives a credit for the rest of the net proceeds.

Market news is not always bad. Securities also rise in value, creating additional equity in long margin accounts.

When Equity Rises Above the Reg T Requirement

When the value of securities in a margin account increases, the equity can rise above the Reg T requirement. The amount by which the equity exceeds the Reg T requirement is the account's *excess*.

When an excess is generated, the brokerage establishes in the account a credit line called the special memorandum account (SMA). The customer can borrow an amount equal to the amount of the excess. By drawing on the SMA, the customer can borrow funds over and above the 50% normally borrowed for margin purposes. The amount of the loan is added to the investor's debit balance.

Investors often use SMA as margin in additional securities purchases. (Note that the term SMA refers to both the credit line and the funds it makes available.) The special memorandum account gives the investor increased buying power; the capability to leverage funds into larger transactions than is otherwise possible. Because the investor needs only to put up 50% of the purchase price under Regulation T, every dollar of SMA gives the investor two dollars of buying power. When a customer purchases securities with SMA funds, the debit value and long market value increase, but the equity remains the same.

Purchasing securities with SMA funds increases debit value and long market value, whereas equity remains the same.

EXAMPLE: The stock in Iona's margin account at Verdura Securities appreciates to $20,000. With a debit balance of $8,000, her equity has grown to $12,000. Because she only needs $10,000 equity to satisfy Reg T, her account has an excess of $2,000. Instead of putting up her own funds as margin, Iona borrows from this credit line to buy $4,000 worth of new securities.

LMV = $20,000 + $4,000 in new securities = $24,000

DR = $8,000 + $2,000 margin borrowed from SMA + $2,000 borrowed from Verdura = $12,000

EQ = $24,000 – $12,000 = $12,000

Because her debit balance and LMV have risen by equal amounts ($4,000), her equity remains unchanged.

As equity in an account increases, the SMA increases. Depositing cash can reduce a debit balance; as the debit balance decreases, equity and SMA increase.

As the equity in an account increases, the SMA increases automatically. In an unrestricted account, every dollar of increased LMV raises the SMA by 50 cents. Investors can raise SMA in other ways as well. Depositing cash reduces the debit balance; as the debit balance decreases, the equity—and along with it, the SMA—increases. In an unrestricted account, SMA increases by 100% of the amount of the cash deposit.

The same is true of interest received on bonds held in the account and cash dividends received on stocks: 100% is applied to pay down the debt balance, thereby increasing the equity and the SMA by the same amount. However, to increase the incentive for customers to reinvest their cash dividends, brokerages add these amounts to SMAs for only 30 days. If a customer does not use the credit within this time, the brokerage subtracts it from the SMA. (The customer retains the actual interest or dividend but loses the chance to borrow an increased amount of SMA.) Stock dividends have no effect on the value of the account, because they leave the total cash value of the security unaffected. Finally, when a customer sells margined securities, 100% of the proceeds is applied to the debit balance, increasing both the equity and the SMA.

Any increase to LMV in a margin account that is currently over the Reg T minimum adds to the SMA.

Decreases in LMV, however, work differently.

SMA and LMV Do Not Fall Together

A decline in an account's long market value does not affect the size of the special memorandum account. An investor can reduce the SMA only by buying additional securities or by withdrawing it.

A customer cannot always use the SMA. If additional borrowing will push the account's equity below the NYSE and NASD minimum maintenance requirement (25% of LMV), the brokerage firm cannot execute the transaction. Because the SMA continues to exist on paper but cannot be used, it is known as a *phantom SMA*.

Investors use long margin accounts to buy on margin—they borrow money, place purchase orders, and receive securities. The process is basically reversed in a short margin account—customers borrow securities, place sell orders, and receive money.

When an investor sells a security short, Reg T requires that the investor deposit 50% of the proceeds of the sale, either in cash or fully paid securities, in his or her margin account. For the investor's first transaction in a margin account, NYSE and NASD rules require the investor to deposit a minimum of $2,000, even if the proceeds for the entire transaction are less than that amount.

Short Margin Accounts

You might wonder why investors need short margin accounts. Because a brokerage firm is extending credit to a customer who borrows a security for a short sale, the transaction must take place in a margin account, not a cash account. Remember the customer is selling the *borrowed security* with the hope that its price will fall so that he or she can buy it back and replace it at a lower price. In a short margin account, a customer's *credit balance* (*CR*) equals the proceeds of any short sale plus whatever margin he or she must deposit for the borrowed security.

EXAMPLE: Luis opens his Verdura Securities margin account by selling short 100 shares of Time & Ink, Inc., at $30. He receives $3,000 from the sale. Reg T requires that he deposit margin of 50% of the proceeds, or $1,500, in his short margin account, but because this is his first transaction in the account, Luis is subject to the NYSE $2,000 minimum margin requirement. He must therefore deposit $2,000 in addition to his proceeds, which makes his credit balance $5,000.

The credit balance does not change until the customer replaces the borrowed security. Just as the debit balance remains constant as the market value of securities in a long account fluctuates, the credit balance remains constant as the market value of borrowed securities in a short account changes.

A debit balance remains constant as the market value of a security in a long account fluctuates and the credit balance remains constant as the market value of a borrowed security changes in a short account.

EXAMPLE: One month after Luis sold Time & Ink short at $30, the company's stock has risen to $36. To cover his short position, Luis needs to spend $3,600. Nonetheless, Verdura Securities keeps his credit balance at the same $5,000—$3,000 from the original short sale plus $2,000 in his margin deposit. A week later, Time & Ink drops to $21. Now Luis can cover his short position for $2,100. His CR remains $5,000.

Investors can deposit margin either in cash or in fully paid, marginable securities. In calculating a credit balance, broker-dealers value marginable securities not at their market price but at their *loan value*. Under Reg T, brokerages can lend customers 50% of the market value of securities, which is their *loan value*.

The current market value of the securities a customer has borrowed for a short sale equals the *short market value* (*SMV*) of the short margin account. Unlike the credit balance, the short market value fluctuates with the prices of the securities. The account's equity equals the credit balance less the SMV. In other words, the equity is what remains after the customer repays the loan of the borrowed securities.

Equity (EQ) = credit balance (CR) – short market value (SMV)

Equity (EQ) equals credit balance (CR) minus short market value (SMV).

Thus, the short seller hopes the SMV—the current price of the borrowed securities—falls as low as possible. When the value of the securities falls, the account's equity increases. However, if the price of the securities rises, the investor will lose equity.

EXAMPLE: Giulio sold short 100 shares of Queue, Inc., at $40, earning $4,000 on the sale and depositing $2,000 margin. His total credit balance stands at $6,000; his equity equals $2,000. Unfortunately for Giulio, Queue rises steadily over the next four weeks, reaching a share price of $45. What is Giulio's equity now? Giulio's equity has dropped to $1,500. Table 21.2 shows how a short margin account loses equity when the price of the stock rises above the original price.

A short margin account loses equity when the stock price rises above the purchase price.

Table 21.2 Equity in an SMA

Giulio's Equity After He Sold Short 100 Shares of Queue at $40		Giulio's Equity When the Price of Queue Rises to $45	
CR	$6,000	CR	$6,000
SMV	– $4,000	SMV	– $4,500
EQ	$2,000	EQ	$1,500

Similar to a long margin account, equity in a short margin account fluctuates as market prices change. The equity can at times fall beneath the level established by Reg T.

When Short Account Equity Drops Under the Reg T Requirement

When the equity in a short market account falls below 50% of the short market value, the account becomes restricted under Reg T. Future short sales are unaffected. When the customer wants to execute a short sale in a restricted account, he or she need not bring the entire account up to the Reg T 50% level, but must simply deposit the required margin for the new short sale. However, when the customer covers prior short positions in a restricted account, he or she must meet the Reg T retention requirement.

By replacing borrowed securities, the customer reduces the account's SMV and also releases funds in the credit balance. Under the retention requirement, the customer must maintain at least 50% of the market value of the replaced securities in the CR, until the equity once again reaches 50% of SMV. The investor can withdraw the remaining 50% of the securities' market value (or use it as margin for other short sales).

> **EXAMPLE:** Andrea's short margin account has a credit balance of $10,000. She has watched its short market value increase to $7,500. This places the account equity at only $2,500, which is below the 50% Reg T requirement. Table 21.3 shows that Andrea's equity is below the Reg T requirement when the account value falls.

Table 21.3 Equity Drops Below Reg T Requirement

Andrea's Account After the Increase in SMV	
CR	$10,000
SMV	–$7,500
EQ	$2,500

Andrea replaces borrowed securities worth $1,000, thereby reducing the account's short market value to $6,500, and potentially releasing $1,000 of her credit balance. Because her account is restricted, however, she must keep at least $500 of this amount in her credit balance. With a new credit balance of $9,500, her equity climbs to $3,000. Andrea can borrow the other $500 for new short sales, or simply withdraw it.

After an account falls below the minimum requirement, the account is restricted and the investor must keep a percentage of the credit balance unavailable for use.

Table 21.4 Equity Rises Above the Reg T Requirement

Andrea's Account After She Replaces $1,000 of Borrowed Securities		Andrea Must Retain $500 of the Released Funds in Her Credit Balance	
CR	$10,000	CR	$9,500
SMV	–$6,500	SMV	–$6,500
EQ	$3,500	EQ	$3,000

Clearly, if the short market value in a margin account increases sufficiently—causing the equity to fall—the account at some point will fail to meet the NYSE and NASD minimum maintenance requirements.

When a Short Market Account Falls Below the Minimum Maintenance Requirement

If the equity in a short margin account falls below 30% of the SMV, the brokerage firm issues the client a margin call.

EXAMPLE: Suzanne sold short 50 shares of Riverview Enterprises at $90 per share, giving her Verdura Securities account an SMV of $4,500. Her credit balance is $6,750. Over the next two months, Riverview rises to $120. The SMV of Suzanne's account also rises, to $6,000. Because her credit balance remains at $6,750, her equity has fallen to just $750, which is far less than the required 30% of SMV, or $1,800. Verdura issues a margin call to Suzanne, who must deposit $1,050 in cash or $2,100 in fully paid, marginable securities. Table 21.5 shows how Suzanne's equity changes as the price of her stock changes.

Table 21.5 Equity Changes

Suzanne's Account When She Sold 50 Shares of Riverview Short at $90		Suzanne's Account After the Price of Riverview Rises to $120		Suzanne's Account After She Deposits Cash to Meet Her Maintenance Requirement	
CR	$6,750	CR	$6,750	CR	$6,750
SMV	–$4,500	SMV	–$6,000	SMV	–$6,000
EQ	$2,250	EQ	$750	EQ (cash deposit)	$750
					+$1,050
				EQ	$1,800

Customers can calculate how high the SMV in their accounts can rise before they receive a margin call by dividing the credit balance by 1.3.

Rise without a margin call = xxx over 1.3 = $5,000

Luckily for short sellers, the market value of securities can also fall. Because an investor can purchase shorted securities for less than he or she borrowed to execute them, the equity in the account increases.

If the equity in a short margin account rises above the Reg T requirement, an excess is created. The brokerage firm then adds an equal amount to the special memorandum account (SMA). For every dollar that the short market value in an unrestricted account decreases, SMA increases by $1.50.

EXAMPLE: In her short margin account, Miranda has a credit balance of $3,900, an SMV of $2,100, and equity of $1,800. This gives her $750 of SMA. Some of her borrowed securities fall again, reducing her SMV by $100. How much does Miranda's SMA increase? Table 21.6 shows the excess in equity in Miranda's account.

If equity rises above the Reg T requirement, excess is created. If equity falls below the requirement, a shortage is created and the investor might receive a margin call to make up the difference. Remember, only 50% of the security value can be purchased on credit. The remaining 50% must be paid for in cash or wholly owned securities.

Table 21.6 Equity Excess			
Miranda's Original Account Balance		**Miranda's Account After Her Borrowed Securities Lose $100**	
CR	$3,900	CR	$3,900
SMV	–$2,100	SMV	+$2,000
EQ	$1,800	EQ	$1,900
Reg T	–$1,050 (SMV × 0.50)	Reg T	–$1,000 (SMV × 0.50)
SMA	$750	SMA	$900

In other words, when her account's SMV declines by $100, Miranda's SMA increases by $150.

The SMA gives the investor *short selling power*, which is the capability to leverage the funds into larger short sales than otherwise possible. With the Reg T requirement set at 50%, an investor has short selling power of two dollars for every dollar of SMA.

Regulation T sets the margin requirement at 50% of the value of the securities that can be purchased on credit.

EXAMPLE: Julian sold short 100 shares of Xyzon, Inc., at $40, leaving his credit balance at $6,000. When Xyzon falls to $36, his equity rises to $2,400. Because this is $600 more than the Reg T minimum requirement, Julian's brokerage increases the available credit in his SMA by $600. For any new short sale, he must deposit 50% margin, thus he can now sell short securities worth $1,200. Table 21.7 shows the short selling power as leverage for funding short sales.

Table 21.7 Leveraging Short Sales				
Julian's Account When Xyzon Trades at $40		**Julian's Account When Xyzon Falls to $36**		**Julian's Selling Power**
CR	$6,000	CR	$6,000	
SMV	–$4,000	SMV	–$3,600	$600 ÷ 0.50 = $1,200
EQ	$2,000	EQ	$2,400	
		Reg T	–$1,800	
		SMA	$600	

Combined Margin Accounts and Special Margin Requirements

Despite the bookkeeping distinction between short and long margin accounts, an investor has only one margin account, in which both long and short transactions take place. Brokerage firms simply find it easier to calculate how much margin a customer must maintain by separating the long and the short transactions. Sometimes the brokerage firm needs to calculate the equity for the entire account. Often this occurs when the customer wants to liquidate the account.

Brokerages total the equity in a margin account simply by adding the equities of the short and long margin accounts.

Combined equity = (LMV – DR) + (CR – SMV)

Some people might prefer to regroup the terms:

Combined equity = (LMV – SMV) + (CR – DR)

Combined equity equals LMV minus DR plus CR minus SMV. Another way to look at it is that combined equity equals LMV minus SMV plus CR minus DR.

EXAMPLE: Danielle has decided to close out her margin account and place all her money in annuities. She has made both purchases and sales in her margin account. At the moment, the account's long market value stands at $12,000 and her debit balance equals $7,000. The credit balance stands at $5,000, whereas the short market value equals $3,000. What is Danielle's combined equity? Danielle's margin account has a total equity of $7,000.

Combined equity = (LMV – DR) + (CR – SMV)
= ($12,000 – $7,000) + ($5,000 – $3,000)
= $5,000 + $2,000 = $7,000

Investors can use margin accounts to trade many kinds of securities. For other securities, brokerages calculate the account's balances the same way, although the securities might have different margin requirements. Both the Federal Reserve and securities exchanges establish margin requirements for investors trading nonequity securities.

Margin Requirements for Nonequity Securities

The NYSE and NASD have mandated the same maintenance margin requirements for nonequity securities as the initial margin requirements. Table 21.8 gives the margin requirements for both types of nonequity securities.

Nonequity securities have different margin requirements as well as an initial and a maintenance requirement; these vary according to the type of security. See Table 21.8 for a list and be familiar with the information.

Table 21.8 Nonequity Securities Margin Requirements

Security	Initial/Maintenance Margin
Corporate bonds	No Reg T margin required for purchase; but the NYSE and NASD require 7% of face value or 20% of market value, whichever is greater.
Government and agency bonds	1% to 6%, depending on the maturity (from 1% for T-bills to 6% for T-bonds with 20 years or more remaining until maturity).
Municipal bonds greater.	7% of face value or 20% of market value, whichever is

Margin Requirements for Options

Options cannot be purchased on margin, but they can be purchased in a margin account—investors must deposit 100% margin for long option positions. For the sale of options, investors must deposit the premium plus part of the market value. According to Reg T, the options held in margin accounts—even fully paid contracts—have no loan value, nor do they increase SMA.

Note that almost all broker-dealers establish margin requirements for option positions that are significantly higher than the Reg T and/or exchange requirements. Investors must deposit margin within two business days of settlement (S+2), although member firms can require that a customer meet an earlier deadline.

Exam Prep Questions

1. Doris trades in a margin account at Serenity Securities. Under NYSE rules, what is the minimum margin she must maintain in her account?
   - ❑ A. 50%
   - ❑ B. 30% on long positions, 25% on short positions
   - ❑ C. 25% on long positions, 30% on short positions
   - ❑ D. 25%

2. Yesterday, the LMV of Doris's long margin account was $40,000; Doris has made no deposits or new trades and today it is $41,000. How did her account acquire the additional $1,000 in value?
   - ❑ A. The securities were marked to market.
   - ❑ B. The brokerage paid interest on her account.
   - ❑ C. The broker borrowed stock for another customer's short sale, temporarily depositing its market value.
   - ❑ D. She requested a revaluation.

3. Hugh purchases 1,000 shares of Horizon on margin at 57. If Horizon rises to 63, what is the equity in his margin account?
   - ❑ A. $63,000
   - ❑ B. $57,000
   - ❑ C. $34,500
   - ❑ D. $31,500

4. After a large fall in the market, Serenity Securities declares Miriam's account restricted. This means that:

   I. The equity in her account has fallen below 50% of its LMV.

   II. She must deposit 100% of the value of any further purchases in the account.

   III. She cannot borrow any additional funds from Serenity.

   IV. She must deposit additional funds.
   - ❑ A. I and IV
   - ❑ B. I and II
   - ❑ C. I, II, and III
   - ❑ D. I only

5. The SMA recorded in Rudy's margin account is $2,500. He uses these funds to purchase $5,000 worth of Robotron stock on margin. What effect does this have on his debit balance and equity?
   - ❑ A. His debit balance increases by $2,500; his equity decreases by $2,500.
   - ❑ B. His debit balance increases by $2,500; his equity remains the same.
   - ❑ C. His debit balance increases by $5,000; his equity remains the same.
   - ❑ D. His debit balance increases by $5,000; his equity decreases by $2,500.

6. Bryn recently opened a margin account. The market value of the securities in the long margin account has risen from $20,000 to $24,000. Which of the following statements are true?

   I. The account's equity has increased by $4,000.

   II. The account's SMA has increased by $2,000.

   III. The account's SMA has increased by $4,000.

   IV. The account's debit balance has increased by $2,000.

   - ❑ A. I and II
   - ❑ B. II and III
   - ❑ C. I and III
   - ❑ D. III and IV

7. Jasper has an SMA of $4,000 in his long margin account. This gives him:

   - ❑ A. Unlimited buying power
   - ❑ B. $2,000 of buying power
   - ❑ C. $4,000 of buying power
   - ❑ D. $8,000 of buying power

8. When the LMV in Jasper's unrestricted margin account increases by $1,000, his SMA:

   - ❑ A. Increases by $1,000
   - ❑ B. Increases by $500
   - ❑ C. Decreases by $500
   - ❑ D. Decreases by $1,000

9. Jenna receives $400 in interest on the Riverview Enterprises bond in her unrestricted margin account. As a result, all the following take place except:

   - ❑ A. The brokerage applies the $400 to Jenna's debit balance.
   - ❑ B. The LMV increases by $400.
   - ❑ C. The equity increases by $400.
   - ❑ D. The SMA increases by $400.

10. The LMV of Gordon's long margin account has risen by $5,000, creating $2,500 in SMA. A sharp drop in the market decreases Gordon's LMV by $5,000. His SMA:

    - ❑ A. Decreases by $5,000
    - ❑ B. Decreases by $2,500
    - ❑ C. Does not decrease
    - ❑ D. Is frozen

11. Scott's short margin account has a credit balance of $3,700, an SMV of $1,900, and equity of $1,800. How much excess does the account contain?
   - ❑ A. None
   - ❑ B. $100
   - ❑ C. $150
   - ❑ D. $850

12. Beatrice's short margin account has an SMV of $22,000 and equity of $9,000. What is her credit balance?
   - ❑ A. $9,000
   - ❑ B. $13,000
   - ❑ C. $22,000
   - ❑ D. $31,000

13. The SMV of Herbert's unrestricted short margin account decreases by $300. His SMA:
   - ❑ A. Does not increase
   - ❑ B. Increases by $150
   - ❑ C. Increases by $300
   - ❑ D. Increases by $450

14. Elmer's margin account has an LMV of $16,000, a DR of $7,000, an SMV of $6,000, and a CR of $11,000. Elmer has:
   - ❑ A. $4,000 in combined equity
   - ❑ B. $5,000 in combined equity
   - ❑ C. $9,000 in combined equity
   - ❑ D. $14,000 in combined equity

15. Sophie purchases 10 $1,000 bonds of Riverview Enterprises at 88. How much margin must she deposit?
   - ❑ A. $700
   - ❑ B. $1,760
   - ❑ C. $2,000
   - ❑ D. $2,700

Exam Prep Answers

1. The correct answer is C. The NYSE and NASD established minimum maintenance margins of 25% for long margin transactions (purchases) and 30% for short margin transactions (short sales).
2. The correct answer is A. Every day, brokerage firms revalue the securities in margin accounts at the closing market rates. This process is called marking to market. The LMV of an account thus rises and falls as the market prices of the securities fluctuate.
3. The correct answer is C. The equity in a long margin account is the difference between its long market value (LMV) and its debit balance (DR). When purchasing the shares on margin, Hugh paid $57,000 ($57 × 1,000 shares). He borrowed 50% of this, or $28,500, from his broker. This is his debit balance. With the shares at 63, the LMV rises to $63,000 ($63 × 1,000 shares). His equity is 34,500 (LMV $63,000 – DR $28,500).
4. The correct answer is D. When the equity in a long margin account drops below the Reg T 50% level, the account becomes restricted. The restriction does not affect future purchases; the customer must simply deposit the required 50% for any new purchase. Miriam thus need not deposit any additional funds. If she decides to sell securities from the account, however, she has to apply 50% of the proceeds towards reducing the debit balance until the equity again equals 50% of LMV.
5. The correct answer is C. The SMA is a credit line that can be used for margin purchases. Normally, for a $5,000 purchase, Rudy has put up 50% (or $2,500) as margin and borrow the rest from the brokerage. If he has $2,500 of SMA, however, he can borrow the margin from the brokerage as well. When he uses the SMA to buy the Robotron stock, the full $5,000 is added to his debit balance. Because this is matched by a $5,000 increase in LMV when the stock is added to his account, there is no change in equity.
6. The correct answer is A. When Bryn purchased $20,000 worth of securities on margin, she put up half the amount and borrowed the rest from her broker. The equity in her account thus stood at (LMV $20,000 – DR $10,000). When the value of the securities rose to $24,000, the account's LMV rose increasing equity by $4,000 (LMV $24,000 – DR $10,000). She borrowed no additional funds, so the debit balance has not changed. However, the Reg T requirement for the account has. At 50% of the value of the securities, it has risen to $12,000 ($24,000 × 50%), producing excess equity of $2,000 (EQ $14,000 – $12,000). The excess is added to her SMA.
7. The correct answer is D. Buying power is the capability to leverage funds into larger transactions. Because Reg T requires a 50% margin,

$4,000 enables him to purchase $8,000 worth of securities. (You calculate buying power by dividing the SMA by the Reg T margin requirement.)

8. The correct answer is B. In an unrestricted margin account, every additional dollar of LMV increases the SMA by 50 cents. It does not raise the SMA by a full dollar, because every additional dollar of LMV also increases the account's Reg T requirement by 50 cents. A $1,000 increase in LMV therefore increases the SMA by $500.
9. The correct answer is B. When interest or dividends are paid to a margin account, the entire amount is applied to pay down the debit balance. Because the cash is immediately applied to the debit balance, the LMV does not increase. Instead, as the debit balance decreases equity and SMA increase by the same amount. However, to provide incentive for customers to reinvest this cash, brokerages apply this credit to SMA for only 30 days.
10. The correct answer is C. A decline in an account's long market value does not affect the size of the special memorandum account. Gordon's SMA decreases only if he uses it to buy additional securities or makes a withdrawal against it.
11. The correct answer is D. The Regulation T requirement for a short margin account is 50% of its short market value. Scott must therefore have equity of $950 (SMV $1,900 × 50%). Because his actual equity is $1,800, he has an excess of $850 (EQ $1,800 –$950).
12. The correct answer is D. The credit balance in a short margin account is the short market value plus the equity. Beatrice's credit balance is therefore $31,000 (SMV $22,000 + EQ $9,000).
13. The correct answer is D. The short market value is the amount that Herbert must currently pay to replace the stocks he borrowed for short sales. Every dollar of decrease in the short market value increases the equity by a dollar and decreases the amount that must be maintained to satisfy Reg T's 50% requirement by 50 cents, generating more excess. For every dollar that the SMV in an unrestricted account decreases, the SMA increases by $1.50. The $300 decrease in SMV therefore results in a $450 increase in SMA ($300 × 1.5).
14. The correct answer is D. Brokerages determine the total equity in a margin account simply by adding the equities of the short and long accounts. The combined equity in the account is $14,000 [(LMV – DR) + (CR – SMV)] or [(16,000 – 7,000) + ($11,000 – $6,000)].
15. The correct answer is B. Reg T does not apply to corporate bonds. For nonequity trades, the NYSE and NASD maintenance requirements are the same as the initial requirements—7% of the bond's face value or 20% of its market value, whichever is greater. Sophie must therefore deposit $1,760 ($880 × 10 × 20%), which is greater than $700 ($1,000 × 10 × 7%).

PART VII
Investment Vehicles

Investment Companies

Terms You Need to Know

- ✓ Closed-end management company
- ✓ Combination REIT
- ✓ Diversification
- ✓ Diversified management company
- ✓ Equity REIT
- ✓ Face-amount certificate company
- ✓ Fixed unit investment trust
- ✓ Investment Company Act of 1940
- ✓ Liquidity
- ✓ Management company
- ✓ Mortgage REIT
- ✓ Net asset value (NAV)
- ✓ Nondiversified management company
- ✓ Omitting prospectus ad
- ✓ Participating unit investment trust
- ✓ Real estate investment trust (REIT)
- ✓ Share of beneficial interest (unit)
- ✓ Sponsor
- ✓ Tombstone ad
- ✓ Unit investment trust (UIT)

Concepts You Need to Understand

- ✓ How investment companies work
- ✓ Unit investment trusts
- ✓ Real estate investment trusts
- ✓ Closed-end management companies
- ✓ Tombstone ads and omitting prospectus ads

Investment Companies

Investment companies are firms that provide smaller investors with greater access to the securities markets, and give those investors three crucial benefits: professional money management, diversification, and liquidity. This chapter discusses various types of investment companies, how they are structured, and the kinds of products they offer.

By pooling the funds of many investors, an investment company gives each investor significantly more market access and clout than he or she can achieve alone. As mentioned in earlier chapters, some securities are sold in minimum denominations that are beyond the capacity of many individuals. Even when this barrier has been passed, small investors face another disadvantage: the owner of 50 shares of General Motors, for example, has much less power to influence company decisions than the holder of several million shares of the company's stock. Investment companies, which enable investors to buy units of $1,000 (or less) and which in turn can purchase large quantities of a given corporation's stock, solve both of these problems.

Advantages of Investment Companies

By placing their money in investment companies, smaller investors hope to gain three fundamental advantages (besides profitability!):

- **Professional management**—Seasoned professionals are more likely to make specific investment choices that are sound, given the investor's goals and the state of the overall market.
- **Diversification**—Their investment portfolio is more spread out over a variety of securities, so that exposure to the risks of any one security is minimized.
- **Liquidity**—Investors can convert their holdings into cash (or some other security) quickly and easily, if necessary.

Investment companies are experienced in making and managing investments. Few ordinary investors have the expertise or time to manage their own portfolios and to consistently turn a profit while doing so. When investors give their money to an investment company, they expect that the money will be better invested than if they had "played" the market themselves. Because the costs of receiving an investment company's professional services are borne by many investors, this kind of management is typically not prohibitively expensive.

Even when a person buys into only one investment company, the nature of the company's business provides the investor with a large degree of diversification.

> **EXAMPLE:** Harold Hille has $10,000 to invest. He is reluctant to put all $10,000 into the stock of one company or into one type of security, no matter how strong a performer that security has been recently. If trouble strikes, Mr. Hille is worried that his savings might be wiped out. On the other hand, even if his investment performed relatively well, it might not grow as rapidly as the rest of the financial market. Mr. Hille seeks diversity. He decides to buy into River CT Investments, which invests in a total of 76 securities, including stocks and corporate bonds, plus Treasury and municipal bonds. So, although Mr. Hille only has a direct interest in River CT, his exposure is spread out over a big pool of widely diversified companies, industries, and securities.

Perfect liquidity simply means that an investor can get out of his or her position in a security whenever desired, without suffering undue capital losses. By their nature, investment company securities are more liquid than most securities. So it is relatively easy for an investor to liquidate his or her interest in an investment company.

All Investment Companies Are Not Alike

Investment companies are distinguished by their products and by how they are capitalized, plus several other factors. Investment companies come in three main types: face-amount certificate companies, unit investment trusts, and management companies.

Face-Amount Certificate Company

A *face-amount certificate company* is an investment company similar to a mutual fund. The company issues certificates that offer a predetermined rate of interest and can be purchased in lump sums, or more commonly, in periodic installments. The installment amount, time period, and face value amount are established at the time of issue. Interest accrues on the amount paid-in each month at the stated rate. The company then invests those funds in a variety of securities. When the certificate reaches maturity, the company pays the investor the face amount of the certificate. The investor's return is the difference between the total payments made and the face amount received—making the certificates similar to zero-coupon bonds.

Investors can also purchase certificates in a single payment at the time of issue. The certificate is purchased for its face value for a specified period of time, typically three, five, seven, or ten years. Interest accrues on the full amount at the stated rate and can be compounded annually. Payments are made at the end of the time period, quarterly, or annually. The issuer agrees to pay the principal investment plus accrued interest based on the agreed time period.

An investor can redeem the certificate prior to maturity, but receives the surrender amount rather than the full face amount. In such a case, the amount payable to the investor is determined by a formula that accounts for the length of time the certificate has been held.

Face-amount certificates are sold primarily by broker-dealers nationwide. Certificates are not traded on exchanges, so do not have market values that fluctuate in response to changes in interest rates or other economic data. Therefore, the value of the certificate, including accrued interest, remains fixed for its entire guarantee period. They are also considered liquid because they can be surrendered back to the issuer for their principal account value, plus interest, less any early withdrawal charges.

Face-amount certificate companies are less common today than in the early 1900s when they first started, although they still exist. They have been replaced by other types of investment companies and products that offer more benefits to both issuers and investors.

There are some benefits in face amount certificates, however. Some of those are:

- No front-end sales charge
- 100% of the investment amount begins to earn interest when purchased
- Higher than typical market yields
- Generally higher interest rates than bank CDs and fixed annuities for terms of comparable durations
- Low minimum investments
- Secured investments backed by reserves

Table 22.1 shows various interest rates, investment amounts, and the return at the end of the period. As you can see, they can be decent investments with little risk. Although this example shows an initial investment of $50,000, it is possible to invest smaller amounts. The return, of course, would be proportionately smaller.

Table 22.1 Investment Certificates at a Glance

Certificate Type	Fully Paid	Fully Paid	Fully Paid	Fully Paid
Hypothetical amount invested (Minimum amount of $1,000 if interest compounded annually or paid annually and $5,000 if paid quarterly)	$50,000	$50,000	$50,000	$50,000
Guarantee period	3 years	5 years	7 years	10 years
Hypothetical interest rate	5.75%	6.15%	6.40%	6.75%
Hypothetical total return at the end of the guarantee period	$59,130	$67,386	$77,190	$96,084

Federal law requires the issuer to maintain reserves for the amounts of the certificate obligations with a third-party custodian at all times. These reserves generally consist of a diversified pool of high-quality equity and fixed income securities, real estate and mortgage loans. This requirement provides security for the purchaser of the certificate. It is important to remember that face amount certificates are not bank products, equity investments, annuities, or life insurance products, and are not guaranteed or insured by the FDIC, any governmental agency or fund, or private third party. Expect to pay an early withdrawal charge if a withdrawal or full surrender is made prior to the end of the guarantee period.

Unit Investment Trusts

A *unit investment trust (UIT)* is an investment company that sells pieces of interest in the income arising from a pool of securities that have been placed in trust. UITs distinguish themselves from other investment companies chiefly by being organized under a trust indenture and by being governed by a board of trustees rather than a board of directors. UITs are not structured like corporations. UITs are created by *sponsors,* which generally are securities firms that specialize in the type of security represented in the underlying pool. Instead of issuing simple shares, UITs issue redeemable shares of beneficial interest.

A *share of beneficial interest* represents an investor's interest in (or ownership of) the income generated by an underlying portfolio of securities. The investor does *not* actually own any of the underlying securities personally. Shares of beneficial interest are sometimes referred to simply as *units*—hence the name, unit investment trusts. The exact nature of a unit depends on whether the trust company is a fixed UIT or a participating UIT.

How Fixed Unit Investment Trusts Operate

The sponsor of a *fixed unit investment trust* purchases a select portfolio of securities, which is fixed for the life of the trust. In other words, no subsequent trades are made in that portfolio—either to add or remove securities. (Because of this, fixed trusts are not considered *managed* investment companies.) The sponsor then sells units to investors, who are buying pieces of the income generated by the underlying portfolio. Fixed trusts are commonly used for repackaging bonds, particularly municipal bonds. As such, given that bonds have maturity dates, most fixed trusts are self-liquidating. That is, the principal repayments on the underlying bonds are used to pay back the unit holders.

Fixed trust unit owners can arrange to receive their share of interest payments from the underlying bonds at regular intervals, such as monthly or quarterly. As the underlying bonds mature or are called (redeemed), principal payments are made to the trust and then used to repay unit holders in the trust, culminating in the liquidation of that trust.

Units in a fixed trust are redeemable with the sponsor at all times. When investors want out early, they are paid the current net asset value for each of their units. A trust's *net asset value (NAV)* is the total market value of its underlying pool of securities, divided by the number of outstanding units in the trust. The NAV represents the current value of one unit in the trust, and is what owners receive when they redeem their units with the sponsor. NAV is an extremely important concept with investment companies, particularly mutual funds.

Net asset value, or NAV, is the total market value of the underlying pool of securities divided by the number of outstanding units in the trust.

net asset value = market value of portfolio/number of outstanding units (or shares)

EXAMPLE: Gene Kelley owns 10,000 units of El Cid Portfolios, a fixed unit trust sponsored by Charisse Investments. Based on advice from his broker at Donen Associates, Mr. Kelley wants to move his money out of El Cid and into Rainy Day Trust, sponsored by Reynolds & Company. How much money will he transfer to Rainy Day? The current market value of the securities in the El Cid portfolio is $184,900,000. There are 172,000 units of El Cid outstanding. El Cid's NAV, therefore, is $1,075. Mr. Kelley will receive $10,750,000 when he redeems his units.

Participating Unit Investment Trusts

A *participating unit investment trust* differs from a fixed trust because its pool of investments is not static. This change is achieved in an indirect manner: the participating trust buys shares in mutual funds, whose own investments can change constantly. After the mutual fund shares are purchased, the participating trust behaves like a fixed trust: no shares are ever added or traded away. Given the variable nature of the investments of the underlying mutual funds, performance of a participating trust is much less predictable than that of a fixed trust. Participating trusts frequently back annuities, which are investment products sold by insurance companies.

Although "participating" and "fixed" denote different structures for unit investment trusts, some trusts are characterized by the type of investment they make. Real estate investment trusts are among the most common investment trusts available.

Real Estate Investment Trusts

Real estate investment trusts (REITs) are trusts that invest in real estate properties, mortgage loans, and short-term construction loans. Like other trusts, they issue shares of beneficial interest to investors; unlike other trusts, however, REITs are listed either on an exchange or on the OTC market. REITs are considered registered securities according to the Securities Act of 1933 and are regulated by the Investment Company Act of 1940. To comply with regulation, REITs must:

- Register with the SEC before commencing operations
- Have no fewer than 100 owners of beneficial interest
- Have less than 50% of the trust controlled by five or fewer investors

There are some benefits to REITs. They do not pay corporate taxes on ordinary income from the underlying portfolio, provided they comply with the following criteria:

- 95% of the REIT's income is distributed to investors (who must then pay taxes on the income)
- 90% of the income comes from rents and interest on real property, or dividends and interest on securities held by the REIT
- 75% of the gross income is from rents and interests on real property
- 75% of the REIT's assets consist of real estate, government securities, or cash

There are several types of REITs: equity, mortgage, and combination.

- *Equity REITs* take equity positions in real estate properties. Unit holders earn income from the rents collected on those properties. If the properties are sold at a profit, the resulting capital gains are distributed to unit holders as well.
- *Mortgage REITs* purchase mortgages and construction loans, passing the income from those loans on to the beneficial owners of the trust.
- *Combination REITs* can buy equity interests in real properties and mortgage loans.

The fact that REITs are traded on exchanges (or OTC) makes them similar to closed-end management companies. Management companies—both closed-end and open-ended—have become the predominant form of investment company today.

Management Companies

A *management company* is a corporation that issues shares of stock, and whose assets consist of one or more portfolios of securities. (Compare this to a unit investment trust, which issues shares of beneficial interest. See Table 22.2.) More important, the directors of a management company actually *manage* the company's portfolios, changing their composition whenever and however they consider it appropriate, given the stated goals of the specific portfolio. Table 22.2 compares a unit investment trust to a management company. Both have advantages and disadvantages. Investors, with advice from a broker, should decide which type best suits their goals.

Table 22.2 Comparison of a Unit Trust and a Management Company

	Unit Investment Trust	Management Company
Structure	Trust	Corporation
Management	Board of trustees	Board of directors
Issues	Shares of beneficial interest	Shares of stock*
Portfolio	Fixed	Variable

* Closed-end management companies can also issue preferred stock and bonds to capitalize themselves.

It is important to thoroughly understand the differences between a unit investment trust and a management company, as well as the types of each, for the exam.

Management companies are differentiated along two lines: investment strategy (diversified versus nondiversified) and capitalization (closed-end versus open-ended).

Investment Strategy Companies

These include diversified and nondiversified management companies. As the name suggests, a *diversified management company* includes a variety of securities in its portfolio. To qualify as diversified, a management company must have:

- At least 75% of its assets invested in securities
- No more than 5% of its assets invested in the securities of one issuer
- No more than 10% of the voting securities of any issuer

  Diversification does not necessarily mean that a portfolio includes different types of securities, or even securities from different industries. A sponsor theoretically can create a diversified pharmaceuticals management company by investing in the stocks of leading drug companies from half-a-dozen countries.

A *nondiversified management company*, on the other hand, concentrates a portion of its investments in one company or in a handful of companies, perhaps investing only in four major U.S. pharmaceuticals companies.

Capitalized Companies

Here, the main distinction is whether the management company is closed-ended or open-ended.

Closed-end management companies are capitalized through one-time offerings of shares. The number of shares that a closed-end management company issues is established in its prospectus. After the predetermined number of shares has been sold, the company is no longer permitted to sell shares directly to investors. All future trading of shares in the management company takes place in the secondary market, either on an exchange or over the counter. If an investor wanted to buy into a closed-ended fund after its original issue date, he or she has to buy shares from an existing shareholder at the prevailing market price.

Open-ended management companies (commonly known as mutual funds) issue new shares. These shares are issued continually and are redeemable from the mutual fund.

Unlike unit investment trusts, closed-end fund shares do not always sell at a price equal to their net asset value. Instead, as with REITs, share prices depend strictly on supply and demand in the market. Thus, a closed-end management company can sell at a premium or discount to its NAV. A well-managed company that shows good returns on investment will attract new demand; its shares thus increase in value. Conversely, a closed-end management company that has consistently picked underperforming stocks can expect to see its share price drop.

Remember: closed-end management companies can sell at a premium or discount to the NAV.

Individuals or businesses that want to establish an investment company must adhere to an array of laws and regulations. Closed-end management companies, because they are considered nonexempt securities, receive close scrutiny from the SEC.

Regulation of Investment Companies

Investment companies are governed primarily by the *Investment Company Act of 1940*. During the 1920s and 1930s, investment companies had a bad reputation. They were noted for over promising, mismanaging customers' funds, and in some cases pocketing clients' money. The 1940 act was designed to curb such abuses and restore public faith in investment companies.

The act requires that investment companies with more than 100 shareholders:

- Register with the SEC and adhere to SEC regulations
- Publicly state their investment objectives
- Offer a prospectus to potential investors
- Report regularly, in writing, to their customers and to the SEC
- Solicit proxies for matters requiring shareholder approval
- Change investment objectives only by majority approval of shareholders

Investment companies must also comply with the dictates of the Securities Act of 1933 and the Securities Exchange Act of 1934, as well as some of the NASD's Conduct Rules. The NASD rules establish guidelines for ethical behavior among member firms, and between member firms and customers. For instance, investment companies must make it clear that their investment practices are not monitored by any governmental body. Similarly, management companies cannot assure their customers a profit.

Perhaps the greatest restriction on investment companies imposed by these various laws is how they are permitted to advertise. The specific requirements for advertising depend on whether the investment company is advertising with—or without—a prospectus.

The Securities Act of 1933 sets the procedures for issuing new securities, whereas the Securities Exchange Act of 1934 regulates the stock exchanges and the trading of securities already issued.

Advertising Restrictions

Advertisements with a prospectus must contain "the whole truth and nothing but the truth." This statement works on two levels. First, a prospectus cannot include outright untruths. Secondly, an investment company cannot leave out facts that might make an investment appear less appealing.

Advertisements with a prospectus *must* contain the truth about the company; otherwise, the company is in violation of federal laws.

To avoid the possibility of investors being misled, a prospectus must carry certain boilerplate disclaimers, such as:

- The fund's past performance might not be indicative of future results
- No one can guarantee that investment goals will be attained
- Most investments carry risks as well as benefits

A company can advertise without a prospectus, however. The SEC lets investment company ads appear without a prospectus in three forms:

- **Tombstone ads**—These ads typically announce the sale of a new issue. They function as headlines—stating the name of the issuer, details about the security, and the amount being offered. Tombstone ads must include standard language about how to obtain a prospectus from the investment company, and cannot discuss the performance of the investments.

- **Omitting prospectus ads**—These are condensed versions of ordinary prospectuses. They can mention fund performance; however, they cannot contain an application to buy into the fund.
- **Generic investment company ads**—These advertisements promote investment companies in general, without naming a particular company. Because no specific trust or fund is mentioned, no prospectus is necessary.

Exam Prep Questions

1. Miser Management is an investment company. All the following are true of Miser except:

❑ A. It pools investors' funds.

❑ B. It offers investors professional management of their investments.

❑ C. It enables investors to pay lower share prices for securities.

❑ D. It maintains diversified investments.

2. All the following statements about face amount certificates are true except:

❑ A. They are backed by investments in high-quality debt securities.

❑ B. They are essentially obsolete.

❑ C. Mortgage holders were required to buy them.

❑ D. Investors can redeem them prior to maturity and receive the full face amount.

3. Moon Units Investments is a UIT. Which of the following are characteristics of Moon Units?

I. It is organized under a trust indenture.

II. A board of directors governs it.

III. A board of trustees governs it.

IV. It issues shares of beneficial interest to investors.

❑ A. I and II

❑ B. I and III

❑ C. I, II, and IV

❑ D. I, III, and IV

4. If Moon Units is a fixed unit investment trust, which of the following statements is true?

❑ A. It is a managed investment company.

❑ B. The trust makes no further trades after the sponsor has selected the portfolio.

❑ C. The investors own the securities in the trust.

❑ D. The sponsor purchases only equity securities.

5. Gillian owns shares of beneficial interest in the fixed trust Moon Units. How can she redeem her units?

❑ A. She cannot redeem them; she must hold them to maturity.

❑ B. She can ask the sponsor to redeem them.

❑ C. She must sell the units on the NYSE.

❑ D. She must sell the units on the secondary market.

6. Unitarian, a UIT, has 190,000 units and a market value of $19.7 million. Unitarian therefore has a net asset value of:
   - ❑ A. $1,000 per unit
   - ❑ B. $1,022.64 per unit
   - ❑ C. $1,036.84 per unit
   - ❑ D. $1,037.00 per unit

7. The difference between a fixed UIT and a participating UIT is that:
   - ❑ A. A fixed trust pays dividends; a participating trust pays interest.
   - ❑ B. A fixed trust cannot change investments; a participating trust can do so indirectly.
   - ❑ C. A fixed trust has a set maturity; a participating trust does not.
   - ❑ D. A fixed trust issues shares of beneficial interest; a participating trust issues certificates.

8. Paydirt Properties is an REIT. Which statements are true of Paydirt?

   I. It must register with the SEC.

   II. It has at least 100 owners of beneficial interest.

   III. Less than 50% of Paydirt is controlled by five or fewer investors.

   IV. It is listed on an exchange or on the OTC market.
   - ❑ A. I and II
   - ❑ B. II and III
   - ❑ C. I, II, and III
   - ❑ D. I, II, III, and IV

9. Paydirt Properties, a REIT, does not pay corporate taxes on ordinary income from its portfolios because, among other requirements, it distributes to its investors:
   - ❑ A. 75% of its income
   - ❑ B. 90% of its income
   - ❑ C. 95% of its income
   - ❑ D. 97% of its income

10. Middle Management is a management company. All of the following are true of Middle except:
    - ❑ A. It was established as a corporation.
    - ❑ B. It issues shares of beneficial interest.
    - ❑ C. A boards of directors manages it.
    - ❑ D. It sometimes changes the securities in its portfolios.

11. Middle Management is a diversified management company. This means that Middle has:

    I. At least 75% of its assets invested in securities.

    II. No more than 5% of its assets invested in the securities of any one issuer.

    III. No more than 10% of the voting securities of any issuer.

    IV. Only one type of security, such as bonds or stocks.

    ❑ A. I and II
    ❑ B. II and III
    ❑ C. I, II, and III
    ❑ D. I, II, III, and IV

12. Lockbox, Inc., is a closed-end management company. Which of the following statements are true of Lockbox?

    I. It issues a fixed number of shares.

    II. It continually issues new shares.

    III. It redeems its shares.

    IV. Its shares trade on the secondary market.

    ❑ A. I and III
    ❑ B. I and IV
    ❑ C. II and III
    ❑ D. II and IV

13. All of the following statements are true of Cul de Sac, a closed-end management company, except:

    ❑ A. It issues a fixed number of shares.
    ❑ B. It does not redeem its own shares.
    ❑ C. Its shares sell at the net asset value.
    ❑ D. Its shares sell in the secondary market.

14. The Investment Company Act of 1940 requires that Lockbox, Inc., an investment company:

    I. Register with the SEC.

    II. Offer a prospectus to all potential investors.

    III. Solicit proxies for matters requiring shareholder approval.

    IV. Change investment objectives by a majority approval of management.

    ❑ A. I and II
    ❑ B. II and III
    ❑ C. I, II, and III
    ❑ D. I, II, III, and IV

15. When Liberal Distribution, an investment company, advertises with a prospectus:

    I. It can make only true statements.

    II. It can tell investors what profits to expect.

    III. It can omit significant facts as long as it does not state an outright untruth.

    IV. It must make clear that its investment practices are not monitored by any governmental body.

    - ❑ A. I only
    - ❑ B. II and III
    - ❑ C. I, II, and III
    - ❑ D. I and IV

Exam Prep Answers

1. The correct answer is C. The market determines the share prices of securities. Investment companies do pool investors' funds to give them more market access and clout. They also provide professional management of investments and offer more diversified portfolios than most individual investors can afford.

2. The correct answer is D. Investors can redeem certificates prior to maturity but do not receive the full face amount. The amount an investor receives is determined by a formula that takes into consideration the length of time the investor held the certificate. A variety of investments underlie the certificates. At one time, mortgage lenders required borrowers to buy face amount certificates, but this concept is now obsolete.

3. The correct answer is D. A UIT, or unit investment trust, is organized under a trust indenture and governed by a board of trustees rather than a board of directors. It issues shares of beneficial interest that represent the investors' interest in, or ownership of, the income generated by the trust's portfolio.

4. The correct answer is B. The sponsor of a fixed unit investment trust purchases a select portfolio of securities, which is fixed for the life of the trust. It makes no subsequent trades on the portfolio. Because of this, fixed trusts are not considered managed investment companies. Fixed trusts are commonly used for repackaging bonds, particularly municipal bonds, not equity securities.

5. The correct answer is B. Because Moon Units is a fixed trust, Gillian can redeem her shares with the sponsor at any time. Sponsors of fixed trusts promise to continuously make a market in the units of their trusts. The sponsor of Moon Units will pay Gillian the current net asset value for each of her units.

6. The correct answer is C. A unit investment trust's net asset value is its portfolio's market value divided by the number of outstanding units. Unitarian's NAV is $1,036.84 ($197,000,000 ÷ 190,000).

7. The correct answer is B. A fixed trust cannot change its pool of investments while a participating unit investment trust can change its pool of investments indirectly. The participating trust buys shares in mutual funds, whose own investments change constantly.

8. The correct answer is D. As a REIT, or real estate investment trust, Paydirt must register with the SEC before commencing operations. It

must have no fewer than 100 owners of beneficial interest, and less than 50% of it can be controlled by five or fewer investors. REITs are traded on exchanges or over the counter.

9. The correct answer is C. REITs, or real estate investment trusts, do not pay corporation taxes on ordinary income from their portfolios (other than capital gains) if they meet certain requirements, including distributing 95% of their income to investors.
10. The correct answer is B. Management companies are corporations that issue shares of stock, not shares of beneficial interest. Their directors actually manage the portfolios, changing their compositions whenever and however they consider appropriate, given the stated goals of the portfolio.
11. The correct answer is C. To qualify as diversified, a management company must have at least 75% of its assets invested in securities, no more than 5% its assets invested in any one security, and no more than 10% of the voting securities of any issuer.
12. The correct answer is B. Closed-end management companies are capitalized through one-time offerings of shares. After the predetermined number of shares has been sold, the company is no longer permitted to sell shares directly to investors. All future trading of shares takes place in the secondary market, either on an exchange or over the counter.
13. The correct answer is C. Closed-end companies do not sell shares at net asset value. After the predetermined number of shares has been sold, the company can no longer sell shares directly to investors. All subsequent trading of shares takes place in the secondary market. Share prices depend on supply and demand, and can sell at a premium or a discount to the company's net asset value.
14. The correct answer is C. Among other things, the Investment Company Act of 1940 requires investment companies to register with the SEC, offer a prospectus to all potential investors, and solicit proxies on matters requiring shareholder approval. Investment companies can change investment objectives only by majority approval of the shareholders.
15. The correct answer is D. Investment companies must make clear that their practices are not monitored by any governmental body. When advertising with prospectus, they must tell "the whole truth and nothing but the truth." The prospectus must not include any outright untruths, and it cannot leave out facts that might make an investment appear less appealing. The advertising must include disclaimers such as ones stating that no one can guarantee that investment goals will be attained.

Mutual Funds

Terms You Need to Know

- ✓ 12b-1 fund
- ✓ Auditor
- ✓ Breakpoint
- ✓ Conduit (or pipeline) theory
- ✓ Custodian
- ✓ Dealer
- ✓ Dividend reinvestment
- ✓ Dollar averaging
- ✓ Dollar cost averaging
- ✓ Exchange privilege
- ✓ Forward price
- ✓ Fund family
- ✓ Investment advisor
- ✓ Letter of discount
- ✓ Load fund
- ✓ Long-term capital gain
- ✓ Net asset value (NAV)
- ✓ No-load fund
- ✓ Open-ended management company
- ✓ Public offering price (POP)
- ✓ Registrar
- ✓ Right of accumulation
- ✓ Short-term capital gain
- ✓ Systematic withdrawal plan
- ✓ Transfer agent
- ✓ Underwriter or sponsor

Concepts You Need to Understand

- ✓ What mutual funds are
- ✓ How mutual funds are set up and managed
- ✓ Different types of mutual funds
- ✓ The responsibilities of the investment advisor and sponsor
- ✓ Functions of the custodian, transfer agent, registrar, and auditor
- ✓ Methods of selling fund shares to investors
- ✓ Load and no-load funds
- ✓ Public offering price and net asset value
- ✓ Selling charges, breakpoints, and dividend reinvestment
- ✓ Taxation questions surrounding redemption
- ✓ How to read mutual fund listings

Mutual Fund Structure

Open-end management companies, better known as mutual funds, serve the same function as the other kinds of investment companies examined in Chapter 22—namely, they provide smaller investors with professional money management along with investment portfolio diversification and liquidity. Mutual funds differ from other investment companies primarily in how they are structured and in their greater liquidity. This chapter explores how mutual funds are organized, who the key players are, the different types of funds, and how fund shares are bought and sold.

Mutual funds are distinguished from closed-end management companies primarily along two lines: capitalization methods and redemption privileges. Closed-end companies issue shares only once, whereas mutual funds issue new shares all the time.

Similarly, after an investor purchases shares in a closed-end company, he or she can only sell those shares on an exchange or over the counter. With mutual funds, investors can always redeem shares with the fund—that is, the fund continuously makes a market in its own shares. Because mutual funds issue and redeem shares at all times, they are considered to be *open-ended management companies.*

In technical terms, a mutual fund share gives the investor an undivided interest in the portfolio of securities held by the issuing fund. It is important to note, however, that mutual fund investors do not actually own any of the individual securities in the portfolio. Rather, investors have purchased an interest in the *income*—including dividends, interest, and capital gains—generated by the securities in the portfolio.

It is important to remember that mutual fund investors do not own any of the securities in the portfolio. They have only purchased an interest in the income from the investments.

Not all mutual funds are alike. Mutual funds can be differentiated according to their investment objectives. Some mutual funds hold a diversified portfolio of securities; others focus on a particular type of security, industry, geographic region, and so forth. In fact, it is a fund's investment objectives, which are stated in its prospectus, that often determine which fund an investor chooses to buy into. Some of the most common types of mutual funds are:

- *Growth funds.* These funds invest primarily in stocks whose price per share is likely to appreciate substantially over time. Growth funds' goal is to realize capital gains over a long-term investment horizon, as opposed to taking in current income in the form of dividends or interest.
- *Income funds.* The opposite of growth funds, income funds seek current gains, not future ones, and therefore concentrate their investments in bonds and stocks with high dividend yields.
- *Balanced fund.* Combining income and growth stocks, a balanced fund's portfolio includes different types of stocks as well as bonds. Indeed, at least 25% of the fund's capital must be invested in bonds for it to qualify as a balanced fund.
- *Money market funds.* An income fund for extremely risk-averse investors: money market funds hold short-term, highly rated, easily liquidated securities such as commercial paper, T-bills, and certificates of deposit. (Money market funds are different from other mutual funds in a variety of ways, including the checks that they enable investors to write against their shares.)
- *Specialized funds.* These funds invest at least 25% of their assets in specific industries, such as transportation, or in specific geographical regions.
- *Tax-exempt funds.* These funds invest primarily in municipal securities, and thus generate income that is not subject to taxation.

It is worth noting that some of the larger investment companies can sponsor a variety of mutual funds, in an attempt to attract more investors. Funds that are sponsored by the same investment company are known as a *fund family.*

According to the Investment Company Act of 1940, mutual funds are nonexempt securities and thus come under SEC supervision. The act requires that mutual funds:

- Provide investors with a prospectus before they buy into the fund
- Revise and update the prospectus as necessary
- Distribute annual reports that include balance sheets, income statements, and lists of all securities held in the fund
- Solicit proxies from shareholders

In addition, mutual funds can only issue common stock (not preferred stock or bonds of any kind), and they cannot borrow from banks in excess of 300% of their total assets.

Key Players in a Mutual Fund

A mutual fund is governed by a board of directors, who are elected by the shareholders of the fund. According to the Investment Company Act of 1940, no more than 60% of the board can be affiliated with the sponsoring investment company; the remaining 40% must be outsiders with no formal affiliation with the fund.

The board is responsible for establishing the fund's investment strategy. Yet, although the board has ultimate authority over the fund's portfolio, it does not handle the day-to-day tasks of managing its assets. An *investment advisor*, appointed by the board of directors, selects the particular securities that compose the fund's portfolio at any given time. An investment advisor is generally hired for a specified time period, with a renewable contract. Although the advisor has considerable freedom to choose what to buy and sell—and when to do so—he or she cannot stray from the stated investment objectives of the fund.

Underwriters

In general, a mutual fund's *underwriter* or *sponsor* is the investment company that is managing the fund. Technically, the investment company purchases shares in the fund at the current net asset value and then resells them to the public at a higher price, which accounts for various fees charged by the fund. (That higher price is called the *public offering price*, explained later in this chapter.) The sponsor is then responsible for advertising the fund and selling its shares to the public. Advertising costs are borne by the underwriter, unless the fund is classified as a *12b-1 fund*. These types of funds, named for section 12b-1 of the Investment Company Act of 1940, are permitted to pass advertising costs on to shareholders in the fund.

Remember, advertising costs are paid for by the underwriter unless it's a 12b-1 fund. 12b-1 funds pass advertising costs to shareholders.

On occasion, however, the sponsor contracts out the marketing of a fund's shares to another securities firm. Known as *dealers*, these firms purchase fund shares from the sponsor, at a discount to the public offering price, and then sell them to investors. Dealers, however, are prohibited from purchasing shares for their own inventory.

Other Important Players in Mutual Funds

The Investment Company Act of 1940 provides a number of checks and balances to make sure that the governance of a mutual fund is not concentrated in a few hands. Of these checks and balances, the three most important functions reside with the fund's custodian, transfer agent, and auditor.

Congress enacted the Investment Company Act of 1940 in response to careless and sometimes criminal behavior on the part of investment companies.

A mutual fund's *custodian* is usually a bank or a trust company charged with keeping the fund's cash and any certificates associated with the fund's securities portfolio.

Transfer agents primarily monitor the purchase and redemption of fund shares by investors—by issuing new shares and canceling redeemed ones. In addition, transfer agents receive payments made by investors and disburse payments, such as dividends, to shareholders.

Twice a year, as required by law, the *auditor*—an independent accounting firm—compiles balance sheets, income statements, and a list of the securities currently held by the fund. This information is then distributed to all shareholders. Table 23.1 is a breakdown of the various players involved in mutual funds and their responsibilities.

Table 23.1 Mutual Fund Positions and Responsibilities

Board of Directors	
60/40 requirement	
Responsible for operation of fund and fulfillment of its investment objectives	
Investment Advisor	**Transfer Agent**
Chooses securities	Issues new shares
Day-to-day management	Cancels redeemed shares
Earns a fee tied to the fund's performance	Receives and makes payments
Sponsor/Underwriter	**Registrar**
Markets fund to the public	Maintains record of shareholders
Sells shares at markup	Mails financial statements and proxies to shareholders

(continued)

Table 23.1 Mutual Fund Positions and Responsibilities *(continued)*

Dealer	**Auditor**
Helps the sponsor market the fund	Hired semiannually
Buys shares from sponsor at discount	Independent of fund
Cannot buy shares for own inventory	Required by law
Custodian	
Safeguards fund assets	

Paying for the Services

Shareholders pay for the services of all the parties involved with mutual funds. Fees for the services of these key players are built into the fund's sales and redemption charges. These charges cannot exceed a combined total of 8.5% of the public offering price. (Redemption fees and how the sales charge is calculated are explained later in this chapter.) Other fees that can also be charged by mutual funds include:

- *Brokerage fees*—Transaction costs to the fund of buying and selling securities in their managed portfolio.
- *Printing fees*—Costs of printing the fund's prospectuses and annual reports.
- *Legal fees*—Costs incurred by hiring lawyers who file registration applications required by the SEC.
- *Administrative fees*—Costs of doing business, including personnel salaries, office rental, and so on.
- *Advertising fees*—Costs of advertising the fund to prospective investors. Only funds with 12b-1 status can pass this cost on to shareholders.

Marketing Mutual Funds

Mutual funds can be marketed to the public in a variety of ways. Perhaps the fundamental distinction is whether a fund is a load fund or a no-load fund. A *no-load fund* is a mutual fund that sells directly to the investor. No-load funds also redeem shares themselves without using an intermediary. As a result, no-load funds carry no sales charges. Money market funds are typically no-load.

It's important to understand that all funds charge fees of one sort or another; no-load funds simply do not have a *sales charge*.

A no-load fund's other costs are deducted before computing its net asset value, which is discussed later in this chapter. Not surprisingly, investors in a *load fund* do pay a sales charge, because the fund does not market and redeem its shares directly.

Mutual fund purchases can be made in a lump sum payment or according to a periodic payment plan. Two of the most common plans are called dollar cost averaging and dollar averaging. Both permit the investor to buy shares on a monthly (or quarterly) basis over a period of months or years.

In *dollar cost averaging*, investors purchase the same dollar amount each period, regardless of the current price of fund shares. In other words, an investor might commit to buying $1,000 worth of shares each month.

Dollar averaging, on the other hand, is a payment plan in which the investor buys the same number of shares each period, regardless of the cost. That is, an investor might agree to purchase 1,000 shares per month.

Assuming that share prices fluctuate in a consistently random way—as opposed, say, to declining continuously—dollar cost averaging results in a lower per-share cost, and consequently the purchase of more shares. In essence, with dollar cost averaging, investors buy more shares when the price is low—and fewer when the price is high—than they do with dollar averaging. Table 23.2 illustrates the benefits of dollar cost averaging.

Remember, dollar cost averaging doesn't guarantee the investor positive returns; it's only relevant to the amount invested.

Table 23.2 Dollar Cost Averaging Versus Dollar Averaging

		Dollar Cost Averaging		Dollar Averaging	
Month	$ Price/Share	$ Paid	Shares Purchased	$ Paid	Shares Purchased
1	$15.00	$1,500	100.00	$1,500	100
2	16.50	1,500	90.91	1,650	100
3	14.03	1,500	106.91	1,403	100
4	12.63	1,500	118.76	1,263	100
5	14.52	1,500	103.31	1,452	100
6	15.97	1,500	93.93	1,597	100
TOTAL		**$9,000**	**613.82**	**$8,865**	**600**
COST PER SHARE		**$14.66**		**$14.78**	

As you can see, the total investment is less with dollar averaging with fewer shares and the cost per share is more. With dollar cost averaging, the total investment is higher, there are more shares, but the cost per share is less than just dollar averaging. Basically, there is little difference between the two. It should be pointed out, however, that neither method guarantees a profit for the investor. And there are disadvantages to both of these methods. Investing either a dollar amount or a share amount each month regardless of the cost of the shares might average out over time but then again, might not.

Two important concepts determine fund share prices and the sales charges that go along with them: net asset value and public offering price.

Net Asset Value

Recall from Chapter 22 that *net asset value (NAV)* represents the current value of a mutual fund share. Mathematically, it is:

Net asset value = market value of the fund portfolio ÷ outstanding units (or share

A fund's NAV is calculated at the end of every trading day and can change daily: the market value of its securities portfolio fluctuates, as does the number of outstanding shares.

The NAV is essentially the starting point for selling mutual fund shares. In a no-load fund, it is the end point, too; the fund sells shares directly to investors at the NAV. If the current NAV is $10.66, the cost to the investor is $10.66 a share. Because NAV is calculated at the end of a trading day, mutual funds charge investors the *forward price*—that is, the NAV at the close of the day on which fund shares are purchased.

Money market funds are somewhat different from other mutual funds, partly because of their NAV. The NAV of a money market fund remains constant at $1 a share. If the value of the fund grows, that growth is not expressed as an increase in the NAV, but rather as an increase in the investor's number of shares.

Load funds use NAV in combination with the sales charge to determine the public offering price.

The Public Offering Price (POP)

The *public offering price (POP)* is the cost to an investor of purchasing a load fund share (remember that a load fund typically hires a sponsor to sell its shares). The POP includes both the fund's NAV and its sales charge.

To determine the POP, the sales charges are expressed as percentages, with the maximum allowable charge being 8.5%. This figure, however, is (somewhat confusingly) based on the POP, not the NAV. Essentially, in determining the POP, funds ask themselves the following question: "What sales charge can we add to NAV so that NAV will represent 91.5% of the POP, with the sales charge accounting for the remaining 8.5%?"

How, you might wonder, does an investor figure the sales charge? An example helps illustrate this.

> **EXAMPLE:** Arthur Rex wants to buy shares of a fund run by Excalibur. He discovers that the current bid price is $22.45 a share and the current ask price is $24.15. The bid price is the NAV—the actual value of the shares, or the price at which the fund redeems shares. The ask price is the POP. For Mr. Rex to find the sales charge percentage, he first must subtract the bid price from the ask price, yielding the dollar amount of the sales charge. In this case, Excalibur has added a sales charge of $1.70 to the NAV ($24.15 – $22.45 = $1.70). Mr. Rex can then determine what percentage the sales charge constitutes. By dividing the sales charge ($1.70) by the POP ($24.15), he finds that the sales charge percentage is 7.04.

How Mutual Funds Determine Sales Charge

Funds work in the opposite direction from their customers. Suppose that Excalibur wants to charge the maximum 8.5%, and that the Excalibur's NAV is $22.45. Excalibur, therefore, wants $22.45 to equal 91.5% (100% less a sales charge of 8.5%) of its POP. Excalibur accomplishes this by dividing the NAV by 91.5%. (This percentage is known as the "complement" of the sales charge percentage—in other words, it is the percentage that, when added to the sales percentage of 8.5, totals 100%.)

POP = NAV ÷ 1.00 – sales charge percentage

POP = $22.45 ÷ 1.00 – 0.085= $22.45 ÷ 0.915

= $24.54

So, to receive a sales charge of 8.5%, Excalibur needs to quote a POP of $24.54.

NAV, POP, and the Sales Charge Relationship

Provided that any two of those figures are known, you can always determine the third. From the POP formula, a fund's NAV can be determined:

NAV = POP × (1.00 – sales charge percentage)

Likewise, the sales charge percentage can be calculated with the following formula:

Sales charge percentage = 1 – NAV/POP

= 1 – 20.00 ÷ 21.75

= 1 – 0.915

= 0.0805 or 8.05%

Breakpoints

Most mutual funds give investors a sales charge discount for bulk purchases, with the discount increasing as the purchase amount increases. The purchase amounts required to receive discounts are called *breakpoints*. However, funds generally have a minimum sales charge. After that floor has been reached, sales charges don't drop any lower no matter what the value of shares purchased totals.

Breakpoints are available only to individuals, although a married couple (along with its dependents) can qualify for this purpose as an "individual." Otherwise, groups cannot get together and pool their money in order to qualify for a breakpoint; one way that mutual funds help their customers reach breakpoints. Other ways include letters of discount and rights of accumulation. With these plans, investors qualify for breakpoints by buying shares over time, rather than by making one lump-sum payment.

Letter of Discount

A *letter of discount* enables the buyer to purchase shares over an interval of 13 months, and to have the total purchase apply toward a breakpoint.

> **EXAMPLE:** Lance Lott wants to buy shares of Excalibur. He plans to purchase $3,000 now and $4,000 in six months, so he signs a letter of discount with the fund. Instead of having to pay an 8.5% sales charge for each purchase, the letter of discount permits him to pay a sales charge of only 7.5%, based on the total payment of $7,000.

If an investor decides not to pay for the full number of shares agreed to, the discount is lost. If Mr. Lott buys only the first $3,000 worth of shares, the sales charge reverts to 8.5% and is factored in when he redeems his shares.

An investor has 90 days to sign a letter of discount. If Gwen Navere buys $3,500 of Excalibur shares on September 1, she has until November 29 to sign a letter of discount that will cover her initial investment.

Remember: an investor has 90 days to sign a letter of discount. If they don't sign it, they lose the discount.

Rights of Accumulation

Rights of accumulation, also called cumulative purchase privileges, are similar to letters of discount, but permit investors to qualify for breakpoints over a longer period—sometimes up to 10 years. If Ms. Navere has already put $8,000 into Excalibur and states her intention to purchase another $25,000 worth over the next 10 years, a right of accumulation then entitles her to a sales charge of 2.5% on both her previous and future purchases.

Rights of accumulation give investors a reduced sales charge on subsequent purchases of shares; that is, they can purchase more shares in a previously purchased fund at a reduced sales charge. The charge is discounted for the entire amount of the purchase, not just the amount over the breakpoint.

Another way for investors to purchase more shares in a mutual fund is to have the dividends they receive reinvested in the fund.

Mutual Funds Dividends

Mutual fund dividends represent the income earned by investors from the fund's securities portfolio. As that portfolio earns capital gains plus dividend and interest income, the fund distributes this income on a pro-rata basis to its shareholders. Some shareholders choose *dividend reinvestment* over receiving cash payments. To encourage investors to reinvest their dividends, many funds enable shareholders to reinvest dividends by buying more shares at NAV, not at the POP.

Redemption of Mutual Fund Shares

All open-end mutual funds make a market in their shares. Thus, shareholders can always liquidate their positions in a fund simply by redeeming their shares—that is, by selling the shares back to the fund itself.

For the most part, the redemption price is the fund's current NAV. Some funds, however, charge a redemption fee, which is usually in the 1% to 2% range. Funds that charge a redemption fee are required to factor that into the initial sales charge. In other words, the total fees charged to an investor—including sales and redemption charges—cannot exceed 8.5%. So, funds that charge redemption fees generally have lower up-front sales charges.

Investors are not required to redeem all their shares at once. Moreover, funds frequently offer *systematic withdrawal plans*, which permit shareholders to liquidate their holding over time. Shareholders sometimes want to redeem their shares in one fund and reinvest the proceeds in another fund of the same family. In such cases, investment companies offer shareholders an exchange privilege.

Exchange privilege permits investors to switch money from one fund to another within the same fund family without incurring a sales charge from the second fund.

Taxes on Mutual Fund Income

Mutual fund shareholders receive no particular tax benefits. Dividends and interest paid by the fund are fully taxable as ordinary income by local, state, and federal governments—whether the dividends and interest are reinvested or paid out by the fund. Capital gains—realized when investors sell shares for more than they paid for them—are also fully taxable, but at different levels depending on the length of time the investor has owned the fund shares. Specifically:

- A *short-term capital gain* results when an investor holds fund shares for less than a year before selling them. A shareholder who purchases fund shares in March for $22 and sells them in July for $25 realizes a short-term capital gain of $3. Short-term gains are taxed at the same rate as the shareholder's ordinary income, up to maximum of 39.6%.
- A *long-term capital gain* applies to shares held longer than 18 months. Long-term gains are taxed at a maximum rate of 20%.

One exception to these rules lies in the tax treatment of capital gains realized by the fund itself. Because it invests in a portfolio of securities whose prices change over time, a fund realizes both capital gains and losses on the portfolio. A fund's net capital gains are bundled together and distributed pro-rata to shareholders once a year. These distributions are considered long-term capital gains regardless of how long shareholders have owned shares in the fund. Thus, shareholders are taxed at the long-term capital gains rate on these distributions.

> **EXAMPLE:** Kay Knight buys 100 shares of Excalibur in July at an NAV of $22.45. In September the fund distributes $3.95 per share in capital gains, giving her $395. In October she redeems her shares at an NAV of $25.45, realizing a capital gains of $3 a share, or $300. This $300 is taxable at Ms. Knight's higher income tax rate, but the $395 distribution in September is taxable at the lower long-term capital gains rate.

Funds Sometimes Pay Taxes

Under Subchapter M of the tax code, investment companies qualify for special treatment if:

- 90% (or more) of their income is generated by portfolio holdings, *and*
- 90% (or more) of their investment income is distributed to shareholders.

So portfolio-based funds that distribute 90% of their income to shareholders do not pay corporate taxes on that income. They only have to pay taxes on the remaining 10%. Indeed, there are further tax advantages to funds that channel more than 90% of their earnings to shareholders. The IRS slaps surcharges on funds that do not pass on at least 97% of their dividend income and 98% of their capital gains. As a result, it's hard to find a fund that keeps more than 2 or 3% of dividend income or capital gains for itself.

The IRS offers these tax breaks to mutual funds on the basis of its *conduit* or *pipeline theory*. That is, if the funds "pipe through" the income earned on a portfolio to investors, who in turn pay taxes on that income, there is no justification for the government to tax this income twice.

Reading Mutual Fund Tables

Table 23.3 is typical of the information that you can find in a daily newspaper regarding mutual funds.

Table 23.3 Mutual Fund Newspaper Listing

Fund Family/ Fund Name	NAV	Qty % Ret. 1 Day	YTD % Ret. from Jan	5-Yr. % Ret. 5 years
BlackRock Svc				
Bal	18.91	–0.4	+10.1	+14.8
CoreBd	9.93	+0.2	+ 5.0	NA
IndexEq	20.90	–0.9	+12.2	+20.8

- The first column lists individual funds within the BlackRock Svc. family.
- The second column lists the NAV of each fund. Remember that NAV is calculated at the end of the business day, so a morning newspaper listing carries the previous day's closing NAV.
- The third column shows the change in the value of the fund's securities from the previous day.
- The fourth column shows the change in the value of the fund's portfolio since the beginning of the calendar year.
- The fifth column calculates the return on the fund's portfolio over the previous five years.

Note that the final column can vary; depending on the day of the week, newspapers can report other data, such as three-month returns, sales charges, or the general fund expenses as a percentage of total assets—the fund's expense ratio.

Exam Prep Questions

1. Steven owns 100 shares of Baker Income Mutual Fund. These shares represent:
   - ❑ A. An ownership interest in the securities underlying the fund.
   - ❑ B. An undivided interest in the income generated by the securities underlying the fund.
   - ❑ C. An ownership interest in the fund.
   - ❑ D. Open-ended ownership of the fund.

2. Marilyn Morone is an investment adviser for Baker Income mutual fund. All of the following are true except:
   - ❑ A. She was appointed by the fund's board of directors.
   - ❑ B. She selects the securities for Baker Income's portfolio.
   - ❑ C. She earns a management fee.
   - ❑ D. She maintains an open-ended contract with Baker Income.

3. McDonough Deals acts as a dealer for Perry Mutual Funds. Which of the following statements is true of McDonough?

   I. It purchases shares from Perry and sells them to investors.

   II. It purchases shares at a discount to the public offering price.

   III. It is prohibited from purchasing shares for its own inventory.

   IV. It sponsors the fund.
   - ❑ A. I and II
   - ❑ B. II and III
   - ❑ C. I, II, and III
   - ❑ D. I, II, III, and IV

4. How do rights of accumulation benefit an investor?
   - ❑ A. New shares can be purchased at a discount.
   - ❑ B. New shares can be purchased at a lower sales charge.
   - ❑ C. Shares can be sold at a premium.
   - ❑ D. Shares can be traded at a lower sales charge.

5. When Perry Mutual Fund charges shareholders for services, the fees cannot exceed:
   - ❑ A. A combined total of 5% of the offering price.
   - ❑ B. A combined total of 7% of the offering price.
   - ❑ C. A combined total of 8.5% of the offering price.
   - ❑ D. Reasonable and customary charges.

6. Which of the following costs can a mutual fund pass on to its shareholders?

   I. Brokerage fees

   II. Advertising fees

   III. Legal fees

   IV. Administrative fees

   ❑ A. I and II
   ❑ B. II and III
   ❑ C. I, II, and IV
   ❑ D. I, III, and IV

7. Brown-Garrett Growth is a no-load mutual fund. All of the following statements are true of Brown-Garrett except:

   ❑ A. It sells shares directly to investors.
   ❑ B. It carries no sales charges.
   ❑ C. It charges no fees to shareholders.
   ❑ D. It redeems its own shares.

8. Carrie purchases 100 shares in the Grand Valley Balanced Mutual Fund each month. This is known as:

   ❑ A. A dollar cost plan.
   ❑ B. Dollar cost averaging.
   ❑ C. Dollar averaging.
   ❑ D. A no-load purchase plan.

9. Which of the following statements are true of Grand Valley Balanced Mutual Fund shares?

   I. Investors can purchase only whole shares.

   II. Investors can purchase fractional shares.

   III. The NAV represents the current value of a share.

   IV. The POP represents the current value of a share.

   ❑ A. I and III
   ❑ B. I, II, and III
   ❑ C. I, III, and IV
   ❑ D. II, III, and IV

10. The POP of a mutual fund share is:

    ❑ A. The NAV
    ❑ B. The NAV plus the sales charge
    ❑ C. The NAV minus the sales charge
    ❑ D. The NAV times 8.5%

11. Brown-Garrett Growth, a mutual fund, has a sales charge of 7% and a NAV of $22. It therefore has a POP of:

❑ A. $20.56
❑ B. $22.00
❑ C. $23.66
❑ D. $24.13

12. Fox Fund mutual fund offers discounts on its sales charges. Which of the following statements are true?

I. Investors receive the discounts on bulk purchases.

II. The discounts increase as the investor's purchase increases.

III. The discounts decrease as the investor's purchase increases.

IV. Fox has a minimum sales charge beyond which it gives no further discounts.

❑ A. I and II
❑ B. I, II, and III
❑ C. I, III, and IV
❑ D. I, II, and IV

13. Devin obtains a letter of discount from Hanley Income, a mutual fund. The letter:

I. Allows Devin's purchases over a period of 12 months to apply toward a breakpoint.

II. Allows Devin's purchases over a period of 13 months to apply toward a breakpoint.

III. Allows Devin to purchase a certain dollar amount of shares.

IV. Legally binds Devin to purchase a certain number of shares.

❑ A. I and III
❑ B. I and IV
❑ C. II only
❑ D. II and III

14. Sharon is a shareholder in Green Growth Mutual Fund. All of the following statements are true except:

❑ A. Sharon receives dividends from income on Green Growth's portfolio.
❑ B. Sharon receives dividends from capital gains on Green Growth's portfolio.
❑ C. Sharon can reinvest her dividends in the fund.
❑ D. When Sharon reinvests her dividends, Green Growth can allow her to purchase shares at the POP rather than at the NAV.

15. Sharon earns income on shares of Green Growth Mutual Fund, which she purchased two years ago. Which of the following statements are true?

    I. Sharon's dividends and interest are fully taxable as ordinary income.

    II. Sharon pays local, state, and federal taxes on her dividends unless they are reinvested.

    III. Sharon pays a maximum of 28% in taxes on long-term capital gains on securities in the fund's portfolio.

    IV. When Sharon sells her shares, she will pay a maximum rate of 20% in taxes on long-term capital gains.

    ❑ A. I and II

    ❑ B. II and III

    ❑ C. I and IV

    ❑ D. I, II, III, and IV

Exam Prep Answers

1. The correct answer is B. A mutual fund share gives an investor an undivided interest in the portfolio of securities held by the issuing fund. Investors in a fund do not actually own any of the individual securities in the portfolio, but rather own an interest in the income generated by the securities.
2. The correct answer is D. Appointed by the board of directors, an investment advisor selects the particular securities that compose the fund's portfolio at any given time. Although they have discretion to buy and sell shares according to their judgment, they must follow the stated goals of the fund. Typically, advisors are hired for two years, with renewable contracts thereafter. Advisors do not receive a management fee but a percentage of the proceeds of the fund, so their compensation is directly affected by the fund's performance.
3. The correct answer is C. The sponsor, or underwriter, is the investment company that manages the fund. Dealers purchase shares from the sponsor at a discount to the public offering price, and then sell them to investors. They are prohibited from purchasing shares for their own inventory. Any purchase they make from the sponsor must be matched with prior orders from investors.
4. The correct answer is B. Rights of accumulation give investors a reduced sales charge if they are purchasing additional shares in a mutual fund in which they have previously invested. ROA is not about selling at a discount or a premium, or about trading shares.
5. The correct answer is C. Fees charged to shareholders for a mutual fund's services cannot exceed a combined total of 8.5% of the public offering price.
6. The correct answer is D. Mutual funds can charge shareholders for a variety of expenses, including brokerage, legal, and administrative fees. Only funds with 12b-1 status can also pass on advertising fees.
7. The correct answer is C. No-load funds sell directly to investors, redeem their shares, and carry no sales charges. They do, however, make other charges for expenses, such as brokerage, printing, legal, or administrative fees.
8. The correct answer is C. Dollar averaging is a payment plan in which the investor buys the same number of shares each period, regardless of the cost. Carrie buys 100 shares of Grand Valley each month, whether the shares cost $10 or $20. In dollar cost averaging, on the other hand, the investor purchases the same dollar amount in shares each period—say, $1,000—regardless of how few or how many shares the money buys. A dollar cost plan and a no-load purchase plan do not exist.

9. The correct answer is B. Investors can purchase both full and fractional shares of mutual funds. The NAV, or net asset value, is the price at which shares can be redeemed and therefore the current value of the shares. The POP, or public offering price, includes both the fund's NAV and its sales charge.
10. The correct answer is B. The POP, or public offering price, of a mutual fund share, includes both the fund's NAV and its sales charge.
11. The correct answer is C. The POP is $23.66. The formula is POP = NAV divided by (1.00 – sales charge percentage). Brown-Garrett's NAV is $22; 1.00 minus the .07 sales charge is .93. $22 divided by .93 equals $23.66.
12. The correct answer is D. Most mutual funds give investors a sales charge discount for bulk purchases, called breakpoints, with the discount increasing as the purchase amount increases. Most funds have a minimum sales charge, after which additional purchases do not receive additional discounts.
13. The correct answer is D. Devin's letter of discount enables him to purchase mutual fund shares over a period of 13 months, and to have the total purchase apply toward a breakpoint. The letter of discount is not legally binding, but if Devin does not buy the full number of shares, the sales charge reverts to a higher percentage, which is factored in when he redeems the shares.
14. The correct answer is D. To encourage shareholders to reinvest, many funds allow investors to use dividends to purchase more shares at the NAV, not the POP. As a mutual fund's portfolio earns capital gains and interest and dividend income, it distributes the income on a pro-rata basis to its shareholders.
15. The correct answer is C. Dividends and interest paid by mutual funds are fully taxable as ordinary income by local, state, and federal governments, even if the dividends are reinvested. Because Sharon has owned her shares for two years, any capital gains she realizes are long-term gains, which are taxable at a maximum rate of 20%. When she pays taxes on capital gains realized on the fund's portfolio, however, these are always considered long-term, regardless of how long the fund owned the securities.

Direct Participation Programs

Terms You Need to Know

✓ Accelerated depreciation
✓ Alternative minimum tax (AMT)
✓ Blind pool
✓ Certificate of limited partnership
✓ Cost depletion
✓ Depletion
✓ Depreciation
✓ Development program
✓ Direct participation program (DPP)
✓ Drilling program
✓ Exploratory program
✓ Fiduciary
✓ General partner
✓ Income program
✓ Limited liability
✓ Limited partner
✓ Limited partnership
✓ Mini-maxi offering
✓ Modified Accelerated Cost Recovery System (MACRS)
✓ Nonrecourse loan
✓ Raw land
✓ Recapture
✓ Recourse loan
✓ Sale-leaseback
✓ Specified pool
✓ Straight-line depreciation
✓ Suitability requirements
✓ Triple net lease

Concepts You Need to Understand

✓ Tax status of partnerships
✓ Differences between general and limited partners
✓ Certificates of limited partnership
✓ Internal Revenue Service definition of a corporation
✓ Different kinds of DPPs
✓ Tax implications of DPPs
✓ Depreciation and depletion

Structure of Direct Participation Programs

Direct participation programs (DPPs) are investment ventures designed to permit investors to become owners of a business—receiving any profits or losses directly, for better or worse. An investor in a DPP receives his or her pro-rata share of the program's income (or accepts a pro-rata share of the loss) each year. Most direct participation programs are organized as partnerships.

According to U.S. tax laws, a partnership is not a taxable entity, so investors in partnerships avoid the additional layer of taxes associated with corporations. When corporations generate revenues, they pay corporate taxes on the income, and then pay stock dividends out of their after-tax earnings. Investors, in turn, must pay personal taxes on their dividend income. Thus, the money that ultimately ends up in an investor's bank account has been taxed twice: once at the corporate level and again at the individual level. Income generated by partnerships flows directly to the partners, who are then taxed as individuals.

Not only are most DPPs organized as partnerships, but they are also generally structured as one specific type—a limited partnership.

Limited and General Partnerships

By law, a *limited partnership* is a business venture consisting of at least one limited partner and one general partner. In practice, most limited partnerships usually have more than one limited partner, and sometimes more than one general partner as well.

The most important distinction between limited and general partners involves liability. *Limited partners* have *limited liability:* in the event of bankruptcy, creditors cannot seek any amount greater than a limited partner's financial stake in the DPP. *General partners*, on the other hand, possess unlimited liability: in theory, a general partner's entire net worth is at risk in a DPP. The two kinds of partners also play different roles in the operation of a DPP.

Theoretically, general partners are at risk of losing their entire net worth in a direct participation program.

The General Partner's Role

The general partner functions as the manager of the DPP—overseeing day-to-day operations, choosing investments, deciding when to buy and sell. Normally, he or she is also in charge of bringing new limited partners into the program. The general partner should also be a person with experience in money management, especially in the type of investment chosen by the DPP.

Depending on the program, the general partner might choose to assume the following roles, or hire other people or firms to do so:

- **Syndicator**—Person who assembles the partnership and files the appropriate documentation in the state where the DPP is headquartered.
- **Underwriter**—Person or firm (often a brokerage) responsible for marketing the program to potential investors.
- **Partnership manager**—Person who chooses the partnership's specific investments and makes business decisions.
- **Property manager**—Individual responsible for managing any properties purchased by a real estate DPP. (The different kinds of DPPs are discussed later in this chapter.)

Under Internal Revenue Code 72-13, a corporation can act as a DPP's general partner, but it must meet certain ownership and net worth requirements. If the contributions to a DPP total $2.5 million or more, the corporate general partner's net worth must total at least 10% of the total contribution. If the total contribution is less than $2.5 million, the corporate general partner must possess a net worth of at least $250,000, or 15% of the total contribution, whichever is less. Corporate general partners are not subject to unlimited liability—their legal obligations are capped by the market value of their corporate assets.

General partners have more responsibilities than rights because of their fiduciary role. A *fiduciary* is someone who has been charged with managing another person's money prudently. Without the approval of the limited partners, a general partner **cannot**:

- Engage or invest in businesses that compete with the partnership (a conflict of interest)
- Bring in another general or limited partner
- Use partnership property for nonpartnership activities
- Continue the partnership after the death, retirement, or incapacity of one of the general partners

- Accept a court judgment against the partnership
- Deviate from the certificate of limited partnership

The Limited Partner's Role

The limited partner's basic role is to provide capital—he or she has little control over the daily management of the DPP. The limited partner is a passive financial backer, whereas the general partner is the professional manager of the program. A limited partner who attempts to become involved in managing a DPP risks losing his or her limited liability. This constitutes a significant drawback of limited partnerships. The profitability of the investment strategy depends to a large degree on the skills of the general partner, and limited partners have little recourse (other than lawsuits) if they are unhappy about how the general partner performs.

Limited partners in a DPP can:

- Inspect the partnership's books
- Receive their share of profits and losses
- Lend funds to the partnership
- Sue to dissolve the partnership
- Sue the general partner, if they believe the general partner is not acting in the program's best interest
- Engage or invest in businesses that compete with the partnership
- Sell or assign their interest in the partnership

The limited partner's basic role is to provide capital with little control over the daily management of the DPP.

The Certificate of Limited Partnership

The *certificate of limited partnership* is the legal agreement between the general and limited partners describing how the DPP is structured and managed. All parties must sign the certificate, vouching for the accuracy of its information. Some of the most important items included are:

- The name of the partnership, its purpose, and its place of business
- The names, addresses, and roles of each participant (general and limited partners)

- How much cash or property each partner has contributed
- How any profits are distributed
- What events cause the dissolution of the partnership
- Whether (and how) a limited partner can sell or assign his or her interest

For potential creditors, a key element of the certificate is the section showing the total financial contribution of each limited partner. Based on this information, creditors can determine the financial strength of the partnership.

Once the certificate is filed with the appropriate state office, any significant changes to the partnership, such as a new limited partner, requires an amendment to the certificate.

The certificate establishes the DPP's tax status as a partnership rather than a corporation. This crucial distinction is based on specific guidelines of the IRS.

How the IRS Distinguishes Between Partnerships and Corporations

The IRS has four criteria for determining whether a business entity is a corporation, regardless of what it calls itself publicly. To be considered a limited partnership by the IRS, a DPP cannot possess more than two of these defining characteristics of a corporation:

- *Continuity of Life.* Death, withdrawal, retirement, or expulsion of a principal does not cause the immediate end of the business entity.
- *Free Transfer of Interests.* The common stock of a corporation is freely transferable; investors need not get the company's permission to sell their shares. Conversely, most limited partnerships require that limited partners secure the approval of the general partner before selling or assigning their interest in a DPP.
- *Limited Liability.* The most that a corporate shareholder—or limited partner in a DPP—can lose is the amount of his or her investment. However, general partners assume unlimited liability in a DPP.
- *Centralized Management.* In a corporation, managerial power is concentrated in a person or group—that is, not all owners of the business have a voice in its operations. Given the role of the general partner, DPPs can seldom get around this corporate characteristic.

How the IRS distinguishes between a partnership and a corporation is important to know.

Types of Direct Participation Programs

Direct participation programs have been created in a wide range of industries. Perhaps the most popular sectors of the economy for DPPs are real estate, oil and gas production, and equipment leasing. Real estate DPPs invest in everything from raw land to the construction or purchase of luxury condominiums and resort hotels. Each has its advantages and disadvantages.

Raw Land

Raw land is simply land that has not yet been developed—it has no real property improvements, such as buildings. Depending on its location, raw land can have strong potential for capital appreciation. A raw land DPP might purchase such property in hopes of eventually developing or selling it.

DPPs are often created to finance the purchase, development, or construction of a variety of properties. Some of the more popular real estate DPPs are:

- *Single tenant net lease*—The program buys a building and leases it to a tenant. When the tenant is the previous owner of the building, this is known as a *sale-leaseback*. In some cases, the tenant is only responsible for the rent. In others, the tenant also pay taxes, insurance, and maintenance costs of the building—an arrangement called a *triple net lease*.

It's important to know the difference between a sale-leaseback and a triple net lease.

- *Shopping centers*—The DPP buys a shopping mall and leases the stores to various tenants. Ideally, the leases go to large tenants who sign long-term leases, giving the program stability and a secure cash flow.
- *Office buildings*—The DPP purchases and leases office buildings. Because office leases tend to be short term, this form of DPP is somewhat risky.

- *Apartment buildings*—Another relatively risky DPP investment, because tenants might fail to pay rent promptly (or at all).
- *Hotels*—Hotel direct participation programs are risky but potentially lucrative. Although management costs are high and changes in the economy can temporarily eliminate profits, successful hotels can bring in huge returns on a program's investment.
- *Warehouse limited partnerships*—This type of program purchases a storage warehouse and rents out space to individual customers.
- *Government assisted housing*—Essentially, this DPP enters into business with the government by building or purchasing housing units for Section 8 tenants. Under Section 8 of the Housing and Community Development Act of 1974, the federal government subsidizes rents for certain low-income, elderly, and otherwise disadvantaged individuals.
- *Registered condominiums*—These DPPs purchase vacation homes in resort areas. As with most real estate projects, location is paramount.

Oil and Gas Production

The search for oil and gas beneath the earth's surface has also been a primary focus of DPPs. The U.S. economy depends on massive quantities of cheap fuel, so the federal government offers many incentives to businesses that search for, drill, and refine oil and gas. Many DPPs are designed to take advantage of these tax incentives.

There are two main types of oil and gas programs: drilling and income.

Drilling Programs

Drilling programs finance the construction of wells in hopes of discovering fuel. These programs can sponsor searches both inside and outside the United States. Drilling costs are substantial—including labor charges, land leases, geological studies, and equipment purchases. Each of these costs offers investors substantial tax deductions. *Exploratory programs* drill wells in unproven ground—an activity referred to as wildcat drilling. Because the ground is unproven, land-lease costs are usually low, but the drilling and exploration costs are relatively high and the risks of failure are large. *Development programs* drill in existing oil fields or in areas adjacent to them. Here land leases are more expensive, but the risk of dry wells is lower.

Exploratory programs drill wells in unproven ground, whereas development programs drill in existing oil fields or adjacent areas.

Income Programs

Income programs pursue the relatively low-risk strategy of purchasing established oil wells. These programs have low drilling costs, because the heavy equipment is already in place and analysis of the field is complete. The program naturally makes its profits by selling the oil or gas reserves. Depletion allowances provide oil and gas DPPs with a means to deduct significant amounts from any revenues, thus lowering tax bills.

Equipment-Leasing Programs

Equipment-leasing programs buy heavy machines and equipment for transportation (buses, trucks, train engines) or construction (cranes, tractors, frontloaders) and then lease them out. A key distinction is the kind of lease: operating or full payout.

With an *operating lease*, the leaseholder pays the DPP a sum less than the cost of the equipment. Normally, these leases are short-term, allowing the program to lease the equipment several times during the machinery's life.

With a *full payout lease*, the leaseholder makes payments that eventually cover the purchase price of the machinery, as well as any debt-financing costs. Full payout leases are typically long term, lasting for the entire life of the equipment.

Direct Participation Programs and Investors

Direct participation programs can raise initial capital in one of two ways:

- Private placements, which require an offering circular under Regulation D of the Securities Act of 1933.
- Public offerings, which require registration with the SEC, a prospectus, and, generally, an underwriter.

Normally underwriters arrange DPP offerings under *mini-maxi agreements*. In a *mini-maxi offering*, the DPP gives the underwriter a certain amount of time to raise a minimum amount of capital. If the underwriter fails to do so, the offering is canceled and whatever money has been collected is returned to investors. Because of the possibility of cancellation, proceeds from the offering are held in an escrow account until the required minimum is reached. Once the minimum has been surpassed, the money is released to the partnership.

A mini-maxi offering in a DPP gives the underwriter time to raise capital. The money is held in escrow until the minimum amount of capital is reached. If the amount of capital is not raised, the offering is cancelled and the proceeds are returned to the investors.

First and foremost, the prospectus must specify which investments the program intends to make. One kind of DPP is known as a *blind-pool investment*, and here the general partner (or sponsor) indicates what *types* of investments will be made, not the specific assets to be purchased or the projects to be financed. The opposite of a blind pool is a *specified pool*, which names specific assets or projects as investment targets.

DPP prospectuses must also include the suitability requirements. Potential investors must meet a *suitability requirement* in order to invest in a direct participation program. Suitability requirements are established mainly to determine the financial status of potential investors; they are based on a variety of factors such as financial capacity and willingness to assume risk.

At the same time, investors need to assess the strengths and weaknesses of DPPs. Prospective investors need to consider the following questions:

- What are the goals of the partnership?
- How qualified is the general partner?
- How long might it likely take for the program to reach its *crossover point*—the moment when revenues exceed expenses?
- Can the investor survive significant economic downturns?
- Can the investor afford to make extraordinary cash infusions that the program might require?
- Can the investor survive the possible loss of his or her entire investment?

Income and Taxes

General partners earn income from DPPs by charging different fees. These include:

- Sales commission, if the general partner acts as the underwriter
- Acquisition fees, for the purchase of assets
- Financing fees, for arranging bank loans
- Management fees

The general partner must also maintain at least a 1% interest in any losses or gains generated by the partnership. Limited partners can benefit from their DPP holdings in three basic manners:

- *Program Income.* For a real-estate program, program income is rent from tenants, whereas for an equipment-leasing program, income comes from lease payments. To the extent that these revenues exceed expenses, the income is passed on to the limited partners.
- *Disposition.* The sale of properties at the end of the partnership's life can also generate income.
- *Tax Deductions.* Losses generated by a DPP are often used to offset income earned from other sources, thus reducing the investor's total tax bill.

Loses and Gains for Tax Purposes

Direct participation programs begin with an investor's tax basis to determine his or her interest in the program. An individual's *tax basis* is his or her total financial contribution to the program, including initial and subsequent cash infusions, real property contributions, and gains in the market value of the investment (if not already withdrawn by the investor).

Remember that DPPs pass both income and losses directly to their limited partners. If these partners earn income from other investments, DPP losses can spell substantial tax relief.

> **EXAMPLE:** Claudia Monay suffers a loss of $60,000 in 1999 from her investment in a cattle-breeding DPP. The same year, however, she receives $100,000 in income from her share in an equipment-leasing DPP. She can offset $60,000 of her equipment-leasing gains with her cattle-breeding losses, thus paying taxes on only $40,000. Had the equipment-leasing DPP created less income for her, say $50,000, Claudia could have

carried forward the remaining $10,000 in cattle-breeding losses, to be applied against income in future years.

Losses from DPPs can only offset passive income. *Passive income* comes from any program investment in which the investor does not participate in the daily management of the business venture. In addition to income from DPPs, the IRS considers income from rental properties to be passive. Other types of income—salaries and wages, and interest and dividend payments from ordinary investments—do not qualify as passive.

Losses from DPPS can only offset passive income—with *one* exception. Losses carried forward from previous years can offset gains and be applied to any type of income when the loss exceeds the gain.

Normally, the proceeds of such a sale are taxed. However, if the partner sells his or her interest for a gain, and has carried forward passive losses from previous years, the losses can be used to shield all or a portion of the gain from the IRS. Moreover, if the past losses exceed the gain from the sale, the difference can be applied to any type of income. This is the *only* case in which DPP losses can be used to offset nonpassive income.

Loans taken out by the DPP can also affect an investor's tax basis, depending on whether the loans are recourse or nonrecourse loans. A limited partner who signs a *recourse loan* has assumed personal responsibility for repaying the loan. If the partnership defaults, the creditor is entitled to pursue the limited partner's personal assets. Therefore, recourse loans are added to an investor's tax basis.

A *nonrecourse loan* prohibits creditors from pursuing the personal assets of partners in a DPP that defaults—only program assets can be liquidated to repay the loan. The most common tax benefits stemming from DPPs are depreciation and depletion allowances, which enable investors to write off certain losses in particular investments.

Writing Off All Taxes

Congress has attempted to prevent wealthy individuals (and companies) from using passive losses to reduce their income-tax liability to zero. Under the federal *alternative minimum tax* (or *AMT*), individuals must add items such as DPP losses to their adjusted gross income, and then proceed to calculate the alternative minimum tax. If this tax bill is larger than an investor's normal one, the investor must pay the alternative tax.

Federal law on the AMT, alternative minimum tax, states that individuals must add items such as DPP loses to their adjusted gross income, and then calculate the alternative minimum tax. If it is larger than the normal tax bill, the alternative tax must be paid.

Depreciation

Depreciation is the annual amount deducted from the original price of a fixed asset (such as machinery, computers, or office furniture) to account for the asset's gradual decline in value. Fixed assets have normal life spans; over time they become worth less and less. The IRS assigns average life spans to different categories of fixed assets, enabling companies to calculate their depreciation easily.

Depreciation can be calculated in several ways; two of the most common are the straight-line method and the accelerated method.

Straight-Line Depreciation

Straight-line depreciation is the simplest: the business writes off equal amounts of the asset's value each year.

> **EXAMPLE:** Consolidated Transport, an equipment-leasing program, bought four heavy trucks last year for $520,000. Assuming that the trucks have a useful life of seven years (approximate life per IRS guidelines), and that Consolidated wants to use the straight-line method, how much can it claim on its tax form as depreciation expense? The program can declare roughly 14% (see IRS tables for exact percentages) or $72,800.

Accelerated Depreciation

Accelerated depreciation enables companies to deduct greater amounts in the early years of the asset's life, and correspondingly less in later years. In 1981 Congress enacted the *Modified Accelerated Cost Recovery System (MACRS)*, and then modified it with the Tax Reform Act of 1986. MACRS stands as the fundamental regulation concerning depreciation, including accelerated methods of calculation. The legislation establishes two categories of property—personal and real—and then sets recovery periods (asset lives) and depreciation methods. Real property—such as commercial buildings and other improvements to land—must be depreciated by the straight-line method. Raw land cannot be depreciated. Personal property includes all assets other than real estate and real property. This category of assets can be depreciated using an accelerated method, with recovery set at 3, 5, 7, or 10 years, depending on the type of asset.

EXAMPLE: Consolidated Transport wants to depreciate their four new trucks by the accelerated depreciation method. With accelerated depreciation, they can write off 50% of the purchase price plus one-half of the usual straight-line depreciation of 14%. This means Consolidated can depreciate their new trucks 50% + 7% = 57%, or $260,000 + $36,400 = $296,400 (this figure is an approximation based on current IRS tables; the reality is that the final amount of depreciation is slightly less once all calculations are made). However, it is still a substantial difference from the 14% allowed for straight-line depreciation.

Depletion

Depletion is another tax benefit given to businesses in the natural-resource sector, such as oil and gas DPPs: in addition to depreciating their manufactured assets each year, mining, oil, and gas companies can write off the cost of their mineral rights. Purchasing the mineral rights below a tract of land is often a major expense, one that is not deductible like a fixed asset. However, a DPP can declare mineral rights as a depletion, thereby reducing its tax bill. The IRS permits two methods of calculating depletion: cost method and percentage-of-income method.

Under *cost depletion*, a program deducts the cost of its mineral rights from its revenues. If, say, the mineral rights for an oil well cost $5 million, and the well has 2.5 million barrels of proven reserves, the DPP can deduct $2.00 of depletion for every barrel it sells. With *percentage-of-income depletion*, the program is allowed to deduct a flat 15% of gross income from each barrel sold. If the price of a barrel of oil stands at $16, the program can declare a depletion of $2.40 per barrel.

Advantages of Depreciation and Depletion for Partners in a DPP

By reducing the program's taxable income, depreciation and depletion allowances can create or increase losses that are passed along to limited partners. Again, such losses permit partners to reduce their tax bills on other investment income. However, when a direct participation program sells real estate or a tangible asset, the IRS disallows depreciation or depletion claimed on it from prior years, treating the deducted amount, at the time of the sale, as ordinary income of the program. This is referred to as *recapture*. Investors need to be aware that if their program sells assets, they will be taxed on this recaptured income.

Exam Prep Questions

1. Most direct participation programs are organized as:
   - ❑ A. Partnerships
   - ❑ B. Corporations
   - ❑ C. Trusts
   - ❑ D. Holding companies

2. Mary is a limited partner in Snow Real Estate, a DPP. Mary may do all of the following EXCEPT:
   - ❑ A. Inspect Snow's books
   - ❑ B. Engage or invest in a business that competes with Snow
   - ❑ C. Sue Snow's general partner
   - ❑ D. Manage the program

3. Glenn and Boris are the general partners of Snow Real Estate, a DPP. Which of the following statements are true of Glenn?

   I. He has unlimited liability.

   II. He can sell real estate for another corporation.

   III. He can use Snow's office and equipment for other business enterprises.

   IV. He can continue the partnership even if Boris dies.

   - ❑ A. I only
   - ❑ B. II and III
   - ❑ C. I, II, and III
   - ❑ D. I, II, III, and IV

4. Barnard Equipment Leasing is a direct partnership. Its certificate of limited partnership states all of the following except:
   - ❑ A. The amount of cash or property contributed by each partner
   - ❑ B. How profits and losses will be distributed
   - ❑ C. Each participant's specific responsibilities
   - ❑ D. Which accounting firm audits the partnership

5. Caracorp, Inc., is a public corporation specializing in developmental drilling. Partnership Drilling is a DPP with one general partner that performs exploratory drilling. Which of the following statements are true of both companies?

   I. Caracorp drills in existing oil fields; Partnership drills in unproven ground.

   II. Caracorp's stock can be traded freely; Partnership's shares cannot be.

   III. Caracorp's shareholders have limited liability; Partnership's partners all have unlimited liability.

   IV. Caracorp's management is centralized; Partnership's is distributed among several partners.

   - ❑ A. I and II
   - ❑ B. II and III
   - ❑ C. III and IV
   - ❑ D. I, II, III, and IV

6. Bianca is thinking of investing in Partnership Drilling, a DPP. About which of the following risks need she be most concerned?

   I. Legislative risk

   II. Systemic risk

   III. Liquidity risk

   IV. Interest rate risk

   - ❑ A. I and II
   - ❑ B. II and III
   - ❑ C. I, II, and III
   - ❑ D. I, II, III, and IV

7. All the following statements are true except:

   - ❑ A. Raw land has no real property improvements.
   - ❑ B. Raw land can have a strong potential for capital appreciation.
   - ❑ C. A raw land DPP can purchase rural land near the site of a proposed freeway interchange.
   - ❑ D. Raw land depreciation offers investors losses to shelter their income from other investments.

8. All of the following are common types of DPPs except:

   - ❑ A. Single-tenant net leases
   - ❑ B. Shopping centers
   - ❑ C. Warehouse corporations
   - ❑ D. Government-assisted housing programs

9. Black Gold Drilling, a DPP which leases land near existing oil fields and drills new wells, is a:
   - ❑ A. Wildcat drilling program
   - ❑ B. Exploratory program
   - ❑ C. Development program
   - ❑ D. Income program

10. A DDP can be sold through a public offering under which type of agreement?
    - ❑ A. A mini-maxi offering
    - ❑ B. Regulation D of the Securities Act of 1933
    - ❑ C. A specified pool
    - ❑ D. A certificate of limited partnership

11. Alaskan Enterprises, a DPP, uses both operating leases and full payout leases in its program. Alaskan Enterprises is:
    - ❑ A. A real estate program
    - ❑ B. A cattle-breeding program
    - ❑ C. An equipment-leasing program
    - ❑ D. A warehouse program

12. Linda is thinking of investing in Wonder Oil, a new blind-pool investment DPP. Wonder Oil is being sold through a public offering. Which of the following statements are true?

    I. The general partner chooses the program's investments.

    II. Before she invests, Linda will not be told what specific investments Wonder Oil makes, only the types of investments.

    III. Before she invests, Linda must be told what specific investments Wonder Oil makes.

    IV. Wonder Oil does not have to provide her with a prospectus.
    - ❑ A. I and II
    - ❑ B. II and III
    - ❑ C. I, II, and IV
    - ❑ D. II, III, and IV

13. Which of the following are considerations for prospective investors?

    I. Qualifications of the general manager

    II. Goals of the partnership

    III. Potential tax law changes that might affect profitability

    IV. Timeframe for reaching the cross-over point
    - ❑ A. I only
    - ❑ B. I and II
    - ❑ C. I, II, and III
    - ❑ D. I, II, III, and IV

14. How do limited partners benefit from their investment?
    - ❑ A. Management fees
    - ❑ B. Program income
    - ❑ C. Selling partnership assets
    - ❑ D. Finance fees

15. Wonder Oil is a DPP run by general partner Max Wonder. Linda Smith, a limited partner in Wonder, has signed a recourse loan on Wonder's behalf. Responsibility for repayment of this loan rests with:
    - ❑ A. All limited partners; if Wonder defaults, creditors can pursue their personal assets.
    - ❑ B. Max Wonder; if Wonder defaults, creditors can pursue his personal assets.
    - ❑ C. Wonder Oil exclusively; if it defaults, creditors can pursue only Wonder's assets.
    - ❑ D. Linda Smith; if Wonder defaults, creditors can pursue her personal assets.

Exam Prep Answers

1. The correct answer is A. Most direct participation programs are organized as partnerships. According to U.S. tax laws, a partnership is not a taxable entity, so investors in partnerships avoid the additional layer of taxes associated with corporations.
2. The correct answer is D. Mary cannot manage the partnership or she risks losing her limited liability status. The general partner is the professional manager of the DPP, while the limited partner is a passive financial backer. She can, however, invest in other companies that compete with Snow, sue the general manager, and sue to end the partnership.
3. The correct answer is A. General partners possess unlimited liability: in theory, Boris's entire net worth is at risk in the DPP. As a general partner, he cannot sell real estate for anyone else because he cannot engage in a business that competes with Snow, and he cannot use partnership property for nonpartnership activities. Partnerships generally do not continue after the death, retirement, or incapacity of one of the general partners.
4. The correct answer is D. It includes information such as the amount of cash or property contributed by each partner, how profits and losses will be distributed, and what events will cause the dissolution of the partnership. It does not include which accounting firm will audit the company.
5. The correct answer is A. Developmental drilling locates in existing oil fields or at least adjacent to them, while exploratory drilling is in unproven ground. Caracorp is a public corporation so its stock can be freely traded while Partnership's DPP stock cannot. Only Partnership's general partner has unlimited liability; its limited partners have limited liability. As a corporation, Caracorp has limited liability. Because Partnership has only one general partner, its management is considered centralized while a corporation can have a number of managers.
6. The correct answer is C. Because investors often select DPPs for the tax advantages they offer, they are fundamentally at the mercy of Congress in its capacity to change federal tax laws. In addition, DPPs expose investors to systemic risk, or the normal risks of the industries in which they operate, particularly in fields such as oil and gas exploration. DPPs are also illiquid investments, so investors need to have other cash sources to weather difficult periods.
7. The correct answer is D. Raw land, or land that has not yet been developed, can have a strong potential for capital appreciation, depending on its location. For example, land on the outskirts of a

growing city, or rural land near the site of a proposed freeway interchange can prove a lucrative investment. However, raw land cannot be depreciated, so raw land DPPs seldom provide investors with losses sufficient to shelter other income.

8. The correct answer is C. Direct participation programs are often created to finance the purchase, development, or construction of a variety of properties. They include single-tenant net leases (in which the program buys a building and leases it to a tenant), shopping centers (in which the DPP buys a mall and leases the stores to various tenants), and government-assisted housing programs (in which the DPP builds or purchases housing for federally-subsidized tenants). Warehouse partnerships are another kind of DPP; however, DPPs are not corporations.
9. The correct answer is C. Development programs drill in existing oil fields or areas adjacent to them. Exploratory programs drill wells in unproven ground, an activity referred to as wildcat drilling. Income programs purchase established oil wells.
10. The correct answer is A. DPPs are sold through mini-maxi offerings under a mini-maxi agreement. An underwriter must raise a minimum amount for the partnership to commence and a maximum amount representing the total value of the potential investments. Regulation D of the Securities Act covers private offerings, not public; a specific pool is a limited partnership announcement of an intended investment; and a certificate of limited partnership is the agreement among the partnership members.
11. The correct answer is C. Equipment-leasing programs buy heavy machines and equipment for transportation or construction and lease them out. They use operating leases or full payout leases. With an operating lease, a shorter-term leaseholder pays the DPP a sum less than the cost of the equipment. With a full payout lease, the leaseholder makes payments that eventually cover the purchase price of the machinery as well as any debt-financing costs.
12. The correct answer is A. The partnership manager chooses the partnership's specific investments. Public offerings of DPPs require registration with the SEC and a prospectus. Although the prospectus of a blind-pool investment must indicate the types of investments to be made, it need not name the specific projects to be financed. For example, Wonder Oil can say that it plans to perform exploratory drilling, but it need not mention in which areas.
13. The correct answer is D. All of the choices are considerations for a potential investor in a DPP. There are certainly others considerations, such as can the investor afford economic downturns or possible loss of the entire investment, what is the economic prognosis for the industry in which the DPP will invest, and many others.

14. The correct answer is B. One of the three main ways for limited partners to benefit from a DPP investment is program income. This could include rent from tenants or equipment lease payments. Other ways for limited partners to benefit are disposition of the partnership properties at the end of its life, or from losses generated by the DPP to offset income earned from other sources, thus giving the investor a tax deduction. Management fees and financing fees are earned by the general manager, not the limited partner. Selling of partnership assets is only correct if it's the end of the partnership.
15. The correct answer is D. A limited partner, such as Smith, who signs a recourse loan has assumed personal responsibility for repaying the loan. If Wonder defaults, the creditor is entitled to pursue Smith's personal assets and not that of the partnership or of Max Wonder's.

Annuities

Terms You Need to Know

- ✓ Accumulation unit
- ✓ Annuitant
- ✓ Annuitization
- ✓ Annuity
- ✓ Annuity certain (or life annuity with period certain)
- ✓ Annuity unit
- ✓ Assumed interest rate (AIR)
- ✓ Cost basis
- ✓ Distribution
- ✓ Expense guarantee
- ✓ Fixed annuity
- ✓ Investment basis
- ✓ Life annuity
- ✓ Lump-sum agreement
- ✓ Mortality guarantee
- ✓ Non-tax qualified plan
- ✓ Separate account
- ✓ Starting date
- ✓ Tax qualified plan
- ✓ Variable annuity

Concepts You Need to Understand

- ✓ What annuities are
- ✓ Fixed annuities versus variable annuities
- ✓ How annuities are sold
- ✓ Accumulation units
- ✓ Growth of variable annuities
- ✓ How payouts are determined
- ✓ Annuity units and taxes
- ✓ Different payment options and their risks

Fixed and Variable Annuities

This chapter covers investment vehicles that enable individuals to accumulate earnings for their retirement years. Annuities, the focus of the present chapter, are insurance company products; however, the SEC considers a major family of annuities (variable annuities) to constitute a securities product and thus regulates it. Although annuities come in various forms, with varying degrees of risk, the basic idea is always the same—a person makes payments to an insurance company for a specified period, the company invests the money (and also reinvests any earnings), and, after the maturity date is reached, the company begins making payments to the customer. This chapter explains the mechanics of annuities—how they are sold and how they eventually pay out.

An *annuity* is a contract between an insurance company and a customer. The customer, called an *annuitant*, most often is seeking to secure retirement income. The customer hopes that the total repayments he or she receives upon retirement are significantly greater than the amount of money invested earlier. This goal is attainable because, except for the amount of the customer contributions, the annuity's growth is tax-deferred by the IRS until retirement distribution begins.

In general, an annuity passes through six basic steps:

1. An insurance company creates a participating trust to collect payments from its customers.
2. The participating trust chooses a management company in which to invest that reflects the investment objectives of its client base.
3. Customers of the insurance company send payments to the trust.
4. The trust places the money in a *separate account* (an account that segregates this money from other company assets), which must be registered with the Securities and Exchange Commission. Annuity funds cannot be combined with other assets of the insurance company.
5. From the separate account, the participating trust invests in the chosen management company.
6. Upon retirement, or at another agreed-upon date, the annuitants begin to receive the money due them from the participating trust.

Fixed Annuities

A *fixed annuity* guarantees the customer a predetermined return on his or her investment upon the contract's maturity. The insurance company carries the bulk of the risk because it must make the agreed-upon payments to the customer regardless of how well the investments have performed. Fixed annuities are attractive to conservative investors, because they minimize risk and let customers know in advance what the overall return will be. However, the value of a fixed annuity might dwindle quickly in times of high inflation. Also note that the annuitant cannot enjoy the extra benefits if the company's investments prove unusually profitable and outperform the market.

> **EXAMPLE:** Winthrop pays $200 per month to his Solid Life fixed annuity, which invests the money in a management company that maintains a diversified bond portfolio. Solid Life guarantees Winthrop monthly payments (beginning when he is 62) that reflect an annual return of 6% on his investments. No matter what happens to bond markets in the intervening years, Winthrop's holdings grow at this annual rate of 6%. From the day he signs his annuity contract, he can determine the size of the monthly check he will receive upon turning 62.

Variable Annuities

A *variable annuity* transfers the investment risks—and benefits—to the customer; the size of the eventual payout depends on the market growth of the annuity's portfolio. A poorly performing portfolio returns less to customers. The opposite is also true, however. If the annuity places its funds in a stellar management company, customers can enjoy above-average returns and a more secure retirement.

> **EXAMPLE:** Amaryllis invests $200 per month in her Transcendental Life variable annuity, which is backed by a portfolio of securities that mirror the S&P 500. Her annuity returns follow the performance of this stock index, some years growing rapidly, other years slowly, and some years even declining. Over the long run, Amaryllis remains confident that the annuity's underlying portfolio will outperform other investment opportunities and provide her with a healthy return on her investments.

How Dividends and Interest Payments Affect an Annuity's Growth

The insurance company reinvests dividend and interest payments; therefore, the separate account has two sources of growth: investors' regular monthly payments and gains from the securities held in the portfolio. Moreover, the IRS does not initially tax these reinvested funds. Although the annuitant's periodic payments are usually taxed, interest and dividend payments—and other sources of internal growth—are tax deferred.

In addition to choosing from annuities with different investment objectives, customers have to make another important choice—between fixed and variable annuities.

The SEC Regulates Annuities

Fixed annuities are deemed an insurance product and thus fall under the purview of the insurance laws of the state in which they operate. Remember with fixed annuities, customers are purchasing a known product and are immune to most market risks. Variable annuities are another matter. Because variable annuities present customers with all the risks of financial market investments, the SEC considers them securities, and thus regulates them under the Investment Company Act of 1940 and the Securities Act of 1933.

The SEC regulates variable annuities because customers risk the same financial fluctuations as any investor in the market; also because variable annuity portfolios are often in stocks and bonds, which fall under the Investment Company Act of 1940 and the Securities Act of 1933.

Congress enacted the Investment Company Act of 1940 to prevent the intentional misuse of clients' money by investment companies. All investment companies with more than 100 shareholders are subject to the act, which requires registration with the SEC and adherence to all SEC regulations.

Variable Annuities: From Sales to Payout

Insurance companies can only sell variable annuities via prospectus. (What the company is actually selling is the separate account, which represents the annuities.) Within an insurance company, only brokers licensed with a Series 7 or a Series 6 can sell annuities. Some states also require that these brokers acquire state securities licenses. The prospectus must include the sales charge, which, according to NASD rules, cannot exceed 8.5% of the capital invested. The prospectus must also describe any extra charges, such as administrative expenses or early withdrawal penalties. In addition, every annuity carries an *expense guarantee*, which ensures that expenses cannot be charged to the customer past a certain predetermined figure.

Potential customers also need to look in the prospectus for the annuity's *assumed interest rate (AIR)*—the projected return based on current market conditions and the historical performance of securities in the portfolio. The AIR is not a guaranteed rate of return, and it generally errs on the conservative side.

Accumulation Units

Accumulation units represent portions of the value of a variable annuity's underlying securities portfolio. Just as investors buy shares in companies or mutual funds, annuitants purchase shares in the separate account. These shares are called accumulation units.

The value of the portfolio owned by the separate account does not stay the same. Securities markets experience normal fluctuations, and securities are constantly being bought and sold. Each price movement or securities transaction affects the value of an accumulation unit. In turn, a customer's regular annuity payment will purchase a different number of units from month to month.

> **EXAMPLE:** For the last year, Rose Arlera's $100 monthly payment to her Granite Life variable annuity has been buying her about five accumulation units per month. Unfortunately, the management company in charge of the annuity has misread the Fed's intentions and loses a significant amount of money on corporate bonds. The portfolio suffers a sharp drop in value; Granite Life's separate account temporarily shrinks. Because the number of accumulation units that Rose and other Granite Life annuitants already posses cannot change, the value of each unit must decline. The following month she notices that her $100 payment to Granite Life now purchases six accumulation units.
>
> A year later, however, the Granite Life annuity begins to enjoy remarkable success with its strong selection of medical technology stocks. The value of the separate account grows rapidly. As the total number of outstanding accumulation units does not change (except through annuitants' monthly payments), the value of each unit must increase. Rose finds that her $100 payment to Granite Life now buys only four units.

To calculate the value of one accumulation unit in a variable annuity, the insurance company must compute the net asset value. Remember, net asset value = market value of assets minus liabilities divided by total accumulation units issued, or:

$$\text{net asset value} = \frac{\text{market value of assets} - \text{liabilities}}{\text{total accumulation units issued}}$$

EXAMPLE: Concrete Life Insurance Company offers a variable annuity with a stock portfolio currently valued at $5 million. Liabilities total $250,000, and customers have so far accumulated 350,000 units. What is the net asset value of the annuity?

$$NAV = \frac{\$5 \text{ million} - \$250{,}000}{350{,}000} = \$13.57$$

Two months later, Concrete's annuity portfolio is valued at $5.34 million, whereas the accumulation units have risen to 371,250. Liabilities remain unchanged. What is the new net asset value?

$$NAV = \frac{\$5.34 \text{ million} - \$250{,}000}{371{,}250} = \$13.71$$

Having kept track of customers' accumulation units over the years, an insurance company is prepared to calculate their eventual monthly payouts.

Determining Payouts

To determine how much it owes a customer upon the maturity of an annuity, the insurance company must convert accumulation units into annuity units—a process called *annuitization.* Like accumulation units, annuity units are an accounting device to make bookkeeping easier for insurance companies. Each *annuity unit* represents a portion of the total amount of money an annuitant receives during *distribution*—the process of paying out the holdings in an annuity account to the customer. Annuity units differ from accumulation units, however, in that they are *not* based simply on the total value the person has accumulated in his or her account. Just as insurance companies use complex statistical tools called actuarial tables to determine prices for life, automobile, and health insurance, they employ the same kinds of tools to determine payouts for annuities. In other words, when a particular annuity matures, the insurance company estimates the client's life expectancy before annuitizing his or her accumulation units. As a result, the customer's annuity units vary not only with the number of accumulation units he or she has acquired, but also with his or her general health and life expectancy.

Annuity units differ from accumulation units because they are NOT based on the total value of the units the customer has accumulated. Instead, the annuity units vary with the number of accumulation units acquired, as well as by the customer's life expectancy. This is calculated with actuary tables.

Why Insurers Estimate Annuitants Life Expectancy

Every annuity includes a contractual provision (described in the prospectus) called a *mortality guarantee*, stating that the annuitant can choose to be paid for life, regardless of how long he or she lives. If a person lives longer than expected, the insurance company nevertheless has to keep making the regular monthly payment. The insurer therefore needs to gather the best information available about a person's projected life span in order to accurately calculate the distribution of annuity units.

When Annuitants Begin Collecting Payments

Annuitants begin receiving distribution payments on the *starting date*, which depends on the wishes and financial needs of the holder as expressed in the original contract. Of course, the longer an annuitant can wait to collect the money, the bigger the separate account grows, and so the larger the customer's distribution. The Internal Revenue Service also has a say in the matter. If a person chooses a starting date that falls before he or she reaches the age of 59½, the IRS charges a penalty tax of 10% on a portion of the payout, creating an incentive to postpone the starting date until that age has been reached. Finally, some annuities carry extra in-house penalties for cashing in accumulation units before the scheduled starting date.

The IRS dictates 59½ as the earliest age an annuitant can begin receiving annuity payments without incurring a 10% penalty.

The Tax Status of Variable Annuities

The IRS labels most variable annuities *non-tax qualified*, meaning that annuitants must make their regular payments (during the accumulation phase) from after-tax income. The value of these initial payments are not taxed again when the annuitant begins *receiving* payments from the insurance company (during the annuity phase). The IRS does regard a few annuities as *tax qualified*, in which case the annuitants' payments during accumulation are made from gross income—before taxes. For a tax-qualified annuity, a customer owes taxes on the entire amount of each payment received during the annuity phase.

Non-tax qualified annuity payments are made from after-tax income. Tax-qualified annuity payments are made from pre-tax income; these annuities are taxed on the payments received when the annuity matures.

EXAMPLE: Charlene, who recently turned 60, has just started to receive monthly annuity payments of about $1,800. During the accumulation phase of her annuity, she paid a total of $70,560 to True Life Insurance. When True Life converted her accumulation units into annuity units, it kept the amount of Charlene's contributions separate. She does not have to pay income taxes on this portion of each annuity check received. Charlene is pleased to discover that the IRS only charges income tax on $1,400 of each payment from True Life.

Charlene's brother Carl recently retired at age 65 and is now collecting approximately $1,000 per month from his tax-qualified annuity. Because his original contributions to the annuity were never taxed, he must pay income taxes on the full amount of each payment received.

Thus, both the insurance company and the IRS need to keep track of an annuitant's cost basis and investment basis. *Cost basis* equals the amount the customer has actually invested in the annuity; which, for most annuities, has already been taxed. *Investment basis* represents the customer's share of the annuity's internal growth (resulting from dividend and interest reinvestment and from securities' appreciation over time), and this amount has enjoyed tax-deferred status throughout the customer's accumulation phase. During a normal payout, the annuitant has to pay taxes on the investment basis, but not the cost basis, of his or her annuity.

A normal payout is taxed on the investment basis of the annuity; meaning the annuitant pays taxes only on the growth portion of the investment.

How Payments Are Made to Annuitants

Annuitants can choose from a menu of payout plans; different options offer different payment amounts and frequencies. Choosing a plan is therefore an important decision for annuity customers. The simplest payout plan is a *lump-sum agreement*, in which the annuitant collects one large payment from the insurance company at the end of the annuity contract.

An annuitant taking a lump-sum payment minimizes his or her risk during retirement. The value of the annuity is determined upon the contract's maturity, and the annuitant collects the full amount. Otherwise, the value of the annuitant's share of the separate account will continue to vary, with the payment checks also varying.

For customers who prefer to assume more risk in exchange for the possibility of receiving additional money, a range of payout plans exists. Recall that the mortality guarantee states that an annuitant can receive payments from the starting date until his or her death. People who take advantage of this provision are betting that they will live to a nice old age, against the insurance company's bet that they will die sooner. These payment options can result in the annuitant getting more money than he or she might normally receive, but they can also mean that the total payout is less than the annuitant's original payments.

If an annuitant opts for a life payment, he or she might receive more or less than expected. The insurance company assumes the annuitant will die sooner rather than later while the annuitant usually expects to live a long time after retirement.

- *Life annuity.* The insurance company pays the client on a regular basis for as long as he or she lives. Payments stop when the annuitant dies.

  Advantages: The annuitant is guaranteed an income; payments are higher; customer might live a long time and receive more money from the insurer than he or she accumulated.

  Disadvantages: Annuitant might die shortly after the starting date, leaving the insurance company with the money remaining in the account.

- *Annuity Certain (or Life Annuity with Period Certain).* The insurance company makes payments for the rest of the customer's life, like life annuity, but the contract also specifies a certain minimum period over which payments will be made, even if the annuitant dies. Payments continue to the heirs up to the period certain if the annuitant dies before the end of the period certain.

  Advantages: The annuitant is guaranteed income; at least a part of the annuity's value will be recovered, either by the annuitant or heirs.

  Disadvantages: The insurer makes lower monthly payments than in a simple life annuity.

  EXAMPLE: Mr. Washburn chose a 10-year period certain life annuity. If he lives only two years beyond the starting date, his heirs will receive either a lump-sum payment for the remainder, or regular payments for the remaining eight years of the contract. If he lives seven years, his heirs will collect three years' worth of payments. If Mr. Washburn dies 12 years after drawing his first check, however, the insurance company does not have to pay any money remaining in the account to his heirs.

- *Joint and Last Survivor Annuity.* The annuity is held jointly by two people and when one dies, the agreed-upon payments continue to the other. Married couples often buy joint and last survivor annuities.

  Advantages: Annuitants are guaranteed an income; the survivor is provided for.

  Disadvantages: The insurer pays a lower monthly amount because the annuity covers two people and is therefore likely to last longer.

- *Unit Refund Life Annuity.* This plan guarantees that either the annuitant or the heirs receive the full value of the annuity account. If the customer dies before collecting all of his or her annuity units, the heirs receive the remainder.

  Advantages: Annuitant is guaranteed an income; the full value of the annuity will be paid out.

  Disadvantages: If the annuitant dies after the annuity is fully paid out, the spouse will not receive benefits; the plan makes lower monthly payments than does a simple life annuity.

- *Combination Annuity (also called a Hybrid Annuity or a Combined Fixed and Variable Annuity).* The customer makes payments into a separate account that funds both a variable annuity and a fixed annuity. Upon the account's maturity, the annuitant receives two income streams.

  Advantages: The fixed annuity acts as a hedge against potential losses in the variable annuity.

  Disadvantages: The combination annuity is riskier than a straight fixed annuity. However, if securities markets boom, the annuitants do not make as much money as they do if all the funds were invested in a variable annuity.

Exam Prep Questions

1. Separate accounts for annuities have which of the following characteristics?

   I. It is the account to which the annuitant will make their payments.

   II. It must register the account with the SEC.

   III. Funds in the account must be segregated from other assets of the insurance company.

   IV. A board of managers oversees the operation of the account.

   ❑ A. I and II

   ❑ B. II and III

   ❑ C. I, II, and III

   ❑ D. I, II, III, and IV

2. The maximum sales charge on a variable annuity is set at which of the following rates?

   ❑ A. There is no preset limit on the sales charge.

   ❑ B. The insurance company is not permitted to charge any sales charge.

   ❑ C. The maximum sales charge is set at 8.5%.

   ❑ D. The maximum sales charge is set at 10%.

3. Accumulation units in an annuity will be representative of which of the following?

   ❑ A. It represents portions of the value of a variable annuity's portfolio.

   ❑ B. It represents the dollar amount invested.

   ❑ C. It represents the number of shares sold of the annuity.

   ❑ D. It represents the total value of the fixed annuity.

4. Which of the following statements are true of accumulation units in a annuity?

   I. Investor monthly payments add to accumulation units.

   II. Accumulation unit value can decline.

   III. Accumulation unit value can increase.

   IV. The total number of units in a client account can decline.

   ❑ A. I and II

   ❑ B. II and III

   ❑ C. I, II, and III

   ❑ D. I, II, III, and IV

5. The value of an accumulation unit in a client account is computed by which of the following?
   - ❑ A. Net asset value
   - ❑ B. Distribution value
   - ❑ C. Cost basis
   - ❑ D. Investment basis
6. Which of the following annuity payout options will guarantee that the full value of an annuity will be paid out by the insurance company?

   I. Unit refund life annuity

   II. Joint and last survivor annuity

   III. Life annuity with period certain

   IV. Life annuity
   - ❑ A. I only
   - ❑ B. II and III
   - ❑ C. I, II, and III
   - ❑ D. I, II, III, and IV
7. Which statement is not true of an annuity contract purchased by an investor?
   - ❑ A. Annuity payments are placed in a separate account.
   - ❑ B. The annuity is considered a security by the SEC.
   - ❑ C. A separate account cannot be combined with other assets of the insurance company.
   - ❑ D. The separate account will invest in a chosen management company.
8. Which of the following are true of an annuity purchased by an investor?

   I. Fixed annuities are considered a security that must register with the SEC.

   II. Variable annuities are considered a security that must register with the SEC.

   III. A separate account is considered a security that must register with the SEC.

   IV. Both fixed and variable annuities can only be sold by prospectus.
   - ❑ A. I and II
   - ❑ B. II and III
   - ❑ C. III only
   - ❑ D. I, II, and IV

9. An investor has commenced distribution from an annuity he has held with a 10-year period certain. Which of the following statements is considered true of the annuity payout?
   - ❑ A. If the investor dies five years after the starting date, the annuity will cease payments.
   - ❑ B. If the investor dies 15 years after the starting date, the annuitant will have stopped receiving payments in the 10th year.
   - ❑ C. If the investor dies 20 years after the starting date, they will have received payments up until their death.
   - ❑ D. If the investor dies 12 years after the starting date, his estate will receive any remaining funds.
10. An assumed interest rate (AIR) on an annuity will have all of the following characteristics *except* for?
   - ❑ A. It is a guaranteed rate of return offered on the annuity.
   - ❑ B. It will be less than the actual expected return of the annuity.
   - ❑ C. The AIR will be found in the annuity's prospectus.
   - ❑ D. It is based on the historical performance of the securities in the annuity's portfolio.
11. The net asset value of an accumulation unit is computed by which of the following?
   - ❑ A. Market value of assets ÷ number of accumulation units issued
   - ❑ B. Market value of assets ÷ number of accumulation units redeemed
   - ❑ C. Market value of assets – liabilities ÷ number of accumulation units issued
   - ❑ D. Market value of assets – liabilities ÷ number of accumulation units redeemed
12. When an insurance company converts accumulation units into annuity units to determine a customer payout, this process is known as?
   - ❑ A. Distribution
   - ❑ B. Annuitization
   - ❑ C. Securitization
   - ❑ D. Cost Basis
13. Under a mortality guarantee in an annuity contract, an annuitant will receive payments from their annuity in which of the following?
   - ❑ A. They will receive payments until all accumulation units are paid.
   - ❑ B. They will receive payments until accumulation units meet the time period agreed upon.
   - ❑ C. They receive payments for as long as they live.
   - ❑ D. They receive payments for the same amount of time they paid into the annuity.

14. An individual chose to begin distribution from an annuity when he is 57 years old. How will the distribution of the annuity payments be taxed?

- ❑ A. As ordinary income
- ❑ B. As tax exempt income
- ❑ C. As ordinary income with a 10% early withdrawal penalty
- ❑ D. As a long-term capital gain

15. An investor has contributed $5,000 per year for 20 years into an non-tax qualified annuity and upon maturity the annuity has accumulation units totaling $250,000. He begins receiving a distribution from his annuity at age 65. Which of the following statements are true of the annuity?

I. The cost basis for the annuity is $100,000 and the investment basis is $150,000.

II. The cost basis for the annuity is $150,000 and the investment basis of the annuity is $100,000.

III. The investment basis is taxable and the cost basis is tax exempt.

IV. The investment basis is tax exempt and the cost basis is taxable.

- ❑ A. I and III
- ❑ B. I and IV
- ❑ C. II and III
- ❑ D. II and IV

Exam Prep Answers

1. The correct answer is D. All of the choices are correct. The separate account is the account into which the annuitants payments are placed by the participating trust; separate accounts must be registered with the SEC. Annuity funds cannot be combined with other assets of the insurance company. A board of managers, elected by the annuitants, oversees the operations of the separate account.
2. The correct answer is C. The maximum sales charge that is printed in the prospectus cannot exceed the NASD rule of 8.5%. Insurance companies can only sell variable annuities via prospectus. The prospectus will also describe any extra charges, such as administrative expenses or early withdrawal penalties permitted by the SEC.
3. The correct answer is A. Accumulation units represent portions of the value of a variable annuity's underlying security portfolio. Investors are purchasing shares in the separate account of the annuity that are called accumulation units.
4. The correct answer is C. The value of the portfolio owned by the separate account does not stay the same. It can rise in value as well as decline in value depending on the securities in the portfolio. These price movements will affect the price of an accumulation unit. The value of units in a clients account may decline, but the total number of units will not.
5. The correct answer is A. To calculate the value of one accumulation unit in a variable annuity, the insurance company must compute the net asset value. The NAV is computed by dividing the number of accumulation units issued into the market value of the assets – the liabilities of the portfolio.
6. The correct answer is A. The only annuity payout plan that will totally guarantee that all of the value of the annuity units will be paid out to the client is the unit refund life annuity. In this payout option, the plan guarantees that either the annuitant or the heirs will receive the full value of the annuity account. If the annuitant dies before collecting all of their annuity, the remaining balance will be paid to the heirs. Each of the other plans will rely on the life expectancy of the annuitant or their spouse, and would not guarantee full payout; even though in some cases, the annuitant receives more than what they paid into the account, because they live far longer then expected.
7. The correct answer is B. It is the separate account, and not the actual annuity, that is considered to be a security by the SEC. Annuity payments are placed in a separate account and a board of managers elected by the annuitants will oversee the operations of the separate account.

8. The correct answer is C. A variable annuity is indirectly considered a security by the SEC. In reality, it is the separate account that is considered a security and that must register with the SEC. What the insurance company is actually selling is the separate account, which represents the annuities. This is a tricky question, but one with only one correct answer.
9. The correct answer is C. A life annuity with a 10-year period certain will enable the annuitant to continue to receive payments from the insurance company for as long as they live. If they should die before the 10-year period certain, the annuity payments will continue to the annuitant's heirs. If the annuitant should die after the period certain, then payments would cease at death.
10. The correct answer is A. An assumed interest rate (AIR) for an annuity is the projected rate of return based on current market conditions and historical performance of securities in the portfolio. The AIR is not a guaranteed rate of return, and would generally err on the conservative side. A company expecting an 8% return on one of its annuities would publish in the prospectus an assumed interest rate of 7%.
11. The correct answer is C. The net asset value of an accumulation unit is determined by the market value of the assets – liabilities ÷ by the total accumulation units issued.
12. The correct answer is B. To determine how much it owes a customer upon the maturity of an annuity, the insurance company must convert the accumulation units into annuity units through a process called annuitization. Like accumulation units, annuity units are an accounting device to make bookkeeping easier for insurance companies.
13. The correct answer is C. Under a mortality guarantee, an annuitant will have signed a contractual agreement that they will receive disbursement payments for life. The annuitant will be paid, regardless of how long he or she lives. If the person lives longer than expected, the insurance company will be required to keep making the monthly payment. If the annuitant should die one year after receiving disbursement payments, the insurance company would not have to make any additional payments, and would keep the remaining funds in the annuity.
14. The correct answer is C. If a person chooses a starting date to begin receiving annuity payments prior to the age of 59½, the Internal Revenue Service will charge a penalty tax of 10% on the portion of the payout. In addition, the disbursed funds will be taxed as ordinary income for the annuitant.

15. The correct answer is A. In a non-tax qualified annuity, the investor has made payments from after tax dollars. When the annuity matures and disbursement begins, the cost basis will be the amount paid into the annuity by the annuitant. In this case, $5,000 for 20 years will have a total cost basis of $100,000, which will not be taxed again. The value of the annuity is now $250,000. The difference of $150,000 is considered the investment basis of the annuity, which upon disbursement will be taxed as ordinary income.

Retirement Accounts

Terms You Need to Know

✓ 401(k) plan
✓ 403(b) plan
✓ Corporate pension plan
✓ Deferred compensation plan
✓ Defined benefit plan
✓ Defined contribution plan
✓ ERISA (Employee Retirement Income Security Act)
✓ ESOP (employee stock ownership plan)
✓ FICA (Federal Insurance Contribution Act)
✓ Individual retirement account (IRA)
✓ IRA rollover
✓ Keogh account
✓ Matching contribution
✓ Non-tax-qualified program
✓ Pension Benefit Guaranty Corporation (PBGC)
✓ Profit-sharing plan
✓ Roth IRA
✓ SEP (simplified employee pension) IRA
✓ Social Security
✓ Tax-deferred
✓ Tax-qualified program
✓ Vesting

Concepts You Need to Understand

✓ Types of retirement plans
✓ Differences between tax-qualified and non-tax-qualified plans
✓ The vesting period
✓ How Social Security programs are funded
✓ How Social Security monies are paid out
✓ The structure of IRAs
✓ Contributions to and disbursements from IRAs
✓ Tax consequences of IRAs
✓ Laws governing retirement programs

Retirement Programs

Most Americans now live long enough to enjoy retirement—often one that lasts many years. Most people want to continue with the same standard of living they enjoyed during their working lives, or at least to approach the same level of economic benefits. Fortunately, government, employers, and businesses now offer an array of investment plans to help people fund their retirement years. This chapter discusses how such retirement plans operate, who is eligible to receive the benefits, and how the plans are regulated.

Retirement programs put a portion of an employee's salary into an investment account, typically over a period of many years. The objective is for the investment to grow large enough to fund the employee's eventual retirement. In the meantime, the IRS allows all investment income to accumulate tax-free until the funds are withdrawn.

Today, employees who want to save for retirement can select from a range of plans. The tax status of different retirement programs is of fundamental importance to potential investors.

Tax-Qualified Retirement Programs

A *tax-qualified program* is one whereby contributions and investment income are *tax-deferred*—taxes are not due until the employee retires and starts withdrawing money from the account. Many retirement programs fit this definition. If an employee earning $25,000 puts $1,000 into a tax-qualified retirement plan, his or her taxable income this year equals $24,000. In this type of program, the employee contributes to a tax-qualified program with pre-tax dollars.

Non-Tax-Qualified Retirement Programs

Non-tax-qualified retirement programs do not offer tax-deferral; rather, the IRS taxes the money invested into these programs as ordinary income. However, the money is not taxed again when the individual withdraws it from the account after retirement. Here the employee is making contributions with after-tax dollars.

Although the sum of the original contributions are not taxed at disbursement, capital gains and interest accrued in the account—which have been allowed to grow tax-deferred—are normally taxed upon withdrawal.

EXAMPLE: For the next 10 years, Bob Smith contributes $1,000 per year to his non-tax-qualified plan. He then retires and begins receiving disbursement checks. His account has grown to $17,000, and he plans to draw down the amount in 10 years, so his gross annual disbursements are for $1,700. On what portion of each disbursement does he owe taxes? Bob owes taxes only on $700 of each disbursement, as the other $1,000 represents his original contribution, on which he has already paid taxes.

Another important question about retirement plans is how long vesting takes.

Vesting

Vesting is the process by which a worker gains the rights to the account benefits accumulated in his or her name. The rules vary according to the type of retirement account. Some programs offer immediate vesting—even though the program's intention is for the employee to receive the money upon retirement, he or she can withdraw it at any time (paying all due taxes, of course).

Most employer-funded programs require a vesting period before employees can claim the accumulated funds. Often the vesting process advances in annual increments of 20%. Thus, if an employee leaves the company after one year, he or she might receive 20% of the funds accumulated under his or her name. After two years, the person will receive 40%. The employee is then fully vested after working for the company for five years.

To avoid early withdrawal tax penalties, employees who leave a company before retirement must transfer their account's money into another qualified retirement plan. Before looking at the tax rules for disbursement, this chapter examines the grandparent of all retirement programs—Social Security.

Social Security

Social Security is a system of federal government programs providing financial assistance to qualifying Americans. Specifically, "Social Security" refers to retirement income for elderly citizens, but the term also commonly refers to such diverse benefit programs as Food Stamps, Medicare, Medicaid, Aid to Families with Dependent Children, Unemployment Insurance, and Public Assistance for the Aged, Blind, and Disabled. In short, Social Security comprises the whole array of "social welfare net" programs created during and after the Great Depression to combat poverty in different segments of the U.S. population.

The Laws Governing Social Security

Congress mandated the basic retirement program with the Social Security Act of 1935. The program is financed through a Social Security Tax, which is authorized by the *Federal Insurance Contributions Act (FICA)*. As of January 1, 2005, FICA requires employers to withhold 6.2% of the first $90,000 of an employee's income, which is paid into a trust fund that finances the various Social Security programs. *Medicare*, the health insurance program for Americans 65 and older, gives rise to the second major Social Security payroll tax: 1.45% of gross income earned.

Funding for Social Security

Social Security actually receives two funding streams: contributions from employees and matching contributions from employers. Self-employed people have to match their own contributions, that is, make a total FICA contribution equal to 12.4% of their income. Washington levies Social Security taxes on a person's wages, tips, and commissions.

Investment income, such as interest and capital gains, is not subject to Social Security taxes.

EXAMPLE: Jay Brown earns $42,500 as a tour guide for Wild West Expeditions. What is his annual FICA contribution? His annual contribution to Social Security amounts to $2,635 (0.062 × $42,500). Because his employer is required to match that amount, the total annual contribution to Jay's future retirement is $5,270.

Jay's wife Holly also works for Wild West Expeditions, where she earns $95,000 as a tour coordinator. Holly's annual FICA payments total $5,580—6.2% of the first $90,000 of her income. (Wild West contributes another $5,580, for a total of $11,160). The remaining portion of Holly's salary ($5,000) is free of the FICA tax.

Social Security Payments

Most of the money collected under FICA goes directly to the various benefit programs financed by the Social Security system, including retirement income for older Americans. What's left over—any surplus between the taxes collected and the benefits paid out—is invested in government debt securities. Ideally, a yearly surplus allows the government to keep investing, and the trust fund continues to grow. At retirement, citizens receive benefit checks according to their total contributions and their life expectancies—regardless of any savings and wealth they have in other sources. Retirees are entitled to receive payments for as long as they live.

IRAs

An *individual retirement account* (or *IRA*) is a tax-qualified retirement plan offered by a private financial company and funded strictly by contributions from the holder of the plan. The investor makes payments to the company (often a bank or a securities firm), which then invests it. When the investor retires, the firm pays back the original contributions, along with any investment earnings (interest payments and capital gains) belonging to the depositor. IRAs provide immediate, full vesting to holders, but the IRS charges a tax penalty if a holder chooses to retire before reaching the age of 59½.

Any person who earns an income can open an IRA, and a nonworking spouse can open a "spousal IRA," provided that the working spouse earned income that year. Married couples can open joint IRAs, but each account must be held in the names of the individuals.

IRAs are permitted to invest in negotiable certificates of deposit (jumbo CDs), mutual funds, certain annuities, bank savings accounts, and securities accounts at brokerage firms. Gold and silver coins minted by the U.S. government are also acceptable investments. IRAs cannot invest in more speculative areas, such as antiques, artwork, jewelry, or precious gemstones.

Under current laws, the most a person can contribute annually to his or her IRAs is $4,000 if under age 50. If age 50 or over, a catch up contribution of $500 is allowed. Remember that a person can open more than one IRA, but the total contributions to all accounts may not exceed $4,000 (or $4,500) in any year. Married couples have an allowance of $4,000 apiece, for a total of $8,000 plus the $500 catch up payment for each spouse. The total contribution is then $9,000. Spouses can distribute their contributions among their accounts as they choose, as long as neither individual's account(s) receives more than $4,500. In 2008, the individual contribution goes up to $5,000, the catch up payment $1,000, and the spouse contributions $10,000.

Tax Rules Affecting IRAs?

Employees not covered by any type of employer pension plan can deduct the full amount of their IRA contributions from their annual income—regardless of their income level. For people who are covered by an employer pension plan, the rules have changed. (Note that IRA contributions must be deposited by April 15 for the account holder to qualify for a tax deduction in the previous calendar year.) The options for married couples aren't as straightforward as for singles. Table 26.1 shows IRA earnings and deductions for 2005.

Table 26.1 2005 IRA Earnings and Deductions

Filling Status	Active Participant Status	Tax Year	Full Deduction	Partial Deduction	No Deduction
Single	Active	2004	$45,000 or less	$45,001–$54,999	$55,000 or more
		2005	$50,000 or less	$50,001–$59.999	$60,000 or more
Married, Joint	Active	2004	$65,000 or less	$65,001–$74,999	$75,000 or more
		2005	$70,000 or less	$70,001–$79,999	$80,000 or more
Married, Joint	Not active but spouse is active	2004 and 2005	$150,000 or less	$150,001–$159,999	$160,000 or more
Married, separate	Active	2004 and 2005	N/A	$0–$9,999	$10,000 or more

Withdrawing IRA Funds

Income invested in tax-qualified retirement programs such as traditional IRAs is not tax-free, but tax-deferred. All withdrawals during the investor's retirement are taxed as regular income, with one exception: contributions made from after-tax dollars (by people whose income exceeded the IRA limits described previously). Upon retirement, most people move into a lower tax bracket, and so the long-term tax deferment offered by IRAs makes the investment attractive.

Money in an IRA can be withdrawn in one lump-sum amount or in periodic payments during retirement. IRA guidelines establish a minimum and maximum age for the commencement of withdrawals. The minimum is set at age 59½. A person who takes money out of an IRA before reaching 59½ must pay a 10% tax penalty—in addition to his or her ordinary income tax. The maximum age to start withdrawing from an IRA is 70½. IRA investors who fail to begin receiving disbursements by that age are subject to a 50% tax on the withdrawals they failed to collect.

The minimum age for withdrawing IRA funds is 59½ and the maximum age to begin withdrawals is 70½. Withdrawing funds before the age of 59½ adds a 10% penalty to the recipient's tax liability; waiting until after the age of 70½ subjects recipients to a 50% tax on withdrawals they failed to collect.

EXAMPLE: When Marsha Spade turns 70½, her life expectancy, based on actuary tables, is 80½. Marsha has saved $100,000 in her IRA, which means she will receive $10,000 a year—as her payments are matched to her life expectancy. If Marsha waits until she is 72½ to begin withdrawing money from her IRA, the IRS will charge a 50% penalty on the $20,000 she has failed to collect (in addition to the normal income tax).

In some instances, investors can free up their IRA money early without incurring a penalty. IRA rules permit an account holder to use IRA funds for medical costs or medical insurance payments. Also, account holders with a disability can remove funds without penalty. Finally, if an IRA holder dies before 59½, funds in the account are released.

The only other way to make early withdrawals without penalty is through an IRA rollover.

IRA Rollovers

An *IRA rollover* is the transfer of money from one tax-qualified IRA to another tax-qualified retirement plan. The IRS permits investors one rollover per year without penalty. An investor who transfers the money out of an IRA must complete the rollover transaction within 60 days. If the disbursement from the old account is not deposited in the new plan within this period, the investor becomes liable for taxes on the full amount of the IRA plus the additional 10% penalty. Normally, investors have their funds sent directly from their old IRAs to the new IRAs in order to avoid any possibility of being taxed, and most large corporations only permit their employees to move funds directly from one qualified plan to another.

IRA Characteristics

- IRAs must be held in an individual's name.
- Maximum IRA contribution is $4,000 per year per person.
- Maximum contribution for married couples is $4,000 per spouse, into separate accounts.
- Contributions are fully deductible for people who are not covered by employer pension plans and for people who earn less than certain income levels.
- Earnings in IRAs are tax deferred until withdrawal, and then taxed as ordinary income.

- Disbursements cannot begin before age $59^1/_2$, and no later than age $70^1/_2$.
- Early withdrawal penalty is 10% of total withdrawal.
- 50% tax penalty is charged on the withdrawal amounts that were not taken at age $70^1/_2$.
- Deposits to IRAs must be made by April 15 to qualify for tax deduction in the previous year.
- Vesting is immediate if you are not covered by an employer plan; vesting could take up to five years for employer plans.
- IRA rollovers, which must be completed within 60 days, are allowed once per year.

In recent years, Congress has established alternatives to traditional IRAs. Roth IRAs are distinguished by their tax status, whereas SEP IRAs require employer contributions.

Roth IRAs

A Roth IRA, named after Delaware Senator William V. Roth Jr., who sponsored its introduction in 1997, turns the normal tax benefits upside down—contributions to the account carry no tax deferral, but retirement disbursements are tax-free. Although it's more costly for a Roth IRA holder to make contributions with after-tax dollars, the possibility of a tax-free income stream during retirement is attractive. Also, investors can make early withdrawals from their Roth IRAs without penalty for the purchase of a first home. Any other use of the funds, however, must wait until the holder reaches age $59^1/_2$.

Roth IRAs

- Maximum IRA contribution is $4,000 per year per person, or $4,500 if over age 50.
- Individuals earning $95,000 or less can make full contributions to Roth IRAs of $4,000 plus $500 additional if over age 50.
- Individuals with an income of $110,000 or more cannot contribute to a Roth IRA.
- Married couples earning $150,000 or less can make the full contribution of $8,000 plus $1,000 additional if over age 50. Couples with a combined income of $160,000 or more cannot contribute to Roth IRAs. Incomes between $150,000 and $160,000 are based on a sliding scale.
- Funds must be held in the account for at least five years before withdrawals can begin.
- Withdrawals from Roth IRAs must start after the minimum age of $59^1/_2$, but there is no maximum age for beginning disbursements (because taxes have already been paid to the government).

SEP IRAs

A *simplified employee plan (SEP) IRA* is a vehicle for small business owners to provide future retirement income for themselves and their employees. A SEP IRA functions as an employee pension plan operating through an IRA. Employers who contribute a percentage of their business income to an SEP IRA must also make the same percentage contribution of each qualified employee's salary. (A qualified employee is one who is at least 21 and has worked with the company a total of three years.) The company can contribute up to 25% of an employer's salary, or $42,000, whichever is less. Contributions up to the maximum are deductible and all are tax-deferred until withdrawn. The employer receives the tax benefit for any contributions made in the employee's name. SEP IRAs allow immediate, full vesting.

Contribution limits and income restrictions make it hard for IRAs to provide full retirement income for many individuals. IRAs are an excellent way to save, but most people who work for companies offering retirement plans also want to make use of them.

Employee Plans

In addition to Social Security, some businesses choose to contribute to private retirement plans for their employees. Although supporting such plans can be expensive to the employer, the advantages are often great—in many industries, the offer of a retirement plan as part of the overall employee benefit package is a key factor in a company's capability to attract and keep qualified workers. Businesses that do not offer some form of retirement plan can find themselves losing the people they need to maintain their competitiveness. Further, part of the money employers pay into retirement plans can be deducted from corporate income taxes, reducing the program's total cost.

Laws Governing Employee Retirement Plans

First and foremost, retirement plans that invest in securities are subject to regulation by the SEC. The IRS also imposes regulations, mainly to determine which plans receive tax-qualified status. But perhaps the most important law pertaining to private retirement programs is the 1974 law known as the *Employee Retirement Income Security Act*, or *ERISA*. Congress created ERISA to safeguard employee pension plans after speculative investments in the early 1970s bankrupted several plans—and left thousands of workers without retirement benefits. The act protects people who work for private employers; plans covering government workers are exempt from ERISA regulations. ERISA's most important provisions include:

- *Equality*. Within a retirement plan, every employee must be treated equally. If an employer offers retirement benefits, it must make them available to all qualified workers.
- *Vesting*. After seven years of employment, an employee must be fully vested in the plan. (Note that many private plans offer earlier vesting.)
- *Fiduciary responsibility*. The plan must be managed by a trustee with fiduciary responsibility to all members of the plan.
- *Prudent man rule*. When making investment decisions, the trustee must follow the "prudent man rule," which states that anyone with fiduciary responsibility must make investment choices that a prudent person would. In effect, ERISA bans speculative investments.

Enforcing ERISA Guidelines

The *Pension Benefit Guaranty Corporation (PBGC)* is the federal agency charged with making sure that private pension plans follow ERISA. When a pension plan goes bankrupt, the PBGC administers basic pension benefits for the affected workers. The agency can also place liens on corporate assets if a business underfunds its workers' plan. Today, the PBGC guarantees pensions for over 45 million workers in the United States.

To achieve tax-qualified status, employee pension plans have to follow ERISA guidelines. Plans that do not meet ERISA standards, such as deferred compensation plans, do not confer tax benefits to the employee or employer.

Deferred Compensation Plans

In a *deferred compensation plan,* the company delays paying part of an employee's salary until after his or her retirement. This type of plan is not tax-deductible, although deferring a portion of salary until after retirement can have the effect of lowering the individual's total tax bill. Deferred compensation plans need not be offered to every worker, and are generally available only to senior executives.

Most retirement plans cover all qualified workers within a company. The most common ones are corporate pension plans and 401(k) plans.

Corporate Pension Plans

Corporate pension plans are tax-qualified retirement programs offered by companies to all employees who work full time. In some cases, only the employer pays into the plan; in others, both the employer and the employee make contributions. Because corporate pension plans are tax qualified, the company and the employee can take deductions for all contributions they make. Normally, employees must work for the company several years to become vested in the plan.

Corporate pension plans are divided into two types: defined contribution plans and defined benefit plans.

In a *defined contribution plan*, the company regularly pays a set amount of money per employee into the plan. The contribution, usually a percentage of corporate income or employee salary, has been pre-determined—an employee's future benefits depend on the size of these defined contributions and on the performance of the plan's investments. The larger the contributions and the longer the employee stays with the company, the higher his or her benefits are likely to be.

Defined contribution plans have a fixed amount paid into the plan per employee. It is usually a pre-determined percentage of corporate income or employee salary.

By contrast, a *defined benefit plan* establishes a desired benefit package and then determines the size of the contributions needed to attain it. Provided an individual works for the company the prescribed number of years, the defined benefits should be attained.

Defined benefit plans establish a benefit package, then determine the size of the contributions to reach the goal.

A corporation can make annual contributions of no more than $42,000 per employee. Whether or not the company earns a profit each year, it must continue to make its established yearly payments to the pension plan. *Profit-sharing plans* are an exception—these programs depend on the amount of profit, if any, the company makes each year. In an unprofitable year, the business makes no contribution to the plan. With certain limitations, corporate contributions to the plan are not taxable as business income or as employee income.

Similar to a profit-sharing plan is an *employee stock ownership plan*, or *ESOP*. Rather than contribute part of its profits, the company buys its own stock on behalf of employees or provides financial assistance to employees who want to purchase the stock. The IRS grants the corporation a tax deduction on the market value of any shares it contributes to the plan. ESOPs are thought to increase business productivity by increasing employees' stake in the future of the company.

401(k) Plans

A *401(k) plan* is another kind of tax-qualified retirement plan. Formally known as a Payroll Deduction Savings Plan, the 401(k) gets its name from the tax code that regulates it. Typically, the employee decides on a level of contribution (a percentage of his or her salary), and the employer makes a *matching contribution* for that or a lesser amount. Some companies don't match contributions exceeding 5% of the employee's salary. Current 401(k) rules allow an employee to contribute as much as $14,000 per year (an amount adjusted annually for inflation; $15,000 for 2006), and still enjoy full deductibility.

Most of the rules for 401(k)s are familiar: contributions are tax deferred, early withdrawals (before the age of 59½) incur a 10% tax penalty, withdrawals must start before the age of 70½. However, 401(k)s do have several differences. For example, employees can borrow against their 401(k) plan without incurring a tax penalty—the plan establishes an interest rate and repayment schedule, typically involving payroll deductions. (Employees who borrow against their 401(k)s and then leave the company must repay the loan within 60 days, or the IRS considers the transaction an early withdrawal.) Vesting rules vary from plan to plan. Normally, the employee is immediately vested for the total of his or her contributions, whereas vesting for the amount of employer contributions takes longer.

Tax deductibility, quick vesting, and matching contributions all help make 401(k) plans attractive to employees. However, they are relatively costly to employers. Smaller businesses sometimes offer different kinds of retirement plans. Some important options are Keogh accounts and 403(b) plans.

Keogh Accounts

Keogh accounts, like SEP IRAs, are retirement plans for small businesses or the self-employed. (Established in 1962, Keogh accounts are named after New York Congressman Eugene Keogh, who sponsored the legislation.) Individuals can contribute up to 25% of their self-employment income or $30,000, whichever is less. Full-time employees of small companies with Keogh plans are entitled to the same percentage contribution that the employer makes for him-self or herself. Deposits are tax-deferred, withdrawals must begin by age 70½ but not before 59½, and disbursements are taxed as ordinary income. The IRS requires specific and extensive reporting for Keogh plans, and also requires the company to continue with its yearly contributions.

403(b) Plans

Also known as tax-deferred annuity plans, *403(b) plans* are retirement programs for employees of nonprofit organizations. A 403(b) plan permits these employees to purchase annuities with contributions that are tax-deferred. Maximum contributions were $14,000 for 2005, with an additional $4,000 for persons over age 50. A comparison of the retirement plans are discussed here in Table 26.2.

Table 26.2 Retirement Plan Comparison

Retirement Plan	Maximum Annual Contribution	Tax Status c = contribution i = investment income	Age When Disbursement Begins (Without Penalty)	Vesting Period
IRA	$4,000 + $500 if over 50	c = deferred with income restrictions i = deferred	59½–70½	Immediate
Roth IRA	$4,000 + $500 if over 50	c = taxed i = tax free	59½–no limit	Immediate
SEP IRA	Company: the lesser of 25% of income or $42,000; for all employees	c = deferred i = deferred	59½–70½	Immediate
Corporate Pension Plan	Lesser of 25% of income or $42,000	c = deferred i = deferred	59½–70½	Varies—no more than seven years
401(k)	Company: usually matches up to a certain amount Employee: $14,000 in 2005; $15,000 in 2006	c = deferred i = deferred	59½–70½	Usually five years for company contribution; immediate for employee contribution

(continued)

Table 26.2 Retirement Plan Comparison *(continued)*

Retirement Plan	Maximum Annual Contribution	Tax Status c = contribution i = investment income	Age When Disbursement Begins (Without Penalty)	Vesting Period
Keogh Account	Lesser of 25% of income or $42,000	c = deferred i = deferred	59½–70½	Immediate
403(b)	$14,000 in 2005 $18,000 if over age 50 $15,000 in 2006	c = deferred i = deferred	59½–70½	Immediate

All of these contributions and deductible limits have planned changes every year until 2008. As an example, an IRA contribution is $5,000 in 2006 with the "catch-up" amount adding $500 per year. So a couple with one working spouse could contribute $10,000 plus a $2,000 catch-up for the 2006 tax year.

Exam Prep Questions

1. Which of the following statements are considered true about FICA payments of an employed individual?

   I. FICA stands for Federal Insurance Contributions Act

   II. FICA contributions have a maximum ceiling of $90,000 per individual, at which point payments into FICA cease

   III. Employee payments to FICA are matched by the employer

   IV. Surplus FICA payments are invested in government securities

   - ❑ A. I and II
   - ❑ B. II and III
   - ❑ C. I, II, and II
   - ❑ D. I, II, III, and IV

2. An individual makes $60,000 per year and wants to open an IRA account with a total contribution of $3,000. What amount of the contribution is deductible for the individual on his taxes?

   - ❑ A. No deduction is allowed
   - ❑ B. A $2,000 maximum deduction is allowed
   - ❑ C. A $2,250 maximum deduction is allowed
   - ❑ D. A $3,000 maximum deduction is allowed

3. An individual is 54 years old and has $440,000 in her IRA account. She takes a disbursement of $20,000 from her account. Which statement is considered true of the IRA disbursement?

   - ❑ A. A disbursement up to 10% is permitted without penalty
   - ❑ B. Any early disbursement will have a 10% penalty
   - ❑ C. There is a 10% penalty for an early withdrawal plus adding the amount of the disbursement to their taxed income for the year
   - ❑ D. The disbursement must be added to taxed income for the year

4. Which of the following statements are considered true of Individual Retirement Accounts?

   I. An IRA account must be in the name of an individual

   II. Disbursements may start at the age of 59½

   III. Disbursements must start by the age of 70½

   IV. IRAs can be rolled over once a year for 30 days

   - ❑ A. I and II
   - ❑ B. II and III
   - ❑ C. I, II, and III
   - ❑ D. I, II, III, and IV

5. A Roth IRA opened for an individual will have which of the following characteristics?

I. There is a maximum contribution of $4,000 allowed

II. An individual can open and deduct a Roth IRA for $4,000 as well as a conventional IRA for $2,000

III. The Roth IRA will pay taxes on the contribution up front

IV. At retirement, all disbursements are nontaxable

❑ A. I and II
❑ B. II and III
❑ C. I, III, and IV
❑ D. I, II, III, and IV

6. Jason Thomas is a self-employed individual earning $150,000 in a calendar year. He has opened a Keogh account for himself. What is his maximum allowable contribution for the year?

❑ A. $2,000
❑ B. $25,000
❑ C. $30,000
❑ D. $37,500

7. A doctor has an established practice with two full-time employees. The doctor makes $300,000 and the employees make $25,000 and $30,000 respectively. The doctor has opened a Keogh account for all of them. Which of the following statements are considered true?

I. The doctor's maximum contribution is $42,000

II. The doctor's maximum contribution is $75,000

III. The doctor must make a contribution for Helen for the amount of $3,500

IV. The doctor must make a contribution for Joann for the amount of $4,200

❑ A. I only
❑ B. I, III, and IV
❑ C. II only
❑ D. II, III, and IV

8. Rich and Christine are a married couple earning $75,000 jointly. Rich is covered by a pension plan at work, but Christine is not. Which of the following statements are considered true?

I. Rich can make a deductible IRA contribution of $4,000

II. Christine can make a deductible IRA contribution of $4,000

III. They can make deductible IRA contributions for both Rich and Christine for $2,000

IV. They can open a joint IRA account and contribute a tax deductible amount of $4,000

- ❑ A. I and II
- ❑ B. II only
- ❑ C. III and IV
- ❑ D. I, II, and III

9. Joseph is employed by a company that does not offer a qualified pension plan. Joseph earns $60,000 for the year and makes a $5,000 contribution to an IRA account. What is his taxable income for the year, including any penalties he must pay?
   - ❑ A. $60,000
   - ❑ B. $58,180
   - ❑ C. $58,000
   - ❑ D. $55,000

10. The allowable limits that are set on corporate pension plan contributions are set at which amount?
    - ❑ A. There is no limit on the contribution a corporation can make
    - ❑ B. The limit is set at $2,000 per employee per year
    - ❑ C. The limit is set at $9,500 per employee per year
    - ❑ D. The limit is set at the lower of $30,000 or 25% of the employee's salary

11. The maximum allowable tax deductible contribution that an employee can make to a 401(k) plan each year is set at which amount?
    - ❑ A. $2,000
    - ❑ B. $9,250
    - ❑ C. $14,000
    - ❑ D. $30,000

12. An employee has taken a loan from his 401(k) plan in the amount of $5,000. After taking the loan, the employee is laid off from his job. Which of the following statements are considered true of the outstanding loan?

    I. The loan is not required to be paid back since the employee was laid off.

    II. The employee has 60 days to pay back the loan in full or it will be considered a disbursement.

    III. If the loan is not paid back in 60 days, it will incur a 10% tax penalty as well as required to be claimed as ordinary taxed income.

    IV. The employee can continue to make payments on the loan.

    - ❑ A. I only
    - ❑ B. II and III
    - ❑ C. III only
    - ❑ D. IV only

13. Conrad is a self-employed individual with a yearly income of $75,000. He decides to plan for his retirement by opening a SEP IRA account. Which of the following statements are considered true of the SEP IRA?

    I. His maximum allowable tax deductible contribution cannot exceed $2,000 each year

    II. His maximum allowable tax deductible contribution cannot exceed $30,000 each year

    III. His maximum allowable tax deductible contribution cannot exceed 25% of his income each year, up to a maximum of $42,000

    IV. Any full-time employees will receive the same percentage contribution that Conrad makes for himself

    - ❑ A. III only
    - ❑ B. II and III
    - ❑ C. II, III, and IV
    - ❑ D. I and IV

14. Ted King is a self-employed professional photographer who earns $150,000 per year. He decides to set up a Keogh account for his retirement. What is his maximum allowable contribution for the year?

    - ❑ A. $2,000 maximum contribution
    - ❑ B. $9,500 maximum contribution
    - ❑ C. $30,000 maximum contribution
    - ❑ D. $37,500 maximum contribution

15. Piper earns $40,000 in a given year, and makes a $3,000 contribution to her IRA account. Which statement is considered true?

    - ❑ A. Piper is permitted to make the $3,000 contribution but cannot take the deduction
    - ❑ B. Piper is only permitted to contribute $2,000 to the IRA
    - ❑ C. Piper is permitted to make the contribution, but must pay a 6% penalty to the IRS on the amount above $2,000
    - ❑ D. Piper can make the $3,000 contribution without penalty and with a full deduction

Exam Prep Answers

1. The correct answer is D. FICA is the Federal Insurance Contribution Act, an employee/employer matching contribution plan. The maximum yearly salary basis for contributions is currently $90,000. Surplus funds collected are invested in government securities.
2. The correct answer is A. An individual earning $60,000 per year has exceeded the allowable deductible earnings amount for an IRA. The individual can make a $3,000 contribution, but because his salary exceeds $55,000, no deduction is given.
3. The correct answer is C. IRA withdrawals are permitted at the age of 59½ without penalty. A person who withdraws funds from an IRA before that time is subject to a 10% penalty on the withdrawn amount, as well as being required to add the withdrawn amount to their ordinary taxable income. There are a few exceptions, none of which are applicable to this individual.
4. The correct answer is C. All Individual Retirement Accounts must be in the name of a single person, as joint accounts are not permitted. Legal disbursements from an IRA can start at age 59½ and are required to begin by the age of 70½. IRAs are permitted to be rolled over once per year within a maximum time frame of 60 days, not 30 days.
5. The correct answer is C. The total contribution to all IRAs, Roth and non-Roth IRAs cannot exceed $4,000 in a given year. If the individual is over 50 years of age, then they are allowed to contribute an additional $500 each year. The Roth IRA holder will pay taxes on the contribution up front, while the disbursement from the Roth IRA at retirement are considered nontaxable.
6. The correct answer is C. The maximum allowable contribution for a self-employed Keogh plan is the lesser of 25% of the individuals' yearly salary or $30,000. In this question, 25% of $150,000 = $37,500. This exceeds the maximum $30,000 contribution, and Jason Thomas will be permitted a maximum contribution to his Keogh account of $30,000.
7. The correct answer is B. The doctor earning $300,000 in a year can contribute the lesser of 25% of his yearly income or $42,000 in a given year to a Keogh account. This gives him a maximum contribution of $42,000, which is 14% of his yearly salary (42,000 ÷ 300,000 = 14%). The doctor will be required to make the same percentage contribution to any full time employees. Helen will receive a contribution of $3,500 and Joann will receive a contribution of $4,200 which represents 14% of their yearly salaries. All three of the plan members are immediately vested of their contribution.

8. The correct answer is A. A married couple earning $75,000 in a single year is permitted to make and deduct a $8,000 contribution to an IRA for each of them. The maximum combined family income cannot exceed $150,000 for a married couple if only one spouse is covered by an employer pension plan.
9. The correct answer is A. In 2005, a $60,000 yearly income for an individual cannot deduct any amount for an IRA contribution. His maximum salary would have to be $45,000; $15,000 less than his current salary.
10. The correct answer is D. The limits on corporate pension plan contributions are considerably higher than IRAs. The maximum contribution is set at 25% of the employee's salary or $42,000, whichever is less. Contributions must be made each year, whether the company turns a profit or not.
11. The correct answer is C. A 401(k) program allows a maximum tax deductible contribution to employees of an amount up to $14,000 for the calendar year 2005. It increases to $15,000 for 2006. Most companies limit their matching contribution to a 401(k) program up to the maximum employee contribution. For example, if an employee decided to contribute $30,000 into their 401(k) plan, a company matching contribution would cease at $14,000.
12. The correct answer is B. A loan from a qualified 401(k) plan is typically organized by the sponsor hired to manage the plan by the corporation. Most loans are paid back by employee payroll deductions. If the individual has been laid off, the sponsor will not continue to service the loan. The individual will now have 60 days to repay the entire loan or it will be considered a disbursement. The disbursement will incur a 10% early withdrawal penalty, as well as required to be claimed on the individuals' tax filing as ordinary income.
13. The correct answer is A. A SEP, Simplified Employee Pension plan, is permitted for small business owners who want to provide for their retirement, as well as the retirement of their employees. Contributions are tax deferred, and an individual opening a SEP IRA can contribute up to 25% of their income earned into the plan, or a maximum amount of $42,000. If the small business owner opens a SEP IRA for himself, they must also contribute the same percentage amount to all full time employees of the business.
14. The correct answer is C. A Keogh account is opened for a self-employed individual. They are very close in structure to SEP IRAs. The maximum Keogh contribution is set at 25% of self-employment income or $30,000, whichever is less. If Ted earned $150,000 for the year he can contribute the lesser of 25% of his income (150,000 × 25% = 37,500) or $30,000. Thus Ted can make a maximum Keogh contribution of $30,000.

15. The correct answer is D. A $30,000 yearly income is under the maximum salary limit to deduct contributions. Any contribution up to $4,000 at an income up to $45,000 is deductible 100%. No individual can contribute more than 100% of their income in a given year, although there are penalties for contributing over the maximum limit. A few exceptions occur; one is for people over 50 years of age who can make extra contributions. The maximum contribution for an individual is actually $42,000 without penalties and $46,000 if over 50 years of age (of which only the original $4,000 is tax-deferred).

PART VIII

Market Analysis and Economics

Taxation and Securities

Terms You Need to Know

- ✓ Accretion
- ✓ Amortization
- ✓ Capital gain/loss
- ✓ Corporate dividend exclusion
- ✓ Cost basis
- ✓ Earned income
- ✓ Estate tax
- ✓ First in, first out (FIFO)
- ✓ Flat tax
- ✓ Gift tax
- ✓ Holding period
- ✓ Investment or portfolio income
- ✓ Long-term gain/loss
- ✓ Married put
- ✓ Municipal bond tax swap
- ✓ Passive income
- ✓ Progressive tax
- ✓ Regressive tax
- ✓ Short against the box
- ✓ Short-term gain/loss
- ✓ Triple exempt
- ✓ Wash sale

Concepts You Need to Understand

- ✓ The types of income
- ✓ The factors that are taken into account in determining taxes
- ✓ The different systems of taxation
- ✓ How different types of securities are taxed
- ✓ How estates and gifts are taxed
- ✓ Short against the box
- ✓ Married put
- ✓ Wash sales
- ✓ Municipal bond tax swaps

Income and Taxation

Investors seek income—whether in the form of dividends, interest, or capital gains—from securities. Each of those forms of income can subject investors to taxation by federal, state, and municipal governments. In fact, how the income from a given security is taxed, and by whom, is very often a deciding factor in investors' specific investment choices. This chapter examines the various types of income, how each is taxed, different theories of taxation, and how different securities are taxed.

To better grasp how income from various securities is taxed, it is important to first understand some principles of taxation in general, and then how income is classified by federal, state, and municipal governments in the United States. Income taxes in this country are a form of progressive taxation, as opposed to a regressive or flat tax.

Progressive Tax

With a *progressive tax*, higher incomes are taxed at higher rates. That is, if Jon Demmy earns $1 million in 2005, and his brother Ted makes $50,000, the government taxes Jon at a higher rate—35%—than it does Ted, who is in a 25% bracket. Tables 27.1 and 27.2 show two of 2005's tax tables available from the IRS.

Table 27.1 Individual Taxable Income

If Taxable Income Is Over	But Not Over	The Tax Is
$0	$7,300	10% of the amount over $0
$7,300	$29,700	$730 plus 15% of the amount over $7,300
$29,700	$71,950	$4,090 plus 25% of the amount over $29,700
$71,950	$150,150	$14,652.50 plus 28% of the amount over $71,950
$150,150	$326,450	$36,548.50 plus 33% of the amount over $150,150
$326,450	no limit	$94,727.50 plus 35% of the amount over $326,450

Table 27.2 Married Filing Jointly or Qualifying Widow(er)

If Taxable Income Is Over	But Not Over	The Tax Is
$0	$14,600	10% of the amount over $0
$14,600	$59,400	$1,460 plus 15% of the amount over $14,600

(continued)

Table 27.2 Married Filing Jointly or Qualifying Widow(er) *(continued)*

If Taxable Income Is Over	But Not Over	The Tax Is
$59,400	$119,950	$8,180 plus 25% of the amount over $59,400
$119,950	$182,800	$23,317.50 plus 28% of the amount over $119,950
$182,800	$326,450	$40,915.50 plus 33% of the amount over $182,800
$326,450	no limit	$88,320 plus 35% of the amount over $326,450

Please note that the various income brackets are not tested on the Series 7, but test-takers are expected to know that the federal income tax is progressive.

Progressive Versus Regressive Taxes

A *regressive tax* takes a larger percentage of a low wage individual's income than it does from a high wage individual. In many instances, taxes that are considered regressive are also *flat taxes*—that is, the same rate is applied to everybody regardless of income. Two examples of regressive taxes are sales taxes and Social Security tax. A sales tax is a flat tax; in New York City, for example, goods and services are taxed at 8.375%, no matter what the cost of the item or service. Sales taxes are also regressive because they consume a larger percentage of a low wage earner's income. In other words, the $8.38 of tax on $100 of groceries hits a New York City bus driver harder than it does a partner in an investment bank.

It is important to remember, too, that people and corporations typically have to pay income taxes to federal, state, and local governments. Each level of government recognizes three main types of income: earned income, passive income, and investment income.

Earned Income

Earned income is the compensation a person or company receives for providing goods or services; it includes wages, salaries, commissions, bonuses, and tips. The cash value of some employee benefits can also be counted as income. Taxpayers can deduct from their earned income certain expenses that were necessary to generate it—such as a traveling salesperson's gas expenses.

Passive Income

Passive income is income generated by a business venture in which the taxpayer has no active managerial role. A limited partner's income from a direct participation program is considered passive income, because the limited partner, by law, cannot participate in the daily operations of the program. In the great majority of cases, losses from passive investments can only be written off against passive income, although they can be carried forward to subsequent years.

Investment Income

Investment or *portfolio income* is income from dividend or interest payments on securities, as well as capital gains (or losses) realized from investments. As with earned income, taxpayers can deduct from this income some of the expenses necessary to earn it.

Capital Gains

Capital gains are profits realized when an asset is sold for more than it was purchased. The capital gain, hence, is the difference between the amount spent on the purchase and the amount received at the sale.

> **EXAMPLE:** Marion's friend Jeff is a sculptor. She buys one of his works for $3,000. Several years later, when he is famous, she is able to sell the sculpture for $30,000. Marion's capital gain is $27,000 (sale price of $30,000 less the original cost of $3,000).

Not surprisingly, a *capital loss* is realized when an asset is sold for less than it originally cost the buyer. In general, capital losses can be written off against capital gains for tax purposes. If capital losses exceed capital gains, a portion of the capital losses can be deducted from other income; an amount that changes from year to year. Any remaining losses can be carried forward to other years.

> **EXAMPLE:** When Marion bought the sculpture from Jeff, she spent another $3,000 on a painting by his younger brother Joe. When Marion sells Jeff's sculpture, she also sells Joe's painting, for $30. This is a capital loss of $2,970 (original cost of $3,000 less the sale price of $30). When Marion fills out her tax return for the year, she writes off this loss against her gain on the sculpture, and pays taxes on a net capital gain of $24,030 (gain of $27,000 minus a loss of $2,970).

Capital losses can be written off against capital gains. If capital losses exceed capital gains, part of the losses can be deducted from other income while the remaining loss amount can be carried forward to other years.

In Marion's case, the original cost of the artwork was simply the price Marion paid; she also received the full sale price. But had she purchased or sold the artwork through an agent, she would have paid commissions—similar to the fees that investors pay when trading most securities. So, in some cases, expenses are involved in purchasing or selling an asset. For this reason, a capital gain or loss is not calculated solely on the purchase and sale prices of an item, but according to its total cost, or cost basis, and the net sale proceeds.

Cost Basis

Cost basis is an asset's cost for tax purposes, which includes the purchase price and expenses such as commissions.

> **EXAMPLE:** Julia buys 100 shares of Oilrich, Inc., at $125 a share. Her broker charges her a commission of $300. The cost basis of the stock, therefore, is $128 a share (purchase price of $125 plus a commission of $3). She later sells the shares at $142, with her broker charging her another $300 commission. For tax purposes, then, her sale proceeds are $139 a share (sale price of $142 minus the $3 commission). Thus, Julia has realized a capital gain of $11 per share, or $1,100 (sale proceeds of $139 per share minus the cost basis of $128 per share times 100 shares).

How capital gains are taxed depends on the owner's holding period for the asset.

A *holding period* is the time during which an investor owned a particular asset or security. In terms of taxes, holding periods are based on trade dates at each end, not settlement dates. The Internal Revenue Service (IRS) has established categories of holding periods for capital gains (and losses).

- *Short-term* gains are gains realized on assets that have been held for up to one year. Short-term gains are taxed at the same rate as the investor's normal tax rate.

- *Long-term* gains are realized on assets held for longer than one year, and are taxed at the same rate as the investor's income, up to a maximum of 15%. Clearly, then, most investors benefit from holding their securities for longer periods.

Taxes on Capital Gains

The IRS includes net capital gains in total income in establishing tax brackets, although the gains themselves are taxed according to the rules outlined earlier. How this works is not tested on the Series 7! What is important to know are the categories of gains and how each is taxed. Table 27.3 shows 2005 tax rates for short-term and long-term gains for various tax brackets and types of assets.

Table 27.3 Capital Gains Tax Rates

Type of Capital Asset	Holding Period	Tax Rate
Short-term capital gains (STCG)	One year or less	Ordinary income tax rates up to 35%
Long-term capital gains (LTCG)	More than one year	**5%** for taxpayers in the 5% and 10% tax brackets **15%** for taxpayers in the 25%, 28%, 33%, and 35% tax brackets
Collectibles	One year or less	STCG tax rates up to 35%
Collectibles	More than one year	28%
Small business stock gains (Section 1202)	More than five years	28% on the gain not excluded
Real estate main home	One year or less More than one year	STCG LTCG taxed at 5% or 15% after any exclusion amount

Having discussed some general principles of income taxes in the United States, it is now important to examine tax regulations for income from specific investment vehicles.

Taxation and Securities

Interest income from debt securities issued by U.S. territories and possessions (such as Puerto Rico or Guam) is exempt from federal, state, and local taxes. Capital gains and losses on these securities, however, are taxed in the same manner as those on other securities.

To a larger extent, the tax treatment of investment income from securities issued outside the United States is the same as for domestic issues. It is worth noting, however, that any taxes that U.S. investors must pay in the issuing country usually can be used as credits on their U.S. tax returns agreements.

Cash dividends paid on stock are part of an investors' investment income, and are taxed in the year they are received (that is, the year the check was issued).

Regulations differ, however, for individuals and corporations in a crucial way. Individuals pay tax on the full dividend. Conversely, the government, in order to encourage corporate investment in other companies, gives corporations a *corporate dividend exclusion*. If the company owns less than 20% of another company, it pays no tax on 70% of dividends received from the second company. If it owns 20% or more, 80% of dividend income is tax-free.

EXAMPLE: Riverview Enterprises owns 25% of Fields, Inc., from which it receives $500,000 in dividends. Because it owns more than 20% of Fields, Riverview does not pay tax on 80% of this amount, or $400,000. It does, however, pay tax on the remaining $100,000.

Stock dividends and splits are treated differently: no tax is paid immediately, but the investor's cost basis in the stock is adjusted accordingly—which affects capital gains down the road.

EXAMPLE: Ellen owns 100 shares of Blue Book, Inc., for which she paid $60 per share. Blue Book decides to pay a 10% stock dividend, giving her a total of 110 shares. Ellen does not pay taxes on this "income." The cost basis of her shares, however, is adjusted downward. Using her original cost basis of $6,000, and dividing that by her new total of 110 shares, yields an adjusted cost basis of $54.55 per share.

As mentioned earlier in this chapter, the cost basis of a security accounts for certain related expenses. For stocks, these include purchase and sales commissions.

Taxing Stock

The cost basis of stock obtained through convertible securities is the same as the cost basis of the original security.

EXAMPLE: Michael bought Adventure, Inc., convertible bonds with a cost basis of $1,000 per bond. Later, he converts each bond to 25 shares of common stock. So, his cost basis in the stock is $40 per share (initial cost basis of $1,000 divided by 25 shares).

Of course, investors frequently purchase shares of a given stock at different times and different prices, creating several cost bases and holding periods. For subsequent sales of this stock, they are allowed to designate the particular shares being sold—which permits them to manage their capital gains income and losses. If the investor does not designate which shares are being traded, the IRS presumes that shares are sold on a *first in, first out (FIFO)* basis, or in the order in which they were purchased.

When selling shares of stock that were purchased at different times, investors can designate the particular shares being sold, permitting them to manage capital gains and losses.

EXAMPLE: Carl has twice purchased 100 shares of Adventure, Inc. The cost basis for the first 100, three years ago, was $48 per share. Six months ago, the second 100 had a cost basis of $50 per share. Now he is selling 100 shares at $55 and has to decide which shares to sell. The $50 shares give him a lesser capital gain ($500 versus $700), but also result in a *short-term* gain. Because Carl is in the 35% tax bracket, he would owe $245 in taxes on this gain ($500 times 35%). Instead, he designates the $48 shares as the shares being sold. This gives him a *long-term* capital gain of $700 on which he pays only 15% tax, or $105 ($700 times 15%).

In many respects, corporate bonds are treated similarly to stocks for tax purposes.

Taxing Corporate Bonds

Interest earned by investors on corporate bonds is considered ordinary taxable income. Like cash dividends, interest income is taxed in the year it is received, at the investor's regular rate.

Investors also often realize capital gains and losses on bonds, although they are treated differently from gains and losses on stocks—which are recognized only at the time of sale. For bonds purchased at a discount, investors must *accrete* the discount annually, on a pro rata basis, over the life of the bond. The annual accretion is then treated as interest income in that year. Each year, the bond's cost basis is adjusted to reflect this accretion. At maturity, the discount has been fully accreted and no capital gain is realized.

EXAMPLE: In 2003, Joyce buys a 10-year, $10,000 Oilrich Corp. bond with a 7% coupon at 90 (or pays $9,000 for the bond). At maturity, she will receive $10,000, theoretically yielding a $1,000 gain. On her tax returns, however, Joyce accretes the $1,000 discount over the 10-year life of the bond. Thus, each year, she will pay taxes on $800 in interest income ($700 of coupon payments plus the $100 annual accretion of the discount). In 2015, the discount will have been fully accreted and no capital gain will be incurred.

Similarly, when an investor purchases a bond at a premium, his or her resulting capital loss is *amortized* over the life of the bond. That is, equal portions of the loss are deducted from interest income each year, with the bond's cost basis adjusted accordingly. Hence, no capital loss is realized at maturity.

> **EXAMPLE:** Fred buys a five-year, $10,000 bond with a coupon of 7% at 110 (or $11,000). His projected loss of $1,000, however, is amortized over the life of the bond. As a result, he subtracts $200 from his coupon payments of $700 each year, and pays taxes on only $500 of interest income. At maturity, no capital loss is realized.

Please note that the government distinguishes between new bonds and bonds purchases on the secondary market. Accretion and amortization are mandatory for new issues, but optional for bonds bought on the secondary market. For the latter, investors can choose to amortize their losses and accrete their gains, or recognize the entire amount at maturity, either as a deduction against interest income (for premium bonds) or as additional interest income (for discount bonds). As confusing as this might be, the relevant fact for the tax treatment of *bonds held to maturity* is that gains and losses are never treated as capital gains income.

For bonds held to maturity, gains and losses are never treated as capital gains income.

Capital gains and losses can be realized on bonds sold prior to maturity. As with stocks, an investor's cost basis in the bonds is crucial in determining the amount of a gain or loss.

Remember that when investors buy bonds, they must pay the seller any accrued interest. This interest is not considered to be part of the buyer's cost basis or the seller's sales proceeds. Instead, it is treated as interest income for the seller, and a deduction against interest income for the buyer, in that year.

> **EXAMPLE:** On September 1, 2004 George buys at par a $1,000 Riverview Enterprises bond, with a 6% coupon, from Gina. She has owned the bond since January 1, 2004; the last interest payment occurred on July 1, 2004. As a result, George pays Gina an additional $10 in accrued interest. (This amount is a rough calculation. Recall that accrued interest on corporate bonds is based on actual days elapsed and a 30/360 basis.) George, therefore, will deduct $10 from his total interest income for the year, whereas Gina will include the $10 with her interest income.

Most rules for corporate bonds apply to government and municipal bonds as well, with a few significant differences.

Taxing Government and Municipal Securities

Treasury and agency securities are taxed in essentially the same way as corporate bonds, but only at the federal level. Because one level of government does not tax another, these securities are not taxable at the state or local level. Remember that there are three crucial exceptions to this rule. Income from securities issued by the housing-related agencies—Fannie Mae, Freddie Mac, and Ginnie Mae—is subject to federal, state, and local taxes. Securities issued by these agencies are based on various types of mortgages, and the mortgagees on these underlying loans already receive federal tax deductions on their interest payments (essentially the income stream for the securities). As a result, investors in Fannie Mae, Freddie Mac, and Ginnie Mae securities pay federal taxes on their income.

Municipal securities are not taxed at federal and local levels. Some are not taxed at the state level either: most states tax only bonds issued by municipalities in other states. Thus, municipals are generally considered to be *triple exempt*, meaning that no taxes are assessed on them. Because no taxes are due, expenses associated with these bonds are not deductible.

Although the same rules regarding gains and losses apply to government securities and corporate bonds, municipal securities differ as to accretion and amortization. Any discount on a municipal issue purchased in the *secondary market* can be accreted or treated as interest income when the bond is sold or matures. That income, however, is taxable, unlike regular interest payments on these securities; the discount can be accreted or it can be reported as taxable interest income when the bond matures or is sold. (Discounts on new municipals must be accreted, with the annual accretion as *nontaxable* income.)

If a municipal bond is purchased at a premium, whether new or in the secondary market, the premium must be amortized. The annual amortization amount reduces the bond's cost basis, and theoretically reduces nontaxable interest income, but obviously this has no effect on the taxes paid by investors.

The taxation of income from investments in mutual funds resembles the treatment of stocks and bonds.

Taxing Mutual Funds

Mutual funds pay dividends. Like dividends from stocks, these are fully taxable at the investor's ordinary income rate in the year in which they are received, even if the dividends are reinvested in the fund.

When the mutual fund shares are sold, the total cost basis is the original price paid for the shares plus the value of all dividends reinvested, plus expenses. Because taxes have already been paid on the dividends that were reinvested, they are not re-taxed as capital gains.

The tax treatment of the securities discussed thus far in this chapter has been relatively uniform. With options, however, the situation is slightly more complex.

Taxing Options

Options are taxed differently depending on whether they are exercised, closed, or allowed to expire. The latter is the least complicated: holders who allow options to expire take a short-term capital loss—the premium paid for the option. Writers of expired options have short-term capital gains.

Capital Gains Treatment of LEAPS

Holders of Long Term Equity Anticipation options (LEAPs) can have long-term capital gains and losses, because LEAPs can have terms of up to 30 months. Tax treatment of these gains and losses, then, depends on the length of the holding period for the LEAP. Please note, however, that writers of LEAPs are never considered to have established a holding period, and so are always considered short sellers, realizing only short-term gains and losses.

EXAMPLE: Sharon buys a call option on Riverview Enterprises stock, giving her the right to buy 100 shares of Riverview at $120 a share within the next three months. For this right, she has paid a premium of $3 per share, or a total of $300. Riverview's stock price never rises above $199, so Sharon allows her option to expire, realizing a short-term capital loss of $300.

Closing open option positions through closing purchases and sales allows investors to lock in a profit or limit a loss. These profits and losses are also considered short-term capital gains and losses.

EXAMPLE: Henry sells a call option on Adventure, Inc. This option gives the holder the right to buy 100 shares of Adventure from Henry at $45 a share during the next six months. Henry receives a premium of $2 per share, or $200 total. When a rumor circulates that Adventure is going to be selected to handle tourism by space shuttle, its stock price climbs. To limit his potential loss, Henry decides to close his position by buying the same option he sold, a call on Adventure at $45, paying a premium of $5 per share, or $500 total. He received $200 for selling the first option and paid $500 to close his position, so his net capital loss is $300.

Should an option holder choose to exercise the option, the tax treatment depends on whether the option is a call or a put.

- *Call option.* When a call option is exercised, the holder purchases stock from the writer at the strike price. The stock is now an asset of the holder; its cost basis is the strike price plus the premium of the option (plus commissions or other expenses). That cost basis is subsequently used to establish the size of any future capital gains or losses. The writer gets the sale proceeds: the strike price plus the premium earned on the option (minus commissions or other expenses). These proceeds are compared to the writer's cost basis for the stock to determine capital gains or losses.

When a call option is exercised, the holder purchases stock from the writer at the strike price. Because the stock is now an asset of the holder, its cost basis is the strike price plus the premium of the option.

EXAMPLE: When Riverview rises to $130 a share, Sharon exercises her option to buy 100 shares at $120. Because she paid a premium of $3 for the option, her cost basis for the stock, excluding commissions, is $123 a share. Chris, the writer who sells her the stock, was a covered writer. That is, he had the 100 shares in his portfolio, with a cost basis of $50 per share. He therefore realizes a long-term capital gain of $73 a share, excluding commissions (strike price of $120 plus a $3 premium minus the cost basis of $50).

Had Chris not been covered, and been forced to buy the shares on the market, he would have taken a short-term capital loss of $7 per share instead (market price of $130 minus sale proceeds of $123).

- *Put option.* When a put option is exercised, the holder sells stock to the writer at the strike price. The sale proceeds for the holder are the cost basis of the stock minus the premium paid for the option (minus commissions and other expenses). This figure is then compared to the holder's cost basis to determine his or her capital gains or losses. The writer is the new owner of the stock; his or her cost basis is the strike price minus the premium earned from writing the option (plus commissions and other expenses).

When the holder sells stock to the writer at the strike price, the sale proceeds for the holder are the cost basis of the stock minus the premium paid for the option (minus commissions and other expenses).

EXAMPLE: When Adventure, Inc., falls to $40 per share, Brad exercises a put option giving him the right to sell 100 Adventure shares for $50 a share. He paid a premium of $2 for the option, so his sale proceeds are $48 a share. Brad, however, did not own the shares; he bought them at market price ($40). This gives him a capital gain, excluding commissions, of $8 a share. The option writer, Alice, is the new owner of the shares. Her cost basis, excluding commissions, is $48 a share (strike price of $50 minus premium earned of $2).

Up to now, this chapter has examined the tax implications of securities that change hands through trading. Not all securities, however, are acquired in that manner; many are received as gifts, or as part of an inherited estate.

Taxing Gifts

The most important tax consideration with gifts is that it is the donor, not the recipient, who is taxed. Individuals can give gifts of up to $11,000 per person per year without paying the federal *gift tax*. (The exclusion is $22,000 for married couples filing jointly.) Gifts to a spouse, however, are not taxed regardless of the amount. A recipient's cost basis for a gifted security is the donor's cost basis or the market value at the time of the gift, whichever is lower.

EXAMPLE: Larry buys 100 shares of ViviVision at $70 a share. He later gives these shares to his nephew Oliver on Oliver's 21st birthday. At that time, ViviVision is selling for $80 a share. The value of the gift, and Oliver's cost basis for the stock, is $70 a share.

Larry also owns 100 shares of Klone-Rite, which he purchased for $101 a share. He gives these to his niece Lolita on her 21st birthday. By that time, Klone-Rite has declined to $75 a share. The value of the gift, and Lolita's cost basis for the stock, is $75 a share.

Because the value of Larry's gifts are $7,000 ($70 times 100 shares) and $7,500 ($75 times 100 shares), respectively, no tax is due on either of them.

Taxing Estates

No *estate tax* is due on an estate bequeathed to a spouse until the death of the surviving spouse. For all other estates in 2005, the first $1.5 million is tax-free. (This amount increases to $2 million in 2006.)

A recipient's cost basis in inherited securities is the current market price at the time of deceased's death. Moreover, capital gains and losses from these securities are treated as long-term, regardless of how long either the deceased or the heir holds them.

Taxing Short Sales

In a short sale, an investor sells a stock that he or she does not own, borrowing it from a broker and replacing it at a later date. The investor is hoping that the stock's price will fall, so that he or she can replace it—repay the broker with an equivalent amount of stock—for less than the sale price. The profit (or loss) on a short sale is a capital gain (or loss), and is measured by the difference between the cost basis and sale proceeds. The government, however, states that no holding period is established by a short seller. Hence, all gains and losses from short sales are short-term.

All gains and losses from short sales are considered short-term for tax purposes.

When an investor sells short a security that he or she owns (has a long position in), this is called a *short against the box*. This strategy was often used by investors who wanted to lock in gains, but postpone paying taxes on them. Because no capital gain or loss can be established in a short sale until the borrowed stock is replaced, an investor can theoretically postpone taxes by selling short in one year and not replacing it until the following year.

The key elements of new legislation, as far as the Series 7 is concerned, are:

- Investors are required to remain at risk for 60 days beyond closing out their short positions, meaning that they cannot realize the gains they had hoped to lock in.

➤ Selling short cannot change short-term capital gains into long-term capital gains. For tax purposes, an investor's holding period in the underlying stock ends on the day of the short sale.

Both short sales and long sales are subject to tax laws on wash sales, another technique formerly used by investors to reduce taxes.

Wash Sales

A *wash sale* is the sale of a security and the repurchase of "substantially the same security" within 30 days. The 30 days extend both before and after the sale. Capital losses from wash sales are not deductible. This is because investors might otherwise sell stocks at the end of a year and claim losses, and then simply repurchase the stocks a few days later at the same price.

Understanding the concept of a wash sale is an important topic to remember.

In a wash sale, the security purchased does not have to be identical to the one sold, only substantially the same. Convertible bonds, convertible preferred stock, or a call option on stock are all substantially the same as the underlying common stock. Preferred stock or ordinary bonds of the same corporation, however, are considered to be substantially different; the basis in the newly acquired stock is its price (including associated transaction costs) *plus* the loss that has been disallowed.

The wash sale rule also applies to short sales: an investor who sells a security short cannot claim a loss if he or she sells the same security short again within 30 days.

Note that the wash sale rule does allow *municipal bond tax swaps*. The significant characteristics of a municipal bond are its issuer, interest rate, and maturity. Investors who sell municipal bonds must purchase other municipals, in which at least two of those three characteristics are different, to not establish a wash sale. If the new bond is considered a different security, it is not considered a wash sale.

Exam Prep Questions

1. Julie purchases 1,000 shares of TNT stock at $50 per share. Her broker charges her a commission of $500 on the transaction. The stock increases in value to $55 per share. What is the cost basis on the stock?

   ❑ A. $49.50 per share
   ❑ B. $50 per share
   ❑ C. $50.50 per share
   ❑ D. $55 per share

2. A tax rate in which investors or corporations pay more taxes on larger incomes is known as:

   ❑ A. Progressive tax
   ❑ B. Regressive tax
   ❑ C. Flat tax
   ❑ D. Exempt tax

3. TNT Corporation owns 25% of the outstanding shares of Acme Corporation. Acme Corporation has issued 1 million shares of stock in the market. Acme pays a dividend of $1 per share. What is the amount that TNT Corporation will have to claim as dividend income on their corporate taxes?

   ❑ A. $250,000 as dividend income
   ❑ B. $75,000 as dividend income
   ❑ C. $200,000 as dividend income
   ❑ D. They will not have to claim any dividend income

4. Robert purchased some GHI stock over the past six months. He purchased 100 shares @ $40, 100 shares @ $42, 100 shares @ $44, and 100 shares @ $46. He then decides to sell 100 shares of the stock. Using the normal IRS designation on the shares, what is the cost basis on the shares he sold?

   ❑ A. $40 cost basis
   ❑ B. $42 cost basis
   ❑ C. $44 cost basis
   ❑ D. $46 cost basis

5. An investor has purchased 10 bonds of a 10-year corporate bond at 90 in the secondary market and holds the bonds to maturity. Which of the following statements are true of the bond?

   ❑ A. The investor will amortize the bonds each year for $100.
   ❑ B. The investor will have a capital gain at maturity of $1,000.
   ❑ C. The investor will accrete the bonds each year for $100.
   ❑ D. The investor will have a capital loss at maturity for $1,000.

6. An investor purchased a 20-year corporate bond at 110 in the secondary market and after five years sells the bond for 120. What is the adjusted cost basis for the bond when it is sold?
   - ❑ A. $1,025 adjusted cost basis
   - ❑ B. $1,075 adjusted cost basis
   - ❑ C. $1,100 adjusted cost basis
   - ❑ D. $1,200 adjusted cost basis

7. Frank purchased the following option: 1 TNT October 60 Call @ 4 in the market. TNT stock goes to $66 in the market and Frank exercises the option. What are his tax implications on the option?
   - ❑ A. He has a short-term gain of $200.
   - ❑ B. He has a short-term gain of $600.
   - ❑ C. He has a capital gain of $200.
   - ❑ D. He has a capital gain of $600.

8. The maximum allowable yearly gift (as of 2005) that can be given to an individual without incurring a gift tax is which amount?
   - ❑ A. $5,000
   - ❑ B. $11,000
   - ❑ C. There is no tax on a gift
   - ❑ D. $22,000

9. A husband gives his wife a gift of a new car valued at $50,000. Under the IRS gift tax rules, how will the gift be taxed?
   - ❑ A. The amount above $10,000 will be taxed as ordinary income.
   - ❑ B. A gift to a spouse is not considered taxable.
   - ❑ C. The donor will pay a gift tax on the full amount, as ordinary income.
   - ❑ D. The gift will be taxed after the car is sold.

10. Frederick purchases 100 shares of VTV stock at $125 per share. He then gives the 100 shares of VTV stock to his nephew on his 21st birthday. The stock is selling at $95 per share at that time. How will the gift of 100 shares of VTV stock be taxed?
    - ❑ A. Frederick will owe a gift tax on $12,500 worth of stock.
    - ❑ B. Frederick will owe a gift tax on $2,500 worth of stock.
    - ❑ C. Frederick will pay no gift tax on the gifted shares of stock.
    - ❑ D. The nephew will pay a gift tax on $9,500 worth of stock.

11. Terry owns 1,000 shares of LTV stock that he purchased on May 17th for $44 per share. Terry passes away on September 1st of the same year and his will leaves the 1,000 shares of LTV stock to his brother Thomas. On September 1st, the LTV shares are selling for $49 per share. A month later, Thomas sells the shares at $52 per share. What is his cost basis for the shares when he sells them?

- ❑ A. $44 per share cost basis
- ❑ B. $49 per share cost basis
- ❑ C. $52 per share cost basis
- ❑ D. The shares will have a cost basis of the average price between the day they were purchased and the day they were sold

12. Barbara sells 100 shares of RTC stock short on January 4, 2004, for $47 per share. On June 25, 2004, she covers her short position by purchasing 100 shares of RTC stock at $35 per share. What are the tax implications on the short sale?

- ❑ A. Barbara has a long-term capital gain of $1,200.
- ❑ B. Barbara has a long-term capital loss of $1,200.
- ❑ C. Barbara has a short-term capital gain of $1,200.
- ❑ D. Barbara has a short-term capital loss of $1,200.

13. Susan purchases 1,000 shares of KLM stock for $50 per share on June 15. After four months, she sells the shares at $42 per share, for a loss of $8,000. Two weeks later she purchases 10 KLM January 40 Calls @ 4. How will the 1,000 shares of KLM stock be taxed?

- ❑ A. Susan will have a capital loss of $8,000 on the stock.
- ❑ B. Susan will have a capital loss of $12,000 on the stock.
- ❑ C. Susan will have a capital loss of $4,000 on the stock.
- ❑ D. Susan will not be able to take a loss on the 1,000 shares of KLM stock.

14. An investor purchases 100 shares of TNT stock at $45 per share on January 10. The investor also purchases 1 TNT April 45 Put @ 3 on the same day. What is the cost basis for the stock, if the investor sells it on June 10th for $54 per share?

- ❑ A. Cost basis of $42
- ❑ B. Cost basis of $45
- ❑ C. Cost basis of $48
- ❑ D. Cost basis of $54

15. Edward purchases 100 shares of Blue Star Enterprises at $50 per share. Blue Star pays a 10% stock dividend to shareholders. Edward then sells his 110 shares of Blue Star for $56 per share. What is his cost basis on the Blue Star shares?

- ❑ A. $45.45 per share
- ❑ B. $50.50 per share
- ❑ C. $55 per share
- ❑ D. $56 per share

Exam Prep Answers

1. The correct answer is C. The cost basis on a stock purchased at $50 per share will be the purchase price plus any commission paid on the purchase. In this question, the purchase price was $50 per share and a total commission of $500 was charged on the purchase of the 1,000 shares. The commission of $500 equals $.50 on each share. This amount will be added to the purchase price to have a cost basis of $50.50 per share.
2. The correct answer is A. A progressive tax imposes higher tax rates on individuals with larger incomes. The U.S. tax system is considered a progressive tax: the more you make, the higher the tax rate and amount due.
3. The correct answer is C. Under the Corporate Dividend Exclusion, if a company owns 25% or more of the outstanding shares of another company, it will pay no tax on 80% of the dividend it receives from the shares. If the company owns less than 20% of the outstanding shares of another company, it will receive an 70% dividend exclusion on the dividend paid.

   EXAMPLE: TNT owns 25% of the outstanding shares of Acme or 250,000 shares (1,000,000 × 25% = 250,000 shares). TNT will receive an 80% dividend exclusion. Acme pays a $1 dividend and TNT receives $250,000 for the shares they own. 80% of this amount is excluded from taxation. $250,000 × 80% = $200,000 is excluded. TNT will pay corporate taxes on the $50,000 that is not excluded.
4. The correct answer is A. If an investor owns numerous shares of a security at different prices and they do not designate which shares they have sold, the IRS will presume that they were sold on the First In First Out basis, or in the order they were purchased. In this case, the first shares in were at $40 each and they will be considered the cost basis on the shares sold.
5. The correct answer is C. This investor purchased $10,000 worth of corporate bonds in the market at 90 for $9,000. Upon maturity, the bonds will pay the holder par value of $10,000. The $1,000 discount will be accreted each year for the life of the bond. $1,000 ÷ 10 years = $100 accreted each year. By accreting the bonds for $100 each year, the investor will not incur a capital gain upon maturity of the bond. The investor is paying the accreted amount on his taxes each year, due to the discount on the bonds.

6. The correct answer is B. This investor purchased a corporate bond at 110 in the market. The bond was purchased at a premium price of $1,100. It is a 20-year bond, and thus it will be amortized over the 20 years. The premium of $100 paid is amortized as: $100 ÷ 20 years = $5 per year amortized or deducted. After five years the bond was sold. The cost basis was $1,100 when it was purchased, but it has been amortized for five years. $5 deducted each year × 5 years = $25. The original cost of $1,100 – $25 = Adjusted cost basis of $1,075.
7. The correct answer is A. All options will always be computed as short-term capital gains. Frank purchased 1 TNT Oct. 60 Call @ 4. His cost for the option was $400. He exercises the option when the stock reaches $66 with the right to buy the stock at $60. His 6 point gain × 100 shares = $600 gain. He can deduct the cost of the option from his gain to realize a short-term gain of $200.
8. The correct answer is B. Individuals may give gifts of up to $11,000 per year in value to another individual without being required to pay a federal gift tax. If the gift is greater than $11,000 then the donor, and not the recipient, will pay the required gift tax. For a married couple filing jointly, the amount of the gift is tax-free up to $22,000.
9. The correct answer is B. A gift to a spouse is considered a nontaxable event to the donor and the beneficiary. Thus, there are no gift taxes owed in this case.
10. The correct answer is C. The 100 shares of VTV stock that Frederick gave to his nephew does not total over $11,000; therefore, there are no gift tax implications on the gift to his nephew.
11. The correct answer is B. The LTV stock will have a cost basis of the attained price on the day that Terry passed away, September 1st. Tom will have a cost basis on that day of $49 per share on the stock he inherited.
12. The correct answer is C. Stock that has been sold short will always have a short-term cost basis, since the stock was never held by the short seller. Selling the RTC stock short at $47 per share and eventually covering the short position at $35 per share will result in a gain of $12 per share or $1,200.
13. The correct answer is D. The IRS disallows a loss on the sale of a security if the investor has repurchased the same stock within a 30-day time period. The purchase of the 10 KLM calls has, in effect, given Susan a new position in KLM once again, disallowing the incurred loss.

14. The correct answer is C. An investor who purchases stock, and on the same day also purchases a protective put option, has in effect married the put to the stock. The IRS allows the cost of the protective or married put to be included in the cost basis for the stock, if done on the same day. The purchase price for the stock was $45 and the put option cost $3 per share. The cost basis is thus considered $48.
15. The correct answer is A. A company that pays a stock dividend of 10% will give the shareholder 10% additional shares. Edward owned 100 shares and now has 110 shares. The stock will be adjusted accordingly for the stock dividend. $50 per share × 100 shares = $5,000 value. The stock dividend now gives the shareholder 110 shares. The stock value will remain the same. $5,000 divided by 110 = $45.45 per share cost basis.

Risk and Client Portfolios

Terms You Need to Know

- ✓ Aggressive portfolio
- ✓ Beta (β)
- ✓ Capital asset pricing model (CAPM)
- ✓ Defensive portfolio
- ✓ Market (or systematic or nondiversifiable) risk
- ✓ Market portfolio
- ✓ Maturity premium
- ✓ Random diversification
- ✓ Risk premium
- ✓ Risk-free return or rate
- ✓ Risk-return tradeoff
- ✓ Selective diversification
- ✓ Standard deviation
- ✓ Unique (or nonsystematic or diversifiable) risk
- ✓ Variance

Concepts You Need to Understand

- ✓ An investor's definition of risk
- ✓ Opportunity cost
- ✓ Degrees of risk: variance and standard deviation
- ✓ Risk-return tradeoff
- ✓ Maturity and risk premiums
- ✓ Market risk versus unique risk
- ✓ Capital asset pricing model (CAPM)
- ✓ Stock betas
- ✓ Different types of risk
- ✓ Investors' various investment objectives
- ✓ Aggressive versus defensive portfolios
- ✓ Selective and random diversification

Risk

A broker-dealer's primary responsibility is tailoring an investment portfolio to the unique needs and objectives of individual clients. Much of that work involves a thorough understanding of the various benefits and risks presented by different types of securities. Not every client is a good candidate for investments in speculative stocks, nor, for that matter, in government securities. This chapter focuses on risk: in terms of investments, how it can be measured, its distinct forms related to securities, and how portfolios are constructed to address risk and an investor's goals.

Nobody disputes that every security brings with it some element of risk. However, what exactly is meant by "risk"? In its broadest terms, to an investor, risk is the possibility of losing money on an investment, commonly referred to as capital risk. Risk is also considered the *opportunity cost* of an investment—the potential income from one investment that was foregone when the investor chose a different investment.

Investors do not judge the merits of an investment in a vacuum, but in relation to the large universe of other possible investments. In that universe, some securities—whether because of the type of security or its issuer—present more risk than others. Again, what is meant by risk?

In this instance, risk refers to the volatility or variability of a given security's returns. For example, in the 1980s fortunes were made *and* lost by investments in junk bonds. Investors who were lucky enough to have selected the bonds of issuers that paid off made a tremendous amount of money—because of the high coupon rates of such bonds. On the other hand, holders of junk bonds from companies that went bankrupt often lost everything.

Measuring Volatility

Thanks to statistics, the variability of the return on a particular security can be quantified. The specific statistical measures are the variance and standard deviation of the given security's returns. We need to understand about variance and standard deviation.

Variance

In the world of statistics, *variance* is the average of squared deviations around an average. Stated simply as it pertains to security returns, variance is the dispersion of actual annual returns around the average return over a given period. Thus, variance represents the risk inherent in a security: how much its actual returns can vary from its historical, or anticipated, returns.

EXAMPLE: Matt Brauderik has $1,000 in his pocket and is given the opportunity to play a game. Two coins will be flipped. For each head that comes up, his $1,000 stake will be increased by 25%; for each tail that comes up, his stake will be reduced by 15%. So the following four outcomes are equally likely:

1. First flip results: head plus head. Brauderik makes 25% plus 25%, or a total gain of 50% (There is no compounding in this game.)
2. Second flip results: head plus tail. Brauderik makes 25% minus 15%, or a net gain of 10%.
3. Third flip results: tail plus head. Brauderik loses 15%, then gains 25%, or a net gain of 10%.
4. Fourth flip results: tail plus tail. Brauderik loses 15% twice, or a total loss of 30%.

What is Mr. Brauderik's expected return from this game? Statistically, there is a 1 in 4 chance he will make 50%, a 2 in 4 chance that he will make 10%, and a 1 in 4 chance he will lose 30%. Mathematically, this can be shown as:

$$\text{Expected return} = \frac{(0.25 \times 50) + (.50 \times 10) + (0.25 \times -30)}{(12.50) + (5) + (-7.50)} = 10\%$$

Each individual outcome listed earlier obviously differs from Mr. Brauderik's expected return. For reasons that are not relevant to this discussion, statisticians square these differences (multiply each difference by itself), then average them to arrive at the variance of returns in this game. Table 28.1 lays it out more clearly.

Table 28.1 Variance from Expected Returns

Rate of Return	Deviation from Exp. Return	Squared Deviation
+50%	+40	1,600
+10%	0	0
+10%	0	0
–30%	–40	1,600

The variance, therefore, equals the sum of those deviations (3,200) divided by four, or 800. Clearly, the variance in Mr. Brauderik's game is difficult to translate into real dollars. After all, what exactly does 800 mean in terms of whether he will make or lose money? This is where standard deviation comes into play.

Standard Deviation

Standard deviation is the square root of the variance. Recall that, in determining the variance, each deviation was squared, which effectively means that the variance is stated in squared percentages. By taking the square root of the variance, standard deviation brings us back to straight percentages—an easier number to grasp. In Mr. Brauderik's investment game, the standard deviation of returns is approximately 28.3% ($\sqrt{800}$). With that information, Mr. Brauderik could compare investments and decide which one he prefers. For example, say that an investment had an expected return of 10%, but its standard deviation was only 15%. An individual might prefer this second investment, which is half as risky as the first game we calculated. To sum up, the larger the standard deviation of a security's returns, the greater the inherent risk. This is because actual returns tend to vary more widely from the expected return. The degree of risk in a certain security is evidenced in the risk-return tradeoff.

Risk-Return Tradeoff

Investors who seek the higher returns of junk bonds, must also take on the increased risk of that type of security. Similarly, purchasers of much safer Treasury bills accept lesser returns on their investment. This *risk-return tradeoff* is demonstrated by historical returns, and the standard deviations of those returns, on T-bills, T-bonds, and common stocks. Average returns and standard deviations for these securities for the period 1926–1996 are shown in Table 28.2.

Table 28.2 Standard Deviations from Returns on Securities

Security	Average Annual Return (Nominal)	Standard Deviation
T-bills	3.8%	3.3%
T-bonds	5.3%	8.0%
Common stocks	12.5%	20.4%

Investors demand a premium for investing in riskier securities such as Treasury bonds and common stocks. In fact, two premiums are at play: a maturity premium and a risk premium.

Maturity Premiums

A *maturity premium* is the additional return required by investors for investing in longer term Treasury bonds, as opposed to Treasury bills. Specifically, from 1926 to 1996, investors received an average additional return of 1.5%

from T-bonds (5.3% minus 3.8%). Because T-bills are short term and guaranteed by the government, the rate on T-bills is sometimes referred to as the *risk-free return*. T-bills have no credit risk and very little or none of the reinvestment and interest rate risk associated with longer term T-bonds—or any longer term bonds, for that matter. Because T-bond purchasers wait longer to get their principal back, exposing themselves to more risk, they demand a maturity premium over the risk-free return.

Risk Premiums

A *risk premium* is the extra return over the risk-free return that investors insist on when purchasing risky securities, such as common stocks. It is clear from Table 28.2 that from 1926 to 1996, investors got a risk premium, or excess return, of 8.7% (12.5% minus 3.8%) for purchasing common stocks instead of T-bills. Issuers of common stock do not have the stability or credit rating of the U.S. government, thus presenting investors with a greater level of risk. As a result, these issuers must reward investors with a risk premium.

To this point, the discussion has focused on risk in terms of what it means to investors: the potential loss of capital or the opportunity cost of one investment versus another. In addition, methods for measuring the degree of risk associated with a specific investment—variance and standard deviation—have been examined. But none of that deals with what makes a given security risky. Risk is not a monolithic, uniform characteristic that securities have to one degree or another. Instead, different types of risk exist that either singly or in combination make a type of security, or a particular issuer's securities, risky. Of those risks, the two most important—in terms of investment portfolio theory—are market risk and unique risk.

Market Risk and Unique Risk

Market or *systematic risk* is the risk that downturns in the economy as a whole, or declines in the larger securities market, might negatively affect the securities of an individual issuer, regardless of that company's own performance over the same period.

Market or systematic risk is a type of risk in which a downturn in the economy might negatively affect the securities of an individual issuer, regardless of the performance of the company in the same period of time.

EXAMPLE: In January 2000, Alex Giness buys 100 shares of Riverview Enterprises, a construction company, for $70 per share. As it turns out, the U.S. economy spends most of 2000 mired in a recession. Riverview, however, has excellent management and is able to eke out a small profit for the year. Nevertheless, stock prices in general fall 10% by year end, and Riverview's is no exception, being quoted at $64 per share in December 2000. So, despite Riverview's stellar managers and profits for the year, its stockholders see their investment lose value.

Not surprisingly, *unique* or *nonsystematic risk* is associated strictly with the issuer. That is, unique risk arises from characteristics of a company such as its industry, location, management, project choices, and so on.

Remember, unique or nonsystematic risk is associated strictly with the issuer.

EXAMPLE: In January 2001, Riverview's CEO, Bill Holdin, dies unexpectedly. His son, Bill Jr., takes over operations. A graduate of the University of Alaska, Bill Jr. does not have the experience or business savvy of his farther, so even though the economy has rebounded and housing demand is climbing steadily, Riverview incurs losses of several million dollars, and stockholders see the value of their shares drop significantly.

The nature of each of these risks contributes to the current understanding of the benefits of portfolio diversification. First, market risk is something that can never be mitigated completely. Even a well-diversified portfolio is subject to swings in the economy. As a result, market risk is sometimes also referred to as *nondiversifiable risk*.

You can eliminate unique risk from a portfolio through diversification. Note that the standard deviation of a security's returns is a measure of the security's unique risk. The impact of one issuer's securities on the value of a portfolio is negligible in a diversified portfolio, leading theorists to describe unique risk as *diversifiable risk*.

Remember, market risk cannot necessarily be avoided; as a result, it is also called nondiversifiable risk. Unique risk, because it can be lessened by portfolio diversification, is known as diversifiable risk.

Theorists go on to say that the only type of risk that need concern an investor is market risk, because all other risk is diversifiable. Specifically, investors need to be aware of how a given security reacts to changes in the economy, and particularly to fluctuations in a market index such as the S&P's

500—frequently referred to as the *market portfolio*. This is the foundation of one of the principal tools for determining expected returns on a stock, called the capital asset pricing model.

The Capital Asset Pricing Model

The capital asset pricing model (CAPM) states that:

$$r = r_f + \beta r_m - r_f$$

whereby:

r = Expected return on a stock

r_f = Risk-free rate (return on T-bills)

β = Beta (factor unique to the given stock)

r_m = Return on the market portfolio (usually the S&P's 500)

Thus, an investor's expected return on a stock should equal the risk-free rate plus a risk premium multiplied by a stock's *beta*, which is explained in detail later in this section. A risk premium is the excess return required by investors for assuming risk on an investment. In CAPM, the term $(r_m - r_f)$ stands in for the risk premium, representing the difference between the return on a market portfolio and the risk-free return. That premium has been 8.7% historically.

Not all stocks react similarly to changes in the overall stock market: some climb and drop faster than the market, others move in directions opposite to the market. This is where a stock's beta comes into play.

A Stock's Beta

Beta (β) is a measure of the sensitivity of a stock's return to fluctuations in the market. A beta of 1.0 means that a stock's returns move with the market; for every 1% swing in the value of the market portfolio, the value of the stock moves 1% in the same direction. The prices of stocks with betas greater than 1.0 fluctuate more widely than the market, but in the same direction; stocks with positive betas less than 1.0 move in the direction as the market, but to a lesser extent. Cyclical stocks—those whose prices tend to follow the business cycle—generally have betas greater than 1.0. Stocks with negative betas (counter-cyclical stocks) move against the market. StockBetas are available from Standard & Poor's or from brokerage houses.

A stock's beta is a measure of the sensitivity of a stock's return to fluctuations in the market. A beta of 1.0 means that a stock's returns move with the market; for every 1% swing in the value of the market portfolio, the value of the stock moves 1% in the same direction. The prices of stocks with betas greater than 1.0 fluctuate higher than the market (a 2% beta means the stock fluctuates two times greater than the market), but in the same direction; stocks with positive betas less than 1.0 move in the direction as the market, but to a lesser extent. Cyclical stocks—those whose prices tend to follow the business cycle—generally have betas greater than 1.0. Stocks with negative betas (counter-cyclical stocks) move against the market.

EXAMPLE: Bob Needermeier, a sophisticated investor, is considering whether to buy the stock of Flounder Seafoods but wants to be sure he will earn a fair return. He calls his broker and asks for Flounder's beta, which turns out to 1.20. The current rate on T-bills is 5.6%. Using CAPM, Mr. Needermeier determines that Flounder's expected return is:

$= 5.6 + 1.2(8.7)$

(Note: 8.7% is the average risk premium for common stocks for the period 1926–1996.)

Mr. Needermeier decides that, given the other securities in his portfolio (some of which have betas less than 1.0), this is a good investment. He will not know until he liquidates his Flounder position whether the stock performed to his expectations.

Alpha Versus Beta

Some financial analysts have developed a measure for the effect of a stock's nonsystematic risk on its expected returns. Called *alpha*, it supposedly quantifies the volatility of a stock's price based on the issuer's unique characteristics. In contrast to beta, the accuracy of alpha has never been established in a real securities market, so it is not a widely used analytical tool.

Market risk and unique risk are by no means the only types of risk that investors encounter in the securities market.

Other Types of Risk

The following risks are also associated with securities:

- **Legislative risk.** The risk that changes in laws, particularly tax regulations, might lower an investor's profits. Direct participation programs are especially prone to legislative risk.
- **Liquidity risk.** Financial risk stemming from the inability to convert a security to cash easily or quickly. Thinly traded securities such as small

capitalization stocks traded on the OTC market commonly have high liquidity risk.

- **Credit risk.** A feature primarily of bonds, credit risk is the risk that a borrower (the issuer) might not have the capacity to make timely interest and principal payments to the lenders (the investors).
- **Interest rate risk.** Another risk characteristic of bonds. Because bonds are fixed-rate instruments, their value is affected by movements in market interest rates. When market rates rise, bondholders see the value of their bonds drop. Bonds with longer maturities are especially prone to interest rate risk.
- **Inflationary** or **purchasing power risk.** The risk that a security's rate of return will not keep pace with inflation, reducing the purchasing power of an investor's proceeds and diluting the overall return. Common stocks historically have outperformed inflation, and are seen as good protection against inflation risk. Given their fixed rate, bonds have high inflationary risk. The longer the maturity of the bond, the greater the inflationary risk.
- **Reinvestment risk.** When investors receive cash from an investment—whether from dividend and interest payments, or from the sale or maturity of the security—they generally want to reinvest those funds. Reinvestment risk is the possibility that they might not be able to purchase securities with an equal or higher rate of return.
- **Sovereign risk.** Persons investing in foreign countries must be alert to sovereign risk. Governments might nationalize industries, repudiate guarantees, limit the flow of cash out of the country, or pursue policies that adversely affect local economies and destroy the value of investments.

After brokers understand the various types and degrees of risk that exist, they are better able to evaluate the many securities available and to construct appropriate portfolios for their clients.

Building a Client's Portfolio

A broker's first consideration in creating a securities portfolio for a client is that client's unique objectives. Investors have distinct investment goals based on their financial capacity, age, family or job situation, and so forth. A young single person, a parent preparing to send three children to college, and a retiree need different things from their investments.

A client's unique investment objectives are a broker's prime consideration in creating a portfolio. Such things as financial capacity, age, family or job situation, affect the goals of the portfolio.

The following list outlines some common investment objectives:

- **Safeguarding of principal.** The investor is less interested in capital growth than in reducing the risk of losing his or her capital. A person with limited investment funds, or nearing retirement, likely has this as a goal. Blue-chip and defensive stocks are frequently purchased by investors with this objective. Defensive stocks are resistant to economic downturns, usually because the issuing companies provide essential products such as medicine or food.
- **Income.** The investor wants to maximize his or her current investment income. Bonds and stocks with high dividend rates compose an income portfolio. Utility companies are known for paying high dividends.
- **Liquidity.** The investor might need funds at short notice, and wants to be able to convert investments into cash at will.
- **Growth.** The investor wants the value of his or her investments to grow at a rate equal to or exceeding the market average. In general, these investors are either risk-takers or younger, with longer-term investment horizons. Growth portfolios present greater degrees of risk than the portfolio types mentioned previously.
- **Speculation.** The investor seeks the greatest possible gain, and is willing to take on any necessary risks to achieve it. Younger investors with large incomes and few commitments, or who are sophisticated about trading strategies, might choose this objective.

The Client's Financial Capacity

Brokers must follow another element of the "Know Your Customer" rule: they should not recommend investments for which their clients clearly lack the experience, sophistication, or temperament.

The "Know Your Customer" rule: a broker must know a client's investment goals and financial capacity to achieve those goals. Never recommending investments for clients who are clearly unable to afford or manage them is of paramount importance for a broker.

Of the investment objectives listed earlier, growth and speculation usually lead to the construction of what is termed an *aggressive portfolio*, in which the potential for high gains is set off by commensurably high degrees of risk.

Conversely, investors who seek to safeguard principal, generate current income, and maintain liquidity prefer *defensive portfolios*, which take on lesser risk in exchange for lower returns. A traditional element of a defensive portfolio is diversification, which eliminates the unique risk generated by individual securities.

Diversification can be either random or selective. With *selective diversification*, a limit is placed on the total amount that is invested in a particular industry or region. *Random diversification* places no constraints on how much money is concentrated in an industry or region, provided that the portfolio, as a whole, remains diversified.

Exam Prep Questions

1. The risk-free rate of return in the United States is defined as which of the following?
   - ❑ A. The value of the Standard & Poor's Index
   - ❑ B. The interest on a T-Bill offering by the Federal Reserve
   - ❑ C. The prime rate offered by the five largest commercial banks in the country
   - ❑ D. The discount rate offered by the Federal Reserve to member banks

2. Which of the following statements are considered true of the risk-return tradeoff?

   I. The longer the maturity the greater return expected

   II. The shorter the maturity, the greater the return expected

   III. T-Bills offer investors a return with no inherent risk

   IV. T-Bonds offer investors a return with no inherent risk
   - ❑ A. I and III
   - ❑ B. II and III
   - ❑ C. I, III, and IV
   - ❑ D. I, II, III, and IV

3. Systematic risk is best defined as which of the following?
   - ❑ A. That an issuer in the marketplace can default
   - ❑ B. That a decline in the bond market has affected the market
   - ❑ C. A downturn in the economy on the whole affects the stock price
   - ❑ D. The Dow average is compared to the Standard & Poor's Index

4. Which of the following statements is considered true of market risk?

   I. Market risk is considered diversifiable

   II. Market risk cannot be diversifiable

   III. Unique risk is the same as nonsystematic risk

   IV. Unique risk is the same a systematic Risk
   - ❑ A. I and III
   - ❑ B. I and IV
   - ❑ C. II and III
   - ❑ D. IV only

5. A stock with a Beta of 3 has which of the following characteristics when compared to the overall movement of prices in the market?

   I. The stock would have a volatility three times the overall market

   II. The stock would move 30% more than the overall market

   III. The stock would move at a rate 3% greater than the market

   IV. The stock would move at a rate of 3% less than the market

   - ❑ A. I and III
   - ❑ B. I and II
   - ❑ C. I only
   - ❑ D. II and IV

6. Which of the following statements would be most accurate about legislative risk?

   I. The government must approve a new issue

   II. The tax laws can change, affecting an issue

   III. Foreign securities have no legislative risk

   IV. Foreign securities have greater legislative risk than American stocks

   - ❑ A. I and III
   - ❑ B. II only
   - ❑ C. II and III
   - ❑ D. II and IV

7. Which of the following risks would be most inherent to an investment made in a security in a new and burgeoning market of a third world nation?

   - ❑ A. Legislative risk
   - ❑ B. Sovereign risk
   - ❑ C. Reinvestment risk
   - ❑ D. Liquidity risk

8. Which statement best describes the importance of a stock's beta?

   - ❑ A. Beta is a measure of a stock's return to fluctuations in the market
   - ❑ B. Beta is a measure of a stock's return compared to other stocks of the same industry
   - ❑ C. Beta is a measure of a stock's return due to legislative risk
   - ❑ D. Beta is a measure of a stock's return due to its own volatility

9. What is *the one* most important responsibility of a broker when building a client's portfolio?
   - ❑ A. Learning the client's name, address, and phone number
   - ❑ B. Learning the names of the client's wife and children
   - ❑ C. Learning the client's golf score
   - ❑ D. Learning the client's financial capabilities and investment goals

10. What is the Capital Asset Pricing Model, or CAPM?
    - ❑ A. The expected return on a security is equal to the rate on a risk-free security plus a risk premium
    - ❑ B. The additional return required by investors for investing in longer term Treasury bonds
    - ❑ C. The extra return that investors want when purchasing risky securities
    - ❑ D. The fluctuations in a market index.

11. Joe buys 100 shares of Parkmont, Inc., a trucking company, for $50 a share. Six months later the market takes a downturn bringing the value of Joe's shares to $25 a share. In spite of the economy, Parkmont managed to make a small profit. Their share price still plummeted. This is an example of:
    - ❑ A. Unique risk
    - ❑ B. Market risk
    - ❑ C. Sovereign risk
    - ❑ D. Nonsystematic risk

12. What constitutes the statistical measure of the volatility of a security?

    I. Variance

    II. Standard deviation of returns

    III. Risk premium

    IV. Unique risk

    - ❑ A. I only
    - ❑ B. III only
    - ❑ C. I and II
    - ❑ D. III and IV

13. What is variance and what does it tell investors about risk?
    - ❑ A. Variance is the percentage of inherent risk of a stock that tells investors the level of risk of a stock
    - ❑ B. Variance is the difference between normal interest rate and premium rate that tells investors the expected percentage of risk of a stock
    - ❑ C Variance is the difference between inherent risk and risk-free returns that tells investors the risk return of a stock
    - ❑ D. Variance is the degree to which a stock's risk deviates from the average, such as Standard & Poor's Index.

14. D & K Sutherland and Bridges & Sons are both manufacturers of diving equipment. For the last five years, the stocks of these companies have yielded the following returns to investors; which is the better recommendation for a cautious investor?

Sutherland	Bridges
10%	18%
17%	7%
8%	16%
16%	8%
9%	11%

- ❑ A. Sutherland
- ❑ B. Bridges
- ❑ C. Both Sutherland and Bridges
- ❑ D. Neither of them

15. Astare Formal Wear, Inc., stock has an expected return of 24%. Treasury bill rates are currently at 6%. The risk premium for the market portfolio for the previous ten years has been 9%. What is Astare's beta? Is Astare stock likely to be part of an aggressive portfolio or a defensive one?

- ❑ A. 1.0, defensive
- ❑ B. 2.0, not defensive, but mildly aggressive
- ❑ C. 3.0, aggressive
- ❑ D. 4.0, very aggressive

Exam Prep Answers

1. The correct answer is B. The risk free rate of return in the United States is the interest rate on T-Bill offerings brought forth by the Federal Reserve Bank. T-bills are considered to be risk free because they are backed by the U.S. government and because they are short-term. Investors don't have to worry about interest rate risk as they would with longer term investments.
2. The correct answer is A. The risk-return tradeoff refers to choosing one investment over another for its degree of risk on the expected return. That is why T-bills are considered the risk-free rate of return in the market because of the short maturity with no inherent risk. While T-Bonds offer some degree of safety, they have maturity risk because they are long-term investments. So investors must decide which level of risk and return they want from their investments. It's a matter of trading off one quality for another with full understanding of what each type of risk offers.
3. The correct answer is B. Systematic risk, also known as market risk, is the risk in which a downturn in the economy might negatively affect the securities of an individual issuer, regardless of the performance of the issuing company.
4. The correct answer is C. Market risk is considered nondiversifiable because it is the market economy that affects the price of securities and stocks; an often unavoidable occurrence. It is also known as systematic risk. Diversifiable risk, or nonsystematic risk, is associated strictly with the issuing company and not the market.
5. The correct answer is A: A stock with a beta of 3 would have an overall volatility that is three times the average movement. It will also increase by 3%. For instance, if the market portfolio increased by 1%, then the stock with a beta of 3 would increase three times the market increase, or 3%. It is stocks with betas of less than 1 that move against the market, or negatively.
6. The correct answer is B. U.S. tax laws can change to affect the overall rate of return on a security. DPPs are especially prone to be affected by changes in the laws; as an example, business taxes could have an adverse affect on profitability or a change to investing in a DPP could seriously affect a DPPs ability to stay in business.
7. The correct answer is B. Sovereign risk would be the greatest inherent risk to an investor of a security in a third world nation. Political instability, nationalizing of business and broken government guarantees can all adversely affect the investment.

8. The correct answer is A. A stock's beta measures its sensitivity to changes in the market, not to other stocks in that industry, to legislative risk, or to its own volatility. These last three choices might to some extent play a role in market fluctuations, but the Beta is primarily how a stock behaves in comparison to the market as a whole.
9. The correct answer is D. It is of the utmost importance to learn and understand the client's investment goals and financial capability to invest. This is known as the "Know Your Customer" rule; it is one rule a broker should *never* forget. Knowing investment goals and the financial ability to reach those goals helps a broker dealer to recommend the right investments for each client. A broker dealer should never recommend an investment that the client is unable to afford, manage, or understand.
10. The correct answer is A. CAPM or capital asset pricing model, says that the expected return on a security is equal to the rate on a risk-free security plus a risk premium. The idea behind CAPM is that investors need to be compensated in two ways: time value of money and risk. The time value of money is represented by the risk-free (rf) rate in the formula and compensates the investors for placing money in any investment over a period of time. The other half of the formula represents risk and calculates the amount of compensation the investor needs for taking on additional risk. This is calculated by taking a risk measure (beta), which compares the returns of the asset to the market over a period of time and compares it to the market premium (Rm-rf).
11. The correct answer is B. Market risk, or systematic risk, is the reason for the drop in the share price of Parkmont, Inc. Even though the business was well enough to make a small profit during an economic downturn, they had no control over the factors affecting their share price. The opposite, nonsystematic risk, would have been unique to the managers and their ability to make a profit. Even if the market was up, Parkmont shares would drop in value if it was poorly managed.
12. The correct answer is C. The statistical measure of the volatility of a security is a calculation with variance and standard deviation of returns for the percentage of volatility of a stock. Calculate the variance, take its square root, and this percentage is the inherent risk of a security. The higher the deviation, the greater the inherent risk because actual returns tend to vary from the expected return. Risk premium is the extra return over the risk-free return when investing in risky securities, and unique risk is nonsystematic risk or risk that is specific to a company.

13. The correct answer is D. Variance is a measure of the volatility of a stock to its average volatility over a given time period. In the example from the chapter, we determined the probabilities of how often heads come up with four flips of a coin. In order to determine the average level of risk, the variance depends on the standard deviation of returns. Taking the square root of 800, our variance number from the game, we arrived at a percentage of risk. This can translate to stocks and the investor's level of risk and rate of expected returns. The larger the standard deviation, the greater the inherent risk. This is because actual returns tend to vary more widely from the expected return. While the variance and deviation calculations give an inherent risk factor for a stock, it is not how you measure variance but more the end result of the calculation.
14. The correct answer is A. The expected, or average, return for both stocks is 12%. Bridges stock, however, is the more variable of the two, as shown by the following variance and standard deviation calculations. Remember, the calculation is: find the mean of the five years of returns, and then subtract each year's return from the mean, and that is the deviation. Then square each deviation, then take the square root of sum of the squared deviations. This gives you the percent of risk, in this case 8.4% for Sutherland and 9.7% for Bridges. The variance is the sum of the squared deviations; 70 for Sutherland and 94 for Bridges. Example for Sutherland:

    Sutherland mean is 12%; 12 – 10 = –2. and so on for each year

    First year deviation = –2. First year deviation squared = 4.

    Sum of the squared deviations = 70 = variance

    Square root of variance is $\sqrt{70}$ = 8.4%

Sutherland		
Rate of Return	Deviation from Exp. Return	Squared Deviation
10%	–2	4
17%	+5	25
8%	–4	16
16%	+4	16
9%	–3	9
Variance = 70	Standard Deviation = 8.5% (70)	

Bridges		
Rate of Return	Deviation from Exp. Return	Squared Deviation
18%	+6	36
7%	–5	25
16%	+4	16
8%	–4	16
11%	–1	1
Variance = 94	Standard Deviation = 9.7% (94)	

So, Sutherland stock, with its lower standard deviation, is a better recommendation for a cautious investor.

15. The correct answer is B. Using the capital asset pricing model, Astare's beta is:

$$r = r(f) + \beta\,(r(m) - r(f))$$

$$24 = 6 + \beta(9)$$

$$18 = \beta(9)$$

$$\beta = 2.0$$

Remember, r = the expected rate of return

f = risk-free rate (return on T-bills)

β = beta (factor unique to the given stock)

R (m) = return on the market portfolio (usually the S&P's 500)

(r(m) – r(f) = CAPM, represents the risk premium, representing the difference between the return on a market portfolio and the risk-free return.

Thus, an investor's expected return on the stock should equal the risk-free rate plus a risk premium multiplied by a stock's beta. Remember, a risk premium is the excess return required by investors for assuming higher risk. With a beta of 2.0, Astare stock is more sensitive to fluctuations in the market portfolio than stock with a beta of 1.0. Its price, therefore, will probably vary somewhat, presenting investors with a greater degree of risk. Astare would probably be part of an aggressive portfolio because of its higher risk.

Macroeconomics

Terms You Need to Know

- ✓ Balance of payments
- ✓ Business cycle
- ✓ Capital account
- ✓ Coincident indicators
- ✓ Conference Board
- ✓ Consumer price index (CPI)
- ✓ Cost-push inflation
- ✓ Credit multiplier
- ✓ Current account
- ✓ Deflation
- ✓ Demand deposits
- ✓ Demand-pull inflation
- ✓ Depression
- ✓ Discount rate
- ✓ Disintermediation
- ✓ Economic indicators
- ✓ Emerging markets
- ✓ Federal funds (or Fed funds)
- ✓ Federal funds rate (or Fed funds rate)
- ✓ Federal Open Market Committee (FOMC)
- ✓ Federal Reserve Board
- ✓ Federal Reserve System (the Fed)
- ✓ Fiscal policy
- ✓ Globalization
- ✓ Gross domestic product (GDP)
- ✓ Gross national product (GNP)
- ✓ Inflation
- ✓ Intermediation
- ✓ Keynesian economics
- ✓ Lagging indicators
- ✓ Leading indicators
- ✓ Matched sale (or match)
- ✓ Monetarist economics
- ✓ Monetary policy
- ✓ Money supply
- ✓ Open market desk
- ✓ Open market operations
- ✓ Recession
- ✓ Reserve requirement
- ✓ Stagflation
- ✓ Time deposits
- ✓ Velocity of money

Concepts You Need to Understand

- ✓ Why investors care about the state of the economy
- ✓ What the business cycle is
- ✓ What economic indicators are
- ✓ Why inflation occurs
- ✓ How the Federal Reserve System controls the money supply
- ✓ What effect the money supply has on prices and interest rates
- ✓ How changing interest rates influence the value of investments
- ✓ How economic problems in one country affect other countries
- ✓ Why international investment is increasing
- ✓ What factors determine exchange rates

The Economy

Financial markets are only one part of a much larger economic system. The prices of stocks, bonds, and other investment products depend in large part on broad economic forces at work in the national and global economies. For this reason, investors should be acquainted with *macroeconomics*, the study of the economy as a whole. Macroeconomics focuses on factors that affect all economic activity within a country, such as inflation, interest rates, investment, and unemployment. Investors need to monitor these and other important macroeconomic indicators, adjusting their investment decisions in accordance with their expectations about the future health of the economy. This brief overview of macroeconomics provides the foundation needed for examining fundamental and technical analyses, which are covered in the following two chapters.

The value of any investment depends on a wide range of factors, including the state of the economy. Stock prices, for example, generally depend on the level of corporate profits—or their expected level in the near future. If the economy as a whole is growing at a fast pace, corporate profits should be rising, and stock prices generally rise with them. Bond prices, on the other hand, depend to a large degree on the level of interest rates and inflation (or their expected levels). During periods of slow economic growth, when interest rates and inflation are normally low, bond prices typically climb.

Many people and financial institutions try to anticipate the future state of the economy in order to adjust their investment strategies, and for this reason markets respond quickly to important economic news. Investors keep a close eye on a wide range of measurements of the economy's health, but the single most important measure is the growth rate of gross domestic product.

Gross Domestic Product

Gross domestic product (GDP) is the total value of all consumer goods and services produced within a country during a given period (usually one year). It adds together all consumer spending, government spending, investments, and net exports to find the total amount of money spent on goods and services. In 2004, for example, the GDP of the United States was about $11.75 trillion, as Table 29.1 shows. This means that the prices of all consumer goods and services produced within the United States during that year added up to $11.75 trillion.

Table 29.1 Five Largest Economies in 2004

Country	GDP (Trillions of Dollars)
United States	$11,750
China	$7,262
Japan	$3,745
India	$3,319
Germany	$2,362

Another measure of national output is *gross national product (GNP)*. GNP includes all the goods and services produced by the residents and companies of a country. Unlike GDP, it does not count goods or services produced within a country by foreign companies, but it does count goods and services produced abroad by domestic companies. Thus, the product sales of an American-owned computer factory in Ireland count toward U.S. gross *national* product, but not toward U.S. gross *domestic* product.

The Business Cycle

The rise and fall of the GDP growth rate over time is known as the *business cycle*. Looking at a graph of a country's GDP growth for a number of years, one normally sees a pattern of "hills" and "valleys," corresponding to the expansion and contraction of business activity. Individual firms, of course, can prosper or fail at any time, but economies show systematic patterns of behavior in the long run. Out of the welter of individual cases, general trends emerge. During certain periods, the nation's economic production increases—businesses do well and GDP increases at a relatively high rate. During other periods, however, economic production decreases—businesses generally do poorly and GDP growth slows or often declines.

The GDP growth rate is compared to the *change* in the inflation rate and the *change* in the unemployment rate. In 2004, for example, the GDP increased at a rate of about 4.2%. At the same time, the inflation rate increased only 1.4%, and the unemployment rate was 5.5%. Putting the data in this form—rates of change—is useful for comparison's sake. Figure 29.2 shows how these numbers have changed in just three years.

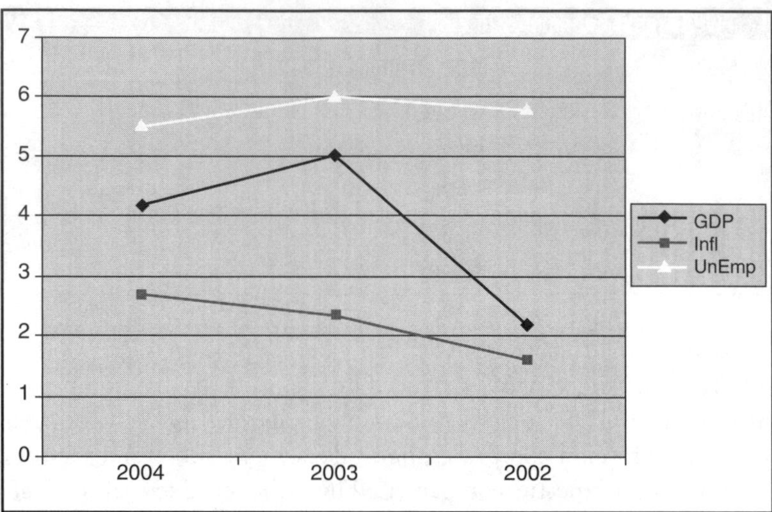

Figure 29.1 GDP comparisons.

Figure 29.1 illustrates the relationship between GDP growth, interest rates, stock prices (shown as NASDAQ composite index), and bond yields. Like the previous one, it shows the rate of change for each variable. In 1999, for example, when GDP was increasing, stock prices and interest rates rose sharply, while long-term bond yields were fairly flat. The graph demonstrates how changes in GDP growth relate to changes in the value of investments. Figure 29.2 shows the changes over a five-year period.

The timing and length of every business cycle is different. Nevertheless, all business cycles do tend to share certain characteristics. Each has five distinct stages. Following is a descriptive outline of an enormously complex series of events, the individual components of which can vary greatly from one cycle to the next.

The five stages of a business cycle is complex but one of the most important concepts a broker dealer needs to understand.

1. *Early expansion*—During this phase, the production of goods and services increases rapidly. Interest rates and inflation are generally low, and, as consumer confidence about the economy rises, people begin to borrow and spend more. Businesses invest to meet growing demand. More workers are added to payrolls, and unemployment decreases. Corporate profits rise, as do stock prices. Bond prices might begin to fall in expectation of higher interest rates and inflation.

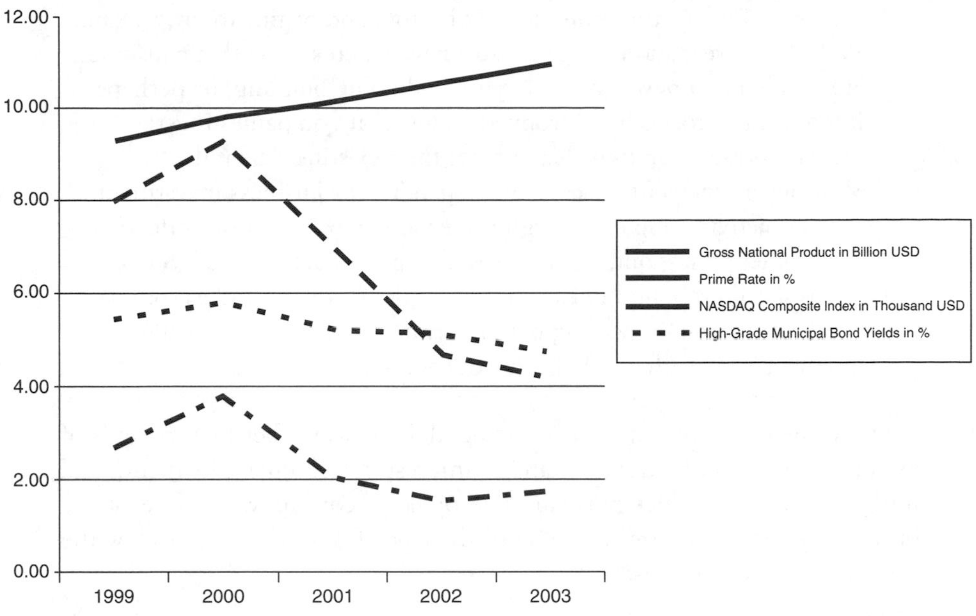

Figure 29.2 GDP comparison over a five-year span.

2. *Late expansion*—As the economy continues to expand, gradually nearing full production capacity, consumer demand might outstrip the supply of goods and services, causing prices to inch upward. Heavy borrowing to finance the expansion can also lead to hikes in interest rates. Stock prices continue to rise because corporate profits remain high. Bond prices often fall due to mounting inflation and interest rates (or the expectation of them).

3. *Peak*—At a certain point, the economy's growth rate reaches a maximum and begins to drop off. Often this peak arrives with a fall in consumer confidence—which might be triggered by higher interest or mortgage rates—and reduced capital spending by businesses.

4. *Recession*—Consumer demand continues to fall, as do business production and employment. When the GDP has contracted for two consecutive quarters, the nation has officially entered a *recession*. Higher unemployment reduces consumer demand, and eventually inflation should fall. Because businesses and consumers are not spending as much, they require less credit from lending institutions, thus leading to a drop in interest rates. Stock prices continue to decline, while bond prices rise. If the downturn continues for 18 months or more, the economy is said to be in a *depression*.

5. *Recovery*—Finally, the economy hits bottom and begins to grow again. Perhaps interest and mortgage rates have fallen so low that consumers are spurred to a new wave of buying and home building, or perhaps business inventories have dropped so low that companies must increase production in order to meet their existing demand. Whichever comes first—consumer spending or business investment—the new activity ripples through the economy with positive effect: employment rises, output increases, and profits are boosted. Stock prices should rebound in expectation of the recovery, and as soon as corporations start reporting better earnings, stock markets will get a powerful boost. The cycle begins once more.

Thus, as the economy experiences its pendulum swings between periods of expansion and contraction, inflation, interest rates, unemployment, and other economic variables normally rise or fall accordingly. Because of the business cycle's impact on the value of their portfolios, investors follow the process with great interest.

Although the contours of the business cycle are often clear with the benefit of hindsight, even the experts find it extremely difficult to predict the timing of future turning points. Investors do the best they can by paying attention to the movement of key economic indicators.

Economic Indicators

Economic indicators are statistical numbers that describe changes in specific sectors of the economy. They are signposts that provide information about the current state of the economy and its future direction. If the government announces, for example, that industrial production is at record-high levels, an investor knows the economy is expanding rapidly, and corporate earnings should be healthy. If, six months later, newspapers report that consumer confidence is faltering, this might be seen as an early indicator that the economy is nearing its peak. Economic indicators track critical information in a wide range of areas, from industrial production, employment, and business inventories, to consumer confidence and inflation. The *Conference Board*, an independent economic research organization, publishes a report each month on the status of the most important indicators. Indicators are divided into three categories—leading, coincident, and lagging. Each category contains a number of indicators that are combined to create a single index value.

Economic indicators are signposts to the current state of the economy and its future direction. Know what the indicators are and how to recognize them.

Leading indicators, listed in Table 29.2, tend to change *before* the economy as a whole changes.

Table 29.2 Leading Indicators of Economic Change

Leading Indicators	Explanation
Average work week of production workers in manufacturing	This number usually changes before factories increase or decrease their work force, and therefore gives an indication of future levels of employment.
Average initial weekly claims for state unemployment insurance	Initial unemployment claims change before total employment changes.
New orders for consumer goods and materials	These orders lead to changes in the production of consumer goods in the near future.
Vendor performance (companies receiving slower deliveries from suppliers)	Slowdowns in deliveries usually mean an increase in demand for manufacturing supplies, which precedes increases in production.
New orders for nonmilitary capital goods	These orders indicate changes in industrial production in the near future.
New building permits issued	Construction activity typically leads to other types of economic production.
Standard & Poor's 500 Stock Index	Investors try to anticipate economic changes, often buying or selling stocks on the basis of companies' projected earnings.
Money supply (M2)	Changes in the money supply indicate that the Federal Reserve Bank is attempting to stimulate growth or counteract inflation.
Spread between yield on 10-year Treasury bonds and the Federal funds rate	A steeper yield curve implies a more rapid growth rate for the economy.
Index of consumer expectations	Because consumer spending represents approximately two-thirds of GDP, people's expectations about how much they intend to spend in the coming year are an important sign of the health of the economy.

Coincident indicators, listed in Table 29.3, describe the *current* state of the economy.

Table 29.3 Coincident Economic Indicators

Coincident Indicators	Explanation
Employees on nonagricultural payrolls	Changes in total employment directly measure a key facet of the nation's economic health.
Personal income minus transfer payments (government entitlementprograms, such as Social Security)	This measures how much consumers have to spend (subtracting transfer payments avoids double-counting that portion of income, which is deducted from gross salaries under the Federal Insurance Contributions Act, or FICA).
Industrial production	This indicator is closely tied to total economic output.
Manufacturing and trade sales	Sales volume measures the economy's business activity.

Lagging indicators, listed in Table 29.4, tend to change *after* the economy has already moved into a new phase.

Table 29.4 Lagging Economic Indicators

Lagging Indicators	Explanation
Average duration of unemployment	Decreases in the length of unemployment usually occur after an expansion gains strength; increases tend to occur after a recession has begun.
Ratio of inventories to sales in manufacturing and trade	Inventories normally increase when the economy slows and corporate sales fail to meet projections. Inventories should decline at the beginning of an expansion, when businesses meet new demand with goods in inventory.
Labor cost per unit of output in manufacturing	Normally, this number peaks during recessions, when output is declining faster than labor costs.
Average prime interest rate	Changes in this interest rate tend to lag behind general economic activities because banks take time to recognize and adjust to new economic conditions.
Commercial and industrial loans	The number of new loans should peak after an expansion peaks, for declining profits continue to boost the demand for loans for a while.

(continued)

Table 29.4 Lagging Economic Indicators *(continued)*

Lagging Indicators	Explanation
Ratio of consumer installment credit to personal income	Consumers tend to hold off new personal borrowing with credit cards until a few months after a recession ends. Conversely, they might continue to build up their installment credit for several months after the economy has peaked.
Consumer price index for services	Service sector inflation normally increases in the initial months of a recession and decreases in the initial months of an expansion.

One of the most closely monitored economic indicators, because of its ramifications for consumers as well as investors, is inflation.

Inflation

Inflation is a general increase in prices for goods and services. For example, in 1968 a gallon of gasoline cost about $0.40, but in 2005 the same gallon cost about $2.50. Inflation therefore represents a decline in the value of money. One dollar in 2005 bought less than one dollar did in 1995. The standard measure of inflation is the *consumer price index (CPI)*, which is based on the current prices of a representative group of consumer goods and services, including food and beverages, transportation, housing, utilities, clothing, medical care, and entertainment. The total price of this basket of goods and services during an arbitrary period in the past (1982–1984) has been given a base value of 100; hence, the current index number describes how prices have changed since the base period. For instance, in 2004, the CPI was 103.4, showing that prices had increased by 3.4% since the early 1980s. If the collection of consumer goods cost $1,200 in the base period, it cost $1,240.80 in 2004 ($1,200 × 1.034 = $1,240.80). Because inflation affects all prices to different degrees, the CPI represents an average rate of inflation. That is, if the CPI is up 3.4 from last year, prices *in general* have risen 3.4%, although individual prices might have risen by different amounts.

How Inflation Affects Investments

Because inflation represents a change in the value of money, it can have important effects on the value of investments. Bonds, for example, generally pay a fixed rate of interest (the coupon). In an inflationary period, the fixed dollar amount of bond payments declines in value.

EXAMPLE: James has just purchased a new 30-year Treasury bond with a face value of $10,000 and a coupon rate of 8¾ %. He will receive coupon payments of $875 annually for 30 years. However, the purchasing power of the interest payment changes because of inflation, which is now at about 5%. If inflation stays constant, his coupon payment next year will be worth only $831.25 (0.05 × $875 = $43.75; $875 – $43.75 = $831.25). The dollar amount of the payment remains the same, of course, but it will purchase 5% less in the economy. Inflation also affects the value of the principal. If inflation averages 5% over the life of the bond, its principal at maturity will be worth only $2,146.39 in James's original dollars.

Because inflation pushes down the value of the coupon payments and the principal, the prices of existing bonds fall during inflationary periods. New bonds are issued with higher coupon rates to compensate for the inflation, thus exerting further downward pressure on existing bond prices. During periods of declining inflation, bond prices tend to rise.

Remember that bond prices and bond yields move in opposite directions.

Although inflation affects the value of stock holdings as well, the relationship between inflation and equity securities is more complicated. Because inflation often occurs during periods of business expansion, stock prices tend to rise at the same time that inflation occurs.

Why Inflation Occurs

Two main schools of economic thought have attempted to explain inflation. One emphasizes the forces of supply and demand in the productive sphere of the economy, the other looks at the expansion and contraction of the money supply. Take the case of economic production. If the demand for goods and services exceeds their supply for a lengthy period, prices will probably rise, because buyers compete for increasingly scarce resources. This can occur in one of two scenarios: dwindling supplies or surging demand. *Cost-push inflation* occurs when businesses attempt to expand production more quickly than the supply of inputs can be increased. When bottlenecks appear, business costs increase. Whenever possible, the higher production costs are passed on to consumers in the form of higher prices. *Demand-pull inflation*, on the other hand, occurs when consumer demand increases more quickly than businesses can expand. Here, prices rise because consumers find themselves with extra disposable income and are willing to pay more for goods and services. Cost-push and demand-pull inflation are most likely to occur during the late expansionary phase and peak of the business cycle. During these stages, consumer demand is increasing, and businesses are trying to increase production.

An alternative explanation of inflation is that the money supply is the key determinant. (The components of the money supply are explained later in this chapter.) If the money supply expands at a faster pace than the rest of the economy, the supply of money exceeds the demand for money. Like any other commodity, its "price" will fall. If money is less valuable, then it takes more money to purchase the same goods, and prices rise. Conversely, if the supply of money increases more slowly than does its demand, the value of money should rise. Now it takes fewer dollars to purchase the same goods, and prices fall. This is known as *deflation*.

Economists and politicians assume that the people, companies, markets, and institutions that compose the modern economy function together in some systematic manner. The challenge is to identify the rules of the system, the key factors that contribute to economic change, and also the proper role for government in promoting a healthy economy. Throughout a succession of schools of economic thought in the years since the second World War, the United States government has employed a range of tools and policies to manage the economy. Both fiscal and monetary policies are important.

Fiscal Policies

A nation's *fiscal policy* is the sum of its taxation and spending programs. After studying the business cycle and the Great Depression, British economist John Maynard Keynes proposed that recessions were caused by insufficient private demand, which could be combated with increased government spending. Inflation, he thought, was caused by excessive demand resulting from economic booms, and could be cured with increased taxation. In very general terms, then, Keynes and his disciples argued for greater government spending during economic downturns, and higher levels of taxation during expansions. This approach is known as *Keynesian economics*.

Keynesian economic theory says that greater government spending is needed during economic downturns and that higher levels of taxation are called for during times of expansion.

Monetary Policies

Monetary policy is the combination of tools used by a country to control its money supply, and thus its economic growth. The school of *monetarist economics* began to gain new adherents in the 1970s with the appearance of *stagflation*, for which there seemed to be no appropriate fiscal response. The economy was faltering, which seemed to call for increased government spending, but at the same time inflation was picking up speed—apparently precluding any added public sector stimulus. Monetarists eschewed fiscal policy in favor of monetary policy, hoping to maintain a steady money supply, low inflation, and favorable interest rates.

Fiscal policy is set by Congress and the president through decisions about taxes and government spending. Because government spending makes up about one-fifth of GDP, the government wields a great deal of power in stimulating or dampening economic activity. Moreover, through its control of taxation, the government can influence the amount and direction of consumer spending. If taxes are reduced, consumers tend to spend more; if taxes are increased, people tend to spend less. And through targeted tax breaks (such as those on home mortgages or retirement investment accounts), the government can encourage consumer spending or investment in particular areas. Fiscal policy, however, is relatively slow to change, for it is inextricably bound up with politics and vested interests. Monetary policy, set by the Federal Reserve Board, may therefore be more important for the economy's short-term and medium-term outlook.

The Federal Reserve System

The *Federal Reserve System (the Fed)* functions as the central bank of the United States. It is made up of a network of 12 regional Federal Reserve banks, 24 branches, and numerous member banks, all under the supervision of the *Federal Reserve Board*, which formulates and executes monetary policy for the nation. The board consists of a chairman and six governors, each appointed by the president and confirmed by the Senate. The governors are appointed for terms of 14 years to ensure their independence from political influence. The Fed controls the money supply and supervises and regulates commercial banking, while serving as the bank for the U.S. government. The policies of the Fed have immediate and far-reaching economic effects, and for that reason it is closely watched by investors the world over.

The Federal Reserve System, known as the Fed, is the central bank of the United States It comprises 12 regional banks, 24 branches, and numerous member banks under the supervision of the Federal Reserve Board, or FRB. The board formulates and executes monetary policy for the nation.

In order to understand how the Fed manipulates the supply of money and credit, it is first necessary to look at the different components of the money supply.

The Money Supply

The *money supply* includes the currency we use every day—the actual bills and coins—as well as deposits in checking accounts, savings accounts, and money market accounts—even Treasury debt securities and Eurodollars. Each of these instruments can be used as money with different degrees of ease. It is easier, for example, to spend a dollar in one's wallet than a dollar that is currently held in a savings account. For this reason, the money supply is divided into a number of different categories. The most liquid portion of the money supply (the most easily spendable part) is called M1. It includes all currency in circulation, plus all demand deposits. *Demand deposits* are deposits at banks that can be drawn on at any time without previous notice. Checking accounts, from which payments can be made directly, represent demand deposits. The next most liquid measure of the money supply is M2, which includes all the money in M1, and time deposits of less than $100,000. *Time deposits* are bank deposits that are left for a specific amount of time in return for interest payments. Savings accounts and certificates of deposit (CDs) are good examples; money must be withdrawn from them before it can be spent, and there is often a penalty for early withdrawals. Other categories of the money supply include less accessible forms of money.

Measures of the Money Supply

M1 = Currency in circulation + demand deposits + traveler's checks

M2 = M1 + time deposits of less than $100,000 + personal balances in money market accounts + overnight repurchase agreements + overnight Eurodollars

M3 = M2 + time deposits of more than $100,000 + money market balances held by institutions + term repurchase agreements

L = M3 + Treasury bills + savings bonds + commercial paper + banker's acceptances + term Eurodollars held by U.S. residents

In the immediate term, the value of money is determined by supply and demand. If the supply of money is larger than the current demand, the value of money should drop. If the situation persists, prices and interest rates start to climb. On the other hand, if the supply shrinks relative to demand, the value of money should rise, leading to lower prices and interest rates. The Fed has a number of tools to increase or decrease the money supply and thus control inflation and interest rates. One of the most powerful implements at its disposal is the capability to set reserve requirements.

Reserve Requirements

Reserve requirements are the mandated level of deposits that a bank must keep on hand (either in its own vault or with a Federal Reserve bank). Money that meets a bank's reserve requirement cannot be loaned out or invested. Banks, of course, earn their profits by taking in customer deposits, on which they pay interest, and then using those deposits to make loans or investments that earn higher rates of interest. But banks cannot use all their deposits—the Fed demands that a certain portion be reserved for depositors to withdraw on short notice. By lowering the reserve requirement, the Fed can increase the amount of money banks can lend, thereby increasing the supply of money in the economy. Conversely, by raising the reserve requirement, the Fed can decrease the amount of money banks are able to lend, and so shrink the country's supply of money.

The influence of any shift in reserve requirements is increased by the credit multiplier.

The Credit Multiplier

The *credit multiplier* is the degree to which an original bank deposit is magnified when the money is re-lent by the bank and redeposited in other banks, which can then loan a portion of the same money out again, and so forth. Through this process of lending and re-lending, a single small deposit can lead to a large amount of new credit and new spending. (The multiplier effect also means that relatively minor adjustments to the reserve requirement can have large consequences, so the Fed is careful not to overuse this tool.)

> **EXAMPLE:** Joe receives a $20,000 inheritance from a long-lost uncle, which he deposits in his checking account at Echo Bank. Because the reserve requirement is set at 10%, Echo must keep $2,000 of Joe's deposit on hand, but it can now make a car loan of $18,000 to Nicole. She pays the car dealer, and the dealer deposits the money in its corporate account at Orion Bank. Orion in turn must keep 10% on reserve, so it can loan out the remaining $16,200. Kent borrows the $16,200 from Orion to pay his

tuition bill at Prestigious University, which deposits this money in its account at Midville Bank. Midville holds $1,620 in reserve, and loans out the remaining $14,580 to Joanne who wants to remodel her kitchen. If economic conditions are just right, this process can continue until there is no money left to lend. The result is that Joe's original $20,000 deposit might create $200,000 in new spending ($18,000 + $16,200 + $14,580 + __ = $200,000). You can determine the multiplier by diving 100% by the reserve requirement. In this case the multiplier is 10 (100% ÷ 10% = 10), so a given deposit leads to 10 times as much money. Suppose that the Fed lowered the reserve requirement to 8%. Now a $20,000 deposit can lead to $250,000 in new spending (100% ÷ 8% = 12.5; 12.5 × $20,000 = $250,000).

In any period, the credit multiplier is affected by economic conditions. Consider two important factors. First, how quickly do people deposit, use, and redeposit money? This is known as the *velocity of money*—the number of times that a dollar is spent in a given period—and it varies with the health of the economy. When the economy is booming, money is spent faster, and banks make loans more quickly, increasing the availability of money. The second factor to keep in mind is the degree to which people put their money into banks rather than directly into investments such as stocks and mutual funds. Depositing money in banks is known as *intermediation* because banks serve as intermediaries between depositors and borrowers. The level of intermediation depends largely on the difference between bank interest rates and the returns available from other investments. If bank rates compare unfavorably, investors move their money out of banks, a process known as *disintermediation.* If intermediation is greater than disintermediation, the credit multiplier's effect should strengthen.

In addition to lending to individuals, banks with funds in excess of reserve requirements can invest them or lend them to other banks.

Federal Funds

Federal funds (or *Fed funds*) are the short-term loans (usually overnight) made between banks to meet the reserve requirement. The rate at which the funds are lent, known as the *Federal funds rate* (or *Fed funds rate*), is determined by the supply of and demand for this overnight money. However, the Fed establishes a target Fed funds rate and attempts to increase or decrease the money supply by the amount necessary to move the actual rate closer to this target rate. (This process is reviewed later in this chapter.)

The Fed can further influence the money supply by changing the discount rate.

Discount Rate

The *discount rate* is the rate at which the Fed itself loans money to banks that are members of the Federal Reserve System. The Fed considers this borrowing a privilege, not a right, and enables banks to borrow at its "discount window" only if they have exhausted all other market sources. Banks can borrow only limited amounts at the discount window, but they enjoy the lowest interest rate available in the economy. Changes in the discount rate are far-reaching, because banks generally set their own rates at a level above the discount rate—when the Fed moves the discount rate, commercial banks follow suit. By raising or lowering the rate, the Fed thus influences how easy it is for all businesses to borrow money. Adjusting the discount rate sends a strong signal to the marketplace about the Fed's current view of the economy and the direction of monetary policy. The Fed uses such adjustments relatively infrequently, compared to its other monetary tools.

Changing reserve requirements or the discount rate has such a strong economic impact that the Fed rarely uses these tools. On a day-to-day basis, the Fed's most effective means to control the money supply is to operate in the open market.

The Fed's most effective means of controlling the money supply on a day-to-day basis is to operate in the open market.

Open Market Operations

In what are called *open market operations*, the Federal Reserve Bank of New York buys and sells Treasury securities. The *Federal Open Market Committee (FOMC)* supervises the procedure, which takes place at the bank's *open market desk*. Each business day, the Fed engages in purchases or sales of Treasury securities with primary dealers in order to fine-tune the money supply and move the Fed funds rate toward its target. Usually, the transactions are for a limited time only.

With a *repurchase agreement* (or *repo*), the Fed buys Treasury securities from a primary dealer, agreeing to sell them back within a short period of time at a set price. In doing so, the Fed temporarily injects money into the banking system. Primary dealers deposit the dollars paid by the Fed into their bank accounts, increasing the amount of money banks have to make new overnight loans. Conversely, the Fed can *sell* Treasury securities to a primary dealer, agreeing to buy them back within a short period of time. This is known as a *reverse repurchase agreement* (or, most commonly, a *matched sale*).

In a matched sale, the primary dealer must withdraw funds from its bank account to purchase the Treasury securities, leaving the banking system with less money to lend overnight.

Repo Versus Reverse Repo

Remember that the terminology of open market operations can be confusing. The difference between a repo and a reverse repo is, after all, one of perspective. When the transaction takes place between a primary dealer and the Fed, the standard practice is to assume the perspective of the *dealer.* Hence, in a repo, the dealer is initially selling securities and receiving cash, and will later repurchase the same securities. In a reverse repo (what the Fed calls a matched sale), the dealer is initially buying securities and spending cash, and will later resell them.

Open market operations are a useful way to temporarily adjust the money supply and thereby influence short-term interest rates. After a repo, for example, money has been taken out of the banking system, and banks must work harder to meet their reserve requirements. The Federal funds rate will tend to increase, moving closer to the Fed's target.

Deciding How to Influence the Economy

The Fed intends to use its tools—open market operations, the Fed funds rate, the discount rate, and reserve requirements—to guide the national economy smoothly through the business cycle. The Fed's directors and chairman closely study a range of economic indicators, and then respond in a way that they believe will maintain growth and keep inflation in check. If the economy looks as if it is growing too quickly and inflation is about to accelerate, the Fed might raise interest rates. In theory, this will dampen the rate of growth, enabling the expansion to continue with stable prices for a while longer. On the other hand, if the economy is in recession, the Fed can lower interest rates in an effort to spur new borrowing and investment, which will lead to renewed growth. Table 29.5 shows the effect of a Fed action and the consequences.

Table 29.5 Fed Actions and Consequences

Action	Immediate Effect	Intended Economic Consequence
Matched sale	Lower banks' reserves	Boost the Fed funds rate
Repurchase agreement	Increase banks' reserves	Lower the Fed funds rate

(continues)

Table 29.5 Fed Actions and Consequences *(continued)*

Action	Immediate Effect	Intended Economic Consequence
Raise Fed funds target rate	Increase the cost of overnight borrowing by banks	Decrease bank lending, slow the economy
Lower Fed funds target rate	Decrease the cost of overnight borrowing by banks	Stimulate the economy
Raise discount rate	Increase the cost of borrowing throughout the economy	Slow the pace of economic activity
Lower discount rate	Decrease the cost of borrowing throughout the economy	Stimulate the economy
Raise reserve requirement	Decrease bank lending (lower the credit multiplier)	Brake the economy
Lower reserve requirement	Boost bank lending (raise the credit multiplier)	Accelerate economic activity

The Global Economy

No economy stands alone—all countries depend to some degree on international trade and global financial markets. As a result, an economic downturn—or upturn—in one country can have critical consequences in trading partners halfway around the globe. Events overseas can also change the value of an investor's portfolio with astonishing—and often dismaying—ease. Many investors now hold foreign stocks and bonds, either directly or indirectly, through vehicles such as mutual funds. Prudent investors must therefore be aware of international events and their possible effects on the domestic economy and financial markets.

Globalization

Globalization is a term used to describe the increasing interdependence and interconnection of national economies. One major force behind globalization is the tremendous increase in international trade. Many countries now depend on imports for essential goods and rely on exports for the sale of domestic products. The greater the dependence of countries on international trade, the greater their sensitivity to conditions in other national economies. Not only has international trade grown in recent decades—both absolutely and as a percentage of global GDP—but it has also become less restricted by barriers such as tariffs and licensing requirements. Goods and services move across national boundaries more easily than they ever have.

A second component of globalization is the rise in international investment. Many countries have removed restrictions on currency exchange, allowed foreign banks and companies to do more domestic business, and made it easier for foreign investors to hold domestic stocks and bonds. Corporations across the spectrum commonly build plants in foreign nations, whose governments and people increasingly rely on their presence for tax revenues and wages. As developing countries have moved to establish modern stock and bond markets, they have succeeded in attracting large numbers of international investors searching for high rates of return. Investment funds that specialize in these *emerging markets* became very popular during the 1990s, both with individual and institutional investors. The risks involved in emerging markets are correspondingly high, however, and foreign money can move out of them as quickly as it moves in.

Finally, advances in telecommunications and computer technology have contributed the means for globalization to occur more rapidly, permitting businesses and investors to better track information from around the world and move their money more efficiently. Traders today can buy and sell stocks, bonds, and other instruments 24 hours a day in nearly every corner of the globe, all without leaving their homes or offices.

To invest successfully overseas, traders must closely watch foreign currency markets. Investments in another country are made in the domestic currency of that country; if the currency loses value relative to other currencies, any investment gains of foreigners can be wiped out.

The value of a foreign currency depends on economic conditions in the issuing country—and on what traders, speculators, and businesses feel about the country's prospects. A country's fiscal and monetary policies, as well as its balance of payments, are therefore crucial determinants of its exchange rate.

The Balance of Payments

The *balance of payments* relates the amount of money that flows into a nation with the amount of money leaving it. Money enters a country when foreigners purchase its exports or invest in its financial instruments. Money leaves the country when its residents purchase imports from other countries or invest in foreign financial instruments. The balance of payments is usually divided into two parts: the current account and the capital account. The *current account* is the difference between imports and exports of goods and services. The *capital account* is the difference between the investment in the country by foreigners and investment in foreign countries by its own residents.

Remember: the *current account* is the difference between imports and exports of goods and services. The *capital account* is the difference between the investment in the country by foreigners and investment in foreign countries by its own residents.

If a country has a favorable balance of payments, its currency tends to strengthen compared to those of its trading partners. To purchase its exports or invest in its markets, foreigners must first buy the country's currency. A balance of payments surplus means increasing demand for the currency, which pushes its price up. If the country has an unfavorable balance of payments—a deficit—international demand for its currency is falling relative to supply, and the value of its currency likely declines.

Exam Prep Questions

1. During periods of slow economic growth, bond prices typically:
   - ❑ A. Climb
   - ❑ B. Fall
   - ❑ C. Remain stable
   - ❑ D. Behave erratically
2. The value of all goods and services produced by companies and persons located in a country is called:
   - ❑ A. GDP
   - ❑ B. GNP
   - ❑ C. Index of leading indicators
   - ❑ D. Capital accounts
3. Unlike the GDP, the GNP does not count:
   - ❑ A. Consumer spending
   - ❑ B. Government spending
   - ❑ C. Net exports
   - ❑ D. Sales within the country by foreign-owned companies
4. A decline in GDP for two consecutive quarters is called:
   - ❑ A. Recession
   - ❑ B. Depression
   - ❑ C. Inflation
   - ❑ D. Deflation
5. Which statement about the index of leading economic indicators is not correct?
   - ❑ A. The index is calculated by the Conference Board.
   - ❑ B. The index is reported monthly.
   - ❑ C. The index is used to signal turning points in the economy.
   - ❑ D. The index consists of 10 indicators of manufacturing activity.
6. All the following are leading economic indicators except:
   - ❑ A. Weekly claims for unemployment insurance
   - ❑ B. New building permits issued
   - ❑ C. New orders for consumer goods
   - ❑ D. Industrial production

7. Inflation caused by competition among consumers for scarce goods and services is:
   - ❑ A. Demand-pull inflation
   - ❑ B. Cost-push inflation
   - ❑ C. Deflation
   - ❑ D. Stagflation

8. The advocacy of government fiscal programs to stimulate or slow the economy is:
   - ❑ A. Keynesian economic theory
   - ❑ B. Monetary policy
   - ❑ C. Moral suasion
   - ❑ D. Globalization

9. Which of the following are included in the M1 definition of money?

   I. Currency in circulation

   II. Demand deposits

   III. Time deposits

   IV. Travelers checks
   - ❑ A. I only
   - ❑ B. I and II
   - ❑ C. I, II, and III
   - ❑ D. I, II, and IV

10. The withdrawal of money from low-yielding bank accounts and the reinvestment into higher-yielding investments is called:
    - ❑ A. The velocity of money
    - ❑ B. Disintermediation
    - ❑ C. Intermediation
    - ❑ D. The multiplier effect of credit

11. When a bank borrows from its local Federal Reserve Bank, it pays the:
    - ❑ A. Federal funds rate
    - ❑ B. Discount rate
    - ❑ C. Call rate
    - ❑ D. Prime rate

12. What are the two accounts associated with the balance of payments?

    I. Line of credit

    II. Current account

    III. Capital account

    IV. Intermediation

    - ❑ A. I only
    - ❑ B. I and II
    - ❑ C. II and IV
    - ❑ D. II and III

13. Which actions of the Fed are consistent with combating recession?

    I. Raising the Fed funds target rate

    II. Lowering the discount rate

    III. Lowering reserve requirements

    IV. Raising the discount rate

    - ❑ A. I and II
    - ❑ B. II and III
    - ❑ C. I and IV
    - ❑ D. I, III, and IV

14. All of the following statements about a country's balance of payments are true except:

    - ❑ A. The balance of payments is a summary of the country's international transactions over a period of time.
    - ❑ B. When foreigners purchase the country's products, money flows into the country.
    - ❑ C. When residents import goods, money leaves the country.
    - ❑ D. There is no effect on the country's balance of payments when residents purchase foreign securities.

15. What is the most effective Fed action in controlling the money supply?

    - ❑ A. Changing the Fed rate
    - ❑ B. Changing the reserve requirement
    - ❑ C. Open market operations
    - ❑ D. Changing the prime rate

Exam Prep Answers

1. The correct answer is A. During periods of slow economic growth, when interest rates and inflation are normally low, bond prices typically climb. Conversely, when the economy grows faster, interest rates and inflation increase causing bonds prices to move lower.
2. The correct answer is A. Gross domestic product (GDP) is the total value of goods and services produced within a country during a given period (usually one year). It includes goods and services produced in the country by foreign-owned firms.
3. The correct answer is D. The GNP measures the value of goods and services produced by residents and companies of a country. It includes goods and services produced abroad but owned by U.S. companies. It does not include foreign businesses located within the United States.
4. The correct answer is A. When the GDP has contracted for two consecutive quarters, the nation has officially entered a recession. If the downturn continues for 18 months or more, the economy is said to be in a depression.
5. The correct answer is D. The index of leading economic indicators is a composite index of 10 indicators of economic activity from different segments of the economy, not just manufacturing. All the other choices are accurate statements about the indicators.
6. The correct answer is D. Industrial production is a coincident indicator. This indicator is closely tied to total economic output but is not one of the leading indicators by itself. Weekly claims for unemployment insurance, new building permits issued, and new orders for consumer goods are all leading economic indicators.
7. The correct answer is A. Demand-pull inflation occurs when consumer demand increases more quickly than businesses can expand. Prices rise because consumers have extra disposable income which leads to increased competition for available goods and services.
8. The correct answer is A. Ascribed to John Maynard Keynes, Keynesian economic theory calls for greater government spending during periods of economic downturns and higher levels of taxation during expansions.
9. The correct answer is D. M1 is made up of types of money commonly used for payment, such as currency, demand deposits, and travelers checks.
10. The correct answer is B. Disintermediation occurs when investors withdraw money from banks to reinvest in higher yielding securities elsewhere.

11. The correct answer is B. The discount rate is the rate at which banks borrow from the Fed. Banks can borrow from the Fed only for specific purposes, such as meeting short-term liquidity needs. The discount rate is the lowest interest rate available in the economy. The Fed funds rate is the rate in which banks borrow among themselves to meet reserve requirements. The call rate is the loan rate in which brokerage houses finance margin accounts, and the prime rate is the rate that commercial banks charge their best customers, usually corporations.
12. The correct answer is D. The current account and the capital account are used to handle the balance of payments between nations. The current account is the difference between imports and exports of goods and services while the capital account is the difference between the investments in the country by foreigners and investments in foreign countries by its own residents.
13. The correct answer is B. Lowering the discount rate decreases the cost of borrowing throughout the economy, thereby providing a stimulus. Lowering reserve requirements boosts bank lending and accelerates economic activity. Recession is combated by lowering rates while raising rates would slow down the economy.
14. The correct answer is D. The capital account of a country's balance of payments is the difference between the investment in the country by foreigners and investment in foreign countries by its own residents. When residents purchase foreign securities, money flows out of the country, which has an unfavorable effect on the balance of payments.
15. The correct answer is C. Open market operations is the day-to-day practice for controlling the economy. When money is short, the Fed buys securities from dealers that sends cash into the economy. When money is in good supply, the Feds sell securities, thus taking money out of the economy. Changing the Fed fund rate is another tool for controlling the money supply, but it is not used on a daily basis. The prime rate, however, is the rate commercial banks charge their customers.

Fundamental Analysis

Terms You Need to Know

- ✓ Accelerated depreciation
- ✓ Asset
- ✓ Balance sheet
- ✓ Bond interest coverage
- ✓ Bond ratio
- ✓ Book value
- ✓ Book value per share
- ✓ Capital in excess of par (capital surplus)
- ✓ Capitalization (capital structure)
- ✓ Cash asset ratio
- ✓ Common equity
- ✓ Common stock ratio
- ✓ Coverage
- ✓ Current assets
- ✓ Current ratio
- ✓ Current yield
- ✓ Cyclical industry
- ✓ Debt-to-equity ratio
- ✓ Defensive industry
- ✓ Depreciation
- ✓ Dividend payout ratio
- ✓ Earnings per share (EPS)
- ✓ Financial statement
- ✓ First-in, first-out method (FIFO)
- ✓ Fully diluted earnings per share
- ✓ Growth stock
- ✓ Income statement (profit and loss statement)
- ✓ Income stock
- ✓ Intangible assets
- ✓ Inventory turnover rate
- ✓ Last-in, first-out method (LIFO)
- ✓ Liability
- ✓ Liquidity
- ✓ Long-term capital
- ✓ Net profit margin
- ✓ Net tangible asset value per bond
- ✓ Net working capital
- ✓ Net worth
- ✓ Operating income
- ✓ Operating profit margin
- ✓ Preferred dividend coverage
- ✓ Preferred stock
- ✓ Preferred stock ratio
- ✓ Price earnings ratio (P/E)
- ✓ Profitability
- ✓ Quick asset ratio (acid test ratio)
- ✓ Retained earnings
- ✓ Return on assets
- ✓ Return on common equity
- ✓ Securities analyst (financial analyst)
- ✓ Statement of changes to retained earnings
- ✓ Stockholders' equity
- ✓ Straight-line depreciation
- ✓ Tangible assets

Concepts You Need to Understand

- ✓ The tasks of a securities analyst
- ✓ Conditions affecting a company's profitability
- ✓ How to read a balance sheet
- ✓ How to read an income statement
- ✓ How securities analysts use financial statements
- ✓ Which ratios are used to describe a company's financial structure

Fundamental Analysis

Although general economic conditions play an important role in any business endeavor, a company's own decisions and actions usually determine its success or failure. With thousands of corporations issuing various kinds of stocks and bonds in numerous markets, most investors cannot hope to individually assess the quality of more than a few securities. The securities analyst does that job.

The prices of stocks and bonds fluctuate according to the state of the economy in general, they also depend on the profitability and financial health of the issuing companies. Securities analysts study companies' financial reports in order to estimate their earning potentials and to determine their creditworthiness. Based on this information, they then estimate the value of stocks and corporate bonds and make investment recommendations to their customers.

Securities analysts (or *financial analysts*) investigate companies' financial health, and then evaluate the companies' stocks and bonds. Investors supply capital to businesses in expectation of returns—fixed rates of return for bondholders and variable rates for stockholders. In order to estimate their risks and assess their returns, investors need information about the issuing company. Bondholders want to know how likely the company is to default on its loans; stockholders want to know how profitable the company is and how much of its future profits are likely to be returned in the form of dividends. The securities analyst attempts to answer these questions by examining a company's assets, liabilities, income, and expenses. Using this information, the analyst attempts to predict how the company's stocks and bonds might perform.

The analyst asks a basic question: how profitable is the company likely to be in the future?

Factors Affecting Profitability

A company's profitability depends on a wide range of factors, including the state of the economy, the state of the company's industry, and the structure of the company itself. The analyst tries to estimate the company's profitability by answering a series of questions.

- How healthy is the economy? When the economy is growing rapidly, most businesses tend to earn larger profits, but when GDP growth falters, many companies see their profits decline.

- To what extent does the industry depend on the state of the economy? The business cycle affects the level of business activity throughout the economy, but it affects particular industries in different ways. Industries are divided into two basic categories: cyclical and defensive.

  Cyclical industries, which are made up of companies such as automobile makers, appliance manufacturers, and suppliers of building materials, follow the business cycle closely. During a recession, people tend to put off purchasing the products of these companies because income is down and borrowing is difficult. As a result, profits fall. When the economy is expanding, however, cyclical industries do well.

Cyclical industries are companies such as automobile, appliance manufacturers, and building suppliers, which are affected negatively by downturns in the economy. On the other side, an expanding economy means more business for these companies.

  Defensive industries, which are composed of companies that produce goods such as energy, food, and pharmaceuticals, do not experience the swings of the business cycle as much as other industries do. Companies in defensive industries sell goods and services that are always needed by consumers. Even if the economy is doing poorly, consumers cannot cut back significantly on these necessities.

Defensive industries are those that are not as affected by changes in the economy; companies such as energy, food, and pharmaceuticals. These companies will experience some level of ups and downs but have relatively little serious financial difficulties like cyclical industries.

- What is the outlook for the company's industry? A company's profitability depends in part on how well its industry is performing. If air travel is increasing rapidly, for example, then most airlines should experience some increase in business. Similarly, if people are buying fewer typewriters, then most typewriter manufacturers will face declining sales.
- How does the company compare to its competitors? Within each industry, of course, businesses are competing for customers. Firms with expanding market share, innovative products, highly trained workers, or more experienced management are more likely to earn profits than firms without these qualities.
- At what stage in its "lifecycle" is the company? Successful businesses pass through different stages as they develop. Normally, they grow

quickly at first, more slowly as their markets are saturated, and then stabilize or eventually decline. To expand rapidly, a company must reinvest most of its profits, which means smaller dividend payments to shareholders. Share prices, however, often increase in expectation of future profits. The stocks of such rapidly expanding companies are known as growth stocks. Mature companies, on the other hand, do not need to reinvest all their earnings and can therefore offer larger dividends to shareholders. Their stocks are known as income stocks.

- *How well is the company using its resources?* Analysts need to determine how quickly companies sell their inventory, how high their overhead costs are, the productivity of their workplaces, and how long it takes to bring new goods to market.
- *Can the company pay its debts?* If a company cannot pay its debts, it cannot very well make a profit. Bondholders and stock investors need to know that a business can at least earn enough to repay its debts. Securities analysts provide this information after a careful study of the company's debt structure, financial situation, and projected earnings.

To respond to these questions, analysts must examine macroeconomic data, industry trends, and, most importantly, the financial statements of individual firms.

Financial Statements

A *financial statement* is a record of the current financial status of a company. All publicly-held corporations are required by the Securities and Exchange Commission to release annual financial reports. These reports enable investors to evaluate the company's financial health and thus make informed investment decisions. The reports are checked by independent accounting firms in order to certify that they are accurate and reveal all necessary information. Financial statements generally include a balance sheet, an income statement, and a statement of changes to retained earnings.

The Balance Sheet

A *balance sheet* records a company's assets, liabilities, and net worth at a particular moment in time. *Assets* are everything owned by the company, such as cash, office equipment, and inventory. *Liabilities* are the company's financial obligations, such as money it has borrowed, or wages it must pay. The difference between what the company owns and what it owes is the *net worth*, also known as the *stockholders' equity*. Stockholders own everything left after the assets have been used to meet the company's liabilities.

Every item on the balance sheet appears twice, once as a credit and once as a debit. For instance, if the company borrows money from a bank to buy new computers, the price of the computers appears under assets, whereas the size of the loan (which equals the price of the computers) appears under liabilities. Or, if the company issues stock and uses the funds to build a new factory, the price of the factory appears as an asset, whereas the same sum appears as a debit termed "stockholders' equity." Total assets therefore must equal total liabilities plus stockholders' equity, because stockholders' equity and liabilities are the *sources* of the capital used to purchase assets.

> **EXAMPLE:** Consider the following balance sheet in Figure 30.1 for RichCo Corporation. It states the financial condition of the company on June 30, 2003.
>
> RichCo's assets total $886,000. They are equal to the sum of RichCo's total liabilities ($459,000) and its stockholders' equity ($427,000). In other words, of the $886,000 worth of goods and cash owned by the company, $459,000 is owed to workers, businesses, governments, banks, and bondholders; and the remaining $427,000 is owed to stockholders.

By looking in more detail at assets, liabilities and stockholders' equity, the company's financial structure becomes clear.

Current Assets

Current assets are possessions the company intends to convert into cash and spend within the next year. Current assets include (in order of liquidity):

- Cash—Money on hand or in bank accounts
- Marketable securities—Stocks and bonds that can be easily sold and converted into cash
- Accounts receivable—Recent billing for merchandise sold, due within 30 to 90 days
- Inventory—Raw material, work in progress, and finished products not yet sold

RichCo Corporation
Balance Sheet
June 30, 2003

ASSETS		**LIABILITIES**	
Current Assets		**Current Liabilities**	
Cash	$28,000		$100,000
Marketable Securities	65,000	Wages Payable	50,000
Accounts Receivable	175,000	Taxes Payable	69,100
Inventory	108,000	Bank Loans Payable	30,000
Total Current Assets	$376,000	Interest Payable	9,900
		Total Current Liabilities	$259,000
Long-Term Assets		**Long-Term Liabilities**	
Notes Receivable After One Year	80,000	7.5% Debentures ($1,000 par) maturing in 2020	200,000
Land, Buildings, Machines, Equipment	500,000	**TOTAL LIABILITIES**	$459,000
Less: Accumulated Depreciation	(100,000)	**STOCKHOLDERS' EQUITY**	
Total Long-Term Assets	$480,000	9% Preferred Stock $100 par, non-convertible	50,000
		Common Stock $1 par	35,000
Intangible Assets		Capital in Excess of Par	152,000
Goodwill	10,000	Retained Earnings	190,000
Patents	20,000	Total Stockholders' Equity	$427,000
Total Intangible Assets	$30,000		
TOTAL ASSETS	$886,000	**TOTAL LIABILITIES AND STOCKHOLDERS' OPTIONS**	$886,000

Figure 30.1 Balance sheet.

Current assets are the possessions a company intends to convert to cash, such as marketable securities, accounts receivable, and inventory.

Although the value of cash, securities, and accounts receivable is easily determined, the value of inventory is more difficult to estimate.

Valuing Inventory

Products in inventory have generally been produced (or purchased) at different times, and, because of inflation or changing production expenses, have different costs. When goods are sold out of inventory, accountants must decide whether the goods sold are the oldest or most recent ones produced. This decision can have important financial repercussions, because the prices of the goods can differ greatly. The *last-in, first-out method (LIFO)* assumes that the last goods to be placed in inventory (the most recently produced or bought) are the first ones sold. The *first-in, first-out method (FIFO)* assumes that the first goods placed in inventory (the earliest produced or bought) are the first ones sold.

LIFO means last inventory purchased by the company but is sold first, whereas FIFO means first inventory purchased is the first sold. These methods of tracking inventory are important concepts to understand.

EXAMPLE: At the beginning of the year, RichCo had 20,000 baseball caps in inventory from the previous year. Then, baseball caps cost $5 each, for a total of $100,000 worth of inventory. During the year, the factory produces another 20,000 caps every three months, but each quarter, the price rises by $.10 per cap. By the end of the year, RichCo has produced 80,000 new caps. The company has also sold 80,000 caps, leaving 20,000 in inventory. How much is the inventory worth? The answer depends on whether RichCo uses the LIFO or FIFO method. Table 30.1 shows the inventory levels as they increase through the year and their total costs; whereas Table 30.2 shows the difference between LIFO and FIFO methods of accounting for the inventory.

Table 30.1 Inventory and Cost

	Quantity	Unit Cost	Total Cost
Beginning Inventory	20,000	$5.00	$100,000
First Quarter	20,000	$5.10	$102,000
Second Quarter	20,000	$5.20	$104,000
Third Quarter	20,000	$5.30	$106,000
Fourth Quarter	20,000	$5.40	$108,000
Total	100,000		$520,000

Table 30.2 Inventory value for LIFO and FIFO

	Quantity	LIFO	FIFO
Total Production	100,000	$520,000	$520,000
Less: Goods Sold	–80,000	–$412,000	–$412,000
Ending Inventory	20,000	$100,000	$108,000

Under the LIFO method, the last caps to come off the assembly line (those produced in the fourth quarter) are the first sold. This means that the caps remaining in inventory must be the ones left over from the previous year, as they were produced first. In this view, the inventory is still worth $100,000 (the price of last year's leftover caps). Under the FIFO method, however, the 20,000 caps produced last year are sold first (because they were the first in). According to this view, the inventory is worth $108,000 (the price of the caps produced in the fourth quarter).

Because prices tend to rise over time, FIFO generally reports a higher value for existing inventories than LIFO, particularly when inflation is high. Both are acceptable methods of accounting, and every company decides which method best suits its needs. But once a company chooses a method, it must continue to use it each year.

Remember, to calculate cost of goods sold:

Beginning Inventory + Net Purchases – Cost of Goods Sold (COGS) = Ending Inventory

FIFO: cost of oldest inventory – cost of oldest inventory sold = ending inventory

Example: $520,000 total inventory – $412,000 sold = $108,000 ending inventory, which consists of the newest goods purchased

LIFO: cost of newest inventory – cost of newest inventory sold = ending inventory

Example: $520,00 total inventory – $412,000 inventory sold = $100,000 ending inventory, which consists of the oldest good purchased

Remember, prices tend to rise over time, so newer inventory costs more for the same items. FIFO generally reports a higher value for existing inventories than LIFO, particularly when inflation is high. Both are acceptable methods of accounting, and every company decides which method best suits its needs. Once a company chooses a method, it must continue to use it each year. The value of ending inventory determines the amount of taxes paid; obviously, the lower ending value of LIFO is appealing.

Long-Term Assets

Long-term assets include notes receivable after one year (long-term loans made by the company) as well as goods owned by the company that are used in the course of business and are not intended to be converted into cash.

They include real estate, buildings, machines, and office equipment. Because all long-term assets (except for land) wear out with use, each year a certain amount, known as *depreciation*, is deducted from their original purchase price. Thus, the reported value of the asset declines until it reaches zero at the end of its useful life. Every item is assigned a useful life by the Internal Revenue Service (IRS). Buildings, for example, have a useful life of 31.5 years. The IRS allows companies to calculate depreciation in two ways—straight line and accelerated. *Straight-line depreciation* subtracts the same percentage of the item's value each year for its entire lifetime, whereas *accelerated depreciation* allows larger deductions in earlier years. A footnote on the balance sheet explains which method is being used.

Straight-line depreciation subtracts the same percentage of the item's value each year for its lifetime, whereas accelerated depreciation allows larger deductions in earlier years.

EXAMPLE: RichCo purchased a $60,000 car for its CEO. Each year on its balance sheet, RichCo must list the car as a $60,000 asset, but because the car (which has a useful life of five years) loses value over time, RichCo can deduct a portion of this price each year. By the straight-line method, RichCo can deduct the same amount each year for five years. The yearly deduction must therefore be equal to $12,000. After the first year, RichCo can subtract $12,000, for a reported asset value of $48,000. After the second year RichCo can subtract $24,000, for a reported value of $36,000, and so on. After the fifth year, the car can no longer have any value as an asset (although it might still be useful for chauffeuring the CEO). If it chooses the accelerated method, RichCo might deduct $20,000 the first year, an additional $16,000 the second, an additional $12,000 the third, and so on. The car might still lose all its value in five years, but it provides larger deductions earlier on, which translates into lower stated income and therefore a smaller corporate tax bill.

All current and long-term assets are *tangible assets*, that is, they are physical goods, such as cash or equipment. Companies can also possess intangible assets.

Intangible Assets

Intangible assets are those possessions of the company that contribute to its worth but are not physical items. Patents, copyrights, and trademarks represent intangible assets. Another intangible asset, known as goodwill, is valued at the amount paid for the company above its book value if the company has been purchased. This is considered to reflect those aspects of the company not represented in its list of assets, such as the experience of its executives, its reputation in the marketplace, or its customer loyalty. Together, the current assets, long-term assets, and intangible assets add up to the total assets of the company.

Liabilities

Liabilities are claims on the assets of the company, and they too can be either current or long-term. Current liabilities are debts that must be paid within one year, generally using funds from current assets. They include:

- Accounts payable—Money owed to creditors (such as suppliers) in the normal course of business
- Wages payable—Wages and salaries owed to employees
- Notes payable—Short-term bank loans that must be repaid within a year
- Taxes payable—Corporate income taxes owed to federal and state governments, payroll withholding taxes, and sales taxes
- Interest payable—Interest owed on outstanding bonds, due within one year

Long-term liabilities, on the other hand, are debts that must be paid more than a year in the future. Such long-term debt often appears in the form of bond issues, for which companies must pay interest each year and repay the principal at maturity. Long-term liabilities are only one source of capital for the firm; stockholders' equity is another.

Stockholders' Equity

Stockholders' equity represents funds acquired by the company through the sale of stock. Many companies issue two types of stock: preferred and common.

Preferred stock is a hybrid between a bond and a stock. It confers ownership rights but pays a fixed annual dividend (a percentage of par, like a bond interest payment). For accounting purposes, preferred stock is given a par value (usually $100) that has no relation to its market price or the price at which it was issued. Because preferred stockholders receive dividends before common stockholders, preferred stock is less risky. However, its returns are also limited to a fixed rate.

Common stock confers ownership rights but pays a dividend that depends on the size of the company's profits. Like preferred stock, common stock is also given an arbitrary par value (often $1) for bookkeeping purposes. Shareholders, however, pay more than par value for the stock when it is issued, and this additional amount must also be accounted for. It is entered on the balance sheet as *capital in excess of par* (or *capital surplus*).

Stockholders are paid out of profits, but sometimes a company reinvests part or all of its profits rather than pay them out as dividends. These profits are known as *retained earnings.* Technically, they are the property of the shareholders, but they are being retained for future use within the company (for activities such as research and development).

In the case of dividends (cash or stock) or stock splits, the stockholders' equity section must be adjusted.

Dividends and Stock Splits

Because dividend payments and stock splits affect the total amount of capital, the number of shares outstanding, and the value of the shares, must be accounted for on the balance sheet. In the case of the announcement of a cash dividend, the number of shares of stock and their par value remain the same, but total retained earnings must be reduced by the amount of the dividend. Total shareholder equity is therefore reduced. In the case of a stock dividend—defined as a distribution of new stock equivalent to less than 25% of outstanding shares—total shareholder equity remains the same. New shares are issued at par value, whereas retained earnings are reduced by an equivalent amount. A stock split, on the other hand, is a distribution of new stock equaling more than 25% of outstanding shares. Here, the par value of the stock is adjusted so that shareholder equity remains the same.

The balance sheet gives a static view of the company's assets and liabilities at a specific point in time. It does not give information about earnings. This information appears in the income statement.

Income Statements

An *income statement* is a yearly summary of revenues, costs, and expenses. It is also known as a *profit and loss statement.* Consider the following example in Table 30.3.

Table 30.3 Profit and Loss Statement

RichCo Corporation Income Statement For the Year Ending June 30, 1999	
Net Sales	$788,900
Less: Cost of Goods Sold	(420,000)
Gross Margin	$368,900
Less: Operating Expenses	(107,200)
Operating Income	$261,700
Less: Depreciation	(36,400)
Earnings Before Interest and Taxes	$225,300
Less: Bond Interest Expense	(15,000)
Earnings Before Taxes	$210,300
Less: Tax	(69,100)
Net Income	$141,200

The statement begins with the total income from sales, and then subtracts all expenses to yield net income or profit. The income statement generally includes the following entries:

- Net sales—Total value of all sales for the period, including those billed for but not yet collected
- Cost of goods sold—Cost to produce the goods sold during the period (including the cost of damaged or stolen goods), calculated on either a LIFO or FIFO basis
- Operating expenses—Costs of conducting business, including rent, depreciation, marketing, administration, salaries, and legal fees
- Depreciation—Accumulated depreciation of long-term operating assets, calculated on either a straight-line or accelerated basis
- Bond interest expense—Interest paid to bondholders, which must be paid regardless of whether the firm makes a profit
- Tax—Corporate income taxes paid to state and federal governments (payroll and property taxes are included in operating expenses)

Although the income statement gives information about expenses and net income, it does not include dividend payments. These appear on the statement of changes to retained earnings.

Statement of Changes to Retained Earnings

The *statement of changes to retained earnings* explains how the net income was used. Net income, or profit, is used to pay dividends to stockholders, or is kept as retained earnings for future use. Consider Table 30.4, which shows RichCo's retained earnings.

Table 30.4 Statement of Retained Earnings

Statement of Changes to Retained Earnings For the Year Ending June 30, 2003	
Beginning of Year Retained Earnings	$83,300
Net Income for the Year	141,200
Less: Preferred Dividend	(4,500)
Common Dividend	(30,000)
End of Year Retained Earnings	$190,000

Balance sheets, income statements, and statements of changes to retained earnings all contain valuable information for securities analysts.

Fundamental Ratios

Although these financial reports contain useful information for assessing a company's creditworthiness and profit potential, they do not always present it in the most useful form. Analysts often rewrite the firm's financial data, creating different ratios to better understand how items in the documents relate to each other. Five categories of ratios are of importance to investors: liquidity, capitalization, coverage, profitability, and earnings. Each group of ratios provides answers to certain questions about the financial status of the firm.

- *Liquidity ratios.* Does the firm have enough income to meet its current expenses?
- *Capitalization ratios.* How large are the firm's long-term debt and equity, and how are they structured?
- *Coverage ratios.* Can the firm meet its annual interest payments?
- *Profitability ratios.* How profitable is the firm?
- *Earnings ratios.* What returns are stockholders' making from dividends? Is the stock underpriced or overpriced?

Liquidity

In this context, *liquidity* describes how well the firm can pay its bills on time; in other words, whether it can meet its current liabilities with its current assets. A company with liquidity problems risks defaulting on short-term debt, and might be managed poorly. Low liquidity, therefore, can have implications for both creditworthiness and profitability. The simplest measure of liquidity is *net working capital*, which is the difference between current assets and current liabilities.

Net working capital = current assets – current liabilities

Working capital is essential for daily operations. If it is positive, the company can pay for all its current liabilities without borrowing more money. If it is negative, the firm must borrow to meet its short-term debts. A more sophisticated measure of liquidity is the *current ratio*, which is the ratio of current assets to current liabilities.

Current ratio = current assets ÷ current liabilities

If the current ratio is greater than one, the company can meet all its current expenses with its current assets.

Some current assets are less liquid than others, however. Inventory, for example, might be difficult to convert to cash quickly, because customers must first buy the goods. Therefore, a more stringent measure of a company's capability to meet its current liabilities quickly is the *quick asset ratio* (also known as the *acid test ratio*), which excludes inventory from current assets.

Quick asset ratio = current assets – inventory ÷ current liabilities

The quick asset ratio compares the company's current supply of cash, marketable securities, and accounts receivable to its current liabilities. A ratio of 1:1 is generally considered safe because it means that the company can pay all its bills, even with no further sales revenue. The quick asset ratio, however, still includes accounts receivable, which depend on the company's capability to collect what it is owed. The most stringent test of liquidity, the *cash asset ratio*, therefore takes into account only cash and marketable securities, the two most liquid forms of assets.

Cash asset ratio = cash + marketable securities ÷ current liabilities

The cash asset ratio focuses on the assets that can be used to pay bills within three business days (the time it takes to convert marketable securities to cash).

Know liquidity ratios: they are very important ratios in determining a company's capability to meet current liabilities with available assets.

EXAMPLE: Looking at RichCo's balance sheet, Julie, a financial analyst at Baylor Austin Securities, begins by calculating its liquidity ratios. She finds net working capital by subtracting total current liabilities from total current assets.

Net working capital = \$376,000 (current assets)
– \$259,000 (current liabilities)
= \$117,000

So, RichCo's current assets exceed its current liabilities by \$117,000. By itself, this number means little, for Julie finds that RichCo's current ratio indicates some liquidity problems.

Current ratio = \$376,000 (current assets)
÷ \$259,000 (current liabilities)
= \$1.45

RichCo has only \$1.45 in current assets for every \$1.00 in current liabilities, less than the recommended 1:1 ratio. If for some reason RichCo's accounts receivable were not paid, it might soon find itself unable to meet its current liabilities. Nonetheless, Julie calculates that the quick asset ratio is in the safe range.

Quick asset ratio = \$376,000 (current assets)
– \$108,000 (inventory)
÷ 259,000 (current liabilities)
= 1.03

RichCo can cover its current liabilities without further sales, using only cash, securities, and accounts receivable. The cash asset ratio, however, is low at 0.36.

Cash asset ratio = \$28,000 (cash) + \$65,000 (marketable securities)
÷ \$259,000
= 0.36

RichCo's most liquid assets therefore cannot cover its current liabilities. Because its liquidity is below what is generally considered safe, Julie decides to investigate further before risking her clients' capital.

Liquidity ratios measure how well the company can meet its current liabilities, but investors also want to know about the long-term obligations represented by the capital structure of the firm.

Capitalization

Capitalization (or *capital structure*) refers to the structure of a company's long-term debt and equity obligations, including bonds, preferred stock, and common stock. The most basic measure of capitalization is *long-term capital*, which is simply the sum of long-term liabilities and stockholders' equity.

Long-term capital = long-term liabilities + stockholders' equity

Analysts also examine how long-term capital is divided among different forms of obligations. The *bond ratio*, for example, describes the portion of long-term capital derived from bonds, whereas the *preferred stock ratio* is the portion represented by preferred stock, and the *common stock ratio* is the portion represented by common equity.

Bond ratio = par value of bonds ÷ long-term capital

Preferred stock ratio = par value of preferred stock ÷ long-term capital

Common stock ratio = common equity ÷ long-term capital

Note that *common equity* is not merely the total par value of the firm's common stock, but also the excess capital and retained earnings, both of which belong to the holders of common stock.

Common equity = common stock + excess capital + retained earnings

Also note that because the sources of long-term capital are bonds, preferred stock, and common stock, these three ratios add up to one.

Another useful measure of capitalization is the *debt-to-equity ratio*, which compares long-term debt in the form of bonds and preferred stock to common equity.

Debt-to-equity ration = bonds + preferred stock ÷ common equity

What are considered appropriate ranges for debt-to-equity vary according to the industry. Most companies have at least a 1:1 ratio, because debt is often cheaper than equity, and because debt represents a fixed yearly cost. Highly leveraged companies, however, can have ratios that approach 2:1.

EXAMPLE: Studying RichCo's balance sheet, Julie finds that total long-term capital amounts to $627,000.

Long-term capital = $200,000 (long-term liabilities)
+ 427,0000 (stockholder's equity)
= $627,000

She then calculates the bond ratio and preferred stock ratios:

Bond ratio = $200,000 (par value of bonds)
÷ $627,000 (long-term capital)
= 0.32

Preferred stock ratio = $50,000 (par value of preferred stock)
÷ $627,000 (long-term capital)
= 0.08

To find the common stock ratio, she first needs to calculate RichCo's common equity.

Common equity = $ 35,000 (par value common stock)
+ 152,000 (excess capital)
+ 190,000 (retained earnings)
= $377,000

The common stock ratio is then:

Common stock ratio = $377,000 (common equity)
÷ $627,000 (long-term capital)
= 0.60

Thus, 32% of the company's long-term capital comes from bonds, 8% from preferred stock, and the remaining 60% from common stock. Julie is also interested in the debt-to-equity ratio:

Debt to equity ratio = \$100,000 (bonds) + \$50,000 (preferred stock)
÷ \$377,000 (common equity)
= 0.66

RichCo has only \$0.66 of debt for each \$1.00 of equity, a low ratio. RichCo is far from overextended in terms of debt, and the firm might even want to consider taking on more debt to expand its operations.

After looking at capitalization ratios, analysts need to examine companies' coverage ratios, which indicate how well the firms can repay their debts.

Coverage

Coverage describes a company's capability to meet its bond and preferred stock obligations. Coverage greatly affects the company's efforts to obtain future credit—the better the coverage, the better its loan terms or the higher its bond rating. One important measure of coverage is *bond interest coverage*, the ratio of earnings (before interest payments and taxes) to annual bond interest. Bond interest coverage shows a company's capability to make annual interest payments on its outstanding bonds.

Bond interest coverage = earnings before interest and taxes ÷ bond interest expense

A ratio of 1:1 demonstrates that the firm had just enough income to cover its obligations, suggesting a high likelihood of default if earnings were to fall. *Preferred dividend coverage* measures the company's capability to make fixed payments to holders of preferred stock.

Preferred dividend coverage = net income ÷ preferred dividends

Note that this ratio is calculated from net income rather than earnings before interest and taxes, because preferred dividend payments are made *after* taxes, whereas bond interest payments are made before taxes.

Another important coverage ratio is the *net tangible asset value per bond*, which gives analysts an idea of the likelihood that bondholders can recover their principal in the event of a company's bankruptcy. When a corporation fails, it is forced to pay off its current liabilities, sell off its tangible assets, and *then* repay bondholders.

Net tangible asset value per bond = tangible assets – current liabilities ÷ number of \$1,000 par bonds outstanding

In other words, this ratio describes the amount of tangible assets backing each bond. A high ratio gives bondholders more security.

EXAMPLE: RichCo's bond interest expense and earnings before interest and taxes can be found on its income statement. Using these figures, Julie learns that the company's bond interest coverage is 14.02.

Bond interest coverage = $225,300 (earnings before interest and taxes)
÷ $15,000 (bond interest expense)
= 14.02

This means that RichCo has $14.02 in income for every dollar it must pay in bond interest. For the present, there is little chance of default on its bond interest payments. Julie then finds that RichCo's preferred dividends total $4,500 ($50,000 par value × 0.09 interest = $4,500), and searches the income statement for net income. With this data, she calculates RichCo's preferred dividend coverage at 31.38.

Preferred dividend coverage = $141,200 (net income)
÷ $4,500 (preferred dividends)
= 31.38

With its low debt burden, RichCo can easily cover both bond interest and preferred dividends (its fixed income charges).

Now Julie finds RichCo's tangible assets:

Tangible assets = $886,000 (total assets)
– $30,000 (intangible assets)
= $856,000

If the company were to go bankrupt, she knows that these tangible assets can be sold to repay bondholders. RichCo has issued 200 bonds with face value of $1,000. The net tangible asset value per bond is therefore $2,985.

Net tangible asset value per bond = $856,000 (tangible assets)
– $259,000 (current liabilities)
÷ 200 (bonds)
= $2,985

With $2,985 of tangible assets behind every $1,000 bond, RichCo enjoys a high credit rating.

Because they receive fixed coupon payments, bondholders are fundamentally interested in the creditworthiness of their bonds' issuers. Common stockholders, on the other hand, are primarily interested in a company's profitability, because they earn returns from dividends and rising share prices.

Measuring Profitability

Profitability can be measured in a number of ways. One basic measure is known as the *operating profit margin*, which is the ratio of operating income to sales.

Operating profit margin = operating income ÷ net sales

Operating income is pretax earnings before depreciation and interest expense. Operating profit margin therefore gives the percentage of every sales dollar available to pay overhead expenses and contribute towards profits. A related ratio is the *net profit margin.* This compares the net income *after* taxes to sales.

Net profit margin = net income ÷ net sales

Net profit is important, but investors also care about how well the firm is using its assets. This can be calculated with return on assets, which compares after-tax income to total tangible assets:

Return on assets = net income ÷ total tangible assets

Return on assets measures how many dollars of profit are generated for each dollar of tangible assets owned by a company. By comparing this percentage to the interest the firm pays on its borrowed funds, analysts can determine whether the company is creating higher returns with its assets than the interest it is paying on its debts.

A related measure is the *return on common equity*, comparing net income, less preferred dividends (because these must be paid before common stock dividends), to the total amount of capital from common stock.

Return on common equity = net income – preferred dividends ÷ common equity

This ratio demonstrates how well the firm uses the capital provided by common stockholders to generate income. Profitability also depends on the efficiency of the firm in turning over its inventory; the more quickly inventory is sold, the more profit the firm can make. The *inventory turnover rate* gauges this.

Inventory turnover rate = cost of goods sold ÷ year end inventory

A high turnover rate shows that products sell quickly, and that relatively little money is spent on storage.

EXAMPLE: The equity customers of Baylor Austin Securities need to know something about RichCo's profitability. Julie looks at the firm's income statement and finds that its operating profit margin is 0.33.

Operating profit margin = $261,700 (operating income)
÷ $788,900 (net sales)
= 0.33

This means that 33% of every dollar earned is left after operating expenses have been paid, and can go toward interest expenses, taxes, and profits. Next Julie determines that RichCo's net profit margin is 0.18.

Net profit margin = $141,200 (net income)
÷ $788,900 (net sales)
= 0.18

That is, after taxes, 18% of RichCo's sales revenue is left for dividends or retained earnings. Julie also calculates profit as return on assets.

Return on assets = $141,200 (net income)
÷ $856,000 (tangible assets)
= 0.16

So RichCo is earning a return of 16% on its tangible assets. If it originally took out loans to buy these assets at a rate of, say, 8%, the company is putting its tangible assets to good use (it is making a spread of 8%). Now Julie turns her analytical eye to return on equity.

Return on common equity = $141,200 (net income)
÷ $377,000 (common equity)
= 0.37

Julie is happy to see that RichCo's profits represent a healthy 37% return on its equity. She wonders how efficiently the company handles its inventory, for warehouse rents have been rising steadily in the last year.

RichCo's inventory turnover looks pretty good.

Inventory turnover = $420,000 (cost of goods sold)
÷ $108,000 (inventory)
= 3.9

In other words, the company sells its entire inventory approximately four times per year.

No matter how profitable and well-managed a company is, potential investors still need to determine whether the stock is trading at an appropriate price. Analysts employ earnings ratios to study the value of stocks.

Valuing Stocks

The market value of a stock depends on a whole range of factors, from macroeconomic conditions to investors' convictions about the company's products. To judge the value of different stocks, securities analysts normally focus on a few fundamental ratios, hoping to determine which are good purchases and which are not. Here, one of the most basic measures is called book value per share. A company's *book value* is the sum of its tangible assets, less total liabilities and preferred stock. Book value gives the assets that are left over to pay common shareholders if the company fails. Therefore, *book value per share* simply describes the amount of assets backing each share of common stock.

Book value per share = tangible assets – total liabilities – preferred stock ÷ number of common shares outstanding

This ratio can be compared to that of other companies in the same industry to determine the relative value of their stocks. Another important measure of a stock's value is the issuing company's *earnings per share (EPS)*, which shows the amount of income that the company generates for each share of common stock.

Earnings per share = net income – preferred dividends ÷ common shares outstanding

Preferred dividends must be subtracted from net income because they are not payable to holders of common stock. It is important to remember that convertible bonds can be exchanged for common stock, so a company that has issued convertible bonds can experience an increase in the number of shares of common stock without a similar increase in earnings. For this reason, EPS is often calculated in two ways: with and without the convertible shares (even if they have not yet been converted). When convertible bonds are included, the ratio is known as *fully diluted EPS.*

Potential investors are also interested in the amount of dividends historically paid to shareholders. The *dividend payout ratio* gives the percentage of earnings that have been distributed as dividends.

Dividend payout ratio = common dividend paid ÷ earnings per share

It is worth mentioning that mature companies tend to have high dividend payout ratios, whereas growth companies typically have low dividend payout ratios.

Investors then need to look at a company's *current yield,* which is the rate of return the dividend represents compared to the stock's current market price.

Current yield = annual dividend per common share ÷ current market price

Clearly, investors can use this ratio to compare stock returns to those from other investments.

Although stock prices depend fundamentally on a company's assets and record of dividend payments, they also depend on investors' expectations about the future. A stock often trades above or below what might be estimated from its book value or current yield, because investors expect either better or worse performance from the issuing company. An important measure of this expectation is the *price earnings ratio (P/E),* relating the stock's current price to the company's earnings per share.

Price earnings ratio (P/E) = market price of stock ÷ earnings per share

EXAMPLE: Julie wants to determine whether RichCo's stock is a good value for Baylor Austin customers. Looking at the corporation's balance sheet, she first calculates the book value per share.

Book value per share = $856,000 – $459,000 – $50,000 ÷ $35,000
= $9.91

One might therefore expect the market price of RichCo stock to be around $10.00. Next the analyst calculates earnings per share.

Earnings per share = $141,200 – $4,500 ÷ $35,000
= $3.91

This shows that RichCo is currently earning $3.91 for each share of common stock outstanding. If RichCo's convertible bonds were exchanged for stock, however, the company would have more shares outstanding, and the earnings per share would be diluted. Julie finds out that RichCo's 200 bonds are convertible at $20 per share—a 50:1 ratio—thus they represent a potential 10,000 shares of additional common stock ($200,000 of bonds ÷ $20 = 10,000 shares). This increases the amount of common stock outstanding to 45,000 shares, but it also increases net income, because interest does not have to be paid to bondholders. Net income now equals $156,200 ($141,200 original income + $15,000 bond interest expense = $156,200). (Of course, this has implications for RichCo's income tax as well—because interest charges are tax deductible but dividends are not.) Now Julie can determine the firm's fully diluted earnings per share.

Fully diluted EPS = $156,200 – $4,500 ÷ 45,000
= $3.37

RichCo's statement of changes to retained earnings show that RichCo paid $30,000 in common stock dividends this year. Stock owners therefore received an $0.86 dividend payment for each share held.

Dividend per common share = $30,000 ÷ $35,000
= $0.86

Julie then investigates how much of the firm's earnings were paid out as dividends.

Dividend payout ratio = $0.86 ÷ $3.91
= $0.22

So RichCo paid out 22% of its earnings to common stock holders. Next the analyst wants to compare the return on RichCo stock with the return on other possible investments. She finds that it is currently $60, and proceeds to compute current yield.

Current yield = $0.86 ÷ $60 = 0.014

The annual dividend payment represents a yield of 1.4% for shareholders, based on the market price of the stock.

Finally, Julie needs to determine the company's P/E ratio.

Price earnings ratio = $60 ÷ $3.91 = $15.4

In general, the Baylor Austin analyst decides, RichCo appears to be a fairly good investment. The company is profitable, it has a reasonable debt burden, and it is returning profits to its shareholders. However, in order to conclude that RichCo's stock is a good value for her customers, Julie also needs to compare the company's P/E ratio with that of other firms in the same industry.

Exam Prep Questions

1. If Ken does not invest in cyclical industries, he still might buy stock in a company that produces:

   ❑ A. Minivans

   ❑ B. Refrigerators

   ❑ C. Bricks and stucco

   ❑ D. Antihistamines

2. Which item does not appear on a company's balance sheet?

   ❑ A. Stockholders' equity

   ❑ B. Net income

   ❑ C. Current assets

   ❑ D. Current liabilities

3. All of the following assets of the Mirabelle Company are current assets except:

   ❑ A. Cash

   ❑ B. Marketable securities

   ❑ C. Accounts receivable

   ❑ D. Office equipment

4. The Mirabelle Company must decide whether to use the LIFO or the FIFO method in evaluating its inventory. Which of the following statements are true?

   I. LIFO assumes that the last goods placed in inventory are the first ones sold.

   II. FIFO assumes that the first goods placed in inventory are the first ones sold.

   III. FIFO generally reports the higher value for existing inventories.

   IV. LIFO generally reports the higher value for existing inventories.

   ❑ A. I and III

   ❑ B. I and IV

   ❑ C. I, II, and III

   ❑ D. I, II, III, and IV

5. Margaret paid $33 a share for common stock issued by Washaw Industries last year. On Washaw's balance sheet, however, common stock is listed at a par value of $1 a share. The additional $32 in value is accounted as:

   ❑ A. Earned surplus

   ❑ B. Capital surplus

   ❑ C. Retained earnings

   ❑ D. Depreciation

6. Tornado, Inc., has 55,000 shares of common stock, par value of $2, outstanding. It splits its stock 2:1. Which of the following statements are true?

   I. Tornado now has 27,500 shares of stock outstanding.

   II. Tornado now has 110,000 shares of stock outstanding.

   III. The stock's par value is now $4.

   IV. The stock's par value is now $1.

   ❑ A. I only
   ❑ B. II only
   ❑ C. I and III
   ❑ D. II and IV

7. Where in its financial statements does Washaw Industries explain how it used its net income?

   ❑ A. In the balance sheet
   ❑ B. In the income statement
   ❑ C. In the statement of changes to retained earnings
   ❑ D. Through its debt-to-equity ratio

8. Zack holds some of Clarabell Investments' bonds, but its falling earnings worry him. To determine whether Clarabell can meet its interest payments, he analyzes the company's:

   ❑ A. Liquidity ratios
   ❑ B. Capitalization ratios
   ❑ C. Profitability ratios
   ❑ D. Coverage ratios

9. How does Marie calculate Washaw Industries' debt-to-equity ratio?

   ❑ A. Bonds + preferred stock ÷ common equity
   ❑ B. Common stock + excess capital + retained earnings
   ❑ C. Common equity ÷ long term capital
   ❑ D. Par value of bonds ÷ long term capital

10. How does Marie calculate Washaw's book value per share?

   ❑ A. (Tangible assets – total liabilities – preferred stock) ÷ number of common shares outstanding
   ❑ B. (Net income – preferred dividends) ÷ number of common shares outstanding
   ❑ C. Common dividend paid ÷ earnings per share
   ❑ D. Annual dividend per common share ÷ current market price

11. The Mirabelle Company paid $75,000 in dividends. With 55,000 common shares outstanding, Mirabelle paid a dividend per share of:
    - ❑ A. $1.36
    - ❑ B. $0.73
    - ❑ C. $2.09
    - ❑ D. $2.82
12. Tornado, Inc., paid a yearly dividend of $0.62 per share. With a market price of $55, what is the current yield on Tornado's stock?
    - ❑ A. 1.13%
    - ❑ B. 11.3%
    - ❑ C. 8.87%
    - ❑ D. 34.1%
13. Which of the following are considered liquidity ratios?

    I.Current assets – current liabilities

    II.Current assets ÷ current liabilities

    III. Common equity ÷ long-term capital

    IV. Net income ÷ preferred dividends
    - ❑ A. I only
    - ❑ B. II and III
    - ❑ C. I and IV
    - ❑ D. I and II
14. How is quick asset ratio calculated?
    - ❑ A. Cash + marketable securities ÷ current liabilities
    - ❑ B. Current assets – inventory ÷ current liabilities
    - ❑ C. Current assets ÷ current liabilities
    - ❑ D. Current assets – current liabilities
15. What are long-term assets and the types of depreciation for them?
    - ❑ A. Real estate, buildings, and machinery can be depreciated by straight-line only.
    - ❑ B. Real estate, buildings, and office equipment can be depreciated by accelerated depreciation only.
    - ❑ C. Real estate, buildings, and machinery can be depreciated by either straight-line or accelerated depreciation.
    - ❑ D. Real estate, buildings, and office equipment cannot be depreciated.

Exam Prep Answers

1. The correct answer is D. Cyclical industries are made up of companies such as automobile makers, appliance manufacturers, and suppliers of building materials, which closely follow the business cycle. Defensive industries, on the other hand, are composed of companies that produce goods like energy, food, and pharmaceuticals. These companies do not experience the swings of the business cycle as much because they sell goods and services that are always needed by consumers.
2. The correct answer is B. A balance sheet records a company's assets, liabilities, and net worth (also known as the stockholders' equity). The income statement shows the company's earnings and expenses.
3. The correct answer is D. Current assets are items that the company intends to convert into cash and spend within the next year. Current assets include (in order of greatest liquidity) cash, marketable securities, accounts receivable, and inventory. Because the company uses its office equipment in the course of business and does not intend to convert it into cash, it is considered a long-term asset.
4. The correct answer is C. The first-in, first-out method (FIFO) assumes that the first goods placed in inventory (the earliest produced or bought) are the first ones sold. The last-in, first-out method (LIFO) assumes that the last goods placed in inventory (the most recently produced or bought) are the first ones sold. Because prices tend to rise over time, FIFO generally reports a higher value for existing inventories than LIFO, particularly when inflation is high.
5. The correct answer is B. Common stock is given an arbitrary par value (often $1) for bookkeeping purposes. The amount paid by shareholders in excess of par value is reflected on the balance sheet in stockholders' equity as capital in excess of par, or capital surplus. Earned surplus is another name for retained earnings, which are the percentage of net earnings not paid out in dividends. Depreciation is the devaluing of an asset over time.
6. The correct answer is D. In a 2:1 stock split, each share of stock becomes two shares. Tornado now has 110,000 shares outstanding. The company must also adjust the par value so that shareholders' equity remains the same. A shareholder who previously owned 100 shares with a par value of $2 now owns 200 shares with a par value of $1.
7. The correct answer is C. The statement of changes to retained earnings explains how a company used its net income. Net income can be used to pay dividends to shareholders, or can be retained earnings for future use. The balance sheet records a company's assets, liabilities,

and net worth at a particular moment in time. The income statement is a yearly summary of revenues, costs, and expenses, whereas the debt-to-equity ratio compares long-term debt in the form of bonds and preferred stock to common equity.

8. The correct answer is D. Coverage is a term that describes a company's capability to meet its bond and preferred stock obligations. Zack will be especially interested in Clarabell's bond interest coverage ratio, which shows the company's capability to make annual interest payments on its outstanding bonds. Liquidity ratios describe how well the firm can meet its current liabilities with its current assets; there are four liquidity ratios. Capitalization ratios determine the amount of a firm's long-term debt and equity, and how are they structured. Profitability ratios determine the degree of a firm's profitability.
9. The correct answer is A. The debt to equity ratio = bonds + preferred stock ÷ common equity. It is a measure of capitalization, or of the company's long-term debt obligations. Most companies have at least a 1:1 debt-to-equity ratio, because debt is often cheaper than equity, and because debt represents a fixed yearly cost. B is common equity ratio, C is the common stock ratio, and D is the bond ratio.
10. The correct answer is A. Book value per share = tangible assets – total liabilities – preferred stock ÷ number of common shares outstanding. The book value per share helps Marie determine whether Washaw's stock is trading at an appropriate price. Book value represents the assets that would be left over to pay common shareholders if the company failed. B represents earnings per share, C is the dividend payout ratio, and D represents the current yield ratio.
11. The correct answer is A. Because Mirabelle's $75,000 in dividends was divided among 55,000 common shares, it paid $1.36 per share ($75,000 × 55,000).
12. The correct answer is A. The current yield measures a company's dividend relative to the market value of its stock. In Tornado's case, the current yield is 1.13% ($0.62 × $55).
13. The correct answer is D. Both I and II are liquidity ratios: net working capital and current ratio. Choosing A is just half the answer, so is incorrect. B is again only half the answer because III is the common stock ratio, not a measure of liquidity but of coverage; and D gives only half the answer because IV is preferred stock ratio. Therefore, the only choice that offers both liquidity ratios is D.
14. The correct answer is B. Quick asset ratio is calculated as current assets – inventory ÷ current liabilities. A is cash asset ratio, C is current ratio, and D is net working capital.

15. The correct answer is C. Long-term assets are those items used in the course of business and are not intended to be converted to cash. They consist of such things as real estate, buildings, machinery, and office equipment. All of these things can be depreciated by either straight-line or accelerated depreciation. The decision for choosing one over the other type of depreciation is made by the company and depends on whether they want to take an equal amount of depreciation each year or a larger amount in the first years, and less in subsequent years. At the end of the life cycle of the asset, the resulting value of the item is the same. A company must determine the benefits of each type of depreciation based on their current financial position.

Technical Analysis

Terms You Need to Know

- ✓ Accumulation area
- ✓ Advance-decline index
- ✓ Advances
- ✓ Bar chart
- ✓ Breakout
- ✓ Chartist
- ✓ Consolidation
- ✓ Contrarian
- ✓ Declines
- ✓ Distribution area
- ✓ Dow theory
- ✓ Downtrend
- ✓ Efficient market
- ✓ Head and shoulders formation
- ✓ Inverse saucer
- ✓ Inverted head and shoulders formation
- ✓ Moving average
- ✓ Odd lot
- ✓ Odd-lot theory
- ✓ Overbought
- ✓ Oversold
- ✓ Put-call ratio
- ✓ Random walk theory
- ✓ Resistance level
- ✓ Saucer
- ✓ Short interest
- ✓ Short interest theory
- ✓ Support level
- ✓ Technical analysis
- ✓ Trading volume
- ✓ Uptrend

Concepts You Need to Understand

- ✓ How to recognize chart patterns
- ✓ Which patterns indicate bullish or bearish markets
- ✓ What kinds of information technical analysts use
- ✓ How different technical theories predict different market behaviors

Technical Analysts

Whereas fundamental analysis begins with the examination of financial statements to develop long-range expectations about a company and its securities, technical analysis focuses on patterns in security prices in order to identify short- and medium-term trends. These market price trends—rather than any information about the company itself—become the basis of the technical analysts' recommended investment strategies.

Technical analysis is the use of price charts and other market information to identify and predict trends in the prices of stocks, stock indexes, bonds, options, commodities, or futures. Because technical analysts spend most of their time analyzing price charts, they are also known as chartists. Some chartists argue that it is unnecessary to know anything about the issuing company or even the kind of securities. Simply by analyzing the patterns of past price changes, these analysts believe they can predict future price movements and recommend the best times to buy or sell.

Technical analysts, or chartists, explain their approach by pointing out that investors' decisions to buy or sell determine the prices of all securities. Technical analysts are simply inferring investors' mindsets from price patterns. How high do investors let the price go before they start selling? How low do they let it drop before they begin to buy? By studying a security's past behavior in the market, analysts try to project its future behavior.

Charts

Charts are an important part of technical analysis. They show changes over time and help investors make informed decisions about an investment. There are numerous types—bar charts, line charts, saucers, and many others. Charts show many different types of information for investors, brokers, bankers, and others. Charts are used to study past performance of a company's stock price in the hopes that past performance is an indicator of future price changes. Some investors believe this absolutely while others are less dependent on past performance as an indicator of future performance. The primary tool of chartists, however, is the bar chart.

Bar Charts

In the financial world, a *bar chart* is a graph that exhibits the price of a security (or group of securities) over a certain period of time. For example, the chart might show the price of a specific bond issue over the course of a month, the price of a stock over the course of a week, or the level of the Dow Jones industrial average over six months, as shown in Figure 31.1.

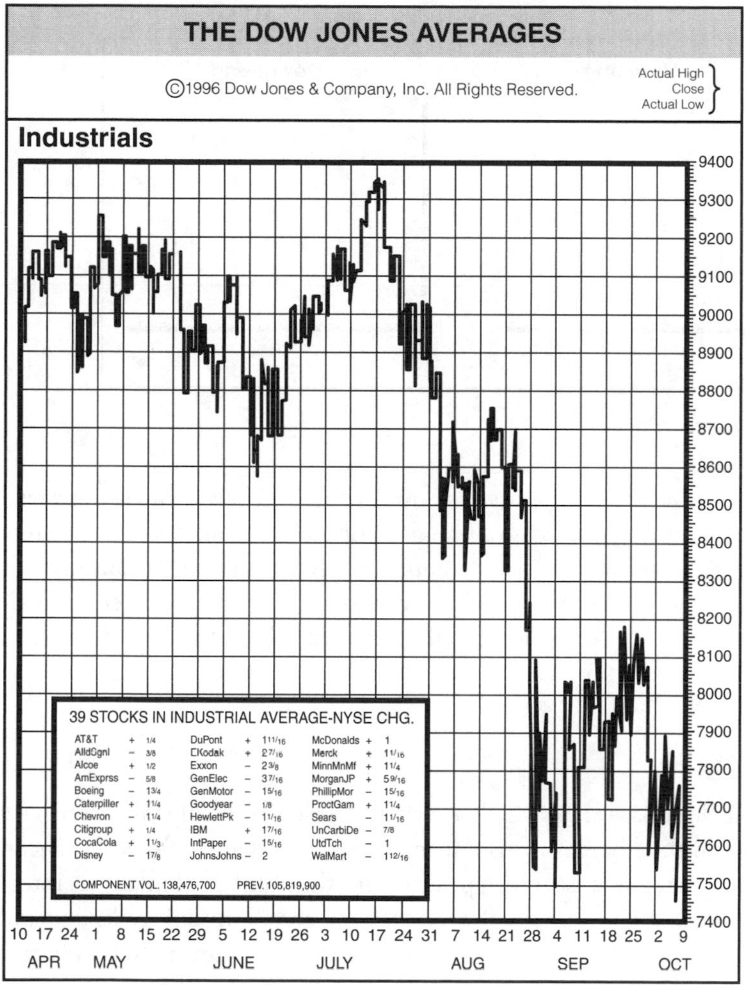

THE DOW JONES AVERAGES
©1996 Dow Jones & Company, Inc. All Rights Reserved.
Actual High
Close
Actual Low
Industrials
9400
9300
9200
9100
9000
8900
8800
8700
8600
8500
8400
8300
8200
8100
8000
7900
7800
7700
7600
7500
7400
39 STOCKS IN INDUSTRIAL AVERAGE-NYSE CHG.
AT&T + 1/4
AlldSgnl − 3/8
Alcoe + 1/2
AmExprss − 5/8
Boeing − 1 3/4
Caterpiller + 1 1/4
Chevron − 1 1/4
Citigroup + 1/4
CocaCola + 1 1/3
Disney − 1 7/8
DuPont + 1 11/16
EKodak + 2 7/16
Exxon − 2 3/8
GenElec − 3 7/16
GenMotor − 1 5/16
Goodyear − 1/8
HewlettPk − 1 1/16
IBM + 1 7/16
IntPaper − 1 5/16
JohnsJohns − 2
McDonalds + 1
Merck + 1 1/16
MinnMnMf + 1 1/4
MorganJP + 5 9/16
PhillipMor − 1 5/16
ProctGam + 1 1/4
Sears − 1 1/16
UnCarbiDe − 7/8
UtdTch − 1
WalMart − 1 12/16
COMPONENT VOL. 138,476,700 PREV. 105,819,900
10 17 24 1 8 15 22 29 5 12 19 26 3 10 17 24 31 7 14 21 28 4 11 18 25 2 9
APR MAY JUNE JULY AUG SEP OCT

Figure 31.1 Bar chart.

High
Open
Close
Low

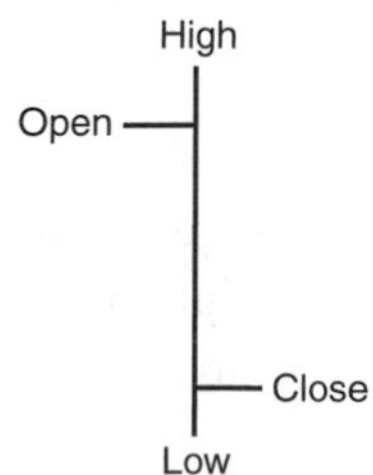

Figure 31.2 Opening and closing price bar chart.

If the daily range of prices gradually rises over time, the path is known as an *uptrend*. If the prices are generally falling, the result is a *downtrend*, as shown in Figure 31.3.

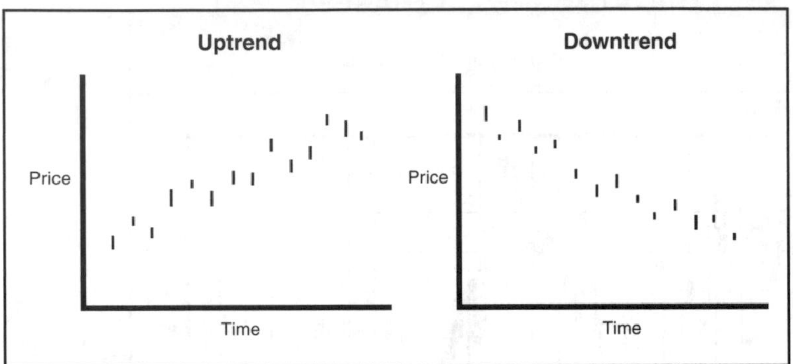

Figure 31.3 Uptrend and downtrend chart.

Of course, just because prices are currently rising (or falling) does not mean that they will continue to do so. The goal of technical analysis is to determine when an uptrend or a downtrend is likely to reverse, because this is when investors want to sell or buy. To accomplish this, analysts need to identify patterns that have often indicated such reversals in the past. One such pattern is known as a saucer.

Saucers

A *saucer* is a chart pattern in which a security's price gradually falls, reaches a minimum, and then begins to rise, forming a shape that resembles a saucer. The pattern occurs because, given price levels, the number of investors interested in buying has slowly risen above those interested in selling. As demand begins to exceed supply, the security's price rises. This pattern often indicates the reversal of a trend—a downtrend ends and an uptrend begins—so the price is likely to continue rising a while. Saucers are thus a bullish sign. After noticing such a pattern, an analyst might want to recommend that his or her customers purchase the security.

An *inverse saucer* is the opposite of a saucer. Here, the price gradually rises, reaches a maximum, and then begins to fall. Inverse saucers suggest the reversal of an uptrend, and are therefore interpreted as a bearish sign. They tell analysts that it is a good time to sell—or sell short—the security. Figure 31.4 is an example of both a saucer and inverse saucer chart.

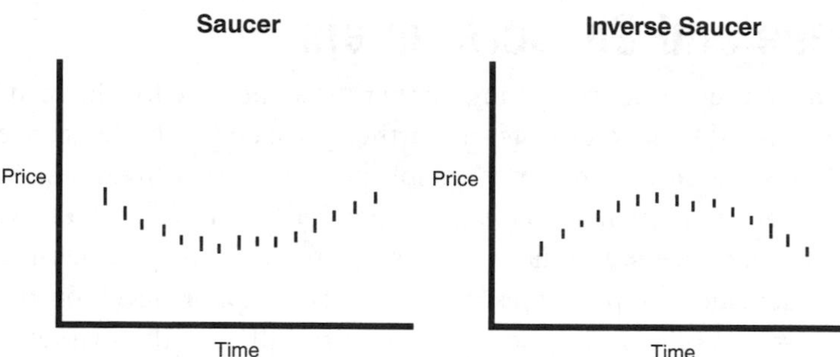

Figure 31.4 Saucer chart.

Head and Shoulders Formation

A *head and shoulders formation*, also signaling the reversal of a trend, occurs when the security price rises to a new peak, falls briefly, rises to an even higher peak, falls again, and then rises to a lower peak. The two lower peaks are the "shoulders" and the high middle peak is the "head." This pattern indicates the close of an uptrend and the beginning of a downtrend, and is therefore bearish. In contrast, an *inverted head and shoulders formation* shows the reversal of a downtrend and, hence, the beginning of an uptrend. Figure 31.5 is an example of a head and shoulders chart; both normal and inverted.

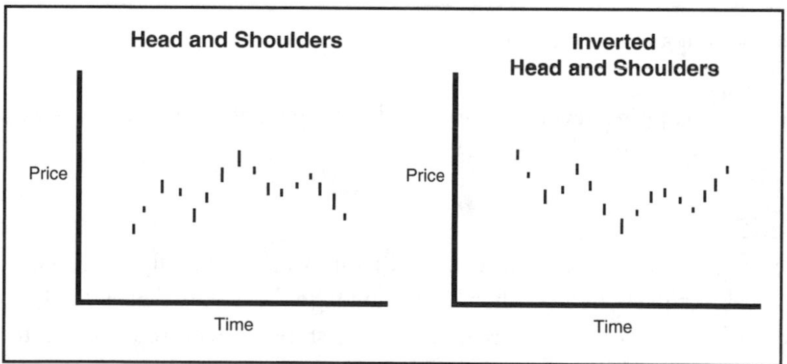

Figure 31.5 Head and shoulders and inverted head and shoulders.

Although security prices sometimes reverse trends, often they bump up against a maximum—or down against a minimum—again and again. These prices are known as resistance and support levels.

Resistance and Support Levels

At a *resistance level*, the market resists any further price increase for the security; at a *support level*, the market resists any further price decrease. Resistance and support levels are because of limits established by market investors. At the resistance level, the price has risen higher than buyers are willing to pay; sellers far outnumber buyers, and the market is said to be *overbought*. Because supply exceeds demand, the price must fall a bit. At a support level, on the other hand, most sellers feel the price is too low to sell, and the market is termed *oversold*. At this price, buyers outnumber sellers, and because demand exceeds supply, the security's price rebounds some. Figure 31.6 charts resistance and support levels.

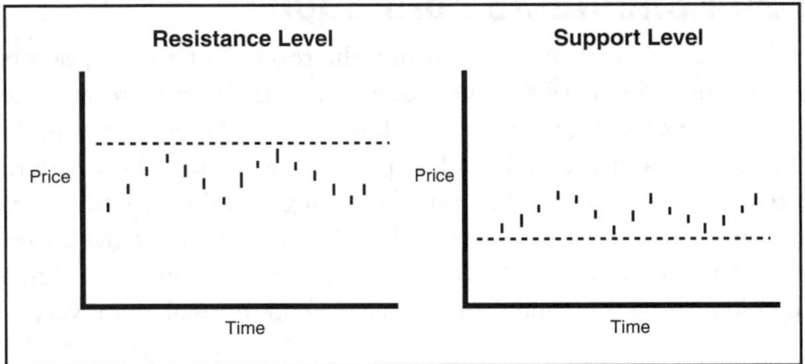

Figure 31.6 Resistance and support chart.

Resistance and support levels do not hold forever. In what is known as a breakout, prices can pass through them.

Breakouts

A *breakout* is the movement of a security through its historical resistance or support level. Analysts believe that breakouts signal a trend that is likely to continue. After the price has reached a resistance level repeatedly, for instance, everyone willing to sell at the resistance price has already sold. When the price finally moves above this point, there is therefore fewer sellers than buyers, leading to a steady climb in prices. Conversely, for a security to fall below its support level, all the buyers who wanted to purchase at that price must be satisfied. When the barrier is crossed, more sellers exist than buyers, leading to a continuing fall in prices. After a breakout, a security will eventually reach a new equilibrium level. Figure 31.7 shows a breakout chart.

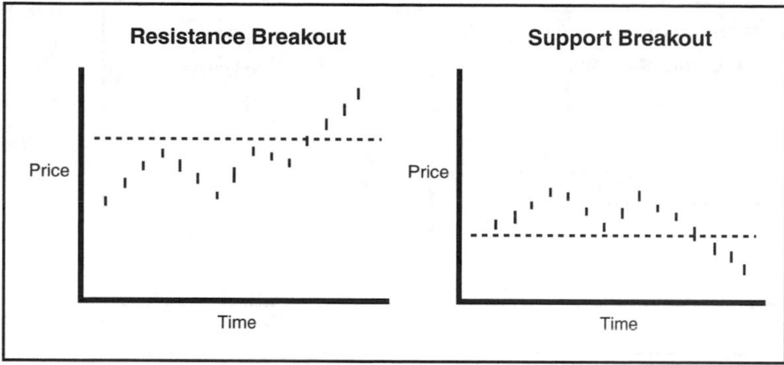

Figure 31.7 Breakout chart.

To pull all this into a simpler format, Table 31.1 shows what each type of chart means for a chartist, and investors as well. Bullish signs are found in saucers, reverse head and shoulder formation, and breakout above resistance levels. Bearish signs are found in an inverse saucer, a head and shoulder formation, and a breakout below support level.

Table 31.1 Summary of Chart Patterns

Bullish Sign	Bearish Sign
Saucer	Inverse saucer
Reverse head and shoulders formation	Head and shoulders formation
Breakout above resistance level	Breakout below support level

Consolidation

In a process known as *consolidation*, the price of a security that has recently broken out begins to level off. During consolidation, the forces of supply and demand are more or less even, as some traders unload the security, whereas others purchase it.

Consolidation has two possible results. In an *accumulation area*, more buyers gradually enter the market than sellers. As the buyers gain force, in expectation of an uptrend, the security's supply diminishes, and its price eventually increases. *Distribution areas* signal the opposite dynamic: more sellers move into the market than buyers. When selling clearly begins to dominate buying, prices fall. Of course, in the midst of consolidation not everyone can foresee whether buying or selling will predominate. It is anyone's bet, until after the fact. Figure 31.8 is an example of a consolidation chart.

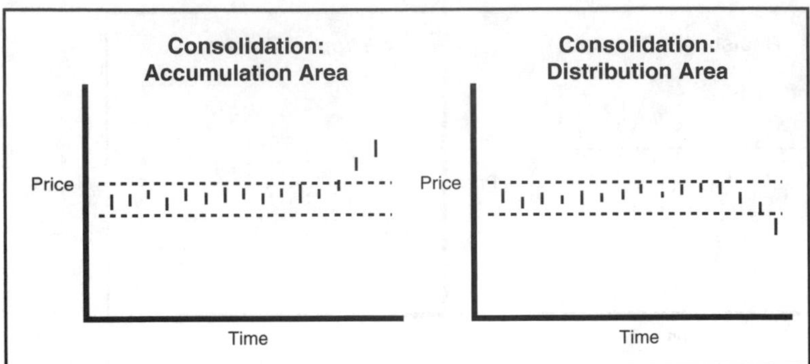

Figure 31.8 Consolidation chart.

Bar charts are very useful for monitoring short-term fluctuations in the prices of securities, but sometimes technical analysts want to look at the long-term trends in prices. Moving averages let them do this.

Moving Averages

A *moving average* is the average price of a security (or index) plotted over time. It is a *moving* average because the figure is recalculated each day as the specified period moves forward. A 200-day moving average thus plots the average price for the past 200 days. Each day, the previous day's price is included in the average, whereas the price that is 201 days old is dropped from the average. Moving average charts result in a smooth line graph that illustrates long-term trends well. Figure 31.9 shows a 200-day moving average.

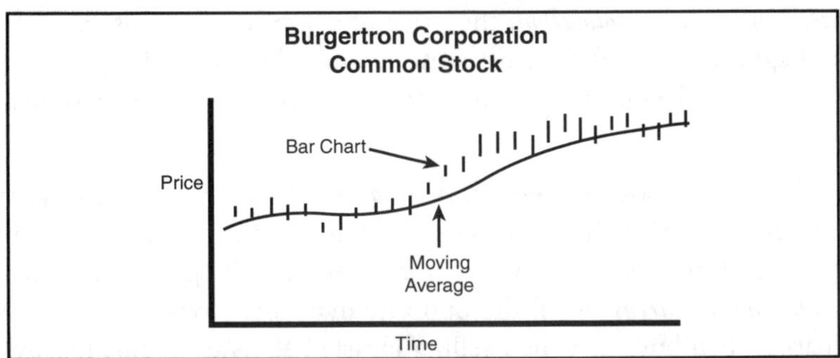

Figure 31.9 Moving average.

Because moving averages demonstrate long-run trends, analysts depend on them to judge whether price changes are temporary, or whether new trends are beginning. If current prices diverge sufficiently from a security's moving average, a new trend might be starting. Technical analysts often study moving averages with different time frames and pay close attention to points where the averages cross.

Technical Theories

No pattern, no matter how strong, guarantees a trend by itself—markets simply are not that predictable. When analysts suspect a new trend is emerging, they look for confirming evidence. In addition to security prices, they often investigate market indexes, trading volumes, short interest, and numbers of advances and declines. Technical analysts have developed theories about the relevance of each of these data sources for future market behavior. Table 31.2 lists the technical theories discussed here and their market indicators.

Table 31.2 Technical Theories and Their Indicators

Theory	Bullish Indicator	Bearish Indicator
Dow theory	DJIA and DJTA reach new peaks	DJIA and DJTA reach new lows
Odd-lot theory	Odd-lot sales increasing	Odd-lot sales decreasing
Odd-lot theory	Odd-lot purchases decreasing	Odd-lot purchases increasing
Random Walk Theory		
Short interest theory	Short interest increasing	Short interest decreasing

Dow Theory

One of the oldest theories in technical analysis is the *Dow theory*, which states that a major market trend is only confirmed when both the Dow Jones industrial average (DJIA) and the Dow Jones transportation average (DJTA) reach a new high or a new low. In other words, if an analyst believes that the market as a whole is experiencing an uptrend, he or she has to confirm this hypothesis by looking for peaks in both the DJIA and the DJTA.

Odd-Lot Theory

The *odd-lot theory* assumes that smaller investors—those who generally trade in *odd lots*, which are trades less than the usual minimum amount for a security in a market—are usually wrong in their market timing. Advocates of the theory argue that odd-lot traders typically buy when prices are near their peak and sell when prices are approaching their low point. That is, the theory goes, small investors are inexperienced—they react too slowly to trends, buying only after an uptrend has become well established, and selling only after a downtrend has become painfully obvious. By that time, the trend might be ready to reverse itself. According to the odd-lot theory, then, a savvy investor should buy when odd-lotters are selling and sell when odd-lotters are buying. They can keep track of odd-lot trading activity by reading any financial newspaper.

Odd-lot theorists believe that odd-lot traders typically buy high and sell low because they are inexperienced and react too slowly to trends, buying only after an uptrend has become well-established, and selling only after a downtrend has become painfully obvious.

EXAMPLE: Maxine has decided to take profits on her Triple Z stock, which has been climbing for five months, but she wants to wait until the price nears its peak. Being of a contrarian nature, she watches the data on odd-lot purchases of Triple Z. After a couple of weeks, she notices that odd-lot purchases are beginning to increase quickly. Small investors are starting to jump on the Triple Z bandwagon, which for Maxine is a sign that the stock's uptrend is about to conclude. She tells her broker to sell her entire holding of Triple Z stock.

Random Walk Theory

Random walk theory posits that the past performance of security prices has no bearing on future performance—that stock prices move in an essentially random and unpredictable manner. All forms of technical analysis are premised on the assumption that stock prices will behave as they have in the past. However, by testing each of the technical theories against historical market data, random walk theorists can show that no strategy works all the time. In fact, the proponents of this theory claim that a portfolio of randomly chosen securities will usually outperform a portfolio managed by technical analysts. Comparisons of the performance of indexes such as the S&P 500 with actively managed mutual funds appear to buttress this position. Despite all their tools and strategies, it has been nearly impossible for fund managers to outperform the S&P 500 for long.

Random walk theorists claim that testing technical theories against historical market data shows that no theory works all the time.

Random walk theory is often paired with efficient market theory. An *efficient market* is an ideal market in which all public information about a company is instantly reflected in the price of its stock. In such a situation, studying the fundamentals of a company cannot uncover any under-priced securities, because perfectly informed investors have already accounted for all potential risks and rewards. People who think that securities markets approach the ideal of the efficient market believe that fundamental analysis is just as misleading as technical analysis. Of course, there are those who have studied the idea of an efficient market at various levels, but the results are not conclusive. Some claim evidence supports an ideal market and others claim evidence rejects it.

Short Interest Theory

Short interest is the number of common stock shares (for a company or a market) that have been sold short and not yet covered. Recall that when investors sell stock short, they are borrowing the shares and must replace them later. A growing short interest might therefore seem like a bearish indicator, because short sellers are betting that stock prices will fall. According to the *short interest theory*, however, the greater the short interest, the greater the number of investors who must eventually purchase stock in order to cover their positions. When they finally do begin to buy, market prices are likely to rise because of the surge in demand. Hence, the greater the short interest, the more likely the price is going to rise in the near future—a bullish sign.

Short interest theory states that the greater the short interest, the more likely the price is going to rise in the near future—a bullish sign, because short sellers must eventually purchase stock to cover their positions. Thus, prices rise.

Advocates of short interest theory are often called *contrarians*, because they assume that most investors are wrong in their reading of the securities markets. Technical analysts employ a wide range of contrarian strategies. The aim of these strategies is to go against the flow, staying one step ahead of other traders to buy when others believe it is a good time to sell, and sell when others believe it is a good time to buy. If they time their transactions correctly, they purchase as securities are sinking toward their low points and sell when securities are rising to their high points—an enviable, although by no means certain, result.

Short interest strategies are not the only contrarian approach to investment. Believers in the odd-lot theory go against the trading patterns set by one particular group of investors, not the entire lot of them.

Perhaps the ultimate contrarians, however, are the disciples of random walk theory, who essentially believe that everyone is wrong.

Other Data Sources

Data sources are other indicators of future price movements just like moving averages and resistance-support levels. Trading volume, the advance-decline index, and the put-call ratio are a few data sources used by technical analysts. Table 31.3 lists the data sources and their market indicators.

Table 31.3 Data Sources and Their Market Indicators

Data Source	Bullish Indicator	Bearish Indicator
Trading volume	Rising prices in conjunction with increasing volume	Rising prices in conjunction with decreasing volume
Trading volume	Falling prices in conjunction with decreasing volume	Falling prices in conjunction with increasing volume
Advance-decline	Advance-decline index positive or increasing	Advance-decline index negative or decreasing
Put-call ratio	Put-call ratio is high	Put-call ratio is low

Trading Volume

Analysts consider *trading volume*, the number of shares or securities traded in a given day, to be an important indicator of future price movements. Volume tends to lead to price trends. If trading volume is steady, price fluctuations are probably temporary. But if trading volume is rising, any new directions in prices might signal a trend. However, if prices are rising but volume is falling, analysts can conclude that the market is overbought (purchasing interest is on the wane), and therefore the uptrend can be expected to end soon. Similarly, if prices are falling in a period of increasing trading volume, the downtrend will probably persist for some time. But if prices are falling while volume is decreasing, the market is oversold, and the downtrend might be nearing its end.

While overall market volume is a crucial tool for analysts searching for major trends, they also want to know the figures for advances and declines.

Advances and Declines

Advances are the stocks in a certain market that have increased in price on a given day; *declines* are the stocks that have decreased in price. The *advance-decline index* measures the proportion of advances and declines.

Advance-decline index = advances – declines ÷ total number of issues

If the index value increases, then advances outnumber declines, and the market is bullish. If the index is decreasing, then declines exceed advances, and the market is considered bearish. Any trends in the index itself are also telling; if the market is rising, and the advance-decline index is also rising, analysts declare that an uptrend is confirmed. If the market is rising while the advance-decline index is falling, however, they forecast a reversal. Financial newspapers list advances and declines for different securities markets each business day.

Put-Call Ratio

The *put-call ratio* is the number of put options compared to the number of call options on a specific index. Some technical analysts believe put-call ratios offer a broad indication of future market behavior. If puts outnumber calls and trading volume is heavy, the bears are driving the market. Although this might appear like a purely bearish situation, many analysts instead take it as a sign that the market is bottoming out, and therefore interpret it as a bullish sign. According to the put-call theory, the market is oversold and will have difficulty going much lower. Conversely, a *low* put-call ratio demonstrates an overbought market, one that is ready for a fall, and hence is seen as a bearish indicator.

A Closing Thought on Pragmatism

No analytical theory can reveal the future, and no method, either fundamental or technical, can guarantee a profitable securities transaction. Smart investors and analysts use all the tools available, however imperfectly they might work. In this light, both fundamental and technical analyses continue to play important roles in the securities industry.

Exam Prep Questions

1. A technical analyst uses which of the following:

   I. Uses charts and graphs to predict trends in the prices of stocks.

   II. Analyzes the financial statements of companies to evaluate investments.

   III. Uses income statements and balance sheets to predict trends in prices of stocks.

   IV. Analyzes patterns of past price movements to predict future price movements of stocks.

   ❑ A. I and II
   ❑ B. II and III
   ❑ C. I, II, and III
   ❑ D. I and IV

2. Fuchsia Fashions stock has fallen, reached a minimum, and then begun to rise again. Maxwell's chart of these price changes reveals:

   ❑ A. A saucer pattern.
   ❑ B. An inverse saucer pattern.
   ❑ C. A head and shoulder formation.
   ❑ D. An reverse head and shoulders formation.

3. Challenger Publishing is trading at its resistance level. At this point:

   I. The market is resisting any further price increase for Challenger stock.

   II. The market is resisting any further price decrease for Challenger stock.

   III. The market is overbought.

   IV. The market is oversold.

   ❑ A. I and III
   ❑ B. I and IV
   ❑ C. II and III
   ❑ D. II and IV

4. On Friday, Challenger Publishing stock is trading at its resistance level. By Monday, the price has risen five points. This increase is known as a:

   ❑ A. Breakout
   ❑ B. Consolidation
   ❑ C. Accumulation
   ❑ D. Distribution

5. When a technical analyst charts the prices of stocks, he considers all the following patterns bullish signs except:
   - ❑ A. Saucers
   - ❑ B. Reverse head and shoulder formations
   - ❑ C. Head and shoulder formations
   - ❑ D. Breakouts above resistance levels

6. Which of the following statements are true of a moving average?

   I. It plots prices over a fixed time frame.

   II. It is recalculated each day.

   III. The oldest prices are dropped as the newest prices are added.

   IV. It plots long-term changes.
   - ❑ A. I only
   - ❑ B. II and III
   - ❑ C. I and IV
   - ❑ D. I, II, III, and IV

7. The Dow theory states that a major market trend is only confirmed when:
   - ❑ A. The Dow Jones transportation average (DJTA) reaches a new high or low.
   - ❑ B. The S&P 500 Index reaches a new high or low.
   - ❑ C. The Dow Jones industrial average reaches a new high or low.
   - ❑ D. Both the Dow Jones industrial average and Dow transportation average reach a new high or low.

8. Emma, a technical analyst, pays considerable attention to trading volume because:

   I. Volume tends to lead to price changes.

   II. A steady volume suggests that price fluctuations are temporary.

   III. A steady volume suggests a new long-term trend.

   IV. Increased volume can signal a new trend.
   - ❑ A. I and II
   - ❑ B. I, III, and IV
   - ❑ C. I, II, and IV
   - ❑ D. I and IV

9. On Tuesday, the NYSE had 2,038 advances and 1,157 declines. What is the advance-decline index for the day?
   - ❑ A. 1.76 to 1
   - ❑ B. .276
   - ❑ C. .637
   - ❑ D. 1.57

10. Deirdre, a technical analyst, believes in the short interest theory. She therefore keeps an eye on the short interest listings, which show:
    - ❑ A. The number of shares of common stock that have been sold short and not yet covered.
    - ❑ B. The number of option contracts that have been sold on a given security.
    - ❑ C. The number of call and put contracts that have been sold on a given security.
    - ❑ D. The number of shorted shares that have been covered.
11. Carl, a successful investor, believes that most investors are wrong in the their reading of the securities market. Carl is a:
    - ❑ A. Short theorist
    - ❑ B. Contrarian
    - ❑ C. Chartist
    - ❑ D. Consolidator
12. The odd-lot theory assumes that smaller investors:

    I. Tend to be right in their timing

    II. Tend to be wrong in their timing

    III. Buy when prices have peaked

    IV. Sell when prices have bottomed out
    - ❑ A. I and IV
    - ❑ B. II, III, and IV
    - ❑ C. II and IV
    - ❑ D. I and III
13. A low put-call ratio indicates all the following except:
    - ❑ A. An overbought market
    - ❑ B. A market ready for a rise
    - ❑ C. A market ready for a fall
    - ❑ D. The approach of a bearish trend
14. Arnold believes that the past performance of security prices has no bearing on future price performance. Arnold believes in:
    - ❑ A. The short interest theory
    - ❑ B. The odd lot theory
    - ❑ C. The random walk theory
    - ❑ D. The advance-decline index
15. Technical analyst Maxwell notices that his chart of Consolidated Cans ends in a head and shoulders formation. To Maxwell, this signals:
    - ❑ A. The reversal of Consolidated's recent downtrend
    - ❑ B. The continuation of Consolidated's recent downtrend
    - ❑ C. The continuation of Consolidated's recent uptrend
    - ❑ D. The reversal of Consolidated's recent uptrend

Exam Prep Answers

1. The correct answer is D. A technical analyst uses price charts and other market information to identify and predict trends in the prices of securities. By analyzing the patterns of past price changes, technical analysts believe they can predict future price movements and recommend the best times to buy and sell.
2. The correct answer is A. A saucer is a chart pattern in which a security's price gradually falls, reaches a minimum, and then begins to rise, forming a shape that resembles a saucer. An inverse saucer is the opposite of a saucer in which the price gradually rises, reaches a maximum, and then begins to fall. A head and shoulders formation signals the reversal of a trend, occurs when the security price rises to a new peak, falls briefly, rises to an even higher peak, falls again, and then rises to a lower peak. A reverse head and shoulders formation shows the reversal of a downtrend and, hence, the beginning of an uptrend.
3. The correct answer is A. At Challenger's resistance level, the market resists any further price increase for Challenger stock. The stock's price has risen higher than buyers are willing to pay. Because sellers now far outnumber buyers, the market is overbought.
4. The correct answer is A. A breakout is the movement of a security through its historical resistance or support level. Analysts believe that a breakout signals a trend that is likely to continue.
5. The correct answer is C. A head and shoulders formation signals the reversal of an uptrend and the beginning of a downtrend. It is thus a bearish sign.
6. The correct answer is D. A moving average is the average price of a security or index plotted over time, from even one day to one, five, and ten-year periods. It is a moving average because the figure is recalculated each day as the specified period moves forward. Each day, the previous day's price is included in the average and the oldest price is dropped. A moving average chart results in a smooth line graph that illustrates long-term trends well.
7. The correct answer is D. The Dow theory states that a major market trend is only confirmed when both the Dow Jones industrial average and the Dow Jones transportation average reach a new high or low. In other words, if an analyst believes that the market as a whole is experiencing an uptrend, he or she must confirm this hypothesis by looking for peaks in both the DJIA and the DJTA.
8. The correct answer is C. Analysts consider trading volume to be an important indicator of future price movements. Volume tends to lead to price trends. If trading volume is steady, then price fluctuations are probably temporary. But if trading volume is rising, new directions in prices may signal a trend.

9. The correct answer is B. The advance-decline index is calculated as advances minus declines, divided by the total number of issues. In this case it is: 2,038 – 1,157 = 881 ÷ (2,038 + 1,157) = .276.
10. The correct answer is A. Short interest is the number of shares of common stock that have been sold short and not yet covered. The greater the short interest, the greater the number of investors who must eventually purchase stock in order to cover their positions. According to the short interest theory, when these investors finally do begin to buy, the surge in demand is likely to raise market prices.
11. The correct answer is B. Carl is a contrarian. Contrarians believe that most investors are wrong in their reading of the securities markets. There are a wide range of contrarian strategies, including those involving short interest, odd-lot trading figures, and the put-call ratio.
12. The correct answer is B. The odd-lot theory assumes that smaller investors—those who generally trade in odd lots of less than the usual minimum amounts—are usually wrong in their market timing. Advocates of this theory argue that odd-lot traders typically buy when prices are near their peak and sell when prices are approaching their low point, reacting too slowly because they are inexperienced.
13. The correct answer is B. The put-call ratio is the number of put options compared to the number of call options on a specific index. Some technical analysts believe this ratio offers a broad indication of future market behavior. To these analysts, a low put-call ratio demonstrates an overbought market (where purchasing interest is on the wane), one that is ready for a fall, and hence a bearish trend in the near future.
14. The correct answer is C. The random walk theory posits that the past performance of security prices has no bearing on future performance—that stock prices move in an essentially random and unpredictable manner. This is contrary to most theories of technical analysis, which hold that stock prices behave as they have in the past.
15. The correct answer is D. A head and shoulders formation occurs when the security price rises to a new peak, falls briefly, rises to an even higher peak, falls again, and then rises to a lower peak. It signals the close of an uptrend and the beginning of a downtrend.

Practice Exam

1. A security that sells in the primary market, and has no further authorized shares to sell, moves on to which of the following?
   - ❑ A. The New York Stock Exchange
   - ❑ B. The OTC market
   - ❑ C. The Amex
   - ❑ D. The exchange where the company will be listed

2. The National Association of Securities Dealers, or NASD, enforces the rules and regulations for which of the following exchanges?

   I. The NYSE

   II. The Amex

   III. The OTC

   IV. The CBOE
   - ❑ A. I only
   - ❑ B. I, II, and III
   - ❑ C. III only
   - ❑ D. III and IV

3. The theorists who believe that all public information about a company is instantly reflected in the price of its stock adhere to which of the following theories?
   - ❑ A. Random walk theory
   - ❑ B. Efficient market theory
   - ❑ C. Dow theory
   - ❑ D. Odd lot theory

4. Which of the following types of retirement accounts requires an individual to become fully vested in order to receive full payment at retirement?
   - ❑ A. IRA accounts
   - ❑ B. Keogh accounts
   - ❑ C. 401(k) program
   - ❑ D. A Roth IRA

5. A price-based option on a T-bill with a premium of 1.00 costs the buyer of the option which of the following amounts?
   - ❑ A. $1,000
   - ❑ B. $2,500
   - ❑ C. $5,000
   - ❑ D. $10,000

6. The holder of one put option has which of the following rights in respect to the option contract? **1 FTD August 60 PUT @ 3**

   I. The right to buy 100 shares of FTD stock at $60

   II. The right to sell 100 shares of FTD stock at $60

   III. The right to receive $300 for the contract

   IV. The right to pay $300 for the contract
   - ❑ A. I and III
   - ❑ B. I and IV
   - ❑ C. II and III
   - ❑ D. II and IV

7. A customer's trade that has been reported on the consolidated tape as 2sGHI 34 s/t is represented by which of the following descriptions?
   - ❑ A. 2,000 shares of GHI at 34 were sold short
   - ❑ B. 200 shares of GHI at 34 were sold short
   - ❑ C. 2,000 shares of GHI at 34 were sold as stopped stock
   - ❑ D. 200 shares of GHI at 34 were sold as stopped stock

8. A Special Tax bond can have all the following sources of income backing it except for which one?
   - ❑ A. Taxes on liquor sales
   - ❑ B. Taxes on tobacco products
   - ❑ C. Taxes on gambling operations
   - ❑ D. The collection of property taxes

9. After the SEC has awarded an effective date for a new issue filing, what can the offering do?

   I. Issue a final prospectus with the offering price

   II. Be offered to the primary market

III. Be sold to the secondary market

IV. The underwriters can begin taking indication on the shares

- ❑ A. I and IV only
- ❑ B. I and II only
- ❑ C. I, II, and III
- ❑ D. I, II, III, and IV

10. Kelly purchases 20-year municipal bonds at 110 in the secondary market with 16 years to maturity. Kelly holds the bonds for 8 years and then sells the bonds at a price of 102 in the market. What are her tax consequences on the bonds?
    - ❑ A. The bonds have no tax consequences because they are tax-free.
    - ❑ B. The bonds have an adjusted cost basis of $10,592.
    - ❑ C. The bonds have an adjusted cost basis of $10,200.
    - ❑ D. The bonds have an adjusted cost basis of $10,800.

11. A broker who attempts to place another broker-dealer into a transaction chain for the execution of a trade to generate additional fees without due cause is guilty of which of the following?
    - ❑ A. Reclamation
    - ❑ B. Interpositioning
    - ❑ C. A multiple listing
    - ❑ D. Marking to the market

12. Strike prices on index options are set at which of the following intervals?
    - ❑ A. 2½ points
    - ❑ B. 5 points
    - ❑ C. 10 points
    - ❑ D. $1.00

13. Which of the following statements are considered true in the valuation of inventories for a company?

    I. LIFO assumes that the last goods to be placed in inventory are the first ones sold.

    II. FIFO assumes that the first goods placed in inventory are the first ones sold.

    III. FIFO generally reports a higher value for existing inventories than LIFO.

    IV. LIFO generally reports a higher value for existing inventories than FIFO.

    - ❑ A. I and III
    - ❑ B. I and IV
    - ❑ C. I, II, and III
    - ❑ D. I, II, III, and IV

14. A holder of an option position who has decided to exercise her option contract asks the Options Clearing Corp. for which of the following?
    - ❑ A. An exercise notice
    - ❑ B. An assignment
    - ❑ C. An option agreement
    - ❑ D. A private placement

15. An agency that has issued modified pass-through certificates can purchase mortgages from lending institutions at which of the following?
    - ❑ A. Purchase mortgages with the same interest rate as the pass-through certificate
    - ❑ B. Purchase mortgages with a lower interest rate than the pass-through certificate
    - ❑ C. Purchase mortgages with a higher interest rate than the pass-through certificate
    - ❑ D. Issue mortgages with the same interest rate as the pass-through certificate

16. Which of the following types of orders is entered at a price above the current market price for the stock?

    I. Sell limit order

    II. Buy stop order

    III. Buy stop limit order

    IV. Buy limit order
    - ❑ A. I only
    - ❑ B. I and II
    - ❑ C. I, II, and III
    - ❑ D. I, II, III, and IV

17. An investor sells 1 HTH April 60 Call @ 5 and buys 1 HTH April 70 Call @ 2. This is an example of which of the following?
    - ❑ A. Long call debit spread
    - ❑ B. Short call debit spread
    - ❑ C. Long call credit spread
    - ❑ D. Short call credit spread

18. All the following statements are true of no-load mutual funds except for?
    - ❑ A. They sell directly to the investor
    - ❑ B. They do not charge a sales fee
    - ❑ C. They do not charge any fees to shareholders
    - ❑ D. They redeem shares for shareholders

19. TNT Corporation has paid out $.62 as a dividend with its share price being $55.00 in the market. What is the current yield on the stock?

- ❑ A. 1.13%
- ❑ B. 11.3%
- ❑ C. 8.87%
- ❑ D. 34.1%

20. Securities that are held in a margin account are required to be kept in which of the following?

- ❑ A. Street name
- ❑ B. Safekeeping
- ❑ C. Segregation
- ❑ D. Registered form

21. A municipal investment trust is best described as which of the following entities?

- ❑ A. An open-ended mutual fund assembled into a large pool of municipal bonds that can be sold to small investors.
- ❑ B. A closed-ended mutual fund assembled into a large pool of municipal bonds that can be sold to small investors.
- ❑ C. Municipal bonds deposited with a trustee as part of a unit trust that sells units to small investors and are representative of all the bonds in the trust.
- ❑ D. Municipal bonds deposited with a trustee as part of a unit trust that enable small investors to purchase smaller increments of the bonds than they can on the market.

22. When the Federal Reserve Bank purchases securities in the market, thereby injecting cash into the money supply, they are conducting which of the following?

- ❑ A. A repurchase agreement
- ❑ B. A reverse repurchase agreement
- ❑ C. An increase in the reserve requirement
- ❑ D. A matched sale purchase

23. An investor purchases 1 STP May 50 Call @ 5 and sells 1 STP May 60 Call @ 2. This is an example of which of the following?

- ❑ A. Long call credit spread
- ❑ B. Long call debit spread
- ❑ C. Short call credit spread
- ❑ D. Short call debit spread

24. Gross National Product can be described as which of the following?

- ❑ A. The measure of all goods and services produced by residents in a country
- ❑ B. The measure of all goods and services produced by residents, companies, and any foreign companies in a country
- ❑ C. The measure of all government spending within a country
- ❑ D. The measure of all corporate, government, and consumer goods and services produced within a country

25. Which of the following statements is true regarding the prime rate in the market?

I. The prime rate is the most volatile of all interest rates.

II. The prime rate is what banks lend to their most credit-worthy customer.

III. The prime rate is a cheaper way for corporations to borrow money than issuing commercial paper.

IV. The prime rate is a cheaper way for corporations to borrow money than issuing debt securities.

- ❑ A. I only
- ❑ B. II only
- ❑ C. I and III
- ❑ D. II and IV

26. An order that has been entered at a specific price and will remain open until the order is either executed or cancelled by the client is known what?

- ❑ A. Day order
- ❑ B. GTC order
- ❑ C. AON order
- ❑ D. FOK order

27. Which of the following is an example of a short put credit bear spread?

- ❑ A. Sell 1 TNT June 60 Put @ 4 / Sell 1 TNT June 50 Put @ 2
- ❑ B. Sell 1 TNT June 60 Put @ 5 / Buy 1 TNT June 50 Put @ 2
- ❑ C. Buy 1 TNT June 60 Put @ 5 / Sell 1 TNT June 50 Put @ 2
- ❑ D. Sell 1 TNT June 60 Put @ 2 / Buy 1 TNT June 50 Put @ 5

28. A long margin account has a market value of $45,000 and equity in the account of $22,500. How low can the market value fall before the account receives a margin call?

- ❑ A. $42,000
- ❑ B. $40,000
- ❑ C. $35,000
- ❑ D. $30,000

29. All the following statements are true about STRIPS (Separate Trading of Registered Interest and Principal) except for?
    - ❑ A. They are only issued in book entry form.
    - ❑ B. They are non-interest bearing securities.
    - ❑ C. They act as zero coupon issues.
    - ❑ D. They no longer are actively traded.

30. A 6.75% corporate bond that is currently selling in the market at a quote of 97 5/8 costs an investor how much to purchase?
    - ❑ A. $97.58
    - ❑ B. $975.80
    - ❑ C. $976.25
    - ❑ D. $970.63

31. When the Federal Reserve Bank lowers the reserve requirement, what effect does this action have?
    - ❑ A. It decreases the available money supply in the economy.
    - ❑ B. It increases the amount that banks must hold in reserve.
    - ❑ C. It enables banks to lend more in the market.
    - ❑ D. It decreases the amount that banks can lend in the market.

32. Which of the following municipal bond issues is considered self-supporting debt?

    I. Water treatment bonds

    II. Bridge and tunnel bonds

    III. School district bonds

    IV. Capital improvement bonds
    - ❑ A. I and II
    - ❑ B. II and III
    - ❑ C. I, II, and III
    - ❑ D. I, II, III, and IV

33. The maximum number of shares that can be sold in a 144 filing is limited to which of the following?
    - ❑ A. The lesser of 1% of the outstanding shares or the average weekly trading volume of the company shares in the four weeks prior to the filing
    - ❑ B. The greater of 1% of the outstanding shares or the average weekly trading volume of the company shares for the four weeks prior to the filing
    - ❑ C. The greater of 5% of the outstanding shares or the average trading volume of the company shares for the 90 days prior to the filing
    - ❑ D. The lesser of 1% of the outstanding shares or the average trading volume of the company shares for the 90 days prior to the filing

34. Which of the following debt securities can be called back by the government if interest rates were to fall sharply?

I. T-bills

II. T-notes

III. T-bonds

IV. Strips

❑ A. I only

❑ B. II and III

❑ C. III only

❑ D. IV only

35. What is the margin requirement for the purchase of a municipal bond in a margin account?

❑ A. 100% of the market value

❑ B. 100% of the face value

❑ C. The greater of 7% par value or 15% of market value

❑ D. The greater of 50% par value or 50% of market value

36. An overbought market has which of the following characteristics?

I. The price of the stock is higher than buyers are willing to pay

II. Sellers outnumber buyers

II. Buyers outnumber sellers

IV. It is a bearish indicator

❑ A. I and II

❑ B. I and III

❑ C. I, II, and IV

❑ D. I, III, and IV

37. Which of the following statements are considered true of a feasibility study requested by a municipality?

I. The study will be for a GO bond issue

II. The study will be conducted by an impartial engineering firm

III. The study will determine the cost of the project

IV. The study will determine the use of the project

❑ A. I and II

❑ B. II, III, and IV

❑ C. I, II, and III

❑ D. I, II, III, and IV

38. An option contract for a index option is represented by which of the following in computing the contract?

- ❑ A. Each contract represents 100 shares
- ❑ B. Each contract represents a multiplier of 100
- ❑ C. Each contract represents $100.00
- ❑ D. Each contract represents $1,000

39. What is considered the truest yield on a bond being considered for purchase by an investor?

- ❑ A. Nominal yield
- ❑ B. Current yield
- ❑ C. Yield to call
- ❑ D. Yield to maturity

40. DTT stock is selling in the market at $42.50. Iris purchases the following option contract: **2 DTT July 40 Calls @ 3**. What is the time value on this option contract?

- ❑ A. $50
- ❑ B. $100
- ❑ C. $500
- ❑ D. $600

41. Which of the following securities cannot be bought or sold on margin?

- ❑ A. NYSE securities
- ❑ B. National market system securities
- ❑ C. OTC pink sheet securities
- ❑ D. Regional listed securities

42. T-bills can be issued in all the following maturities except for which?

- ❑ A. 13 weeks
- ❑ B. 26 weeks
- ❑ C. 39 weeks
- ❑ D. 52 weeks

43. Which of the following statements is true regarding a trust account?

I. A trustee manages the assets of the individual named in the account.

II. The court can appoint a trustee.

III. The person named in the trust account can be alive or deceased.

IV. Transactions in the account can be performed only when outlined in the trust agreement.

- ❑ A. I and II
- ❑ B. II and III
- ❑ C. I, II, and III
- ❑ D. I, II, III, and IV

44. Which of the following accounts has an individual other than the beneficial owner making investment decisions in the account?

I. Custodian account

II. Discretionary account

III. Omnibus account

IV. Fiduciary account

❑ A. I only

❑ B. I and II

❑ C. I, II, and IV

❑ D. I, II, III, and IV

45. Which of the following statements is characteristic of operating income for a company?

I. Operating income is determined before taxes are paid.

II. Operating income is determined before interest expense.

III. Operating income is determined before depreciation.

IV. Operating income is found on the balance sheet.

❑ A. I and II

❑ B. II and III

❑ C. I, II, and III

❑ D. I, II, III, and IV

46. A markup on an OTC security conducted in a principal transaction has to be disclosed to the customer on the trade confirmation for which of the following securities?

I. NMS listed securities

II. SmallCap NASDAQ securities

III. Bulletin Board stocks

IV. Pink Sheet stocks

❑ A. I only

❑ B. I and II

❑ C. I, II, and III

❑ D. I, II, III, and IV

47. An investor has purchased five municipal bonds in the market with a market price of 96½. What is the total cost of the transaction for the customer?

❑ A. $960.50

❑ B. $965.00

❑ C. $4,802.50

❑ D. $4,825.00

48. Interest income that is earned from municipal bond issues is taxed in which of the following manners?

❑ A. Owes federal taxes, but not state and local taxes
❑ B. Owes state and local taxes, but not federal taxes
❑ C. Owes federal, state, and local taxes
❑ D. Does not owe federal, state, or local taxes

49. Which of the following procedures favors the small investor as opposed to the large investor in a company?

I. Statutory voting rights
II. Cumulative voting rights
III. A forward stock split
IV. A reverse stock split

❑ A. I only
❑ B. II and III
❑ C. I and III
❑ D. II and IV

50. Which of the following statements are considered true of municipal bond offerings?

I. GO bond offerings are done on a competitive bid basis.
II. GO bond offerings are done on a negotiated bid basis.
III. Revenue bond offerings are done on a competitive bid basis.
IV. Revenue bond offerings are done on a negotiated bid basis.

❑ A. I and III
❑ B. I and IV
❑ C. II and III
❑ D. II and IV

51. The crossover point for a direct participation program is best defined as which of the following?

❑ A. The point at which revenues exceed the expenses of the program
❑ B. The point at which the DPP has sold out its shares to investors
❑ C. The point at which the DPP liquidates its assets
❑ D. The point at which the DPP is dissolved as partnership

52. Which of the following industries is not considered a cyclical industry?

❑ A. Automobile manufacturers
❑ B. Appliance manufacturers
❑ C. Building material manufacturers
❑ D. Pharmaceutical manufacturers

53. Nancy sells 100 shares of PDQ stock short in the market at $58. She also purchases 1 PDQ April 60 Call @ 4 in the market. PDQ stock goes to $72 in the market at expiration. What is the profit or loss on this account?

❑ A. Gain of $1,800
❑ B. Gain of $3,200
❑ C. Loss of $200
❑ D. Loss of $600

54. The Standard & Poor's 500 Index tracks 500 stocks as an index for securities on which of the following markets?

I. The NYSE

II. The AMEX

III. The NASDAQ market

IV. The Bulletin Board

❑ A. I only
❑ B. I and II
❑ C. I, II, and III
❑ D. I, II, III, and IV

55. Which of the following statements are considered true of the listed municipal bond offering?

50 California Highway 6.175% 1/1/15 C05 6.485% Merrill Lynch

I. The bonds have a nominal yield of 6.485%

II. The bonds are revenue bonds

III. The bonds are callable

IV. The bonds mature in the year 2015

❑ A. I and II
❑ B. II and III
❑ C. II, III, and IV
❑ D. I, II, III, and IV

56. An investor purchases 1 FTD May 55 Call @ 4 and also sells 1 FTD May 65 Call @ 2. What is the breakeven point on the long call if the market price of FTD is $56?

❑ A. $57
❑ B. $59
❑ C. $60
❑ D. $61

57. All exercise notices that have been sent to the Options Clearing Corporation are handled in which of the following manner?

- ❑ A. Last in first out basis
- ❑ B. First in first out basis
- ❑ C. Random basis
- ❑ D. Largest position basis

58. Treasury bills can be purchased in which of the following minimum denominations?

- ❑ A. $1,000 minimum purchase with increments of $1,000 thereafter
- ❑ B. $5,000 minimum purchase with increments of $1,000 thereafter
- ❑ C. $10,000 minimum purchase with increments of $1,000 thereafter
- ❑ D. $10,000 minimum purchase with increments of $5,000 thereafter

59. Which is the only true statement about Fannie Mae's capability to borrow from the Federal Reserve Bank?

- ❑ A. It can borrow from the Fed at the discount window.
- ❑ B. It can borrow from the Fed at the Fed Funds rate.
- ❑ C. It can borrow from the Fed at the call rate.
- ❑ D. It can borrow from the Fed at the prime rate.

60. The largest securities that are listed on the over-the-counter market are found on which part of the NASDAQ system?

- ❑ A. National Market System
- ❑ B. The bulletin board
- ❑ C. The pink sheets
- ❑ D. The blue market

61. A fixed annuity has all the following characteristics except for which one?

- ❑ A. Guarantees the annuitant a predetermined rate of return
- ❑ B. The insurance company takes on the bulk of the risk in the annuity
- ❑ C. The annuitant incurs the risk in the annuity
- ❑ D. High inflation cannot decrease the value of the annuity

62. Which of the following municipal bond issues best protects a bondholders' interest and principal repayment?

- ❑ A. A 10-year municipal revenue bond with a net revenue pledge
- ❑ B. A 20-year municipal revenue bond with a net revenue pledge
- ❑ C. A 10-year municipal revenue bond with a gross revenue pledge
- ❑ D. A 20-year municipal revenue bond with a gross revenue pledge

63. A broker who borrows from a bank to make a loan to a customer in a margin account is permitted to pledge what value of the securities to secure the loan?

- ❑ A. 140% of the debit balance
- ❑ B. 100% of the market value
- ❑ C. 100% of the debit balance
- ❑ D. 50% of the market value

64. Which of the following statements would most be accurate about legislative risk?

I. The government must approve a new issue.

II. The tax laws can change, affecting an issue.

III. Foreign securities have no legislative risk.

IV. Foreign securities have greater legislative risk than American stocks.

- ❑ A. I and III
- ❑ B. II only
- ❑ C. II and III
- ❑ D. II and IV

65. If the New York Stock Exchange had 2,038 advances and 1,157 declines for the day, what is the advance decline index for the day?

- ❑ A. 1.76 to 1
- ❑ B. .276
- ❑ C. .637
- ❑ D. 1.57

66. Sal purchases 10 DVD May 45 Puts @ 3. What is the maximum amount he can make on this investment, and the maximum amount he can lose?

- ❑ A. Maximum gain is $4,200; maximum loss is $3,000
- ❑ B. Maximum gain is $3,000; maximum loss is $4,200
- ❑ C. Maximum gain is $42,000; maximum loss is $3,000
- ❑ D. Maximum gain is unlimited; maximum loss is $3,000

67. The managing underwriter of a syndicate handles all the following responsibilities except?

- ❑ A. Making all investment decisions for the offering
- ❑ B. Settling the account with all syndicate members
- ❑ C. Choosing the members of the syndicate
- ❑ D. Registering the security offering with the SEC

68. Which of the following information is written on an order ticket for a trade to be entered for a customer?

I. The security and number of shares

II. The customers account number

III. The registered representative's name or AE number

IV. Whether the trade was solicited

❑ A. I and II

❑ B. I and III

❑ C. I, II, and III

❑ D. I, II, III, and IV

69. The settlement terms on price-based options is set at which of the following terms?

❑ A. Same day settlement

❑ B. Next day settlement

❑ C. Trade date + 3

❑ D. Trade date + 5

70. What is the difference between a fixed unit investment trust and a participating unit investment trust?

❑ A. A fixed trust pays a dividend and a participating trust pays interest.

❑ B. A fixed trust cannot directly change investments, whereas a participating trust can indirectly.

❑ C. A fixed trust has a set maturity, whereas a participating trust does not.

❑ D. A fixed trust issues shares of beneficial interest, whereas a participating trust does not.

71. An agency debt bond quoted at 102.12 has a current selling price of which of the following?

❑ A. $1,020.12

❑ B. $1,020.09

❑ C. $1,021,20

❑ D. $1,023.75

72. Which of the following statements are characteristic of Long Term Equity Anticipation Securities (LEAPS)?

I. They have expiration terms of up to three years.

II. They can be American-style options.

III. They can be European-style options.

IV. They expire in December of each year.

❑ A. I and II

❑ B. I and III

❑ C. I, II, and III

❑ D. I, II, III, and IV

73. Piper earns $50,000 per year in her current job and has decided to open a tax qualified retirement plan to which she will contribute 5% of her salary. What is Piper's taxable income?

- ❑ A. $50,000
- ❑ B. $47,500
- ❑ C. $45,000
- ❑ D. $40,000

74. Which of the following statements are considered true of 403-B retirement plan?

I. A 403-B plan is established for employees of nonprofit organizations.

II. The maximum tax deductible contribution allowed is set at $9,500.

III. 403-B plans are known as tax deferred annuity plans.

IV. The maximum tax deductible contribution allowed is set at 25% of the individuals' yearly income.

- ❑ A. I and II
- ❑ B. II and III
- ❑ C. I, II, and III
- ❑ D. I, III, and IV

75. Which of the following statements is true of a corporate bond that has been purchased at a premium?

- ❑ A. The bond is accreted each year.
- ❑ B. The bond is amortized each year.
- ❑ C. The bond pays the premium at maturity.
- ❑ D. The bond pays a discount at maturity.

76. Market risk negatively impacts securities during downturns in the economy. Which of the following statements is considered true of market risk?

I. Market risk is considered diversifiable.

II. Market risk cannot be diversified against.

III. Unique risk is the same as nonsystematic risk.

IV. Unique risk is the same a systematic risk.

- ❑ A. I and III
- ❑ B. I and IV
- ❑ C. II and III
- ❑ D. IV only

77. The number of option contracts that an investor can have on an underlying security depends on which of the following?

I. The number of shares outstanding on the stock

II. The trading volume of the underlying security

III. The side of the market the contract is on

IV. The expiration cycle of the security

❑ A. I only
❑ B. I and II
❑ C. I, II, and III
❑ D. I, II, III, and IV

78. Which of the following best describes the strategy of a short call option writer?

❑ A. Hopes the market will rise to buy the stock at the lower strike
❑ B. Hopes the market will rise to keep the premium on the expiring worthless option
❑ C. Hopes the market will drop to be able to sell the stock at the higher strike price
❑ D. Hopes the market will drop to keep the premium on the expiring worthless option

79. Which of the following is considered to be bearish on the underlying security?

I. Long call spread

II. Long put spread

III. Short call spread

IV. Short put spread

❑ A. I and III
❑ B. I and IV
❑ C. II and III
❑ D. II and IV

80. All the following are true of stock index options except for?

❑ A. An index is a statistically derived number that reflects changes in the individual stocks.
❑ B. An index is a single number that reflects daily movements in the prices of the large group of stocks.
❑ C. Stocks are not always weighted the same.
❑ D. An index can be a good indicator of the market as a whole.

81. Which of the following yield-based options statements is considered true?

- ❑ A. Yield-based options do not have an actual security that is representative of the option contract.
- ❑ B. Yield-based options have strike prices with intervals of five points.
- ❑ C. Settlement on yield-based options is the trade date + 3.
- ❑ D. All yield-based options are American style options.

82. Which of the following statements is considered true regarding a broker-dealer who is holding customer securities in street name?

I. Dividends are retained by the broker.

II. The securities are in the customer's name, but held by the broker.

III. The securities are in the name of the broker.

IV. The customer is considered the nominal owner.

- ❑ A. I and II
- ❑ B. II and III
- ❑ C. III and IV
- ❑ D. I, II, III, and IV

83. A parent has opened a custodial account for a child. The parent deposited $50,000 worth of securities in the account. The parent incurs financial hardship several years down the road and wants to withdraw funds from the account. Which statements are considered true about the account?

I. The parent needs the child's approval to withdraw any funds.

II. Under hardship, the custodian can remove 20% of the holdings in the account and be taxed as ordinary income.

III. The parent or guardian is not permitted to remove funds unless they petition a probate court for authorization.

IV. The holdings in the account are irrevocable and cannot be removed.

- ❑ A. I and II
- ❑ B. I, II, and III
- ❑ C. III
- ❑ D. IV

84. What is the maximum coverage for a brokerage account that is covered by the Securities Investor Protection Corporation?

- ❑ A. $1,000,000 in combined securities and cash
- ❑ B. $500,000 in securities with $100,000 in cash
- ❑ C. $400,000 in securities with $100,000 in cash
- ❑ D. $900,000 in securities with $100,000 in cash

85. The constant update and revaluation of securities in a margin account is known as?

- ❑ A. Mark to market
- ❑ B. Short interest
- ❑ C. Long market value
- ❑ D. Short market value

86. A long margin account has a market value of $18,000, a debit balance of $9,000, and equity balance of $9,000. What is the minimum maintenance level of this account?

- ❑ A. $16,000
- ❑ B. $12,000
- ❑ C. $9,000
- ❑ D. $4,500

87. Under the Investment Company Act of 1940, investment companies are required to do which of the following?

I. Register with the SEC

II. Offer a prospectus to all investors

III. Solicit proxies from all investors

IV. Change the investment objectives without shareholder approval

- ❑ A. I and II
- ❑ B. II and III
- ❑ C. I, II, and III
- ❑ D. I, II, III, and IV

88. Which of the following privatized agencies are listed on the New York Stock Exchange?

I. GNMA

II. FNMA

III. Sallie Mae

IV. Freddie Mac

- ❑ A. I and II
- ❑ B. II and III
- ❑ C. I, II, and III
- ❑ D. IV

89. If two separate and distinct municipal broker-dealers have complaints against each other, under MSRB rules they have to resolve the matter in which manner?

- ❑ A. Via arbitration
- ❑ B. Via an outside court to resolve the matter
- ❑ C. Via the NASD for a resolution
- ❑ D. Via the MSRB for a resolution

90. If an investor sells 400 shares of PDQ Stock short @ $59 per share and purchases 4 PDQ July 60 Calls @ 5, what is the maximum potential loss the investor has in this account?

❑ A. Maximum loss of $100
❑ B. Maximum loss of $600
❑ C. Maximum loss of $2,400
❑ D. Maximum loss is unlimited

91. Which statements are true regarding Real Estate Investment Trusts (REITS)?

I. They must register with the SEC

II. Must have at least 100 owners of beneficial interest

III. Cannot have 50% of the trust controlled by five or fewer investors

IV. They are listed on a stock exchange or over-the-counter market

❑ A. I and II
❑ B. II and III
❑ C. I, II, and III
❑ D. I, II, III, and IV

92. In an attempt to slow down a runaway economy, the Federal Reserve Bank performs which of the following actions?

❑ A. Sells securities in the market
❑ B. Purchases securities in the market
❑ C. Lowers the reserve requirement
❑ D. Lowers the discount rate

93. A buyer and a seller of the same option contract has which of the following relationships?

❑ A. They always match up as the opposite sides of each other.
❑ B. There is a direct one-to-one relationship between buyer and seller.
❑ C. Each side of the trade settles with the options clearing corp.
❑ D. Each side of the trade settles if and when the option is exercised.

94. A moving average has which of the following characteristics?

I. It looks at a specific time frame and never changes.

II. It is recalculated each day as the specified time period is recalculated.

III. It drops the oldest day and adds the newest day.

IV. Moving averages demonstrate long changes.

❑ A. I only
❑ B. II and III
❑ C. I and IV
❑ D. II, III, and IV

95. Which of the following statements are true of dealers who market mutual fund shares?

I. The dealers purchase shares from the fund and then sell to investors.

II. They purchase shares at a discount to the public offering price.

III. They are prohibited from purchasing shares for their own inventory.

IV. They are considered the sponsor of the mutual fund.

- ❑ A. I and II
- ❑ B. II and III
- ❑ C. I, II, and III
- ❑ D. I, II, III, and IV

96. Which of the following securities issued by a company has the highest claim on assets if a company went bankrupt?

- ❑ A. Common stock
- ❑ B. Warrants
- ❑ C. Rights
- ❑ D. Options

97. Which of the following are characteristics of the role of technical analysts?

I. They predict trends of prices of stocks by use of charts and graphs.

II. They analyze financial ratios of companies to determine trends.

III. They use income statements and balance sheets to identify trends.

IV. They analyze patterns of past price changes to predict future price movements of stocks.

- ❑ A. I and II
- ❑ B. II and III
- ❑ C. I, II, and III
- ❑ D. I and IV

98. GHI convertible bonds have a conversion ratio of 20 to 1. The bonds are selling in the market at 92. At what price are the common shares selling in order to trade at parity?

- ❑ A. $40
- ❑ B. $42
- ❑ C. $44
- ❑ D. $46

99. A markup on an OTC security conducted in a principal transaction has to be disclosed to the customer on the trade confirmation for which of the following securities?

I. NMS listed securities

II. SmallCap NASDAQ securities

III. Bulletin Board stocks

IV. Pink Sheet stocks

- ❑ A. I only
- ❑ B. I and II
- ❑ C. I, II, and III
- ❑ D. I, II, III, and IV

100. The main way that the Student Loan Marketing Association assists the educational sector of the economy is by which of the following?

- ❑ A. Issuing low-cost tuition loans to students
- ❑ B. Issuing low-cost tuition loans to students who meet grade requirements
- ❑ C. Purchasing student loans from financial institutions
- ❑ D. Selling student loans to financial institutions

101. Based on the following Level II NASDAQ table, what is the current spread on TNT stock?

Dealer	**Bid**	**Ask**
MP	15	15.50
ACE	15.12	15.62
GB	15.25	15.62
WLE	15.12	15.75

- ❑ A. .25 point spread
- ❑ B. .50 point spread
- ❑ C. .75 point spread
- ❑ D. .62 point spread

102. Which of the following best describes the strategy of long put option holders?

- ❑ A. Hope the market will rise so that they can keep the premium on the expiring worthless option
- ❑ B. Hope the market will rise so that they can purchase the stock at the lower strike price
- ❑ C. Hope the market declines so that they can sell the stock at the higher strike price
- ❑ D. Hope the market declines so that they can keep the premium on the expiring worthless option

103. Which of the following items is part of a customer confirm?

I. The security and number of shares

II. Trade and settlement dates

III. The role of the broker as agent or principal

IV. The commission charged to the client

- ❑ A. I and II
- ❑ B. I, II, and III
- ❑ C. II, III, and IV
- ❑ D. I, II, III, and IV

104. In a negotiated bid for a municipal bond offering, which of the following statements are considered true?

I. It is conducted for a revenue bond issue.

II. It is conducted for a GO bond issue.

III. The municipality commits to one underwriter to issue the bonds.

IV. The municipality is guaranteed the lowest possible interest rate.

- ❑ A. I and III
- ❑ B. II and III
- ❑ C. II, III, and IV
- ❑ D. I, III, and IV

105. If a new issue of a non-listed security is brought to the market for the first time ever by a corporation, the final prospectus must be sent to customers for the period of how many days?

- ❑ A. 40 days
- ❑ B. 60 days
- ❑ C. 90 days
- ❑ D. 25 days

106. An individual who has secured a 30-year mortgage to purchase a home, can do which of the following with the loan?

- ❑ A. Depreciate the mortgage
- ❑ B. Accrete the mortgage
- ❑ C. Amortize the mortgage
- ❑ D. Appreciate the mortgage

107. A municipality has issued a short-term note in the market to finance its short-term needs. Which of the following is considered the highest credit rating that Moody's assigns to municipal notes?

- ❑ A. aaa
- ❑ B. AAA
- ❑ C. MIG-1
- ❑ D. MIG-4

108. Which of the following types of orders are entered below the current market price of the stock?

I. Buy limit order

II. Buy stop order

III. Sell stop order

IV. Sell stop limit order

❑ A. I only
❑ B. I and II
❑ C. I, II, and III
❑ D. I, III, and IV

109. If an investor sells 400 shares of PDQ Stock short @ $59 per share and purchases 4 PDQ July 60 Calls @ 5, at what price does PDQ stock have to be for the investor to break even on this account?

❑ A. $54
❑ B. $55
❑ C. $64
❑ D. $65

110. What is the equity in a long margin account when the investor purchases 1,000 shares of TNT @ $57, and the price of TNT goes to $63 per share?

❑ A. $63,000
❑ B. $57,000
❑ C. $34,500
❑ D. $31,500

111. Insurance companies are permitted to sell variable annuities only under which of the following rules?

I. They must issue a prospectus to potential investors.

II. They are regulated under the Investment Company Act of 1940.

III. They are regulated under the Securities Act of 1933.

IV. They are considered a security by the Securities & Exchange Commission.

❑ A. I and II
❑ B. I and III
❑ C. I and IV
❑ D. I, II, III, and IV

112. Revenue bonds that have been issued by a municipality are directly backed by which of the following sources of income?

I. Ad valorem taxes

II. Sales taxes

III. Income taxes

IV. Project revenues

❑ A. I and IV
❑ B. II and IV
❑ C. III and IV
❑ D. IV

113. The rules and regulations that the MSRB have created for the municipal securities market apply to which of the following?

I. Municipal brokers and dealers

II. Commercial banks that deal in municipal underwriting

III. Thrift institutions

IV. Municipalities bringing new issues to the market

❑ A. I only
❑ B. I and II
❑ C. I, II, and III
❑ D. I, II, III, and IV

114. An investor who wants to purchase a NASDAQ listed security for fewer than 1,000 shares can use which of the following automated computer systems?

❑ A. The Designated Order Turnaround system
❑ B. The SUPER DOT system
❑ C. The SOES system
❑ D. The Bulletin Board

115. The following option contract is considered in the money at which of the following market prices?

1 CBC May 45 Call @ 3

I. CBC is selling at $42

II. CBC is selling at $48

III. CBC is selling at $52

IV. CBC is selling at $40

❑ A. I and II
❑ B. II and III
❑ C. III only
❑ D. I and IV

116. An investment advisor is managing a portfolio of computer technology stocks. What type of index option should the advisor choose to hedge the portfolio?

- ❑ A. Broad based
- ❑ B. Narrow based
- ❑ C. LEAPS
- ❑ D. CAPS

117. The New York Stock Exchange can impose its own margin requirements on member firms. Which of the following statements is considered true?

I. NYSE rules can be less strict than the Federal Reserve Bank rules.

II. NYSE rules also apply to NASD firms.

III. NYSE rules can be the same as the Federal Reserve Bank rules.

IV. NYSE rules can be more strict than the Federal Reserve Bank rules.

- ❑ A. I and II
- ❑ B. II and III
- ❑ C. I, II, and III
- ❑ D. III and IV

118. A mutual fund is not required to pay corporate taxes on portfolio income if it distributes what percentage of its investment income to shareholders?

- ❑ A. 75% of its income
- ❑ B. 80% of its income
- ❑ C. 90% of its income
- ❑ D. 97% of its income

119. Which of the following statements are true about the expansion phase of the business cycle?

I. Production of goods and services are increasing

II. Interest rates are high

III. Inflation is low

IV. Unemployment decreases

- ❑ A. I and II
- ❑ B. II and III
- ❑ C. I, II, and III
- ❑ D. I, III, and IV

120. If a NYSE-listed company failed to issue an annual report for the year, which of the following actions will likely occur?

I. The exchange might delist the security.

II. The SEC would conduct an investigation as to why.

III. The company could continue their business unaffected.

IV. Their credibility in the market is severely jeopardized.

- ❑ A. I and II
- ❑ B. III only
- ❑ C. I and IV
- ❑ D. I, II, and IV

121. If the city of Gainesville was attempting to issue municipal bonds to finance commercial redevelopment in its municipality, they need to issue which type of municipal bond?

- ❑ A. Moral obligation bonds
- ❑ B. Special assessment bond
- ❑ C. Special tax bonds
- ❑ D. Tax allocation bonds

122. A municipality has issued insured revenue bonds in the market that pay an interest rate of 6.60%. Investors who have purchased these bonds are protected against which of the following?

- ❑ A. The bonds cannot default
- ❑ B. Interest and principal payments are paid by the insurer in the event of default
- ❑ C. The bonds have a revenue source, thus are not insured
- ❑ D. The cancellation of the revenue project

123. All NYSE member firms are required to provide which of the following to prevent fraud or embezzlement by the firm's employees?

- ❑ A. A surety bond
- ❑ B. A blanket fidelity bond
- ❑ C. A flower bond
- ❑ D. A zero tolerance bond

124. Treasury bonds can be purchased in which of the following minimum denominations?

- ❑ A. $5,000 minimum purchase with increments of $5,000 thereafter
- ❑ B. $5,000 minimum purchase with increments of $1,000 thereafter
- ❑ C. $1,000 minimum purchase with increments of $1,000 thereafter
- ❑ D. $10,000 minimum purchase with increments of $1,000 thereafter

125. John sells 1 FTD May 60 Call @ 4 and 1 FTD May 60 Put @ 3. What is the maximum potential gain that John can have with this transaction?

- ❑ A. Unlimited potential gain
- ❑ B. $700 potential gain
- ❑ C. $5,700 potential gain
- ❑ D. $6,700 potential gain

126. Which of the following are considered major market indexes that are considered broad-based?

I. The Consumer Price Index

II. The Major Market Index

III. The Standard & Poor's 100 Index

IV. The Standard & Poor's 500 Index

- ❑ A. I and II
- ❑ B. II and III
- ❑ C. II, III, and IV
- ❑ D. I, II, III, and IV

127. What is the pricing method for T-bills used by the U.S. Treasury known as?

- ❑ A. Competitive basis
- ❑ B. Non-competitive basis
- ❑ C. Discount-to-yield basis
- ❑ D. Premium yield basis

128. A customer has opened an option account and has begun trading in the account. After 15 days, the customer has still not signed and returned the option agreement. What happens to this account?

- ❑ A. The account is already opened and can continue to trade
- ❑ B. The account is immediately closed
- ❑ C. The account is restricted to closing transactions
- ❑ D. The client can only purchase options, not write them

129. A customer wants to purchase $5,000 worth of stock on margin. The Regulation T requirement is 50%. Which of the following meets the Reg T Requirement?

I. A deposit of $2,500 worth of marginable securities

II. A deposit of $2,500 in cash

III. A deposit of $5,000 worth of marginable securities

IV. A deposit of $5,000 in cash

- ❑ A. I and II
- ❑ B. I, II, and III
- ❑ C. II and III
- ❑ D. II, III, and IV

130. Which of the following statements are true of a Regulation T restricted margin account?

I. The equity in the account has fallen below 50%

II. Further purchases in the account require a 100% deposit

III. The account cannot borrow any additional funds

IV. The customer is not required to bring in any additional funds

- ❑ A. I and IV
- ❑ B. I and II
- ❑ C. I, II, and III
- ❑ D. IV only

131. A mutual fund that is permitted to pass advertising costs on to its shareholders is known as what type of fund?

- ❑ A. A no-load fund
- ❑ B. A 12-b-1 fund
- ❑ C. A 1099 fund
- ❑ D. A 401(k) fund

132. Annuities are most commonly used for which of the following purposes by investors?

- ❑ A. To invest in mutual funds
- ❑ B. To invest in income stocks
- ❑ C. To secure retirement income
- ❑ D. To arrange insurance coverage

133. Which of the following affects the rate of inflation in the economy?

I. The supply and demand for goods and services produced

II. The expansion of the money supply

III. The contraction of the money supply

IV. The value of money

- ❑ A. I and II
- ❑ B. I and III
- ❑ C. I, II, and III
- ❑ D. I, II, III, and IV

134. An individual who investigates a company's financial health by examining the assets, liabilities, income, and expenses is called which of the following?

- ❑ A. A technical analyst
- ❑ B. A fundamental analyst
- ❑ C. A chartist
- ❑ D. A portfolio theorist

135. Which of the following agencies funds the short-term needs of the farming sector?

I. Federal Land Banks

II. Federal Intermediate Credit Banks

III. Banks for Cooperatives

IV. They all fund long term needs of the farming sector

❑ A. I only
❑ B. II only
❑ C. II and III
❑ D. IV

136. An investor living in Illinois has decided to purchase $20,000 worth of 6.5% Washington, D.C., municipal improvement bonds. How is the interest income on this high-yielding municipal bond taxed?

❑ A. The interest is exempt from federal taxes
❑ B. The interest is exempt from state and local taxes
❑ C. The interest is exempt from federal, state, and local taxes
❑ D. The income from the bonds doesn't receive any exemption because the investor does not live in Washington, D.C.

137. Which of the following instances allows an OTC Member firm to charge a markup or commission on a customer trade in excess of the 5% NASD policy?

I. The size of the trade

II. The number of market makers contacted

III. The price of the underlying security

IV. The marketability of the underlying security

❑ A. I only
❑ B. I and II
❑ C. I, II, and III
❑ D. I, II, III, and IV

138. Which of the following statements are true regarding investment companies and advertising?

I. Investment companies are not permitted to advertise for customers

II. Investment companies can only advertise with a prospectus

III. Investment companies can advertise without a prospectus

IV. Investment companies can advertise with or without a prospectus

❑ A. I and II
❑ B. II and III
❑ C. III and IV
❑ D. II, III, and IV

139. Which of the following authorities can raise capital through a municipal bond issue?

I. School districts

II. Water districts

III. Public utilities

IV. Sewage treatment plants

- ❑ A. I and II
- ❑ B. I, II, and III
- ❑ C. I, II, and IV
- ❑ D. I, II, III, and IV

140. An accredited investor is considered to be someone or some entity meeting which of the following requirements?

I. Having a net worth of $1 million

II. Having made $200,000 per year for the past two years, or having a net worth of $1 million

III. An officer or director of the issuing company

IV. A bank or an insurance company with assets greater than $3 million

- ❑ A. I only
- ❑ B. I, II, and III
- ❑ C. I, III, and IV
- ❑ D. IV only

141. The Super DOT system on the NYSE is designed to route which of the following to the specialist?

- ❑ A. Market orders up to 99,999 shares to the specialist
- ❑ B. Market orders up to 30,999 shares to the specialist
- ❑ C. Limit orders up to 99,999 shares to the specialist
- ❑ D. Limit orders up to 30,999 shares to the specialist

142. Yield-base interest rate options have which of the following characteristics?

I. Are American-style options

II. Are European-style options

III. Settlement is in cash on the trade date + 3

IV. Settlement is in cash on the next day

- ❑ A. I only
- ❑ B. II only
- ❑ C. I and III
- ❑ D. II and IV

143. Which of the following are considered leading economic indicators?

I. Average work week for production workers in manufacturing

II. Weekly claims on unemployment insurance

III. New building permits issued

IV. New orders for consumer goods

❑ A. I and II

❑ B. I, II, and III

❑ C. I, III, and IV

❑ D. I, II, III, and IV

144. Arthur purchases 100 shares of GHI stock in the market at $44. Arthur also purchases 1 GHI October 45 Put @ 3 in the market. GHI stock goes to $48 in the market at expiration. What is Arthur's profit or loss on these positions?

❑ A. Profit of $100

❑ B. Profit of $400

❑ C. Loss of $100

❑ D. Loss of $300

145. Corporations that have already issued shares in the market place or have been listed, and are now coming out with a new issue, must send a final prospectus to potential customers for which period of time?

❑ A. 25 days

❑ B. 40 days

❑ C. 90 days

❑ D. 120 days

146. The role of the market maker on the over-the-counter market is most closely associated with which of the following individuals working on the floor of the NYSE?

❑ A. The floor broker

❑ B. The specialist

❑ C. The $2.00 broker

❑ D. The floor reporter

147. A first mortgage bond using the real property of the issuer as collateral would have a lien on the property held by whom?

❑ A. The bondholders

❑ B. The trustee

❑ C. The executor

❑ D. The issuer

148. Which of the following government agencies pays the lowest interest rates to bondholders when they all came out with debt issues at the same time?

- ❑ A. FNMA
- ❑ B. GNMA
- ❑ C. Freddie Mac
- ❑ D. Sallie Mae

149. Individuals currently participating in a municipal apprenticeship program are permitted to do which of the following?

I. Represent their firms to public customers

II. Receive remuneration in the form of commissions

III. Represent their firms to other municipal broker-dealers

IV. None of the above, because they are still apprentices

- ❑ A. I and II
- ❑ B. II and III
- ❑ C. III
- ❑ D. IV

150. An over-the-counter dealer who has sold a NASDAQ listed security out of its inventory account charges which of the following?

- ❑ A. A commission
- ❑ B. A markdown
- ❑ C. A markup
- ❑ D. A nominal spread

151. What is the maximum potential gain for the writer and the holder of the following option contract? **5 DTT April 70 Calls @ 5**

- ❑ A. Writer can gain $500; holder can gain $6,500
- ❑ B. Writer can gain $2,500; holder can gain $6,500
- ❑ C. Writer can gain $2,500; holder can gain unlimited
- ❑ D. Writer can gain $2,500; holder can gain $32,500

152. The maximum number of expiration cycles that any one option can possibly have for an underlying security is?

- ❑ A. One
- ❑ B. Three
- ❑ C. Four
- ❑ D. Five

153. An investor is long an index option with a strike price of 500. At 10:00 a.m., the holder exercises her option with the index value at 510. The index option closes at the end of business at 535. What value does the holder receive?

❑ A. 500

❑ B. 510

❑ C. 530

❑ D. 535

154. Which of the following regulations governs the broker loan that is secured for a customer from a bank?

❑ A. Regulation T

❑ B. Regulation Q

❑ C. Regulation G

❑ D. Regulation U

155. Which of the following entities are closely associated with the governance of mutual funds?

I. Custodians

II. Transfer agents

III. Registrar

IV. Auditors

❑ A. I and II

❑ B. II and III

❑ C. I, II, and III

❑ D. I, II, III, and IV

156. When a bond is purchased at a premium by an investor, the amount of the premium over the remaining life of the bond can be which of the following?

❑ A. Amortized

❑ B. Accreted

❑ C. Adjusted

❑ D. Appreciated

157. When a security has moved through its historical resistance or support level, it is known as a what?

❑ A. Breakout

❑ B. Consolidation

❑ C. Accumulation

❑ D. Distribution

158. Which of the following statements are true regarding the New York Stock Exchange?

I. The NYSE is an auction market

II. The NYSE is a negotiated market

III. The NYSE is also known as the Curb Market

IV. The NYSE is also known as the Big Board

- ❑ A. I and III
- ❑ B. II and IV
- ❑ C. I and IV
- ❑ D. II and III

159. A rise in the discount rate impacts the overall economy in which of the following ways?

- ❑ A. A rise in the discount rate makes interest rates on loans increase.
- ❑ B. A rise in the discount rate makes banks lower their reserve requirements.
- ❑ C. A rise in the discount rate makes it easier for banks to borrow money.
- ❑ D. A rise in the discount rate gives a needed boost to a stagnant economy.

160. An investor has purchased five call option contracts and has the right to do which of the following?

- ❑ A. Sell five shares of the underlying stock at the strike price
- ❑ B. Buy five shares of the underlying stock at the strike price
- ❑ C. Sell 500 shares of the underlying stock at the strike price
- ❑ D. Buy 500 shares of the underlying stock at the strike price

161. Which of the following direct treasury instruments pays interest to the purchaser of the security?

I. A 30-year 6.65% Treasury bond

II. A 10-year 6.18% Treasury note

III. A 20-year 6.44% Treasury bond

IV. A 52-week 5.25% Treasury bill

- ❑ A. I and II
- ❑ B. I, II, and III
- ❑ C. II and III
- ❑ D. I, II, III, and IV

162. Which of the following statements are true of limited partnerships?

I. Limited partners have limited liability

II. Limited partners have unlimited liability

III. General partners have limited liability

IV. General partners have unlimited liability

- ❑ A. I and III
- ❑ B. I and IV
- ❑ C. II and III
- ❑ D. II and IV

163. Which of the following tax sources can be used to service a Kansas State Municipal bond issue with a 7% tax-free yield?

I. State income taxes

II. State sales taxes

III. Ad valorem taxes

IV. Special assessment taxes

- ❑ A. I only
- ❑ B. I and II
- ❑ C. I, II, and III
- ❑ D. I, III, and IV

164. Christopher was participating in a municipal apprenticeship program and has successfully passed his licensing exam in 21 days. How long does the apprenticeship program last for Christopher?

- ❑ A. 21 days
- ❑ B. 30 days
- ❑ C. 60 days
- ❑ D. 90 days

165. Fred Buys 1 TNT June 70 Call @ 4 and also sells 1 TNT June 80 Call @ 1. What is the maximum possible gain and maximum possible loss on this long call spread?

- ❑ A. Max gain is $1,000; max loss is $400
- ❑ B. Max gain is $1,000; max loss is $300
- ❑ C. Max gain is $ 700; max loss is $400
- ❑ D. Max gain is $ 700; max loss is $300

166. Harry has opened a Roth IRA account at his local brokerage. Which of the following statements are considered true of the account?

I. Any IRA contributions are considered tax deductible

II. All IRA contributions are considered taxable

III. Disbursement is permitted at the age of 59½

IV. Disbursement must begin by the age of 70½

- ❑ A. I and III
- ❑ B. II and III
- ❑ C. II, III, and IV
- ❑ D. I, III, and IV

167. Which of the following acts of Congress were designed specifically to regulate the over-the-counter market?
- ❑ A. Securities Act of 1933
- ❑ B. Securities Act of 1934
- ❑ C. The Maloney Act of 1938
- ❑ D. The Investment Act of 1940

168. A mutual fund purchase plan whereby the investor purchases the same number of mutual fund shares each month is known as?
- ❑ A. Dollar cost plan
- ❑ B. Dollar cost averaging plan
- ❑ C. Dollar averaging plan
- ❑ D. A no-load purchase plan

169. The portion of a municipality's debt that is backed by the collection of tax revenues is considered which of the following?
- ❑ A. Gross direct debt
- ❑ B. Net direct debt
- ❑ C. Gross revenue debt
- ❑ D. Net revenue debt

170. A member firm that does not accept the ruling of the District Business Conduct Committee of the NASD in handling a customer complaint can appeal their ruling to which of the following?

I. The NASD Adjudication Council

II. The SEC

III. An outside civil court

IV. The MSRB

- ❑ A. I only
- ❑ B. I and II
- ❑ C. I, II, and III
- ❑ D. I, II, III, and IV

171. All call options that have been issued for ABC stock are best described as which of the following?
- ❑ A. The option series
- ❑ B. The option type
- ❑ C. The option class
- ❑ D. The option cycle

172. All trades that have been marked discretionary for an account by a registered representative must have which of the following by the end of business each day?

- ❑ A. The approval of the principal in the branch office
- ❑ B. The cash to settle the trade in the account by the end of the day
- ❑ C. The approval of the customer by the end of the day
- ❑ D. The approval of one other broker in the office

173. When underwriters have submitted a competitive bid for a municipal bond offering, they enter which of the following to the municipality?

- ❑ A. All their pre-sale orders
- ❑ B. The net interest cost of the bonds
- ❑ C. The true interest cost of the bonds
- ❑ D. The scale on the bonds

174. What is the breakeven point on this option for the writer and the holder? 50 TCI March 75 Puts @ 6

- ❑ A. Breakeven point for the writer is $81; breakeven point for the holder is $69
- ❑ B. Breakeven point for the writer is $69; breakeven point for the holder is $81
- ❑ C. Breakeven point for the writer is $69; breakeven point for the holder is $69
- ❑ D. Breakeven point for the writer is $81; breakeven point for the holder is $81

175. Which of the following constitutes a good delivery of municipal bonds under MSRB rules?

I. If the bonds are in bearer form, they must have all unpaid coupons attached.

II. They must have serial numbers that have not been called by the issuer.

III. The bond's legal opinion must be attached.

IV. The issuers debt statement must be attached.

- ❑ A. I and II
- ❑ B. II and III
- ❑ C. I, II, and III
- ❑ D. I, II, III, and IV

176. A client has deposited securities with her brokerage firm and requested that the securities be held in safekeeping. What does the broker do with these securities?

- ❑ A. The broker holds the fully registered securities for the client by depositing them with a trustee.
- ❑ B. The broker takes the securities out of the customer's name and holds them in their name for ease of transfer.
- ❑ C. The broker holds the securities in street name for the client.
- ❑ D. The broker holds the securities in the customer's name.

177. For an initial transaction in a margin account, the minimum deposit required is which of the following?

- ❑ A. 50% of the transaction cost
- ❑ B. 75% of the transaction cost
- ❑ C. The greater of a $2,000 minimum or 75% of the transaction cost
- ❑ D. The greater of a $2,000 minimum or 100% of the transaction cost

178. Which of the following risks are most closely associated with limited partnerships?

I. Legislative risk

II. Systemic risk

III. Liquidity risk

IV. Interest rate risk

- ❑ A. I and II
- ❑ B. II and III
- ❑ C. I, II, and III
- ❑ D. I, II, III, and IV

179. When a firm purchases securities in the OTC market for its own inventory account, it is acting as what?

- ❑ A. Broker
- ❑ B. Dealer
- ❑ C. Trader
- ❑ D. Specialist

180. Which of the following statements are true in regards to the issuance of preferred stock by a company?

I. Preferred stock owners have limited voting rights

II. Preferred stock has a higher par value than common stock

III. Preferred stock owners maintain pre-emptive rights

IV. Preferred stock market value must always be higher than common stock

- ❑ A. I only
- ❑ B. I and II
- ❑ C. I and III
- ❑ D. I, II, and IV

181. The United States government has decided to issue $5 billion worth of T-bills in the coming week. There are $3 billion worth of competitive bids and $4 billion worth of noncompetitive bids for the issue. How will the government allocate the bids?

❑ A. The $3 billion of competitive bids will be filled and the $2 billion of the noncompetitive bids will be filled.

❑ B. The government will change the auction to issue $7 billion worth of T-bills.

❑ C. The $4 billion of noncompetitive bids will be filled and $1 billion of the competitive bids will be filled.

❑ D. The government will allow $2.5 billion of the competitive bids to be filled and $2.5 billion of the noncompetitive bids to be filled.

182. Which of the following statements are considered true of a stock index option expiring?

I. The underlying stocks changes hands between buyer and seller.

II. Only cash changes hands between buyer and seller.

III. The seller earns a premium.

IV. The buyer either makes a profit or loses the premium paid.

❑ A. I and III

❑ B. I and IV

❑ C. I, III, and IV

❑ D. II, III, and IV

183. The law that created Social Security and disability benefits for individuals is known as what?

❑ A. SIPC

❑ B. FDIC

❑ C. FICA

❑ D. FSLIC

184. Syndicate members of a municipal bond syndicate earn which of the following for each bond that they sell?

❑ A. Management fee

❑ B. Concession

❑ C. Takedown fee

❑ D. Reallowance fee

185. A municipal broker's broker has offered bonds in the market for an institutional client. Which type of quote is required of the broker's broker?

❑ A. Workable quote

❑ B. Bona fide quote

❑ C. Nominal quote

❑ D. Subject quote

186. A municipal dealer has made a political contribution to the campaign of an elected official in excess of MSRB rules. How is the dealer censured?

- ❑ A. It is fined 100 times the amount of the contribution.
- ❑ B. It is fined 1,000 times the amount of the contribution.
- ❑ C. It is prevented from being a negotiated bid underwriter for the next five years.
- ❑ D. It is prevented from being a negotiated bid underwriter for the next two years.

187. Which of the following statements are considered true of a life annuity contract?

I. If the annuitant dies before the separate account is fully paid, his estate receives the remaining payments.

II. If the annuitant dies before the separate account is fully paid, only his spouse can receive the remaining funds.

III. The annuitant receives payments for as long as he lives.

IV. Upon the death of the annuitant, the annuity ceases payments.

- ❑ A. I only
- ❑ B. II only
- ❑ C. III and IV
- ❑ D. II, III, and IV

188. The Federal Home Loan Mortgage Corporation issues stock that has which of the following characteristics?

I. The stock is traded on the NYSE.

II. The stock is sold to savings institutions.

III. The stock issued is only preferred stock.

IV. The stock is held in trust by the Federal Home Loan Bank System.

- ❑ A. I and II
- ❑ B. II and III
- ❑ C. II and IV
- ❑ D. III and IV

189. Richard purchases 5 DTT May 40 Calls @ 3 and purchases 5 DTT May 40 Puts @ 4 in the market. What is the maximum potential gain and maximum potential loss this account has?

- ❑ A. Max gain is $3,500; max loss is $20,000
- ❑ B. Max gain is $21,500; max loss is $3,500
- ❑ C. Max gain is unlimited; max loss is $3,500
- ❑ D. Max gain is unlimited; max loss is $16,500

190. Which of the following statements is considered true regarding the opening of an option account?

I. There are no restrictions on an individual opening an options account.

II. The broker needs to determine whether the client understands how options work.

III. The broker needs to determine whether the client can afford to incur potential losses in options.

IV. The client needs to understand the risks involved with options.

- ❑ A. I only
- ❑ B. II only
- ❑ C. II and III
- ❑ D. II, III, and IV

191 Customer margin is best defined as which of the following?

- ❑ A. The portion of the value of the securities that investors must deposit in their account when they buy or sell securities on credit.
- ❑ B. The portion of the value of the securities that investors can borrow from the Federal Reserve Bank when buying or selling securities on credit.
- ❑ C. The portion of the value of the securities that investors can borrow from the broker when buying or selling securities on credit.
- ❑ D. The portion of the value of the securities that investors can borrow from the NYSE when buying or selling securities on credit.

192. If interest rates were to rise sharply in the market, which of the following pass-through risks would be most affected?

- ❑ A. Prepayment risk
- ❑ B. Default risk
- ❑ C. Market risk
- ❑ D. Extension risk

193. A T-note that an investor is considering buying in the secondary market is quoted at 94. What will an investor pay for this T-note?

- ❑ A. $940
- ❑ B. $904
- ❑ C. $9,400
- ❑ D. $9.40

194 The money supply as measured by M1 includes which of the following figures?

I. Currency in circulation

II. Demand deposits

III. Time deposits

IV. Travelers checks

- ❑ A. I only
- ❑ B. I and II
- ❑ C. I, II, and III
- ❑ D. I, II, and IV

195. What is the method for tracking open interest on options on an underlying security?
    - ❑ A. By the short interest positions
    - ❑ B. By the number of open interest
    - ❑ C. By the amount of the call rate
    - ❑ D. By the when issued number

196. Which is true of a company that has issued guaranteed bonds?
    - ❑ A. Bonds are issued with a AAA rating.
    - ❑ B. Bonds are issued by a subsidiary and backed by the parent company.
    - ❑ C. Corporate bonds use government subsidies as a guarantee.
    - ❑ D. Bonds are issued by a Blue Chip company.

197. An investor who purchased 1 XYZ April 50 Call @ 4 can do which of the following with the option position?

    I. Exercise the option

    II. Allow the option to expire

    III. Conduct a closing purchase

    IV. Conduct a closing sale

    - ❑ A. I only
    - ❑ B. II only
    - ❑ C. I, II, and III
    - ❑ D. I, II, and IV

198. An account that has been established by court appointment for a minor who earns a substantial amount of money is called which of the following?
    - ❑ A. Conservator account
    - ❑ B. A guardian account
    - ❑ C. A receivership account
    - ❑ D. A trust account

199. Which of the following statements are true of the rights of a general partner in a direct participation program?

    I. They have unlimited liability.

    II. They can engage in a business that competes with the limited partnership.

    III. They can use partnership property for their own personal use.

    IV. They can continue the partnership after the death of one of the general partners.

- ❑ A. I only
- ❑ B. II and III
- ❑ C. I, II, and III
- ❑ D. I, II, III, and IV

200. Which of the following short-term municipal issues can be used to pull forward income to be used before it is collected?

I. Tax anticipation notes (TANS)

II. Revenue anticipation notes (RANS)

III. Tax and revenue anticipation notes (TRANS)

IV. Project notes

- ❑ A. I only
- ❑ B. II only
- ❑ C. I, II, and III
- ❑ D. I, II, III, and IV

201. If a holder of an STP option contract exercises the option position with 30 days left to expiration against a writer, open interest increases or decreases by what amount?

- ❑ A. Open interest increases by 1
- ❑ B. Open interest increases by 100
- ❑ C. Open interest decreases by 1
- ❑ D. Open interest decreases by 100

202. All the following statements are true of long and short margin accounts, except for:

- ❑ A. The only constant in a long margin account is the debit balance.
- ❑ B. The only constant in a short margin account is the credit balance.
- ❑ C. The equity in a long account increases if the market value increases.
- ❑ D. The equity in a short account increases if the market value increases.

203. Which of the following practices is considered manipulation by the SEC on a new issue?

I. The underwriter sells the shares to its best clients.

II. The underwriter solicits a wash trade with a sister company.

III. The underwriter uses a stabilizing bid ½ point below the public offering price.

IV. The company sends a correspondence to clients stating that the company is on the verge of signing a multi-million dollar contract with another company, when in fact the contract is being held up in litigation.

- ❑ A. I and II
- ❑ B. III
- ❑ C. II and IV
- ❑ D. I, II, III, and IV

204. The maximum potential profit for an opening put purchase is realized when which of the following occurs?

- ❑ A. The stock rises to an unlimited amount.
- ❑ B. The stock declines to zero.
- ❑ C. The market price rises above the strike and the premium is retained.
- ❑ D. The market price falls below the strike and the premium is retained.

205. When a company decides to raise additional capital through the sale of a rights offering, which of the following statements is considered true?

I. Rights are priced higher than the market price.

II. Rights are priced lower than the market price.

III. A rights offering must offer proportionate ownership to existing shareholders.

IV. A rights offering can be used to dilute the percentage of ownership a shareholder will have after the offering.

- ❑ A. I only
- ❑ B. II only
- ❑ C. I and IV
- ❑ D. II and III

206. An investor owns the following option contract. 1 HTH May 50 Call @ 3. The market price of HTH currently is at $48. Which of the following statements is true regarding this contract?

- ❑ A. The option is in the money.
- ❑ B. Thc option has a breakeven point of $47.
- ❑ C. The option is out of the money.
- ❑ D. The option has a breakeven point of $51.

207. Ryan sells 50 NCR August 80 Puts @ 6. To be considered a covered writer of these puts, Ryan needs what in his account?

- ❑ A. Long 5,000 shares NCR stock
- ❑ B. Long 500 shares NCR stock
- ❑ C. Long 50,000 shares NCR stock
- ❑ D. Short 5,000 shares NCR stock

208. An investor writes 15 HTH Feb 110 Calls @ 5 and also writes 15 HTH Feb 110 Puts @ 6. What is the maximum profit that the investor can make on this short straddle?

- ❑ A. $7,500
- ❑ B. $9,000
- ❑ C. $16,500
- ❑ D. Unlimited profit

209. A customer has an account at a broker-dealer that has failed. The client has $450,000 in securities and $100,000 in cash in the account. To what amount is the customer covered by SIPC insurance?

- ❑ A. $450,000 in stock and $100,000 in cash
- ❑ B. $400,000 in stock and $100,000 in cash
- ❑ C. $450,000 in stock and $50,000 in cash
- ❑ D. $400,000 in stock and $50,000 in cash

210. Which of the following statements are considered true of annuities offered by insurance companies?

I. Fixed annuities must register with the Securities & Exchange Commission.

II. Variable annuities must register with the Securities and Exchange Commission.

III. Fixed annuities are considered insurance products.

IV. Variable annuities are considered securities.

- ❑ A. I and II
- ❑ B. II and III
- ❑ C. I, III, and IV
- ❑ D. II, III, and IV

211. Which of the following are considered to be capital gains for an individual?

I. An increase in salary from $40,000 to $50,000

II. Purchasing 1,000 shares of stock for $20.00 and selling them for $35.00

III. Purchasing a painting for $20,000 and then selling it for $50,000

IV. A company building a factory for $1 million and then selling it for $3 million

- ❑ A. I only
- ❑ B. II and III
- ❑ C. IV only
- ❑ D. II, III, and IV

212. A seat on the New York Stock Exchange according to NYSE rules must be in the name of which of the following?

- ❑ A. The member firm
- ❑ B. The specialist
- ❑ C. The floor broker
- ❑ D. The CEO of the member firm

213. What is the maximum potential gain and the maximum potential loss the writer of the following option can incur on the following? Write 10 CBC June 50 Calls @ 3.

❑ A. Maximum gain is $300; maximum loss is $4,700

❑ B. Maximum gain is $4,700; maximum loss is $300

❑ C. Maximum gain is $3,000; maximum loss is $47,000

❑ D. Maximum gain is $3,000; maximum loss is unlimited

214. Mary Sells 1 BTO Jan 50 Put @ 6 and also Buys 1 BTO Jan 40 Put @ 3 This is an example of which of the following?

❑ A. Long put debit spread

❑ B. Short put debit spread

❑ C. Long put credit spread

❑ D. Short put credit spread

215. Which of the following agencies and their issues are directly backed by the United States government?

I. Federal National Mortgage Association

II. Government National Mortgage Association

III. The Export Import Bank

IV. Federal Home Loan Mortgage Company

❑ A. I and II

❑ B. II and III

❑ C. II only

❑ D. I, II, III, and IV

216. Pass-through certificates have all the following characteristics except for which?

❑ A. The underlying mortgages are pooled

❑ B. The mortgages are repackaged

❑ C. The mortgages have been securitized

❑ D. The mortgages are government guaranteed

217. An investor has purchased a variable annuity to fund their retirement. Which statements are true of the annuity purchased?

I. The risk of the annuity is borne by the annuitant.

II. The risk of the annuity is borne by the insurance company.

III. The rate of return on the annuity is guaranteed.

IV. The rate of return on the annuity is not guaranteed.

❑ A. I and III

❑ B. I and IV

❑ C. II and III

❑ D. II and IV

218. Shareholders who have paid more than stated par value for common stock when it is issued have this additional amount accounted for on the balance sheet as what?

- ❑ A. Earned surplus
- ❑ B. Capital surplus
- ❑ C. Retained earnings
- ❑ D. Depreciation

219. Which of the following bonds have the highest market risk for an investor?

- ❑ A. A 10-year 8% debenture
- ❑ B. A 20-year 5% debenture
- ❑ C. A 30-year 9% debenture
- ❑ D. A 30-year 5% debenture

220. The main goal of agencies that issue pass-through certificates is to perform which of the following?

- ❑ A. Make loans to qualified homeowners
- ❑ B. Purchase mortgages from lenders so that they can make additional loans
- ❑ C. Make loans to lending institutions
- ❑ D. None of the above

221. A trade that has been executed on the floor of the NYSE between a broker and a contra-broker typically appears on the consolidated tape how quickly?

- ❑ A. Within five seconds
- ❑ B. Within 30 seconds
- ❑ C. Within 60 seconds
- ❑ D. Within 90 seconds

222. Which of the following is characteristic of the Options Clearing Corporation?

I. They clear all option trades.

II. They set the strike price and expiration on contracts.

III. They set maximum position limits on options.

IV. They guarantee all contracts.

- ❑ A. I and II
- ❑ B. II and III
- ❑ C. I, II, and III
- ❑ D. I, II, III, and IV

223. Which statement is considered true regarding a fixed unit investment trust?

- ❑ A. The fund is managed by an investment company.
- ❑ B. After the portfolio has been selected it cannot be changed.
- ❑ C. The investor owns the securities in the trust.
- ❑ D. Unit trusts only purchase equity securities.

224. What is the term for a security whose price has recently broken out and begun to level off?

- ❑ A. Accumulation
- ❑ B. Distribution
- ❑ C. Consolidation
- ❑ D. Breakpoint

225. Which of the following protective covenants are designed to protect the bondholder from the issuer diluting the collateral of the revenue project?

- ❑ A. Maintenance covenant
- ❑ B. Rate covenant
- ❑ C. Additional bonds covenant
- ❑ D. Non-discrimination covenant

226. The New York Stock Exchange Composite Index represents which of the following?

- ❑ A. A select 100 stocks listed on the NYSE
- ❑ B. A select 500 stocks listed on the NYSE
- ❑ C. All common and preferred stocks listed on the NYSE
- ❑ D. All common stocks listed on the NYSE

227. Municipal bonds of a new bond issue targeted for allocation accounts, such as municipal investment trusts, are part of which type of order?

- ❑ A. Pre-sale orders
- ❑ B. Designated orders
- ❑ C. Group net orders
- ❑ D. Member takedown orders

228. Annuitization of an annuity for an investor has all the following characteristics except for which?

- ❑ A. The insurance company converts accumulation units into annuity units.
- ❑ B. The process of annuitization is done at maturity of the annuity.
- ❑ C. Annuity units vary over the life expectancy of the investor.
- ❑ D. Annuity units are based on the total value of the accumulation units in the client account.

229. An investor conducts a short call option in the market for an underlying security. Which of the following statements is considered true about a short call?

- ❑ A. The investor doing the short call is bullish
- ❑ B. The investor doing the short call can make an unlimited amount of profit
- ❑ C. The investor doing the short call can only make the premium received
- ❑ D. The investor doing the short call has a maximum potential loss if the stock dropped to zero

230. If Action Securities is the lead underwriter for an offering and they have negotiated a management fee of .25 as part of the total takedown of 1.00 and they have sold 1 million shares directly to their clients, what is their fee for the sale of the securities?

- ❑ A. $250,000
- ❑ B. $750,000
- ❑ C. $1,000,000
- ❑ D. $100,000

231. Which of the following credit ratings is considered to be a speculative rating issued by either Standard & Poor's or Moody's?

I. Baa

II. BBB

III. Ba

IV. BB

- ❑ A. I and II
- ❑ B. III and IV
- ❑ C. I, II, and III
- ❑ D. I, II, III, and IV

232. When searching for a municipal bond underwriter for a general obligation bond issue, a municipality performs which of the following?

I. Places an advertisement for the bonds in the *Daily Bond Buyer*

II. Arranges an agreement with one underwriter to issue the bonds

III. Offers the bonds out to a competitive bidding process

IV. Takes the lowest interest rate costs as the winning bid from an underwriter

- ❑ A. I only
- ❑ B. II only
- ❑ C. I and III
- ❑ D. I, III, and IV

233. An investor purchases 500 shares of TNT stock on margin at $44.00 per share. The stock rises in value to $48.00 per share. What is the new equity in the account?

- ❑ A. $11,000
- ❑ B. $12,000
- ❑ C. $13,000
- ❑ D. $24,000

234. A riskless trade conducted by an OTC broker-dealer occurs when they do what?

- ❑ A. Sell a stock from their inventory to a customer
- ❑ B. Buy a stock for their inventory, and immediately sell it to a customer for a profit
- ❑ C. Sell a stock short for the customer when the customer is short against the box
- ❑ D. Buy a married put for a customer on the same day that they buy shares for the customer

235. Hank writes 1 HPO May 40 Call @ 3. Which of the following positions consider him a covered writer?

I. Long 100 shares of HPO

II. Short 100 shares of HPO

III. Long 4 HPO convertible debentures with a 25 to 1 conversion ratio

IV. Long 1 HPO May 40 Put

- ❑ A. I only
- ❑ B. II only
- ❑ C. I and III
- ❑ D. II and IV

236. Brian purchases 5 BBC May 55 Calls @ 4 and Purchases 5 BBC May 55 Puts @ 3. Which of the following prices of BBC stock causes a loss for Brian?

I. BBC selling at $60

II. BBC selling at $63

III. BBC selling at $48

IV. BBC selling at $44

- ❑ A. I only
- ❑ B. I and II
- ❑ C. I and IV
- ❑ D. I, II, III, and IV

237. All the following are characteristics of demand deposits except?

- ❑ A. They are deposits at banks that can be drawn on at any time.
- ❑ B. A checking account is considered a demand deposit.
- ❑ C. A bank certificate of deposit is considered a demand deposit.
- ❑ D. There are no penalties for early withdrawal.

238. An investor writes 5 QRT April 70 Calls @ 6. The investor is also long 500 shares of QRT stock at $68 per share. If QRT stock goes to $97 in the market, what is the profit or loss for the account?

- ❑ A. Profit of $4,000
- ❑ B. Profit of $14,500
- ❑ C. Loss of $10,500
- ❑ D. Loss of $11,500

239. Which of the following are used to create debt-based options on government securities?

I. Yield based options

II. Equity based options

III. Price based options

IV. Derivative based options

- ❑ A. I only
- ❑ B. II only
- ❑ C. I and III
- ❑ D. II and IV

240. Which of the following statements are considered true regarding management companies?

I. Open-end management companies are considered exempt securities.

II. Close-end management companies are considered exempt securities.

III. Open-end management companies are required to register with the SEC.

IV. Close-end management companies are required to register with the SEC.

- ❑ A. I only
- ❑ B. I and II
- ❑ C. II and III
- ❑ D. III and IV

241. Larkin Securities is currently the financial advisor for the city of Hope, Arkansas. The city of Hope has decided to issue $10 million worth of general obligation bonds on a competitive bid basis. Which of the following statements is considered true?

- ❑ A. Larkin Securities cannot bid on the bond issue.
- ❑ B. Larkin Securities would have to resign as financial advisor to bid on the bond issue.
- ❑ C. Larkin Securities is the only broker-dealer that can bid on the bonds.
- ❑ D. Other broker-dealers in the state cannot bid on the bond issue.

242. A NASDAQ National Market System security with a daily trading volume of 5,000 shares quoted by a market maker must offer a minimum of how many shares in their quote?

- ❑ A. 100
- ❑ B. 200
- ❑ C. 500
- ❑ D. 1,000

243. Which of the following methods of holding customer securities is considered non-negotiable in a margin account?

- ❑ A. Street name
- ❑ B. Segregation
- ❑ C. Safekeeping
- ❑ D. Beneficial securities

244. Unit investment trusts have which of the following characteristics?

I. They are organized under a trust indenture

II. They are governed by a board of directors

III. They are governed by a board of trustees

IV. They issue shares of beneficial interest to investors

- ❑ A. I and II
- ❑ B. I and III
- ❑ C. I, II, and IV
- ❑ D. I, III, and IV

245. An individual residing in California has a net worth of $5 million and in the 40% tax bracket has decided to purchase either a AAA 20-year corporate bond with a coupon rate of 7.80% or a AAA Puerto Rico Municipal bond at 5.28%. His financial advisor would advise him to purchase which of the bonds and for what reason?

- ❑ A. Purchase the 7.80% corporate bond because the yield is 2.52% higher.
- ❑ B. Purchase the 7.80% corporate bond because the after-tax yield will be higher.
- ❑ C. Purchase the 5.28% municipal bond because the after-tax yield will be 30 basis points higher.
- ❑ D. Purchase the 7.80% corporate bond, because he is a resident of California, and by purchasing Puerto Rican bonds, he loses his triple tax exempt status on the bonds.

246. All the following terms are considered a purchased option position except for?

- ❑ A. Long an option
- ❑ B. An opening purchase
- ❑ C. An opening sale
- ❑ D. Holder of an option

247. Frank purchases 1 PDQ April 45 Call @ 4 and 1 PDQ April 45 Put @ 3 with PDQ selling in the market at $46. What is the breakeven point on the call and the put in this account?

- ❑ A. Breakeven point on the call is $49; breakeven point on the put is $42
- ❑ B. Breakeven point on the call is $52; breakeven point on the put is $38
- ❑ C. Breakeven point on the call is $38; breakeven point on the put is $52
- ❑ D. Breakeven point on the call is $50; breakeven point on the put is $43

248. A money market fund that currently holds $5 million worth of 10-year Treasury notes wants to hedge the position. Which of the following can most effectively accomplish this strategy?

- ❑ A. Buy T-note calls
- ❑ B. Buy T-note puts
- ❑ C. Sell T-note calls
- ❑ D. Sell T-note puts

249. A price-based interest rate option with a strike price of 96.06 has a value of which of the following amounts?

- ❑ A. $960.06
- ❑ B. $960.60
- ❑ C. $961.88
- ❑ D. $966.00

250. A client purchases a 30-year $100,000 Treasury bond in a margin account selling at 104. What is the margin requirement on the T-bond?

- ❑ A. $2,000
- ❑ B. $6,000
- ❑ C. $6,240
- ❑ D. $104,000

Answers and Explanations

1. The correct answer is D. After the shares have sold out of the primary market they move on to sell in the respective market, where the new offering is registered to trade. This can be any one of the three exchanges listed.
2. The correct answer is C. The NASD, or the National Association of Security Dealers, was created by the SEC to oversee the over-the-counter market specifically.
3. The correct answer is B. The *efficient market theory* states that the market is an ideal market where all public information about a company is instantly reflected in the price of its stock. In such a situation, studying the fundamentals of a company cannot uncover any underpriced securities, because perfectly informed investors have already accounted for all potential risks and rewards on the stock. None of the other theories looks at the price of a stock as an ideal model.
4. The correct answer is C. The only choice that requires the individual to become vested is the 401(k) program. A 401(k) typically has matching employer contributions that enable the individual to be fully vested after a maximum number of years. All the other choices are fully vested immediately by the individual.
5. The correct answer is B. T-bill options have a premium value of $2,500 for each point of the premium. The investor purchased the T-bill for 1 point, thus it cost him $2,500; therefore, the other answers are not correct.
6. The correct answer is D. The holder of a put option has the right to sell 100 shares of FTD stock at the price of $60, hoping that the price of the stock drops below the strike of $60. The holder realizes that he will pay the writer $300 for 1 FTD Put option @ 3.

7. The correct answer is D. A trade shown on the consolidated tape as 2sGHI 34 s/t means that 200 shares of GHI were sold at 34 as stopped stock. Stopped stock is a courtesy function that a specialist will perform for a floor broker. It means that the specialist is stopping the price at 34. Other brokers entering the market will pay the market price of the stock. Because there might be a difference between the two prices, it is reported on the tape as stopped stock.
8. D is the correct answer. A special tax bond taxes are collected on such items as liquor, gambling, or tobacco sales. The backing comes from taxes that are not directly derived from the project being built. They cannot have property taxes as a source of revenue.
9. The correct answer is B. The SEC effective date allows the issuer to issue a final prospectus with the final offering price and begin selling the security in the primary market. Indications of interest occur prior to the effective date and sales in the secondary market occur after the issue sells out of the primary market.
10. The correct answer is D. A 20-year muni bond purchased at 110 in the secondary market with 16 years to maturity, held for 8 years, and then sold at 102 has the adjusted cost basis of the bond computed to determine whether the investor has a capital gain or a capital loss. The adjusted cost basis is:

    Cost + time since issued/life of bond × par value – cost basis

    11,000 + 4/20 × 10,000 – 11,000 =

    11,000 + .2 × –$1,000

    11,000 + (–$200) = $10,800 adjusted cost basis
11. The correct answer is B. A broker who attempts to bring an additional broker or dealer into a transaction without just cause is guilty of interpositioning. The charging of additional transaction fees is acceptable only when another broker legitimately needs to be part of a trade.
12. The correct answer is B. Strike prices established on Stock Index Options are set at five point intervals, which is different from equity options where strike price intervals can be set at 2½ points, 5 points, or 10 points. Strike prices are set in points, not dollars.
13. The correct answer is C. The LIFO accounting system assumes that the last goods placed in inventory are the first ones sold. The FIFO accounting system assumes that the first goods placed in inventory are the first ones sold. FIFO generally reports a higher value for existing inventories than the LIFO system.
14. The correct answer is B. When investors decide to exercise their option contract, they will notify their broker to enter an exercise notice. The exercise notice is sent to the Options Clearing Corp. for assignment. The OCC finds the other side of the option trade for the

client wanting to exercise. If there are not enough sellers, the market maker steps in to be the other side of the trade.

15. The correct answer is C. The agency that has issued a pass-through certificate purchase mortgages that have a higher interest rate than the rate offered to the pass-through holder. This difference in interest rates or spread is the profit that the agency earns. For instance, they issue 7% pass-through certificates and purchase corresponding mortgages that are paying 7.5%. The .5% spread is the profit for the agency. Thus, all other choices are incorrect.
16. The correct answer is C. Sell limit orders, buy stop orders, and buy stop limit orders are all entered above the current market price for execution. After the limit has been reached on each, the price depends on the designated order. A buy limit order is at current market price or below.
17. The correct answer is D. If the investor who sold 1 HTH April 60 Call @ 5 and bought 1 HTH April 70 Call @ 2, he or she will have created a Short Call Credit Spread. The short means the dominant part of the spread is the one that was sold, because the investor took in more than they paid for the call they purchased. The credit exists because they took in $5 in premiums on the April 60 call while paying out only $2 in premium on the April 70 call.
18. The correct answer is C. A no-load fund sells directly to the investor, does not charge a sales fee to purchase the fund's shares, and redeems shares for shareholders. They are permitted, however, to charge other fees such as legal, brokerage, printing and administrative fees, that can be passed on to shareholders.
19. The correct answer is A. A company with a market price of $55.00 and a dividend payment of $.62 pays shareholders a rate of return on each share of 1.13%. This is computed as .62 divided by 55.00 = 1.13 current yield.
20. The correct answer is A. Securities that are purchased in a margin account are held in street name by the broker. The securities are considered owned by the customer and entitle the customer to dividends. They remain in street name until the customer pays off the debit balance for ease of selling.
21. The correct answer is C. A municipal investment trust is an accumulation of various municipal bonds, typically from the same state of issuance, that have been deposited with a trustee. The trust sells incremental units of the total portfolio of bonds to investors, typically in $1,000 increments. The investors do not actually own any one bond, but rather they own a portion of the entire MIT. The MIT pays the holders interest from the pooled bonds on a monthly basis, as opposed to semi-annual payments that are paid for individual bonds that are not in the trust.

22. The correct answer is A. When the Fed wants to purchase securities in the market to expand the money supply, they do so with the use of repurchase agreements. They buy the securities from primary dealers and inject funds into the market. By expanding the money supply, borrowing from banks becomes easier.
23. The correct answer is B. A purchase of 1 STP May 50 Call @ 5 and the sale of 1 STP May 60 call @ 2 is considered a long call debit spread. It is long because the purchased call is more important to the investor than the short call. It is a debit spread because the investor paid more in premium ($5) than he took in from the sale of the May 60 Call ($2).
24. The correct answer is A. Gross national product is a measure of national output that includes all the goods and services produced by the residents and companies of a country. GNP does not count goods and services produced abroad by domestic companies, nor does it count goods that are produced within a country by foreign companies.
25. The correct answer is B. The prime rate is set by major commercial banks in lending to their highest credit-rated borrowers. It is not considered the most volatile rate in the market; that distinction is held by the Fed funds rate for overnight borrowing. Corporations typically issue debt securities at a lower rate then the prime rate.
26. The correct answer is B. A good till cancelled order is a limit order that is considered open until it is either executed or cancelled by the customer. All GTC orders are held by the specialist for execution after the limit price has been reached. A day order is for the day only and an AON (all or none order) is to be completed for the entire order or none of it. An FOK order is a fill it or kill it order, in which the order is to be filled immediately and completely or not at all.
27. The correct answer is B. A short put credit bear spread is the sale of the first put that took in more than the purchase of the second put for the investor. It is this credit that makes the first put more important to the investor. He is bearish on the stock because he has sold a put for more than the put he purchased in the spread. B is the only example of a short put credit bear spread because he took in $5 in premium and paid out only $2 in premiums.
28. The correct answer is D. To determine the amount that a long margin account can fall before it is required to bring in additional funds (through a margin call), an investor can simply divide the debit balance by the complement of the 25% minimum maintenance requirement for a long account, which is .75. A debit balance of $22,500 ÷ .75 = $30,000. The account can fall to a market value of $30,000 before it will be at the minimum maintenance level. LMV of

$30,000 – Debit Balance of $22,500 = Equity of $7,500. The account is now sitting exactly at 25%.

29. The correct answer is D. Strips are still actively traded. They are considered non-interest bearing securities that are issued in book entry form only and are repackaged government debt that have been created as zero coupon bonds. They are also considered non-interest bearing securities because as zero coupon bonds they do not pay interest to holders.
30. The correct answer is C. A corporate bond quoted at 97⅝ is selling in the market at $976.25. The 97 equals $970 and the ⅝ths equals $6.25. ($970 + $6.25 = $976.25.) All the other calculations are incorrect.
31. The correct answer is C. If the Federal Reserve Bank lowers the reserve requirement, banks can lend more in the market. Lower reserve requirements enable banks to lend out additional funds that are normally held in reserve.
32. The correct answer is A. Revenue bonds for such items as water treatment plants and bridge and/or tunnel construction are considered to be self-supporting. An analyst needs to look closely at the debt service coverage ratio to determine whether the project is generating enough income to cover the required debt service. School districts or capital improvements are not self-supporting debts.
33. The correct answer is B. The maximum number of shares that can be sold every 90 days under the dribble rule is the greater of 1% of the outstanding shares or the average weekly volume for the previous four weeks to the 144 filing.
34. The correct answer is C. T-bonds are the only Treasury security that are callable by the U.S. government in the last five years prior to maturity. T-notes, T-bills, and strips are not callable securities.
35. The correct answer is C. A municipal bond purchased on margin has a margin requirement of the greater of 7% of the par value or 15% of the market value to meet the margin requirement.
36. The correct answer is C. The market is said to be overbought when the price of the security is higher than what buyers are willing to pay, sellers far outnumber buyers, and supply exceeds demand causing the price to drop. This indicates a bearish sign.
37. The correct answer is B. A Feasibility study is required when a municipality wants to issue a revenue bond to finance a revenue producing project. The study is conducted by an impartial engineering firm (not the engineer for the project). The study determines the projected cost of the project and the projected use of the project to support the debt. It does not make any determination for a GO bond issue.

38. The correct answer is B. Stock index options use a multiplier of 100 when computing the value of the contract and the premium for the contract. Thus, an index that cost an investor a premium of 3½ is multiplied by 100 to equal a dollar amount of $350 for the premium.
39. The correct answer is D. The truest yield measure is the yield to maturity. The YTM takes into consideration any premium paid or discount earned on a bond, as well as the remaining time left to maturity.
40. The correct answer is B. The DTT call options are 2.50 points in the money, which represents intrinsic value. The remaining value of the premium is .50 point of time value × 200 shares = $100.
41. The correct answer is C. Over the counter pink sheet securities are not considered marginable unless they are on the Federal Reserve Bank's "margin list" of allowable securities.
42. The correct answer is C. Bills are issued in 13, 26, or 52 week duration. 39 weeks is the only incorrect answer.
43. The correct answer is D. All the statements are true. A trust account is typically established by a court appointed trustee to manage the account. The trustee has a duty to manage the assets in the account for the individual named in the account. That individual can either be alive or deceased. The trustee is required to follow the instructions set forth in the trust agreement outlined.
44. The correct answer is D. A custodian account, discretionary account, omnibus account, and fiduciary account each has a designated individual assigned to trade on behalf of the beneficial owner of the account. Each of these accounts except for an Omnibus account have limits on the types of investments that can be made in the account.
45. The correct answer is C. Operating income is determined before taxes are paid, before interest expense, and before depreciation. Interest expense, depreciation, and taxes are all deducted from operating income to determine net income. It is found on the income statement of a company, not the balance sheet.
46. The correct answer is B. Markups must be reported to customers on a trade confirmation for all NASDAQ listed securities. This include the National Market System (NMS) and the Small Cap Marketplace, which comprise the NASDAQ. The bulletin board and pink sheet stocks are considered small securities or penny stocks and are not required to report markups to customers on the confirm.
47. The correct answer is D. A municipal bond that has been quoted in the market at 96½ has a per bond cost of $965.00 (1,000 × 96.5% = $965.00) The investor has purchased a round lot of five bonds, thus the total cost is $965.00 × 5 = $4,825.00.

48. The correct answer is D. Interest that is earned on municipal bond issues is, in most cases, exempt from federal, state, and local taxes for the bondholder. The municipal market is a thin market that enables investors from their state of residence to purchase municipal issues from that state to receive a triple tax exemption on interest earned.
49. The correct answer is B. Small investors are best served with cumulative voting rights and a forward stock split. Cumulative voting gives the smaller shareholder the capability to put more weight of their voting right behind any one board member that is up for election. A forward stock split adjusts the stock price downward, which in the event of a high priced stock, makes it more attractive to the small investor.
50. The correct answer is B. When a municipality offers a new bond issue, the type of bid depends on the type of bonds being issued. A general obligation bond issue is based on a competitive bid basis because the municipality must be able to show the public that they have secured the lowest possible financing for the bonds. A revenue bond is conducted on a negotiated bid basis. The municipality commits to one underwriter and negotiates the parameters of the bond issue. The negotiated bid is typically done using an underwriter whom the municipality has done business with in the past.
51. The correct answer is A. A direct participation program is typically a long-term investment in a rather risky and illiquid entity. The crossover point for a DPP is determined to be the point when the revenues generated from the program exceed the expenses that are incurred. This point might not be realized for investors as the program weathers economic conditions.
52. The correct answer is D. Cyclical industries are made up of companies such as automobile makers, appliance manufacturers, and suppliers of building materials. A pharmaceutical company is considered a defensive industry because it sells goods that are always needed by consumers. Even if the economy is doing poorly, consumers cannot cut back on a necessity such as drug prescriptions.
53. The correct answer is D. Nancy sells short 100 shares of PDQ at $58. The stock went to $72 in the market for a loss of $1,400 on the short position. She also bought 1 PDQ April 60 Call @ 4 in the market. The call allows her to buy PDQ at $60. She makes $1,200 on the call less the premium paid of $400 = $800 gain on the call. She lost $1,400 on the short sale and made $800 on the option for a total loss of $600 to the account.
54. The correct answer is C. The S&P's 500 index is a measure of 500 select stocks from the NYSE, the AMEX, and the over-the-counter market. Bulletin board stocks are very small stocks listed on the pink

sheets or bulletin board of the OTC market and are too small to be considered for the S&P's 500 index.

55. The correct answer is C. When reading a municipal bond offering, the first interest rate quoted is considered the nominal yield for the bond. The second interest rate is the yield to maturity for the bond. These are California Highway bonds that are more than likely to be revenue bonds supported by tolls from the project. The bonds are callable, starting in the year 2005 (C 05) and the bonds mature on 1/1/15.
56. The correct answer is A. An investor Buys 1 FTD May 55 Call @ 4 and also sells 1 FTD May 65 Call @ 2. The breakeven point on the long call is $57. If FTD only goes to $57, the investor makes 2 points on the May 55 Call he purchased at $4. He will only have a $2 loss on the May 55 Call. But he will also keep the $2 premium received on the short May 65 Call, which would not be exercised against him for a gain of the premium received of $2. Thus at $57 he lost $2.00 on the May 55 Call but makes $2.00 on the May 65 Call to break even.
57. The correct answer is C. The OTC handles exercise notices on a random basis. The firm that has received the assignment can choose a client on any basis of their choice, including LIFO or FIFO.
58. The correct answer is A. All direct government obligations are issued in minimum denominations of $1,000.00 with increments of $1,000.00 thereafter. T-bills use to have a minimum denomination of $10,000.00, but this was changed in 1998.
59. The correct answer is A. Fannie Mae can borrow from the Federal Reserve Bank at their discount window. This provides short-term low-cost borrowing to the agency if needed. The discount rate is the lowest rate in the market and is offered by the Fed to its members and related agencies, such as FNMA.
60. The correct answer is A. The larger more well-known securities listed on the OTC market are also found on the level of NASDAQ known as the National Market System. The bulletin board and pink sheets provide information to investors on the smaller OTC issues. The blue market suggests municipal listings, but is commonly known as the blue list.
61. The correct answer is C. The insurance company, not the annuitant, takes on the bulk of the risk involved in the fixed annuity contract. A fixed annuity guarantees the customer a predetermined return on their investment upon the contract's maturity. Fixed annuities are attractive to conservative investors because they minimize risk for the investor by letting the customer know in advance what their rate of return is. Inflation does not decrease the value of the annuity because

the insurance company guarantees both earnings and principal to the annuitant.

62. The correct answer is C. A 10-year gross revenue pledge bond pays the bondholder interest and principal first, before operation and maintenance of the project, making it the safest investment. A net revenue pledge pays operation and maintenance first, before bondholder interest and principal payments, thus it's not the best protection of interest and principal.

63. The correct answer is A. A broker securing a margin loan for a customer is permitted to pledge 140% of the debit balance to the bank in order to secure the loan for the margin customer. The debit balance is considered the amount of the loan.

64. The correct answer is D. U.S. tax laws can change to affect the overall rate of return on a security. Foreign securities have greater legislative risk than U.S. stocks because of the sovereign risk that also comes hand in hand with government changes.

65. The correct answer is B. The advance decline index is computed by: Advances – declines divided by the total number of issues. 2,038 advances – 1,157 declines = 881. 881 is then divided by the total number of issues (2,038 + 1,157 = 3,195). 881 divided by 3,195 equals .276.

66. The correct answer is C. A holder of 10 DVD May 45 Puts @ 3 has a maximum potential gain of the strike price of the option less the premium paid. A $45 strike less $3 premium equals $42 total possible gain per share if the stock declined to zero. $42 × 1,000 shares = $42,000 maximum gain. The most the holder can lose on the contract is the premium paid. The premium of $3.00 × 1,000 shares = $3,000 maximum potential loss.

67. The correct answer is D. The lead underwriter makes all the investment decisions of the offering, settles the account at the end of the offering with all syndicate members, and chooses members of the syndicate. He cannot register with the SEC; the issuing company is required to take on the task of registering with the SEC.

68. The correct answer is D. A customer order ticket includes the security, the number of shares bought or sold, the customers account number, the AE number, and a designation of a solicited trade.

69. The correct answer is B. Settlement date on price-based options are set at the next business day.

70. The correct answer is B. The difference between a fixed unit investment trust and a participating unit investment trust is that the fixed unit trust cannot change investments once established and the participating trust can indirectly change investments through the underlying mutual fund it has purchased. None of the other choices is correct.

71. The correct answer is D. The Federal agency bond with a maturity date of May 2001 has a selling price of the lowest asking price of 102.12, or 102 12/32. Each point is worth $10.00. Thus, 102 pts × $10.00 = $1,020.00, and 12/32 = $3.75, for a total of $1,023.75.
72. The correct answer is D. LEAPS, or Long Term Equity Anticipation Securities, have terms of up to three years, enabling investors to create long-term options strategies. LEAPS can either be American-style or European-style in their exercise. All LEAPS have expirations in the month of December.
73. The correct answer is B. A tax qualified retirement plan enables the individual to deduct contributions into the plan from their yearly salary. A 5% contribution on a $50,000 salary totals a contribution of $2,500 (50,000 × 5%). The individual has a taxable income of $47,500.
74. The correct answer is D. A 403-B Plan is known as a tax deferred annuity plan for employees of nonprofit organizations. The plan enables these employees to purchase annuities in which the contributions are tax deferred. The maximum contribution is set at 25% of yearly income or $14,000 whichever is less.
75. The correct answer is B. A corporate bond purchased at a premium means that the investors have paid more for the bond than they will eventually receive at maturity. This will be a loss for the bondholder and a portion of this loss can be deducted from the interest received each year. The premium paid on the bond can be amortized (or deducted) each year by the bondholder.
76. The correct answer is C. Market risk cannot be diversified against and is also known as unique or nonsystematic risk in the markets.
77. The correct answer is C. The OCC set parameters regulating the number of contracts that any one investor is permitted to have on an underlying security on either side of the market. The number of contracts permitted is determined by the number of outstanding shares, the trading volume, and which side of the market the option is on (bullish or bearish). An investor who bought calls and sold puts on the same security is actually on the same side of the market (bullish). Selling calls and buying puts are also on the same side of the market (bearish).
78. The correct answer is D. A short call writer is considered bearish on the underlying security. The short call writer hopes that the price of the underlying security falls below the strike price of the call option. If the market price is below the strike price, the call writer keeps the premium received on the sale of the calls.
79. The correct answer is C. The long put spread and the short call spread are both considered bullish for an investor using option spreads. The short call means the investor sold call options. If the

stock goes up in value, the investor loses money. If it declines, the investor keeps the premium of the expiring worthless option. Thus, they are bearish on the underlying stock. The long put spread means the investor purchased a put option hoping the market goes down in value so they can put the stock back to the writer at the higher strike price.

80. The correct answer is A. A stock index is a single number whose daily movement reflects changes in the prices of the group of stocks within the index, not in any specific individual stocks. There are various calculations for weighting stocks within an index, however, all measure the diversity of their underlying securities. An index can be an indicator of the market of that particular industry but does not necessarily indicate good performance of any specific stocks within the index. Some stocks perform better than the index and some worse.
81. The correct answer is A. Yield-base options are not representative of the actual security positions of the underlying government instrument being used. Strike prices are in intervals of 2½ points and they settle in funds the next business day. Yield-base options are also European style as opposed to price-base options, which are American style.
82. The correct answer is C. Securities that kept in street name are kept in the broker's name with the customer designated as nominal owner. Information or dividends that are distributed by a company are sent to the registered owner, which in this case is the broker. They must be forwarded to the client by the proxy department.
83. The correct answer is D. Parents who have opened a custodian account for their child have given an irrevocable gift to the minor. Removal of funds from the account is not permitted under any circumstances short of the death of the minor.
84. The correct answer is B. Securities and Investors Protection Corporation cover a customer account up to an amount of $500,000 of which $100,000 can be in cash. Most brokers offer an enhanced version of this insurance coverage, but the maximum coverage offered by SIPC is the $500,000 coverage of assets.
85. The correct answer is A. At the end of each day, a brokerage firm revalues each security in a margin account at the closing market price in a process called "mark to market." It is done to make sure margin requirements are met; if not, the trader will face a margin call. The short market value is the value of all short sales in the account at the end of the day only. The long market value of the account will rise and fall as the market prices of the securities change and is calculated by the previous day's closing price of each security in the account. Short interest is the total number of shares of a security that have been sold short.

86. The correct answer is B. To determine the minimum value that a long margin account can reach before it has to bring in additional funds (through a margin call), an investor can simply divide the debit balance by the complement of the 25% minimum maintenance requirement for a long account, which is .75.

    A debit balance of $9,000 ÷ .75 = $12,000. The account can fall in market value to $12,000 before it will be at the minimum maintenance level.

    LMV of $12,000 – Debit Balance of $9,000 = Equity of $3,000. The account is now sitting at exactly 25%.

87. The correct answer is C. The Investment Company Act of 1940 requires that investment companies register the issue with the SEC, offer a prospectus to all investors, and solicit proxies on matters requiring shareholder approval. They are not permitted to change investment objectives without the majority approval of shareholders.

88. The correct answer is B. Only Fannie Mae and Sallie Mae are privatized and have stock that is listed on the NYSE. Freddie Mac also issues stock, but it is only sold to savings and loan institutions across the United States, and held in trust by the federal home loan bank system. GNMA is a government corporation within HUD and thus not private.

89. The correct answer is A. Under MSRB rules, broker-dealer complaints against each other are required to go to arbitration. Failure to submit to arbitration can result in censure and fines by the MSRB.

90. The correct answer is C. The most the investor can lose is the 1 point increase on the short shares to the maximum of the strike price, plus the premium of $5 per share on the calls = $6 total × 400 shares = $2,400 possible loss.

91. The correct answer is D. Real estate investment trusts are required to registered with the SEC before commencing operations. They must have no fewer than 100 owners of beneficial interest, and must have less than 50% of the trust controlled by five or fewer investors. REITS are either listed on a stock exchange or the OTC for traders.

92. The correct answer is A. In an attempt to slow down a runaway economy, the Federal Reserve sells securities in the market. This takes funds out of the market, making borrowing more expensive. The other choices do not help slow down an economy.

93. The correct answer is C. The buyer and seller of an option contract actually settles with the Options Clearing Corporation and not each other next business day. There really is no direct relationship between buyer and seller because of the exercising of options. No writer ever knows exactly when they will be assigned an option, and for this reason, the OCC has to act as the clearing agent for all options.

94. The correct answer is D. A moving average is the average price of a security or index plotted over time. It is a moving average because the figure is recalculated each day, dropping the oldest day and adding the newest day, as the specified period moves forward. Moving averages illustrate long term trends fairly well.
95. The correct answer is C. Dealers will purchase mutual fund shares from the sponsor, at a discount to the public offering price. They will then sell the shares to investors but are not permitted to purchase shares for their own inventory accounts. Any purchase they make from the sponsor must be matched with prior orders from investors. They are not the sponsors of the fund.
96. The correct answer is A. From this selection of corporate securities, only common shareholders have any claim on the assets of a company in a liquidation process. Warrants, rights, and options have no claim on the assets of a company.
97. The correct answer is D. Technical analysis is the use of price charts and other market information to identify and predict trends in the prices of securities. By analyzing patterns of past price changes, technical analysts believe that they can predict future price movements and recommend the best times to buy and sell.
98. The correct answer is D. A convertible bond selling in the market at 92 ($920) with a conversion ratio of 20 to 1 needs for the common shares to be selling at $46 per share to trade at parity. $46 \times 20 = 920$.
99. The correct answer is B. Markups must be reported to customers on a trade confirmation for all NASDAQ listed securities. This includes the National Market System and the Small Cap Marketplace, which comprise the NASDAQ. The bulletin board and pink sheet stocks are considered small securities or penny stocks, and are not required to report markups to customers on the confirm.
100. The correct answer is C. The Student Loan Marketing Association is a government sponsored agency that purchases student loans from financial institutions by selling short and medium term notes to the public. The loans that they purchase provide lenders with additional funds to lend to students.
101. The correct answer is A. The current spread on TNT stock as reported on the NASDAQ Level II screen is the difference between the highest bid price and the lowest ask price. The market is 15.25 Bid × 15.50 ask or a spread of .25 point for TNT stock.
102. The correct answer is C. A long put holder is bearish on the underlying security. They hope that the market price of the stock drops below the strike price of the option, so that they can put the stock back to the writer at the higher strike price. The most they can lose is the premium paid, and the most they can make is the stock declining in value to zero.

103. The correct answer is D. A customer confirm lists the security and number of shares bought or sold, designates the trade date and settlement date, notes any commission or markup charged to the customer, and designates the broker as either principal or agent.

104. The correct answer is A. In a negotiated bid, the municipality issues a revenue bond. In doing so, the municipality has committed to one underwriter that they have done business with in the past. The negotiated bid determines the call schedule, protective covenants, bond denominations, spread, and other parameters of the issue between the underwriter and municipality. Conversely, GO bond issues are conducted on a competitive bid basis.

105. The correct answer is C. New issues brought to the market for the first time, and non-listed, must send a final prospectus to customers for a period of 90 days. For already exchange listed securities, the requirement is 25 days. For nonexchange, listed, and second offering securities, the requirement is 40 days.

106. The correct answer is C. Homeowners who have secured a 30-year mortgage can amortize the payments over the life of the loan as they make payments to the mortgage issuer.

107. The correct answer is C. Moody's will rate municipal notes on a scale of Moody's Investment Grade or MIG. The highest rating they give to short term debt of municipalities is MIG-1, with their lowest rating being MIG-4. AAA and aaa are not Moody ratings.

108. The correct answer is D. Buy limit orders, sell stop orders, and sell stop limit orders are all entered below the current market price for execution. A buy stop order is entered above the current market price for execution.

109. The correct answer is A. The investor breaks even on this account when the price of PDQ stock goes to $54 per share. At $54 per share, the investor makes 5 points × 400 shares on the short sale = $2,000 gain. The call options that the investor purchased to protect their upside loss potential are at a market price of $54 less the entire premium paid of $5 × 400 shares = $2,000 loss.

110. The correct answer is C. The equity in a long margin account is determined by the market value – the debit balance. The investor purchased 1,000 shares of TNT stock at $57.00. The account is set at: LMV =$57,000 – Debit Balance of Reg. T 50% amount borrowed = $28,500 = Equity of $28,500.

If the LMV increased to $63,000 minus the debit balance of $28,500 = Equity of $34,500. In a long account, an increase in the LMV also increases the equity by the same amount.

111. The correct answer is D. Insurance companies can only sell variable annuities via prospectus. Variable annuities present customers with all

the risks of financial market investments and are required to register with the SEC as a security. As securities, a variable annuity will fall under the regulations of the Investment Company Act of 1940 and the Securities Act of 1933.

112. The correct answer is D. A revenue bond is typically backed by the revenues or tolls generated from the proposed project such as a bridge, tunnel, or highway.

113. The correct answer is B. The MSRB rules and regulations that have been established apply only to those entities that deal in municipal securities. They do not apply to the issuing municipality. The municipal market is different than the corporate market, when it applies to underwriting. Municipal securities can be underwritten by both securities dealers as well as commercial banks and savings banks. Thrift institutions do not underwrite municipal issues, thus the MSRB rules does not apply to them. Issuers are not subject to MSRB rules, either by design or by inference.

114. The correct answer is C. The Small Order Execution System, or SOES, is the OTC computerized system that automatically matches buyer and seller of OTC stocks under 1,000 shares. The bulletin board is another OTC reporting system that is used for non-NASDAQ listed securities (pink sheet stocks). The Super Dot and DOT are used by the NYSE for small order entries, limit orders, and basket and program trades.

115. The correct answer is B. Call options are considered in the money if the market price of the underlying security is higher than the strike price for the underlying security. 1 CBC May 45 Call @ 3 is considered in the money by three points with a market price of $48, and in the money by seven points if the market price were at $52. Market prices below the strike price of $45 are considered out of the money.

116. The correct answer is B. A narrow-based index option reflects the price movements of a narrow group of stocks, such as those in one particular sector or industry. Computer technology stocks are in one sector, and thus are narrow-based. Broad-based indexes, on the other hand, reflect the price movements in a group of industries and market sectors, such as the S&P's 500 index. LEAPS are a type of option contract and CAPS are a type of preferred stock.

117. The correct answer is D. The New York Stock Exchange margin rules can either be the same as the Federal Reserve Bank margin rules or stricter than the Fed's rules. NYSE rules can never be less lenient than those established by the Federal Reserve Bank.

118. The correct answer is C. Under Subchapter M of the IRS tax code, portfolio-based mutual funds are not required to pay corporate taxes on their income if they distribute 90% of their earnings to shareholders. The IRS charges a tax surcharge on funds that do not pass on at

least 97% of their dividend income and 98% of their capital gains to shareholders. Most funds retain only 2 or 3% of their earnings in order to meet these IRS requirements.

119. The correct answer is D. The expansion phase of the business cycle denotes an increase in the production of goods and services while interest rates and inflation remain generally low. More workers are hired to meet the expansion, and unemployment decreases.
120. The correct answer is D. Failure to issue an annual report can lead to a delisting of the stock, an investigation by the SEC, and might lead to a lack of credibility in the market with potential investors. They cannot continue business unaffected; at least to some degree.
121. The correct answer is D. Tax allocation bonds are used to finance commercial redevelopment in a municipality, whereas the others are not used for this purpose.
122. The correct answer is B. An insured municipal bond issue only guarantees that interest and principal are paid to the holder in the event of the default of the bond issue. If the bonds go into default, the insurance pays the bondholders.
123. The correct answer is B. NYSE member firms are required to provide a blanket fidelity bond to guard against fraud and embezzlement by employees when becoming a member of the NYSE. What are the others and why not?
124. The correct answer is C. Treasury bonds are issued in a minimum purchase amount of $1,000.00, with increments of $1,000.00 thereafter.
125. The correct answer is B. The writer of this option can have a possible gain of the premiums received on the options. In this case, the writer received a premium of $4.00 on the call option and $3.00 on the put option for a total possible gain of $700. This straddle position gains if the stock remains constant in price at the strike price, thus retaining the premiums received on each option.
126. The correct answer is C. All the major stock indexes are considered broad based. Major stock indexes include the Dow Jones industrial average, the Major Market Index, and the S&P's 100 and the S&P's 500. Broad-based indexed a large number of stocks from a variety of companies and sectors. The Consumer Price Index is not a broad-based index as such but a measure of goods and service produced.
127. The correct answer is C. Treasury bills are purchased on a discount-to-yield basis. Instead of actually paying interest like T-notes and T-bonds, Treasury bills are discounted and based on the maturity of 13, 26, or 52 weeks and mature at par value. Competitive and noncompetitive bids are not pricing methods.

128. C is correct. A client who has failed to sign the option agreement after 15 days is restricted to closing transactions in the account. The client cannot write or purchase any new options. Even though the account is open and the client cannot continue to trade, the account is not immediately closed.
129. The correct answer is D. An investor purchasing $5,000 worth of securities in a margin account is required to deposit 50% of their value, or in this case, a deposit of cash in a minimum of $2,500. If the customer is depositing marginable securities, the value of the securities must be $5,000, because only 50% of their value is considered.
130. The correct answer is A. When the long market value of the securities falls to the point where the equity drops below the Reg T 50% level, the account is considered restricted. In a restricted account, future purchases are not affected; the customer must simply deposit the required 50% for any new securities. The customer is not required to bring the entire account up to Reg T, just any new purchases.
131. The correct answer is B. A 12-b-1 mutual fund is named after the section of the Investment Company Act of 1940 that permits certain classified mutual funds to pass on advertising costs to investors in the form of fees charged.
132. The correct answer is C. Most annuities are designed to secure retirement income for the individual. The customer pays money to the insurance company, which the company invests, and then later pays to the customer. Mutual funds and stocks do not, in general, provide the safe return most annuitants look for. Insurance coverage is not a function of an annuity.
133. The correct answer is D. Inflation can be explained as the general increase in prices for goods and services produced. The forces of supply and demand in the productive sphere of the economy change during the business cycle. If the demand for goods and services exceeds the supply, prices rise. Inflation is also explained as the value of money and the external expansion and contraction of the money supply in the economy. If the money supply expands or contracts too quickly, it affects the value of money and what it can buy for a consumer.
134. The correct answer is B. A fundamental analyst investigates a company's financial health by looking at the company's assets, liabilities, income and expenses. The analyst tries to determine how profitable the company is likely to be in the future.
135. The correct answer is C. The Federal Intermediate Credit Banks and Banks for Cooperatives finance short-term farming needs, whereas Federal Land Banks arrange financing for longer-term needs.

136. The correct answer is C. Interest earned on a territorial municipal bond issue such as Washington, D.C. (District of Columbia), is exempt from federal, state, and local taxes regardless of the investor's state of residence.

137. The correct answer is D. The NASD 5% markup policy is a guideline that member firms need to follow. In certain instances, a firm can charge more if they have gone to extraordinary measures to execute a trade for a client. Measures include the size of the trade, the number of market makers that had to be contacted, the price of the security, and the marketability of the security.

138. The correct answer is C. In most cases, investment companies are required to advertise with a prospectus. The SEC, however, does allow advertising without a prospectus in certain cases, such as through a tombstone ad in a financial publication.

139. The correct answer is D. Municipal bonds can be issued through any state, county, township, or village. They can also be issued for a municipal entity such as a school district. This can include public utilities and water and sewage districts.

140. The correct answer is B. An accredited investor is an individual who has a net worth of $1 million, has an income of $200,000 for the past two years, or is an insider of the issuing company. A bank or investment company must have assets greater than $5 million and not $3 million to qualify as an accredited investor.

141. The correct answer is C. The Super Dot System will handle limit orders up to 99,999 shares for execution directly to the specialist. The DOT system handles market orders up to 30,999 shares.

142. The correct answer is D. Yield-base interest rate options are considered to be European style and have a settlement of the next business day. American-style options are price based but also settle next business day. Neither settle at trade date + 3 as equity securities do.

143. The correct answer is D. Leading economic indicators include the average work week of production workers in manufacturing, the average weekly claims for unemployment insurance, the issuance of new building permits, and new orders for consumer goods and materials. These leading indicators tend to change before the economy changes in the business cycle.

144. The correct answer is A. Arthur is long 100 shares of GHI at $44 and the stock goes to $48 in the market. He has made $400 on the stock. He also purchases 1 GHI Oct. 45 Put @ 3. If the stock rises above the strike price on the put, it would be worthless to Arthur. It went to $48, thus he will lose the premium paid of $300. He made $400 on the stock and lost $300 on the put, for a total gain of $100.

145. The correct answer is A. New offerings for a company with shares already listed must send a final prospectus for a period of 25 days to meet mandatory requirements. A second offering non-listed period is 40 days and the first offering non-listed period is 90 days.

146. The correct answer is B. A market maker in the OTC market is suggestive of the role the specialist carries in the NYSE auction market. They both make a market in the underlying securities they trade in.

147. The correct answer is B. Property that has been pledged to secure debt issued would have a lien on the property held by the trustee overseeing the bond indenture. In the event of default, the trustee would liquidate the property and pay the bondholders back.

148. The correct answer is B. This question is best answered by determining which of the choices have the most secure guarantee. Only GNMA is backed by the government and guarantees the mortgages purchased. FNMA, Freddie Mac, and Sallie Mae are government agencies with the implicit backing of the government, but not a guarantee. Thus, GNMA is considered the safest investment, and can issue debt securities with the lowest interest rate.

149. The correct answer is C. The apprenticeship program allows individuals to represent their firm to other municipal dealers, as long as they are not earning a commission on any business they bring to the firm. They can be paid by salary, but not on commission while participating in an apprentice program.

150. The correct answer is C. When an OTC dealer trades a stock out of their own inventory account, they are permitted to mark up the stock as their profit on the transaction. If they were buying from a client, they would mark the stock down to earn a profit. A commission is earned when they go to another market maker to secure the stock for a client.

151. The correct answer is C. The maximum gain for the writer of 5 DTT April 70 Calls @ 5 is the premium that has been received ($5.00 × 500 shares = $2,500). The maximum gain for the holder of the contract is the unlimited amount that the market price of the stock can rise above the strike price of the underlying option.

152. The correct answer is C. The OCC issues options on a predetermined cycle that the security has been assigned to. A cycle of February, May, August, and November can have options on any given date with four expiration dates. For instance, February would be the spot expiration, with an option for March then being issued, followed by the next two months of the expiration cycle (May and August) for a maximum total of four expiration dates at any given time.

153. The correct answer is D. The exercise settlement value for an index option is the closing value of the index for the day and not its value at

the moment of exercise. In this question, the investor receives a value of 535, which is the closing value at the end of the day.

154. The correct answer is D. Regulation U governs the amount that a broker can borrow from a bank using pledged securities to secure a margin loan for a customer. Brokers pledge 140% of the debit balance and banks are permitted to lend 70% of that amount to the broker for a margin loan.

155. The correct answer is D. All the entities listed have a role in the governance of mutual funds. The custodian is usually a bank or trust company charged with keeping the fund's cash and any securities associated with the fund's securities portfolio. A transfer agent monitors the purchase and redemption of fund shares by investors. A registrar maintains records of all shareholders and mails any financial statements or proxies. An auditor is required by law to act as an independent accounting firm in verifying all financial statements and performance of the fund's portfolio.

156. The correct answer is A. Investors purchasing a bond at a premium have paid more for the bond than they receive at maturity. This added amount reflects a drop in interest rates in the market. The amount of the premium can be amortized (or deducted) for the bondholder over the life of the bond.

157. The correct answer is A. A breakout is the movement of a security through its historical resistance or support level. Technical analysts believe that a breakout signals a trend that is likely to continue.

158. The correct answer is C. The NYSE is considered the largest auction market in the world. The NYSE is commonly nicknamed the "Big Board," whereas the Amex is known as the Curb market. The OTC market is considered a negotiated market.

159. The correct answer is A. When the Federal Reserve Bank raises the discount rate, it becomes more expensive for member banks to borrow directly from the Fed at the discount window. This action makes it more expensive for banks to borrow, and in turn, makes it more expensive for corporations to borrow from banks. This slows down borrowing, and the overall economy.

160. The correct answer is D. An investor purchasing 5 Call option contracts has the right to buy 500 shares (or 100 shares per contract) of the underlying security. The investor also has the right to purchase the shares of the underlying security at the strike or exercise price. The buyer of a call option wants the stock to go up in value, so investors can purchase the shares at the lower strike price.

161. The correct answer is B. Treasury notes and treasury bonds pay interest on a semi-annual basis. Treasury bills are considered to be non-interest bearing securities. They are sold at a discount to yield basis,

and any income derived from the T-bill is considered a discount, not interest.

162. The correct answer is B. Limited partnerships have limited liability based on the amount of their investment. General partners, on the other hand, possess unlimited liability up to their entire net worth.

163. The correct answer is B. State municipal bond issues can use many different taxes to back a general obligation bond. They can use state income and state sales taxes to back the issue. Ad valorem (property taxes) taxes can only be used on a local level.

164. The correct answer is D. The apprenticeship program for a new employee of a municipal dealer is 90 days. During that time period, the apprentice prepares to qualify and pass the appropriate licensing exam required. If the individual is in an apprentice program, and receives their license prior to the 90 day completion of the program, they are still required to complete the entire 90 day program.

165. The correct answer is D. This long call spread has a maximum possible gain of $700 and a maximum possible loss of $300. The spread is 10 points (70 to 80) and the debit is the cost of the June 70 Call @ $4 less the $1 premium received on the short TNT June 80 Call ($3). The most he can lose is the $300 in premiums, whereas the most he can make is the spread of $10 less the debit of $3 = $7 × 100 shares = $700.

166. The correct answer is B. Contributions to a Roth IRA are considered taxable to the individual. Retirement withdrawals from the Roth IRA are tax-free. An individual opening a Roth IRA is not permitted to take early withdrawal from the plan without a penalty up to the age of $59^1/_2$, at which time he can withdraw without penalty. The one exception to this penalty is for first-time home buyers using a disbursement from the Roth IRA without incurring the 10% penalty. Contributions to Roth IRAs are tax-free because taxes were paid up front, so there is no need to wait until age $70^1/_2$ to withdraw.

167. The correct answer is C. Congress implemented the Maloney Act of 1938 to deal with the over-the-counter securities market when they realized that this market was not being adequately regulated. They gave the enforcement power to the NASD to set the rules and enforce them on member firms.

168. The correct answer is C. Dollar averaging is a payment plan in which the investor purchases the same number of mutual fund shares each period, regardless of the changing cost. For example, an investor might agree to purchase 100 mutual fund shares each month, regardless of the net asset value changing.

169. The correct answer is B. Net direct debt is computed after all self-supporting debt (revenue bonds) have been deducted and any sinking fund provision on outstanding debt. This leaves the issuer with that

portion of their debt that must be met through general obligation issues. These issues are backed by property taxes and other taxes collected by the issuer.

170. The correct answer is C. Depending on the complaint, any member firm that does not accept the ruling of District Business Conduct Committee can take the ruling to additional appeal levels such as the NASD Adjudication council, the SEC, or an outside civil court.

171. The correct answer is C. All call options for one company represent one class of options. The class of an option is all options of the same type for a company. The option series represents all calls for ABC stock that expire in the same month with the same strike price, such as a May expiration date at $40. All ABC calls that expire in May with a strike price of $45 represent another series. The option cycle represents the expiration cycle the option follows.

172. The correct answer is A. Discretionary trades require the approval of a registered principal in the office at the end of business each day. The principal of the office is responsible for making sure the broker is conducting suitable trades and to make sure the broker is not churning the customer's account. Some explanation of the others needed.

173. The correct answer is C. The final bid that has been entered by an underwriter for a competitive bid is the issuers expected cost of the bond issue. The true interest cost of the bid takes into consideration the time value of the interest payments and discounting their future value into today's dollars. This is the cost that the issuer is most interested in when accepting competitive bids for the bond issue. And the other choices?

174. The correct answer is C. The breakeven point on 50 TCI March 75 Puts @ 6 is determined by the strike price less the premium. $75 Strike price less $6 premium = $69 breakeven point. Remember, the writer and holder always have the same breakeven point.

175. The correct answer is C. A good delivery of municipal bonds requires that all unpaid coupons for the bonds are attached and serial numbers of the bonds that have not been called. Clients must also receive a copy of the bonds legal opinion for the delivery to be considered a good delivery. An issuer's debt statement is not required.

176. The correct answer is D. Customer securities that are held in safekeeping by a broker are held in the customer's name. The broker is responsible for the safe keeping of the actual stock certificates for the client as a brokerage service.

177. The correct answer is D. An initial transaction in a margin account requires the greater of a $2,000.00 minimum or 100% of the transaction cost. Thus, if a client were to purchase 100 shares of stock at $34, the margin requirement is $2,000 for an initial transaction.

178. The correct answer is B. Limited partnerships experience legislative risk because the government can change tax laws that might not be beneficial to limited partnerships. They also expose investors to the systemic risk of the industries in which they operate (such as oil and gas exploration).

179. The correct answer is B. When an OTC firm purchases securities for their own inventory account, they are acting in the role of a dealer. A broker execute an order for a client, whereas a trader works on a trading desk for a firm, and a specialist works on the NYSE floor making a market in securities.

180. The correct answer is B. Preferred stock has limited voting rights if any, and always has a higher par value than common stock, which normally has a very low par value. Preferred stock does not have preemptive right like common stock. Lastly, common stock can have a market value higher than preferred stock, which tends to range in price not far from par value.

181. The correct answer is C. In a $5 billion T-bill auction, the Federal Reserve Bank honors all noncompetitive bids first. If noncompetitive bids total $3 billion, the remaining competitive bids are honored up to $2 billion in total.

182. The correct answer is D. Investors in index options are betting on the rise or fall of an index, rather than an individual stock. They are not dealing in shares of stock, but rather cash. The seller of an stock index receives a premium, and the holder or buyer either makes a profit, or loses the premium that has been paid.

183. The correct answer is C. The Federal Insurance Contributions Act, or FICA, created Social Security and Disability benefits for employed individuals. FICA requires employee contributions each year up to a maximum salary of $60,600, with employer matching contributions.

184. The correct answer is C. Syndicate members in a underwriting syndicate share in the overall spread that has been arranged in the winning bid. Each syndicate member receives a portion of the spread for each bond that they sell in a remuneration known as a takedown fee. Because syndicate members are invited to be part of a syndicate by the lead underwriter, they earn the entire spread less the lead underwriter management fee, for each bond they sell.

185. The correct answer is B. All quotes given by a broker's broker are considered bona fide quotes. A broker's broker is a specialized firm that buys or sells bonds for large institutional clients. They do not make an inventory in the bonds, but rather represent their customer on an anonymous basis to secure the best possible price for them. The municipal market is a thinly traded market and a large block of bonds that come to the market by an institution can send a message that they are desperate to move the bonds, thus affecting the price.

186. The correct answer is D. Any political contribution that has been made by a broker-dealer to a political candidate in excess of $250 prohibits the broker-dealer from being a negotiated bid underwriter for that municipality for a period of two years.

187. The correct answer is C. In a life annuity contract, the insurance company continues to pay the annuitant for as long as they live. The annuity payments cease upon the death of the annuitant (whether after five years or 25 years). Any monies remaining in the account revert to the insurance company.

188. The correct answer is C. Freddie Mac issues stock but it is only sold to savings and loan institutions across the United States. The stock is held in trust by the Federal Home Loan Bank System.

189. The correct answer is C. The maximum gain on the purchase of 5 DTT May 40 Calls @ 3 and 5 DTT May 40 Puts @ 4 is an unlimited amount because of the calls. The maximum loss equals the premiums paid if both of the options expired worthless. Therefore, the maximum gain is unlimited and the maximum loss is the total $7 premium × 500 shares = $3,500.

190. The correct answer is D. The opening of an option account for a client must be approved by a registered options principal. The client must be capable of handling the risk involved with options, as well as understand how options work as an investment. The financial position of the client is something that the broker wants to know, to ensure that the client can incur potential losses when dealing in options.

191. The correct answer is A. Margin is a portion of the value of the securities that the investor must deposit into their account before they can buy or sell securities on credit. Currently, it is 50% of the value of the securities.

192. The correct answer is D. Extension risk is most affected when interest rates rise sharply in the market. Homeowners are then more likely to hold on to their current lower interest rate mortgages.

193. The correct answer is A. A Treasury note with a quote of 94 tells an investor the note is selling for 94% of par or face value. Par value is $1,000×94% = $940.00 purchase price.

194. The correct answer is D. The money supply as measured by M1 includes currency in circulation, demand deposits such as checking accounts, and travelers checks used by individuals. M1 does not include time deposits such as bank certificate of deposits (CDs), which are established for a set period of time, and are not considered liquid.

195. The correct answer is B. Open interest is the number of open option positions on an underlying security. As each option contract is bought and sold, it increases open interest by one.

196. The correct answer is B. Guaranteed bonds are best described as bonds issued by a subsidiary and backed by the parent company. The credit rating for the issue takes on the parent company rating, and not the issuer's rating.
197. The correct answer is D. Purchasers of a call option contract can do one of three things with their option contracts. They can exercise their option and buy the shares at the strike price, they can allow the option to expire at the expiration date, or they can perform a closing sale of their opening purchase, to close out the option.
198. The correct answer is B. A guardian account is established by a court for a minor who is incapable of managing their own assets. If a minor was an actor with considerable earnings, the court appoints a guardian to protect the assets of the minor until they reach the age of majority. A conservatorship is established for a mentally incompetent individual, whereas a receivership is used for liquidation of a bankrupt company.
199. The correct answer is A. A general partner in a direct participation program has unlimited liability to the extent of their entire net worth. They are not permitted to invest in other investments that compete with the program they manage, nor can they use DPP property for their own personal use. Typically, a partnership cannot continue after the death or retirement of one of the partners.
200. The correct answer is C. A municipality that issues short term notes such as TANS, RANS, and TRANS is "pulling forward" anticipated funds to be collected from municipal property taxes, revenues, and other taxes. Project notes do not bring forward anticipated revenues.
201. The correct answer is C. Investors who have closed out their option position by exercising their option will have in effect decreased open interest on the stock by one. By exercising the option, the opposite side or seller is assigned. The option positions are matched up, and this decreases open interest on STP by one.
202. The correct answer is D. Equity in a short account increases by a decline in the short market value of the account. Short sellers make money when the securities drop in market value, not rise. If the market value increases in a short account, the equity decreases.
203. The correct answer is C. Soliciting a wash trade and sending out false or misleading information to clients constitutes manipulation and is illegal. Selling shares of a new issue to their best clients is not considered manipulation, nor is a stabilizing bid considered manipulation as long as the bid is at the public offering price or below.
204. The correct answer is B. The holder of an opening put option hopes that the market value of the underlying security drops below the strike price of the option. The maximum profit to a put holder occurs

when the stock drops to zero, making it possible to put the option back to the writer at the higher strike price.

205. The correct answer is D. A rights offering is offered at a lower price to shareholders than the current market price. Existing shareholders must receive their proportionate ownership in a rights offering. The rights offered cannot be used to dilute the percentage ownership that any one investor maintains in the company.

206. The correct answer is C. 1 HTH May 50 Call @ 3 with a market price of $48 is considered out of the money by two points (50 strike price – 48 market price = 2 points out of money). The breakeven point for a call option is the strike price plus the amount of the premium paid by the holder. In this case, the breakeven point is $50 strike price + $3 premium paid = $53.

207. The correct answer is D. To be considered a covered writer of put options, the seller needs to be short the number of shares indicated by the option contract. In this case, Ryan needs to be short 5,000 shares of NCR stock to be a covered writer (50 contracts × 100 shares per contract = 5,000 shares of stock). If the put options went down in value, the loss would be offset by the gain from the shorted shares of NCR stock. Remember, writers want the market price of the put option to rise above the strike price, so that they can keep the premium received and the put will expire worthless to the holder. A put writer loses money if the stock declines in value. A short seller makes money on the decline in market value of the stock. The two positions cancel each other out, and the writer is considered covered.

208. The correct answer is C. A writer of 15 HTH Feb 110 Calls @ 5 and also 15 HTH Feb 110 Puts @ 6 would have a maximum potential profit in this account of the two premiums received. The premium on the call is $5 + the premium on the put of $6 = $11 × 1,500 shares = $16,500 maximum potential profit to the writer. The maximum loss is the unlimited amount to which the call option can rise.

209. The correct answer is C. A customer with $450,000 in securities and $100,000 in cash is covered up to $500,000 in assets, with a maximum of $100,000 being in cash. The customer is covered for the entire $450,000 in securities and only $50,000 in cash. The remaining $50,000 in cash becomes a general creditor of the failed firm.

210. The correct answer is D. Fixed annuities are deemed an insurance product, and thus fall under the purview of the insurance laws of the state in which they operate. Variable annuities on the other hand are considered securities that must be registered by the SEC because they present customers with all the risks of the financial markets. In particular, the separate account of the variable annuity registers as a security with the SEC.

211. The correct answer is D. Capital gains are the profits made when an asset is sold for more than it cost to purchase. Examples of capital gains are purchasing a stock for a price, and then selling it for a higher price. Any asset purchased at a price and then resold at a higher price will represent a capital gain.

212. The correct answer is C. Seats on the floor of the NYSE are required under NYSE rules to be in the name of an individual, and not the member firm. This means that only the broker who has the seat is permitted to conduct business on the floor of the exchange. If the floor broker were ill, and cannot work, the firm cannot replace them with another individual.

213. The correct answer is D. The maximum gain for a writer of a call option is the premium received. In this question the premium received was $3.00 × 1,000 shares (10 contracts) = $3,000. The maximum exposure to loss that the writer of an uncovered option has is the amount that the market price of the stock can go up above the strike price. In theory, the maximum loss is unlimited, because the stock can rise to any price.

214. The correct answer is D. Mary Sells 1 BTO Jan 50 Put @ 6 and also Buys 1 BTO Jan 40 Put @ 3. This is an example of a short put credit spread. The short is the sale of the Jan 50 option that took in premiums of $6 as opposed to the purchase of the Jan 40 put that cost them $3 that created a $3 credit for the investor. In effect this investor cannot make more than $300, nor can he lose more than $700 on the spread. 10 point spread less credit of 3 = 7 × 100 shares = $ 700 maximum loss.

215. The correct answer is B. Only the Government National Mortgage Association and the Export Import Bank are backed directly by the U.S. government in the securities that they issue. FNMA and Freddie Mac have only an implicit backing, not a direct backing, of the U.S. government in the securities that they issue.

216. The correct answer is D. Pass-through certificates are not government guaranteed. They are created by the pooling of mortgages that have been purchased from lending institutions and they are repackaged and securitized (made into a negotiable security).

217. The correct answer is B. An investor who has purchased a variable annuity will take on the risk of the investment portfolio. There is no guarantee on the rate of return that the annuity will earn. If the annuity portfolio fares well, the investor will receive the entire return. If the annuity does poorly, the investor bears this risk also.

218. The correct answer is B. Shareholders who have paid more than par value for the stock when it is issued have a capital surplus accounted for on the balance sheet as capital in excess of par.

219. The correct answer is D. Bonds that have longer maturities and lower coupon rates would be most affected by market risk (the market value of the bond as it reacts to interest rate changes). In this example, the 30 year bond with a low 5% coupon rate has the highest market risk.
220. The correct answer is B. Pass-through certificates were created by agencies to provide necessary funds to the mortgage lenders in the country. They provide new funds to a needed segment of the economy so that the public can continue to secure mortgages to purchase homes.
221. The correct answer is D. Normal trade reporting from the time of execution to reporting on the consolidated tape takes an average of 90 seconds to be disseminated to the public forum.
222. The correct answer is D. The Options Clearing Corp. has a wide variety of responsibilities over option contracts. They set the parameters on all options such as the strike price, expiration, and initial premium. They guarantee all contracts and handle the clearing of all trades on the next business day. The OCC also sets the limits on the number of contracts that any one investor can exercise in any five-day period.
223. The correct answer is B. A fixed unit investment trust purchases a select portfolio of securities, which are fixed for the life of the trust. The portfolio neither adds nor removes securities after they have been chosen.
224. The correct answer is C. Consolidation is when a security price has recently broken out and begun to level off. During consolidation, the forces of supply and demand are more or less even—some investors sell the stock, whereas others buy it. It will follow a steady consolidating flow.
225. The correct answer is C. An additional bonds covenant requires that the issuer receive bondholder approval before they can issue new bonds against the revenue project. Without this protective covenant, using the project as collateral to secure additional debt can easily jeopardize the project.
226. The correct answer is D. The New York Composite Index is an index that measures all the common stocks listed on the NYSE. It is a broadly based index that measures about 75% of all the stocks listed on the NYSE.
227. The correct answer is D. The lead underwriter in a municipal underwriting allocates a portion of the bonds for sale to an allocation account destined for a Municipal Investment Trust. The MIT can be an allocation account that one of the syndicate members has sponsored. These bonds are allocated only if any remain and would be sold through member takedown orders, or last in the sale of the bonds.

228. The correct answer is D. To determine how much it owes a customer upon the maturity of an annuity, the insurance company must convert accumulation units into annuity units, through a process called annuitization. Each annuity unit is based on a portion of the total amount of money an annuitant will receive during distribution. It does not represent the value of the accumulation units in the client account.

229. The correct answer is C. The sale of a call would make the writer bearish on the underlying security. The writer wants the market to decline below the strike price, so that they can make a maximum of the premium received. A writer of a call has an unlimited exposure to loss because the stock can rise to any price above the strike price.

230. The correct answer is C. Action negotiated a management fee of .25 and they directly sold 1 million shares to their clients. In this example, they retain the entire 1 point spread/takedown of the syndicate for each share they sold directly to their customers, which is $1 million.

231. The correct answer is B. Standard & Poor's uses all capital letters in their ratings, whereas Moody's uses upper- and lowercase letters in their ratings. The highest rating for a municipal bond considered speculative is BB for S&P's and Ba for Moodys.

232. The correct answer is D. A competitive bid is almost always required for a general obligation bond issue. When seeking an underwriter, the municipality places an advertisement in the *Daily Bond Buyer* for interested municipal dealers. The interested dealer enters a competitive bid to the issuer, and if they have submitted the lowest interest cost to the municipality, they are awarded the issue. Working with one underwriter to issue bonds is used for revenue bonds that are negotiated.

233. The correct answer is C. A long margin account with 500 shares of TNT at $44 is established as: LMV = 22,000 – Debit Balance ($11,000) = Equity ($11,000). If the LMV increases to $48 per share: LMV = $24,000 – Debit Balance ($11,000) = Equity ($13,000).

234. The correct answer is B. A riskless trade is when a broker-dealer purchases a stock for their own inventory, and immediately sells it for a profit to a customer.

235. The correct answer is C. To be considered a covered writer of 1 HPO May 40 Call @ 3, the writer needs to be long the 100 shares of HPO stock. He can also be long the 4 HPO convertible debentures that can be converted into 100 shares of HPO stock (25 to 1 ratio). Being short the 100 shares of HPO stock does not cover the writer. The writer loses money if the price of the stock goes up in value. The writer also loses money on the short shares if the market goes up. This incurs twice the loss, and would not cover the writer. Being long 1 put would not cover the writer, because the put holder would want

the stock to go down in value to make money. If the stock goes up in value, they lose on the sale of the calls, and they would lose on the premium paid for the purchase of the put.

236. The correct answer is C. We need to determine the breakeven point on the call option and put option for this question. Brian purchased 5 BBC May 55 Calls @ 4 and also purchased 5 BBC May 55 Puts @ 3. The total premiums added together total $4 + $3 = $7. We add this to the call side strike price of $55 + $7 premiums = $62 breakeven point. We subtract this from the put side strike price of $55 – $7 = $48 breakeven point. Any prices between the $48 and $62 amounts would be a loss for Brian. Any amounts below or above these breakeven points would make him money. Don't count $48 as a loss for the account, because at this amount the holder breaks even.

237. The correct answer is C. A bank certificate of deposit is not considered a demand deposit, but rather a time deposit for an investor. Demand deposits include checking accounts, accounts that can be drawn on at any time, and account for which there are no penalties for early withdrawal.

238. The correct answer is A. If QRT stock went to $97 the investor would have made $29 per share on the 500 long shares for a profit of $14,500. The investor would then lose $27 per share on the call options less the premium received of $6.00 = $21 per share loss × 500 shares = $10,500 loss on the calls. The investor would then have a total gain of $4,000 for the account.

239. The correct answer is C. Direct government obligations have interest rate options written on them that can either be yield-based or price-based options. Equity options are issued on corporate securities and derivative-based options are another term for equity options. Yield-base options are settled in cash, whereas price-based options can be settled in the actual underlying security representative of the option.

240. The correct answer is D. Management companies are required to register with the SEC when being issued. This includes both open end and close end funds, neither of which are considered exempt securities.

241. The correct answer is B. A municipal broker-dealer acting as a financial advisor to a municipality and wanting to be a negotiated underwriter for a general obligation bond issue is required to resign as the financial advisor and receive written permission from the municipality to bid on the GO bond issue.

242. The correct answer is D. A market maker for a NASDAQ listed security that has a daily trading volume of at least 5,000 shares is required to offer a minimum of at least 1,000 shares of the underlying security in their quotes as a market maker for the security.

243. The correct answer is C. Securities that are held in safekeeping are held in registered form by the broker in the client's name. These securities are considered non-negotiable. The broker is providing a service to the client, by holding their fully owned securities for them in safekeeping.

244. The correct answer is D. A unit investment trust is organized under a trust indenture and governed by a board of trustees. The unit trust issues shares of beneficial interest to investors.

245. The correct answer is C. The investor is best served if he were to purchase the 5.28% municipal issue, because in the long run after taxes, he will earn 30 basis points more on this investment. The 7.80% corporate bond pays 40% in taxes. 7.80 ×.60 = 4.68 The investor would only retain a yield of 4.68% on the corporate bonds, whereas he can earn 5.28% on the municipal bonds, tax-free. Purchasing Puerto Rico bonds and living in California does not matter, because Puerto Rico is considered a territory of the United States and can be purchased by residents in any state and still retain their tax-exempt status.

246. The correct answer is C. There are many terms used for being long or short an option contract. A writer or seller of an option has conducted an opening sale. The holder of an option is also considered the buyer of the contract. They are also considered long the option, or have conducted an opening purchase.

247. The correct answer is B. The breakeven point on a straddle option is computed by adding the premiums paid together and adding them to the call option, while subtracting them from the put option. Thus the premiums paid were $4 on the call and $3 on the put = $7 total premium. The strike price on the call is $45 + $7 premium = $52 breakeven. The strike price on the put is $45 – $7 = $38 breakeven.

248. The correct answer is B. A money market fund that wants to hedge their portfolio can purchase T-note puts to protect against a drop in interest rates. If the rates were to decline, the long puts can be exercised and force the writer to purchase the T-notes at the higher strike price, which in effect locks in an interest rate for the fund.

249. The correct answer is C. A T-note or T-bond price based interest rate option with a strike price of 96.06 is worth 96 = 960 and 6/32nds or a price of $961.88. (6 ÷ 32 = .1875 = $1.88.)

250. The correct answer is C. A $100,000 30-year Treasury bond purchased at 104 on margin requires 6% of the market value margin requirement deposit. The bonds were selling at 104 for a value of $104,000 × 6% = $6,240.00 margin requirement.

PART IX
Appendixes

What's on the CD-ROM

The CD features a complete Series 7 exam with 120 questions in an innovative practice test engine powered by MeasureUp, giving you yet another effective tool to assess your readiness for the exam. The CD also includes a helpful "Need to Know More?" appendix that breaks down by chapter extra resources you can visit if some of the topics in this book are still unclear to you, as well as a PDF of the entire text of the book.

Multiple Test Modes

MeasureUp practice tests are available in Study, Certification, Custom, Adaptive, Missed Question, and Non-Duplicate question modes.

Study Mode

Tests administered in Study Mode allow you to request the correct answer(s) and explanations for each question during the test. These tests are not timed. You can modify the testing environment *during* the test by clicking the Options button.

Certification Mode

Tests administered in Certification Mode closely simulate the actual testing environment you will encounter when taking a certification exam. These tests do not allow you to request the answer(s) or explanation for each question until after the exam.

Custom Mode

Custom Mode enables you to specify your preferred testing environment. Use this mode to specify the objectives you want to include in your test, the timer length, and other test properties. You can also modify the testing environment *during* the test by clicking the Options button.

Adaptive Mode

Tests administered in Adaptive Mode closely simulate the actual testing environment you will encounter when taking an adaptive exam. After answering a question, you are not allowed to go back; you are only allowed to move forward during the exam.

Missed Question Mode

Missed Question Mode allows you to take a test containing only the questions you missed previously.

Non-Duplicate Mode

Non-Duplicate Mode allows you to take a test containing only questions not displayed previously.

Question Types

The practice question types simulate the real exam experience.

Random Questions and Order of Answers

This feature helps you learn the material without memorizing questions and answers. Each time you take a practice test, the questions and answers appear in a different randomized order.

Detailed Explanations of Correct and Incorrect Answers

Here, you receive automatic feedback on all correct and incorrect answers. The detailed answer explanations are a superb learning tool in their own right.

Attention to Exam Objectives

MeasureUp practice tests are designed to appropriately balance the questions within each technical area covered by a specific exam.

Installing the CD

The minimum system requirements for the CD-ROM are as listed here:

- Windows 95, 98, ME, NT4, 2000, or XP
- 7MB disk space for testing engine
- An average of 1MB disk space for each test

If you need technical support, please contact MeasureUp at 678-356-5050 or email **support@measureup.com**. Additionally, you can find Frequently Asked Questions (FAQs) at **www.measureup.com**.

To install the CD-ROM, follow these instructions:

1. Close all applications before beginning this installation.
2. Insert the CD into your CD-ROM drive. If the setup starts automatically, go to step 6. If the setup does not start automatically, continue with step 3.
3. From the Start menu, select Run.
4. Click Browse to locate the MeasureUp CD. In the Browse dialog box, from the Look In drop-down list, select the CD-ROM drive.

5. In the Browse dialog box, double-click on `Setup.exe`. In the Run dialog box, click OK to begin the installation.
6. On the Welcome Screen, click Next.
7. To agree to the Software License Agreement, click Yes.
8. On the Choose Destination Location screen, click Next to install the software to `C:\Program Files\MeasureUp Practice Tests\Launch`.

If you cannot locate MeasureUp Practice Tests through the Start menu, see the section later in this appendix titled "Creating a Shortcut to the MeasureUp Practice Tests."

9. On the Setup Type screen, select Individual Typical Setup. Click Next to continue.
10. On the Select Features screen, click the check box next to the test(s) you purchased. After you have checked your test(s), click Next.
11. On the Enter Text screen, type the password provided in this receipt, and click Next. Follow this step for any additional tests.
12. On the Select Program Folder screen, verify that the Program Folder is set to MeasureUp Practice Tests, and click Next.
13. After the installation is complete, verify that Yes, I Want to Restart My Computer Now is selected. If you select No, I Will Restart My Computer Later, you will not be able to use the program until you restart your computer.
14. Click Finish.
15. After restarting your computer, choose Start, Programs, MeasureUp Practice Tests, Launch.
16. On the MeasureUp welcome screen, click Create User Profile.
17. In the User Profile dialog box, complete the mandatory fields and click Create Profile.
18. Select the practice test you want to access and click Start Test.

Creating a Shortcut to the MeasureUp Practice Tests

To create a shortcut to the MeasureUp Practice Tests, follow these steps:

1. Right-click on your desktop.
2. From the shortcut menu select New, Shortcut.
3. Browse to `C:\Program Files\MeasureUp Practice Tests` and select the `MeasureUpCertification.exe` or `Localware.exe` file.
4. Click OK.
5. Click Next.
6. Rename the shortcut MeasureUp.
7. Click Finish.

After you have completed step 7, use the MeasureUp shortcut on your desktop to access the MeasureUp products you ordered.

Technical Support

If you encounter problems with the MeasureUp test engine on the CD-ROM, you can contact MeasureUp at 678-356-5050 or email `support@measureup.com`. Technical support hours are from 8 a.m. to 5 p.m. EST Monday through Friday. Additionally, you'll find Frequently Asked Questions (FAQs) at `www.measureup.com`.

If you want to purchase additional MeasureUp products, telephone 678-356-5050 or 800-649-1MUP (1687), or visit `www.measureup.com`.

Need to Know More?

The purpose of this book is to help you prepare for the Series 7 licensing exam. It is not intended as a replacement for a Series 7 training session or as your only source for study. The focus of this book is to review information you already know or are very familiar with. The topics discussed are all important, but you might not have exam questions on all of them. The following additional resources can help you prepare:

- National Association of Securities Dealers, NASD, www.nasd.com, and www.nasd-institute.com, have links for e-learning, professional development, conferences, as well as a full list of the rules and procedures of the NASD.
- The Chicago Board of Trade, www.cbot.com, provides information about the over-the-counter market, including market data, products, clearing, education, and news. It is considered one of the best resources for OTC information.
- NASDAQ, www.nasdaq.com, gives a concise overview of the stock market, lots of statistical information, and investor information. It is aimed mostly toward investors, but does offer some instructional information.
- The New York Stock Exchange, NYSE, is found at www.nyse.com. This website provides an overview of the market, a glossary, some educational materials, reference data, and news.
- Investopedia, found at www.Investopedia.com, is a good resource on the OTC, with articles, tutorials, a dictionary, exam prep materials, an exam simulator, and a research link.

- The Municipal Securities Rulemaking Board, MRSB, found at `www.msrb.org`, offers an overview of the board, its rules, information about the various forms, reporting to the board, political contributions, a glossary, general news, and much more.
- The Securities Exchange Commission, found at `www.sec.gov`, offers links to other informational sites, news, information about filings, and other general information.

Glossary

12b-1 fund
Mutual fund that is permitted to pass the costs of advertising through to its shareholders.

401(k) plan
Retirement plan whereby employees contribute part of their pre-tax income to a qualified tax-deferred program. Generally, the employer can match part or all the employee contributions to the plan.

403(b) plan
Tax-deferred annuity plan for employees of nonprofit organizations.

5% policy
Element of the Rules of Fair Practice, which states that in most cases dealers need to restrict their fees to 5% of the transaction amount.

Accelerated depreciation
Method of depreciating an asset by writing off greater amounts in earlier years, and lesser amounts in later years.

Accredited investor
Certain financial and nonprofit institutions, and persons who meet established net worth or annual income criteria.

Accretion
Annual allocation of the capital gains earned on a discount bond, calculated for tax and yield purposes.

Accrued interest
Interest owed to the seller of a bond by its buyer. Using a 30-day month/360-day year calendar, the accrued interest is calculated from the date of the last interest payment up to, but not including, the settlement date.

Accumulation area
Consolidation pattern in which buyers gradually begin to outnumber sellers, leading to an uptrend.

Accumulation unit
Unit of measurement for ownership in an annuity. Each payment made by an annuitant goes to purchase a certain number of accumulation units.

Ad valorem taxes
Taxes collected on the value of property, goods, or services. Revenues from ad valorem property taxes often service general obligation bonds.

Adjusted cost basis
Sliding adjustment over time, for tax purposes, of the nominal price of a bond bought at a premium or discount.

Adjustable preferred
Preferred stock whose dividend rate is periodically reset to reflect changes in market interest rates.

Adjustment bond (income bond)
Bond issued by a company in bankruptcy. These bonds replace existing bonds, have a higher face value than the original bonds (that is, have been adjusted), and pay interest only when the company generates sufficient income.

Administrator account
Fiduciary account whereby a court appoints an individual to settle the affairs of a person who died intestate (without a will).

Advance-decline index
Number of stocks advancing, minus the number of stocks declining, divided by the total number of issues. A trend is considered confirmed when the advance-decline index moves in the same direction as the market.

Advances
Number of stocks in a market that have increased in price on a given day.

After-tax yield
Rate of return on a bond after all income taxes on the interest have been paid.

Agency
Organization created (and either owned or sponsored) by the U.S. government.

Agent
Broker-dealer who acts as an intermediary in a transaction, helping an investor purchase stocks from—or sell them to—a second dealer.

Aggressive portfolio
A securities portfolio that stresses capital growth, and perhaps speculation.

Agreement among underwriters
Contract among members of a syndicate, stating their commitment and the structure of fees.

All or none (AON)
Instruction to fill the entire order at a certain price, or not at all (several attempts are allowed).

Alternative minimum tax (AMT)

Federal income tax designed to prevent wealthy individuals from employing passive income losses to reduce their tax bills to zero.

American depositary receipts (ADRs)

Certificates representing the common stock of a foreign company. ADRs are traded in the United States, whereas the actual shares are held in the country of origin by an American bank.

American Stock Exchange (Amex)

Second major New York exchange; noted for its listings of oil and gas companies and for its foreign securities; lists close to 1,000 medium-sized companies.

American-style exercise

Contract provision in all equity options that permits holders to exercise at any time until the Friday before expiration.

American-style option

An option that can be exercised by the holder at any time before expiration.

Amortization

The annual deduction from interest income of a portion of the premium paid on a bond. If the bond is held to maturity, no capital loss is incurred.

Annuitant

Purchaser of an annuity.

Annuitization

Conversion of accumulation units into annuity units, enabling the individual to begin collecting payments from the insurer.

Annuity

Contract sold by an insurance company that guarantees a return to the investor (usually upon retirement) in exchange for regular payments made earlier in the investor's life.

Annuity certain (or life annuity with period certain)

Contract that ensures the annuitant receives payments until his or her death, and also guarantees payments for a certain period to survivors if the annuitant dies before the end of the stated period.

Annuity unit

Unit of measurement for the amount of money an insurance company owes to an investor upon an annuity's maturity.

Arbitrage

Trading the same security in different markets simultaneously to take advantage of price differences.

Arbitrage account

Account in which a customer takes both a long and a short position in the same security (for tax purposes).

Arbitrage trade

In the OTC (over the counter) market, a transaction in which a dealer takes advantage of the difference between quotations given by two market makers, thereby earning a profit.

Arbitration
The settling of a dispute through nonjudicial means; all parties must accept the decision of an arbitrator.

Ask price (or offered price, or asked)
Lowest price a potential seller is prepared to accept for a stock.

Ask quote
Price at which a market maker is willing to sell stock.

Assessed valuation
Value that a municipality assigns to a parcel of property for purposes of computing taxes owed on that property.

Asset
Anything of value owned by a business.

Assignment
The match of a holder who wants to exercise an option with a writer of the identical option. After being notified by the holder's broker, the OCC randomly assigns the option to a broker-dealer representing an appropriate writer. This broker, in turn, selects a particular writer, either randomly or on a "first in, first out" (FIFO) basis.

Associated person (or AP)
Employee who is registered with a securities firm and has passed the required licensing exams.

Assumed interest rate (AIR)
Insurance company's nonbinding estimate of the expected return on a variable annuity.

At the close
Order intended to be executed as close to the day's closing price as possible.

At the money
For put options, when the strike price is the same as the market price of the underlying security.

At the opening
Order intended to be executed at a stock's opening price (or as close as possible) on a given day.

Auction market
Securities marketplace that has a physical trading floor, where prices are established by competitive bids and offers. One specialist creates an orderly market for each stock and operates from a trading post on the floor.

Auditor
Independent accounting firm hired by a mutual fund to compile its financial statements and a list of the securities in its portfolio.

Authorized stock
Amount of stock a corporation's charter allows it to sell.

Average life
Expected maturity of a pool of mortgages, given the prepayment speed predicted by the PSA model.

Away from the market
Term for any order that is not at the current market price.

Backing away
Illegal practice in which a dealer fails to honor a firm price quote.

Balance of payments
Difference between the amount of money that a country spends overseas and the amount it receives from overseas. The balance of payments is often divided into the current account and the capital account.

Balance sheet
Portion of a financial statement detailing a company's assets, liabilities, and stockholders' equity on a particular date.

Bank-qualified issues
Municipal bonds with a feature attractive to banks: 80% of the interest that a bank pays on deposits that have been used to buy bank-qualified bonds is tax deductible.

Banker's acceptance
Post-dated check sent by a domestic importer to a foreign exporter, when the check has been "accepted" (or guaranteed) by a bank. Exporters also initiate banker's acceptances to transact their international business.

Bar chart
Graph that exhibits the changing price of a security or group of securities over a certain period. Daily high and low prices are connected by a vertical bar, whereas opening and closing prices are often indicated by horizontal marks.

Basis point
One one-hundredth of a percent (0.01%); the smallest unit of measure for bond yields.

Bear spread
A spread designed to bet that the price of the underlying stock will remain the same or fall. Short call spreads and long put spreads are bearish.

Beneficial owner
Individual who owns the assets in an account, and who receives the profits or losses from trading in the account.

Beta
A number that indicates the price volatility of a stock or group of stocks compared to that of the market as a whole. The price of a stock with a beta of 1 is exactly as volatile as the market. The price of a stock with a beta of 2 is twice as volatile as the market.

Bid price (or bid)
Highest price a potential buyer is willing to pay for a stock.

Bid quote
Price at which a market maker is willing to buy stock.

Bid wanted (BW)
Dealer's request for a potential stock purchaser to suggest a price.

Big Board
Popular term for the New York Stock Exchange.

Blanket fidelity bond
An insurance policy that NYSE member firms must purchase to protect their investors against fraud or embezzlement by firm employees.

Blind pool investment
An investment program specifying only the kind of investments it will make, not the actual investments.

Block trade
A trade involving 10,000 shares or more.

Blue sky laws
State laws with which a company must comply in order to sell its securities within the state's boundaries.

Board broker
Exchange member who helps OBOs with trades for the most active options.

Bona fide quote
Price given on a security by a broker who is prepared to honor it at that time, but who can change the quote prior to the transaction if market conditions change.

Bond
Transferable long-term debt instrument that pays a fixed interest rate. Issuers must repay the principal at maturity to bondholders, who do not have ownership rights in the issuing firm.

Bond (or coupon) equivalent yield
Measure of an investor's return on a bill, comparable to yield to maturity. This yield helps investors compare the returns on T-bills with those of Treasury notes, Treasury bonds, and other interest-bearing securities.

Bond interest coverage
Ratio of earnings before interest and taxes to bond interest expense.

Bond rating
Evaluation by independent rating company of corporation's financial strength and capability to repay its bonds, as well as the indenture provisions of each bond issue.

Bond ratio
Ratio of par value of bonds to long-term capital.

Book value
Portion of a corporation's assets that are used to pay common stockholders in the event of bankruptcy. Book value equals tangible assets, minus total liabilities and preferred stockholders' equity.

Book value per share
Ratio of book value to number of common shares.

Book-entry method
Manner of conducting stock transactions without certificates changing hands; the transfers are recorded as changes in customers' accounts.

Borrowed security
Security that a customer borrows from a brokerage to make a short sale. The customer must eventually replace the security, which normally the brokerage has borrowed (under a loan agreement) from another customer's account.

Breakeven point
Market price of the underlying security at which either the writer or the buyer will not make or lose money on the option. For an uncovered call, it equals the strike price plus the premium.

Breakout
Action of a security whose price has risen above a resistance level or fallen below a support level. Typically, the price will continue moving in the direction of the breakout.

Breakpoint
Amount of money that must be invested in a fund in order for a customer to qualify for a lower sales charge.

Breeding program
Direct participation program that buys cattle and breeds them for future sale.

Broad-based index
An index that reflects the price movements of a diverse or widely held group of stocks.

Broker loan rate (or call rate)
Interest rate at which a broker-dealer can borrow funds from a bank to lend to a customer in a margin transaction.

Broker-dealer
Firm that buys and sells securities for customers (as a broker) and for itself (as a dealer).

Bull spread
A spread designed to bet that the price of the underlying stock will rise. Long call spreads and short put spreads are bullish.

Business cycle
The cyclical expansion and contraction of economic activity. Each full business cycle has five phases: early expansion, late expansion, peak, recession, and recovery.

Buttonwood Agreement
1792 pact between 24 brokers and merchants that is cited as the origin of the NYSE. The name comes from the buttonwood tree under which it was signed.

Buying in
Purchase of a shorted security by a brokerage to cover a fail-to-deliver.

Buying power
Purchasing leverage afforded by the SMA of a margin account. With Reg T set at 50%, one dollar of SMA equals two dollars of buying power.

Call option
Contract that provides the right to buy a number of shares of a security at a fixed price at any time until a certain date

Call premium
For callable bonds, the amount by which the call price exceeds the bond's face value.

Call protection
Feature of some callable bonds that prevents the issuer from redeeming the bond before a certain date, usually 10 or more years after the issue.

Call provision
Measure in some bond indentures that enables the issuing company to buy back ("call in") the bond before maturity.

Call rate (or broker loan rate)
Interest rate charged by banks to brokerage houses for their clients' margin accounts.

Call risk
Risk that the issuer of a callable bond might redeem the bond prior to maturity, thereby reducing an investor's expected return.

Callable preferred
Preferred stock that the issuer can call (buy back) if interest rates fall; typically pays a higher dividend rate because of the call feature.

Capital account
Difference between the amount foreigners invest in a country and the amount that residents of the country invest abroad.

Capital asset pricing model (CAPM)
Financial model that states that the expected return on a stock must equal the risk-free rate plus a risk premium multiplied by the stock's beta.

Capital gain/loss
A profit or loss resulting from the sale of an asset. The gain or loss represents the difference between the asset's cost basis and its sale proceeds.

Capital in excess of par (capital surplus)
Difference between the total issue price of a stock offering and its total par value.

Capitalization (capital structure)
A corporation's long-term financial structure, including long-term debt, preferred stock, and common stock.

CAPS (capped index options)
A European-style option in which a limit is placed on the maximum profit, similar to a vertical spread. The option is automatically exercised when the index reaches the cap price (generally 30 points above or below the strike price), or the holder can exercise it on the last business day before expiration.

Cash account
Account for which all trades must be paid in full at the time of settlement.

Cash asset ratio
Ratio of cash and marketable securities to current liabilities.

Cash settlement
Securities transaction that is finalized, or settled, the same day the trade is made.

Cashier's department
Department that accepts customer deposits and issues checks to them.

CATS (Certificates of Accrual on Treasury Securities)
Devised by dealers at Salomon Brothers, this product created a zero-coupon bond from the principal portion of the underlying Treasury bond.

Certificate of limited partnership
Agreement signed by the members of a partnership. The certificate names each partner, his or her financial contribution and obligation, and outlines the partnership's investment objectives.

Chartist
Individual who examines the movement of security prices in order to recommend trading strategies (as opposed to a fundamental analyst, who studies the company and its financial statements).

Chicago Board Options Exchange (CBOE)
Largest options exchange in the country. Established in 1973, the CBOE was the first exchange to trade listed, standardized options.

Churning
Excessive trading in a customer's account, given the customer's investment goals and risk tolerance.

Circuit breakers
NYSE regulations that temporarily shut the market down after the Dow falls 10%, 20%, and 30%.

Class
Division of a company's equity securities into different categories of stock (usually class A and class B), with different voting powers or other privileges.

Class
Group of all options of the same type with the same underlying security (for example, all the puts on Xyron Corporation stock).

Clearing member
Brokerage firm officially associated with the OCC, allowing it to trade options. Clearing members are responsible for covering their customers' options positions.

Closed-end management company
A management company that raises capital through a one-time offering of stock. Shares are subsequently traded either on an exchange or over the counter.

Closing purchase
Purchase of an option identical to one already written. The purpose is to reduce or eliminate the original short position in order to lock in a profit or limit a loss.

Closing sale
Sale of an option identical to one already held. The purpose is to reduce or eliminate the original long position in order to lock in a profit or limit a loss.

Code of Arbitration
NASD rules pertaining to arbitration of monetary disputes between NASD member firms and between broker-dealers and clients.

Code of Procedure
NASD rules governing complaints of wrongdoing by member firms.

Coincident indicators
Indicators for parts of the economy that tend to change at the same time as the economy enters a new phase of the business cycle.

Collateral trust certificate
Bond secured by a portfolio of negotiable securities, such as equity stocks and government bonds.

Collateralized mortgage obligation (CMO)
Security that resembles a pass-through, but that has been divided into sections (tranches) to distribute cash flows.

Combination
The purchase or sale of both a call and a put on the same underlying stock (as in a straddle), but with different strike prices and/or different expirations. Combinations enable investors to tailor straddles to their specific expectations about the stock's future market price movement.

Combination REIT
Real estate investment trust that combines the goals of equity and mortgage REITs.

Commercial paper
Debt security issued by corporations, finance companies, and bank holding companies with a maturity of fewer than 270 days.

Commission
Fee charged by a broker to its customers, a percentage of the total cost of the securities that were sold or bought.

Commitment
Degree and kind of responsibility an underwriter assumes for the sale of a securities issue.

Common equity
Sum of par value of common stock, excess capital, and retained earnings.

Common stock
Security that represents ownership in a corporation, and might, depending on the firm's profitability, pay a variable dividend.

Common stock ratio

Ratio of common equity to long-term capital.

Companion tranche

Tranche designed to absorb prepayment or extension risk.

Competitive bid

Treasury auction bid placed by a primary dealer. The bid states the price the dealer is willing to pay for a given issue and the dollar amount of the issue the dealer wants to purchase.

Competitive (or registered) trader

A securities trader who trades for his or her own account.

Compliance registered options principal (CROP)

Person at a brokerage firm who must approve all advertising and educational material pertaining to options trading. Such material must also be approved by one of the options exchanges.

Comptroller of the Currency

Agency of the U.S. Treasury Department that enforces regulations—including those set by the MSRB—on national banks.

Conduit (or pipeline) theory

Principle of taxation in which the income from a mutual fund's portfolio is passed through to investors, who in turn pay taxes on it. This eliminates the need for the fund to pay corporate taxes on that income.

Conference Board

Independent economic research group that collects and reports data on the state of the economy, including the major economic indicators.

Confirmation (or confirm)

Report from a broker-dealer to a customer showing all relevant details of a trade, including the security, amount, price, and counter-party. It must be sent by the business day following the trade's execution.

Conflict of interest

Situation in which a broker-dealer assumes two roles that have conflicting goals or that might provide an opportunity to make an unfair profit.

Conservator account

Fiduciary account in which a person appointed by a court manages the assets of an individual who is judged incompetent.

Consolidated tape system (CTS)

Computerized system that displays transactions in stocks listed on the NYSE, AMEX, and regional exchanges.

Consolidation

Period after an uptrend or downtrend during which a security's price reaches a new equilibrium level. During consolidation, the price tends to stay within a limited range.

Consumer price index (CPI)
Measures the percentage difference between the prices of a collection of consumer goods at some arbitrary date in the past and their prices today. The CPI is one of the most common measures of inflation.

Contrarian
Individual who assumes that most investors are wrong in their reading of the market. Contrarian investors buy when most people are selling and sell when most are buying.

Control relationship
Situation in which a municipality and a broker-dealer can influence each other through issuing, servicing, or investing in a municipal bond.

Control stock
Securities owned by a director or officer of a corporation, or by a shareholder with 10% or more of the company's stock.

Conversion parity
A share price of common stock at which convertible securities can be exchanged without any loss of value.

Conversion ratio
Number of preferred shares needed to acquire one share of common stock.

Convertible bond (or convertible debenture)
Bond that can be exchanged for the issuing company's common stock at a predetermined conversion rate.

Convertible preferred
Preferred stock that can be converted into common stock at a set ratio.

Cooling-off period
Period following the filing date (minimum of 20 days), during which the corporation and its underwriter must fulfill certain obligations while waiting for the registration to become effective.

Corporate account
Account owned by a corporation; a corporate resolution specifies who is allowed to trade in the account.

Corporate dividend exclusion
Tax rule that reduces taxes on dividends paid to corporations. If a corporation owns less than 20% of another company, it pays no tax on 70% of dividends received from that company; if it owns 20% or more, it pays no tax on 80% of dividends received.

Corporate pension plan
Basic type of tax-qualified retirement plan.

Cost basis
For tax purposes, the purchase price of a bond. Investors use this value to compute potential capital gains or capital losses when they sell or redeem the bond.

Cost depletion

Method of calculating depletion in which the costs of the mineral rights are divided by the proven reserves, and then subtracted from each unit of oil or gas sold.

Cost-push inflation

Inflation because of competition among businesses for scarce inputs. As companies bid the input prices up, their costs increase, often leading the companies to increase the prices of their finished products, thus producing inflation.

Coupon (coupon rate)

Fixed rate of interest on a bond, payable every year in semiannual installments.

Coverage

Capability of a corporation to meet its fixed obligations, such as bond interest payments and preferred stock dividends, out of its earnings.

Covered call

Call option for which the writer owns the necessary shares of the underlying stock, or can otherwise cover potential losses.

Covered call writer

Writer who owns (is long) the number of shares covered by the option.

Covered put

Put option for which the writer sold short the necessary shares of the underlying stock, or can otherwise cover potential losses.

Covered put writer

Writer who is short the shares of stock specified by the option.

Credit agreement

Agreement setting forth the terms of the margin loan from a brokerage to a customer, including the interest rate charged.

Credit balance (or CR)

The short market value plus the equity in a short margin account. Unless the customer repays part of the loaned securities, the credit balance remains constant.

Credit multiplier

Measure of how a relatively small change in bank deposits can lead to a relatively large change in the money supply.

Credit risk

Risk that the issuing company will default on bond interest and principal payments.

Crossed trade

Transaction in which a dealer matches two clients as opposite sides of the trade. The dealer earns two commissions: one from buying the security from the first client, and another from selling it to the second client.

Crossover point

Moment when a limited partnership's program revenues begin to exceed its expenses.

Cum dividend
How a stock is sold before the record date of a dividend payment—with the dividend.

Cum rights
How a stock is sold before the record date of a rights offering—with the rights attached.

Cumulative preferred
Preferred stock requiring that any previously missed dividend payments be paid before dividends are paid to common stockholders.

Cumulative voting
Form of voting that enables shareholders to distribute their total votes—still calculated by one vote per share, per voting matter—as they see fit.

Current account
Difference between the value of goods and services a country imports and the value of goods and services it exports.

Current assets
Assets that a company plans to spend or use in the next year, including cash, marketable securities, bills to be received within 90 days, and inventory.

Current ratio
Ratio of current assets to current liabilities.

Current yield
Ratio of annual dividend per common share to current market price of stock.

Custodian
Bank or trust company hired by a mutual fund to safeguard its securities certificates.

Custodian account
Account that a parent or other adult manages for a minor. Assets placed in a custodian account cannot be legally removed, and the account must be reregistered in the minor's name when he or she reaches the age of majority.

Customer suitability
Appropriateness of a muni bond for a client, based on an evaluation of the client's tax status, financial holdings, and investment goals.

Cycle
Regular schedule on which options are issued, traded, and expired. Every option is assigned to one of three cycles. At any one time, options are only traded for the current month, the following month, and the next two established months of the option's cycle.

Cyclical industry
Industry composed of companies that tend to be profitable when the economy is growing strongly and unprofitable when the economy is growing at a slow rate, or is declining.

Day order
Order that is valid only for the current trading day.

Dealer
Securities firm hired by the sponsor to help market a fund's shares to the public.

Debenture
An unsecured bond.

Debit balance (or DR)
Amount a customer owes to his or her brokerage in a long margin account. The debit balance remains constant unless the customer pays back a portion of the margin loans.

Debt-to-equity ratio
Ratio of par value of bonds and preferred stock to common equity.

Declines
Number of stocks in a market that have decreased in price on a given day.

Defeasance
Method of removing debt from a corporation's books by purchasing new, higher-yielding securities that cover both the interest and principal payments of the original debt.

Defensive industry
Industry composed of companies whose profitability does not depend closely on the business cycle.

Defensive portfolio
A securities portfolio that focuses on some combination of safeguarding principal, maximizing current income, and maintaining liquidity.

Deferred compensation plan
Nonqualified plan offered to senior employees of a company in which a portion of the employees' salaries are paid at a later date, typically after retirement.

Defined benefit plan
Pension plan that guarantees employees a certain benefit package (tied to their years of employment), to be paid during retirement. To accomplish this, the upfront contributions are set at an appropriate level.

Defined contribution plan
Pension plan in which the upfront payments are predetermined, whereas the payout amounts depend on the size and the number of contributions, as well as the plan's investment earnings.

Deflation
General decrease in prices.

Demand deposits
Customer bank deposits that can be withdrawn on "demand," without previous notice (for example, checking accounts).

Demand-pull inflation
Inflation because of competition among consumers for scarce goods and services. Here, consumer demand exceeds the capacity of business production.

Depletion
For tax purposes, deduction as a business expense of the mineral rights of a natural resource asset, such as oil in a well.

Depreciation
Decline in the value of fixed assets, such as machinery and buildings, because of normal wear and tear. Depreciation is calculated using either a straight-line or accelerated method.

Depression
Period of decreased business activity in which GDP declines for at least six consecutive quarters.

Derivative
Financial instrument whose price is related to, or derived from, the price of an underlying security.

Designated Order Turnaround (DOT)
A computerized system that sends market orders directly to the specialist, bypassing the floor broker.

Development program
Drilling program in or near proven oil and gas fields.

Diagonal spread
A spread in which both the strike prices and the expirations of the two options differ.

Direct obligations
Securities issued directly by the Treasury Department of the United States through the Federal Reserve.

Direct participation program (DPP)
Investment vehicle in which profits and losses from a business venture are passed directly on to investors, often for tax objectives.

Discount
Amount by which a bond's market price has dropped below its par value.

Discount bond
Bond currently priced lower than its par value.

Discount rate
Interest rate that the Federal Reserve charges banks and other depository institutions for emergency or seasonal loans (from its "discount window") to meet reserve requirements or liquidity needs.

Discount to yield
Pricing method used for trading T-bills. The price is stated in terms of the annualized discount as a percentage of face value.

Discretionary account
Account about which a registered rep decides the kinds and amounts of securities to trade on behalf of the owner.

Disintermediation
Technical term for withdrawing money from a bank account and investing it directly in financial products. Disintermediation tends to occur when bank rates are no longer competitive with other investment products.

Distribution
Payments of annuity funds to an annuitant.

Distribution area
Consolidation pattern in which sellers gradually begin to outnumber buyers, leading to a downtrend.

District Business Conduct Committee (DBCC)
Body that hears and rules on complaints filed against NASD member firms.

Diversification
The act of spreading an investor's risk over a variety of securities, industries, or geographic regions.

Diversified management company
An investment company that purchases a wide range of securities, perhaps spread among industries or geographic regions.

Dividend
Periodic payment (either in cash or stock) made to a company's common or preferred shareholders.

Dividend payout ratio
Ratio of common dividends paid to earnings per share.

Dividend reinvestment
Use of dividend payments from a mutual fund to purchase additional shares in the same fund.

Do not reduce (DNR) order
Instruction not to reduce the price of a limit or stop order by the amount that a stock's current price is reduced on its ex-dividend date.

Dollar averaging
Term for a purchasing plan in which a constant number of mutual fund shares is purchased at regular intervals regardless of fluctuations in share price.

Dollar cost averaging
Term for a purchasing plan in which a constant number of dollars is invested, at regular intervals, in a mutual fund.

Dow Jones Industrial Average
A stock index that tracks price changes in large companies or blue-chip stocks listed on the NYSE.

Dow theory
Theory stating that a major stock market trend is only confirmed when both the Dow Jones industrial average and the Dow Jones transportation average reach a new high or a new low.

Downtrend
Succession of decreases in the price of a security (or market index).

Drilling program
Direct participation program that invests in exploration projects for oil and gas.

Dual agency transaction
Trade in which a customer sells one security and uses the proceeds to buy another.

Dual listing
Listing of a security on both a regional and a national exchange.

Due bill

Statement that the upcoming dividend is owed to the buyer of a stock. This is used when the trade took place before the ex-dividend date, but the seller has failed to deliver the stock by the record date.

Due diligence meeting

Meeting held at the end of the cooling-off period, in which the issuer, lead underwriter, and syndicate members make sure that all securities laws have been met.

Duplicate confirms

Second set of transaction confirmations that a broker must send to the employer of any client who works for another securities firm.

Earned income

Compensation for work performed, such as salaries, wages, tips, commissions (and, in some cases, employee benefits).

Earnings per share (EPS)

Ratio of net income, less preferred dividends, to number of common shares.

Eastern account (or undivided account)

Underwriting syndicate in which each member is responsible for selling a specific portion of the issue, plus that same portion of any shares left unsold by other members.

Economic indicators

Statistically derived numbers that describe changes in certain sectors, thus providing information about the current state of the economy and its future direction.

Effective date

Date on which the SEC tells the issuer that the registration statement is effective and that the offering can begin.

Efficient market

Market in which, theoretically, all public information about a company is instantly reflected in the price of its securities, making it impossible to find undervalued securities or to forecast market movements.

Either/or (OCO)

Instruction to execute one of two orders and to cancel the remaining order (executing one cancels the other).

Emerging markets

Securities markets in countries with recent industrial development and/or little history of such financial institutions. Emerging markets can provide high returns for investors, but they also carry high risk.

Equipment trust certificate (ETC)

Bond secured for equipment that the company purchases with the proceeds of the bond issue.

Equity
Amount by which the assets of an account exceed the total debt. If the account were liquidated, the customer would receive the equity.

Equity option
Contract giving the purchaser the right to buy or sell a stock at a given price before a certain date.

Equity REIT
Real estate investment trust that takes an equity position in real properties, distributing income from the rents to its shareholders.

ERISA (Employee Retirement Income Security Act)
1974 law that governs the operation of private retirement plans, safeguarding employees' monies and their rights to the pension, while ensuring that all employees are treated equally.

ESOP (employee stock ownership plan)
Retirement plan in which employees acquire stock in the company for which they work.

Estate tax
Tax due on an inheritance. Estates transferred to a spouse are tax-free, as per the preset limits.

Eurobond
Bond issued in the denomination of one country and sold in another country.

Eurodollar bond
Bond issued outside the United States, but denominated in U.S. dollars.

Eurodollars
U.S. dollars deposited in banks, either U.S. or foreign, outside the United States.

European-style exercise
Contract provision in some non-equity options (such as index options) that lets holders exercise only on the last business day before expiration.

European-style option
An option that can be exercised only at expiration.

Ex date
Date on (and after) which purchasers of a stock are no longer eligible to receive a declared dividend; also the date on which an exchange adjusts the price of a company's stock downward to account for the dividend.

Ex dividend
How a stock is sold after the record date of a dividend payment—without the dividend.

Ex rights
How a stock is sold after the record date of a rights offering—without the rights attached.

Excess
Equity in a margin account above the Reg T requirement.

Exchange privilege
Right given to an investor to switch money from one fund to another fund managed by the same company, without paying a sales charge.

Executor account
Fiduciary account in which a person, designated in a will, administers an estate and executes the will by collecting assets, paying debts and taxes, and distributing the remaining assets to heirs.

Exempt security
Security not subject to most provisions of the Securities Act of 1933 (for example, government bonds). Exempt securities do not have to meet the Fed's margin requirements under Reg T.

Exercise
To use an option. For a put, the holder exercises the option by selling the shares of stock specified by the option contract.

Exercise limit
Maximum number of options contracts an investor can exercise on a given class over five consecutive business days. The actual number depends on the trading volume of the underlying security.

Expense guarantee
Insurance company promise that it will not charge more than a limited amount of expenses to a customer.

Exploratory program
Drilling program that establishes itself in unproven oil and gas fields.

Export-Import Bank (Eximbank)
Bank established by the U.S. government to promote trade with other nations.

Extension risk
Risk that homeowners will pay off their mortgages later than anticipated (but not after the maturity date).

Face value (par value)
The principal of a bond (or other debt security). The holder receives this amount at maturity. Interest-paying bonds pay out a fixed rate of interest based on par value.

Face-amount certificate company
A largely obsolete type of investment company that issues a certificate with a maturity date and interest rate. Investors make either lump-sum or periodic payments; at maturity, the company pays the investor the face amount, which is greater than the sum of the payments.

Fail to deliver
Failure by an investor to place a security in a margin account within 10 days after settlement in order to cover a sale.

Feasibility study
Report by an independent engineering firm to determine the soundness of the plan for a proposed revenue bond project.

Federal Deposit Insurance Corporation (FDIC)

Federal agency that guarantees deposits at commercial banks against loss and enforces regulations—including those set by the MSRB—on state-chartered banks that are not members of the Federal Reserve System.

Federal Farm Credit System (FFCS)

Network of government agencies created to provide low-cost financing for farming and farming-related businesses. Through the Federal Farm Credit Bank, the FFCS issues debt securities to fund the operations of a Federal Land Bank, a Federal Intermediate Credit Bank, and a Bank for Cooperatives in each of 12 Farm Credit districts.

Federal funds (or Fed funds)

Money deposited by commercial banks at Federal Reserve Banks to meet the mandated reserve requirement. The term also refers to money lent or borrowed overnight between banks in order to meet the same reserve requirement.

Federal funds rate (or Fed funds rate)

Interest rate that banks charge each other for overnight loans to meet reserve requirements (the most volatile of all money market rates). This is the key target of the Fed's open market operations in its efforts to control inflation and economic growth.

Federal Home Loan Bank System (FHLBS)

Network of 12 regional Federal Home Loan Banks that provide credit reserves to U.S. savings and loan companies and cooperative banks. The FHLBS supports the government's goal of providing affordable homeownership.

Federal Home Loan Mortgage Corporation (Freddie Mac)

Government-sponsored independent corporation that buys and resells residential mortgage loans.

Federal National Mortgage Association (Fannie Mae)

Government-sponsored independent corporation that supports home ownership by buying mortgages from local lenders and reselling them to investors.

Federal Open Market Committee (FOMC)

Group of senior Federal Reserve officials who supervise the Fed's open market operations. The FOMC sets target interest rates and determines the amount of government securities to be bought or sold.

Federal Reserve Board

Governing body of the Federal Reserve System, consisting of a chairman and six governors, who together establish monetary policy for the United States.

Federal Reserve System (the Fed)

Central bank of the United States. The Federal Reserve Board, in conjunction with a network of 12 Federal Reserve banks (plus their branches), regulates banking, executes monetary policy, and performs banking services for the nation.

Feeding program

Program that buys cattle for subsequent slaughter.

FICA (Federal Insurance Contribution Act)

Law requiring employers to withhold and match a portion of their employees' wages in order to fund Social Security retirement and other programs.

Fiduciary

Individual charged with managing others' money and assets in a sound manner.

Fiduciary account

Account in which one individual trades or otherwise acts on behalf of another.

Filing date

Day the SEC receives a corporation's registration statement to sell a new issue.

Fill or kill (FOK)

Instruction to execute the entire order immediately or cancel it (one attempt is made).

Final prospectus

Document that describes the issuer and the offering, including the public offering price. This document is delivered to buyers.

Financial operations principal (or FINOP)

Individual in a securities firm who oversees the production of financial reports to regulatory authorities.

Financial statement

Document that accounts for the financial status of a business. Financial statements generally include a balance sheet, an income statement, and a statement of changes to retained earnings.

First market

Component of the secondary market that includes the stock exchanges and the exchanges that trade equity options.

First mortgage bond

Bond secured by a lien on real estate.

First-in, first-out method (FIFO)

Cost accounting method that assumes that the first goods entered into a company's inventory are the first goods to be sold.

Fiscal agents

Broker-dealers contracted to sell agency securities at the time of original issue.

Fiscal policy
A government's taxation and spending programs, often designed to help promote economic growth and maintain high levels of employment.

Fixed annuity
Annuity whose yield is determined in the original contract and agreed to by both parties, thus placing the financial risk on the insurer.

Fixed unit investment trust
A unit trust that typically purchases a portfolio of debt securities that remains in place for the life of the trust. No subsequent trades are made into or out of the portfolio.

Flat tax
A tax that applies the same rate to all incomes or amounts.

Flat yield curve
Yield curve with little or no slope, indicating that short- and long-term yields are roughly equal.

Floor broker
Exchange member used by a brokerage firm to execute orders from investors (public orders) or for the firm's own account.

Flow-of-funds
Structure of priorities for allocating the money generated by a revenue bond project.

Forced conversion
Conversion initiated by bond issuer when the bond's market value as converted stock is higher than the bond's call price. Bondholders must convert in order to avoid taking a loss.

Form 10-K
Annual report that issuers of registered securities must file with the SEC, detailing the company's financial situation.

Forward price
Fund's NAV at the close of business on the day that an investor purchases shares in the fund. The forward price is used to calculate the public offering price, which is the investor's cost.

Fourth market
Securities trading that occurs directly among big institutional investors, allowing the participants to avoid brokerage commissions.

Freeriding
Illegal practice in which an underwriter allocates shares of a hot issue to business associates, friends, family members, or other proscribed individuals.

Front running
Illegal practice in which a dealer executes a transaction for his or her own account ahead of a similar transaction for a customer.

Full payout lease
Long-term lease for heavy machinery and equipment in which the lease payments cover all costs of purchasing the equipment.

Fully diluted earnings per share
Earnings per share calculated for the case in which all convertible bonds are converted to shares of common stock.

Fund family
Group of funds with a variety of investment objectives that are run by the same investment company.

Futures contract
A legally binding agreement to buy or sell a specific commodity (or security) at a set price at an agreed-upon date in the future. Futures and options on futures are regulated by the Commodity Futures Trading Commission.

General obligation (GO) bond
Municipal bond backed by the good faith, credit, and taxing capability of the issuing municipality. General obligation bonds are the safest municipal bonds.

General partner
Manager of a limited partnership; a role that assumes unlimited liability in the partnership.

Gift tax
Tax due on gifts (to persons other than the donor's spouse) with a value of more than $10,000. Tax is paid by the donor, not the recipient.

Globalization
General trend toward increasing flows of international trade and investment capital.

Good delivery
Delivery of securities to a client by a broker-dealer in an acceptable form by the transaction settlement date.

Good till cancelled (GTC or open) order
Instruction to keep the order active until the customer either executes or cancels it.

Government National Mortgage Association (Ginnie Mae)
Agency in the U.S. Department of Housing and Urban Development that buys and repackages mortgage loans.

Government-sponsored entity
The term for an agency that is not part of the federal government, but works to achieve one of the government's policy objectives.

Green shoe clause
Provision of most underwriting agreements stating that, in the face of strong public demand for an offering, the corporation will issue an additional number of shares.

Gross domestic product (GDP)
Total value of all goods and services produced within a country during a certain period (usually one year). GDP consists of consumer spending, government spending, investment, and net exports.

Gross national product (GNP)
Total value of all goods and services produced by residents of a country, both domestically and abroad.

Gross revenue pledge
Flow-of-funds that pays bondholder interest and principal before allocating money to the operations and maintenance of the project.

Growth stock
Stock issued by a company aiming for rapid expansion. Growth stocks are associated with companies that normally reinvest most of their profits and therefore rarely pay dividends.

Guaranteed bond
Bond issued by one company and guaranteed by another, generally the parent company of the issuer.

Guaranteed mortgage
Mortgage guaranteed by a government agency such as the Veterans' Administration or the Federal Housing Administration.

Guardian account
Fiduciary account in which a legal guardian protects the assets of another person, typically a minor.

Head and shoulders formation
Bearish chart pattern in which prices rise to a new peak, fall briefly, rise to an even higher peak, fall again, and then rise to a lower peak. (The two lower peaks are the "shoulders"; the high middle peak is the "head.")

Hedging strategy
Buying an option (or other security) to offset the risk of adverse price movements on a stock position (or other investment).

Holder
Buyer of an option.

Holding period
The time during which an asset is owned. For securities, the holding period is based on trade dates, not settlement dates.

Horizontal spread (calendar spread)
A credit spread in which the strike prices of the two options are the same, but the expirations differ.

Hot issue
Public offering for which demand is so great (or the price so low) that the security quickly sells out of the primary market and starts selling in the secondary market at a premium.

Hypothecation
Pledge of securities bought on margin as collateral for the loan financing the purchase.

Hypothecation agreement
Agreement by which a customer pledges any securities bought on margin to the brokerage house as collateral for the funds loaned.

Immediate or cancel (IOC)
Instruction to execute as much of the order as possible immediately, and to cancel any portion that is not filled.

In the money

For call options, when the strike price is below the market price of the underlying security; for put options, when the strike price is higher than the market price of the underlying security.

Income program

Oil and gas direct participation program that invests in existing producing wells.

Income statement (profit and loss statement)

Summary of a company's revenues, expenses, and net income during a certain period.

Income stock

Stock issued by a mature, stable company in an established industry. Income stocks are associated with companies that pay out a significant portion of their earnings as dividends.

Indenture

Legal agreement between a company issuing bonds and bond purchasers. The indenture provides for the appointment of a trustee to protect the rights of the bondholders.

Index

A statistically derived number designed to measure changes in a larger group of data, generally expressed in terms of the percentage change from a certain base period. The Consumer Price Index, for example, measures the percentage difference between the prices of a collection of consumer goods at some arbitrary date in the past and their prices today—inflation.

Index option

An option based on an index rather than on a single underlying stock. The strike price of the option refers to the value of the index rather than to the price of a particular stock.

Individual retirement account (IRA)

Tax-deferred retirement account that can be started by an individual to supplement retirement income.

Inflation

General increase in prices for goods and services.

Initial public offering (IPO)

Company's first attempt to raise capital by selling securities to the public.

Initial requirement

Amount of money that must be deposited in order for the first purchase or sale in a margin account to take place. For instance, the NYSE requires a $2,000 margin deposit to open a margin account.

Initial transaction

First transaction in a margin account, which actually opens the account.

Inside market

Highest bid quote and the lowest ask quote among all the market makers in a given stock.

Insider
Officer, director, or individual who owns at least 10% of the shares of a corporation. These persons are considered to have access to privileged "inside" information about the corporation.

Instinet, Inc.
Computer network (run by Institutional Networks Corporation and owned by Reuters) used by large institutional investors for trading in the fourth market.

Intangible assets
Nonphysical corporate assets, such as copyrights, patents, trademarks, and goodwill.

Interest and dividend department
Department in a brokerage house that pays bond interest and equity dividends to beneficial owners of securities that are held in street name.

Interest rate option (debt option)
An option based on a Treasury bill, note, or bond. Debt options can be price based or yield based.

Interest rate risk
Risk that a bond will lose value when interest rates rise.

Intermediation
Technical term for depositing money into an account at a bank, which acts as a financial intermediary by investing the funds.

Interpositioning
Illegal maneuver in which two dealers act as agents in the same transaction, thereby earning two commissions on one transaction.

Intrinsic value
Difference between the market price of the underlying stock and the strike price of the option. For a call, if the stock price is less than or equal to the strike price, the option has an intrinsic value of zero.

Inventory turnover rate
Ratio of the cost of goods sold to inventory.

Inverse saucer
Chart pattern in which prices gradually rise, reach a maximum, and then begin to fall. Inverse saucers suggest the reversal of an uptrend, and are therefore a bearish sign.

Inverted head and shoulders formation
Bullish chart pattern in which prices fall to a new minimum, rise briefly, fall to an even lower minimum, rise again, and then fall to a less extreme minimum. (The two smaller valleys are the "shoulders"; the deeper valley is the "head.")

Inverted yield curve
Yield curve with a descending slope, showing that short-term yields are actually higher than long-term yields. (This situation is rare, occurring only in highly inflationary periods when the Federal Reserve has greatly reduced available short-term credit in the market.)

Investment adviser
Person who manages other people's money, making trades on their behalf in return for a commission or fee; or one who manages a mutual fund's portfolio.

Investment banking
Business of helping companies carry out mergers, acquisitions, reorganizations, other financial matters, and the underwriting of security issues.

Investment basis
Customer's share of the annuity's internal growth; usually as a result of dividend and interest reinvestment as well as securities appreciation. The investment basis is tax-deferred during the accumulation phase.

Investment Company Act of 1940
The federal law that governs the activities of investment companies.

Investment or portfolio income
Income received from investments, including dividends, interest, and capital gains.

Investors
People, institutions, and businesses who buy securities (or other assets) in hopes of seeing the value of their holdings increase.

IRA rollover
Transfer of funds from an IRA to another qualified retirement plan. A 10% tax penalty is assessed on the full amount of the rollover if the transfer is not completed within a 60-day period.

Issued stock
Stock that has been sold to investors.

Issuer
The company selling its securities.

Joint account
Account held in common by two or more people.

Joint tenants with rights of survivorship account (JTWROS)
Joint account in which, if one party dies, his or her portion of the account passes to the remaining account holder.

Junk bond
High-risk, high-yield bond that has received a speculative rating.

Keogh account
Retirement plan for self-employed individuals, allowing tax-deductible contributions up to $30,000 per year, or 25% of the person's income, whichever is less.

Keynesian economics
Influential body of economic theory largely derived from the work of John Maynard Keynes. Keynesian economists believe that government fiscal policy can effectively moderate the ups and downs of the business cycle.

Kiddie tax
Federal tax owed on the interest and dividends (in excess of $1,300) earned by a custodian account for a child under the age of 14. The Kiddie tax is levied at the top rate of the parents.

Lagging indicators

Indicators for parts of the economy that tend to change after the economy has already entered a new phase of the business cycle.

Last-in, first-out method (LIFO)

Cost accounting method that assumes that the last goods entered into a company's inventory are the first goods to be sold. During inflationary periods, LIFO results in higher costs (and lower profits) than the first-in, first-out method.

Leading indicators

Indicators for parts of the economy that tend to change before the economy as a whole enters a new phase of the business cycle.

LEAPS (Long-term Equity AnticiPation Securities)

Equity or index options with terms of up to three years.

Legal list

Set of investments that are permitted for persons managing custodian or fiduciary accounts. The legal list is used by states that do not employ the prudent man rule.

Legislative risk

Risk that state or federal governments will change, in an adverse way for bond investors, how interest income or capital gains and losses are taxed.

Letter of discount

Method of earning a discount on the sales charge. Investors agree to purchase a certain number of shares over 13 months, and the mutual fund gives them credit for the total purchase in determining the proper breakpoint.

Letter of intent

Underwriter's plan for making a public offering of a company's securities.

Levels One, Two, and Three of the NASDAQ system

Separate levels of the NASDAQ computer quotation system. Each level provides different information, to which different participants in the OTC market have access.

Leverage

Use of credit to buy or sell securities with a greater value than the cash an investor has on hand.

Liability

The debt obligations of a business.

LIBOR (London Interbank Offered Rate)

Interest rate that overseas banks charge for international loans of Eurodollars.

Life annuity

Annuity that makes payments to the holder from the date of the contract's maturity until the annuitant's death.

Limit order
Order to buy or sell securities at a specified price (or better) other than the current market price.

Limited liability
Term describing the financial obligation of a limited partner, which cannot exceed his or her total contribution to the partnership.

Limited partner
Passive investor in a partnership, with limited liability.

Limited partnership
Most common form of direct participation program, in which at least one limited partner and one general partner share the risks and gains of a business investment.

Liquidity
Capability to convert an asset to cash quickly and without significant losses. For a firm, liquidity refers to its capability to meet its current liabilities with current assets.

Liquidity risk
Risk that selling the bond will involve above-average transaction costs. Generally, short-term and highly rated bonds are more liquid than long-term and low-rated bonds.

Load fund
Mutual fund with a sales charge.

Loan consent agreement
Agreement in which a customer gives a brokerage the right to lend the customer's securities for short sales. (Some broker-dealers make this agreement optional.)

Loan value
Part of the value of a fully paid, marginable security that a brokerage can accept as margin. Under Reg T, loan value is half of the marginable security's current market value.

Long call spread
A long spread composed of two call options with different strike prices. The trader hopes to make money on a moderate rise in the stock's price.

Long margin account
Part of a margin account in which a customer can purchase securities.

Long market value (or LMV)
Current market value of the securities in a long margin account.

Long position (or simply long)
The situation of an option holder, who is said to be "long the option" or to have opened a long position.

Long put spread
A long spread composed of two put options with different strike prices. The trader is hoping to make money on a moderate fall in the stock's price.

Long spread (debit spread)

A spread in which the premium of the option purchased is larger than the premium of the option sold, for a net debit on the investor's position.

Long straddle

Holding a call and a put on the same underlying stock, with both options having the same strike price and expiration. Long straddles are profitable if the stock's price fluctuates widely.

Long-term capital

Sum of long-term liabilities and stockholders' equity.

Long-term Equity AnticiPation Securities (LEAPS)

Equity options with a lifetime of up to 36 months rather than the nine month maximum of most equity options.

Long-term gain/loss

A gain or loss on an asset held for more than 18 months.

Lump-sum agreement

Payout option in which the insurance company pays the annuitant the full amount of the account all at once.

Maintenance margin

Amount an investor must retain in a margin account to cover the value of securities not yet paid for.

Major Market Index

An index calculated from the prices of 20 blue-chip stocks. Its value almost exactly mirrors the Dow.

Management company

An investment company that is governed by a board of directors and sells shares of stock, which represent investors' interest in the income generated by an underlying pool of securities. Management companies are distinguished from investment trusts because the underlying portfolio is professionally managed, as opposed to being static.

Margin

Amount an investor must deposit to buy or sell securities on credit. The remainder of the securities' value is loaned to the investor by the brokerage firm.

Margin account

Account in which a customer can trade without immediately paying the full amount of a transaction; instead, the customer deposits a required amount (often a percentage of the funds needed), and the broker-dealer lends the remainder.

Margin agreement

The agreement customers must sign to open a margin account, usually consisting of three separate documents: a credit agreement, a hypothecation agreement, and a loan consent agreement.

Margin call

Notice to a customer that his or her margin account has fallen below the required level. The customer must deposit additional funds to fulfill the requirement.

Margin department
Department that monitors margin accounts and ensures that margin and minimum maintenance requirements are met.

Marginable securities
Securities that can be traded using margin.

Mark to market
The process of calculating the current market value of securities in an account or a portfolio.

Mark-down
Fee that a dealer acting as a principal in a transaction charges a customer who sells an OTC stock.

Mark-up (or mark-down)
Fee charged by a dealer to its customers, added to (or subtracted from) the current market price of shares sold (or bought).

Market (or systematic or nondiversifiable) risk
The risk that downturns in the economy, or the securities market, will cause the value of an individual issuer's securities to decline, regardless of the issuer's performance. Market risk cannot be avoided, making it nondiversifiable.

Market maker
Exchange member registered to trade specific options for his or her own account. When needed, market makers take the opposite side of public orders, ensuring that options always have a market.

Market order
Order to buy or sell securities at the current market price.

Market portfolio
Term for a well diversified portfolio like the S&P's 500 index.

Market risk
Risk that a bond's value will vary greatly with movements in interest rates. This risk is particularly strong for bonds with long maturities or low coupons, because their prices move more dramatically with changes in interest rates.

Market value
Current price of a share of stock in the market where it trades.

Marketability risk
Risk that a bond might be difficult to sell in the future. This depends on demand for the bond—the more actively traded an issue is, the easier it is to sell.

Married put
A put purchased as a hedge on the same day as the underlying security. The premium for a married put is treated as part of the underlying security's cost basis.

Matched sale (or match)
Reverse repo negotiated between a primary dealer and the Federal Reserve. The Fed uses matched sales to temporarily contract banks' reserves, thereby raising the Fed funds rate.

Matching contribution
Amount paid into an employee's 401(k) plan by an employer, usually equaling the amount contributed by the employee.

Maturity date
Date on which the issuer must repay the principal to the bondholder.

Maturity premium
The extra return that investors demand for purchasing longer term Treasury bonds instead of short-term Treasury bills.

Medicare
Part of Social Security that provides medical insurance to individuals over the age of 65.

Mill rate
Tax rate on property within a municipality. One mill is equal to 0.1% (1/1,000) of the assessed valuation of the property.

Mini-maxi offering
Public offering of a DPP (or other security) in which the underwriter has a limited amount of time to sell a minimum dollar amount, or the offering is canceled.

Minimum maintenance requirement
Amount of maintenance margin a customer must retain in an account at all times, or face a margin call. The NYSE and NASD set minimum maintenance requirements. Also, the amount of margin an options trader must maintain in his or her account when writing uncovered calls or puts.

Modified Accelerated Cost Recovery System (MACRS)
Set of Internal Revenue Service rules for depreciation, in which property is divided into classes and each class is assigned a number of years over which depreciation expenses can be taken.

Modified pass-through
Pass-through that carries a direct government guarantee.

Monetarist economics
Economic theory that advocates the use of monetary policy (rather than fiscal policy) to manage the economy.

Monetary policy
Methods used by a country's central bank to control the money supply. Changes in the money supply strongly affect market interest rates and inflation, and therefore economic growth.

Money center bank
Large bank located in one of the financial centers of the world (New York, London, or Tokyo, for example). These banks are major players in the money market.

Money market
Part of the debt market where companies, banks, and the federal government can issue and trade short-term debt securities to raise immediate cash—or to dispose of extra funds. Some longer-term securities can be traded, but always within a short-term agreement (see repurchase agreement).

Money market fund
Mutual fund that invests primarily in money market instruments.

Money supply
Quantity of money in the economy, including cash, bank deposits, and other forms of money. The Fed manipulates the size of the money supply to control inflation and interest rates.

Moral suasion
Public statements made by members of the Federal Reserve Board to influence the actions of banks and other financial institutions.

Mortality guarantee
Insurance company promise that an annuitant will continue to be paid for as long as he or she lives.

Mortgage loan (mortgage or conventional mortgage)
Loan extended to a property buyer by a bank or other lending institution, collateralized by the property itself.

Mortgage pool
Group of mortgages with the same interest rate and maturity.

Mortgage REIT
Real estate investment trust that purchases mortgages and construction loans, passing on to its shareholders the income from the interest payments on those loans.

Moving average
Line graph representing an average of daily security prices or index values over a certain period, such as 30 days or 200 days, that moves forward daily. Each day the average price is recalculated to include the most recent range of values.

Municipal bond (or muni)
Debt instrument issued by a state or municipality to raise money for needed expenditures.

Municipal bond tax swap
The sale of one municipal bond and the immediate repurchase of another. To qualify as a tax swap, and not a wash sale, the new bond must differ from the original in at least two of the following categories: issuer, maturity, or interest rate.

Municipal investment trust (or MIT)
Fund that specializes in investing in a variety of municipal bond offerings.

Municipal securities principal
Employee who manages or supervises operations in a municipal securities firm. Broker-dealers with muni desks must employ at least one principal at each branch office.

Municipal Securities Rulemaking Board (MSRB)
Self-regulatory organization established by federal law in 1975 that sets rules and guidelines to govern the municipal debt market.

Narrow-based index

An index that reflects the price movements of a narrow group of stocks, usually those of a certain country, market segment, or industry.

NASDAQ (National Association of Securities Dealers Automated Quotation System)

Arm of the NASD that is both a securities market (with some 5,500 stocks listed) and a computerized system with price quotes used for trading most over-the-counter stocks.

NASDAQ National Market System (NMS)

Stock market that lists the 2,500 largest over-the-counter stocks.

NASDAQ SmallCap Market

Stock market that lists 3,000 smaller over-the-counter stocks.

NASDAQ Stock Market

NASDAQ entity that combines the National Market System and the SmallCap Market.

National Arbitration Committee

Body that arbitrates disputes between NASD member firms and other firms or their customers. Three arbitrators are assigned to each case.

National Association of Securities Dealers (NASD)

Self-regulating organization that governs the OTC market.

Negotiable certificates of deposit (or jumbo CDs)

Short or medium-term debt securities, issued by banks, with a minimum face value of $100,000, and traded in the money market.

Negotiable securities

Securities pledged under a hypothecation agreement and kept in street name, which the broker-dealer can therefore sell if the customer defaults on the margin loan.

Negotiated (or dealer) market

Securities marketplace that has no physical trading floor, instead using a network of telephones and computers to connect buyers and sellers who negotiate prices among themselves. Negotiated markets are also distinguished by their use of multiple market makers for each security.

Net asset value (NAV)

A measure of the value of one share in a unit trust (or mutual fund), obtained by dividing the market value of the investment company's portfolio by the number of shares issued. Also, the current value of one accumulation unit. Net asset value is determined by subtracting liabilities from the market value of the annuity's assets, and then dividing by the total number of units held by customers.

Net profit margin

Ratio of net income after tax to net sales.

Net revenue pledge
Flow-of-funds that gives priority to operations and maintenance costs before payments to bondholders.

Net tangible asset value per bond
Ratio of tangible assets, less current liabilities, to the number of $1,000 bonds outstanding.

Net working capital
Current assets minus current liabilities.

Net worth
Difference between a firm's assets and liabilities.

New issue
Securities that have not been offered for sale previously. New issues are sold either in an initial public offering or in a primary offering.

New York Stock Exchange (NYSE)
Largest and busiest exchange on the globe, the "Big Board" is where the stocks of many of the most important U.S. corporations are traded.

Next month
Month after spot. If the current month's options have expired, the next month is actually two calendar months in the future.

Nine-bond rule (NYSE Rule 396)
Requirement that any NYSE member firm that is executing an order for nine bonds or fewer must place the order on the floor of the NYSE for one hour before sending the order to the OTC market.

No-load fund
Mutual fund with no sales charge.

Nominal owner
Owner of a security in name only. For securities held in street name, the nominal owner is the brokerage, which is not entitled to the benefits of ownership, such as dividends or voting rights.

Nominal quote
Price given as a starting point to test the market for the best available price on a municipal security.

Nominal yield
Fixed interest rate on a bond, guaranteed in the indenture.

Noncompetitive bid
Treasury auction bid placed by an individual investor.
Noncompetitive bids state only the dollar amount of the issue that the investors want to purchase, because the price that they pay is determined by the average of the winning competitive bids.

Nondiversified management company
An investment company that concentrates its investments in a particular security, industry, or geographic region.

Noninterest-bearing securities
Securities that do not make periodic interest payments. The investor's return is based solely on the discount, the difference between the purchase price and the par value.

Nonrecourse loan
Loan taken out by a limited partnership in which liability is restricted to the partnership itself.

Nontax-qualified program
Retirement plan in which contributions are made from after-tax income, but disbursement payments are tax-free.

Normal yield curve
Yield curve with a positive, ascending slope, showing that bond yields increase as time to maturity lengthens.

Not held (NH)
Instruction that gives the broker discretion about when to execute the trade, in the hopes that the broker will get the best price. The broker is not held liable if the client does not like the price.

Numbered account
Account in which, for reasons of confidentiality, the owner is identified by a number rather than by name (which is known only by the registered rep and the branch manager).

Odd-lot theory
Theory stating that sophisticated investors should act contrary to small, odd-lot investors, who are assumed to enter and get out of markets at the wrong time.

Odd-lot trades
Trades involving fewer than 100 shares.

Off-the-floor trading
Buying and selling exchange-listed securities (principally from the NYSE) by OTC firms, away from the exchange "floor."

Offer wanted (OW)
Dealer's request for a potential stock seller to suggest a price.

Office of supervisory jurisdiction (OSJ)
Branch of every NASD member firm that ensures the firm and its employees comply with all applicable securities regulations.

Omnibus account
Account set up by an investment adviser who trades with the aggregate funds of many clients, although the assets of the account remain the property of the various clients.

Open interest
Number of option contracts for an underlying security that are still open; that is, have not expired, been exercised, or been closed out.

Open market desk
Where the Fed, through the New York Federal Reserve Bank, buys and sells government securities as a means to control the nation's money supply.

Open market operations
The Fed's purchases and sales of government securities in order to adjust the money supply.

Open-end management company

Technical term for a mutual fund. Open-end funds, in contrast to closed-end companies, issue and redeem shares continuously.

Opening purchase

Purchase of a new option. The holder opens (or increases) a long position.

Opening sale

Sale of a new option. The writer opens (or increases) a short position.

Operating income

Earnings before depreciation, interest expense, and taxes.

Operating lease

Short-term lease for heavy machinery and equipment in which the full cost of the equipment is not covered by the lessee's payments.

Operating profit margin

Ratio of operating income to net sales.

Opportunity cost

The potential income foregone by having chosen a lesser yielding investment over a higher yielding one.

Option

Contract that gives the buyer the right to buy or sell a number of shares of a security at a fixed price at any time until a certain date.

Option account

Account in which options are traded.

Options Clearing Corporation (OCC)

Company that issues, processes, and guarantees all options. Owned by the exchanges where options trade, and overseen by the SEC, the OCC acts as a clearing house for all options transactions.

Order book official (OBO)

Exchange employee who holds public limit orders that cannot be filled immediately. The OBO executes the orders later, if and when the market price moves to the desired level.

Order ticket

The form completed by a broker for his or her client that contains information about a trade, including the type of order and any special instructions.

Original issue discount (OID)

Muni bond issued at a discount. The discount on an OID is accreted annually over the life of the bond (added to the bond's cost basis and treated as interest), and thus remains tax-exempt for a buyer who holds the bond until maturity.

Original issue discount bond

Bond issued at a discount (rather than at par value).

OTC Bulletin Board

NASDAQ-operated computerized system for obtaining price quotes on Pink Sheet stocks.

Out of the money
For call options, when the strike price is above the market price of the underlying security; for put options, when the strike price is lower than the market price of the underlying security.

Outstanding stock
Stock that is currently owned by investors.

Over-the-counter (OTC) market
Not a physical location, but a system for trading securities by means of individual negotiations, usually over computer and telephone lines.

Overbought
Market situation after buyers have temporarily driven up the price of a security. Because sellers now outnumber buyers, the price is likely to fall.

Oversold
Market situation after sellers have temporarily driven down the price of a security. Because buyers now outnumber sellers, the price is likely to rise.

Par value (face value)
Principal amount of the bond, typically $1,000 for corporate bonds; or arbitrary price assigned by a corporation to each share of its common or preferred stock; essentially meaningless for common stock, but significant for preferred stock.

Parity price of stock
Share price of common stock at which a convertible bond can be converted without any loss (or gain) in value.

Participating preferred
Preferred stock that lets the shareholder receive any "extraordinary" dividends declared by the company in a particularly strong year.

Participating unit investment trust
A unit trust that purchases shares in one or more management companies. Because the investments of the management company change over time, the return on a participating trust is less predictable than that on a fixed trust.

Partnership account
Securities account owned by a legal partnership; the account agreement specifies who can trade in the account.

Partnership manager
Individual who chooses investments for a limited partnership.

Pass-through certificate
Security that directs the cash flow from a pool of mortgages through an agency and on to investors.

Passive income
Income received from business ventures in which the recipient did not play an active management role, such as limited partnerships.

Penalty bid clause

Provision of many underwriting agreements that cancels the fee earned by a member of an underwriting syndicate if its customers are found to be selling their shares back to the lead underwriter (who has just placed a stabilizing bid).

Penny stocks

Stocks with a market value of less than $5. Penny stocks are volatile and considered speculative.

Pension Benefit Guaranty Corporation (PBGC)

Federal agency charged with ensuring that private pension plans follow ERISA rules.

Percentage of par

Pricing method used for trading Treasury notes and bonds. Prices are stated as a percentage of the security's par value.

Percentage-of-income depletion

Method to calculate depletion in which a flat percentage of gross income (15%) is deducted from each unit of oil or gas sold.

Phantom interest

Accretion of the capital gain on a zero-coupon bond.

Phantom SMA

SMA that cannot be used because if it were, the account's equity would fall below the minimum maintenance requirement.

Pink Sheets

National Quotation Bureau publication that provides quotes for the 4,500 over-the-counter stocks not included in the NASDAQ Stock Market. These stocks are sometimes referred to as Pink Sheet stocks.

Plain vanilla CMO

Original form of a CMO (contrast with later CMOs, whose tranches are matched with companion tranches).

Planned amortization class bond (PAC)

CMO that includes two companion tranches for every PAC tranche (or regular tranche), thus giving the PAC tranche protection against both prepayment and extension risk.

Point

100 basis points (1%). Each point represents $10 in the price of a bond.

Position limit

Maximum number of options contracts that any one investor (or group of investors working together) can buy or sell on a given stock on a single side of the market.

Power of attorney

Legal document in which a person gives another the right to act on his or her behalf. A power of attorney must be signed by a customer and notarized before giving a registered rep discretion to trade in the customer's account.

Preemptive right
Right of existing shareholders to maintain their proportionate share of equity during a new issue.

Preferred dividend coverage
Ratio of net income to preferred dividends.

Preferred stock
Equity security that pays a fixed dividend, based on a percentage of its par value. Preferred stock does not usually confer voting rights, but it has preference over common stock in the payment of dividends and in the liquidation of assets.

Preferred stock ratio
Ratio of par value of preferred stock to long-term capital.

Preliminary prospectus (or red herring)
Document, prepared by a lead underwriter, that describes a public offering and is intended to elicit the interest of other underwriters and potential customers.

Premium
Amount by which a bond's market price exceeds its par value. Premiums are amortized annually over the life of the bond (subtracted from the bond's cost basis and treated as a reduction in interest).

Prepayment risk
Risk that homeowners might pay off their mortgage loans earlier than expected, exposing investors to reinvestment risk.

Present value
How much a specified dollar amount in the future is worth to an investor today.

Price earnings ratio (P/E)
Ratio of market price of stock to earnings per share.

Price-based option
An interest rate option based on the price of a specific issue of Treasury securities. The contract holder can buy or sell the underlying bill, note, or bond at the strike price, quoted as a percentage of par value.

Primary dealer
Large securities firm or financial institution that has qualified to place competitive bids at Treasury auctions. These dealers must maintain a certain presence in all Treasury auctions and also must make a secondary market for Treasury securities.

Primary market
Market where corporations raise capital by selling their equity (or debt) securities to investors.

Primary offering
Any subsequent attempt by a company to raise capital in the primary market.

Prime rate
Interest rate charged by banks on loans to their largest and safest corporate customers.

Principal
Dealer who trades stock from its own inventory (note second use of the word: principal as a partner or manager in a securities firm). Also, the partner or manager in a securities firm (to be distinguished from a dealer "acting as a principal" in a transaction).

Private activity bonds
Municipal bonds that do not qualify for triple-tax exemption because their proceeds are used for certain private enterprise projects (such as a new sports stadium).

Private placement (Regulation D or Reg D placement)
Issue sold through private channels, mainly to accredited investors. Because it is not offered on the public market, a Reg D placement is not subject to the normal SEC requirements.

Profit-sharing plan
Retirement plan in which the employee shares in part of the company's profits (typically the employee's share accumulates until he or she retires or leaves the company).

Profitability
Capability of a business to generate income in excess of its expenses.

Program trading
A form of computerized stock trading widely used by large institutional traders, such as mutual and pension funds. Transactions are triggered automatically when the market crosses preset thresholds.

Progressive tax
A tax that applies higher tax rates to larger incomes or amounts.

Property manager
Person responsible for managing properties in a real estate DPP.

Protective call
Call option purchased by an investor who has sold the underlying stock short. The call hedges against an unforeseen increase in the price of the stock.

Protective covenants
Features or agreements written into a revenue bond contract that are designed to protect the interests of bondholders.

Protective put
Put option purchased by an investor who owns the underlying stock. The put hedges against a fall in the stock's price.

Proxy
Means by which a shareholder who does not attend the annual corporate meeting can vote via mail-in ballot.

Proxy department
Department charged with keeping track of beneficial owners of securities that are held in street name.

Prudent man rule
Guideline adopted by many states requiring that persons trading on behalf of others make investment judgments that a careful person ("prudent man") would make when trading on behalf of a fiduciary account.

Public offering price
Price per share of a new issue.

Public Securities Association (PSA) model
Statistical model created by analysts at the PSA to predict the rate of prepayments for mortgages, based on their interest rates and maturities.

Purchase and sales (P&S) department
Department in a brokerage house that sends customer confirms and reconciles trading errors.

Purchasing power risk
Risk that inflation will mount over the life of the bond, thereby leading interest rates to rise and bond prices to fall.

Put option
Contract that gives the holder the right to sell a number of shares of a security at a fixed price at any time until a certain date.

Put provision
Measure in some bond indentures that gives holders the right to sell the bond back to the issuer prior to maturity. (Usually the put price is set at par value.)

Put-call ratio
Volume of put options divided by volume of call options. A high ratio indicates that options traders are bearish, generally taken as a sign that the market is about to turn bullish. A low ratio is a bearish sign.

Quick asset ratio (acid test ratio)
Ratio of current assets, less inventory, to current liabilities.

Quotation
Combination of the highest bid price and the lowest ask price available for any particular security at any time.

Random walk theory
Theory stating that the past performance of security prices has no bearing on future performance. In other words, stock prices move in an essentially random manner and cannot be predicted.

Raw land
Undeveloped land, with no real property improvements that cannot be depreciated

Real estate investment trust (REIT)
A trust that invests in real estate properties, mortgages, and construction loans. REIT shares are traded on an exchange or over the counter.

Recapture
Taxing claimed tax deductions, such as accelerated depreciation, as ordinary income when a property is sold.

Receivership account
Fiduciary account in which a person takes control of the assets of a business or estate in bankruptcy. This person, who does not take title to the assets, is charged with managing them and the affairs of the business until a court makes a final disposition of the assets.

Recession
Period of decreased business activity in which GDP declines for at least two consecutive quarters.

Reciprocal dealing
Prohibited situation in which two broker-dealers agree that one will sell the products of the second in return for the second funneling trading in that product through the first.

Reclamation
Customer's right to recover losses when a delivery of purchased securities arrives in unacceptable condition (for example, with mutilated bonds or missing coupons).

Record date
Date by which any purchase of shares must be settled in order for the buyer to either participate in a rights offering or receive a dividend payment.

Recourse loan
Loan taken out by a limited partnership in which the partners are personally responsible for any remaining debt should the partnership default.

Refunding
Issuing a new bond to retire an existing bond issue or to purchase securities to defease the existing bond.

Regional exchange
One of the U.S. stock exchanges located outside of New York City. The regional exchanges generally specialize in smaller, local companies, as well as in dual listings with major exchanges.

Registered options principal (ROP)
Person at a brokerage firm who approves new options accounts. The ROP is responsible for evaluating whether an investor is qualified to assume the risks of options trading.

Registered representative
Employee of a securities firm who solicits business, or otherwise handles customer accounts and investments.

Registrar
Person or business who works with a company's transfer agent to maintain records of stock (and bond) owners. The registrar's duties include ensuring that outstanding stock does not exceed the amount authorized in the corporate charter.

Regressive tax
A tax that consumes proportionately more of a low wage earner's income than that of a high wage earner.

Regular way settlement (T+3)
The standard required completion of a securities transaction on the third full business day after the trade.

Regulation A (or small issue exemption)

Regulation allowing companies to make public offerings of up to $5 million without meeting the normal SEC registration requirements.

Regulation T (or Reg T)

Federal Reserve regulation that controls brokerages' extension of credit to customers, specifying the minimum amounts or percentages of the value of securities that must be supplied by the investor.

Regulation U (or Reg U)

Federal Reserve regulation that controls banks' extensions of credit to brokerages for margin transactions.

Rehypothecation

Repledging of a customer's margined securities by a broker-dealer to a bank as collateral for a broker loan.

Reinvestment risk

Risk that an investor will not be able to reinvest interest or principal receipts at an equal or higher rate (because of falling interest rates).

Reorganization department

Department that notifies customers of changes in the corporate ownership of companies whose securities the customer holds.

Repackaging

Using Treasuries as underlying securities to create new products for investors. Repackaging primarily consists of stripping apart the interest and principal cash flows of a T-bond, and creating a series of zero-coupon bonds.

Repurchase agreement (repo)

Sale of securities (usually Treasuries) in which the seller agrees to buy back the securities at a later date for a specified price. When primary dealers engage in repurchase agreements with the Federal Reserve, banks' reserves are temporarily expanded, and the Fed funds rate should fall.

Reserve requirement

Percentage of customer deposits that commercial banks must maintain in cash, either in their own safes or in a Federal Reserve Bank. By raising and lowering reserve requirements, the Fed adjusts the supply of money and thus the pace of economic activity.

Resistance level

Security price at which the market resists any further increase, because of high selling pressure.

Restricted account

Account that has fallen below the Reg T 50% margin requirement.

Restricted stock

Unregistered securities, normally purchased in a private placement.

Retained earnings

Profits made by a company that are retained for future use rather than paid out as dividends.

Retention requirement

Reg T requirement that 50% of the proceeds from any sale in a restricted account be applied to paying down the debit balance in a long margin account (or be maintained in the credit balance of a short margin account).

Return on assets

Ratio of net income after tax to total tangible assets.

Return on common equity

Ratio of net income after tax, less preferred dividends, to common equity.

Revenue anticipation note (RAN)

Short-term municipal debt issued in anticipation of income from a revenue-producing project.

Revenue bond

Bond used to finance a specific revenue-generating project, such as a bridge or tunnel. Income from the project (such as tolls collected at the bridge) services the revenue bond.

Reverse repurchase agreement (or reverse repo)

Purchase of securities (usually Treasuries) in which the buyer agrees to sell them back at a later date for a specified price.

Reverse split

Stock split in which the number of a company's outstanding shares is reduced by a certain ratio, while the market price of the stock rises accordingly.

Right of accumulation

Similar to a letter of discount, except that the purchase period can extend up to 10 years.

Rights offering

Opportunity for shareholders of record on a certain date to buy newly issued company stock at a discounted price.

Risk premium

The excess return that investors require for buying securities such as common stocks.

Risk-free return or rate

Term used by financial theorists for the rate on new issue Treasury bills, which, given the issuer and time frame, are considered practically risk-free.

Risk-return tradeoff

The relationship between risk and return in the securities market. The higher the return, the greater the risk.

Riskless trade

Trade in which a dealer buys stock for its own account and immediately sells it at a profit.

Road show

Presentations to develop interest in a new offering, made by the issuer and lead underwriter to members of the investment community around the country.

Roth IRA

IRA in which initial contributions are made from after-tax dollars, whereas all withdrawals during retirement are tax-free.

Round-lot trades

Trades involving multiples of 100 shares.

Rule 144 (or dribble rule)

SEC regulation permitting company insiders to sell a limited number of restricted and control shares to the public—at a "dribble"—every 90 days.

Rule 144a

Provision of federal securities law that enables large institutional investors to trade unregistered securities among themselves without abiding by the limits of Rule 144.

Rule 147 (or intrastate exemption)

Securities law provision allowing a corporation to sell securities within the borders of a state (if the company is based primarily in that state) without meeting the normal SEC registration requirements.

Rule 405 ("Know Your Customer" rule)

A NYSE regulation requiring brokers to find out enough about their customers to judge whether investments are suitable for them. Although Rule 405 officially only applies to NYSE member firms, it has been adopted as a standard throughout the securities industry.

Rules of Fair Practice (or Conduct Rules)

Set of rules designed to ensure ethical behavior by NASD members toward customers.

Safekeeping

Holding securities in the customer's own name at a broker-dealer.

Sale-leaseback

Transaction in which an investor purchases a building from its current owner-occupant, and then leases it back to the same party.

Same-day substitution

Purchase and sale in a restricted account of securities on the same day for the same amount. For same-day substitutions, the investor need not deposit additional Reg T margin.

Saucer

Chart pattern in which prices gradually fall, reach a minimum, and then begin to rise. Saucers indicate the reversal of a downtrend, and are therefore a bullish sign.

Seat
Common name for a membership on the NYSE.

Second market
Over-the-counter (OTC) market; another component of the broader, secondary market.

Second mortgage bond
Bond secured by real estate that acts as collateral for a prior mortgage bond. Second mortgage bondholders are junior (subordinate) to first mortgage bondholders.

Secondary market
Market where investors buy and sell securities among themselves. Gains and losses accrue to these investors rather than to the stock's issuing company.

Secured debt
Debt issue for which a tangible asset has been pledged as collateral. If the company defaults on its debt, the asset is sold, and the proceeds are used to pay the interest and principal.

Securities Act of 1933
Federal law that sets the rules and procedures for selling new issues.

Securities analyst (financial analyst)
Individual who examines the financial condition of a company (or group of companies) in order to recommend strategies for trading stocks, bonds, and other securities.

Securities and Exchange Commission (SEC)
Federal agency charged with enforcing the rules and regulations of the securities markets.

Securities Exchange Act of 1934
Main body of federal laws regulating the stock exchanges and the trading of already-issued securities.

Securities Investor Protection Corporation (SIPC)
U.S. government entity that provides insurance coverage for customer accounts at securities firms that fail.

Securitization
act of making a nonnegotiable instrument (such as a mortgage) into a negotiable security (such as a bond).

Selective diversification
Method of diversifying a securities portfolio, in which limits are placed on the total amount that can be invested in a given industry or region.

Selling group
Broker-dealers organized by the lead underwriter to sell a portion of a public offering. Selling group members receive a smaller compensation than syndicate members but carry no financial liability.

Selling out
The point at which, according to the terms of the underwriting contract, an issue has been fully placed on the primary market and can therefore begin trading in the secondary market.

Selling short
Selling a security borrowed from a broker-dealer. If the security's price later falls, the seller can replace the borrowed security for less money than he or she received for its sale.

Senior registered options principal (SROP)
Person at a broker-dealer who has a Series 8 license and who must review and approve all customer applications to trade options.

SEP (simplified employee pension) IRA
IRA into which small businesses or self-employed individuals can make contributions to qualified pension plans.

Separate account
Account into which the annuity customers make their payments. The insurance company must keep this account's assets separate from its other assets.

Series
Group of all options in a class with the same strike price and expiration date (for example, all the puts on Xyron Corp. stock with a strike price of $45 and an expiration in November).

Series 27
License for financial operations principals.

Series 52
License for municipal securities representatives, who must attain it in conjunction with a 90-day apprenticeship at a municipal securities firm.

Series 53
License for municipal securities principals.

Share of beneficial interest (or unit)
One piece of investors' interest in the income produced by a unit trust's portfolio of securities. Units do not constitute ownership of the underlying securities.

Shareholder of record
Any investor who owns stock in a company as of the record date.

Shelf registration
Process in which a company registers a new issue with the SEC but can delay selling all or part of the stock for up to two years.

Short against the box
The short sale of a security the investor currently owns. Formerly, this was a strategy for locking in gains and postponing taxes; under current tax laws, taxes usually cannot be postponed.

Short call spread
A short spread composed of two call options with different strike prices. The trader hopes to retain the difference in premiums, expecting no movement or a moderate fall in the stock's price.

Short interest
Number of shares of a company's common stock that have been sold short and have not yet been covered.

Short interest theory
Theory stating that the greater the short interest, the more likely that prices are going to rise in the near future. Short sellers must eventually cover their sales, and their buying will exert upward pressure on prices.

Short margin account
Part of a margin account in which a customer can sell securities short.

Short market value
Current market value of the borrowed securities in a short margin account.

Short position (or simply short)
The situation of an option writer, who is said to be "short the option" or to have opened a short position.

Short put spread
A short spread composed of two put options with different strike prices. The trader hopes to retain the difference in premiums, expecting no movement or a moderate rise in the stock's price.

Short selling power
Selling leverage afforded a customer by the SMA in a short margin account.

Short spread (credit spread)
A spread in which the premium of the option sold is greater than the premium of the option purchased, for a net credit on the investor's position.

Short straddle
Writing a call and a put on the same underlying stock, with both options having the same strike price and expiration. Short straddles are profitable when the stock's price remains within certain bounds.

Short-sale rule (or uptick rule)
Provision of the Securities Exchange Act of 1934 that prohibits selling a security short if its price has declined. Investors can only sell short after a security's price has increased (an uptick) or remained steady after an increase (a zero uptick).

Short-term capital gain
Gain resulting from the sale of mutual fund shares (or other assets) that have been held for less than one year.

Short-term gain/loss
A gain or loss on an asset held for one year or less.

Short-term municipal debt (municipal notes)
Municipal debt securities with maturities of less than five years (and usually less than one year). Municipalities often issue these bonds in anticipation of revenue from long-term bonds, or to even out cash flow.

Simplified arbitration
Alternative for arbitrating disputes involving less than $10,000. One arbitrator decides the case.

Sinking fund
Cash fund created to ensure that a bond issuer can repay the principal to its bondholders.

Size of the market
Indication from a specialist to a floor broker of what the bid and ask prices are for a security, and of how many shares are desired or offered at those prices.

Small Order Execution System (SOES)
Automated system for buying OTC stocks in lots of less than 1,000 shares.

Social Security
Federal government program providing financial assistance and other benefits to retired people and other qualified individuals.

Special memorandum account (or SMA)
Credit line associated with a margin account, allowing a customer to borrow funds over and above those normally borrowed for margin purposes.

Specialist
A person who oversees the market for a particular security, often acting as a buyer or seller to maintain a fair and orderly market.

Specialist's book
Book in which a specialist records all orders that are above or below the current market price ("away from the market"), and which therefore cannot be executed immediately.

Specified pool
Limited partnership that announces its intended investments in a prospectus.

Sponsor
The firm or individual who creates and markets a unit investment trust or other type of investment company.

Spot
Current month, for options trading. After the month's options have expired (on the Saturday following the third Friday), the following calendar month is considered the spot.

Spread
Holding and writing two call options (or two put options) on the same underlying stock, with each option having a different strike price and/or expiration. Spreads limit risk on the primary option in exchange for reduced potential profits.

Stabilizing bid
Tactic used by a lead underwriter to support a sticky issue by setting a price floor at or just below the public offering price (without exceeding any independent bid in the market).

Stagflation
The combination of economic stagnation (low or negative growth rates plus high unemployment) and high inflation. First experienced in the 1970s, stagflation went against the received opinion that higher growth rates brought on inflation.

Standard & Poor's 100
An index calculated from the prices of a portfolio of 100 stocks on the NYSE, weighted to include more shares of stock from companies that have a larger number of shares outstanding.

Standard & Poor's 500 (Standard and Poor's Composite)
An index calculated from the prices of a portfolio of 500 stocks on the NYSE, weighted to include more shares of stock from companies that have a larger number of shares outstanding.

Standard deviation
The square root of the variance, another common measure of the risk inherent in a security.

Standby commitment
Obligation of an investment banker to purchase any rights that the shareholders of record do not buy during a rights offering.

Standing orders
Instructions from a customer that are valid for all trades in a particular account of the customer.

Starting date
Date on which the annuitant begins to receive payments from the insurance company. According to IRS guidelines, the minimum age at which an annuitant can begin receiving payments without incurring tax penalties is 59½.

Statement
Report on a securities account that includes all trades made during the period and the value of all holdings in the account at the closing price on the statement date.

Statement of changes to retained earnings
Statement of a company's net income and dividend payments for a given year.

Statutory voting
Most common form of shareholder voting, in which stockholders receive one vote for each ballot item.

Sticky issue
Offering that has been priced too high (or for which demand is too low), meaning that it will sell in the secondary market at a discount—if it reaches the secondary market.

Stock (or equity security)
Ownership of a corporation. The company sells shares of its stock to investors in the primary market.

Stock dividend
Dividend payment of stock shares rather than cash.

Stock exchange
Place where brokers and dealers gather to take part in auctions to trade securities.

Stock index
An index based on the market prices of a specific group of stocks, used to measure changes in the market as a whole or in specific sectors.

Stock split
Corporate action that multiplies the number of a company's outstanding shares by a certain ratio. The market price of the stock is adjusted downward accordingly.

Stockholders' equity
Net worth of a corporation.

Stop order
A buy or sell order that becomes a market order after a certain price called the stop price is reached.

Stop-limit order
A buy or sell order that becomes a limit order after the stop price is reached.

Stopping stock
A specialist's guarantee to a floor broker that the best price currently available will remain available to that broker for a certain period, usually 15 minutes.

Straddle
The purchase or sale of both a call and a put on the same underlying stock, with both options having the same strike price and expiration.

Straight pass-through
Pass-through that does not carry a direct government guarantee.

Straight-line depreciation
Method of depreciating an asset in equal amounts each year.

Straight-line method
Method to calculate a bond's adjusted cost basis evenly over the time remaining until maturity.

Street name
In the name of the broker-dealer. Securities purchased on margin are held in street name until the customer has paid for them in full. Also, securities are often held in street name to facilitate the process of transferring them after a sale.

Strike price (or exercise price)
The price at which the option can be exercised. For a put option, the holder has the right to sell the security to the writer at the strike price.

STRIPS (Separate Trading of Registered Interest and Principal of Securities)

Zero-coupon bonds created from the interest and principal portions of underlying Treasuries. STRIPS are the Treasury Department's response to the dealer profits generated by CATS and TIGERS.

Student Loan Marketing Association (Sallie Mae)

Government-sponsored, independent corporation created to expand the availability of low-cost financing for higher education.

Subchapter S corporation

Corporation with 35 or fewer shareholders, which, for tax purposes, is treated as a partnership.

Subject quote

Dealer's nonbinding price quote on a stock, subject to confirmation with a market maker in that stock.

Subordinated debenture

Unsecured bond that takes a junior position to prior debentures.

Subscription price

Price at which either rights or warrants can be exercised. The price is set below market for rights, and above market for warrants.

Suitability requirement

Criterion that investors must meet to join a direct participation program. Suitability is based on a variety of factors, including financial capacity and willingness to assume risk.

Super DOT

A computerized system that sends limit orders directly to the specialist.

Support level

Security price at which the market resists any further decrease, because of high buying pressure.

Syndicate of underwriters

Group of underwriters working together to sell a company's securities.

Syndicator

Organizer of a direct participation program. The syndicator, who is often the general partner, is responsible for registering the partnership with the proper authorities.

Systematic risk (market risk)

The risk of a stock falling in value because the entire market is falling.

Systematic withdrawal plan

Method of withdrawing money at regular intervals from a mutual fund, generally in order to liquidate an investor's holdings.

Taking indication

Process of shopping around a red herring to underwriters, dealers, and clients to gauge interest.

Tangible assets

Physical items owned by (or owed to) a company.

Targeted amortization class bond (TAC)

CMO that gives each regular tranche a companion tranche to offset prepayment risk, but not one to cover extension risk.

Tax anticipation note (TAN)

Short-term municipal debt issued in anticipation of income from property, sales, or other general taxes.

Tax assessment

Amount of property tax that an owner owes to a municipality on a piece of real estate. Municipalities calculate the tax assessment by multiplying the property's assessed valuation by the local mill rate.

Tax basis

Financial stake of an investor in a limited partnership, typically used to determine how much an investor can claim as losses on his or her tax returns. Tax basis is affected both by contributions and withdrawals from the partnership.

Tax qualified plan

Annuity in which the customer's regular payments are made from pretax income; the annuitants defer taxes on the money until they receive their distributions.

Tax-deferred

Investment in which taxes are not due until returns are withdrawn (in this case, after retirement).

Tax-qualified program

Retirement plan in which some or all contributions can be deducted from the individual's income taxes.

Taxable equivalent yield (or tax-equivalent yield)

Higher interest rate that is needed on a taxable bond (such as a corporate bond) to equal the return earned on a tax-exempt municipal bond.

Technical analysis

Examination of price charts, trading volumes, moving averages, and other market information to identify and predict trends in security prices. Generally, technical analysis is used for short-or medium-term predictions.

Tenancy-in-common account

Joint account whereby, if one party dies, his or her portion of the account passes to his or her estate.

Third market

Trading of exchange-listed securities by an OTC firm, rather than by a member of the exchange. The OTC firm necessarily carries out such transactions "off the floor."

TIGERS (Treasury Investment Growth Receipts)

Zero-coupon bonds created from both the interest and principal portions of an underlying Treasury bond.

Time deposits
Customer bank deposits that are left for a specific amount of time in return for interest payments (for example, savings accounts and certificates of deposit).

Time value
Value derived from the time remaining until the option expires and investors' expectations about what might happen during that period. Time value is calculated by subtracting the intrinsic value from the premium. All options have some time value until they expire.

Tombstone advertisement
Notice placed in a financial newspaper that announces a new issue of securities. It names the issuer, the size of the offering, the price of a share, and the syndicate members

Trading post
Location on the exchange floor where trading for a certain stock takes place.

Trading volume
Total number of securities traded in a given day, reported for individual issues as well as for entire exchanges. Technical analysts watch trading volume closely, because it measures investor interest and offers an important clue about future price movements.

Tranche
Section of a CMO (Collateralized mortgage obligation) that has a particular repayment rate and maturity, based on management of the cash flows from a pool of mortgages.

Transfer agent
Firm that maintains records of a corporation's stock (and bond) owners, mailing and canceling stock certificates as needed.

Treasuries
Blanket term for Treasury bills, notes, and bonds.

Treasury bills (T-bills)
Short-term debt by the U.S. government with maturities of 13, 26, or 52 weeks. T-bills are sold at a discount and are non-interest bearing; paying face value at maturity.

Treasury bonds (T-bonds)
Long-term debt issued by the U.S. government with maturities of 11 to 30 years. T-bonds are sold on a percentage of par basis, pay a fixed rate of interest, and repay the principal at maturity.

Treasury notes (T-notes)
Intermediate-term debt issued by the U.S. government with maturities of 1 to 10 years. T-notes are sold on a percentage of par basis, pay a fixed rate of interest, and repay the principal at maturity.

Treasury receipts
Alternate name for both CATS and TIGERS.

Treasury security (or Treasury)
Debt issued by the federal government. Treasuries include bills, notes, and bonds.

Treasury stock
Stock that has been issued and then repurchased by the corporation.

Triple exempt
Term that refers to securities, primarily municipal bonds, that are not taxed by federal, state, or local governments.

Triple net lease
Real estate lease in which the tenant pays all rents, taxes, insurance, and maintenance costs.

Triple tax exemption
Freedom from federal, state, and local taxation on the interest earned on most municipal bonds. Triple tax exemption helps make the returns of munis competitive with those of federal and corporate bonds.

Trust account
Fiduciary account in which a trustee oversees the account under the guidance of a trust agreement.

Trust Indenture Act of 1939
Federal legislation requiring that bonds be issued under an agreement—the indenture—that protects bondholders and meets specific SEC requirements.

Two-dollar (or independent) broker
A broker who executes trades for floor brokers who have more orders than they can process, or for member firms who do not have a representative on the floor at the time.

Type
One of the two kinds of options: a call or a put.

Uncovered call or put writer (or naked writer)
Writer who does not own the number of shares covered by the option, cannot guarantee potential losses, and must deposit margin upon the sale of the option.

Underlying security
The security specified by an option.

Underwriter
A firm that assists a company to issue its securities, often by purchasing them (taking on risk) and then reselling them. An underwriter can be a full-fledged investment bank or, in some cases, a smaller firm engaged only in this one aspect of investment banking.

Underwriting spread
Difference between the public offering price of a security and the amount that the issuing company receives.

Uniform Gifts to Minors Act (UMGA)
Federal law regulating how adults can give money and property to people less than 18 years of age. The UMGA allows for custodian accounts in securities trading, while regulating the taxation of any investment income earned by those minors.

Uniform Practice Code
NASD rules that govern dealings between member firms and outline the proper handling of OTC transactions.

Unique (or nonsystematic or diversifiable) risk

The risk that arises from an issuer's individual characteristics, such as management and project selection. Diversification eliminates unique risk.

Unit investment trust (UIT)

An investment company organized under an indenture and governed by a board of trustees. Unit trusts sell shares of beneficial interest in the income that is derived from an underlying pool of securities.

Unsolicited trade

Trade that a customer wants to make, without a broker's recommendation.

Unsystematic risk

The risk of a stock falling in value for reasons specific to that particular stock, such as poor management by the issuing company, competition, or a decline in the company's business sector.

Uptrend

Succession of increases in the price of a security (or market index).

Variable annuity

Annuity whose yield is determined by the performance of the underlying portfolio of securities. Therefore, the financial risk is assumed by the annuitant.

Variance

The average of squared deviations around another average. Variance measures the variability of a security's returns, and hence the degree of risk associated with the security.

Velocity of money

Number of times a dollar is spent in a specific period. The velocity of money is an important factor in determining the level of economic activity that a given supply of money can support.

Vertical spread (price spread)

A spread in which the strike prices of the two options differ, but the expirations are the same.

Vesting

Process by which an employee acquires the right to receive benefits from an employer-paid retirement plan. Vesting typically requires that a person work for a company for a certain period of time.

Voting trust certificates (VTCs)

Certificates that replace common stock and are issued to shareholders of a company in financial difficulties. VTCs have all the rights of common stock except voting privileges.

Warrant (or subscription warrant)

Transferable security that allows the holder to buy common stock at some point in the future—at a price higher than the current market price.

Wash sale
The sale of a security and the repurchase within 30 days of a substantially similar security. Tax losses from wash sales are disallowed.

Western account
Underwriting syndicate in which each member is responsible for selling a specific portion of the issue.

Wire and order department
Department in a brokerage house that communicates between brokers and the exchanges about the execution of trades.

Withholding
Illegal practice in which an underwriter holds back part of a hot issue in order to resell it later at a price above the initial offering price.

Workout quote
Dealer's nonbinding price quote on a particular amount of a given stock, subject to confirmation with a client of the dealer who earlier had expressed an interest in trading the same amount of that stock.

Writer
Seller of an option.

Yankee bond
Bond issued in the United States in U.S. dollars by a foreign company or government.

Yellow Sheets
National Quotation Bureau publication, named for the color of the paper used, that gives the ask and bid prices for bonds traded on the OTC market.

Yield
What an investor earns from his or her bonds (or other investments).

Yield curve
Graph showing the relationship between maturities and yields for bonds of similar quality.

Yield to call (YTC)
Similar to yield to maturity, this rate of return uses the call date and price (rather than its maturity and par value) to calculate the bondholder's capital gain or loss.

Yield to maturity
The most complete way of calculating a bond's rate of return. Yield to maturity takes into account the bond's fixed interest payments, current market price, and any capital gains or losses at maturity.

Yield to put (YTP)
Similar to yield to maturity, this rate of return uses the put date and price (rather than its maturity and par value) to calculate the bondholder's capital gain or loss. Often yield to put differs from yield to maturity only because redemption takes place before maturity.

Yield-based option

An interest rate option based on the yield of Treasury securities with a particular maturity. Yield-based options are settled in cash, the amount being calculated from the difference between the current market yield and the strike price yield.

Yield-spread basis

Method of quoting prices of bonds that compares the difference in yield between two similar securities.

Zero-coupon bond

Bond that does not pay interest and is sold at a deep discount, but is redeemable at par upon maturity.

Index

NUMBERS

C

D

E

G

H

I

J - K

L

N

How can we make this index more useful? Email us at indexes@quepublishing.com

P

Q - R

S

U

V - W

X - Y - Z

How can we make this index more useful? Email us at indexes@quepublishing.com